# This is

## power source
### given by:

### date:

### occasion:

KU-021-554

'I pray that you will begin to understand the incredible greatness of his power for us who believe in him.'

Ephesians 1:19

Dedicated to Katie, my beautiful daughter.

# ACKNOWLEDGEMENTS

With a project like this where do you start? Simple, you start with your wife! Thank you, Michelle, for your patience, encouragement and keen eye throughout the many late nights and early mornings and for your deep reservoir of love that keeps me going. Thank you to the Scottish Bible Society (Doug, Colin & Sharon) for your integrity, passion and commitment to get the Word of God into the world of sport, in Scotland and around the world. Thank you to all those experts that helped shape and encourage the project including: Mary MacLeod, Barry Nicholson, Emma Cromwell, Alan Gray and the KICK TEAM, Dr Peter Walters, Christians in Sport, Gordon Thiessen, Doug Reese - tothenextlevel.org....

A massive thanks to Graeme Hewitson, our graphic designer: for all your hard work, most excellent design, indefatigable coolness and continuous friendship - your creative heart is a reflection of your Creator.

The nt:sport New Testament is an extract of the New Testament from the *Holy Bible*, New Living Translation, British Text, © 2000, an anglicised version of the Holy Bible, New Living Translation.

Holy Bible, New Living Translation, © 1996 by Tyndale Charitable Trust. All rights reserved.

The nt:sport illustrations, pictures, editorial and all text matter relating to them have been created by Rev Steve Connor, Sports Outreach Association © 2004. All rights reserved.

The text of the Holy Bible, New Living Translation, may be quoted in any form (written, visual, electronic, or audio) up to and inclusive of two hundred and fifty (250) verses without express written permission of the publisher, provided that the verses quoted do not account for more than 20 per cent of the work in which they are quoted, and provided that a complete book of the Bible is not quoted.

When the Holy Bible, New Living Translation, is quoted, one of the following three credit lines must appear on the copyright page or title page of the work:

Scripture quotations marked NLT are taken from the Holy Bible, New Living Translation copyright 1996. Used by permission of Tyndale House Publishers, Inc., Wheaton, Illinois 60169, United States of America. All rights reserved.

Scripture quotations are taken from the Holy Bible, New Living Translation, copyright 1996. Used by permission of Tyndale House Publishers, Inc., Wheaton, Illinois 60169, United States of America. All rights reserved.

Unless otherwise indicated, all Scripture quotations are taken from the Holy Bible, New Living Translation, copyright 1996. Used by permission of Tyndale House Publishers, Inc., Wheaton, Illinois 60169, United States of America. All rights reserved.

When quotations from the NLT text are used in non-saleable media, such as church bulletins, orders of service, newsletters, transparencies, or similar media, a complete copyright notice is not required, but the initials NLT must appear at the end of each quotation.

Quotations in excess of two hundred and fifty (250) verses or 20 per cent of the work, or other permission requests, must be directed to and approved in writing by Tyndale House Publishers, Inc., PO Box 60, Wheaton, Illinois 60169, United States of America.

Publication of any commentary or other Bible reference work produced for commercial sale that uses the New Living Translation requires written permission for use of the NLT text.

*New Living*, *NLT*, and the New Living Translation logo are trademarks of Tyndale House Publishers, Inc.

Graphic Design by Graeme Hewitson of Viewfield Design, Glasgow.
Typeset by Stewart Rollo.
Published by The Scottish Bible Society © 2004. All rights reserved.
Printed in Italy by Legoprint s.p.a.

nt:sport ISBN 0 9015 1845 X

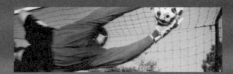

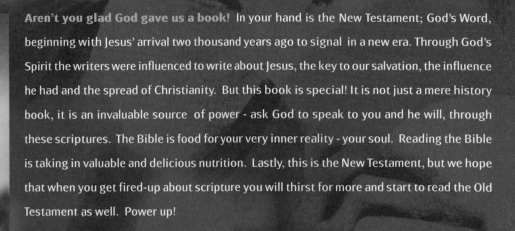

# A NOTE FROM THE EDITOR

**Aren't you glad God gave us a book!** In your hand is the New Testament; God's Word, beginning with Jesus' arrival two thousand years ago to signal in a new era. Through God's Spirit the writers were influenced to write about Jesus, the key to our salvation, the influence he had and the spread of Christianity. But this book is special! It is not just a mere history book, it is an invaluable source of power - ask God to speak to you and he will, through these scriptures. The Bible is food for your very inner reality - your soul. Reading the Bible is taking in valuable and delicious nutrition. Lastly, this is the New Testament, but we hope that when you get fired-up about scripture you will thirst for more and start to read the Old Testament as well. Power up!

**Of course the writers of the Bible did not use 21 Century English;** the books of the Bible were originally written in Hebrew (Old Testament), Greek and Aramaic. This edition of the Bible: *New Living Translation* has been meticulously translated - by loads of scholars - into our modern language. It has been seriously scrutinised and the result is The Word of God in a modern accurate understandable version.

Read this!

**The Coloured Sidebars** (Count On It, What Does It Mean, Stats, Tips, Bible Hits....) are interspersed throughout the scripture to add insight into your sport and your faith in Christ. Many of the Sidebars will have a Bible verse in the box along with brief commentary to encourage you to live out your faith and understand the scriptures better - but they are not the scriptures! I hope the 'sidebars' give you insight and bring clarity to the Word of God, but make sure they do not distract you. Put simply, the most powerful part of your book will be in black letters on the white pages!

## All God's Best!

*Steve*

Steve Connor is International Director of Sports Outreach Association. The past eighteen years he has been helping develop sports ministry in USA, England and Scotland. Steve became a Christian when he was invited to a sports camp by his high school football coach. He was an NAIA two-time All American at Azusa Pacific University and had a

If you aim at **nothing**
you will achieve it - nothing

A **goal**
not written down
is merely a **wish**

**a good coach**
will help the player do what
they **do not want** to do
(like train hard) so they will
do what **they want** to do
(achieve their potential)

who am I?
where am I going?
how am I going to get there? ▶

# MONTHLY ACTION PLAN

## PLANNING GUIDE

### Developing a healthy game plan for life:

It is good to develop healthy habits that will help you to achieve your priorities and goals throughout your entire life. The Monthly Action Plan helps you map-out a strategy for achieving your priorities and goals in a balanced healthy exercise.

1) Ask God to help you with this planning exercise.

2) Look at the pages in the back of your Bible (Spiritual Disciplines, Prayer List, Personal Goals and Sports Goals) and fill them in where appropriate.
   *If you need help it is good to get a parent, coach, friend, or minister to help you plan your Monthly Action Plan.

3) As a monthly exercise fill in the four boxes at the bottom of your Monthly Action Plan, from the lists at the back of your Bible.

4) If you know you have a competition, church event or other events already fixed in your year, mark them into your calendar above the boxes.

5) Review your Monthly Action Plan (Spiritual Disciplines, Prayer List, Personal Goals and Sports Goals) daily then honestly mark the boxes that you have worked on or prayed through during that day.

## EXAMPLES:

### Spiritual Disciplines

**Prayer** I will aim to pray every morning

**Faith Community** I am going to not only attend my church weekly, I want to contribute 2 hours a week to the Sunday school.

**Bible Reading** I will aim at reading the Gospel of John this month, every morning before training and work hard at living out what I learn from it.

### Prayer List

**Friends** I am going to pray for three friends from my list in the back of my Bible every day. (see back pages for bigger lists)

**World** I am going to pray for my political leaders and a section of the world every day for this month. (see back pages for bigger lists)

**Personal** I am going to pray (from my back list) that 'Thy will' not 'my will' be done in certain areas of my life every day. (see back pages for bigger lists)

### Personal Goals

**Family** This month I am going to work hard on encouraging my sister.

**Work/School/Social** This month I am going to focus on getting to work on time.

**Challenge** This month I am going to work hard on memorising John 14:6

### Sport Goals

**Training** This month I am going to focus on my ball handling skills.

**Performance** This month I am going to work on staying focused throughout the competition.

**Competition Results** This month I am going to do my best to keep the team unified throughout the competition.

# TABLE OF CONTENTS

Introduction pages:

Acknowledgements

Note from the Editor

Monthly Action Plan: Planning Guide

Final Section:

Notes

Monthly Action Plan: Goals Lists

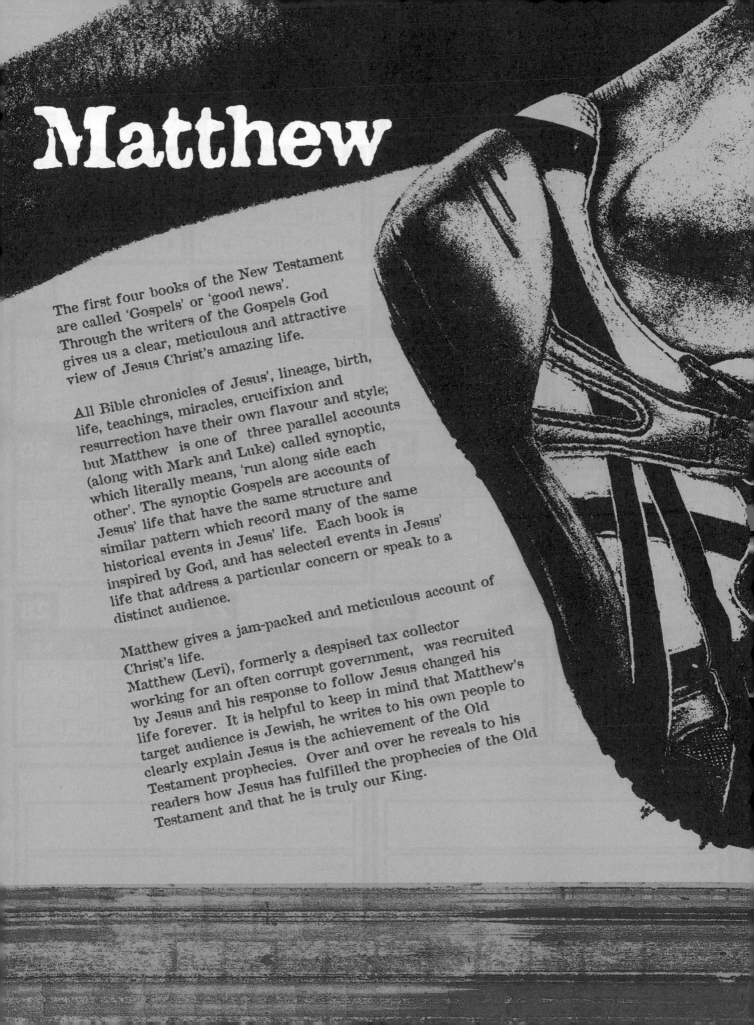

# Matthew

The first four books of the New Testament are called 'Gospels' or 'good news'. Through the writers of the Gospels God gives us a clear, meticulous and attractive view of Jesus Christ's amazing life.

All Bible chronicles of Jesus', lineage, birth, life, teachings, miracles, crucifixion and resurrection have their own flavour and style; but Matthew is one of three parallel accounts (along with Mark and Luke) called synoptic, which literally means, 'run along side each other'. The synoptic Gospels are accounts of Jesus' life that have the same structure and similar pattern which record many of the same historical events in Jesus' life. Each book is inspired by God, and has selected events in Jesus' life that address a particular concern or speak to a distinct audience.

Matthew gives a jam-packed and meticulous account of Christ's life.

Matthew (Levi), formerly a despised tax collector working for an often corrupt government, was recruited by Jesus and his response to follow Jesus changed his life forever. It is helpful to keep in mind that Matthew's target audience is Jewish, he writes to his own people to clearly explain Jesus is the achievement of the Old Testament prophecies. Over and over he reveals to his readers how Jesus has fulfilled the prophecies of the Old Testament and that he is truly our King.

# JANUARY M.A.P.

## 1
| S.D. | P.L. | P.G. | S.G. |
|------|------|------|------|
| P. ☐ | F. ☐ | F. ☐ | T. ☐ |
| F. ☐ | W. ☐ | W. ☐ | P. ☐ |
| B. ☐ | P. ☐ | C. ☐ | C. ☐ |

## 2
| S.D. | P.L. | P.G. | S.G. |
|------|------|------|------|
| P. ☐ | F. ☐ | F. ☐ | T. ☐ |
| F. ☐ | W. ☐ | W. ☐ | P. ☐ |
| B. ☐ | P. ☐ | C. ☐ | C. ☐ |

## 3
| S.D. | P.L. | P.G. | S.G. |
|------|------|------|------|
| P. ☐ | F. ☐ | F. ☐ | T. ☐ |
| F. ☐ | W. ☐ | W. ☐ | P. ☐ |
| B. ☐ | P. ☐ | C. ☐ | C. ☐ |

## 4
| S.D. | P.L. | P.G. | S.G. |
|------|------|------|------|
| P. ☐ | F. ☐ | F. ☐ | T. ☐ |
| F. ☐ | W. ☐ | W. ☐ | P. ☐ |
| B. ☐ | P. ☐ | C. ☐ | C. ☐ |

## 9
| S.D. | P.L. | P.G. | S.G. |
|------|------|------|------|
| P. ☐ | F. ☐ | F. ☐ | T. ☐ |
| F. ☐ | W. ☐ | W. ☐ | P. ☐ |
| B. ☐ | P. ☐ | C. ☐ | C. ☐ |

## 10
| S.D. | P.L. | P.G. | S.G. |
|------|------|------|------|
| P. ☐ | F. ☐ | F. ☐ | T. ☐ |
| F. ☐ | W. ☐ | W. ☐ | P. ☐ |
| B. ☐ | P. ☐ | C. ☐ | C. ☐ |

## 11
| S.D. | P.L. | P.G. | S.G. |
|------|------|------|------|
| P. ☐ | F. ☐ | F. ☐ | T. ☐ |
| F. ☐ | W. ☐ | W. ☐ | P. ☐ |
| B. ☐ | P. ☐ | C. ☐ | C. ☐ |

## 12
| S.D. | P.L. | P.G. | S.G. |
|------|------|------|------|
| P. ☐ | F. ☐ | F. ☐ | T. ☐ |
| F. ☐ | W. ☐ | W. ☐ | P. ☐ |
| B. ☐ | P. ☐ | C. ☐ | C. ☐ |

## 17
| S.D. | P.L. | P.G. | S.G. |
|------|------|------|------|
| P. ☐ | F. ☐ | F. ☐ | T. ☐ |
| F. ☐ | W. ☐ | W. ☐ | P. ☐ |
| B. ☐ | P. ☐ | C. ☐ | C. ☐ |

## 18
| S.D. | P.L. | P.G. | S.G. |
|------|------|------|------|
| P. ☐ | F. ☐ | F. ☐ | T. ☐ |
| F. ☐ | W. ☐ | W. ☐ | P. ☐ |
| B. ☐ | P. ☐ | C. ☐ | C. ☐ |

## 19
| S.D. | P.L. | P.G. | S.G. |
|------|------|------|------|
| P. ☐ | F. ☐ | F. ☐ | T. ☐ |
| F. ☐ | W. ☐ | W. ☐ | P. ☐ |
| B. ☐ | P. ☐ | C. ☐ | C. ☐ |

## 20
| S.D. | P.L. | P.G. | S.G. |
|------|------|------|------|
| P. ☐ | F. ☐ | F. ☐ | T. ☐ |
| F. ☐ | W. ☐ | W. ☐ | P. ☐ |
| B. ☐ | P. ☐ | C. ☐ | C. ☐ |

## 25
| S.D. | P.L. | P.G. | S.G. |
|------|------|------|------|
| P. ☐ | F. ☐ | F. ☐ | T. ☐ |
| F. ☐ | W. ☐ | W. ☐ | P. ☐ |
| B. ☐ | P. ☐ | C. ☐ | C. ☐ |

## 26
| S.D. | P.L. | P.G. | S.G. |
|------|------|------|------|
| P. ☐ | F. ☐ | F. ☐ | T. ☐ |
| F. ☐ | W. ☐ | W. ☐ | P. ☐ |
| B. ☐ | P. ☐ | C. ☐ | C. ☐ |

## 27
| S.D. | P.L. | P.G. | S.G. |
|------|------|------|------|
| P. ☐ | F. ☐ | F. ☐ | T. ☐ |
| F. ☐ | W. ☐ | W. ☐ | P. ☐ |
| B. ☐ | P. ☐ | C. ☐ | C. ☐ |

## 28
| S.D. | P.L. | P.G. | S.G. |
|------|------|------|------|
| P. ☐ | F. ☐ | F. ☐ | T. ☐ |
| F. ☐ | W. ☐ | W. ☐ | P. ☐ |
| B. ☐ | P. ☐ | C. ☐ | C. ☐ |

## Spiritual Disciplines

**Prayer**

**Faith Community**

**Bible Reading**

## Prayer List

**Friends**

**World**

**Personal**

(For designing your MAP - Monthly Action Plan - see introduction pages)

Who am I....
Where am I going....
How am I going to get there?

# nt:spor†
## MONTHLY ACTION PLAN

### 5
| S.D. | P.L. | P.G. | S.G. |
|---|---|---|---|
| P. ☐ | F. ☐ | F. ☐ | T. ☐ |
| F. ☐ | W. ☐ | W. ☐ | P. ☐ |
| B. ☐ | P. ☐ | C. ☐ | C. ☐ |

### 6
| S.D. | P.L. | P.G. | S.G. |
|---|---|---|---|
| P. ☐ | F. ☐ | F. ☐ | T. ☐ |
| F. ☐ | W. ☐ | W. ☐ | P. ☐ |
| B. ☐ | P. ☐ | C. ☐ | C. ☐ |

### 7
| S.D. | P.L. | P.G. | S.G. |
|---|---|---|---|
| P. ☐ | F. ☐ | F. ☐ | T. ☐ |
| F. ☐ | W. ☐ | W. ☐ | P. ☐ |
| B. ☐ | P. ☐ | C. ☐ | C. ☐ |

### 8
| S.D. | P.L. | P.G. | S.G. |
|---|---|---|---|
| P. ☐ | F. ☐ | F. ☐ | T. ☐ |
| F. ☐ | W. ☐ | W. ☐ | P. ☐ |
| B. ☐ | P. ☐ | C. ☐ | C. ☐ |

### 13
| S.D. | P.L. | P.G. | S.G. |
|---|---|---|---|
| P. ☐ | F. ☐ | F. ☐ | T. ☐ |
| F. ☐ | W. ☐ | W. ☐ | P. ☐ |
| B. ☐ | P. ☐ | C. ☐ | C. ☐ |

### 14
| S.D. | P.L. | P.G. | S.G. |
|---|---|---|---|
| P. ☐ | F. ☐ | F. ☐ | T. ☐ |
| F. ☐ | W. ☐ | W. ☐ | P. ☐ |
| B. ☐ | P. ☐ | C. ☐ | C. ☐ |

### 15
| S.D. | P.L. | P.G. | S.G. |
|---|---|---|---|
| P. ☐ | F. ☐ | F. ☐ | T. ☐ |
| F. ☐ | W. ☐ | W. ☐ | P. ☐ |
| B. ☐ | P. ☐ | C. ☐ | C. ☐ |

### 16
| S.D. | P.L. | P.G. | S.G. |
|---|---|---|---|
| P. ☐ | F. ☐ | F. ☐ | T. ☐ |
| F. ☐ | W. ☐ | W. ☐ | P. ☐ |
| B. ☐ | P. ☐ | C. ☐ | C. ☐ |

### 21
| S.D. | P.L. | P.G. | S.G. |
|---|---|---|---|
| P. ☐ | F. ☐ | F. ☐ | T. ☐ |
| F. ☐ | W. ☐ | W. ☐ | P. ☐ |
| B. ☐ | P. ☐ | C. ☐ | C. ☐ |

### 22
| S.D. | P.L. | P.G. | S.G. |
|---|---|---|---|
| P. ☐ | F. ☐ | F. ☐ | T. ☐ |
| F. ☐ | W. ☐ | W. ☐ | P. ☐ |
| B. ☐ | P. ☐ | C. ☐ | C. ☐ |

### 23
| S.D. | P.L. | P.G. | S.G. |
|---|---|---|---|
| P. ☐ | F. ☐ | F. ☐ | T. ☐ |
| F. ☐ | W. ☐ | W. ☐ | P. ☐ |
| B. ☐ | P. ☐ | C. ☐ | C. ☐ |

### 24
| S.D. | P.L. | P.G. | S.G. |
|---|---|---|---|
| P. ☐ | F. ☐ | F. ☐ | T. ☐ |
| F. ☐ | W. ☐ | W. ☐ | P. ☐ |
| B. ☐ | P. ☐ | C. ☐ | C. ☐ |

### 29
| S.D. | P.L. | P.G. | S.G. |
|---|---|---|---|
| P. ☐ | F. ☐ | F. ☐ | T. ☐ |
| F. ☐ | W. ☐ | W. ☐ | P. ☐ |
| B. ☐ | P. ☐ | C. ☐ | C. ☐ |

### 30
| S.D. | P.L. | P.G. | S.G. |
|---|---|---|---|
| P. ☐ | F. ☐ | F. ☐ | T. ☐ |
| F. ☐ | W. ☐ | W. ☐ | P. ☐ |
| B. ☐ | P. ☐ | C. ☐ | C. ☐ |

### 31
| S.D. | P.L. | P.G. | S.G. |
|---|---|---|---|
| P. ☐ | F. ☐ | F. ☐ | T. ☐ |
| F. ☐ | W. ☐ | W. ☐ | P. ☐ |
| B. ☐ | P. ☐ | C. ☐ | C. ☐ |

**Psalm 25:5**

Lead me by your truth and teach me, for you are the God who saves me. All day long I put my hope in you.

## Personal Goals

**Family**

**Work/School/Social**

**Challenge**

## Sport Goals

**Training**

**Performance**

**Competition Results**

# Direction
## FOLLOW it

Trust in the Lord with all your heart; do not depend on your own understanding. Seek His will in all you do, and he will direct your paths.

PROVERBS 3:5-6

# MATTHEW

## The Record of Jesus' Ancestors

# 1

This is a record of the ancestors of Jesus the Messiah, a descendant of King David and of Abraham:

²Abraham was the father of Isaac.

Isaac was the father of Jacob.

Jacob was the father of Judah and his brothers.

³Judah was the father of Perez and Zerah (their mother was Tamar).

Perez was the father of Hezron.

Hezron was the father of Ram.

⁴Ram was the father of Amminadab.

Amminadab was the father of Nahshon.

Nahshon was the father of Salmon.

⁵Salmon was the father of Boaz (his mother was Rahab).

Boaz was the father of Obed (his mother was Ruth).

Obed was the father of Jesse.

⁶Jesse was the father of King David.

David was the father of Solomon (his mother was Bathsheba, the widow of Uriah).

⁷Solomon was the father of Rehoboam.

Rehoboam was the father of Abijah.

Abijah was the father of Asaph.

⁸Asaph was the father of Jehoshaphat.

Jehoshaphat was the father of Jehoram.

Jehoram was the father of Uzziah.

⁹Uzziah was the father of Jotham.

Jotham was the father of Ahaz.

Ahaz was the father of Hezekiah.

¹⁰Hezekiah was the father of Manasseh.

Manasseh was the father of Amos.

Amos was the father of Josiah.

¹¹Josiah was the father of Jehoiachin and his brothers (born at the time of the exile to Babylon).

¹²After the Babylonian exile:

Jehoiachin was the father of Shealtiel.

## Bible Facts

**John Wycliffe translated the first English Bible in 1382.**

Shealtiel was the father of Zerubbabel.

¹³Zerubbabel was the father of Abiud.

Abiud was the father of Eliakim.

Eliakim was the father of Azor.

¹⁴Azor was the father of Zadok.

Zadok was the father of Akim.

Akim was the father of Eliud.

¹⁵Eliud was the father of Eleazar.

Eleazar was the father of Matthan.

Matthan was the father of Jacob.

¹⁶Jacob was the father of Joseph, the husband of Mary. Mary was the mother of Jesus, who is called the Messiah.

¹⁷All those listed above include fourteen generations from Abraham to King David, and fourteen from David's time to the Babylonian exile, and fourteen from the Babylonian exile to the Messiah.

God helps your habits: Good habits come with understanding what God wants of you. Ask for God's help and have a determination to follow his plan for your life. Fill your life with good habits.

"And you yourself must be an example to them by doing good deeds of every kind. Let everything you do reflect the integrity and seriousness of your teaching."

Titus 2:7

## The Birth of Jesus the Messiah

¹⁸Now this is how Jesus the Messiah was born. His mother, Mary, was engaged to be married to Joseph. But while she was still a virgin, she became pregnant by the Holy Spirit. ¹⁹Joseph, her fiancé, being a just man, decided to break the engagement quietly, so as not to disgrace her publicly.

²⁰As he considered this, he fell asleep, and an angel of the Lord appeared to him in a dream. "Joseph, son of David," the angel said, "do not be afraid to go ahead with your marriage to Mary. For the child within her has been conceived by the Holy Spirit. ²¹And she will have a son, and you are to name him Jesus, for he will save his people from their sins."

²²All of this happened to fulfil the Lord's message through his prophet:

²³"Look! The virgin will conceive a child!

She will give birth to a son,

and he will be called Immanuel

(meaning, God is with us)."

²⁴When Joseph woke up, he did what the angel of the Lord commanded. He brought Mary home to be his wife, ²⁵but she remained a virgin until her son was born. And Joseph named him Jesus.

## The Visit of the Wise Men

# 2

Jesus was born in the town of Bethlehem in Judea, during the reign of King Herod. About that time some wise men from eastern lands arrived in Jerusalem, asking, ²"Where is the newborn king of the Jews? We have seen his star as it arose, and we have come to worship him."

³Herod was deeply disturbed by their question, as was all of Jerusalem. ⁴He called a meeting of the leading priests and teachers of religious law. "Where did the prophets say the Messiah would be born?" he asked them.

⁵"In Bethlehem," they said, "for this is what the prophet wrote:

⁶'O Bethlehem of Judah,

you are not just a lowly village in Judah,

for a ruler will come from you

who will be the shepherd for my people Israel.'"

⁷Then Herod sent a private message to the wise men, asking them to come and see him. At this meeting he learned the exact time when they first saw the star. ⁸Then he told them, "Go to Bethlehem and search carefully for the child. And when you find him, come back and tell me so that I can go and worship him, too!"

⁹After this interview the wise men went their way. Once again the star appeared to them, guiding them to Bethlehem. It

# profiles

## Adam & Eve: They had it all!

God ended his creation with a spectacular finish, he created men and women in His own image. First, Adam, who was in charge of caring for and nurturing God's creation. Next, he made Eve, knowing it was not good for man to be alone. They had all the privileges of the Garden of Eden (paradise) and they enjoyed perfect companionship with God. He gave them full reign over all creation with one clear directive: *"You can enjoy all things, but death will come to you if you eat of the 'tree of the knowledge of good and evil.'"* One day Satan in the form of a serpent shifted Eve's focus and desire from all the wonderful privileges she possessed to the one thing she was not allowed, the very thing that would hurt her. Eve willingly broke God's rules and listened to a serpent instead of God. Adam, sadly, also accepted the forbidden fruit and not only broke his relationship to God but all his descendants would inherit the same devastating fate – separation from God, death.

But God already had a plan in restoring his people; as the Gospel writer Luke emphasises, there will be a New Adam, sinless, who will take away the sin of the world. God's plan is Jesus.

went ahead of them and stopped over the place where the child was. ¹⁰When they saw the star, they were filled with joy! ¹¹They entered the house where the child and his mother, Mary, were, and they fell down before him and worshipped him. Then they opened their treasure chests and gave him gifts of gold, frankincense, and myrrh. ¹²But when it was time to leave, they went home another way, because God had warned them in a dream not to return to Herod.

## The Escape to Egypt

¹³After the wise men had gone, an angel of the Lord appeared to Joseph in a dream. "Get up and flee to Egypt with the child and his mother," the angel said. "Stay there until I tell you to return, because Herod is going to try to kill the child."

¹⁴That night Joseph left for Egypt with the child and Mary, his mother, ¹⁵and they stayed there until Herod's death. This fulfilled what the Lord had spoken through the prophet: "I called my Son out of Egypt."

¹⁶Herod was furious when he learned that the wise men had outwitted him. He sent soldiers to kill all the boys in and around Bethlehem who were two years old and under, because the wise men had told him that the star first appeared to them about two years earlier. ¹⁷Herod's brutal action fulfilled the prophecy of Jeremiah:

¹⁸"A cry of anguish is heard in Ramah—
weeping and mourning unrestrained.
Rachel weeps for her children,
refusing to be comforted—for they are dead."

## The Return to Nazareth

¹⁹When Herod died, an angel of the Lord appeared in a dream to Joseph in Egypt and told him, ²⁰"Get up and take the child and his mother back to the land of Israel, because those who were trying to kill the child are dead." ²¹So Joseph returned immediately to Israel with Jesus and his mother. ²²But when he learned that the new ruler was Herod's son Archelaus, he was afraid. Then, in another dream, he was warned to go to Galilee. ²³So they went and lived in a town called Nazareth. This fulfilled what was spoken by the prophets concerning the Messiah: "He will be called a Nazarene."

## John the Baptist Prepares the Way

# 3

In those days John the Baptist began preaching in the Judean wilderness. His message was, ²"Turn from your sins and turn to God, because the Kingdom of Heaven is near." ³Isaiah had spoken of John when he said,

"He is a voice shouting in the wilderness:
'Prepare a pathway for the Lord's coming!
Make a straight road for him!'"

⁴John's clothes were woven from camel hair, and he wore a leather belt; his food was locusts and wild honey. ⁵People from Jerusalem and from every section of Judea and from all over the Jordan Valley went out to the wilderness to hear him preach.

⁶And when they confessed their sins, he baptized them in the River Jordan.

⁷But when he saw many Pharisees and Sadducees coming to be baptized, he denounced them. "You brood of snakes!" he exclaimed. "Who warned you to flee God's coming judgement?

⁸Prove by the way you live that you have really turned from your sins and turned to God. ⁹Don't just say, 'We're safe—we're the descendants of Abraham.' That proves nothing. God can change these stones here into children of Abraham. ¹⁰Even now the axe of God's judgement is poised, ready to sever your roots. Yes, every tree that does not produce good fruit will be chopped down and thrown into the fire.

¹¹"I baptize with water those who turn from their sins and turn to God. But someone is coming soon who is far greater than I am—so much greater that I am not even worthy to be his slave. He will baptize you with the Holy Spirit and with fire. ¹²He is ready to separate the chaff from the grain with his winnowing fork. Then he will clean up the threshing area, storing the grain in his barn but burning the chaff with never-ending fire."

## The Baptism of Jesus

¹³Then Jesus went from Galilee to the River Jordan to be baptized by John. ¹⁴But John didn't want to baptize him. "I am the one who needs to be baptized by you," he said, "so why are you coming to me?"

¹⁵But Jesus said, "It must be done, because we must do everything that is right." So then John baptized him.

¹⁶**After his baptism, as Jesus came up out of the water, the heavens were opened and he saw the Spirit of God descending like a dove and settling on him. ¹⁷And a voice from heaven said, "This is my beloved Son, and I am fully pleased with him."**

## The Temptation of Jesus

# 4

Then Jesus was led out into the wilderness by the Holy

**'Temptation' MATTHEW CH 4**
The 'Temptation' of Jesus is a preface to the start of his formal ministry and follows forty days and nights fasting and praying in the desert of Judea. This is a tough test with Satan trying to sever Jesus' relationship with his Father. It was a brutal challenge but with a victorious result for Christ and a shining example for us. Note how Jesus relies on his Father and the Holy Spirit for strength. It is also important to understand how Satan falsely uses scripture to tempt Jesus but fails as Jesus refutes him with scripture in right context.

Spirit to be tempted there by the Devil. [2]For forty days and forty nights he ate nothing and became very hungry. [3]Then the Devil came and said to him, "If you are the Son of God, change these stones into loaves of bread."

[4]But Jesus told him, "No! The Scriptures say,
'People need more than bread for their life;
they must feed on every word of God.'"

[5]Then the Devil took him to Jerusalem, to the highest point of the Temple, [6]and said, "If you are the Son of God, jump off! For the Scriptures say,
'He orders his angels to protect you.
And they will hold you with their hands
to keep you from striking your foot on a stone.'"

[7]Jesus responded, "The Scriptures also say, 'Do not test the Lord your God.'"

[8]Next the Devil took him to the peak of a very high mountain and showed him the nations of the world and all their glory. [9]"I will give it all to you," he said, "if you will only kneel down and worship me."

[10]"Get out of here, Satan," Jesus told him. "For the Scriptures say,
'You must worship the Lord your God;
serve only him.'"

[11]Then the Devil went away, and angels came and cared for Jesus.

## The Ministry of Jesus Begins

[12]When Jesus heard that John had been arrested, he left Judea and returned to Galilee. [13]But instead of going to Nazareth, he went to Capernaum, beside the Sea of Galilee, in the region of Zebulun and Naphtali. [14]This fulfilled Isaiah's prophecy:

[15]"In the land of Zebulun and of Naphtali, beside the sea, beyond the River Jordan—
in Galilee where so many Gentiles live—
[16]the people who sat in darkness
have seen a great light.
And for those who lived in the land where death casts its shadow, a light has shined."

[17]From then on, Jesus began to preach, "Turn from your sins and turn to God, because the Kingdom of Heaven is near."

## The First Disciples

[18]One day as Jesus was walking along the shore beside the Sea of Galilee, he saw two brothers—Simon, also called Peter, and Andrew—fishing with a net, for they were commercial fishermen. [19]**Jesus called out to them, "Come, be my disciples, and I will show you how to fish for people!" [20]And they left their nets at once and went with him.**

[21]A little farther up the shore he saw two other brothers, James and John, sitting in a boat with their father, Zebedee, mending their nets. And he called them to come, too. [22]They immediately followed him, leaving the boat and their father behind.

## The Ministry of Jesus in Galilee

[23]Jesus travelled throughout Galilee teaching in the synagogues, preaching everywhere the Good News about the Kingdom. And he healed people who had every kind of sickness and disease. [24]News about him spread far beyond the borders of Galilee so that the sick were soon coming to be healed from as far away as Syria. And whatever their illness and pain, or whether they were possessed by demons, or were epileptics, or were paralysed—he healed them all. [25]Large crowds followed him wherever he went-people from Galilee, the Ten Towns, Jerusalem, from all over Judea, and from east of the River Jordan.

## The Sermon on the Mount

## 5

[1]One day as the crowds were gathering, Jesus went up the mountainside with his disciples and sat down to teach them.

## The Beatitudes

[2]This is what he taught them:
[3]"God blesses those who realize their need for him,
for the Kingdom of Heaven is given to them.
[4]God blesses those who mourn,
for they will be comforted.
[5]God blesses those who are gentle and lowly,
for the whole earth will belong to them.
[6]God blesses those who are hungry and thirsty for justice,
for they will receive it in full.
[7]God blesses those who are merciful,
for they will be shown mercy.
[8]God blesses those whose hearts are pure,
for they will see God.
[9]God blesses those who work for peace,
for they will be called the children of God.
[10]God blesses those who are persecuted because they live for God,
for the Kingdom of Heaven is theirs.
[11]"God blesses you when you are mocked and persecuted and lied about because you are my followers. [12]Be happy about

**My closest friend is really messed-up, but who am I to tell them to straighten out their life?**

First, it is not your job to straighten out anybody's life. It is God's job and he has been doing it for a long time. You do have a responsibility to pray for your friends and team-mates and to have Jesus' life reflected in your life. Guide your friends to God when the opportunity arises, tell them you are praying for them and, when it is appropriate, tell them that some of their actions are breaking God's heart. Read the Parable of the Lost Son (Luke 15:11-32). Remember prayer changes things.

it! Be very glad! For a great reward awaits you in heaven. And remember, the ancient prophets were persecuted, too.

action

**CH 5:1-12 WHAT'S IT SAYING?**

**WHAT AM I GOING TO DO ABOUT IT?**

## Teaching about Salt and Light

13"You are the salt of the earth. But what good is salt if it has lost its flavour? Can you make it useful again? It will be thrown out and trampled underfoot as worthless. 14You are the light of the world—like a city on a mountain, glowing in the night for all to see. 15Don't hide your light under a basket! Instead, put it on a stand and let it shine for all. 16In the same way, let your good deeds shine out for all to see, so that everyone will praise your heavenly Father.

## Teaching about the Law

17"Don't misunderstand why I have come. I did not come to abolish the law of Moses or the writings of the prophets. No, I came to fulfil them. 18I assure you, until heaven and earth disappear, even the smallest detail of God's law will remain until its purpose is achieved. 19So if you break the smallest commandment and teach others to do the same, you will be the least in the Kingdom of Heaven. But anyone who obeys God's laws and teaches them will be great in the

Kingdom of Heaven.
20"But I warn you—unless you obey God better than the teachers of religious law and the Pharisees do, you can't enter the Kingdom of Heaven at all!

## Teaching about Anger

21"You have heard that the law of Moses says, 'Do not murder. If you commit murder, you are subject to judgement.'
22But I say, if you are angry with someone, you are subject to judgement! If you call someone an idiot, you are in danger of being brought before the high council. And if you curse someone, you are in danger of the fires of hell.
23"So if you are standing before the altar in the Temple, offering a sacrifice to God, and you suddenly remember that someone has something against you, 24leave your sacrifice there beside the altar. Go and be reconciled to that person. Then come and offer your sacrifice to God. 25Come to terms quickly with your enemy before it is too late and you are dragged into

## count on it

### Get some rest!
There are times when you will feel stressed by your performance on and off the pitch or field. Sometimes you will feel so exhausted that you feel you can't recharge: mentally, physically, spiritually and socially. What does God say? 'Come to me... and I will give you rest!' Count on it! "Come to me, all of you who are weary and carry heavy burdens, and I will give you rest." Matthew 11:28
**Count on it!**

court, handed over to an officer, and thrown in jail. 26I assure you that you won't be free again until you have paid the last penny.

## Teaching about Adultery

27"You have heard that the law of Moses says, 'Do not commit adultery.' 28But I say, anyone who even looks at a woman with lust in his eye has already committed adultery with her in his heart. 29So if your eye—even if it is your good eye—causes you to lust, gouge it out and throw it away. It is better for you to lose one part of your body than for your whole body to be thrown into hell. 30And if your hand—even if it is your stronger hand—causes you to sin, cut it off and throw it away. It is better for you to lose one part of your body than for your whole body to be thrown into hell.

## Teaching about Divorce

31"You have heard that the law of Moses says, 'A man can divorce his wife by merely giving her a letter of divorce.' 32But I say that a man who divorces his wife, unless she has been unfaithful, causes her to commit adultery. And anyone who marries a divorced woman commits adultery.

## Teaching about Vows

33"Again, you have heard that the law of Moses says, 'Do not break your vows; you must carry out the vows you have made to the Lord.' 34But I say, don't make any vows! If you say, 'By heaven!' it is a sacred vow because heaven is God's throne. 35And if you say, 'By the earth!' it is a sacred vow because the earth is his footstool. And don't swear, 'By Jerusalem!' for Jerusalem is the city of the great King. 36Don't even swear, 'By my head!' for you can't turn one hair white or black. 37Just say a simple, 'Yes, I will,' or 'No, I won't.' Your word is enough. To strengthen your promise with a vow shows that something is wrong.

## Teaching about Revenge

38"You have heard that the law of Moses says, 'If an eye is injured, injure the eye of the person who did it. If a tooth gets knocked out, knock out the tooth of the person who did it.' 39But I say, don't resist an evil person! If you are slapped on the right cheek, turn the other, too.
40If you are ordered to court and your shirt is taken from you, give your coat, too. 41If a soldier demands that you carry his gear for a kilometre, carry it two kilometres. 42Give to those who ask, and don't turn away from those who want to borrow.

## Teaching about Love for Enemies

43"You have heard that the law of Moses says, 'Love your neighbour' and hate your enemy. 44But I say, love your enemies! Pray for those who persecute you!" 45In that

**5:44** Some manuscripts add *Bless those who curse you. Do good to those who hate you.* Compare Luke 6:27-28.

What are the five most significant things you could do with your life?

1
2
3
4
5

BIG FIVE

action

way, you will be acting as true children of your Father in heaven. For he gives his sunlight to both the evil and the good, and he sends rain on the just and on the unjust, too. **⁴⁶If you love only those who love you, what good is that? Even corrupt tax collectors do that much. ⁴⁷If you are kind only to your friends, how are you different from anyone else? Even pagans do that.** ⁴⁸But you are to be perfect, even as your Father in heaven is perfect.

## Teaching about Giving to the Needy

# 6

"Take care! Don't do your good deeds publicly, to be admired, because then you will lose the reward from your Father in heaven. ²When you give a gift to someone in need, don't shout about it as the hypocrites do—blowing trumpets in the synagogues and streets to call attention to their acts of charity! I assure you, they have received all the reward they will ever get. ³But when you give to someone, don't tell your left hand what your right hand is doing. ⁴Give your gifts in secret, and your Father, who knows all secrets, will reward you.

## Teaching about Prayer and Fasting

⁵"And now about prayer. When you pray, don't be like the hypocrites who love to pray publicly on street corners and in the synagogues where everyone can see them. I assure you, that is all the reward they will ever get. ⁶But when you pray, go away by yourself, shut the door behind you, and pray to your Father secretly. Then your Father, who knows all secrets, will reward you. ⁷"When you pray, don't babble on and on as people of other religions do. They think their prayers are answered only by repeating their words again and again. ⁸Don't be like them, because your Father knows exactly what you need before you ask him! ⁹Pray like this:

Our Father in heaven,
may your name be honoured.
¹⁰May your Kingdom come soon.
May your will be done here on earth,
just as it is in heaven.
¹¹Give us our food for today,
¹²and forgive us our sins,
just as we have forgiven those who have sinned against us.
¹³And don't let us yield to temptation,
but deliver us from the evil one.*

**¹⁴"If you forgive those who sin against you, your heavenly Father will forgive you. ¹⁵But if you refuse to forgive others, your Father will not forgive your sins.** ¹⁶"And when you fast, don't make it obvious, as the hypocrites do, who try to look pale and dishevelled so people will admire them for their fasting. I assure you, that is the only reward they will ever get. ¹⁷But

when you fast, comb your hair and wash your face. ¹⁸Then no one will suspect you are fasting, except your Father, who knows what you do in secret. And your Father, who knows all secrets, will reward you.

**CH 6:14-18 WHAT'S IT SAYING?**

**WHAT AM I GOING TO DO ABOUT IT?**

## Teaching about Money and Possessions

¹⁹"Don't store up treasures here on earth, where they can be eaten by moths and get rusty, and where thieves break in and steal. ²⁰Store your treasures in heaven, where they will never become moth-eaten or rusty and where they will be safe from thieves. ²¹Wherever your treasure is, there your heart and thoughts will also be.

²²"Your eye is a lamp for your body. A pure eye lets sunshine into your soul. ²³But an evil eye shuts out the light and plunges you into darkness. If the light you think you have is really darkness, how deep that darkness will be!

²⁴"No one can serve two masters. For you will hate one and love the other, or be devoted to one and despise the other. You cannot serve both God and money.

²⁵"So I tell you, don't worry about everyday life—whether you have enough food, drink, and clothes. Doesn't life consist of more than food and clothing?

6:13 Some manuscripts add *For yours is the kingdom and the power and the glory forever. Amen.*

**TIPS**

**Progress:**

By using balanced training principles, eating a nutrient-rich diet, and by getting proper amounts of rest, almost every person can make incredible changes in his or her performance.

²⁶Look at the birds. They don't need to plant or harvest or put food in barns, for your heavenly Father feeds them. And you are far more valuable to him than they are. ²⁷Can all your worries add a single moment to your life? Of course not.

²⁸"And why worry about your clothes? Look at the lilies and how they grow. They don't work or make their clothing, ²⁹yet Solomon in all his glory was not dressed as beautifully as they are.

³⁰And if God cares so wonderfully for flowers that are here today and gone tomorrow, won't he more surely care for you? You have so little faith!

³¹"So don't worry about having enough food or drink or clothing. ³²Why be like the pagans who are so deeply concerned about these things? Your heavenly Father already knows all your needs,

³³**and he will give you all you need from day to day if you live for him and make the Kingdom of God your primary concern.**

³⁴"**So don't worry about tomorrow, for tomorrow will bring its own worries. Today's trouble is enough for today.**

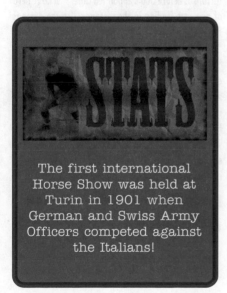

**STATS**

The first international Horse Show was held at Turin in 1901 when German and Swiss Army Officers competed against the Italians!

## Don't Condemn Others

# 7

"Stop judging others, and you will not be judged. ²For others will treat you as you treat them. Whatever measure you use in judging others, it will be used to measure how you are judged.

³And why worry about a speck in your friend's eye when you have a log in your own? ⁴**How can you think of saying, 'Let me help you get rid of that speck in your eye,' when you can't see past the log in your own eye?** ⁵Hypocrite! First get rid of the log from your own eye; then perhaps you will see well enough to deal with the speck in your friend's eye.

⁶"Don't give what is holy to unholy people. Don't give pearls to swine! They will trample the pearls, then turn and attack you.

## Effective Prayer

⁷"Keep on asking, and you will be given what you ask for. Keep on looking, and you will find. Keep on knocking, and the door will be opened. ⁸For everyone who asks, receives. Everyone who seeks, finds. And the door is opened to everyone who knocks. ⁹You parents—if your children ask for a loaf of bread, do you give them a stone instead? ¹⁰Or if they ask for a fish, do you give them a snake? Of course not! ¹¹If you sinful people know how to give good gifts to your children, how much more will your heavenly Father give good gifts to those who ask him.

## The Golden Rule

¹²"**Do for others what you would like them to do for you. This is a summary of all that is taught in the law and the prophets.**

## The Narrow Gate

¹³"You can enter God's Kingdom only through the narrow gate. The highway to hell is broad, and its gate is wide for the many who choose the easy way. ¹⁴But the gateway to life is small, and the road is narrow, and only a few ever find it.

**action**

**CH 7:7–12 WHAT'S IT SAYING?**

**WHAT AM I GOING TO DO ABOUT IT?**

## The Tree and Its Fruit

¹⁵"Beware of false prophets who come disguised as harmless sheep, but are really wolves that will tear you apart. ¹⁶You can detect them by the way they act, just as you can identify a tree by its fruit. You don't pick grapes from thorn bushes, or figs from thistles. ¹⁷A healthy tree produces good fruit, and an unhealthy tree produces bad fruit. ¹⁸A good tree can't produce bad fruit, and a bad tree can't produce good fruit. ¹⁹So every tree that does not produce good fruit is chopped down and thrown into the fire. ²⁰Yes, the way to identify a tree or a person is by the kind of fruit that is produced.

## True Disciples

²¹"Not all people who sound religious are really godly. They may refer to me as 'Lord,' but they still won't enter the

'Lord of the harvest' MATTHEW 9:35 - 10:42

Jesus so far in his ministry has recruited disciples, taught and performed miracles. At the end of chapter 9 we see Jesus very upset as he sees his people who are helpless and without someone to lead them safely. A weak analogy could be a gifted athlete who had no encouragement, guidance or coaching and was spoiling their health by stupid and poor training. Jesus is concerned with his people and urges prayer to his Father, the 'Lord of the harvest' to send out workers. It is no coincidence that in the next passage we see Jesus training and mobilizing his top guys to do ministry.

Kingdom of Heaven. The decisive issue is whether they obey my Father in heaven. ²²On judgement day many will tell me, 'Lord, Lord, we prophesied in your name and cast out demons in your name and performed many miracles in your name.' ²³But I will reply, 'I never knew you. Go away; the things you did were unauthorized.'

## Building on a Solid Foundation

²⁴"Anyone who listens to my teaching and obeys me is wise, like a person who builds a house on solid rock.

²⁵Though the rain comes in torrents and the floodwaters rise and the winds beat against that house, it won't collapse, because it is built on rock. ²⁶But anyone who hears my teaching and ignores it is foolish, like a person who builds a house on sand.

²⁷When the rains and floods come and the winds beat against that house, it will fall with a mighty crash."

²⁸After Jesus finished speaking, the crowds were amazed at his teaching, ²⁹for he taught as one who had real authority—quite unlike the teachers of religious law.

## Jesus Heals a Man with Leprosy

Large crowds followed Jesus as he came down the mountainside.

²Suddenly, a man with leprosy approached Jesus. He knelt before him, worshipping. "Lord," the man said, "if you want to, you can make me well again."

³Jesus touched him. "I want to," he said. "Be healed!" And instantly the leprosy disappeared. ⁴Then Jesus said to him, "Go straight over to the priest and let him examine you. Don't talk to anyone along the way. Take along the offering required in the law of Moses for those who have been healed of leprosy, so everyone will have proof of your healing."

## Faith of the Roman Officer

⁵When Jesus arrived in Capernaum, a Roman officer came and pleaded with him, ⁶"Lord, my young servant lies in bed, paralysed and racked with pain."

⁷Jesus said, "I will come and heal him."

⁸Then the officer said, "Lord, I am not worthy to have you come into my home. Just say the word from where you are, and my servant will be healed! ⁹I know, because I am under the authority of my superior officers and I have authority over my soldiers. I only need to say, 'Go,' and they go, or 'Come,' and they come. And if I say to my slaves, 'Do this or that,' they do it."

¹⁰When Jesus heard this, he was amazed. Turning to the crowd, he said, "I tell you the truth, I haven't seen faith like this in all the land of Israel! ¹¹And I tell you this, that many Gentiles will come from all over the world and sit down with Abraham, Isaac, and Jacob at the feast in the Kingdom of Heaven.

¹²But many Israelites—those for whom the Kingdom was prepared—will be cast into outer darkness, where there will be weeping and gnashing of teeth."

¹³Then Jesus said to the Roman officer, "Go on home. What you have believed has happened." And the young servant was healed that same hour.

## Jesus Heals Many People

¹⁴When Jesus arrived at Peter's house, Peter's mother-in-law was in bed with a high fever. ¹⁵But when Jesus touched her hand, the fever left her. Then she got up and prepared a meal for him.

¹⁶That evening many demon-possessed people were brought to Jesus. All the spirits fled when he commanded them to leave; and he healed all the sick. ¹⁷This fulfilled the word of the Lord through Isaiah, who said, "He took our sicknesses and removed our diseases."

## The Cost of Following Jesus

¹⁸When Jesus noticed how large the crowd was growing, he instructed his disciples to cross to the other side of the lake.

¹⁹Then one of the teachers of religious law said to him, "Teacher, I will follow you no matter where you go!"

²⁰But Jesus said, "Foxes have dens to live in, and birds have nests, but I, the Son of Man, have no home of my own, not even a place to lay my head."

²¹Another of his disciples said, "Lord, first let me return home and bury my father."

²²But Jesus told him, "Follow me now! Let those who are spiritually dead care for their own dead."

## Jesus Calms the Storm

²³Then Jesus got into the boat and started across the lake with his disciples. ²⁴Suddenly, a terrible storm came up, with waves breaking into the boat. But Jesus was sleeping. ²⁵The disciples went to him and woke him up, shouting,

"Lord, save us! We're going to drown!"

²⁶And Jesus answered, "Why are you afraid? You have so little faith!" Then he stood up and rebuked the wind and waves, and suddenly all was calm. ²⁷The disciples just sat there in awe. "Who is this?" they asked themselves. "Even the wind and waves obey him!"

## Jesus Heals Two Demon-Possessed Men

²⁸When Jesus arrived on the other side of the lake in the land of the Gadarenes, two men who were possessed by demons met him. They lived in a cemetery and were so dangerous that no one could go through that area. ²⁹They began screaming at him, "Why are you bothering us, Son of God? You have no right to torture us before God's appointed time!" ³⁰A large herd of pigs was feeding in the distance, ³¹so the demons begged,

"If you cast us out, send us into that herd of pigs."

³²"All right, go!" Jesus commanded them. So the demons came out of the men and entered the pigs, and the whole herd plunged down the steep hillside into the lake and drowned in the water.

³³The herdsmen fled to the nearby city, telling everyone what happened to the demon-possessed men. ³⁴The entire town came out to meet Jesus, but they begged him to go away and leave them alone.

## Jesus Heals a Paralysed Man

Jesus climbed into a boat and went back across the lake to his own town. ²Some people brought to him a

paralysed man on a mat. Seeing their faith, Jesus said to the paralysed man,
"Take heart, my child! Your sins are forgiven."
[3]"Blasphemy! This man talks as if he were God!" some of the teachers of religious law said among themselves. [4]Jesus knew what they were thinking, so he asked them, "Why are you thinking such evil thoughts? [5]Is it easier to say,
'Your sins are forgiven' or 'Get up and walk'?
[6]I will prove that I, the Son of Man, have the authority on earth to forgive sins." Then Jesus turned to the paralysed man and said, "Stand up, take your mat, and go on home, because you are healed!"
[7]And the man jumped up and went home! [8]Fear swept through the crowd as they saw this happen right before their eyes. They praised God for sending a man with such great authority.

## Jesus Calls Matthew

[9]**As Jesus was going down the road, he saw Matthew sitting at his tax-collection booth. "Come, be my disciple," Jesus said to him. So Matthew got up and followed him.**
[10]That night Matthew invited Jesus and his disciples to be his dinner guests, along with his fellow tax collectors and many other notorious sinners. [11]The Pharisees were indignant. "Why does your teacher eat with such scum?" they asked his disciples.
[12]When he heard this, Jesus replied, "Healthy people don't need a doctor—sick people do." [13]Then he added, "Now go and learn the meaning of this Scripture: 'I want you to be merciful; I don't want your sacrifices.' For I have come to call sinners, not those who think they are already good enough."

## A Discussion about Fasting

[14]One day the disciples of John the Baptist came to Jesus and asked him, "Why do we and the Pharisees fast, but your disciples don't fast?"
[15]Jesus responded, "Should the wedding guests mourn while celebrating with the groom? Someday he will

be taken from them, and then they will fast. [16]And who would patch an old garment with unshrunk cloth? For the patch shrinks and pulls away from the old cloth, leaving an even bigger hole than before.
[17]And no one puts new wine into old wineskins. The old skins would burst from the pressure, spilling the wine and ruining the skins. New wine must be stored in new wineskins. That way both the wine and the wineskins are preserved."

## Jesus Heals in Response to Faith

[18]As Jesus was saying this, the leader of a synagogue came and knelt down before him. "My daughter has just died," he said, "but you can bring her back to life again if you just come and lay your hand upon her."
[19]As Jesus and the disciples were going to the official's home, [20]a woman who had had a haemorrhage for twelve years came up behind him. She touched the fringe of his robe, [21]for she thought, "If I can just touch his robe, I will be healed."
[22]Jesus turned around and said to her, "Daughter, be

encouraged! Your faith has made you well." And the woman was healed at that moment.
[23]When Jesus arrived at the official's home, he noticed the noisy crowds and heard the funeral music. [24]He said, "Go away, for the girl isn't dead; she's only asleep." But the crowd laughed at him. [25]When the crowd was finally outside, Jesus went in and took the girl by the hand, and she stood up! [26]The report of this miracle swept through the entire countryside.

## Jesus Heals the Blind and Mute

[27]After Jesus left the girl's home, two blind men followed along behind him, shouting, "Son of David, have mercy on us!"
[28]They went right into the house where he was staying, and Jesus asked them, "Do you believe I can make you see?"
"Yes, Lord," they told him, "we do."
[29]Then he touched their eyes and said, "Because of your faith, it will happen." [30]And suddenly they could see! Jesus sternly warned them, "Don't tell anyone about this."
[31]But instead, they spread his fame all over the region.
[32]When they left, some people brought to him a man who couldn't speak because he was possessed by a demon. [33]So

**I know I am supposed to have peace but I just keep feeling anxious.**
You are definitely not alone on this one! Anxiety is a bell to remind us to pray. Ask God for help and keep asking him. Sometimes it is good to make a list of everything that is making you anxious and pray about each item on the list. Know that God wants what is best for you.

## STAND POINT

**When your performance is poor**

**10:31**

So don't be afraid; you are more valuable to him than a whole flock of sparrows

Jesus cast out the demon, and instantly the man could talk. The crowds marvelled.

"Nothing like this has ever happened in Israel!" they exclaimed.

[34]But the Pharisees said, "He can cast out demons because he is empowered by the prince of demons."

### The Need for Workers

[35]Jesus travelled through all the cities and villages of that area, teaching in the synagogues and announcing the Good News about the Kingdom. And wherever he went, he healed people of every sort of disease and illness. [36]He felt great pity for the crowds that came, because their problems were so great and they didn't know where to go for help. They were like sheep without a shepherd.

[37]He said to his disciples, "The harvest is so great, but the workers are so few. [38]So pray to the Lord who is in charge of the harvest; ask him to send out more workers for his fields."

### Jesus Sends Out the Twelve Apostles

## 10

Jesus called his twelve disciples to him and gave them authority to cast out evil spirits and to heal every kind of disease and illness. [2]Here are the names of the twelve apostles:

first Simon (also called Peter), then Andrew (Peter's brother), James (son of Zebedee), John (James's brother),

[3]Philip, Bartholomew, Thomas, Matthew (the tax collector),

James (son of Alphaeus), Thaddaeus, [4]Simon (the Zealot),

Judas Iscariot (who later betrayed him).

[5]Jesus sent the twelve disciples out with these instructions: "Don't go to the Gentiles or the Samaritans, [6]but only to the people of Israel—God's lost sheep. [7]Go and announce to them that the Kingdom of Heaven is near. [8]Heal the sick, raise the dead, cure those with leprosy, and cast out demons. Give as freely as you have received!

[9]"Don't take any money with you.

[10]Don't carry a traveller's bag with an extra coat and sandals or even a walking stick. Don't hesitate to accept hospitality, because those who work deserve to be fed. [11]Whenever you enter a city or village, search for a worthy man and stay in his home until you leave for the next town. [12]When you are invited into someone's home, give it your blessing. [13]If it turns out to be a worthy home, let your blessing stand; if it is not, take back the blessing. [14]If a village doesn't welcome you or listen to you, shake off the dust of that place from your feet as you leave. [15]I assure you, the wicked cities of Sodom and Gomorrah will be better off on the judgement day than that place will be.

[16]"Look, I am sending you out as sheep among wolves. Be as wary as snakes and harmless as doves. [17]But beware! For you will be handed over to the courts and beaten in the synagogues.

[18]And you must stand trial before governors and kings because you are my followers. This will be your opportunity to tell them about me—yes, to witness to the world. [19]When you are arrested, don't worry about what to say in your defence, because you will be given the right words at the right time. [20]For it won't be you doing the talking—it will be the Spirit of your Father speaking through you.

[21]Brother will betray brother to death, fathers will betray their own children, and children will rise against their parents and cause them to be killed. [22]And everyone will hate you because of your allegiance to me. But those who endure to the end will be saved. [23]When you are persecuted in one town, flee to the next. I assure you that I, the Son of Man, will return before you have reached all the towns of Israel.

[24]"A student is not greater than the teacher. A servant is not greater than the master. [25]The student shares the teacher's fate. The servant shares the master's fate. And since I, the master of the household, have been called the prince of demons, how much more will it happen to you, the members of the household! [26]But don't be afraid of those who threaten you. For the time is coming when everything will be revealed; all that is secret will be made public. [27]What I tell you now in the darkness, shout abroad when daybreak comes. What I whisper in your ears, shout from the housetops for all to hear!

[28]"**Don't be afraid of those who want to kill you. They can only kill your body; they cannot touch your soul. Fear only God, who can destroy both soul and body in hell.** [29]Not even a sparrow, worth only half a penny, can fall to the ground without your Father knowing it. [30]And the very hairs on your head are all numbered. [31]So don't be afraid; you are more valuable to him than a whole flock of sparrows.

[32]"If anyone acknowledges me publicly here on earth, I will openly acknowledge that person before my Father in heaven. [33]But if anyone denies me here on

## Winners walk the talk!

Why is it, we can painstakingly live out our faith in every aspect of our life, then completely ignore Christ in our sport? If we do not 'practise what we preach,' - the character and qualities of Christ working in us - then we slash the throat of our gospel message. We must live it on the pitch, in the locker rooms and on the road. The best way to teach a concept is to model it. Make sport your mission! "In the same way, encourage the young men to live wisely in all they do. And you yourself must be an example to them by doing good deeds of every kind." Titus 2:6-7a

Winners - live it!

earth, I will deny that person before my Father in heaven.

34"Don't imagine that I came to bring peace to the earth! No, I came to bring a sword. 35I have come to set a man against his father, and a daughter against her mother, and a daughter-in-law against her mother-in-law. 36Your enemies will be right in your own household! 37If you love your father or mother more than you love me, you are not worthy of being mine; or if you love your son or daughter more than me, you are not worthy of being mine.

38If you refuse to take up your cross and follow me, you are not worthy of being mine. 39If you cling to your life, you will lose it; but if you give it up for me, you will find it.

40"Anyone who welcomes you is welcoming me, and anyone who welcomes me is welcoming the Father who sent me. 41If you welcome a prophet as one who speaks for God, you will receive the same reward a prophet gets. And if you welcome good and godly people because of their godliness, you will be given a reward like theirs.

42And if you give even a cup of cold water to one of the least of my followers, you will surely be rewarded."

**CH 10:40-42 WHAT'S IT SAYING?**

**WHAT AM I GOING TO DO ABOUT IT?**

# WHAT DOES IT MEAN?

'Unpardonable sin'
Jesus assures us that all our sins can be forgiven, even blasphemy (to speak irreverently and disrespectfully about or to God), except the deliberate refusal to acknowledge God's power, the Holy Spirit, in Christ. Many people have been worried that they have accidentally committed the 'unpardonable sin'. The very fact of being concerned about committing the 'unpardonable sin', the blaspheming of the Holy Spirit, would suggest they haven't. To blaspheme is to wilfully know God's truth and to speak or attribute the action of the Holy Spirit to Satan, not to speak out of ignorance or unbelief.

## Jesus and John the Baptist

# 11

When Jesus had finished giving these instructions to his twelve disciples, he went off teaching and preaching in towns throughout the country.

2John the Baptist, who was now in prison, heard about all the things the Messiah was doing. So he sent his disciples to ask Jesus, 3"Are you really the Messiah we've been waiting for, or should we keep looking for someone else?"

4Jesus told them, "Go back to John and tell him about what you have heard and seen—5the blind see, the lame walk, the lepers are cured, the deaf hear, the dead are raised to life, and the Good News is being preached to the poor. 6And tell him: 'God blesses those who are not offended by me.'"

7When John's disciples had gone, Jesus began talking about him to the crowds. "Who is this man in the wilderness that you went out to see? Did you find him weak as a reed, moved by every breath of wind? 8Or were you expecting to see a man dressed in expensive clothes? Those who dress like that live in palaces, not out in the wilderness. 9Were you looking for a prophet? Yes, and he is more than a prophet. 10John is the man to whom the Scriptures refer when they say,

'Look, I am sending my messenger before you,
and he will prepare your way before you.'

11"I assure you, of all who have ever lived, none is greater than John the Baptist. Yet even the most insignificant person in the Kingdom of Heaven is greater than he is! 12And from the time John the Baptist began preaching and baptizing until now, the Kingdom of Heaven has been forcefully advancing, and violent people attack it. 13For before John came, all the teachings of the Scriptures looked forward to this present time. 14And if you are willing to accept what I say, he is Elijah, the one the prophets said would come. 15Anyone who is willing to hear should listen and understand! 16How shall I describe this generation? These people are like a group of children playing a game in the public square. They complain to their friends, 17'We played wedding songs, and you weren't happy, so we played funeral songs, but you weren't sad.' 18For John the Baptist didn't drink wine and he often fasted, and you say, 'He's demon possessed.' 19And I, the Son of Man, feast and drink, and you say, 'He's a glutton and a drunkard, and a friend of the worst sort of sinners!' But wisdom is shown to be right by what results from it."

## Judgement for the Unbelievers

20Then Jesus began to denounce the cities where he had done most of his miracles, because they hadn't turned from their sins and turned to God. 21"What horrors await you, Korazin and Bethsaida! For if the miracles I did in you had been done in wicked Tyre and Sidon, their people would have sat in deep repentance long ago, clothed in sackcloth and throwing ashes on their heads to show their remorse. 22I assure you, Tyre and Sidon will be better off on the judgement day than you! 23And you people of Capernaum, will you be exalted to heaven? No, you will be brought down to the place of the dead. For if the miracles I did for you had been done in Sodom, it would still be here today. ²⁴I assure you, Sodom will be better off on the judgement day than you."

## Jesus' Prayer of Thanksgiving

²⁵Then Jesus prayed this prayer: "O Father, Lord of heaven and earth, thank you for hiding the truth from those who think themselves so wise and clever, and for revealing it to the childlike. ²⁶Yes, Father, it pleased you to do it this way! ²⁷"My Father has given me authority over everything. No one really knows the Son except the Father, and no one really knows the Father except the Son and those to whom the Son chooses to reveal him."

²⁸**Then Jesus said, "Come to me, all of you who are weary and carry heavy burdens, and I will give you rest.** ²⁹Take my yoke upon you. Let me teach you, because I am humble and gentle, and you will find rest for your souls. ³⁰For my yoke fits perfectly, and the burden I give you is light."

## Controversy about the Sabbath

# 12

At about that time Jesus was walking through some cornfields on the Sabbath. His disciples were hungry, so they began breaking off heads of wheat and eating the grain. ²Some Pharisees saw them do it and protested, "Your disciples shouldn't be doing that! It's against the law to work by harvesting corn on the Sabbath."

³But Jesus said to them, "Haven't you ever read in the Scriptures what King David did when he and his companions

## When you need to keep your cool

### 12:28-30

But if I am casting out demons by the Spirit of God, then the Kingdom of God has arrived among you. Let me illustrate this. You can't enter a strong man's house and rob him without first tying up. Only then can his house be robbed!' ³⁰Anyone who isn't helping me opposes me, and anyone who isn't working with me is actually working against me

were hungry? ⁴He went into the house of God, and they ate the special bread reserved for the priests alone. That was breaking the law, too. ⁵And haven't you ever read in the law of Moses that the priests on duty in the Temple may work on the Sabbath? ⁶I tell you, there is one here who is even greater than the Temple! ⁷But you would not have condemned those who aren't guilty if you knew the meaning of this Scripture:

'I want you to be merciful; I don't want your sacrifices.' ⁸For I, the Son of Man, am master even of the Sabbath." ⁹Then he went over to the synagogue, ¹⁰where he noticed a man with a deformed hand. The Pharisees asked Jesus,

"Is it legal to work by healing on the Sabbath day?" (They were, of course, hoping he would say yes, so they could bring charges against him.)

¹¹**And he answered, "If you had one sheep, and it fell into a well on the Sabbath, wouldn't you get to work and pull it out? Of course you would.** ¹²And how much more valuable is a person than a sheep! Yes, it is right to do good on the Sabbath."

¹³Then he said to the man, "Reach out your hand." The man reached out his hand, and it became normal, just like the other one. ¹⁴Then the Pharisees called a meeting and discussed plans for killing Jesus.

## Jesus, God's Chosen Servant

¹⁵But Jesus knew what they were planning. He left that area, and many people followed him. He healed all the sick among them, ¹⁶but he warned them not to say who he was. ¹⁷This fulfilled the prophecy of Isaiah concerning him:

¹⁸"Look at my Servant,
whom I have chosen.
He is my Beloved,

and I am very pleased with him.
I will put my Spirit upon him,
and he will proclaim justice to the nations.
¹⁹He will not fight or shout;
he will not raise his voice in public.
²⁰He will not crush those who are weak,
or quench the smallest hope,
until he brings full justice with his final victory.
²¹And his name will be the hope
of all the world."

## Jesus and the Prince of Demons

²²Then a demon-possessed man, who was both blind and unable to talk, was brought to Jesus. He healed the man so that he could both speak and see. ²³The crowd was amazed.

"Could it be that Jesus is the Son of David, the Messiah?" they wondered out loud.

²⁴But when the Pharisees heard about the miracle, they said,

"No wonder he can cast out demons. He gets his power from Satan, the prince of demons."

²⁵Jesus knew their thoughts and replied, "Any kingdom at war with itself is doomed. A city or home divided against itself is doomed. ²⁶And if Satan is casting out Satan, he is fighting against himself. His own kingdom will not survive. ²⁷And if I am empowered by the prince of demons, what about your own followers? They cast out demons, too, so they will judge you for what you have said. ²⁸But if I am casting out demons by the Spirit of God, then the Kingdom of God has arrived among you. ²⁹Let me illustrate this. You can't enter a strong man's house and rob him without first tying him up. Only then can his house be robbed! ³⁰Anyone who isn't helping me opposes me, and anyone who isn't working with me is actually working against me. ³¹"Every sin or blasphemy can be forgiven—except blasphemy against the Holy Spirit, which can never be forgiven. ³²Anyone who blasphemes against me, the Son of Man, can be forgiven, but blasphemy against the Holy Spirit will never be forgiven, either in this world or in the world to come.

³³"A tree is identified by its fruit. Make a tree good, and its fruit will be good. Make a tree bad, and its fruit will be bad. ³⁴You brood of snakes! How could evil men like you speak what is good and right? For whatever is in your heart determines what you say. ³⁵A good person produces good words from a good heart, and an evil person produces evil words from an evil heart. ³⁶And I tell you this, that you must give an account on judgement day of every idle word you

speak. [37]The words you say now reflect your fate then; either you will be justified by them or you will be condemned."

## The Sign of Jonah

[38]One day some teachers of religious law and Pharisees came to Jesus and said, "Teacher, we want you to show us a miraculous sign to prove that you are from God."

[39]But Jesus replied, "Only an evil, faithless generation would ask for a miraculous sign; but the only sign I will give them is the sign of the prophet Jonah. [40]For as Jonah was in the belly of the great fish for three days and three nights, so I, the Son of Man, will be in the heart of the earth for three days and three nights. [41]The people of Nineveh will rise up against this generation on judgement day and condemn it, because they repented at the preaching of Jonah. And now someone greater than Jonah is here—and you refuse to repent. [42]The queen of Sheba will also rise up against this generation on judgement day and condemn it, because she came from a distant land to hear the wisdom of Solomon. And now someone greater than Solomon is here—and you refuse to listen to him.

[43]"When an evil spirit leaves a person, it goes into the desert, seeking rest but finding none. [44]Then it says, 'I will return to the person I came from.' So it returns and finds its former home empty, swept, and clean. [45]Then the spirit finds seven other spirits more evil than itself, and they all enter the person and live there. And so that person is worse off than before. That will be the experience of this evil generation."

## The True Family of Jesus

[46]As Jesus was speaking to the crowd, his mother and brothers were outside, wanting to talk with him. [47]Someone told Jesus, "Your mother and your brothers are outside, and they want to speak to you."

[48]Jesus asked, "Who is my mother? Who are my brothers?" [49]Then he pointed to his disciples and said, "These are my mother and brothers. [50]**Anyone who does the will of my Father in heaven is my brother and sister and mother!**"

## Story of the Farmer Scattering Seed

# 13

Later that same day, Jesus left the house and went down to the shore, [2]where an immense crowd soon gathered. He got into a boat, where he sat and taught as the people listened on the shore. [3]He told many stories such as this one:

"A farmer went out to plant some seed. [4]As he scattered it across his field, some seeds fell on a footpath, and the birds came and ate them. [5]Other seeds fell on shallow soil with underlying rock. The plants sprang up quickly, [6]but they soon wilted beneath the hot sun and died because the roots had no nourishment in the shallow soil. [7]Other seeds fell among thorns that shot up and choked out the tender blades. [8]But some seeds fell on fertile soil and produced a crop that was thirty, sixty, and even a hundred times as much as had been planted. [9]Anyone who is willing to hear should listen and understand!"

[10]His disciples came and asked him, "Why do you always tell stories when you talk to the people?"

[11]Then he explained to them, "You have been permitted to understand the secrets of the Kingdom of Heaven, but others have not. [12]To those who are open to my teaching, more understanding will be given, and they will have an abundance of knowledge. But to those who are not listening, even what they have will be taken away from them. [13]That is why I tell these stories, because people see what I do, but they don't really see. They hear what I say, but they don't really hear, and they don't understand. [14]This fulfils the prophecy of Isaiah, which says:

'You will hear my words,
but you will not understand;
you will see what I do,
but you will not perceive its meaning.
[15]For the hearts of these people are hardened,
and their ears cannot hear,
and they have closed their eyes—
so their eyes cannot see,
and their ears cannot hear,
and their hearts cannot understand,
and they cannot turn to me
and let me heal them.'

[16]"But blessed are your eyes, because they see; and your ears, because they hear. [17]I assure you, many prophets and godly people have longed to see and hear what you have seen and heard, but they could not.

[18]"Now here is the explanation of the story I told about the farmer sowing grain: [19]The seed that fell on the hard path represents those who hear the Good News about the Kingdom and don't understand it. Then the evil one comes and snatches the seed away from their hearts. [20]The rocky soil represents those who hear the message and receive it with joy. [21]But like young plants in such soil, their roots don't go very deep. At first they get along fine, but they wilt as soon as they have problems or are persecuted because they believe the word. [22]The thorny ground represents those who hear and accept the Good News, but all too quickly the message is crowded out by the cares of this life and the lure of wealth, so no crop is produced. [23]The good soil represents the hearts of those who truly accept God's message and produce a huge harvest—thirty, sixty, or even a hundred times as much as had been planted."

## Story of the Wheat and Weeds

[24]Here is another story Jesus told: "The Kingdom of Heaven is like a farmer who planted good seed in his field. [25]But that night as everyone slept, his enemy came and planted weeds among the wheat. [26]When the crop began to grow and produce grain, the weeds also grew. [27]The farmer's servants came and told him, 'Sir, the field where you planted that good seed is full of weeds!'

[28]"'An enemy has done it!' the farmer exclaimed.

"'Shall we pull out the weeds?' they asked.

[29]"He replied, 'No, you'll hurt the wheat if you do. [30]Let both grow together until the harvest. Then I will tell the harvesters to sort out the weeds and burn them and to put the wheat in the barn.'"

## Illustration of the Mustard Seed

[31]Here is another illustration Jesus used: "The Kingdom of Heaven is like a mustard seed planted in a field. [32]It is the smallest of all seeds, but it becomes the largest of garden plants and grows into a tree where birds can come and find shelter in its branches."

## Illustration of the Yeast

[33]Jesus also used this illustration: "The Kingdom of Heaven is like yeast used by a woman making bread.

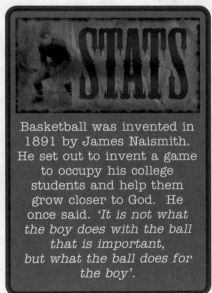

STATS

Basketball was invented in 1891 by James Naismith. He set out to invent a game to occupy his college students and help them grow closer to God. He once said, *'It is not what the boy does with the ball that is important, but what the ball does for the boy'.*

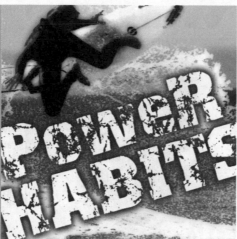

Keep Your focus positive! Think about people or things that are truthful and good and try to do things the right way. When in doubt, think about the life of Jesus. "Fix your thoughts on what is true and honourable and right. Think about things that are pure and lovely and admirable. Think about things that are excellent and worthy of praise."

Philippians 4:8

Even though she used a large amount of flour, the yeast permeated every part of the dough."

³⁴Jesus always used stories and illustrations like these when speaking to the crowds. In fact, he never spoke to them without using such parables. ³⁵This fulfilled the prophecy that said,

"I will speak to you in parables.
I will explain mysteries hidden since the creation of the world."

## The Wheat and Weeds Explained

³⁶Then, leaving the crowds outside, Jesus went into the house. His disciples said, "Please explain the story of the weeds in the field."

³⁷"All right," he said. "I, the Son of Man, am the farmer who plants the good seed. ³⁸The field is the world, and the good seed represents the people of the Kingdom. The weeds are the people who belong to the evil one. ³⁹The enemy who planted the weeds among the wheat is the Devil. The harvest is the end of the world, and the harvesters are the angels.

⁴⁰"Just as the weeds are separated out and burned, so it will be at the end of the world. ⁴¹I, the Son of Man, will send my angels, and they will remove from my Kingdom everything that causes sin and all who do evil, ⁴²and they will throw them into the furnace and burn them. There will be weeping and gnashing of teeth. ⁴³Then the godly will shine like the sun in their Father's Kingdom. Anyone who is willing to hear should listen and understand!

## Illustration of the Hidden Treasure

⁴⁴"The Kingdom of Heaven is like a treasure that a man discovered hidden in a field. In his excitement, he hid it again and sold everything he owned to get enough money to buy the field—and to get the treasure, too!

CH 13:44-45 WHAT'S IT SAYING?

WHAT AM I GOING TO DO ABOUT IT?

## Illustration of the Pearl Merchant

⁴⁵"Again, the Kingdom of Heaven is like a pearl merchant on the lookout for choice pearls. ⁴⁶When he discovered a pearl of great value, he sold everything he owned and bought it!

## Illustration of the Fishing Net

⁴⁷"Again, the Kingdom of Heaven is like a fishing net that is thrown into the water and gathers fish of every kind. ⁴⁸When the net is full, they drag it up onto the shore, sit down, sort the good fish into crates, and throw the bad ones away.

⁴⁹That is the way it will be at the end of the world. The angels will come and separate the wicked people from the godly, ⁵⁰throwing the wicked into the fire. There will be weeping and gnashing of teeth.

⁵¹Do you understand?"

"Yes," they said, "we do."

⁵²Then he added, "Every teacher of religious law who has become a disciple in the Kingdom of Heaven is like a person who brings out of the storehouse the new teachings as well as the old."

## Jesus Rejected at Nazareth

⁵³When Jesus had finished telling these stories, he left that part of the country. ⁵⁴He returned to Nazareth, his home town. When he taught there in the synagogue, everyone was astonished and said, "Where does he get his wisdom and his miracles? ⁵⁵He's just a carpenter's son, and we know Mary, his mother, and his brothers—James, Joseph, Simon, and Judas. ⁵⁶All his sisters live right here among us. What makes him so great?" ⁵⁷And they were deeply offended and refused to believe in him.

Then Jesus told them, "A prophet is honoured everywhere except in his own home town and among his own family." ⁵⁸And so he did only a few miracles there because of their unbelief.

## The Death of John the Baptist

# 14

When Herod Antipas heard about Jesus, ²he said to his advisers, "This must be John the Baptist come back to life again! That is why he can do such miracles." ³For Herod had arrested and imprisoned John as a favour to his wife Herodias (the former wife of Herod's brother Philip). ⁴John kept telling Herod, "It is illegal for you to marry her." ⁵Herod would have executed John, but he was afraid of a riot, because all the people believed John was a prophet.

⁶But at a birthday party for Herod, Herodias's daughter performed a dance that greatly pleased him, ⁷so he promised with an oath to give her anything she wanted. ⁸At her mother's urging, the girl asked, "I want the head of John the Baptist on a tray!" ⁹The king was sorry, but because of his oath and because he didn't want to back down in front of his guests, he issued the necessary orders. ¹⁰So John was

beheaded in the prison, [11]and his head was brought on a tray and given to the girl, who took it to her mother. [12]John's disciples came for his body and buried it. Then they told Jesus what had happened.

## Jesus Feeds Five Thousand

[13]As soon as Jesus heard the news, he went off by himself in a boat to a remote area to be alone. But the crowds heard where he was heading and followed by land from many villages.

[14]A vast crowd was there as he stepped from the boat, and he had compassion on them and healed their sick.

[15]That evening the disciples came to him and said, "This is a desolate place, and it is getting late. Send the crowds away so they can go to the villages and buy food for themselves."

[16]But Jesus replied, "That isn't necessary - you feed them."

[17]"Impossible!" they exclaimed. "We have only five loaves of bread and two fish!"

[18]"Bring them here," he said. [19]Then he told the people to sit down on the grass. And he took the five loaves and two fish, looked up towards heaven, and asked God's blessing on the food. Breaking the loaves into pieces, he gave some of the bread and fish to each disciple, and the disciples gave them to the people. [20]They all ate as much as they wanted, and they picked up twelve baskets of leftovers. [21]About five thousand men had eaten from those five loaves, in addition to all the women and children!

## Jesus Walks on Water

[22]Immediately after this, Jesus made his disciples get back into the boat and cross to the other side of the lake while he sent the people home. [23]Afterwards he went up into the hills by himself to pray. Night fell while he was there alone. [24]Meanwhile, the disciples were in trouble far away from land, for a strong wind had risen, and they were fighting heavy waves.

[25]About three o'clock in the morning Jesus came to them, walking on the water. [26]When the disciples saw him, they screamed in terror, thinking he was a ghost. [27]But Jesus spoke to them at once. "It's all right," he said. "I am here! Don't be afraid."

[28]Then Peter called to him, "Lord, if it's really you, tell me to come to you by walking on the water."

[29]"All right, come," Jesus said.

So Peter went over the side of the boat and walked on the water towards Jesus. [30]But when he looked around at the high waves, he was terrified and began to sink. "Save me, Lord!" he shouted.

[31]Instantly Jesus reached out his hand and grabbed him. "You don't have much faith," Jesus said. "Why did you doubt me?" [32]And when they climbed back into the boat, the wind stopped.

What does it mean to be **'salt and light?'** Jesus is giving us a very positive action-oriented challenge in the word picture of salt and light. These are two things we may take for granted but in Jesus' day they were really valuable and harder to come by. Salt was used to keep food from rotting and bring out its flavour. And light obviously helps us see and keeps us safely on the right path. Much the same as we Christians are to have a positive influence in the world around us and impede the evil that rots God's creation. Also, we are to be proactive in shedding light on God's plan, which illuminates the path which God has desired the world to travel.

[33]Then the disciples worshipped him. "You really are the Son of God!" they exclaimed.

[34]After they had crossed the lake, they landed at Gennesaret.

[35]The news of their arrival spread quickly throughout the whole surrounding area, and soon people were bringing all their sick to be healed. [36]The sick begged

him to let them touch even the fringe of his robe, and all who touched it were healed.

## Jesus Teaches about Inner Purity

# 15

Some Pharisees and teachers of religious law now arrived from Jerusalem to interview Jesus. [2]"Why do your disciples disobey our age-old traditions?" they demanded. "They ignore our tradition of ceremonial hand washing before they eat."

[3]Jesus replied, "And why do you, by your traditions, violate the direct commandments of God? [4]For instance, God says, 'Honour your father and mother,' and 'Anyone who speaks evil of father or mother must be put to death.'

[5]But you say, 'You don't need to honour your parents by caring for their needs if you give the money to God instead.'

[6]And so, by your own tradition, you nullify the direct commandment of God. [7]You hypocrites! Isaiah was prophesying about you when he said,

[8]'These people honour me with their lips,
but their hearts are far away.

[9]Their worship is a farce,
for they replace God's commands with their own man-made teachings.'"

[10]Then Jesus called to the crowds and said, "Listen to what I say and try to understand. [11]You are not defiled by what you eat; you are defiled by what you say and do."

[12]Then the disciples came to him and asked, "Do you realize you offended the Pharisees by what you just said?"

[13]Jesus replied, "Every plant not planted by my heavenly Father will be rooted up, [14]so ignore them. They are blind guides leading the blind, and if one blind person guides another, they will both fall into a ditch."

[15]Then Peter asked Jesus, "Explain what you meant when you said people aren't defiled by what they eat."

[16]"Don't you understand?" Jesus asked him. [17]**"Anything you eat passes through the stomach and then goes out of the body. [18]But evil words come from an evil heart and defile the person who says them.** [19]For from the heart come evil thoughts, murder, adultery, all other sexual immorality, theft, lying, and slander. [20]These are what defile you. Eating with unwashed hands could never defile you and make you unacceptable to God.

## Bible

There are 30,442 verses—about 845,000 words—in the English Bible.

**action**

**CH 15:1-20 WHAT'S IT SAYING?**

**WHAT AM I GOING TO DO ABOUT IT?**

### The Faith of a Gentile Woman

²¹Jesus then left Galilee and went north to the region of Tyre and Sidon. ²²A Gentile woman who lived there came to him, pleading, "Have mercy on me, O Lord, Son of David! For my daughter has a demon in her, and it is severely tormenting her."

²³But Jesus gave her no reply—not even a word. Then his disciples urged him to send her away. "Tell her to leave," they said. "She is bothering us with all her begging."

²⁴Then he said to the woman, "I was sent only to help the people of Israel—God's lost sheep—not the Gentiles."

²⁵But she came and worshipped him and pleaded again, "Lord, help me!"

²⁶"It isn't right to take food from the children and throw it to the dogs," he said.

²⁷"Yes, Lord," she replied, "but even dogs are permitted to eat crumbs that fall beneath their master's table."

²⁸**"Woman," Jesus said to her, "your faith is great. Your request is granted."** And her daughter was instantly healed.

### Jesus Heals Many People

²⁹Jesus returned to the Sea of Galilee and climbed a hill and sat down. ³⁰A vast crowd brought him the lame, blind, crippled, mute, and many others with physical difficulties, and they laid them before Jesus. And he healed them all. ³¹The crowd was amazed! Those who hadn't been able to speak were talking, the crippled were made well, the lame were walking around, and those who had been blind could see again! And they praised the God of Israel.

### Jesus Feeds Four Thousand

³²Then Jesus called his disciples to him and said, "I feel sorry for these people. They have been here with me for three days, and they have nothing left to eat. I don't want to send them away hungry, or they will faint along the road."

³³The disciples replied, "And where would we get enough food out here in the wilderness for all of them to eat?"

³⁴Jesus asked, "How many loaves of bread do you have?"

They replied, "Seven, and a few small fish." ³⁵So Jesus told all the people to sit down on the ground. ³⁶Then he took the seven loaves and the fish, thanked God for them, broke them into pieces, and gave them to the disciples, who distributed the food to the crowd. ³⁷They all ate until they were full, and when the scraps were picked up, there were seven large baskets of food left over! ³⁸There were four thousand men who were fed that day, in addition to all the women and children. ³⁹Then Jesus sent the people home, and he got into a boat and crossed over to the region of Magadan.

### Leaders Demand a Miraculous Sign

# 16

One day the Pharisees and Sadducees came to test Jesus' claims by asking him to show them a miraculous sign from heaven.

²He replied, "You know the saying, 'Red sky at night means fair weather tomorrow, ³red sky in the morning means foul weather all day.' You are good at reading the weather signs in the sky, but you can't read the obvious signs of the times! ⁴Only an evil, faithless generation would ask for a miraculous sign, but the only sign I will give them is the sign of the prophet Jonah." Then Jesus left them and went away.

### Yeast of the Pharisees and Sadducees

⁵Later, after they crossed to the other side of the lake, the disciples discovered they had forgotten to bring any food. ⁶"Watch out!" Jesus warned them. "Beware of the yeast of the Pharisees and Sadducees."

⁷They decided he was saying this because they hadn't brought any bread. ⁸Jesus knew what they were thinking, so he said, "You have so little faith! Why are you worried about having no food? ⁹Won't you ever understand? Don't you remember the five thousand I fed with five loaves, and the baskets of food that were left over? ¹⁰Don't you remember the four thousand I fed with seven loaves, with baskets of food left over?

¹¹How could you even think I was talking about food? So again I say, 'Beware of the yeast of the Pharisees and Sadducees.'"

¹²Then at last they understood that he wasn't speaking about yeast or bread but about the false teaching of the Pharisees and Sadducees.

### Peter's Declaration about Jesus

¹³When Jesus came to the region of Caesarea Philippi, he asked his disciples, "Who do people say that the Son of Man is?"

¹⁴"Well," they replied, "some say John the Baptist, some say Elijah, and others say Jeremiah or one of the other prophets." ¹⁵Then he asked them, "Who do you say I am?"

¹⁶**Simon Peter answered, "You are the Messiah, the Son of the living God."**

¹⁷Jesus replied, "You are blessed, Simon son of John, because my Father in heaven has revealed this to you. You did not learn this from any human being. ¹⁸Now I say to you that

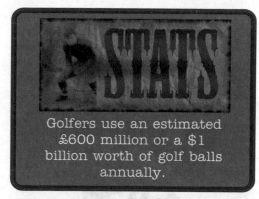

Golfers use an estimated £600 million or a $1 billion worth of golf balls annually.

you are Peter, and upon this rock I will build my church, and all the powers of hell will not conquer it. ¹⁹And I will give you the keys of the Kingdom of Heaven. Whatever you lock on earth will be locked in heaven, and whatever you open on earth will be opened in heaven." ²⁰Then he sternly warned them not to tell anyone that he was the Messiah.*

**action**

CH 16:24-28 WHAT'S IT SAYING?

WHAT AM I GOING TO DO ABOUT IT?

## Jesus Predicts His Death

²¹From then on Jesus began to tell his disciples plainly that he had to go to Jerusalem, and he told them what would happen to him there. He would suffer at the hands of the leaders and the leading priests and the teachers of religious law. He would be killed, and he would be raised on the third day.

²²But Peter took him aside and began to reprimand him. "Heaven forbid, Lord," he said. "This will never happen to you!"

²³**Jesus turned to Peter and said, "Get away from me, Satan! You are a dangerous trap to me. You are seeing things merely from a human point of view, and not from God's."**

²⁴Then Jesus said to the disciples, "If any of you wants to be my follower, you must put aside your selfish ambition, shoulder your cross, and follow me. ²⁵If you try to keep your life for yourself, you will lose it. But if you give up your life for me, you will find true life. ²⁶And how do you benefit if you gain the whole world but lose your own soul in the process? Is anything worth more than your soul? ²⁷For I, the Son of Man, will come in the glory of my Father with his angels and will judge all people according to their deeds. ²⁸And I assure you that some of you standing here right now will not die before you see me, the Son of Man, coming in my Kingdom."

## The Transfiguration

# 17

Six days later Jesus took Peter and the two brothers, James and John, and led them up a high mountain. ²As the men watched, Jesus' appearance changed so that his face shone like the sun, and his clothing became dazzling white. ³Suddenly, Moses and Elijah appeared and began talking with Jesus. ⁴Peter blurted out, "Lord, this is wonderful! If you want me to, I'll make three shrines, one for you, one for Moses, and one for Elijah."

⁵But even as he said it, a bright cloud came over them, and a voice from the cloud said, "This is my beloved Son, and I am fully pleased with him. Listen to him." ⁶The disciples were terrified and fell face down on the ground.

⁷Jesus came over and touched them. "Get up," he said, "don't be afraid." ⁸And when they looked, they saw only Jesus with them. ⁹As they descended the mountain, Jesus commanded them, "Don't tell anyone what you have seen until I, the Son of Man, have been raised from the dead."

¹⁰His disciples asked, "Why do the teachers of religious law insist that Elijah must return before the Messiah comes?"

¹¹Jesus replied, "Elijah is indeed coming first to set everything in order. ¹²But I tell you, he has already come, but he wasn't recognized, and he was badly mistreated. And soon the Son of Man will also suffer at their hands." ¹³Then the disciples realized he had been speaking of John the Baptist.

## Jesus Heals a Demon-Possessed Boy

¹⁴When they arrived at the foot of the mountain, a huge crowd was waiting for them. A man came and knelt before Jesus and said, ¹⁵"Lord, have mercy on my son, because he has seizures and suffers terribly. He often falls into the fire or into the water. ¹⁶So I brought him to your disciples, but they couldn't heal him."

¹⁷Jesus replied, "You stubborn, faithless people! How long must I be with you until you believe? How long must I put up with you? Bring the boy to me." ¹⁸Then Jesus rebuked the demon in the boy, and it left him. From that moment the boy was well.

¹⁹Afterwards the disciples asked Jesus privately, "Why couldn't we cast out that demon?"

²⁰"You didn't have enough faith," Jesus told them. "I assure you, even if you had faith as small as a mustard seed you could say to this mountain, 'Move from here to there,' and it would move. Nothing would be impossible."

## Jesus Again Predicts His Death

²²One day after they had returned to Galilee, Jesus told them, "The Son of Man is going to be betrayed. ²³He will be killed, but three days later he will be raised from the dead." And the disciples' hearts were filled with grief.

## Payment of the Temple Tax

²⁴On their arrival in Capernaum, the tax collectors for the Temple tax came to Peter and asked him, "Doesn't your teacher pay the Temple tax?"

²⁵"Of course he does," Peter replied. Then he went into the house to talk to Jesus about it.

But before he had a chance to speak, Jesus asked him, "What do you think, Peter? Do kings tax their own people or the foreigners they have conquered?" ²⁶"They tax the foreigners," Peter replied.

"Well, then," Jesus said, "the citizens are free! ²⁷However, we don't want to offend them, so go down to the lake and throw in a line. Open the mouth of the first fish you catch, and you will find a coin. Take the coin and pay the tax for both of us."

## The Greatest in the Kingdom

# 18

About that time the disciples came to Jesus and asked, "Which of us is greatest in the Kingdom of Heaven?" ²Jesus called a small child over to him and put the child among them. ³Then he said, "I assure you, unless you turn from your sins and become as little children, you will never get into the Kingdom of Heaven. ⁴Therefore, anyone who becomes as humble as this little child is the greatest in the Kingdom of Heaven. ⁵And anyone who welcomes a little child like this on

17:20 Some manuscripts add verse 21, *But this kind of demon won't leave except by prayer and fasting.* Compare Mark 9:29.

## Over-training:

'The more you work out, the stronger & fitter you will get.' No! No! No! This is one of the most damaging myths that ever reared its ugly head. Most professionals will admit that at some time they made this mistake. When you train your body needs rest to allow it to regenerate. In order to maximise a training week a lot of athletes will plan their training programme so that they focus on different muscle groups on alternate days (i.e. Monday – focus on lower body, Tuesday – focus on upper body). It is important to note that while this allows an athlete to train every day, one complete day should be given over to relaxation to allow the body to recover.

my behalf is welcoming me. **⁶But if anyone causes one of these little ones who trusts in me to lose faith, it would be better for that person to be thrown into the sea with a large millstone tied around the neck.**

⁷"How terrible it will be for anyone who causes others to sin. Temptation to do wrong is inevitable, but how terrible it will be for the person who does the tempting. ⁸So if your hand or foot causes you to sin, cut it off and throw it away. It is better to enter heaven crippled or lame than to be thrown into the unquenchable fire with both of your hands and feet. ⁹And if your eye causes you to sin, gouge it out and throw it away. It is better to enter heaven half blind than to have two eyes and be thrown into hell.

¹⁰"Beware that you don't despise a single one of these little ones. For I tell you that in heaven their angels are always in the presence of my heavenly Father."

### Story of the Lost Sheep

¹²"If a shepherd has a hundred sheep, and one wanders away and is lost, what will he do? Won't he leave the ninety-nine others and go out into the hills to search for the lost one? ¹³And if he finds it, he will surely rejoice over it more than over the ninety-nine that didn't wander away!

¹⁴In the same way, it is not my heavenly Father's will that even one of these little ones should perish.

### Correcting a Fellow Believer

¹⁵"If another believer sins against you, go privately and point out the fault. If the other person listens and confesses it, you have won that person back. ¹⁶But if you are unsuccessful, take one or two others with you and go back again, so that everything you say may be confirmed by two or three witnesses. ¹⁷If that person still refuses to listen, take your case

to the church. If the church decides you are right, but the other person won't accept it, treat that person as a pagan or a corrupt tax collector. ¹⁸I tell you this: Whatever you prohibit on earth is prohibited in heaven, and whatever you allow on earth is allowed in heaven.

¹⁹"I also tell you this: If two of you agree here on earth concerning anything you ask, my Father in heaven will do it for you.

²⁰For where two or three gather together because they are mine, I am there among them."

action

CH 18:1-6 WHAT'S IT SAYING?

WHAT AM I GOING TO dO ABOUT IT?

### Story of the Unforgiving Debtor

²¹Then Peter came to him and asked, "Lord, how often should I forgive someone who sins against me? Seven times?"

²²"No!" Jesus replied, "seventy times seven!

²³"For this reason, the Kingdom of Heaven can be compared to a king who decided to bring his accounts up to date with servants who had borrowed money from him. ²⁴In the process, one of his debtors was brought in who owed him millions of pounds. ²⁵He couldn't pay, so the king ordered that he, his wife, his children, and everything he had be sold to pay the debt. ²⁶But the man fell down before the king and begged him, 'Oh, sir, be patient with me, and I will pay it all.' ²⁷Then the king was filled with pity for him, and he released him and forgave his debt.

²⁸"But when the man left the king, he went to a fellow servant who owed him a few thousand pounds. He grabbed him by the throat and demanded instant payment. ²⁹His fellow servant fell down before him and begged for a little more time. 'Be patient and I will pay it,' he pleaded. ³⁰But his creditor wouldn't wait. He had the man arrested and jailed until the debt could be paid in full.

³¹"When some of the other servants saw this, they were very upset. They went to the king and told him what had happened. ³²Then the king called in the man he had forgiven and said, 'You evil servant! I forgave you that tremendous debt because you pleaded with me. ³³Shouldn't you have mercy on your fellow servant, just as I had mercy on you?'

³⁴Then the angry king sent the man to prison until he had paid every penny.

³⁵"**That's what my heavenly Father will do to you if you refuse to forgive your brothers and sisters in your heart.**"

18:10 Some manuscripts add verse 11, *And the Son of Man came to save those who are lost.* Compare Luke 19:10.

## Discussion about Divorce and Marriage

# 19

After Jesus had finished saying these things, he left Galilee and went southward to the region of Judea and into the area east of the River Jordan. [2]Vast crowds followed him there, and he healed their sick.

[3]Some Pharisees came and tried to trap him with this question:

"Should a man be allowed to divorce his wife for any reason?"

[4]"Haven't you read the Scriptures?" Jesus replied. "They record that from the beginning 'God made them male and female.' [5]And he said, 'This explains why a man leaves his father and mother and is joined to his wife, and the two are united into one.' [6]Since they are no longer two but one, let no one separate them, for God has joined them together."

[7]"Then why did Moses say a man could merely write an official letter of divorce and send her away?" they asked.

[8]Jesus replied, "Moses permitted divorce as a concession to your hard-hearted wickedness, but it was not what God had originally intended. [9]And I tell you this, a man who divorces his wife and marries another commits adultery—unless his wife has been unfaithful."*

[10]Jesus' disciples then said to him, "Then it is better not to marry!"

[11]"Not everyone can accept this statement," Jesus said. "Only those whom God helps. [12]Some are born as eunuchs, some have been made that way by others, and some choose not to marry for the sake of the Kingdom of Heaven. Let anyone who can, accept this statement."

## Jesus Blesses the Children

[13]Some children were brought to Jesus so he could lay his hands on them and pray for them. The disciples told them not to bother him. [14]**But Jesus said, "Let the children come to me. Don't stop them! For the Kingdom of Heaven belongs to such as these."** [15]And he put his hands on their heads and blessed them before he left.

**CH 19:27-30 WHAT'S IT SAYING?**

**WHAT AM I GOING TO DO ABOUT IT?**

## The Rich Young Man

[16]Someone came to Jesus with this question: "Teacher, what good things must I do to have eternal life?"

[17]"Why ask me about what is good?" Jesus replied. "Only God is good. But to answer your question, you can receive eternal life if you keep the commandments."

[18]"Which ones?" the man asked.

And Jesus replied: "'Do not murder. Do not commit adultery. Do not steal. Do not testify falsely. [19]Honour your father and mother. Love your neighbour as yourself.'"

[20]"I've obeyed all these commandments," the young man replied. "What else must I do?"

[21]Jesus told him, "If you want to be perfect, go and sell all you have and give the money to the poor, and you will have treasure in heaven. Then come, follow me." [22]But when the young man heard this, he went away sadly because he had many possessions.

[23]Then Jesus said to his disciples, "I tell you the truth, it is very hard for a rich person to get into the Kingdom of Heaven. [24]I say it again—it is easier for a camel to go through the eye of a needle than for a rich person to enter the Kingdom of God!"

[25]**The disciples were astounded. "Then who in the world can be saved?" they asked.**

[26]**Jesus looked at them intently and said, "Humanly speaking, it is impossible. But with God everything is possible."**

[27]Then Peter said to him, "We've given up everything to follow you. What will we get out of it?"

[28]And Jesus replied, "I assure you that when I, the Son of Man, sit upon my glorious throne in the Kingdom, you who have been my followers will also sit on twelve thrones, judging the twelve tribes of Israel. [29]And everyone who has given up houses or brothers or sisters or father or mother or children or property, for my sake, will receive a hundred times as much in return and will have eternal life. [30]But many who seem to be important now will be the least important then, and those who are considered least here will be the greatest then.

## Story of the Vineyard Workers

# 20

"For the Kingdom of Heaven is like the owner of an estate who went out early one morning to hire workers for his vineyard.

[2]He agreed to pay the normal daily wage and sent them out to work.

---

'The Rich Young Man' Matthew 19:16-30

Along comes what would seem to many a top recruit for Jesus' movement. He had morality, he had authority, he had bravado and he had cash. Seem like all the ingredients to be headhunted for a top spot on God's team? Wrong! The man was trying to justify himself to God by his own good works. In God's economy the rich young man's good works were pretty weak. He was probably a good guy in many ways but Jesus looked deep into his heart and saw him for who he was, a sinner who loved his possessions more than obedience to God. Jesus does not ask anyone else to give up all their possessions, but if he gave you a direct command, could you obey? The disciples were pretty shocked at Jesus' response to the 'rich' guy and asked 'who in the world can be saved?' Of course Jesus' reply is clear, 'Humanly speaking it is impossible. But with God, all things are possible!'

---

19:9 Some manuscripts add *And anyone who marries a divorced woman commits adultery.* Compare Matt 5:32.

³"At nine o'clock in the morning he was passing through the marketplace and saw some people standing around doing nothing. ⁴So he hired them, telling them he would pay them whatever was right at the end of the day. ⁵At noon and again around three o'clock he did the same thing. ⁶At five o'clock that evening he was in town again and saw some more people standing around. He asked them, 'Why haven't you been working today?'

⁷"They replied, 'Because no one hired us.'

"The owner of the estate told them, 'Then go on out and join the others in my vineyard.'

⁸"That evening he told the foreman to call the workers in and pay them, beginning with the last workers first. ⁹When those hired at five o'clock were paid, each received a full day's wage. ¹⁰When those hired earlier came to get their pay, they assumed they would receive more. But they, too, were paid a day's wage. ¹¹When they received their pay, they protested, ¹²Those people worked only one hour, and yet you've paid them just as much as you paid us who worked all day in the scorching heat.'

¹³"He answered one of them, 'Friend, I haven't been unfair! Didn't you agree to work all day for the usual wage? ¹⁴Take it and go. I wanted to pay this last worker the same as you. ¹⁵Is it against the law for me to do what I want with my money? Should you be angry because I am kind?'

¹⁶"And so it is, that many who are first now will be last then; and those who are last now will be first then."

## Jesus Again Predicts His Death

¹⁷As Jesus was on the way to Jerusalem, he took the twelve disciples aside privately and told them what was going to happen to him. ¹⁸"When we get to Jerusalem," he said, "the Son of Man will be betrayed to the leading priests and the teachers of religious law. They will sentence him to die. ¹⁹Then they will hand him over to the Romans to be mocked, whipped, and crucified. But on the third day he will be raised from the dead."

## Jesus Teaches about Serving Others

²⁰Then the mother of James and John, the sons of Zebedee, came to Jesus with her sons. She knelt respectfully to ask a favour. ²¹"What is your request?" he asked.

She replied, "In your Kingdom, will you let my two sons sit in places of honour next to you, one at your right and the other at your left?"

²²But Jesus told them, "You don't know what you are asking! Are you able to drink from the bitter cup of sorrow I am about to drink?"

"Oh yes," they replied, "we are able!"

²³"You will indeed drink from it," he told them.

"But I have no right to say who will sit on the thrones next to mine. My Father has prepared those places for the ones he has chosen."

²⁴When the ten other disciples heard what James and John had asked, they were indignant. ²⁵But Jesus called them together and said, "You know that in this world kings are tyrants, and officials lord it over the people beneath them. ²⁶But among you it should be quite different. Whoever wants to be a leader among you must be your servant, ²⁷and whoever wants to be first must become your slave. **²⁸For even I, the Son of Man, came here not to be served but to serve others, and to give my life as a ransom for many."**

## Jesus Heals Two Blind Men

²⁹As Jesus and the disciples left the city of Jericho, a huge crowd followed behind. ³⁰Two blind men were

**It's not easy!**
It never says in the scriptures you are going to have an easy life. Families break up, friends blow it, teams lose and stuff happens. What God does promise is that he will comfort you in the tough times when you are hurting if you draw on him. "God blesses those who mourn, for they will be comforted." Matthew 5:4
**Count on it!**

sitting beside the road. When they heard that Jesus was coming that way, they began shouting, "Lord, Son of David, have mercy on us!" ³¹The crowd told them to be quiet, but they only shouted louder, "Lord, Son of David, have mercy on us!"

³²Jesus stopped in the road and called, "What do you want me to do for you?"

³³"Lord," they said, "we want to see!" ³⁴Jesus felt sorry for them and touched their eyes. Instantly they could see! Then they followed him.

## The Triumphal Entry

# 21

As Jesus and the disciples approached Jerusalem, they came to the town of Bethphage on the Mount of Olives. Jesus sent two of them on ahead. ²"Go into the village over there," he said, "and you will see a donkey tied there, with its colt beside it. Untie them and bring them here. ³If anyone asks what you are doing, just say, 'The Lord needs them,' and he will immediately send them." ⁴This was done to fulfil the prophecy,

⁵"Tell the people of Israel,
'Look, your King is coming to you.
He is humble, riding on a donkey—
even on a donkey's colt.'"

⁶The two disciples did as Jesus said. ⁷They brought the animals to him and threw their garments over the colt, and he sat on it.

⁸Most of the crowd spread their coats on the road ahead of Jesus, and others cut branches from the trees and spread them on the road. ⁹He was in the centre of the procession, and the crowds all around him were shouting,
"Praise God for the Son of David!
Bless the one who comes in the name of the Lord!
Praise God in highest heaven!"

¹⁰The entire city of Jerusalem was stirred as he entered. "Who is this?" they asked.

¹¹And the crowds replied, "It's Jesus, the prophet from Nazareth in Galilee."

## Jesus Clears the Temple

¹²Jesus entered the Temple and began to drive out the merchants and their customers. He knocked over the tables of the money changers and the stalls of those selling doves. ¹³He said, "The Scriptures declare, 'My Temple will be called a place of prayer,' but you have turned it into a den of thieves!"

¹⁴The blind and the lame came to him, and he healed them there in the Temple. ¹⁵The leading priests and the teachers of religious law saw these wonderful miracles and heard even the little children in the Temple shouting, "Praise God for

the Son of David." But they were indignant [16]and asked Jesus, "Do you hear what these children are saying?"

"Yes," Jesus replied. "Haven't you ever read the Scriptures? For they say, 'You have taught children and infants to give you praise.'" [17]Then he returned to Bethany, where he stayed overnight.

## Jesus Curses the Fig Tree

[18]In the morning, as Jesus was returning to Jerusalem, he was hungry, [19]and he noticed a fig tree beside the road. He went over to see if there were any figs on it, but there were only leaves. Then he said to it, "May you never bear fruit again!" And immediately the fig tree withered up.

[20]The disciples were amazed when they saw this and asked, "How did the fig tree wither so quickly?"

[21]Then Jesus told them, "I assure you, if you have faith and don't doubt, you can do things like this and much more. You can even say to this mountain, 'May God lift you up and throw you into the sea,' and it will happen. [22]If you believe, you will receive whatever you ask for in prayer."

## The Authority of Jesus Challenged

[23]When Jesus returned to the Temple and began teaching, the leading priests and other leaders came up to him. They demanded, "By whose authority did you drive out the merchants from the Temple? Who gave you such authority?" [24]"I'll tell you who gave me the authority to do these things if you answer one question," Jesus replied. [25]"Did John's baptism come from heaven or was it merely human?"

They talked it over among themselves. "If we say it was from heaven, he will ask why we didn't believe him. [26]But if we say it was merely human, we'll be mobbed, because the

changed his mind and went anyway. [30]Then the father told the other son, 'You go,' and he said, 'Yes, sir, I will.' But he didn't go. [31]Which of the two was obeying his father?"

They replied, "The first, of course."

Then Jesus explained his meaning: "I assure you, corrupt tax collectors and prostitutes will get into the Kingdom of God before you do. [32]For John the Baptist came and showed you the way to life, and you didn't believe him, while tax collectors and prostitutes did. And even when you saw this happening, you refused to turn from your sins and believe him.

## Story of the Evil Farmers

[33]"Now listen to this story. A certain landowner planted a vineyard, built a wall around it, dug a pit for pressing out the grape juice, and built a lookout tower. Then he leased the vineyard to tenant farmers and moved to another country. [34]At the time of the grape harvest he sent his servants to collect his share of the crop. [35]But the farmers grabbed his servants, beat one, killed one, and stoned another. [36]So the landowner sent a larger group of his servants to collect for him, but the results were the same.

[37]"Finally, the owner sent his son, thinking, 'Surely they will respect my son.'

[38]"But when the farmers saw his son coming, they said to one another, 'Here comes the heir to this estate. Come on, let's kill him and get the estate for ourselves!' [39]So they grabbed him, took him out of the vineyard, and murdered him.

[40]"When the owner of the vineyard returns," Jesus

'The stone rejected by the builders
has now become the cornerstone.
This is the Lord's doing,
and it is marvellous to see.'

[43]What I mean is that the Kingdom of God will be taken away from you and given to a nation that will produce the proper fruit. [44]Anyone who stumbles over that stone will be broken to pieces, and it will crush anyone on whom it falls."

[45]When the leading priests and Pharisees heard Jesus, they realized he was pointing at them—that they were the farmers in his story. [46]They wanted to arrest him, but they were afraid to try because the crowds considered Jesus to be a prophet.

## Story of the Great Feast

# 22

Jesus told them several other stories to illustrate the Kingdom. He said, [2]"The Kingdom of Heaven can be illustrated by the story of a king who prepared a great wedding feast for his son. [3]Many guests were invited, and when the banquet was ready, he sent his servants to notify everyone that it was time to come. But they all refused! [4]So he sent other servants to tell them, 'The feast has been prepared, and choice meats have been cooked. Everything is ready. Hurry!' [5]But the guests he had invited ignored them and went about their business, one to his farm, another to his store. [6]Others seized his messengers and treated them shamefully, even killing some of them.

## Basic Lifts are Best:

Using simple free weights (barbells and dumbbells) on basic multi-joint exercises, like the squat, bench press, shoulder press, and deadlift, is still the most effective means of resistance exercise ever invented. Scientific research has shown that many exercise machines lack the proper eccentric component of an exercise that's necessary to stimulate muscle strength and growth.

people think he was a prophet." [27]So they finally replied, "We don't know."

And Jesus responded, "Then I won't answer your question either.

## Story of the Two Sons

[28]"But what do you think about this? A man with two sons told the older boy, 'Son, go out and work in the vineyard today.' [29]The son answered, 'No, I won't go,' but later he

asked, "what do you think he will do to those farmers?"

[41]The religious leaders replied, "He will put the wicked men to a horrible death and lease the vineyard to others who will give him his share of the crop after each harvest."

[42]Then Jesus asked them, "Didn't you ever read this in the Scriptures?

[7]"Then the king became furious. He sent out his army to destroy the murderers and burn their city. [8]And he said to his servants, 'The wedding feast is ready, and the guests I invited aren't worthy of the honour. [9]Now go out to the street corners and invite everyone you see.'

[10]"So the servants brought in everyone they could find, good and bad alike, and the banquet hall was filled

with guests. ¹¹But when the king came in to meet the guests, he noticed a man who wasn't wearing the proper clothes for a wedding. ¹²'Friend,' he asked, 'how is it that you are here without wedding clothes?' And the man had no reply. ¹³Then the king said to his aides, 'Bind him hand and foot and throw him out into the outer darkness, where there is weeping and gnashing of teeth.' **¹⁴For many are called, but few are chosen."**

## Taxes for Caesar

¹⁵Then the Pharisees met together to think of a way to trap Jesus into saying something for which they could accuse him. ¹⁶They decided to send some of their disciples, along with the supporters of Herod, to ask him this question: "Teacher, we know how honest you are. You teach about the way of God regardless of the consequences. You are impartial and don't have favourites.

¹⁷Now tell us what you think about this: Is it right to pay taxes to the Roman government or not?"

¹⁸But Jesus knew their evil motives. "You hypocrites!" he said. "Whom are you trying to fool with your trick questions? ¹⁹Here, show me the Roman coin used for the tax." When they handed him the coin, ²⁰he asked, "Whose picture and title are stamped on it?"

²¹"Caesar's," they replied.

"Well, then," he said, "give to Caesar what belongs to him. But everything that belongs to God must be given to God." ²²His reply amazed them, and they went away.

## Discussion about Resurrection

²³That same day Jesus was approached by some Sadducees—a group of Jews who say there is no resurrection after death. They posed this question: ²⁴"Teacher, Moses said,

'If a man dies without children, his brother should marry the widow and have a child who will be the brother's heir.'

²⁵Well, there were seven brothers. The oldest married and then died without children, so the second brother married the widow. ²⁶This brother also died without children, and the wife was married to the next brother, and so on until she had been the wife of each of them. ²⁷And then she also died. ²⁸So tell us, whose wife will she be in the resurrection? For she was the wife of all seven of them!"

²⁹Jesus replied, "Your problem is that you don't know the Scriptures, and you don't know the power of God. ³⁰For when the dead rise, they won't be married. They will be like the angels in heaven. ³¹But now, as to whether there will be a resurrection of the dead—haven't you ever read about this in the Scriptures? Long after Abraham, Isaac, and Jacob had died, God said, ³²'I am the God of Abraham, the God of Isaac, and the God of Jacob.' So he is the God of the living, not the dead."

³³When the crowds heard him, they were impressed with his teaching.

## The Most Important Commandment

³⁴But when the Pharisees heard that he had silenced the Sadducees with his reply, they thought up a fresh question of their own to ask him. ³⁵One of them, an expert in religious law, tried to trap him with this question: ³⁶"Teacher, which is the most important commandment in the law of Moses?"

³⁷Jesus replied, "'You must love the Lord your God with all your heart, all your soul, and all your mind.' ³⁸This is the first and greatest commandment. **³⁹A second is equally important: 'Love your neighbour as yourself.' ⁴⁰All the other commandments and all the demands of the prophets are based on these two commandments."**

## Whose Son Is the Messiah?

⁴¹Then, surrounded by the Pharisees, Jesus asked them a question: ⁴²"What do you think about the Messiah? Whose son is he?"

They replied, "He is the son of David."

⁴³Jesus responded, "Then why does David, speaking under the inspiration of the Holy Spirit, call him Lord? For David said,

⁴⁴'The LORD said to my Lord,
Sit in honour at my right hand
until I humble your enemies beneath your feet.'

⁴⁵Since David called him Lord, how can he be his son at the same time?"

⁴⁶No one could answer him. And after that, no one dared to ask him any more questions.

## Jesus Warns the Religious Leaders

# 23

Then Jesus said to the crowds and to his disciples, ²"The teachers of religious law and the Pharisees are the official interpreters of the Scriptures. ³So practise and obey whatever they say to you, but don't follow their example. For they don't practise what they teach.

⁴They crush you with impossible religious demands and never lift a finger to help ease the burden.

⁵"Everything they do is for show. On their arms they wear extra wide prayer boxes with Scripture verses inside, and they wear extra long tassels on their robes. ⁶And how they love to sit at the head table at banquets and in the most prominent seats in the synagogue! ⁷They enjoy the attention they get on the streets, and they enjoy being called 'Rabbi.' ⁸Don't ever let anyone call you 'Rabbi,' for you have only one teacher, and all of you are on the same level as brothers and sisters. ⁹And don't address anyone here on earth as 'Father,' for only God in heaven is your spiritual Father. ¹⁰And don't let anyone call you 'Master,' for there is only one master, the Messiah. **¹¹The greatest among you must be a servant.** ¹²But those who exalt themselves will be humbled, and those who humble themselves will be exalted.

¹³"How terrible it will be for you teachers of religious law and you Pharisees. Hypocrites! For you won't let others enter the Kingdom of Heaven, and you won't go in yourselves.*

¹⁵Yes, how terrible it will be for you teachers of religious law and you Pharisees. For you cross land and sea to make one convert, and then you turn him into twice the son of hell as you yourselves are.

¹⁶"Blind guides! How terrible it will be for you! For you say that it means nothing to swear 'by God's Temple'—you can break that oath. But then you say that it is binding to swear 'by the gold in the Temple.' ¹⁷Blind fools! Which is greater, the gold, or the Temple that makes the gold sacred? ¹⁸And you say that to take an oath 'by the altar' can be broken, but to swear 'by the gifts on the altar' is binding! ¹⁹How blind! For which is greater, the gift on the altar, or the altar that makes the gift sacred? ²⁰When you swear 'by the altar,' you are swearing by it and by everything on it. ²¹And when you swear 'by the Temple,' you are swearing by it and by God, who lives in it. ²²And when you swear 'by heaven,' you are swearing by the throne of God and by God, who sits on the throne.

²³"How terrible it will be for you teachers of religious law and you Pharisees. Hypocrites! For you are careful to tithe even the tiniest part of your income, but you ignore the important things of the law—justice, mercy, and faith. You should tithe, yes, but you should not leave undone the more important things. ²⁴Blind guides! You strain your water so you won't accidentally swallow a gnat; then you swallow a camel!

²⁵"How terrible it will be for you teachers of religious law and you Pharisees. Hypocrites! You are so careful to clean the outside of the cup and the dish, but inside you are filthy—full of greed and self-indulgence! ²⁶Blind Pharisees! First wash the inside of the cup, and then the outside will become clean, too.

---

23:13 *Some manuscripts add verse 14, What sorrow awaits you teachers of religious law and you Pharisees. Hypocrites! You shamelessly cheat widows out of their property and then pretend to be pious by making long prayers in public. Because of this, you will be severely punished. Compare Mark 12:40 and Luke 20:47.*

# FEBRUARY M.A.P.

## 1
| S.D. | P.L. | P.G. | S.G. |
|------|------|------|------|
| P. ☐ | F. ☐ | F. ☐ | T. ☐ |
| F. ☐ | W. ☐ | W. ☐ | P. ☐ |
| B. ☐ | P. ☐ | C. ☐ | C. ☐ |

## 2
| S.D. | P.L. | P.G. | S.G. |
|------|------|------|------|
| P. ☐ | F. ☐ | F. ☐ | T. ☐ |
| F. ☐ | W. ☐ | W. ☐ | P. ☐ |
| B. ☐ | P. ☐ | C. ☐ | C. ☐ |

## 3
| S.D. | P.L. | P.G. | S.G. |
|------|------|------|------|
| P. ☐ | F. ☐ | F. ☐ | T. ☐ |
| F. ☐ | W. ☐ | W. ☐ | P. ☐ |
| B. ☐ | P. ☐ | C. ☐ | C. ☐ |

## 4
| S.D. | P.L. | P.G. | S.G. |
|------|------|------|------|
| P. ☐ | F. ☐ | F. ☐ | T. ☐ |
| F. ☐ | W. ☐ | W. ☐ | P. ☐ |
| B. ☐ | P. ☐ | C. ☐ | C. ☐ |

## 9
| S.D. | P.L. | P.G. | S.G. |
|------|------|------|------|
| P. ☐ | F. ☐ | F. ☐ | T. ☐ |
| F. ☐ | W. ☐ | W. ☐ | P. ☐ |
| B. ☐ | P. ☐ | C. ☐ | C. ☐ |

## 10
| S.D. | P.L. | P.G. | S.G. |
|------|------|------|------|
| P. ☐ | F. ☐ | F. ☐ | T. ☐ |
| F. ☐ | W. ☐ | W. ☐ | P. ☐ |
| B. ☐ | P. ☐ | C. ☐ | C. ☐ |

## 11
| S.D. | P.L. | P.G. | S.G. |
|------|------|------|------|
| P. ☐ | F. ☐ | F. ☐ | T. ☐ |
| F. ☐ | W. ☐ | W. ☐ | P. ☐ |
| B. ☐ | P. ☐ | C. ☐ | C. ☐ |

## 12
| S.D. | P.L. | P.G. | S.G. |
|------|------|------|------|
| P. ☐ | F. ☐ | F. ☐ | T. ☐ |
| F. ☐ | W. ☐ | W. ☐ | P. ☐ |
| B. ☐ | P. ☐ | C. ☐ | C. ☐ |

## 17
| S.D. | P.L. | P.G. | S.G. |
|------|------|------|------|
| P. ☐ | F. ☐ | F. ☐ | T. ☐ |
| F. ☐ | W. ☐ | W. ☐ | P. ☐ |
| B. ☐ | P. ☐ | C. ☐ | C. ☐ |

## 18
| S.D. | P.L. | P.G. | S.G. |
|------|------|------|------|
| P. ☐ | F. ☐ | F. ☐ | T. ☐ |
| F. ☐ | W. ☐ | W. ☐ | P. ☐ |
| B. ☐ | P. ☐ | C. ☐ | C. ☐ |

## 19
| S.D. | P.L. | P.G. | S.G. |
|------|------|------|------|
| P. ☐ | F. ☐ | F. ☐ | T. ☐ |
| F. ☐ | W. ☐ | W. ☐ | P. ☐ |
| B. ☐ | P. ☐ | C. ☐ | C. ☐ |

## 20
| S.D. | P.L. | P.G. | S.G. |
|------|------|------|------|
| P. ☐ | F. ☐ | F. ☐ | T. ☐ |
| F. ☐ | W. ☐ | W. ☐ | P. ☐ |
| B. ☐ | P. ☐ | C. ☐ | C. ☐ |

## 25
| S.D. | P.L. | P.G. | S.G. |
|------|------|------|------|
| P. ☐ | F. ☐ | F. ☐ | T. ☐ |
| F. ☐ | W. ☐ | W. ☐ | P. ☐ |
| B. ☐ | P. ☐ | C. ☐ | C. ☐ |

## 26
| S.D. | P.L. | P.G. | S.G. |
|------|------|------|------|
| P. ☐ | F. ☐ | F. ☐ | T. ☐ |
| F. ☐ | W. ☐ | W. ☐ | P. ☐ |
| B. ☐ | P. ☐ | C. ☐ | C. ☐ |

## 27
| S.D. | P.L. | P.G. | S.G. |
|------|------|------|------|
| P. ☐ | F. ☐ | F. ☐ | T. ☐ |
| F. ☐ | W. ☐ | W. ☐ | P. ☐ |
| B. ☐ | P. ☐ | C. ☐ | C. ☐ |

## 28
| S.D. | P.L. | P.G. | S.G. |
|------|------|------|------|
| P. ☐ | F. ☐ | F. ☐ | T. ☐ |
| F. ☐ | W. ☐ | W. ☐ | P. ☐ |
| B. ☐ | P. ☐ | C. ☐ | C. ☐ |

## Spiritual Disciplines

**Prayer**

**Faith Community**

**Bible Reading**

## Prayer List

**Friends**

**World**

**Personal**

Who am I....
Where am I going....
How am I going to get there?

**nt:sport**

MONTHLY ACTION PLAN

### 5
| S.D. | P.L. | P.G. | S.G. |
|------|------|------|------|
| P. ☐ | F. ☐ | F. ☐ | T. ☐ |
| F. ☐ | W. ☐ | W. ☐ | P. ☐ |
| B. ☐ | P. ☐ | C. ☐ | C. ☐ |

### 6
| S.D. | P.L. | P.G. | S.G. |
|------|------|------|------|
| P. ☐ | F. ☐ | F. ☐ | T. ☐ |
| F. ☐ | W. ☐ | W. ☐ | P. ☐ |
| B. ☐ | P. ☐ | C. ☐ | C. ☐ |

### 7
| S.D. | P.L. | P.G. | S.G. |
|------|------|------|------|
| P. ☐ | F. ☐ | F. ☐ | T. ☐ |
| F. ☐ | W. ☐ | W. ☐ | P. ☐ |
| B. ☐ | P. ☐ | C. ☐ | C. ☐ |

### 8
| S.D. | P.L. | P.G. | S.G. |
|------|------|------|------|
| P. ☐ | F. ☐ | F. ☐ | T. ☐ |
| F. ☐ | W. ☐ | W. ☐ | P. ☐ |
| B. ☐ | P. ☐ | C. ☐ | C. ☐ |

### 13
| S.D. | P.L. | P.G. | S.G. |
|------|------|------|------|
| P. ☐ | F. ☐ | F. ☐ | T. ☐ |
| F. ☐ | W. ☐ | W. ☐ | P. ☐ |
| B. ☐ | P. ☐ | C. ☐ | C. ☐ |

### 14
| S.D. | P.L. | P.G. | S.G. |
|------|------|------|------|
| P. ☐ | F. ☐ | F. ☐ | T. ☐ |
| F. ☐ | W. ☐ | W. ☐ | P. ☐ |
| B. ☐ | P. ☐ | C. ☐ | C. ☐ |

### 15
| S.D. | P.L. | P.G. | S.G. |
|------|------|------|------|
| P. ☐ | F. ☐ | F. ☐ | T. ☐ |
| F. ☐ | W. ☐ | W. ☐ | P. ☐ |
| B. ☐ | P. ☐ | C. ☐ | C. ☐ |

### 16
| S.D. | P.L. | P.G. | S.G. |
|------|------|------|------|
| P. ☐ | F. ☐ | F. ☐ | T. ☐ |
| F. ☐ | W. ☐ | W. ☐ | P. ☐ |
| B. ☐ | P. ☐ | C. ☐ | C. ☐ |

### 21
| S.D. | P.L. | P.G. | S.G. |
|------|------|------|------|
| P. ☐ | F. ☐ | F. ☐ | T. ☐ |
| F. ☐ | W. ☐ | W. ☐ | P. ☐ |
| B. ☐ | P. ☐ | C. ☐ | C. ☐ |

### 22
| S.D. | P.L. | P.G. | S.G. |
|------|------|------|------|
| P. ☐ | F. ☐ | F. ☐ | T. ☐ |
| F. ☐ | W. ☐ | W. ☐ | P. ☐ |
| B. ☐ | P. ☐ | C. ☐ | C. ☐ |

### 23
| S.D. | P.L. | P.G. | S.G. |
|------|------|------|------|
| P. ☐ | F. ☐ | F. ☐ | T. ☐ |
| F. ☐ | W. ☐ | W. ☐ | P. ☐ |
| B. ☐ | P. ☐ | C. ☐ | C. ☐ |

### 24
| S.D. | P.L. | P.G. | S.G. |
|------|------|------|------|
| P. ☐ | F. ☐ | F. ☐ | T. ☐ |
| F. ☐ | W. ☐ | W. ☐ | P. ☐ |
| B. ☐ | P. ☐ | C. ☐ | C. ☐ |

### 29
| S.D. | P.L. | P.G. | S.G. |
|------|------|------|------|
| P. ☐ | F. ☐ | F. ☐ | T. ☐ |
| F. ☐ | W. ☐ | W. ☐ | P. ☐ |
| B. ☐ | P. ☐ | C. ☐ | C. ☐ |

**Psalm 43:3**

Send out your light and your truth; let them guide me. Let them lead me to your holy mountain, to the place where you live.

## Personal Goals

**Family**

**Work/School/Social**

**Challenge**

## Sport Goals

**Training**

**Performance**

**Competition Results**

(For designing your MAP - Monthly Action Plan - see introduction pages)

27"How terrible it will be for you teachers of religious law and you Pharisees. Hypocrites! You are like whitewashed tombs—beautiful on the outside but filled on the inside with dead people's bones and all sorts of impurity. 28You try to look like upright people outwardly, but inside your hearts are filled with hypocrisy and lawlessness.

29"How terrible it will be for you teachers of religious law and you Pharisees. Hypocrites! For you build tombs for the prophets your ancestors killed and decorate the graves of the godly people your ancestors destroyed. 30Then you say, 'We never would have joined them in killing the prophets.' 31"In saying that, you are accusing yourselves of being the descendants of those who murdered the prophets. 32Go ahead. Finish what they started. 33Snakes! Sons of vipers! How will you escape the judgement of hell? 34I will send you prophets and wise men and teachers of religious law. You will kill some by crucifixion and whip others in your synagogues, chasing them from city to city. 35As a result, you will become guilty of murdering all the godly people from righteous Abel to Zechariah son of Barachiah, whom you murdered in the Temple between the altar and the sanctuary.

36I assure you, all the accumulated judgement of the centuries will break upon the heads of this very generation.

## Jesus Grieves over Jerusalem

37"O Jerusalem, Jerusalem, the city that kills the prophets and stones God's messengers! How often I have wanted to gather your children together as a hen protects her chicks beneath her wings, but you wouldn't let me. 38And now look, your house is left to you, empty and desolate. 39For I tell you this, you will never see me again until you say, 'Bless the one who comes in the name of the Lord!'"

## Jesus Foretells the Future

# 24

As Jesus was leaving the Temple grounds, his disciples pointed out to him the various Temple buildings. 2But he told them, "Do you see all these buildings? I assure you, they will be so completely demolished that not one stone will be left on top of another!"

3Later, Jesus sat on the slopes of the Mount of Olives. His disciples came to him privately and asked, "When will all this take place? And will there be any sign ahead of time to signal your return and the end of the world?"

4Jesus told them, "Don't let anyone mislead you. 5For many will come in my name, saying, 'I am the Messiah.' They will lead many astray. 6And wars will break out near and far, but don't panic. Yes, these things must come, but the end won't follow immediately. 7The nations and kingdoms will proclaim war against each other, and there will be famines and earthquakes in many parts of the world. 8But all this will be only the beginning of the horrors to come.

9"Then you will be arrested, persecuted, and killed. You will be hated all over the world because of your allegiance to me.

10And many will turn away from me and betray and hate each other. 11And many false prophets will appear and will lead many people astray. 12Sin will be rampant everywhere, and the love of many will grow cold. 13But those who endure to the end will be saved. 14And the Good News about the Kingdom will be preached throughout the whole world, so that all nations will hear it; and then, finally, the end will come.

15"The time will come when you will see what Daniel the prophet spoke about: the sacrilegious object that causes desecration standing in the Holy Place"— reader, pay attention! 16"Then those in Judea must flee to the hills. 17A person outside the house must not go inside to pack. 18A person in the field must not return even to get a coat. 19How terrible it will be for pregnant women and for mothers nursing their babies in those days. 20And pray that your flight will not be in winter or on the Sabbath. 21For that will be a time of greater horror than anything the world has ever seen or will ever see again.

22In fact, unless that time of calamity is shortened, the entire human race will be destroyed. But it will be shortened for the sake of God's chosen ones.

23"Then if anyone tells you, 'Look, here is the Messiah,' or 'There he is,' don't pay any attention. 24For false messiahs and false prophets will rise up and perform great miraculous signs and wonders so as to deceive, if possible, even God's chosen ones. 25See, I have warned you.

26"So if someone tells you, 'Look, the Messiah is out in the desert,' don't bother to go and look. Or, 'Look, he is hiding here,' don't believe it! 27For as the lightning lights up the entire sky, so it will be when the Son of Man comes. 28Just as the gathering of vultures shows there is a carcass nearby, so these signs indicate that the end is near.

29"Immediately after those horrible days end, the sun will be darkened, the moon will not give light, the stars will fall from the sky, and the powers of heaven will be shaken.

30And then at last, the sign of the coming of the Son of Man will appear in the heavens, and there will be deep mourning among all the nations of the earth. And they will see the Son of Man arrive on the clouds of heaven with power and great glory. 31**And he will send forth his angels with the sound of a mighty trumpet blast, and they will gather together his chosen ones from the farthest ends of the earth and heaven.**

32"Now learn a lesson from the fig tree. When its buds become tender and its leaves begin to sprout, you know without being told that summer is near. 33Just so, when you see the events I've described beginning to happen, you can know his return is very near, right at the door. 34I assure you, this generation will not pass from the scene before all these things take place. 35Heaven and

## Lean Gut Myth:

Even though you see it on television there is no such thing as spot-reduction; making one specific part of your body lean! (We are not talking about getting rid of pimples by weight lifting). Doing thousands and thousands of sit-ups will give you tight abdominal muscles, but they will do nothing to rid your midsection of fat. Nothing will rid the body of fat, unless it is a carefully orchestrated reduction in your daily energy intake; in other words, if you burn more calories than you actually take in.

earth will disappear, but my words will remain for ever.

<sup>36</sup>"However, no one knows the day or the hour when these things will happen, not even the angels in heaven or the Son himself. Only the Father knows.

<sup>37</sup>"When the Son of Man returns, it will be like it was in Noah's day. <sup>38</sup>In those days before the Flood, the people were enjoying banquets and parties and weddings right up to the time Noah entered his boat. <sup>39</sup>People didn't realize what was going to happen until the Flood came and swept them all away. That is the way it will be when the Son of Man comes.

<sup>40</sup>"Two men will be working together in the field; one will be taken, the other left. <sup>41</sup>Two women will be grinding flour at the mill; one will be taken, the other left. <sup>42</sup>So be prepared, because you don't know what day your Lord is coming.

<sup>43</sup>"Know this: A home-owner who knew exactly when a burglar was coming would stay alert and not permit the house to be broken into. <sup>44</sup>You also must be ready all the time. For the Son of Man will come when least expected.

<sup>45</sup>"Who is a faithful, sensible servant, to whom the master can give the responsibility of managing his household and feeding his family? <sup>46</sup>If the master returns and finds that the servant has done a good job, there will be a reward. <sup>47</sup>I assure you, the master will put that servant in charge of all he owns. <sup>48</sup>But if the servant is evil and thinks, 'My master won't be back for a while,' <sup>49</sup>and begins oppressing the other servants, partying, and getting drunk—<sup>50</sup>well, the master will return unannounced and unexpected. <sup>51</sup>He will tear the servant apart and banish him with the hypocrites. In that place there will be weeping and gnashing of teeth.

## Story of the Ten Bridesmaids

# 25

"The Kingdom of Heaven can be illustrated by the story of ten bridesmaids who took their lamps and went to meet the bridegroom.

<sup>2</sup>Five of them were foolish, and five were wise. <sup>3</sup>The five who were foolish took no oil for their lamps, <sup>4</sup>but the other five were wise enough to take along extra oil. <sup>5</sup>When the bridegroom was delayed, they all laid down and slept. <sup>6</sup>At midnight they were roused by the shout, 'Look, the bridegroom is coming! Come out and welcome him!'

<sup>7</sup>"All the bridesmaids got up and prepared their lamps. <sup>8</sup>Then the five foolish ones asked the others,

'Please give us some of your oil because our lamps

are going out.' <sup>9</sup>But the others replied, 'We don't have enough for all of us. Go to a shop and buy some for yourselves.'

<sup>10</sup>"But while they were gone to buy oil, the bridegroom came, and those who were ready went in with him to the marriage feast, and the door was locked. <sup>11</sup>Later, when the other five bridesmaids returned, they stood outside, calling, 'Sir, open the door for us!' <sup>12</sup>But he called back, 'I don't know you!'

<sup>13</sup>**"So stay awake and be prepared, because you do not know the day or hour of my return.**

**CH 25:14-30 WHAT'S IT SAYING?**

**WHAT AM I GOING TO DO ABOUT IT?**

## Story of the Three Servants

<sup>14</sup>"Again, the Kingdom of Heaven can be illustrated by the story of a man going on a trip. He called together his servants and gave them money to invest for him while he was gone. <sup>15</sup>He gave five bags of gold to one, two bags of gold to another, and one bag of gold to the last—dividing it in proportion to their abilities—and then left on his trip. <sup>16</sup>The servant who received the five bags of gold began immediately to invest the money and soon doubled it. <sup>17</sup>The servant with two bags of gold also went right to work and doubled the money. <sup>18</sup>But the servant who received the one bag of gold dug a hole in the ground and hid the master's money for safe keeping.

<sup>19</sup>"After a long time their master returned from his trip and called them to give an account of how they had used his money.

<sup>20</sup>The servant to whom he had entrusted the five bags of gold said, 'Sir, you gave me five bags of gold to invest, and I have doubled the amount.' <sup>21</sup>The master was full of praise. 'Well done, my good and faithful servant. You have been faithful in handling this small amount, so now I will give you many more responsibilities. Let's celebrate together!'

<sup>22</sup>"Next came the servant who had received the two bags of gold, with the report, 'Sir, you gave me two bags of gold to invest, and I have doubled the amount.' <sup>23</sup>The master said, 'Well done, my good and faithful servant. You have been faithful in handling this small amount, so now I will give you many more responsibilities. Let's celebrate together!'

<sup>24</sup>"Then the servant with the one bag of gold came and said, 'Sir, I know you are a hard man, harvesting crops you didn't plant and gathering crops you didn't cultivate. <sup>25</sup>I was afraid I would lose your money, so I hid it in the earth and here it is.'

<sup>26</sup>"But the master replied, 'You wicked and lazy servant! You think I'm a hard man, do you, harvesting crops I didn't plant and gathering crops I didn't cultivate? <sup>27</sup>Well, you should at least have put my money into the bank so I could have some interest. <sup>28</sup>Take the money from this servant and give it to the one with the ten bags of gold. <sup>29</sup>To those who use well what they are given, even more will be given, and they will have an abundance. But from those who are unfaithful, even what little they have will be taken away. <sup>30</sup>Now throw this useless servant into outer darkness, where there will be weeping and gnashing of teeth.'

## The Final Judgement

<sup>31</sup>"But when the Son of Man comes in his glory, and all the angels with him, then he will sit upon his glorious throne. <sup>32</sup>All the nations will be gathered in his presence, and he will separate them as a shepherd separates the sheep from the goats.

**STAND POINT**

**When you are dating**

**26:41**

Keep alert and pray. Otherwise temptation will overpower you. For though the spirit is willing enough, the body is weak!

## count on it

**Get cleaned up!**

Have you ever done something so bad you hope nobody will ever find out about it? Have you ever done something so bad you feel you can never be forgiven? God is in the business of forgiveness. Also, when you ask, he will make you totally clean. "If we confess our sins to him, he is faithful and just to forgive us and to cleanse us from every wrong." 1 John 1:9
**Count on it!**

³³**He will place the sheep at his right hand and the goats at his left. ³⁴Then the King will say to those on the right, 'Come, you who are blessed by my Father, inherit the Kingdom prepared for you from the foundation of the world. ³⁵For I was hungry, and** you fed me. I was thirsty, and you gave me a drink. I was a stranger, and you invited me into your home. ³⁶I was naked, and you gave me clothing. I was sick, and you cared for me. I was in prison, and you visited me.'

³⁷"Then these righteous ones will reply, 'Lord, when did we ever see you hungry and feed you? Or thirsty and give you something to drink? ³⁸Or a stranger and show you hospitality? Or naked and give you clothing? ³⁹**When did we ever see you sick or in prison, and visit you?'** ⁴⁰And the King will tell them, 'I assure you, when you did it to one of the least of these my brothers and sisters, you were doing it to me!'

⁴¹"Then the King will turn to those on the left and say, 'Away with you, you cursed ones, into the eternal fire prepared for the Devil and his demons! ⁴²For I was hungry, and you didn't feed me. I was thirsty, and you didn't give me anything to drink. ⁴³I was a stranger, and you didn't invite me into your home. I was naked, and you gave me no clothing. I was sick and in prison, and you didn't visit me.'

⁴⁴"Then they will reply, 'Lord, when did we ever see you hungry or thirsty or a stranger or naked or sick or in prison, and not help you?' ⁴⁵And he will answer, 'I assure you, when you refused to help the least of these my brothers and sisters, you were refusing to help me.' ⁴⁶And they will go away into eternal punishment, but the righteous will go into eternal life."

## The Plot to Kill Jesus

# 26

When Jesus had finished saying these things, he said to his disciples, ²"As you know, the Passover celebration begins in two days, and I, the Son of Man, will be betrayed and crucified."

³At that same time the leading priests and other leaders were meeting at the residence of Caiaphas, the high priest, ⁴to discuss how to capture Jesus secretly and put him to death. ⁵"But not during the Passover," they agreed, "or there will be a riot."

## Jesus Anointed at Bethany

⁶Meanwhile, Jesus was in Bethany at the home of Simon, a man who had leprosy. ⁷During supper, a woman came in with a beautiful jar of expensive perfume and poured it over his head. ⁸The disciples were indignant when they saw this. "What a waste of money," they said. ⁹"She could have sold it for a fortune and given the money to the poor."

¹⁰But Jesus replied, "Why berate her for doing such a good thing to me? ¹¹You will always have the poor among you, but I will not be here with you much longer. ¹²She has poured this perfume on me to prepare my body for burial. ¹³I assure you, wherever the Good News is preached throughout the world, this woman's deed will be talked about in her memory."

## Judas Agrees to Betray Jesus

¹⁴Then Judas Iscariot, one of the twelve disciples, went to the leading priests ¹⁵and asked, "How much will you pay me to betray Jesus to you?" And they gave him thirty pieces of silver. ¹⁶From that time on, Judas began looking for the right time and place to betray Jesus.

## action

CH 26:26-30 WHAT'S IT SAYING?

**WHAT AM I GOING TO DO ABOUT IT?**

## The Last Supper

¹⁷On the first day of the Festival of Unleavened Bread, the disciples came to Jesus and asked, "Where do you want us to prepare the Passover supper?"

¹⁸"As you go into the city," he told them, "you will see a certain man. Tell him, 'The Teacher says: My time has come, and I will eat the Passover meal with my disciples at your house.'" ¹⁹So the disciples did as Jesus told them and prepared the Passover supper there.

²⁰When it was evening, Jesus sat down at the table with the twelve disciples. ²¹While they were eating, he said, "The truth is, one of you will betray me."

²²Greatly distressed, one by one they began to ask him, "I'm not the one, am I, Lord?"

²³He replied, "One of you who is eating with me now will betray me. ²⁴For I, the Son of Man, must die, as the Scriptures declared long ago. But how terrible it will be for my betrayer. Far better for him if he had never been born!"

²⁵Judas, the one who would betray him, also asked, "Teacher, I'm not the one, am I?"

And Jesus told him, "You have said it yourself."

²⁶As they were eating, Jesus took a loaf of bread and asked God's blessing on it. Then he broke it in pieces and gave it to the disciples, saying, "Take it and eat it, for this is my body." ²⁷And he took a cup of wine

and gave thanks to God for it. He gave it to them and said, "Each of you drink from it, ²⁸for this is my blood, which seals the covenant between God and his people. It is poured out to forgive the sins of many. ²⁹Mark my words—I will not drink wine again until the day I drink it new with you in my Father's Kingdom." ³⁰Then they sang a hymn and went out to the Mount of Olives.

## Jesus Predicts Peter's Denial

³¹"Tonight all of you will desert me," Jesus told them. "For the Scriptures say,

'God will strike the Shepherd,
and the sheep of the flock will be scattered.'

³²But after I have been raised from the dead, I will go ahead of you to Galilee and meet you there."

³³Peter declared, "Even if everyone else deserts you, I never will."

³⁴"Peter," Jesus replied, "the truth is, this very night, before the cock crows, you will deny me three times."

³⁵"No!" Peter insisted. "Not even if I have to die with you! I will never deny you!" And all the other disciples vowed the same.

## Jesus Prays in Gethsemane

³⁶Then Jesus brought them to an olive grove called Gethsemane, and he said, "Sit here while I go on ahead to pray."

³⁷He took Peter and Zebedee's two sons, James and John, and he began to be filled with anguish and deep distress. ³⁸He told them, "My soul is crushed with grief to the point of death. Stay here and watch with me."

³⁹He went on a little farther and fell face down on the ground, praying, "My Father! If it is possible, let this cup of suffering be taken away from me. Yet I want your will, not mine." ⁴⁰Then he returned to the disciples and found them asleep. He said to Peter, "Couldn't you stay awake and watch with me even one hour?

⁴¹Keep alert and pray. Otherwise temptation will overpower you. For though the spirit is willing enough, the body is weak!"

⁴²Again he left them and prayed, "My Father! If this cup cannot be taken away until I drink it, your will be done."

⁴³He returned to them again and found them sleeping, for they just couldn't keep their eyes open.

⁴⁴So he went back to pray a third time, saying the same things again. ⁴⁵Then he came to the disciples and said, "Still sleeping? Still resting? Look, the time has come. I, the Son of Man, am betrayed into the hands of sinners. ⁴⁶Up, let's be going. See, my betrayer is here!"

## Jesus Is Arrested

⁴⁷And even as he said this, Judas, one of the twelve disciples, arrived with a mob that was armed with swords and clubs. They had been sent out by the leading priests and other leaders of the people. ⁴⁸Judas had given them a prearranged signal:

"You will know which one to arrest when I go over and give him the kiss of greeting." ⁴⁹So Judas came straight to Jesus.

"Greetings, Teacher!" he exclaimed and gave him the kiss.

⁵⁰Jesus said, "My friend, go ahead and do what you have come for." Then the others grabbed Jesus and arrested him. ⁵¹One of the men with Jesus pulled out a sword and slashed off an ear of the high priest's servant.

⁵²"Put away your sword," Jesus told him. "Those who use the sword will be killed by the sword. **⁵³Don't you realize that I could ask my Father for thousands of angels to protect us, and he would send them instantly? ⁵⁴But if I did, how would the Scriptures be fulfilled that describe what must happen now?"**

⁵⁵Then Jesus said to the crowd, "Am I some dangerous criminal, that you have come armed with swords and clubs to arrest me? Why didn't you arrest me in the Temple? I was there teaching every day. ⁵⁶But this is all happening to fulfil the words of the prophets as recorded in the Scriptures." At that point, all the disciples deserted him and fled.

## Jesus before the Council

⁵⁷Then the people who had arrested Jesus led him to the home of Caiaphas, the high priest, where the teachers of religious law and other leaders had gathered. ⁵⁸Meanwhile, Peter was following far behind and eventually came to the courtyard of the high priest's house. He went in, sat with the guards, and waited to see what was going to happen to Jesus.

⁵⁹Inside, the leading priests and the entire high council were trying to find witnesses who would lie about Jesus, so they could put him to death. ⁶⁰But even though they found many who agreed to give false witness, there was no testimony they could use. Finally, two men were found ⁶¹who declared, "This man said, 'I am able to destroy the Temple of God and rebuild it in three days.'"

⁶²Then the high priest stood up and said to Jesus, "Well, aren't you going to answer these charges? What do you have to say for yourself?" ⁶³But Jesus remained silent. Then the high priest said to him, "I demand in the name of the living God that you tell us whether you are the Messiah, the Son of God."

**⁶⁴Jesus replied, "Yes, it is as you say. And in the future you will see me, the Son of Man, sitting at God's right hand in the place of power and coming back on the clouds of heaven."**

⁶⁵Then the high priest tore his clothing to show his horror, shouting, "Blasphemy! Why do we need other witnesses? You have all heard his blasphemy. ⁶⁶What is your verdict?"

"Guilty!" they shouted. "He must die!"

⁶⁷Then they spat in Jesus' face and hit him with their fists. And some slapped him, ⁶⁸saying, "Prophesy to us, you Messiah! Who hit you that time?"

## Peter Denies Jesus

⁶⁹Meanwhile, as Peter was sitting outside in the courtyard, a servant girl came over and said to him, "You were one of those with Jesus the Galilean."

⁷⁰But Peter denied it in front of everyone. "I don't know what you are talking about," he said.

⁷¹Later, out by the gate, another servant girl noticed him and said to those standing around, "This man was with Jesus of Nazareth."

⁷²Again Peter denied it, this time with an oath. "I don't even know the man," he said.

⁷³A little later some other bystanders came over to him and said, "You must be one of them; we can tell by your Galilean accent."

⁷⁴Peter said, "I swear by God, I don't know the man." And immediately the cock crowed. **⁷⁵Suddenly, Jesus' words flashed through Peter's mind: "Before the cock crows, you will deny me three times." And he went away, crying bitterly.**

## Judas Hangs Himself

# 27

Very early in the morning, the leading priests and other leaders met again to discuss how to persuade the Roman government to sentence Jesus to death. ²Then they bound him and took him to Pilate, the Roman governor.

³When Judas, who had betrayed him, realized that Jesus had been condemned to die, he was filled with remorse. So he took the thirty pieces of silver back to the leading priests and other leaders. ⁴"I have sinned," he declared, "for I have betrayed an innocent man."

"What do we care?" they retorted. "That's your problem."

⁵Then Judas threw the money onto the floor of the Temple and went out and hanged himself. ⁶The leading priests picked up the money. "We can't put it in the Temple treasury," they said, "since it's against the law to accept money paid for

murder." [7]After some discussion they finally decided to buy the potter's field, and they made it into a cemetery for foreigners. [8]That is why the field is still called the Field of Blood. [9]This fulfilled the prophecy of Jeremiah that says,
"They took the thirty pieces of silver—
the price at which he was valued by the people of Israel—
[10]and purchased the potter's field,
as the Lord directed."

## Jesus' Trial before Pilate

[11]Now Jesus was standing before Pilate, the Roman governor. "Are you the King of the Jews?" the governor asked him. Jesus replied, "Yes, it is as you say."
[12]But when the leading priests and other leaders made their accusations against him, Jesus remained silent. [13]"Don't you hear their many charges against you?" Pilate demanded. [14]But Jesus said nothing, much to the governor's great surprise.
[15]Now it was the governor's custom to release one prisoner to the crowd each year during the Passover celebration—

anyone they wanted. [16]This year there was a notorious criminal in prison, a man named Barabbas. [17]As the crowds gathered before Pilate's house that morning, he asked them, "Which one do you want me to release to you—Barabbas, or Jesus who is called the Messiah?" [18](He knew very well that the Jewish leaders had arrested Jesus out of envy.)
[19]Just then, as Pilate was sitting on the judgement seat, his wife sent him this message: "Leave that innocent man alone, because I had a terrible nightmare about him last night."
[20]Meanwhile, the leading priests and other leaders persuaded the crowds to ask for Barabbas to be released and for Jesus to be put to death. [21]So when the governor asked again, "Which of these two do you want me to release to you?" the crowd shouted back their reply: "Barabbas!"
[22]"But if I release Barabbas," Pilate asked them, "what should I do with Jesus who is called the Messiah?"

And they all shouted, "Crucify him!"
[23]"Why?" Pilate demanded. "What crime has he committed?"
But the crowd only roared the louder, "Crucify him!"
[24]Pilate saw that he wasn't getting anywhere and that a riot was developing. So he sent for a bowl of water and washed his hands before the crowd, saying, "I am innocent of the blood of this man. The responsibility is yours!"
[25]And all the people yelled back, "We will take responsibility for his death—we and our children!"
[26]So Pilate released Barabbas to them. He ordered Jesus flogged with a lead-tipped whip, then turned him over to the Roman soldiers to crucify him.

## The Soldiers Mock Jesus

[27]Some of the governor's soldiers took Jesus into their headquarters and called out the entire battalion. [28]They stripped him and put a scarlet robe on him. [29]They made a crown of long, sharp thorns and put it

PERSONAL ASSESSMENTS

## Not just on Sundays!

God does not want us to be part-time Christians. It is not starting the race that counts, but how we finish. He wants us to persevere to the end.

He also wants every area of our lives to be under his care and control. God knows that we cannot change on our own - we need help from others to encourage us and, more importantly, we need power from God. But he promised he would stay close. *"And be sure of this: I am with you always, even to the end of the age." Mt 28:20*

Is my faith affecting every area of my life?

|  | Not at all | a little | things are happening | God is in control |
|---|---|---|---|---|
|  | 1——2——3——4——5——6——7——8——9——10 | | | |
| Mental: | 1——2——3——4——5——6——7——8——9——10 | | | |
| Physical: | 1——2——3——4——5——6——7——8——9——10 | | | |
| Social | 1——2——3——4——5——6——7——8——9——10 | | | |
| Spiritual: | 1——2——3——4——5——6——7——8——9——10 | | | |

on his head, and they placed a stick in his right hand as a sceptre. Then they knelt before him in mockery, yelling, "Hail! King of the Jews!" [30]And they spat on him and grabbed the stick and beat him on the head with it. [31]When they were finally tired of mocking him, they took off the robe and put his own clothes on him again. Then they led him away to be crucified.

## The Crucifixion

[32]Along the way, they came across a man named Simon, who was from Cyrene, and they forced him to carry Jesus' cross. [33]Then they went out to a place called Golgotha (which means Skull Hill). [34]The soldiers gave him wine mixed with bitter gall, but when he had tasted it, he refused to drink it.

[35]After they had nailed him to the cross, the soldiers gambled for his clothes by throwing dice.* [36]Then they sat around and kept guard as he hung there. [37]A signboard was fastened to the cross above Jesus' head, announcing the charge against him. It read: "This is Jesus, the King of the Jews."

[38]Two criminals were crucified with him, their crosses on either side of his. [39]And the people passing by shouted abuse, shaking their heads in mockery. [40]"So! You can destroy the Temple and build it again in three days, can you? Well then, if you are the Son of God, save yourself and come down from the cross!"

[41]The leading priests, the teachers of religious law, and the other leaders also mocked Jesus. [42]"He saved others," they scoffed, "but he can't save himself! So he is the king of Israel, is he? Let him come down from the cross, and we will believe in him! [43]He trusted God—let God show his approval by delivering him! For he said, 'I am the Son of God.'"

[44]And the criminals who were crucified with him also shouted the same insults at him.

## The Death of Jesus

[45]At noon, darkness fell across the whole land until three o'clock. [46]At about three o'clock, Jesus called out with a loud voice, *"Eli, Eli, lema sabachthani?"* which means, "My God, my God, why have you forsaken me?"

[47]Some of the bystanders misunderstood and thought he was calling for the prophet Elijah. [48]One of them ran and filled a sponge with sour wine, holding it up to him on a stick so he could drink. [49]But the rest said, "Leave him alone. Let's see whether Elijah will come and save him."*

[50]Then Jesus shouted out again, and he gave up his spirit.

[51]At that moment the curtain in the Temple was torn in two, from top to bottom. The earth shook, rocks split apart, [52]and tombs opened. The bodies of many godly men and women who had died were raised from the dead [53]after Jesus' resurrection. They left the cemetery, went into the holy city of Jerusalem, and appeared to many people.

[54]**The Roman officer and the other soldiers at the crucifixion were terrified by the earthquake and all that had happened. They said,**

"Truly, this was the Son of God!"

[55]And many women who had come from Galilee with Jesus to care for him were watching from a distance. [56]Among them were Mary Magdalene, Mary (the mother of James and Joseph), and Zebedee's wife, the mother of James and John.

## The Burial of Jesus

[57]As evening approached, Joseph, a rich man from Arimathea who was one of Jesus' followers, [58]went to Pilate and asked for Jesus' body. And Pilate issued an order to release it to him. [59]Joseph took the body and wrapped it in a long linen cloth. [60]He placed it in his own new tomb, which had been carved out of the rock. Then he rolled a great stone across the entrance as he left. [61]Both Mary Magdalene and the other Mary were sitting nearby watching.

## The Guard at the Tomb

[62]The next day—on the first day of the Passover ceremonies—the leading priests and Pharisees went to see Pilate. [63]They told him, "Sir, we remember what that deceiver once said while he was still alive: 'After three days I will be raised from the dead.' [64]So we request that you seal the tomb until the third day. This will prevent his disciples from coming and stealing his body and then telling everyone he came back to life! If that happens, we'll be worse off than we were at first."

[65]**Pilate replied, "Take guards and secure it the best you can." [66]**So they sealed the tomb and posted guards to protect it.

## The Resurrection

# 28

Early on Sunday morning, as the new day was dawning, Mary Magdalene and the other Mary went out to see the tomb. [2]Suddenly there was a great earthquake, because an angel of the Lord came down from heaven and rolled aside the stone and sat on it. [3]His face shone like lightning, and his clothing was as white as snow.

[4]The guards shook with fear when they saw him, and they fell into a dead faint.

[5]Then the angel spoke to the women. "Don't be afraid!" he said. "I know you are looking for Jesus, who was crucified. [6]He isn't here! He has been raised from the dead, just as he said would happen. Come, see where his body was lying. [7]And now, go quickly and tell his disciples he has been raised from the dead, and he is going ahead of you to Galilee. You will see him there. Remember, I have told you."

[8]The women ran quickly from the tomb. They were very frightened but also filled with great joy, and they rushed to find the disciples to give them the angel's message. [9]And as they went, Jesus met them. "Greetings!" he said. And they ran to him, held his feet, and worshipped him. [10]Then Jesus said to them,

"Don't be afraid! Go tell my brothers to leave for Galilee, and they will see me there."

## The Report of the Guard

[11]As the women were on their way into the city, some of the men who had been guarding the tomb went to the leading priests and told them what had happened. [12]A meeting of all the religious leaders was called, and they decided to bribe the soldiers. [13]They told the soldiers, "You must say, 'Jesus' disciples came during the night while we were sleeping, and they stole his body.' [14]If the governor hears about it, we'll stand up for you and everything will be all right." [15]So the guards accepted the bribe and said what they were told to say. Their story spread widely among the Jews, and they still tell it today.

## The Great Commission

[16]Then the eleven disciples left for Galilee, going to the mountain where Jesus had told them to go. [17]When they saw him, they worshipped him—but some of them still doubted! [18]**Jesus came and told his disciples, "I have been given complete authority in heaven and on earth. [19]**Therefore, go and make disciples of all the nations, baptizing them in the name of the Father and the Son and the Holy Spirit. [20]Teach these new disciples to obey all the commands I have given you. And be sure of this: I am with you always, even to the end of the age."

27:35 A few late manuscripts add *This fulfilled the word of the prophet: "They divided my garments among themselves and cast lots for my robe."* See Ps 22:18.
27:49 Some manuscripts add *And another took a spear and pierced his side, and out flowed water and blood.* Compare John 19:34.

# Change your Form

'Don't forget to pray for us, too, that God will give us many opportunities to preach about his secret plan- that Christ is also for you Gentiles. That is why I am here in chains. Pray that I will proclaim this message as clearly as I should.' Colossians 4:3-4

Good coaches can sustain the big picture while being flexible enough to adapt the teams' strategy. Can we help the church do the same? One summer morning I found myself in the vestry (back room) of an ancient Scottish Church waiting to preach at a 'special evangelistic service'. Sitting next to me was the old 'Beadle' (church caretaker) preparing himself to lead the procession (me) to the sanctuary! I was already a bit disheartened after peeking at the congregation — it was a sea of grey hair, not a young person in sight! I thought 'my father-in-law would love this place because it would make him feel young.' I asked the Beadle, 'How long have you served this church?' He paused, pondered, protruded his lower lip, squinted his eyes, shook his head and said, 'Eh, just over thirty years.' I replied, 'Wow! Over thirty years you must have seen a lot of changes here!' The old man again paused, pondered, protruded his lower lip, squinted his eyes, shook his head and replied matter-of-factly, 'No!' After the service, I thought to myself that if that old Beadle had served that church for two hundred years he would not have seen any change!

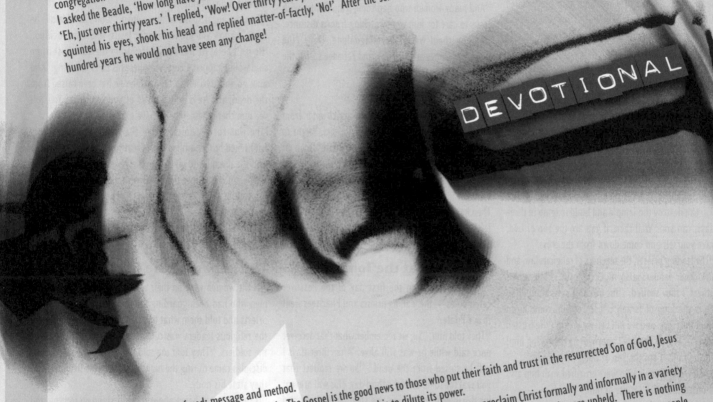

Two components of Christianity get confused: message and method.
The message must be biblically based and convey spiritual truth: The Gospel is the good news to those who put their faith and trust in the resurrected Son of God, Jesus Christ. This message must never, ever change or be watered down. To dilute the Gospel is to dilute its power. However, the method is different, and open to change. There is no biblical mandate for sharing our faith. You may proclaim Christ formally and informally in a variety of ways. You can proclaim the Gospel through speech, word, picture, song, and drama… as long as biblical reliability and compassion are upheld. There is nothing sacred about the method. When one style of transmitting the method becomes more important than the message, your traditions are more important than the people outside the church.

If a coach or business person had the same results as many of our churches they would have a team of sports people who had not changed their style in generations. Imagine golfing with wooden shaft clubs, high jumping into a sandpit, sprinting on cinders, pole-vaulting with a wooden pole. If that does not hit home, how about living without penicillin or smallpox vaccinations?

## Reflection
Do we value sitting in comfortable pews more than making disciples? Hold tight to the message not the method.

## Prayer
Father, help me to understand the difference between truth and style.

'Disregard the immaterial.'
Blake's dictum

Nicked from:A Sporting Guide to Eternity, Steve Connor,
Christian Focus Publications - ISBN 1-85792-746-X

# Mark

Mark is the second of the four 'Gospels' of Christ. Having four Gospels gives us a distinct view of Christ's life from different angles yet, at the same time, all the books are consistent and harmonious. Having four Gospels gives us a powerful, vivid and distinct look at Jesus' life. Remarkably these books are written by very different men, yet all the Gospels have a complementary power, inspired by God, which reveal Jesus' life, character, mission, power and purpose. Each account reveals a special aspect to Jesus' history and lineage. Each writer starts Jesus' history from a different branch of His family tree to emphasise particular aspects of his life and authority.

John takes us back right to the beginning of time and the foundation of the world to reveal Jesus was with his Father as the Creator and Sustainer of 'all things'. Jesus is God.

Luke traces his account of Jesus back to Adam to explain that Jesus is the new Adam. Jesus is our Saviour.

Matthew starts Jesus' life with King David to reveal that Jesus is the fulfilment of the Old Testament prophecies, 'a saviour and new king will come from the line of King David'. Jesus is our King.

Mark cuts to the quick and starts recording Christ's life as an adult: the Messiah-deliverer. This is a fast-paced, action-packed look at Jesus' life and ministry. Jesus calmed the sea, healed the sick, drove out demons, fed the 4,000, debated with religious leaders and recruited, trained and mobilised his followers. This is the shortest Gospel - most Bible scholars consider that Matthew and Luke both used Mark as their model for their own book. Mark's target audience is the Gentiles (non-Jews), which would arguably have been mainly Roman. Mark, inspired by the Holy Spirit, deliberately selects and omits sections of Jesus' ministry that we find in the other Gospels, which would have had little meaning to his unique audience. Mark keeps a very intense pace, emphasising Jesus' action in the face of spiritual adversity. This Gospel emphasises Jesus' servant-hood and sacrifice throughout and we are challenged to do the same in complete surrender and commitment to Christ.

**Improvement**
LIVE it

# MARK

## John the Baptist Prepares the Way

# 1

Here begins the Good News about Jesus the Messiah, the Son of God.

[2]In the book of the prophet Isaiah, God said,
"Look, I am sending my messenger before you,
and he will prepare your way.
[3]He is a voice shouting in the wilderness:
'Prepare a pathway for the Lord's coming!
Make a straight road for him!'"

[4]This messenger was John the Baptist. He lived in the wilderness and was preaching that people should be baptized to show that they had turned from their sins and turned to God to be forgiven. [5]People from Jerusalem and from all over Judea travelled out into the wilderness to see and hear John. And when they confessed their sins, he baptized them in the River Jordan. [6]His clothes were woven from camel hair, and he wore a leather belt; his food was locusts and wild honey. [7]**He announced: "Someone is coming soon who is far greater than I am—so much greater that I am not even worthy to be his slave.** [8]I baptize you with water, but he will baptize you with the Holy Spirit!"

## The Baptism of Jesus

[9]One day Jesus came from Nazareth in Galilee, and he was baptized by John in the River Jordan. [10]And when Jesus came up out of the water, he saw the heavens split open and the Holy Spirit descending like a dove on him. [11]And a voice came from heaven saying, "You are my beloved Son, and I am fully pleased with you."

## The Temptation of Jesus

[12]Immediately the Holy Spirit compelled Jesus to go into the wilderness. [13]He was there for forty days, being tempted by Satan. He was out among the wild animals, and angels took care of him.

## The First Disciples

[14]Later on, after John was arrested by Herod Antipas, Jesus went to Galilee to preach God's Good News. [15]"At last the time has come!" he announced. "The Kingdom of God is near! Turn from your sins and believe this Good News!"

[16]One day as Jesus was walking along the shores of the Sea of Galilee, he saw Simon and his brother,

**STATS**

The first International football played between non-British sides took place in 1902 at Vienna when Austria beat Hungary 5-1.

Andrew, fishing with a net, for they were commercial fishermen. [17]Jesus called out to them, "Come, be my disciples, and I will show you how to fish for people!" [18]And they left their nets at once and went with him. [19]A little farther up the shore Jesus saw Zebedee's sons, James and John, in a boat mending their nets. [20]He called them, too, and immediately they left their father, Zebedee, in the boat with the hired men and went with him.

## Jesus Casts Out an Evil Spirit

[21]Jesus and his companions went to the town of Capernaum, and every Sabbath day he went into the synagogue and taught the people. [22]They were amazed at his teaching, for he taught as one who had real authority—quite unlike the teachers of religious law. [23]A man possessed by an evil spirit was in the synagogue, [24]and he began shouting, "Why are you bothering us, Jesus of Nazareth? Have you come to destroy us? I know who you are—the Holy One sent from God!"
[25]Jesus cut him short. "Be silent! Come out of the man." [26]At that, the evil spirit screamed and threw the man into a convulsion, but then he left him.
[27]Amazement gripped the audience, and they began to discuss what had happened. "What sort of new teaching is this?" they asked excitedly. "It has such authority! Even evil spirits obey his orders!" [28]The news of what he had done spread quickly through that entire area of Galilee.

## Jesus Heals Many People

[29]After Jesus and his disciples left the synagogue, they went over to Simon and Andrew's home, and James and John were with them. [30]Simon's mother-in-law was sick in bed with a high fever. They told Jesus about her right away. [31]He went to her bedside, and as he took her by the hand and helped her to sit up, the fever suddenly left, and she got up and prepared a meal for them.
[32]That evening at sunset, many sick and demon-possessed people were brought to Jesus. [33]And a huge crowd of people from all over Capernaum gathered outside the door to watch. [34]So Jesus healed great numbers of sick people who had many different kinds of diseases, and he ordered many demons to come out of their victims. But because they knew who he was, he refused to allow the demons to speak.

## Jesus Preaches in Galilee

[35]The next morning Jesus awoke long before daybreak and went out alone into the wilderness to pray. [36]Later Simon and the others went out to find him. [37]They said, "Everyone is asking for you."
[38]But he replied, "We must go on to other towns as well, and I will preach to them, too, because that is why I came." [39]So he travelled throughout the region of Galilee, preaching in the synagogues and expelling demons from many people.

## Jesus Heals a Man with Leprosy

[40]A man with leprosy came and knelt in front of Jesus, begging to be healed. "If you want to, you can make me well again," he said. [41]Moved with pity, Jesus touched him. "I want to,"

Make time for God: Excuses are like elbows - we all have two of them! If you can make time for sport, time for friends and entertainment, you can make time for God. It will be the best thing you do all day. "The next morning Jesus awoke long before daybreak and went out alone into the wilderness to pray."
**Mark 1:35**

POWER HABITS

he said. "Be healed!" [42] Instantly the leprosy disappeared—the man was healed. [43] Then Jesus sent him on his way and told him sternly, [44]"Go right over to the priest and let him examine you. Don't talk to anyone along the way. Take along the offering required in the law of Moses for those who have been healed of leprosy, so everyone will have proof of your healing."

[45] But as the man went on his way, he spread the news, telling everyone what had happened to him. As a result, such crowds soon surrounded Jesus that he couldn't enter a town anywhere publicly. He had to stay out in the secluded places, and people from everywhere came to him there.

**CH 2:1-5 WHAT'S IT SAYING?**

**WHAT AM I GOING TO DO ABOUT IT?**

## Jesus Heals a Paralysed Man

**2**

Several days later Jesus returned to Capernaum, and the news of his arrival spread quickly through the town. [2] Soon the house where he was staying was so packed with visitors that there wasn't room for one more person, not even outside the door. And he preached the word to them. [3] Four men arrived carrying a paralysed man on a mat. [4] They couldn't get to Jesus through the crowd, so they dug through the clay roof above his head. Then they lowered the sick man on his mat,

right down in front of Jesus. [5] Seeing their faith, Jesus said to the paralysed man, "My child, your sins are forgiven."

[6] But some of the teachers of religious law who were sitting there said to themselves, [7]"What? This is blasphemy! Who but God can forgive sins!"

[8] Jesus knew what they were discussing among themselves, so he said to them, "Why do you think this is blasphemy? [9] Is it easier to say to the paralysed man, 'Your sins are forgiven' or 'Get up, pick up your mat, and walk'?

[10] I will prove that I, the Son of Man, have the authority on earth to forgive sins." Then Jesus turned to the paralysed man and said, [11]"Stand up, take your mat, and go on home, because you are healed!"

[12] The man jumped up, took the mat, and pushed his way through the stunned onlookers. Then they all praised God. "We've never seen anything like this before!" they exclaimed.

## Jesus Calls Levi (Matthew)

[13] Then Jesus went out to the lakeshore again and taught the crowds that gathered around him. [14] As he walked along, he saw Levi son of Alphaeus sitting at his tax-collection booth.

"Come, be my disciple," Jesus said to him. So Levi got up and followed him.

[15] That night Levi invited Jesus and his disciples to be his dinner guests, along with his fellow tax collectors and many other notorious sinners. (There were many people of this kind among the crowds that followed Jesus.) [16] But when some of the teachers of religious law who were Pharisees saw him eating with people like that, they said to his disciples, "Why does he eat with such scum?"

[17] When Jesus heard this, he told them, "Healthy people don't need a doctor—sick people do. I have come to call sinners, not those who think they are already good enough."

## A Discussion about Fasting

[18] John's disciples and the Pharisees sometimes fasted. One day some people came to Jesus and asked, "Why do John's disciples and the Pharisees fast, but your disciples don't fast?"

[19] Jesus replied, "Do wedding guests fast while celebrating with the groom? Of course not. They can't fast while they are with the groom. [20] But someday he will be taken away from them, and then they will fast. [21] And who would patch an old garment with unshrunk cloth? For the new patch shrinks and pulls away from the old cloth, leaving an even bigger hole than before.

# WHAT DOES IT MEAN?

### Sea of Galilee

The Sea of Galilee, is a lake 12.5 miles long, and over 7 wide and about 60 miles north-east of Jerusalem with access to all nations and countries. It attracted the Lord Jesus, and induced him to make this spot the centre of his public ministry, his "own city" (Matt. 9:1).

It was famous for its fishing and attracted a large cross-section of people. Capernaum was a coastal city where Jesus chose fishermen, Peter and his brother Andrew, and James and John, to be disciples, and mobilised them to be "fishers of men" (Matt. 4:18,22; Mark 1:16-20; Luke 5: 1-11). Jesus showed his power by calming a horrific storm and here also he showed himself to his disciples after his resurrection (John 21). It is also called, 'Lake of Gennesareth' and the 'Sea of Tiberias'.

²²And no one puts new wine into old wineskins. The wine would burst the wineskins, spilling the wine and ruining the skins. New wine needs new wineskins."

## A Discussion about the Sabbath

²³One Sabbath day as Jesus was walking through some cornfields, his disciples began breaking off heads of wheat.

²⁴But the Pharisees said to Jesus, "They shouldn't be doing that! It's against the law to work by harvesting corn on the Sabbath."

²⁵But Jesus replied, "Haven't you ever read in the Scriptures what King David did when he and his companions were hungry? ²⁶He went into the house of God (during the days when Abiathar was high priest), ate the special bread reserved for the priests alone, and then gave some to his companions. That was breaking the law, too." ²⁷Then he said to them, **"The Sabbath was made to benefit people, and not people to benefit the Sabbath.** ²⁸And I, the Son of Man, am master even of the Sabbath!"

## Jesus Heals on the Sabbath

# 3

Jesus went into the synagogue again and noticed a man with a deformed hand. ²Since it was the Sabbath, Jesus' enemies watched him closely. Would he heal the man's hand on the Sabbath? If he did, they planned to condemn him. ³Jesus said to the man, "Come and stand in front of everyone." ⁴Then he turned to his critics and asked, "Is it legal to do good deeds on the Sabbath, or is it a day for doing harm? Is this a day to save life or to destroy it?" But they wouldn't answer him. ⁵He looked around at them angrily, because he

was deeply disturbed by their hard hearts. Then he said to the man, "Reach out your hand." The man reached out his hand, and it became normal again! ⁶At once the Pharisees went away and met with the supporters of Herod to discuss plans for killing Jesus.

## Crowds Follow Jesus

⁷Jesus and his disciples went out to the lake, followed by a huge crowd from all over Galilee, Judea, ⁸Jerusalem, Idumea, from east of the River Jordan, and even from as far away as Tyre and Sidon. The news about his miracles had spread far and wide, and vast numbers of people came to see him for themselves. ⁹Jesus instructed his disciples to bring around a boat and to have it ready in case he was crowded off the beach. ¹⁰There had been many healings that day. As a result, many sick people were crowding around him, trying to touch him. ¹¹And whenever those possessed by evil spirits caught sight of him, they would fall down in front of him shrieking, "You are the Son of God!" ¹²But Jesus strictly warned them not to say who he was.

**There are 66 books in the Bible, 39 in the Old Testament and 27 in the New Testament.**

## Jesus Chooses the Twelve Apostles

¹³Afterwards Jesus went up on a mountain and called the ones he wanted to go with him. And they came to

him. ¹⁴Then he selected twelve of them to be his regular companions, calling them apostles. He sent them out to preach, ¹⁵and he gave them authority to cast out demons. ¹⁶These are the names of the twelve he chose:

Simon (he renamed him Peter),
¹⁷James and John (the sons of Zebedee, but Jesus nicknamed them "Sons of Thunder"),
¹⁸Andrew,
Philip,
Bartholomew,
Matthew,
Thomas,
James (son of Alphaeus),
Thaddaeus,
Simon (the Zealot),
¹⁹Judas Iscariot (who later betrayed him).

## Jesus and the Prince of Demons

²⁰When Jesus returned to the house where he was staying, the crowds began to gather again, and soon he and his disciples couldn't even find time to eat. ²¹When his family heard what was happening, they tried to take him home with them. "He's out of his mind," they said.

²²But the teachers of religious law who had arrived from Jerusalem said, "He's possessed by Satan, the prince of demons. That's where he gets the power to cast out demons." ²³Jesus called them over and said to them by way of illustration, "How can Satan cast out Satan? ²⁴A kingdom at war with itself will collapse. ²⁵A home divided against itself is doomed. ²⁶And if Satan is fighting against himself, how can he stand? He would never survive. ²⁷Let me illustrate this. You can't enter a strong man's house and rob him without first tying him up. Only then can his house be robbed! ²⁸I assure you that any sin can be forgiven, including blasphemy; ²⁹but anyone who blasphemes against the Holy Spirit will never be forgiven. It is an eternal sin." ³⁰He told them this because they were saying he had an evil spirit.

---

'Choose your side!' MARK 3:23-29

The Christian life is a competition, a fight, and a war in which we are the soldiers. As sportspeople we prepare mentally and physically, often at great sacrifice of time and effort, in order to win games. How much more, having identified our opponent, should we be prepared for a lifetime in the service of Christ? In a delightful illustration Jesus talked about a strong man (the devil) defending his possessions until an even stronger man (Jesus) comes along, overpowers and disarms him. We were all playing in the devil's team, but Christ has transferred us into his team. The transfer fee was his precious blood. Come the final whistle Satan's defeat is certain. CHOOSE YOUR SIDE - 'He who is not with me is against me, and he who does not gather with me scatters.' Imagine being on a rugby field, let us say Western Samoa v New Zealand; perhaps you are a hooker and just as the scrum goes down you think 'I don't know what side I'm on!' In the middle of that set scrum there would be no room for neutrality. Jesus says there is no room for neutrality in the spiritual battle. If you are not with him gathering into Heaven, you are with the enemy scattering into Hell.

# STAND
# POINT

## When you have doubts

### 4:41

They were filled with awe and said among themselves, "Who is this man, that even the wind and waves obey him?"

## The True Family of Jesus

[31]Jesus' mother and brothers arrived at the house where he was teaching. They stood outside and sent word for him to come out and talk with them. [32]There was a crowd around Jesus, and someone said, "Your mother and your brothers and sisters are outside, asking for you."

[33]Jesus replied, "Who is my mother? Who are my brothers?" [34]Then he looked at those around him and said, "These are my mother and brothers. [35]Anyone who does God's will is my brother and sister and mother."

## Story of the Farmer Scattering Seed

# 4

Once again Jesus began teaching by the lakeshore. There was such a large crowd along the shore that he got into a boat and sat down and spoke from there. [2]He began to teach the people by telling many stories such as this one:

[3]"Listen! A farmer went out to plant some seed. [4]As he scattered it across his field, some seed fell on a footpath, and the birds came and ate it. [5]Other seed fell on shallow soil with underlying rock. The plant sprang up quickly, [6]but it soon wilted beneath the hot sun and died because the roots had no nourishment in the shallow soil. [7]Other seed fell among thorns that shot up and choked out the tender blades so that it produced no grain. [8]Still other seed fell on fertile soil and produced a crop that was thirty, sixty, and even a hundred times as much as had been planted." Then he said, [9]"Anyone who is willing to hear should listen and understand!"

[10]Later, when Jesus was alone with the twelve disciples and with the others who were gathered around, they asked him, "What do your stories mean?"

[11]He replied, "You are permitted to understand the secret about the Kingdom of God. But I am using these stories to conceal everything about it from outsiders, [12]so that the

Scriptures might be fulfilled:
'They see what I do,
but they don't perceive its meaning.
They hear my words,
but they don't understand.
So they will not turn from their sins
and be forgiven.'

[13]"But if you can't understand this story, how will you understand all the others I am going to tell? [14]The farmer I talked about is the one who brings God's message to others. [15]The seed that fell on the hard path represents those who hear the message, but then Satan comes at once and takes it away from them. [16]The rocky soil represents those who hear the message and receive it with joy. [17]But like young plants in such soil, their roots don't go very deep. At first they get along fine, but they wilt as soon as they have problems or are persecuted because they believe the word. [18]**The thorny ground represents those who hear and accept the Good News, [19]but all too quickly the message is crowded out by the cares of this life, the lure of wealth, and the desire for nice things, so no crop is produced.** [20]But the good soil represents those who hear and accept God's message and produce a huge harvest—thirty, sixty, or even a hundred times as much as had been planted."

## Illustration of the Lamp

[21]Then Jesus asked them, "Would anyone light a lamp and then put it under a basket or under a bed to shut out the light? Of course not! A lamp is placed on a stand, where its light will shine.

[22]"Everything that is now hidden or secret will eventually be brought to light. [23]Anyone who is willing to hear should listen and understand! [24]And be sure to pay attention to what you hear. The more you do this, the more you will understand—and even more, besides. [25]To those who are open to my teaching, more understanding will be given. But to those who are not

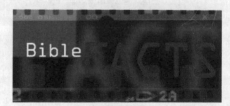

Bible FACTS

**The word "Christian" appears only three times in the Bible: Acts 11:26; 26:28; 1 Peter 4:16.**

listening, even what they have will be taken away from them."

## action

### CH 4:21-25 WHAT'S IT SAYING?

### WHAT AM I GOING TO DO ABOUT IT?

## Illustration of the Growing Seed

[26]Jesus also said, "Here is another illustration of what the Kingdom of God is like: A farmer planted seeds in a field, [27]and then he went on with his other activities. As the days went by, the seeds sprouted and grew without the farmer's help, [28]because the earth produces crops on its own. First a leaf blade pushes through, then the heads of wheat are formed, and finally the grain ripens. [29]And as soon as the grain is ready, the farmer comes and harvests it with a sickle."

## Illustration of the Mustard Seed

[30]Jesus asked, "How can I describe the Kingdom of God? What story should I use to illustrate it? [31]It is like a tiny mustard seed. Though this is one of the smallest of seeds, [32]it grows to become one of the largest of plants, with long branches where birds can come and find shelter."

[33]He used many such stories and illustrations to teach the people as much as they were able to understand.

## The Stretch is Not Enough:

Stretching is often incorrectly considered a complete warm-up because it is commonly done during the first stage of training. In addition to the stretch, a walk to run that gradually increases heart rate will help prepare the body for action by raising body temperatures and blood flow.

[34]In fact, in his public teaching he taught only with parables, but afterwards when he was alone with his disciples, he explained the meaning to them.

## Jesus Calms the Storm

[35]As evening came, Jesus said to his disciples, "Let's cross to the other side of the lake." [36]He was already in the boat, so they started out, leaving the crowds behind (although other boats followed). [37]But soon a fierce storm arose. High waves began to break into the boat until it was nearly full of water.

[38]Jesus was sleeping at the back of the boat with his head on a cushion. Frantically they woke him up, shouting, "Teacher, don't you even care that we are going to drown?"

[39]**When he woke up, he rebuked the wind and said to the water, "Silence! Be still!" Suddenly the wind stopped, and there was a great calm. [40]And he asked them, "Why are you so afraid? Do you still not have faith in me?"**

[41]And they were filled with awe and said among themselves, "Who is this man, that even the wind and waves obey him?"

## Jesus Heals a Demon-Possessed Man

# 5

So they arrived at the other side of the lake, in the land of the Gerasenes. [2]Just as Jesus was climbing from the boat, a man possessed by an evil spirit ran out from a cemetery to meet him. [3]This man lived among the tombs and could not be restrained, even with a chain. [4]Whenever he was put into chains and shackles—as he often was—he snapped the chains from his wrists and smashed the shackles. No one was strong enough to control him. [5]All day long and throughout the night, he would wander among the tombs and in the hills, screaming and hitting himself with stones.

[6]When Jesus was still some distance away, the man saw him. He ran to meet Jesus and fell down before him. [7]He gave a terrible scream, shrieking, "Why are you bothering me, Jesus, Son of the Most High God? For God's sake, don't torture me!" [8]For Jesus had already said to the spirit, "Come out of the man, you evil spirit."

[9]Then Jesus asked, "What is your name?"

And the spirit replied, "Legion, because there are many of us here inside this man." [10]Then the spirits begged him again and again not to send them to some distant place. [11]There happened to be a large herd of pigs feeding on the hillside nearby. [12]"Send us into those pigs," the evil spirits begged. [13]Jesus gave them permission. So the evil spirits came out of the man

and entered the pigs, and the entire herd of two thousand pigs plunged down the steep hillside into the lake, where they drowned.

[14]The herdsmen fled to the nearby city and the surrounding countryside, spreading the news as they ran. Everyone rushed out to see for themselves. [15]A crowd soon gathered around Jesus, but they were frightened when they saw the man who had been demon possessed, for he was sitting there fully clothed and perfectly sane. [16]Those who had seen what happened to the man and to the pigs told everyone about it, [17]and the crowd began pleading with Jesus to go away and leave them alone.

[18]When Jesus got back into the boat, the man who had been demon possessed begged to go, too. [19]But Jesus said, "No, go home to your friends, and tell them what wonderful things the Lord has done for you and how merciful he has been." [20]So the man started off to visit the Ten Towns of that region and began to tell everyone about the great things Jesus had done for him; and everyone was amazed at what he told them.

## Jesus Heals in Response to Faith

[21]When Jesus went back across to the other side of the lake, a large crowd gathered around him on the shore. [22]A leader of the local synagogue, whose name was Jairus, came and fell down before him, [23]pleading with him to heal his little daughter. "She is about to die," he said in desperation. "Please come and place your hands on her; heal her so she can live."

[24]Jesus went with him, and the crowd thronged behind. [25]**And there was a woman in the crowd who had had a haemorrhage for twelve years. [26]She had**

'Pro-active player & Pro-active prayer" Mark 6:46

Again we see Jesus in action. Jesus knows one of the most important parts of his life is to stay in complete harmony with his Father. Prayer is action! Prayer gets God's purpose done. Before every big and many small events we see Jesus get away and pray. One great thing about athletes is you are pro-active. You don't just sit around and talk about life, you live it! God wants you not only to be a pro-active 'player' - but a pro-active 'prayer'. How are your goals being achieved in your training schedule?

BIBLE HIT

suffered a great deal from many doctors through the years and had spent everything she had to pay them, but she had got no better. In fact, she was worse. ²⁷She had heard about Jesus, so she came up behind him through the crowd and touched the fringe of his robe. ²⁸For she thought to herself, "If I can just touch his clothing, I will be healed." ²⁹Immediately the bleeding stopped, and she could feel that she had been healed!

³⁰Jesus realized at once that healing power had gone out from him, so he turned around in the crowd and asked, "Who touched my clothes?"

³¹His disciples said to him, "All this crowd is pressing around you. How can you ask, 'Who touched me?'"

³²But he kept on looking around to see who had done it. ³³Then the frightened woman, trembling at the realization of what had happened to her, came and fell at his feet and told him what she had done. ³⁴And he said to her, "Daughter, your faith has made you well. Go in peace. You have been healed." ³⁵While he was still speaking to her, messengers arrived from Jairus's home with the message, "Your daughter is dead. There's no use troubling the Teacher now."

³⁶But Jesus ignored their comments and said to Jairus, "Don't be afraid. Just trust me." ³⁷Then Jesus stopped the crowd and wouldn't let anyone go with him except Peter and James and John. ³⁸When they came to the home of the synagogue leader, Jesus saw the commotion and the weeping and wailing. ³⁹He went inside and spoke to the people. "Why all this weeping and commotion?" he asked. "The child isn't dead; she is only asleep."

⁴⁰The crowd laughed at him, but he told them all to go outside. Then he took the girl's father and mother and his three disciples into the room where the girl was lying. ⁴¹Holding her hand, he said to her, "Get up, little girl!" ⁴²And the girl,

count on it

**God will keep His promise**

Friends, teams, coaches and you yourself will sometime eventually be let down. But Jesus Christ will never, never, never let you down. He is flawless! 'For all of GOD'S promises have been fulfilled in HIM. That is why we say "Amen" when we give glory to God through CHRIST.'
2 Corinthians 1:20
**Count on it!**

who was twelve years old, immediately stood up and walked around! Her parents were absolutely overwhelmed. ⁴³Jesus commanded them not to tell anyone what had happened, and he told them to give her something to eat.

## Jesus Rejected at Nazareth

### 6

Jesus left that part of the country and returned with his disciples to Nazareth, his home town. ²The next Sabbath he began teaching in the synagogue, and many who heard him were astonished. They asked, "Where did he get all his wisdom and the power to perform such miracles? ³He's just the carpenter, the son of Mary and brother of James, Joseph, Judas, and Simon. And his sisters live right here among us." They were deeply offended and refused to believe in him. ⁴Then Jesus told them, "A prophet is honoured everywhere except in his own home town and among his relatives and his own family." ⁵And because of their unbelief, he couldn't do any mighty miracles among them except to place his hands on a few sick people and heal them. ⁶And he was amazed at their unbelief.

## Jesus Sends Out the Twelve Apostles

Then Jesus went out from village to village, teaching. ⁷And he called his twelve disciples together and sent them out two by two, with authority to cast out evil spirits. ⁸He told them to take nothing with them except a walking stick—no food, no traveller's bag, no money. ⁹He told them to wear sandals but not to take even an extra coat. ¹⁰"When you enter each village, be a guest in only one home," he said. ¹¹"And if a village won't welcome you or listen to you, shake off its dust from your feet as you leave. It is a sign that you have abandoned that village to its fate."

¹²So the disciples went out, telling all they met to turn from their sins. ¹³And they cast out many demons and healed many sick people, anointing them with olive oil.

## The Death of John the Baptist

¹⁴Herod Antipas, the king, soon heard about Jesus, because people everywhere were talking about him. Some were saying, "This must be John the Baptist come back to life again. That is why he can do such miracles." ¹⁵Others thought Jesus was the ancient prophet Elijah. Still others thought he was a prophet like the other great prophets of the past. ¹⁶When Herod heard about Jesus, he said, "John, the man I beheaded, has come back from the dead." ¹⁷For Herod had sent soldiers to arrest and imprison John as a favour to Herodias. She had been his brother Philip's wife, but Herod had married her. ¹⁸John kept telling Herod, "It is illegal for you to marry your brother's wife." ¹⁹Herodias was enraged and wanted John killed in

Who are the five top people from history you admire?

1
2
3
4
5

BIG FIVE

revenge, but without Herod's approval she was powerless. [20]And Herod respected John, knowing that he was a good and holy man, so he kept him under his protection. Herod was disturbed whenever he talked with John, but even so, he liked to listen to him.

[21]Herodias's chance finally came. It was Herod's birthday, and he gave a party for his palace aides, army officers, and the leading citizens of Galilee. [22]Then his daughter, also named Herodias, came in and performed a dance that greatly pleased them all. "Ask me for anything you like," the king said to the girl, "and I will give it to you." [23]Then he promised, "I will give you whatever you ask, up to half of my kingdom!"

[24]She went out and asked her mother, "What should I ask for?"

Her mother told her, "Ask for John the Baptist's head!"

[25]So the girl hurried back to the king and told him, "I want the head of John the Baptist, right now, on a tray!"

[26]Then the king was very sorry, but he was embarrassed to break his oath in front of his guests. [27]So he sent an executioner to the prison to cut off John's head and bring it to him. The soldier beheaded John in the prison, [28]brought his head on a tray, and gave it to the girl, who took it to her mother. [29]When John's disciples heard what had happened, they came for his body and buried it in a tomb.

## Jesus Feeds Five Thousand

[30]The apostles returned to Jesus from their ministry tour and told him all they had done and what they had taught. [31]Then Jesus said, "Let's get away from the crowds for a while and rest." There were so many people coming and going that Jesus and his apostles didn't even have time to eat. [32]They left by boat for a quieter spot. [33]But many people saw them leaving, and people from many towns ran ahead along the shore and met them as they landed. [34]A vast crowd was there as he stepped from the boat, and he had compassion on them because they were like sheep without a shepherd. So he taught them many things. [35]Late in the afternoon his disciples came to him and said, "This is a desolate place, and it is getting late. [36]Send the crowds away so they can go to the nearby farms and villages and buy themselves some food."

[37]But Jesus said, "You feed them."

"With what?" they asked. "It would take a small fortune to buy food for all this crowd!"

[38]"How much food do you have?" he asked. "Go and find out."

They came back and reported, "We have five loaves of bread and two fish." [39]Then Jesus told the crowd to sit down in groups on the green grass. [40]So they sat in groups of fifty or a hundred.

[41]Jesus took the five loaves and two fish, looked up towards heaven, and asked God's blessing on the food. Breaking the loaves into pieces, he kept giving the bread and fish to the disciples to give to the people. [42]They all ate as much as they wanted, [43]and they picked up twelve baskets of leftover bread and fish. [44]Five thousand men had eaten from those five loaves!

## Jesus Walks on Water

[45]Immediately after this, Jesus made his disciples get back into the boat and head out across the lake to Bethsaida, while he sent the people home. [46]**Afterwards he went up into the hills by himself to pray.**

[47]During the night, the disciples were in their boat out in the middle of the lake, and Jesus was alone on land. [48]He saw that they were in serious trouble, rowing hard and struggling against the wind and waves. About three o'clock in the morning he came to them, walking on the water. He started to go past them, [49]but when they saw him walking on the water, they screamed in terror, thinking he was a ghost. [50]They were all terrified when they saw him. But Jesus spoke to them at once. "It's all right," he said. "I am here! Don't be afraid." [51]Then he climbed into the boat, and the wind stopped. They were astonished at what they saw. [52]They still didn't understand the significance of the miracle of the multiplied loaves, for their hearts were hard and they did not believe.

[53]When they arrived at Gennesaret on the other side of the lake, they anchored the boat [54]and climbed out. The people standing there recognized him at once, [55]and they ran throughout the whole area and began

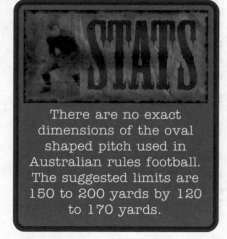

There are no exact dimensions of the oval shaped pitch used in Australian rules football. The suggested limits are 150 to 200 yards by 120 to 170 yards.

carrying sick people to him on mats. [56]Wherever he went—in villages and cities and out on the farms—they laid the sick in the market-places and streets. The sick begged him to let them at least touch the fringe of his robe, and all who touched it were healed.

## Jesus Teaches about Inner Purity

# 7

One day some Pharisees and teachers of religious law arrived from Jerusalem to confront Jesus. [2]They noticed that some of Jesus' disciples failed to follow the usual Jewish ritual of hand washing before eating. [3](The Jews, especially the Pharisees, do not eat until they have poured water over their cupped hands, as required by their ancient traditions. [4]Similarly, they eat nothing bought from the market unless they have immersed their hands in water. This is but one of many traditions they have clung to—such as their ceremony of washing cups, pitchers, and kettles. ) [5]So the Pharisees and teachers of religious law asked him, "Why don't your disciples follow our age-old customs? For they eat without first performing the hand-washing ceremony."

[6]Jesus replied, "You hypocrites! Isaiah was prophesying about you when he said,

[7]'These people honour me with their lips, but their hearts are far away. Their worship is a farce, for they replace God's commands with their own man-made teachings.'

[8]For you ignore God's specific laws and substitute your own traditions."

[9]Then he said, "You reject God's laws in order to hold on to your own traditions. [10]For instance, Moses gave you this law from God: 'Honour your father and mother,' and 'Anyone who speaks evil of father or mother must be put to death.' [11]But you say it is all right for people to say to their parents, 'Sorry, I can't help you. For I have vowed to give to God what I could have given to you.' [12]You let them disregard their needy parents. [13]As such, you break the law of God in order to protect your own tradition. And this is only one example. There are many, many others."

[14]**Then Jesus called to the crowd to come and hear. "All of you listen," he said, "and try to understand. [15]You are not defiled by what you eat; you are defiled by what you say and do!"** *

[17]Then Jesus went into a house to get away from the crowds, and his disciples asked him what he meant by the statement he had made. [18]"Don't you understand either?" he asked. "Can't you see that what you eat won't defile you? [19]Food doesn't come in contact with your heart, but only passes

7:15 Some manuscripts add verse 16, *Anyone with ears to hear should listen and understand.* Compare 4:9, 23.

MARK

**'Prophecies fulfilled' Mark 8:22**

In the Old Testament a prophet called Isaiah made several predictions about Christ, 700 years before he was born. Here is one of them: Isaiah 35:4-5 says: 'Be strong and do not fear, for your God is coming to destroy your enemies. He is coming to save you. And when he comes, he will open the eyes of the blind and unstop the ears of the deaf.' Jesus fulfilled all of Isaiah's predictions including helping the blind and deaf, both the physically blind and deaf and the spiritually blind and deaf.

through the stomach and then comes out again." (By saying this, he showed that every kind of food is acceptable.) [20]And then he added, "It is the thought-life that defiles you. [21]For from within, out of a person's heart, come evil thoughts, sexual immorality, theft, murder, [22]adultery, greed, wickedness, deceit, eagerness for lustful pleasure, envy, slander, pride, and foolishness. [23]All these vile things come from within; they are what defile you and make you unacceptable to God."

**CH 7:7-23 WHAT'S IT SAYING?**

**WHAT AM I GOING TO DO ABOUT IT?**

## The Faith of a Gentile Woman

[24]Then Jesus left Galilee and went north to the region of Tyre. He tried to keep it secret that he was there, but he couldn't. As usual, the news of his arrival spread fast. [25]Right away a woman came to him whose little girl was possessed by an evil spirit. She had heard about Jesus, and now she came and fell at his feet. [26]She begged him to release her child from the demon's control. Since she was a Gentile, born in Syrian Phoenicia, [27]Jesus told her, "First I should help my own family, the Jews. It isn't right to take food from the children and throw it to the dogs."

[28]She replied, "That's true, Lord, but even the dogs under the table are given some crumbs from the children's plates."

[29]"Good answer!" he said. "And because you have answered so well, I have healed your daughter." [30]And when she arrived home, her little girl was lying quietly in bed, and the demon was gone.

## Jesus Heals a Deaf and Mute Man

[31]Jesus left Tyre and went to Sidon, then back to the Sea of Galilee and the region of the Ten Towns. [32]A deaf man with a speech impediment was brought to him, and the people begged Jesus to lay his hands on the man to heal him. [33]Jesus led him to a private place away from the crowd. He put his fingers into the man's ears. Then, spitting onto his own fingers, he touched the man's tongue with the spittle. [34]And looking up to heaven, he sighed and commanded, "Be opened!" [35]Instantly the man could hear perfectly and speak plainly! [36]Jesus told the crowd not to tell anyone, but the more he told them not to, the more they spread the news, [37]for they were completely amazed. Again and again they said, **"Everything he does is wonderful. He even heals those who are deaf and mute."**

## Jesus Feeds Four Thousand

# 8

About this time another great crowd had gathered, and the people ran out of food again. Jesus called his disciples and told them, [2]"I feel sorry for these people. They have been here with me for three days, and they have nothing left to eat. [3]And if I send them home without feeding them, they will faint along the road. For some of them have come a long distance."

[4]"How are we supposed to find enough food for them here in the wilderness?" his disciples asked.

[5]"How many loaves of bread do you have?" he asked. "Seven," they replied. [6]So Jesus told all the people to sit down on the ground. Then he took the seven loaves, thanked God for them, broke them into pieces, and gave them to his disciples, who distributed the bread to the crowd. [7]A few small fish were found, too, so Jesus also blessed these and told the disciples to pass them out.

[8]They ate until they were full, and when the scraps were picked up, there were seven large baskets of food left over! [9]There were about four thousand people in the crowd that day, and he sent them home after they had eaten. [10]Immediately after this, he got into a boat with his disciples and crossed over to the region of Dalmanutha.

## Pharisees Demand a Miraculous Sign

[11]When the Pharisees heard that Jesus had arrived, they came to argue with him. Testing him to see if he was from God, they demanded, "Give us a miraculous sign from heaven to prove yourself."

[12]When he heard this, he sighed deeply and said, "Why do you people keep demanding a miraculous sign? I assure you, I will not give this generation any such sign." [13]So he got back into the boat and left them, and he crossed to the other side of the lake.

## Yeast of the Pharisees and Herod

[14]But the disciples discovered they had forgotten to bring any food, so there was only one loaf of bread with them in the boat. [15]As they were crossing the lake, Jesus warned them, "Beware of the yeast of the Pharisees and of Herod."

[16]They decided he was saying this because they hadn't brought any bread. [17]Jesus knew what they were thinking, so he said, "Why are you so worried about

having no food? Won't you ever learn or understand? Are your hearts too hard to take it in? [18]You have eyes—can't you see? You have ears—can't you hear?' Don't you remember anything at all? [19]What about the five thousand men I fed with five loaves of bread? How many baskets of leftovers did you pick up afterwards?"

"Twelve," they said.

[20]"And when I fed the four thousand with seven loaves, how many large baskets of leftovers did you pick up?"

"Seven," they said.

[21]"Don't you understand even yet?" he asked them.

## Jesus Heals a Blind Man

[22]When they arrived at Bethsaida, some people brought a blind man to Jesus, and they begged him to touch and heal the man. [23]Jesus took the blind man by the hand and led him out of the village. Then, spitting on the man's eyes, he laid his hands on him and asked, "Can you see anything now?"

[24]The man looked around. "Yes," he said, "I see people, but I can't see them very clearly. They look like trees walking around."

[25]Then Jesus placed his hands over the man's eyes again. As the man stared intently, his sight was completely restored, and he could see everything clearly. [26]Jesus sent him home, saying, "Don't go back into the village on your way home."

## Peter's Declaration about Jesus

[27]Jesus and his disciples left Galilee and went up to the villages of Caesarea Philippi. As they were walking along, he asked them, "Who do people say I am?"

[28]"Well," they replied, "some say John the Baptist, some say Elijah, and others say you are one of the other prophets."

[29]Then Jesus asked, "Who do you say I am?" Peter replied, "You are the Messiah." [30]But Jesus warned them not to tell anyone about him.

## Jesus Predicts His Death

[31]Then Jesus began to tell them that he, the Son of Man, would suffer many terrible things and be rejected by the leaders, the leading priests, and the teachers of religious law. He would be killed, and three days later he would rise again. [32]As he talked about this openly with his disciples, Peter took him aside and told him he shouldn't say things like that.

[33]Jesus turned and looked at his disciples and then said to Peter very sternly, "Get away from me, Satan! You are seeing things merely from a human point of view, not from God's."

## count on it

### Keep your focus

If you feel like you are floundering and need to make sense out of your life, remember you have a purpose: that purpose is to worship God. In all you do you are to worship God. In worship, you will find focus and happiness! "The devil took (Jesus) to the peak of a mountain and showed him the nations of the world and all their glory. 'I will give it all to you,' he said, 'if you will only kneel down and worship me.' 'Get out of here, Satan,' Jesus told him. 'For the Scriptures say,
You must worship the LORD your God; serve only him.'"
Matt. 4: 8-10
**Count on it!**

[34]**Then he called his disciples and the crowds to come over and listen. "If any of you wants to be my follower," he told them, "you must put aside your selfish ambition, shoulder your cross, and follow me.** [35]If you try to keep your life for yourself, you will lose it. But if you give up your life for my sake and for the sake of the Good News, you will find true life. [36]And how do you benefit if you gain the whole world but lose your own soul in the process? [37]Is anything worth more than your soul? [38]If a person is ashamed of me and my message in these adulterous and sinful days, I, the Son of Man, will be ashamed of that person when I return in the glory of my Father with the holy angels."

## 9

Jesus went on to say, "I assure you that some of you standing here right now will not die before you see the Kingdom of God arrive in great power!"

## The Transfiguration

[2]Six days later Jesus took Peter, James, and John to the top of a mountain. No one else was there. As the men watched, Jesus' appearance changed, [3]and his clothing became dazzling white, far whiter than any earthly process could ever make it. [4]Then Elijah and Moses appeared and began talking with Jesus.

[5]"Teacher, this is wonderful!" Peter exclaimed. "We will make three shrines—one for you, one for Moses, and one for Elijah." [6]He didn't really know what to say, for they were all terribly afraid.

[7]Then a cloud came over them, and a voice from the cloud said, "This is my beloved Son. Listen to him." [8]Suddenly they looked around, and Moses and Elijah were gone, and only Jesus was with them. [9]As they descended the mountainside, he told them not to tell anyone what they had seen until he, the Son of Man, had risen from the dead. [10]So they kept it to themselves, but they often asked each other what he meant by "rising from the dead."

[11]Now they began asking him, "Why do the teachers of religious law insist that Elijah must return before the Messiah comes?"

[12]Jesus responded, "Elijah is indeed coming first to set everything in order. Why then is it written in the Scriptures that the Son of Man must suffer and be treated with utter contempt? [13]But I tell you, Elijah has already come, and he was badly mistreated, just as the Scriptures predicted."

## Jesus Heals a Boy Possessed by an Evil Spirit

[14]At the foot of the mountain they found a great crowd surrounding the other disciples, as some teachers of religious

## STAND POINT

### When you feel like quitting

### 9:23-24

"What do you mean, 'If I can'?" Jesus asked. "Anything is possible if a person believes." The father instantly replied, "I do believe, but help me not to doubt!"

law were arguing with them. [15]The crowd watched Jesus in awe as he came towards them, and then they ran to greet him. [16]"What is all this arguing about?" he asked.

[17]One of the men in the crowd spoke up and said, "Teacher, I brought my son for you to heal him. He can't speak because he is possessed by an evil spirit that won't let him talk. [18]And whenever this evil spirit seizes him, it throws him violently to the ground and makes him foam at the mouth and grind his teeth and become rigid. So I asked your disciples to cast out the evil spirit, but they couldn't do it."

[19]Jesus said to them, "You faithless people! How long must I be with you until you believe? How long must I put up with you? Bring the boy to me." [20]So they brought the boy. But when the evil spirit saw Jesus, it threw the child into a violent convulsion, and he fell to the ground, writhing and foaming at the mouth. [21]"How long has this been happening?" Jesus asked the boy's father.

He replied, "Since he was very small. [22]The evil spirit often makes him fall into the fire or into water, trying to kill him. Have mercy on us and help us. Do something if you can."

[23]"What do you mean, 'If I can'?" Jesus asked. "Anything is possible if a person believes."

[24]The father instantly replied, "I do believe, but help me not to doubt!"

[25]When Jesus saw that the crowd of onlookers was growing, he rebuked the evil spirit. "Spirit of deafness and muteness," he said, "I command you to come out of this child and never enter him again!" [26]Then the spirit screamed and threw the boy into another violent convulsion and left him. The boy lay there motionless, and he appeared to be dead. A murmur ran through the crowd, "He's dead." [27]But Jesus took him by the hand and helped him to his feet, and he stood up.

[28]Afterwards, when Jesus was alone in the house with his disciples, they asked him, "Why couldn't we cast out that evil spirit?"

[29]Jesus replied, "This kind can be cast out only by prayer."

## Jesus Again Predicts His Death

[30]**Leaving that region, they travelled through Galilee. Jesus tried to avoid all publicity [31]in order to spend more time with his disciples and teach them. He said to them, "The Son of Man is going to be betrayed. He will be killed, but three days later he will rise from the dead." [32]**But they didn't understand what he was saying, and they were afraid to ask him what he meant.

## The Greatest in the Kingdom

[33]After they arrived at Capernaum, Jesus and his disciples settled in the house where they would be staying. Jesus asked them, "What were you discussing out on the road?"

[34]But they didn't answer, because they had been arguing about which of them was the greatest. [35]He sat down and called the twelve disciples over to him. Then he said, "Anyone who wants to be the first must take last place and be the servant of everyone else."

[36]Then he put a little child among them. Taking the child in his arms, he said to them, [37]"Anyone who welcomes a little child like this on my behalf welcomes me, and anyone who welcomes me welcomes my Father who sent me."

**action**

**CH 9:33-37 WHAT'S IT SAYING?**

**WHAT AM I GOING TO DO ABOUT IT?**

## Using the Name of Jesus

[38]John said to Jesus, "Teacher, we saw a man using your name to cast out demons, but we told him to stop because he isn't one of our group."

[39]"Don't stop him!" Jesus said. "No one who performs miracles in my name will soon be able to speak evil of me. [40]Anyone who is not against us is for us. [41]**If anyone gives you even a cup of water because you belong to the Messiah, I assure you, that person will be rewarded.**

[42]"But if anyone causes one of these little ones who trusts in me to lose faith, it would be better for that person to be thrown into the sea with a large millstone tied around the neck. [43]If your hand causes you to sin, cut it off. It is better to enter heaven with only one hand than to go into the unquenchable fires of hell with two hands.* [45]If your foot causes you to sin, cut it off. It is better to enter heaven with only one foot than to be thrown into hell with two feet.* [47]And if your eye causes you to sin, gouge it out. It is better to enter the Kingdom of God half blind than to have two eyes and be thrown into hell, [48]'where the worm never dies and the fire never goes out.'

[49]"For everyone will be purified with fire. [50]Salt is good for seasoning. But if it loses its flavour, how do you make it salty again? You must have the qualities of salt among yourselves and live in peace with each other."

## Discussion about Divorce and Marriage

# 10

Then Jesus left Capernaum and went southward to the region of Judea and into the area east of the River Jordan. As always there were the crowds, and as usual he taught them.

[2]Some Pharisees came and tried to trap him with this question: "Should a man be allowed to divorce his wife?" [3]"What did Moses say about divorce?" Jesus asked them.

[4]"Well, he permitted it," they replied. "He said a man merely has to write his wife an official letter of divorce and send her away."

[5]But Jesus responded, "He wrote those instructions only as a concession to your hard-hearted wickedness. [6]But God's plan was seen from the beginning of creation, for 'He made them male and female.' [7]This explains why a man leaves his father and mother and is joined to his wife, [8]and the two are united into one.' Since they are no longer two but one, [9]let no one separate them, for God has joined them together."

[10]Later, when he was alone with his disciples in the house, they brought up the subject again. [11]He told them, "Whoever divorces his wife and marries someone else commits adultery against her. [12]And if a woman divorces her husband and remarries, she commits adultery."

## Jesus Blesses the Children

[13]One day some parents brought their children to Jesus so he could touch them and bless them, but the disciples told them not to bother him. [14]But when Jesus saw what was happening, he was very displeased with his disciples. He said to them, "Let the children come

9:43 Some manuscripts add verse 44, 'where the maggots never die and the fire never goes out.' See 9:48.
9:45 Some manuscripts add verse 46, 'where the maggots never die and the fire never goes out.' See 9:48.

to me. Don't stop them! For the Kingdom of God belongs to such as these. [15]I assure you, anyone who doesn't have their kind of faith will never get into the Kingdom of God." [16]**Then he took the children into his arms and placed his hands on their heads and blessed them.**

### The Rich Man

[17]As he was starting out on a trip, a man came running up to Jesus, knelt down, and asked, "Good Teacher, what should I do to get eternal life?"

[18]"Why do you call me good?" Jesus asked. "Only God is truly good. [19]But as for your question, you know the commandments: 'Do not murder. Do not commit adultery. Do not steal. Do not testify falsely. Do not cheat. Honour your father and mother.'"

[20]"Teacher," the man replied, "I've obeyed all these commandments since I was a child."

[21]Jesus felt genuine love for this man as he looked at him. "You lack only one thing," he told him. "Go and sell all you have and give the money to the poor, and you will have

## If You Don't Use It You Lose It:

Improving and retaining flexibility depend on numerous variables, including genetic factors, age, and the state of training. Thus, your muscles' responses to regular stretching are a function of these factors and are dependent on which muscle group you stretch. Generally, for healthy individuals, the longer, more frequently, and more intensely you stretch, the faster and more significant your improvement in flexibility will be. Likewise, once you stop your stretching programme, the flexibility gains will be lost over time.

treasure in heaven. Then come, follow me." ²²At this, the man's face fell, and he went sadly away because he had many possessions.

²³Jesus looked around and said to his disciples, "How hard it is for rich people to get into the Kingdom of God!" ²⁴This amazed them. But Jesus said again, "Dear children, it is very hard to get into the Kingdom of God. ²⁵It is easier for a camel to go through the eye of a needle than for a rich person to enter the Kingdom of God!"

²⁶**The disciples were astounded. "Then who in the world can be saved?" they asked.**

²⁷**Jesus looked at them intently and said, "Humanly speaking, it is impossible. But not with God. Everything is possible with God."**

²⁸Then Peter began to mention all that he and the other disciples had left behind. "We've given up everything to follow you," he said.

²⁹And Jesus replied, "I assure you that everyone who has given up house or brothers or sisters or mother or father or children or property, for my sake and for the Good News, ³⁰will receive now in return, a hundred times over, houses, brothers, sisters, mothers, children, and property—with persecutions. And in the world to come they will have eternal life. ³¹But many who seem to be important now will be the least important then, and those who are considered least here will be the greatest then."

## Jesus Again Predicts His Death

³²They were now on the way to Jerusalem, and Jesus was walking ahead of them. The disciples were filled with dread and the people following behind were overwhelmed with fear. Taking the twelve disciples aside, Jesus once more began to describe everything that was about to happen to him in Jerusalem. ³³"When we get to Jerusalem," he told them, "the Son of Man will be betrayed to the leading priests and the teachers of religious law. They will sentence him to die and hand him over to the Romans. ³⁴They will mock him, spit on him, beat him with their whips, and kill him, but after three days he will rise again."

## Jesus Teaches about Serving Others

³⁵Then James and John, the sons of Zebedee, came over and spoke to him. "Teacher," they said, "we want you to do us a favour."

³⁶"What is it?" he asked.

³⁷"In your glorious Kingdom, we want to sit in places of honour next to you," they said, "one at your right and the other at your left."

³⁸But Jesus answered, "You don't know what you are asking! Are you able to drink from the bitter cup of sorrow I am about to drink? Are you able to be baptized with the baptism of suffering I must be baptized with?"

³⁹"Oh yes," they said, "we are able!"

And Jesus said, "You will indeed drink from my cup and be baptized with my baptism, ⁴⁰but I have no right to say who will sit on the thrones next to mine. God has prepared those places for the ones he has chosen."

⁴¹When the ten other disciples discovered what James and John had asked, they were indignant. ⁴²So Jesus called them together and said, "You know that in this world kings are tyrants, and officials lord it over the people beneath them. ⁴³But among you it should be quite different. Whoever wants to be a leader among you must be your servant, ⁴⁴and whoever wants to be first must be the slave of all. ⁴⁵**For even I, the Son of Man, came here not to be served but to serve others, and to give my life as a ransom for many."**

## Jesus Heals Blind Bartimaeus

⁴⁶And so they reached Jericho. Later, as Jesus and his disciples left town, a great crowd was following. A blind beggar named Bartimaeus (son of Timaeus) was sitting beside the road as Jesus was going by. ⁴⁷When Bartimaeus heard that Jesus from Nazareth was nearby, he began to shout out, "Jesus, Son of David, have mercy on me!"

⁴⁸"Be quiet!" some of the people yelled at him. But he only shouted louder, "Son of David, have mercy on me!"

⁴⁹When Jesus heard him, he stopped and said, "Tell him to come here."

So they called the blind man. "Cheer up," they said. "Come on, he's calling you!" ⁵⁰Bartimaeus threw aside his coat, jumped up, and came to Jesus.

⁵¹"What do you want me to do for you?" Jesus asked.

"Teacher," the blind man said, "I want to see!"

⁵²And Jesus said to him, "Go your way. Your faith has healed you." And instantly the blind man could see! Then he followed Jesus down the road.

## The Triumphal Entry

# 11

As Jesus and his disciples approached Jerusalem, they came to the towns of Bethphage and Bethany, on the Mount of Olives. Jesus sent two of them on ahead. ²"Go into that village over there," he told them, "and as soon as you enter it, you will see a colt tied there that has never been ridden. Untie it and bring it here. ³If anyone asks what you are doing, just say, 'The Lord needs it and will return it soon.'"

⁴The two disciples left and found the colt standing in the street, tied outside a house. ⁵As they were untying it, some bystanders demanded, "What are you doing, untying that colt?" ⁶They said what Jesus had told them to say, and they were permitted to take it. ⁷Then they brought the colt to Jesus and threw their garments over it, and he sat on it. ⁸Many in the crowd spread their coats on the road

## I really want to share my faith but I do not know how to start?

Great question! Follow Jesus' example and ask a pointed question. This shows you are interested in that person and you are willing to listen to them. You cannot give good directions until you know where they are coming from. A good starting point is: 'do you know for sure that if you died tonight, you would go to heaven?'

## I hate feeling like a hypocrite. I have a church life and a life with the pals. Any suggestions?

Facing the fact that trying to live two different lives will make you miserable, is a good start. Jesus had strong words for those pretending to be genuine Christians. Find a friend to encourage you and hold you accountable. Be honest with your unchurched friends, be a genuine Christian 24/7. If they do not like you for your faith, they are loser friends.

# Winners live it out!

It is powerful to watch an athlete stay in control, especially when they are under pressure. It is often shocking that some of the most mature Christians, many of whom are leaders in their own churches, think that they can indulge themselves in improper behaviour in competition. People who would never dream of being rude, cheating, fighting or having a temper tantrum in their neighbourhood, place of work, school or church, act like idiots in sport. Why is it that often we feel we have licence to exhibit poor sportsmanship? Don't compete like a fool, hold it together.
"A fool gives full vent to anger, but a wise person quietly holds it back." Proverbs 29:11

Winners – live it!

ahead of Jesus, and others cut leafy branches in the fields and spread them along the way. [9]He was in the centre of the procession, and the crowds all around him were shouting,
"Praise God!
Bless the one who comes in the name of the Lord!
[10]Bless the coming kingdom of our ancestor David! Praise God in highest heaven!"
[11]So Jesus came to Jerusalem and went into the Temple. He looked around carefully at everything, and then he left because it was late in the afternoon. Then he went out to Bethany with the twelve disciples.

## Jesus Curses the Fig Tree

[12]The next morning as they were leaving Bethany, Jesus felt hungry. [13]He noticed a fig tree a little way off that was in full leaf, so he went over to see if he could find any figs on it. But there were only leaves because it was too early in the season for fruit. [14]Then Jesus said to the tree, "May no one ever eat your fruit again!" And the disciples heard him say it.

## Jesus Clears the Temple

[15]When they arrived back in Jerusalem, Jesus entered the Temple and began to drive out the merchants and their customers. He knocked over the tables of the money changers and the stalls of those selling doves, [16]and he stopped everyone from bringing in merchandise. [17]He taught them, "The Scriptures declare, 'My Temple will be called a place of prayer for all nations,' but you have turned it into a den of thieves."
[18]When the leading priests and teachers of religious law heard what Jesus had done, they began planning how to kill him. But they were afraid of him because the people were so enthusiastic about Jesus' teaching. [19]That evening Jesus and the disciples left the city.

[20]The next morning as they passed by the fig tree he had cursed, the disciples noticed it was withered from the roots. [21]Peter remembered what Jesus had said to the tree on the previous day and exclaimed, "Look, Teacher! The fig tree you cursed has withered!" [22]Then Jesus said to the disciples, "Have faith in God. [23]I assure you that you can say to this mountain, 'May God lift you up and throw you into the sea,' and your command will be obeyed. All that's required is that you really believe and do not doubt in your heart. [24]Listen to me! You can pray for anything, and if you believe, you will have it. **[25]But when you are praying, first forgive anyone against whom you are holding a grudge, so that your Father in heaven will forgive your sins, too."***

## The Authority of Jesus Challenged

[27]By this time they had arrived in Jerusalem again. As Jesus was walking through the Temple area, the leading priests, the teachers of religious law, and the other leaders came up to him. They demanded, [28]"By whose authority did you drive out the merchants from the Temple? Who gave you such authority?"
[29]"I'll tell who gave me authority to do these things if you answer one question," Jesus replied. [30]"Did John's baptism come from heaven or was it merely human? Answer me!"
[31]They talked it over among themselves. "If we say it was from heaven, he will ask why we didn't believe him. [32]But do we dare say it was merely human?" For they were afraid that the people would start a riot, since everyone thought that John was a prophet. [33]So they finally replied, "We don't know."
And Jesus responded, "Then I won't answer your question either."

## Story of the Evil Farmers

# 12

Then Jesus began telling them stories: "A man planted a vineyard, built a wall around it, dug a pit for pressing out the grape juice, and built a lookout tower. Then he leased the vineyard to tenant farmers and moved to another country. [2]At grape-picking time he sent one of his servants to collect his share of the crop. [3]But the farmers grabbed the servant, beat him up, and sent him back empty-handed.
[4]"The owner then sent another servant, but they beat him over the head and treated him shamefully. [5]The next servant he sent was killed. Others who were sent were either beaten or killed, [6]until there was only one left—his son whom he loved dearly. The owner finally sent him, thinking, 'Surely they will respect my son.'
[7]"But the farmers said to one another, 'Here comes the heir to this estate. Let's kill him and get the estate for ourselves!' [8]So they grabbed him and murdered him and threw his body out of the vineyard.
[9]"What do you suppose the owner of the vineyard will do?"

## STAND POINT

### When you need an example of strength: 14:36

"Abba,* Father," he said, "everything is possible for you. Please take this cup of suffering away from me. Yet I want your will, not mine."

11:25 Some manuscripts add verse 26, *But if you refuse to forgive, your Father in heaven will not forgive your sins.* Compare Matt 6:15.

MARK

Jesus asked. "I'll tell you—he will come and kill them all and lease the vineyard to others. [10]Didn't you ever read this in the Scriptures?

'The stone rejected by the builders
has now become the cornerstone.
[11]This is the Lord's doing,
and it is marvellous to see.'"

[12]The Jewish leaders wanted to arrest him for using this illustration because they realized he was pointing at them— they were the wicked farmers in his story. But they were afraid to touch him because of the crowds. So they left him and went away.

## Taxes for Caesar

[13]The leaders sent some Pharisees and supporters of Herod to try to trap Jesus into saying something for which he could be arrested. [14]"Teacher," these men said, "we know how honest you are. You are impartial and don't have favourites. You sincerely teach the ways of God. Now tell us—is it right to pay taxes to the Roman government or not? [15]Should we pay them, or should we not?"

Jesus saw through their hypocrisy and said, "Whom are you trying to fool with your trick questions? Show me a Roman coin, and I'll tell you." [16]When they handed it to him, he asked, "Whose picture and title are stamped on it?"

"Caesar's," they replied.

[17]"Well, then," Jesus said, "give to Caesar what belongs to him. But everything that belongs to God must be given to God." This reply completely amazed them.

## Discussion about Resurrection

[18]Then Jesus was approached by some Sadducees—a group of Jews who say there is no resurrection after death. They posed this question: [19]"Teacher, Moses gave us a law that if a man dies, leaving a wife without children, his brother should marry the widow and have a child who will be the brother's heir. [20]Well, there were seven brothers. The oldest of them married and then died without children. [21]So the second brother married the widow, but soon he too died and left no children. Then the next brother married her and died without children. [22]This continued until all the brothers had married her and died, and still there were no children. Last of all, the woman died, too. [23]So tell us, whose wife will she be in the resurrection? For all seven were married to her."

[24]Jesus replied, "Your problem is that you don't know the Scriptures, and you don't know the power of God. [25]For when the dead rise, they won't be married. They will be like the angels in heaven. [26]But now, as to whether the dead will be raised—haven't you ever read about this in the writings of Moses, in the story of the burning bush? Long after Abraham, Isaac, and Jacob had died, God said to Moses, 'I am the God of Abraham, the God of Isaac, and the God of Jacob.' [27]So he

is the God of the living, not the dead. You have made a serious error."

## The Most Important Commandment

[28]One of the teachers of religious law was standing there listening to the discussion. He realized that Jesus had answered well, so he asked, "Of all the commandments, which is the most important?"

[29]Jesus replied, "The most important commandment is this: 'Hear, O Israel! The Lord our God is the one and only Lord. [30]And you must love the Lord your God with all your heart, all your soul, all your mind, and all your strength.' [31]The second is equally important: 'Love your neighbour as yourself.' No other commandment is greater than these."

[32]The teacher of religious law replied, "Well said, Teacher. You have spoken the truth by saying that there is only one God and no other. [33]And I know it is important to love him with all my heart and all my understanding and all my strength, and to love my neighbours as myself. This is more important than to offer all of the burnt offerings and sacrifices required in the law."

[34]Realizing this man's understanding, Jesus said to him, "You are not far from the Kingdom of God." And after that, no one dared to ask him any more questions.

## Whose Son Is the Messiah?

[35]Later, as Jesus was teaching the people in the Temple, he asked, "Why do the teachers of religious law claim that the Messiah will be the son of David? [36]For David himself, speaking under the inspiration of the Holy Spirit, said,

'The LORD said to my Lord,
Sit in honour at my right hand

until I humble your enemies beneath your feet.'
[37]Since David himself called him Lord, how can he be his son at the same time?" And the crowd listened to him with great interest.

[38]Here are some of the other things he taught them at this time: "Beware of these teachers of religious law! For they love to parade in flowing robes and to have everyone bow to them as they walk in the marketplaces. [39]And how they love the seats of honour in the synagogues and at banquets. [40]But they shamelessly cheat widows out of their property, and then, to cover up the kind of people they really are, they make long prayers in public. Because of this, their punishment will be the greater."

## The Widow's Offering

[41]Jesus went over to the collection box in the Temple and sat and watched as the crowds dropped in their money. Many rich people put in large amounts. [42]Then a poor widow came and dropped in two pennies. [43]He called his disciples to him and said, "I assure you, this poor widow has given more than all the others have given. [44]For they gave a tiny part of their surplus, but she, poor as she is, has given everything she has."

CH 12:28-31 WHAT'S IT SAYING?

WHAT AM I GOING TO DO ABOUT IT?

Today's Olympic gold medals actually are sterling silver covered with a thin coat of gold.

## Jesus Foretells the Future

# 13

As Jesus was leaving the Temple that day, one of his disciples said, "Teacher, look at these tremendous buildings! Look at the massive stones in the walls!" [2]Jesus replied, "These magnificent buildings will be so completely demolished that not one stone will be left on top of another."

[3]Later, Jesus sat on the slopes of the Mount of Olives across the valley from the Temple. Peter, James, John,

object that causes desecration standing where it should not be"—reader, pay attention! "Then those in Judea must flee to the hills. [15]A person outside the house must not go back into the house to pack. [16]A person in the field must not return even to get a coat. [17]How terrible it will be for pregnant women and for mothers nursing their babies in those days. [18]And pray that your flight will not be in winter. [19]For those will be days of greater horror than at any time since God created the world. And it will never happen again. [20]In fact, unless the Lord shortens that time of calamity, the entire human race will be destroyed.

the Son himself. Only the Father knows. [33]And since you don't know when they will happen, stay alert and keep watch. [34]"The coming of the Son of Man can be compared with that of a man who left home to go on a trip. He gave each of his employees instructions about the work they were to do, and he told the gatekeeper to watch for his return. [35]So keep a sharp lookout! For you do not know when the home-owner will return—at evening, midnight, early dawn, or late daybreak. [36]Don't let him find you sleeping when he arrives without warning. [37]What I say to you I say to everyone: Watch for his return!"

## Your Pace is Great:

Athletes all have a different capacity to learn skill and strategy. Work hard on staying focused, and feel free to ask the coach at an appropriate time for extra help.

and Andrew came to him privately and asked him, [4]"When will all this take place? And will there be any sign ahead of time to show us when all this will be fulfilled?"

[5]Jesus replied, "Don't let anyone mislead you, [6]because many will come in my name, claiming to be the Messiah. They will lead many astray. [7]And wars will break out near and far, but don't panic. Yes, these things must come, but the end won't follow immediately. [8]Nations and kingdoms will proclaim war against each other, and there will be earthquakes in many parts of the world, and famines. But all this will be only the beginning of the horrors to come. [9]But when these things begin to happen, watch out! You will be handed over to the courts and beaten in the synagogues. You will be accused before governors and kings of being my followers. This will be your opportunity to tell them about me. [10]And the Good News must first be preached to every nation. [11]But when you are arrested and stand trial, don't worry about what to say in your defence. Just say what God tells you to. Then it is not you who will be speaking, but the Holy Spirit.

[12]"Brother will betray brother to death, fathers will betray their own children, and children will rise against their parents and cause them to be killed. [13]And everyone will hate you because of your allegiance to me. But those who endure to the end will be saved.

[14]"The time will come when you will see the sacrilegious

But for the sake of his chosen ones he has shortened those days.

[21]"And then if anyone tells you, 'Look, here is the Messiah,' or, 'There he is,' don't pay any attention. [22]For false messiahs and false prophets will rise up and perform miraculous signs and wonders so as to deceive, if possible, even God's chosen ones. [23]Watch out! I have warned you!

[24]"At that time, after those horrible days end,
the sun will be darkened,
the moon will not give light,
[25]the stars will fall from the sky,
and the powers of heaven will be shaken.

[26]Then everyone will see the Son of Man arrive on the clouds with great power and glory. [27]And he will send forth his angels to gather together his chosen ones from all over the world—from the farthest ends of the earth and heaven.

[28]"Now, learn a lesson from the fig tree. When its buds become tender and its leaves begin to sprout, you know without being told that summer is near. [29]Just so, when you see the events I've described beginning to happen, you can be sure that his return is very near, right at the door. [30]I assure you, this generation will not pass from the scene until all these events have taken place. [31]**Heaven and earth will disappear, but my words will remain for ever.**

[32]"However, no one knows the day or hour when these things will happen, not even the angels in heaven or

## Jesus Anointed at Bethany

# 14

It was now two days before the Passover celebration and the Festival of Unleavened Bread. The leading priests and the teachers of religious law were still looking for an opportunity to capture Jesus secretly and put him to death. [2]"But not during the Passover," they agreed, "or there will be a riot." [3]Meanwhile, Jesus was in Bethany at the home of Simon, a man who had leprosy. During supper, a woman came in with a beautiful jar of expensive perfume. She broke the seal and poured the perfume over his head. [4]Some of those at the table were indignant. "Why was this expensive perfume wasted?" they asked. [5]"She could have sold it for a small fortune and given the money to the poor!" And they scolded her harshly.

[6]But Jesus replied, "Leave her alone. Why berate her for doing such a good thing to me? [7]You will always have the poor among you, and you can help them whenever you want to. But I will not be here with you much longer. [8]She has done what she could and has anointed my body for burial ahead of time. [9]**I assure you, wherever the Good News is preached throughout the world, this woman's deed will be talked about in her memory.**"

## Judas Agrees to Betray Jesus

[10]Then Judas Iscariot, one of the twelve disciples, went to the leading priests to arrange to betray Jesus to them. [11]The

# MARCH M.A.P.

## 1
| S.D. | P.L. | P.G. | S.G. |
|---|---|---|---|
| P. ☐ | F. ☐ | F. ☐ | T. ☐ |
| F. ☐ | W. ☐ | W. ☐ | P. ☐ |
| B. ☐ | P. ☐ | C. ☐ | C. ☐ |

## 2
| S.D. | P.L. | P.G. | S.G. |
|---|---|---|---|
| P. ☐ | F. ☐ | F. ☐ | T. ☐ |
| F. ☐ | W. ☐ | W. ☐ | P. ☐ |
| B. ☐ | P. ☐ | C. ☐ | C. ☐ |

## 3
| S.D. | P.L. | P.G. | S.G. |
|---|---|---|---|
| P. ☐ | F. ☐ | F. ☐ | T. ☐ |
| F. ☐ | W. ☐ | W. ☐ | P. ☐ |
| B. ☐ | P. ☐ | C. ☐ | C. ☐ |

## 4
| S.D. | P.L. | P.G. | S.G. |
|---|---|---|---|
| P. ☐ | F. ☐ | F. ☐ | T. ☐ |
| F. ☐ | W. ☐ | W. ☐ | P. ☐ |
| B. ☐ | P. ☐ | C. ☐ | C. ☐ |

## 9
| S.D. | P.L. | P.G. | S.G. |
|---|---|---|---|
| P. ☐ | F. ☐ | F. ☐ | T. ☐ |
| F. ☐ | W. ☐ | W. ☐ | P. ☐ |
| B. ☐ | P. ☐ | C. ☐ | C. ☐ |

## 10
| S.D. | P.L. | P.G. | S.G. |
|---|---|---|---|
| P. ☐ | F. ☐ | F. ☐ | T. ☐ |
| F. ☐ | W. ☐ | W. ☐ | P. ☐ |
| B. ☐ | P. ☐ | C. ☐ | C. ☐ |

## 11
| S.D. | P.L. | P.G. | S.G. |
|---|---|---|---|
| P. ☐ | F. ☐ | F. ☐ | T. ☐ |
| F. ☐ | W. ☐ | W. ☐ | P. ☐ |
| B. ☐ | P. ☐ | C. ☐ | C. ☐ |

## 12
| S.D. | P.L. | P.G. | S.G. |
|---|---|---|---|
| P. ☐ | F. ☐ | F. ☐ | T. ☐ |
| F. ☐ | W. ☐ | W. ☐ | P. ☐ |
| B. ☐ | P. ☐ | C. ☐ | C. ☐ |

## 17
| S.D. | P.L. | P.G. | S.G. |
|---|---|---|---|
| P. ☐ | F. ☐ | F. ☐ | T. ☐ |
| F. ☐ | W. ☐ | W. ☐ | P. ☐ |
| B. ☐ | P. ☐ | C. ☐ | C. ☐ |

## 18
| S.D. | P.L. | P.G. | S.G. |
|---|---|---|---|
| P. ☐ | F. ☐ | F. ☐ | T. ☐ |
| F. ☐ | W. ☐ | W. ☐ | P. ☐ |
| B. ☐ | P. ☐ | C. ☐ | C. ☐ |

## 19
| S.D. | P.L. | P.G. | S.G. |
|---|---|---|---|
| P. ☐ | F. ☐ | F. ☐ | T. ☐ |
| F. ☐ | W. ☐ | W. ☐ | P. ☐ |
| B. ☐ | P. ☐ | C. ☐ | C. ☐ |

## 20
| S.D. | P.L. | P.G. | S.G. |
|---|---|---|---|
| P. ☐ | F. ☐ | F. ☐ | T. ☐ |
| F. ☐ | W. ☐ | W. ☐ | P. ☐ |
| B. ☐ | P. ☐ | C. ☐ | C. ☐ |

## 25
| S.D. | P.L. | P.G. | S.G. |
|---|---|---|---|
| P. ☐ | F. ☐ | F. ☐ | T. ☐ |
| F. ☐ | W. ☐ | W. ☐ | P. ☐ |
| B. ☐ | P. ☐ | C. ☐ | C. ☐ |

## 26
| S.D. | P.L. | P.G. | S.G. |
|---|---|---|---|
| P. ☐ | F. ☐ | F. ☐ | T. ☐ |
| F. ☐ | W. ☐ | W. ☐ | P. ☐ |
| B. ☐ | P. ☐ | C. ☐ | C. ☐ |

## 27
| S.D. | P.L. | P.G. | S.G. |
|---|---|---|---|
| P. ☐ | F. ☐ | F. ☐ | T. ☐ |
| F. ☐ | W. ☐ | W. ☐ | P. ☐ |
| B. ☐ | P. ☐ | C. ☐ | C. ☐ |

## 28
| S.D. | P.L. | P.G. | S.G. |
|---|---|---|---|
| P. ☐ | F. ☐ | F. ☐ | T. ☐ |
| F. ☐ | W. ☐ | W. ☐ | P. ☐ |
| B. ☐ | P. ☐ | C. ☐ | C. ☐ |

## Spiritual Disciplines

**Prayer**

**Faith Community**

**Bible Reading**

## Prayer List

**Friends**

**World**

**Personal**

**(For designing your MAP - Monthly Action Plan - see introduction pages)**

Who am I....
Where am I going....
How am I going to get there?

nt:sport
MONTHLY ACTION PLAN

## 5

| S.D. | P.L. | P.G. | S.G. |
|------|------|------|------|
| P. ☐ | F. ☐ | F. ☐ | T. ☐ |
| F. ☐ | W. ☐ | W. ☐ | P. ☐ |
| B. ☐ | P. ☐ | C. ☐ | C. ☐ |

## 6

| S.D. | P.L. | P.G. | S.G. |
|------|------|------|------|
| P. ☐ | F. ☐ | F. ☐ | T. ☐ |
| F. ☐ | W. ☐ | W. ☐ | P. ☐ |
| B. ☐ | P. ☐ | C. ☐ | C. ☐ |

## 7

| S.D. | P.L. | P.G. | S.G. |
|------|------|------|------|
| P. ☐ | F. ☐ | F. ☐ | T. ☐ |
| F. ☐ | W. ☐ | W. ☐ | P. ☐ |
| B. ☐ | P. ☐ | C. ☐ | C. ☐ |

## 8

| S.D. | P.L. | P.G. | S.G. |
|------|------|------|------|
| P. ☐ | F. ☐ | F. ☐ | T. ☐ |
| F. ☐ | W. ☐ | W. ☐ | P. ☐ |
| B. ☐ | P. ☐ | C. ☐ | C. ☐ |

## 13

| S.D. | P.L. | P.G. | S.G. |
|------|------|------|------|
| P. ☐ | F. ☐ | F. ☐ | T. ☐ |
| F. ☐ | W. ☐ | W. ☐ | P. ☐ |
| B. ☐ | P. ☐ | C. ☐ | C. ☐ |

## 14

| S.D. | P.L. | P.G. | S.G. |
|------|------|------|------|
| P. ☐ | F. ☐ | F. ☐ | T. ☐ |
| F. ☐ | W. ☐ | W. ☐ | P. ☐ |
| B. ☐ | P. ☐ | C. ☐ | C. ☐ |

## 15

| S.D. | P.L. | P.G. | S.G. |
|------|------|------|------|
| P. ☐ | F. ☐ | F. ☐ | T. ☐ |
| F. ☐ | W. ☐ | W. ☐ | P. ☐ |
| B. ☐ | P. ☐ | C. ☐ | C. ☐ |

## 16

| S.D. | P.L. | P.G. | S.G. |
|------|------|------|------|
| P. ☐ | F. ☐ | F. ☐ | T. ☐ |
| F. ☐ | W. ☐ | W. ☐ | P. ☐ |
| B. ☐ | P. ☐ | C. ☐ | C. ☐ |

## 21

| S.D. | P.L. | P.G. | S.G. |
|------|------|------|------|
| P. ☐ | F. ☐ | F. ☐ | T. ☐ |
| F. ☐ | W. ☐ | W. ☐ | P. ☐ |
| B. ☐ | P. ☐ | C. ☐ | C. ☐ |

## 22

| S.D. | P.L. | P.G. | S.G. |
|------|------|------|------|
| P. ☐ | F. ☐ | F. ☐ | T. ☐ |
| F. ☐ | W. ☐ | W. ☐ | P. ☐ |
| B. ☐ | P. ☐ | C. ☐ | C. ☐ |

## 23

| S.D. | P.L. | P.G. | S.G. |
|------|------|------|------|
| P. ☐ | F. ☐ | F. ☐ | T. ☐ |
| F. ☐ | W. ☐ | W. ☐ | P. ☐ |
| B. ☐ | P. ☐ | C. ☐ | C. ☐ |

## 24

| S.D. | P.L. | P.G. | S.G. |
|------|------|------|------|
| P. ☐ | F. ☐ | F. ☐ | T. ☐ |
| F. ☐ | W. ☐ | W. ☐ | P. ☐ |
| B. ☐ | P. ☐ | C. ☐ | C. ☐ |

## 29

| S.D. | P.L. | P.G. | S.G. |
|------|------|------|------|
| P. ☐ | F. ☐ | F. ☐ | T. ☐ |
| F. ☐ | W. ☐ | W. ☐ | P. ☐ |
| B. ☐ | P. ☐ | C. ☐ | C. ☐ |

## 30

| S.D. | P.L. | P.G. | S.G. |
|------|------|------|------|
| P. ☐ | F. ☐ | F. ☐ | T. ☐ |
| F. ☐ | W. ☐ | W. ☐ | P. ☐ |
| B. ☐ | P. ☐ | C. ☐ | C. ☐ |

## 31

| S.D. | P.L. | P.G. | S.G. |
|------|------|------|------|
| P. ☐ | F. ☐ | F. ☐ | T. ☐ |
| F. ☐ | W. ☐ | W. ☐ | P. ☐ |
| B. ☐ | P. ☐ | C. ☐ | C. ☐ |

**Psalm 48:14**

For that is what God is like. He is our God forever and ever, and he will be our guide until we die.

## Personal Goals

**Family**

**Work/School/Social**

**Challenge**

## Sport Goals

**Training**

**Performance**

**Competition Results**

leading priests were delighted when they heard why he had come, and they promised him a reward. So he began looking for the right time and place to betray Jesus.

## The Last Supper

[12]On the first day of the Festival of Unleavened Bread (the day the Passover lambs were sacrificed), Jesus' disciples asked him, "Where do you want us to go to prepare the Passover supper?"

[13]So Jesus sent two of them into Jerusalem to make the arrangements. "As you go into the city," he told them, "a man carrying a pitcher of water will meet you. Follow him. [14]At the house he enters, say to the owner, 'The Teacher asks: Where is the guest room where I can eat the Passover meal with my disciples?' [15]He will take you upstairs to a large room that is already set up. That is the place; go ahead and prepare our supper there." [16]So the two disciples went on ahead into the city and found everything just as Jesus had said, and they prepared the Passover supper there.

[17]In the evening Jesus arrived with the twelve disciples.

[18]As they were sitting around the table eating, Jesus said, "The truth is, one of you will betray me, one of you who is here eating with me."

[19]Greatly distressed, one by one they began to ask him, "I'm not the one, am I?"

[20]He replied, "It is one of you twelve, one who is eating with me now. [21]For I, the Son of Man, must die, as the Scriptures declared long ago. But how terrible it will be for my betrayer. Far better for him if he had never been born!"

[22]As they were eating, Jesus took a loaf of bread and asked God's blessing on it. Then he broke it in pieces and gave it to the disciples, saying, "Take it, for this is my body."

[23]And he took a cup of wine and gave thanks to God for it. He gave it to them, and they all drank from it. [24]And he said to them, "This is my blood, poured out for many, sealing the covenant between God and his people. [25]I solemnly declare that I will not drink wine again until that day when I drink it new in the Kingdom of God." [26]Then they sang a hymn and went out to the Mount of Olives.

## Jesus Predicts Peter's Denial

[27]"All of you will desert me," Jesus told them. "For the Scriptures say,
'God will strike the Shepherd,
and the sheep will be scattered.'
[28]**But after I am raised from the dead, I will go ahead of you to Galilee and meet you there.**"

[29]Peter said to him, "Even if everyone else deserts you, I never will."

[30]"Peter," Jesus replied, "the truth is, this very night, before the cock crows twice, you will deny me three times."

[31]"No!" Peter insisted. "Not even if I have to die with you! I

will never deny you!" And all the others vowed the same.

**action**

CH 14:35-42 WHAT'S IT SAYING?

WHAT AM I GOING TO DO ABOUT IT?

## Jesus Prays in Gethsemane

[32]And they came to an olive grove called Gethsemane, and Jesus said, "Sit here while I go and pray." [33]He took Peter, James, and John with him, and he began to be filled with horror and deep distress. [34]He told them, "My soul is crushed with grief to the point of death. Stay here and watch with me."

[35]He went on a little farther and fell face down on the ground. He prayed that, if it were possible, the awful hour awaiting him might pass him by. [36]"Abba, Father," he said, "everything is possible for you. Please take this cup of suffering away from me. Yet I want your will, not mine."

[37]Then he returned and found the disciples asleep. "Simon!" he said to Peter. "Are you asleep? Couldn't you stay awake and watch with me for even one hour? [38]Keep alert and pray. Otherwise temptation will overpower you. For though the spirit is willing enough, the body is weak."

[39]Then Jesus left them again and prayed, repeating his pleadings. [40]Again he returned to them and found them sleeping, for they just couldn't keep their eyes open. And they didn't know what to say.

[41]When he returned to them the third time, he said,

"Still sleeping? Still resting? Enough! The time has come. I, the Son of Man, am betrayed into the hands of sinners. [42]Up, let's be going. See, my betrayer is here!"

## Jesus Is Betrayed and Arrested

[43]And immediately, as he said this, Judas, one of the twelve disciples, arrived with a mob that was armed with swords and clubs. They had been sent out by the leading priests, the teachers of religious law, and the other leaders. [44]Judas had given them a prearranged signal: "You will know which one to arrest when I go over and give him the kiss of greeting. Then you can

## count on it

### Little things matter!

Put in that extra effort to obey the Holy Spirit - that voice, that small voice from God. Work hard at keeping your motives pure: you may be tempted to cheat or cut corners. Don't! It will catch up with you. God is interested in the little things - they become big things! "Don't be misled. Remember that you can't ignore God and get away with it. You will always reap what you sow! Those who live only to satisfy their own sinful desires will harvest the consequences of decay and death. But those who live to please the Spirit will harvest everlasting life from the Spirit." Galatians 6: 7-8
**Count on it!**

take him away under guard."

⁴⁵As soon as they arrived, Judas walked up to Jesus. "Teacher!" he exclaimed, and gave him the kiss. ⁴⁶Then the others grabbed Jesus and arrested him. ⁴⁷But someone pulled out a sword and slashed off an ear of the high priest's servant.

⁴⁸Jesus asked them, "Am I some dangerous criminal, that you come armed with swords and clubs to arrest me? **⁴⁹Why didn't you arrest me in the Temple? I was there teaching every day. But these things are happening to fulfil what the Scriptures say about me."**

⁵⁰Meanwhile, all his disciples deserted him and ran away. ⁵¹There was a young man following along behind, clothed only in a linen nightshirt. When the mob tried to grab him, ⁵²they tore off his clothes, but he escaped and ran away naked.

## Jesus before the Council

⁵³Jesus was led to the high priest's home where the leading priests, other leaders, and teachers of religious law had gathered. ⁵⁴Meanwhile, Peter followed far behind and then slipped inside the gates of the high priest's courtyard. For a while he sat with the guards, warming himself by the fire.

⁵⁵Inside, the leading priests and the entire high council were trying to find witnesses who would testify against Jesus, so they could put him to death. But their efforts were in vain. ⁵⁶Many false witnesses spoke against him, but they contradicted each other.

⁵⁷Finally, some men stood up to testify against him with this lie: ⁵⁸"We heard him say, 'I will destroy this Temple made with human hands, and in three days I will build another, made without human hands.'" ⁵⁹But even then they didn't get their stories straight!

⁶⁰Then the high priest stood up before the others and asked Jesus, "Well, aren't you going to answer these charges? What do you have to say for yourself?" ⁶¹Jesus made no reply. Then the high priest asked him, **"Are you the Messiah, the Son of the blessed God?"**

**⁶²Jesus said, "I am, and you will see me, the Son of Man, sitting at God's right hand in the place of power and coming back on the clouds of heaven."**

⁶³Then the high priest tore his clothing to show his horror and said, "Why do we need other witnesses? ⁶⁴You have all heard his blasphemy. What is your verdict?" And they all condemned him to death.

⁶⁵Then some of them began to spit at him, and they blindfolded him and hit his face with their fists. "Who hit you that time, you prophet?" they jeered. And even

the guards were hitting him as they led him away.

## Peter Denies Jesus

⁶⁶Meanwhile, Peter was below in the courtyard. One of the servant girls who worked for the high priest ⁶⁷noticed Peter warming himself at the fire. She looked at him closely and then said, "You were one of those with Jesus, the Nazarene."

⁶⁸Peter denied it. "I don't know what you're talking about," he said, and he went out into the entryway. Just then, a cock crowed.

⁶⁹The servant girl saw him standing there and began telling the others, "That man is definitely one of that group!" ⁷⁰Peter denied it again.

A little later some other bystanders began saying to Peter, "You must be one of that group because you are from Galilee."

⁷¹Peter said, "I swear by God, I don't know this man you're talking about." ⁷²And immediately the cock crowed the second time. Suddenly, Jesus' words flashed through Peter's mind: "Before the cock crows twice, you will deny me three times." And he broke down and cried.

## Jesus' Trial before Pilate

# 15

Very early in the morning the leading priests, other leaders, and teachers of religious law—the entire high council—met to discuss their next step. They bound Jesus and took him to Pilate, the Roman governor.

²Pilate asked Jesus, "Are you the King of the Jews?" Jesus replied, "Yes, it is as you say."

³Then the leading priests accused him of many crimes, ⁴and Pilate asked him, "Aren't you going to say something? What about all these charges against you?" ⁵But Jesus said nothing, much to Pilate's surprise.

⁶Now it was the governor's custom to release one prisoner each year at Passover time—anyone the people requested. ⁷One of the prisoners at that time was Barabbas, convicted along with others for murder during an insurrection. ⁸The mob began to crowd in towards Pilate, asking him to release a prisoner as usual. ⁹"Should I give you the King of the Jews?" Pilate asked. ¹⁰(For he realized by now that the leading priests had arrested Jesus out of envy.) ¹¹But at this point the leading priests stirred up the mob to demand the release of Barabbas instead of Jesus. ¹²"But if I release Barabbas," Pilate asked them, "what should I do with this man you call the King of the Jews?"

¹³They shouted back, "Crucify him!"

¹⁴"Why?" Pilate demanded. "What crime has he committed?" But the crowd only roared the louder, "Crucify him!"

¹⁵So Pilate, anxious to please the crowd, released Barabbas to them. He ordered Jesus flogged with a lead-tipped whip, then turned him over to the Roman soldiers to crucify him.

## The Soldiers Mock Jesus

¹⁶The soldiers took him into their head-quarters and called out the entire battalion. ¹⁷They dressed him in a purple robe and made a crown of long, sharp thorns and put it on his head. ¹⁸Then they saluted, yelling, "Hail! King of the Jews!" ¹⁹And they beat him on the head with a stick, spat on him, and dropped to their knees in mock worship. ²⁰When they were finally tired of mocking him, they took off the purple robe and put his own clothes on him again. Then they led him away to be crucified.

## The Crucifixion

²¹A man named Simon, who was from Cyrene, was coming in from the country just then, and they forced him to carry Jesus' cross. (Simon was the father of Alexander and Rufus.) ²²And they brought Jesus to a place called Golgotha (which means Skull Hill). ²³They offered him wine drugged with myrrh, but he refused it. ²⁴Then they nailed him to the cross. They gambled for his clothes, throwing dice to decide who would get them.

²⁵It was nine o'clock in the morning when the crucifixion took place. ²⁶A signboard was fastened to the cross above Jesus' head, announcing the charge against him. It read: "The King of the Jews." ²⁷Two criminals were crucified with him, their crosses on either side of his.* ²⁹And the people passing by shouted abuse, shaking their heads in mockery. "Ha! Look at you now!" they yelled at him. "You can destroy the Temple and rebuild it in three days, can you? ³⁰Well then, save yourself and come down from the cross!"

³¹The leading priests and teachers of religious law also mocked Jesus. "He saved others," they scoffed, "but he can't save himself! ³²Let this Messiah, this king of Israel, come down from the cross so we can see it and believe him!" Even the two criminals who were being crucified with Jesus ridiculed him.

## The Death of Jesus

³³At noon, darkness fell across the whole land until three o'clock. ³⁴Then, at that time Jesus called out with a loud voice, "Eloi, Eloi, lema sabachthani?" which means, "My God, my God, why have you forsaken me?"

³⁵Some of the bystanders misunderstood and thought he was calling for the prophet Elijah. ³⁶One of them ran and filled a sponge with sour wine, holding it up to him on a stick so he could drink. "Leave him alone. Let's see whether Elijah will come and take him down!" he said.

---

15:27 Some manuscripts add verse 28, And the Scripture was fulfilled that said, "He was counted among those who were rebels." See Isa 53:12; also compare Luke 22:37.

# profiles

## John the Baptist:

'He (Jesus) must become greater and greater, and I must become less and less.' John the Baptist (not to be confused with John the Apostle) was related to Jesus and commissioned by God to usher in a new era, the era of Jesus, the Saviour of the world. He was given a unique task, to be the 'voice in the wilderness, to prepare the way of the Lord', a prophesy proclaimed by Isaiah hundreds of years earlier. Through the Gospels and other historical evidence we find John fulfilling his task flawlessly. The Baptist was a rugged individual who stayed focused on his task and attracted quite a crowd and baptised hundreds of followers. He was asked often, 'Are you the Messiah?' John constantly plays down his role. He announced: "Someone is coming soon who is far greater than I am – so much greater that I am not even worthy to be his slave." John's mission was to announce the forthcoming of God's Kingdom through Jesus and the need for you now to turn from your sin, which was symbolised in baptism. He was bold and did not apologise for his message. His boldness cost him his life, and his cousin Jesus mourned his death. John understood Jesus' ministry and his role in God's purpose. You also have a purpose; Jesus wants to live in you. Can you say in your life: 'He must become greater and greater and I must become less and less'?

[37]Then Jesus uttered another loud cry and breathed his last. [38]And the curtain in the Temple was torn in two, from top to bottom. [39]**When the Roman officer who stood facing him saw how he had died, he exclaimed, "Truly, this was the Son of God!"** [40]Some women were there, watching from a distance, including Mary Magdalene, Mary (the mother of James the younger and of Joseph), and Salome. [41]They had been followers of Jesus and had cared for him while he was in Galilee. Then they and many other women had come with him to Jerusalem.

## The Burial of Jesus

[42]This all happened on Friday, the day of preparation, the day before the Sabbath. As evening approached, [43]an honoured member of the high council, Joseph from Arimathea (who was waiting for the Kingdom of God to come), gathered his courage and went to Pilate to ask for Jesus' body. [44]Pilate couldn't believe that Jesus was already dead, so he called for the Roman military officer in charge and asked him. [45]The officer confirmed the fact, and Pilate told Joseph he could have the body. [46]Joseph bought a long sheet of linen cloth, and taking Jesus' body down from the cross, he wrapped it in the cloth and laid it in a tomb that had been carved out of the rock. Then he rolled a stone in front of the entrance. [47]Mary Magdalene and Mary the mother of Joseph saw where Jesus' body was laid.

## The Resurrection

# 16

The next evening, when the Sabbath ended, Mary Magdalene and Salome and Mary the mother of James went out and purchased burial spices to put on Jesus' body. [2]Very early on Sunday morning, just at sunrise, they came to the tomb. [3]On the way they were discussing who would roll the stone away from the entrance to the tomb. [4]But when they arrived, they looked up and saw that the stone—a very large one—had already been rolled aside. [5]So they entered the tomb, and there on the right sat a young man clothed in a white robe. The women were startled, [6]**but the angel said, "Do not be so surprised. You are looking for Jesus, the Nazarene, who was crucified. He isn't here! He has been raised from the dead! Look, this is where they laid his body.** [7]Now go and give this message to his disciples, including Peter: Jesus is going ahead of you to Galilee. You will see him there, just as he told you before he

died!" [8]The women fled from the tomb, trembling and bewildered, saying nothing to anyone because they were too frightened to talk.

## (Shorter Ending of Mark)

Then they reported all these instructions briefly to Peter and his companions. Afterwards Jesus himself sent them out from east to west with the sacred and unfailing message of salvation that gives eternal life. Amen.

## (Longer Ending of Mark)

[9]It was early on Sunday morning when Jesus rose from the dead, and the first person who saw him was Mary Magdalene, the woman from whom he had cast out seven demons. [10]She went and found the disciples, who were grieving and weeping. [11]But when she told them that Jesus was alive and she had seen him, they didn't believe her.

[12]Afterwards he appeared to two who were walking from Jerusalem into the country, but they didn't recognize him at first because he had changed his appearance. [13]When they realized who he was, they rushed back to tell the others, but no one believed them.

[14]Still later he appeared to the eleven disciples as they were eating together. He rebuked them for their unbelief—their stubborn refusal to believe those who had seen him after he had risen.[*]

[15]And then he told them, "Go into all the world and preach the Good News to everyone, everywhere. [16]Anyone who believes and is baptized will be saved. But anyone who refuses to believe will be condemned. [17]These signs will accompany those who believe: They will cast out demons in my name, and they will speak new languages. [18]They will be able to handle snakes with safety, and if they drink anything poisonous, it won't hurt them. They will be able to place their hands on the sick and heal them."

[19]When the Lord Jesus had finished talking with them, he was taken up into heaven and sat down in the place of honour at God's right hand. [20]And the disciples went everywhere and preached, and the Lord worked with them, confirming what they said by many miraculous signs.

16:14 Some early manuscripts add: And they excused themselves, saying, "This age of lawlessness and unbelief is under Satan, who does not permit God's truth and power to conquer the evil [unclean] spirits. Therefore, reveal your justice now." This is what they said to Christ. And Christ replied to them, "The period of years of Satan's power has been fulfilled, but other dreadful things will happen soon. And I was handed over to death for those who have sinned, so that they may return to the truth and sin no more, and so they may inherit the spiritual, incorruptible, and righteous glory in heaven."

Luke was interested in the BIG PICTURE! He is not only credited with writing the Gospel we see before us but he also wrote the book of Acts which is a, 'what happened next', sequel to Luke. This Gospel tells the story of Jesus' life and has special emphasis on the power of prayer and the power of the Holy Spirit. Luke reveals the special attention Jesus pays the poor and his 'Power Habit' of praying before every tough decision or challenge he faces. As a historian he places special emphasis on the Old Testament prophecies which Jesus fulfils. We also get a great insight to Jesus' childhood, some of which is not recorded in the other Gospels.

Luke was commissioned to seek-out and interview intimate friends of Jesus as well as people who had been directly impacted by his ministry and write a special account of Jesus' life. The list could have included Mary the mother of Jesus, James - Jesus brother, disciples of John the Baptist, and Jesus very own top guys, including John and Peter. Luke became a close friend of the Apostle Paul who calls Luke, 'Dear Doctor Luke' (Col. 4:14), this would makes sense, because his writing style is clearly that of an educated man and there are small hints that he wrote from a physician's point of view. 'Dear Doctor Luke's attention to detail and accuracy are present along with a structure that corresponds with the Gospels of Matthew and Mark.

# Luke

# LUKE

## Introduction

# 1

Most honourable Theophilus:
Many people have written accounts about the events that took place among us. ²They used as their source material the reports circulating among us from the early disciples and other eyewitnesses of what God has done in fulfilment of his promises. ³**Having carefully investigated all of these accounts from the beginning, I have decided to write a careful summary for you, ⁴to reassure you of the truth of all you were taught.**

## The Birth of John the Baptist Foretold

⁵It all begins with a Jewish priest, Zechariah, who lived when Herod was king of Judea. Zechariah was a member of the priestly order of Abijah. His wife, Elizabeth, was also from the priestly line of Aaron. ⁶Zechariah and Elizabeth were righteous in God's eyes, careful to obey all of the Lord's commandments and regulations. ⁷They had no children because Elizabeth was barren, and now they were both very old.

⁸One day Zechariah was serving God in the Temple, for his order was on duty that week. ⁹As was the custom of the priests, he was chosen by lot to enter the sanctuary and burn incense in the Lord's presence. ¹⁰While the incense was being burned, a great crowd stood outside, praying.

¹¹Zechariah was in the sanctuary when an angel of the Lord appeared, standing to the right of the incense altar. ¹²Zechariah was overwhelmed with fear. ¹³But the angel said, "Don't be afraid, Zechariah! For God has heard your prayer, and your wife, Elizabeth, will bear you a son! And you are to name him John. ¹⁴You will have great joy and gladness, and many will rejoice with you at his birth, ¹⁵for he will be great in the eyes

The longest chapter in the Bible is Psalm 119, a celebration of God's Word.

of the Lord. He must never touch wine or strong drink, and he will be filled with the Holy Spirit, even before his birth. ¹⁶And he will persuade many Israelites to turn to the Lord their God. ¹⁷He will be a man with the spirit and power of Elijah, the prophet of old. He will precede the coming of the Lord, preparing the people for his arrival. He will turn the hearts of the fathers to their children, and he will change disobedient minds to accept godly wisdom."

¹⁸Zechariah said to the angel, "How can I know this will happen? I'm an old man now, and my wife is also getting on in years."

¹⁹Then the angel said, "I am Gabriel! I stand in the very presence of God. It was he who sent me to bring you this good news! ²⁰And now, since you didn't believe what I said, you won't be able to speak until the child is born. For my words will certainly come true at the proper time."

²¹Meanwhile, the people were waiting for Zechariah to come out, wondering why he was taking so long. ²²When he finally did come out, he couldn't speak to them. Then they realized from his gestures that he must have seen a vision in the Temple sanctuary.

²³He stayed at the Temple until his term of service was over, and then he returned home. ²⁴Soon afterwards his wife, Elizabeth, became pregnant and went into seclusion for five months. ²⁵"How kind the Lord is!" she exclaimed. "He has taken away my disgrace of having no children!"

## The Birth of Jesus Foretold

²⁶In the sixth month of Elizabeth's pregnancy, God sent the angel Gabriel to Nazareth, a village in Galilee, ²⁷to a virgin named Mary. She was engaged to be married to a man named Joseph, a descendant of King David. ²⁸Gabriel appeared to her and said, "Greetings, favoured woman! The Lord is with you!"*

²⁹Confused and disturbed, Mary tried to think what the angel could mean. ³⁰"Don't be frightened, Mary," the angel told her, "for God has decided to bless you! ³¹You will become pregnant and have a son, and you are to name him Jesus. ³²He will be very great and will be called the Son of the Most High. And the Lord God will give him the throne of his ancestor David. ³³And he will reign over Israel for ever; his Kingdom will never end!"

³⁴Mary asked the angel, "But how can I have a baby? I am a virgin."

³⁵The angel replied, "The Holy Spirit will come upon you, and the power of the Most High will overshadow you. So the baby born to you will be holy, and he will be called the Son of God. ³⁶What's more, your relative

Elizabeth has become pregnant in her old age! People used to say she was barren, but she's already in her sixth month. ³⁷For nothing is impossible with God."

³⁸Mary responded, "I am the Lord's servant, and I am willing to accept whatever he wants. May everything you have said come true." And then the angel left.

## Mary Visits Elizabeth

³⁹A few days later Mary hurried to the hill country of Judea, to the town ⁴⁰where Zechariah lived. She entered the house and greeted Elizabeth. ⁴¹At the sound of Mary's greeting, Elizabeth's child leaped within her, and Elizabeth was filled with the Holy Spirit.

⁴²Elizabeth gave a glad cry and exclaimed to Mary, "You are blessed by God above all other women, and your child is blessed. ⁴³What an honour this is, that the mother of my Lord should visit me! ⁴⁴When you came in and greeted me, my baby jumped for joy the instant I heard your voice! ⁴⁵You are blessed, because you believed that the Lord would do what he said."

## The Magnificat: Mary's Song of Praise

⁴⁶Mary responded,
"Oh, how I praise the Lord.
⁴⁷How I rejoice in God my Saviour!
⁴⁸For he took notice of his lowly servant girl,
and now generation after generation
will call me blessed.
⁴⁹For he, the Mighty One, is holy,
and he has done great things for me.
⁵⁰His mercy goes on from generation to generation,
to all who fear him.
⁵¹His mighty arm does tremendous things!
How he scatters the proud and haughty ones!
⁵²**He has taken princes from their thrones and exalted the lowly.**
⁵³He has satisfied the hungry with good things
and sent the rich away with empty hands.
⁵⁴And how he has helped his servant Israel!
He has not forgotten his promise to be merciful.
⁵⁵For he promised our ancestors—Abraham and his children—
to be merciful to them for ever."

⁵⁶Mary stayed with Elizabeth about three months and then went back to her own home.

## The Birth of John the Baptist

⁵⁷Now it was time for Elizabeth's baby to be born, and it was a boy. ⁵⁸The word spread quickly to her neighbours and relatives that the Lord had been very kind to her, and everyone rejoiced with her.

1:28 Some manuscripts add *Blessed are you among women.*

# profiles

## Peter:

Jesus asked Peter, 'Do you love me more than these?' It was a painful time in Peter's amazing relationship with His master. Christ's original commission for Peter was, 'come follow me and I will make you a fisher of men.' Now Jesus had been crucified, resurrected and had revealed himself to Peter on many occasions. It seemed that Peter was to return to his old life of fishing. His three-year dream of following this King seemed to be over. When Jesus appears to Peter (Jesus had renamed Him Peter, which means rock) we see this impetuous man who had bragged that he would follow him to death, then denied him three times that very night. Now Jesus asks him again do you love me more than these? What was around Peter at this scene? His friends, fish and boats. Jesus slowly draws the poison and grief Peter held inside him, asking him three more times, 'do you love me?' Jesus met Peter where he was at the time and reinstated him. Jesus also asks you, 'do you love me more than these?' Look around. What is more important than Jesus? He wants your allegiance to him to be first in your life. Peter was not a perfect man, but God used him in great ways. He was the recognized leader of the church movement; he became a fearless messenger of Jesus and writer of 1 and 2 Peter.

[59]When the baby was eight days old, all the relatives and friends came for the circumcision ceremony. They wanted to name him Zechariah, after his father. [60]But Elizabeth said, "No! His name is John!"

[61]"What?" they exclaimed. "There is no one in all your family by that name." [62]So they asked the baby's father, communicating to him by making gestures. [63]He motioned for a writing tablet, and to everyone's surprise he wrote, "His name is John!" [64]Instantly Zechariah could speak again, and he began praising God.

[65]Wonder fell upon the whole neighbourhood, and the news of what had happened spread throughout the

Judean hills. [66]Everyone who heard about it reflected on these events and asked, "I wonder what this child will turn out to be? For the hand of the Lord is surely upon him in a special way."

## Zechariah's Prophecy

[67]Then his father, Zechariah, was filled with the Holy Spirit and gave this prophecy:

[68]"Praise the Lord, the God of Israel,
because he has visited his people and redeemed them.
[69]He has sent us a mighty Saviour
from the royal line of his servant David,
[70]just as he promised
through his holy prophets long ago.
[71]Now we will be saved from our enemies
and from all who hate us.
[72]He has been merciful to our ancestors
by remembering his sacred covenant with them,

[73]the covenant he gave to our ancestor Abraham.
[74]We have been rescued from our enemies,
so we can serve God without fear,
[75]in holiness and righteousness for ever.
[76]"And you, my little son,
will be called the prophet of the Most High,
because you will prepare the way for the Lord.
[77]You will tell his people how to find salvation
through forgiveness of their sins.
[78]Because of God's tender mercy,
the light from heaven is about to break upon us,
[79]to give light to those who sit in darkness and in the shadow of death,

and to guide us to the path of peace."
[80]John grew up and became strong in spirit. Then he lived out in the wilderness until he began his public ministry to Israel.

## The Birth of Jesus

# 2

At that time the Roman emperor, Augustus, decreed that a census should be taken throughout the Roman Empire. [2](This was the first census taken when Quirinius was governor of Syria.)
[3]All returned to their own towns to register for this census.
[4]And because Joseph was a descendant of King David, he had to go to Bethlehem in Judea, David's ancient home. He travelled there from the village of Nazareth in Galilee. [5]He took with him Mary, his fiancée, who

was obviously pregnant by this time.

⁶And while they were there, the time came for her baby to be born. ⁷She gave birth to her first child, a son. She wrapped him snugly in strips of cloth and laid him in a manger, because there was no room for them in the village inn.

## The Shepherds and Angels

⁸That night some shepherds were in the fields outside the village, guarding their flocks of sheep. ⁹Suddenly, an angel of the Lord appeared among them, and the radiance of the Lord's glory surrounded them. They were terribly frightened, ¹⁰but the angel reassured them. "Don't be afraid!" he said. "I bring you good news of great joy for everyone!

¹¹The Saviour—yes, the Messiah, the Lord—has been born tonight in Bethlehem, the city of David! ¹²And this is how you will recognize him: You will find a baby lying in a manger, wrapped snugly in strips of cloth!"

¹³Suddenly, the angel was joined by a vast host of others—the armies of heaven—praising God:

¹⁴"Glory to God in the highest heaven,
and peace on earth to all whom God favours."

¹⁵When the angels had returned to heaven, the shepherds said to each other, "Come on, let's go to Bethlehem! Let's see this wonderful thing that has happened, which the Lord has told us about."

¹⁶They ran to the village and found Mary and Joseph. And there was the baby, lying in the manger. ¹⁷Then the shepherds told everyone what had happened and what the angel had said to them about this child. ¹⁸All who heard the shepherds' story were astonished, ¹⁹but Mary quietly treasured these things in her heart and thought about them often. ²⁰The shepherds went back to their fields and flocks, glorifying and praising God for what the angels had told them, and because they had seen the child, just as the angel had said.

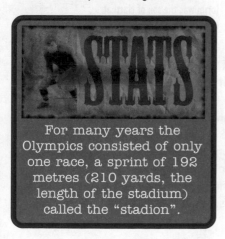

For many years the Olympics consisted of only one race, a sprint of 192 metres (210 yards, the length of the stadium) called the "stadion".

Be joyful always! This is a tough habit! To have that deep down in your gut happiness (joy) even when you've blown it or lost a match. How can you do it? By knowing no matter what your circumstances, God totally loves you. "Always be joyful. Keep on praying. No matter what happens, always be thankful, for this is God's will for you who belong to Christ Jesus."

1 Thessalonians 5:16-18

## Jesus Is Presented in the Temple

²¹Eight days later, when the baby was circumcised, he was named Jesus, the name given him by the angel even before he was conceived.

²²Then it was time for the purification offering, as required by the law of Moses after the birth of a child; so his parents took him to Jerusalem to present him to the Lord. ²³The law of the Lord says, "If a woman's first child is a boy, he must be dedicated to the Lord." ²⁴So they offered a sacrifice according to what was required in the law of the Lord—"either a pair of turtle-doves or two young pigeons."

## The Prophecy of Simeon

²⁵Now there was a man named Simeon who lived in Jerusalem. He was a righteous man and very devout. He was filled with the Holy Spirit, and he eagerly expected the Messiah to come and rescue Israel. ²⁶The Holy Spirit had revealed to him that he would not die until he had seen the Lord's Messiah. ²⁷That day the Spirit led him to the Temple. So when Mary and Joseph came to present the baby Jesus to the Lord as the law required, ²⁸Simeon was there. He took the child in his arms and praised God, saying,

²⁹"Lord, now I can die in peace!
As you promised me,
³⁰I have seen the Saviour
³¹you have given to all people.
³²He is a light to reveal God to the nations,
and he is the glory of your people Israel!"

³³Joseph and Mary were amazed at what was being said about Jesus. ³⁴Then Simeon blessed them, and he said to Mary, "This child will be rejected by many in Israel, and it will be their undoing. But he will be the greatest joy to many others. ³⁵Thus, the deepest thoughts of many hearts will be revealed. And a sword will pierce your very soul."

## The Prophecy of Anna

³⁶Anna, a prophet, was also there in the Temple. She was the daughter of Phanuel, of the tribe of Asher, and was very old. She was a widow, for her husband had died when they had been married only seven years. ³⁷She was now eighty-four years old. She never left the Temple but stayed there day and night, worshipping God with fasting and prayer. ³⁸She came along just as Simeon was talking with Mary and Joseph, and she began praising God. She talked about Jesus to everyone who had been waiting for the promised King to come and deliver Jerusalem.

³⁹When Jesus' parents had fulfilled all the requirements of the law of the Lord, they returned home to Nazareth in Galilee.

⁴⁰There the child grew up healthy and strong. He was filled with wisdom beyond his years, and God placed his special favour upon him.

## Jesus Speaks with the Teachers

⁴¹Every year Jesus' parents went to Jerusalem for the Passover festival. ⁴²When Jesus was twelve years old, they attended the festival as usual. ⁴³After the celebration was over, they started home to Nazareth, but Jesus stayed behind in Jerusalem. His parents didn't miss him at first, ⁴⁴because they assumed he was with friends among the other travellers. But when he didn't show up that evening, they started to look for him among their relatives and friends. ⁴⁵When they couldn't find him, they went back to Jerusalem to search for him there. ⁴⁶Three days later they finally discovered him. He was in the Temple, sitting among the religious teachers, discussing deep questions with them. ⁴⁷And all who heard him were amazed at his understanding and his answers. ⁴⁸His parents didn't know what to think. "Son!" his mother

said to him. "Why have you done this to us? Your father and I have been frantic, searching for you everywhere."

⁴⁹"But why did you need to search?" he asked. "You should have known that I would be in my Father's house."

⁵⁰But they didn't understand what he meant.

⁵¹Then he returned to Nazareth with them and was obedient to them; and his mother stored all these things in her heart. **⁵²So Jesus grew both in height and in wisdom, and he was loved by God and by all who knew him.**

## John the Baptist Prepares the Way

# 3

It was now the fifteenth year of the reign of Tiberius, the Roman emperor. Pilate was governor over Judea; Herod Antipas was ruler over Galilee; his brother Philip was ruler over Iturea and Traconitis; Lysanias was ruler over Abilene. ²Annas and Caiaphas were the high priests. At this time a message from God came to John son of Zechariah, who was living out in the wilderness. ³Then John went from place to place on both sides of the River Jordan, preaching that people should be baptized to show that they had turned from their sins and turned to God to be forgiven. ⁴Isaiah had spoken of John when he said,

"He is a voice shouting in the wilderness:
'Prepare a pathway for the Lord's coming!
Make a straight road for him!
⁵Fill in the valleys,
and level the mountains and hills!
Straighten the curves,
and smooth out the rough places!
⁶And then all people will see
the salvation sent from God.'"

⁷Here is a sample of John's preaching to the crowds that came for baptism: "You brood of snakes! Who warned you to flee God's coming judgement? ⁸Prove by the way you live that you have really turned from your sins and turned to God. Don't just say, 'We're safe—we're the descendants of Abraham.' That proves nothing. God can change these stones here into children of Abraham. ⁹Even now the axe of God's judgement is poised, ready to sever your roots. Yes, every tree that does not produce good fruit will be chopped down and thrown into the fire."

¹⁰The crowd asked, "What should we do?"

¹¹John replied, "If you have two coats, give one to the poor. If you have food, share it with those who are hungry."

¹²Even corrupt tax collectors came to be baptized and asked,

"Teacher, what should we do?"

¹³"Show your honesty," he replied. "Make sure you collect no more taxes than the Roman government requires you to."

¹⁴"What should we do?" asked some soldiers.

John replied, "Don't extort money, and don't accuse people of things you know they didn't do. And be content with your pay."

¹⁵Everyone was expecting the Messiah to come soon, and they were eager to know whether John might be the Messiah.

¹⁶John answered their questions by saying, "I baptize with water; but someone is coming soon who is greater than I am—so much greater that I am not even worthy to be his slave. He will baptize you with the Holy Spirit and with fire. ¹⁷He is ready to separate the chaff from the grain with his winnowing fork. Then he will clean up the threshing area, storing the grain in his barn but burning the chaff with never-ending fire." ¹⁸John used many such warnings as he announced the Good News to the people.

¹⁹John also publicly criticized Herod Antipas, ruler of Galilee, for marrying Herodias, his brother's wife, and for many other wrongs he had done. ²⁰So Herod put John in prison, adding this sin to his many others.

## The Baptism of Jesus

²¹One day when the crowds were being baptized, Jesus himself was baptized. As he was praying, the heavens opened, ²²and the Holy Spirit descended on him in the form of a dove. And a voice from heaven said, "You are my beloved Son, and I am fully pleased with you."

## The Record of Jesus' Ancestors

²³Jesus was about thirty years old when he began his public ministry.

Jesus was known as the son of Joseph.
Joseph was the son of Heli.
²⁴Heli was the son of Matthat.
Matthat was the son of Levi.
Levi was the son of Melki.
Melki was the son of Jannai.
Jannai was the son of Joseph.
²⁵Joseph was the son of Mattathias.
Mattathias was the son of Amos.
Amos was the son of Nahum.
Nahum was the son of Esli.
Esli was the son of Naggai.
²⁶Naggai was the son of Maath.
Maath was the son of Mattathias.
Mattathias was the son of Semein.
Semein was the son of Josech.
Josech was the son of Joda.
²⁷Joda was the son of Joanan.
Joanan was the son of Rhesa.
Rhesa was the son of Zerubbabel.
Zerubbabel was the son of Shealtiel.
Shealtiel was the son of Neri.
²⁸Neri was the son of Melki.
Melki was the son of Addi.
Addi was the son of Cosam.
Cosam was the son of Elmadam.
Elmadam was the son of Er.
²⁹Er was the son of Joshua.
Joshua was the son of Eliezer.
Eliezer was the son of Jorim.
Jorim was the son of Matthat.
Matthat was the son of Levi.

**Is competition wrong? When you compete at the top level, how do you keep everything in perspective? How do you give it your best shot without treating it like World War Three?**

First, in serious competition, we are to give our best and give God the praise for our effort, win, lose or draw. The Christian's purpose is to live out the presence of Christ. For athletes it's in the world of sport - the idea of demonstrating Christ's presence in us and through us in competition to the best of our ability. It is the 'What Would Jesus Do?' attitude, applied to our sport. It is to love our neighbour (our team-mate, our opponent and even the officials) as ourselves. No one is saying that this is easy. However, it is in the way that we conduct ourselves in the heat of the battle that will show the difference Christ makes in our lives.

## Don't Just Diet:

Hundreds of research studies have shown that the slow down in metabolism is due to a loss of muscle tissue. And the loss of muscle tissue is directly related to a lack of hard physical activity!

[30]Levi was the son of Simeon.
Simeon was the son of Judah.
Judah was the son of Joseph.
Joseph was the son of Jonam.
Jonam was the son of Eliakim.
[31]Eliakim was the son of Melea.
Melea was the son of Menna.
Menna was the son of Mattatha.
Mattatha was the son of Nathan.
Nathan was the son of David.
[32]David was the son of Jesse.
Jesse was the son of Obed.
Obed was the son of Boaz.
Boaz was the son of Salmon.
Salmon was the son of Nahshon.

[33]Nahshon was the son of Amminadab.
Amminadab was the son of Admin.
Admin was the son of Arni.
Arni was the son of Hezron.
Hezron was the son of Perez.
Perez was the son of Judah.
[34]Judah was the son of Jacob.
Jacob was the son of Isaac.
Isaac was the son of Abraham.
Abraham was the son of Terah.
Terah was the son of Nahor.
[35]Nahor was the son of Serug.
Serug was the son of Reu.
Reu was the son of Peleg.
Peleg was the son of Eber.

Eber was the son of Shelah.
[36]Shelah was the son of Cainan.
Cainan was the son of Arphaxad.
Arphaxad was the son of Shem.
Shem was the son of Noah.
Noah was the son of Lamech.
[37]Lamech was the son of Methuselah.
Methuselah was the son of Enoch.
Enoch was the son of Jared.
Jared was the son of Mahalalel.
Mahalalel was the son of Kenan.
[38]Kenan was the son of Enosh.
Enosh was the son of Seth.
Seth was the son of Adam.
Adam was the son of God.

## The Temptation of Jesus

# 4

Then Jesus, full of the Holy Spirit, left the River Jordan. He was led by the Spirit to go out into the wilderness, [2]where the Devil tempted him for forty days. He ate nothing all that time and was very hungry.

[3]Then the Devil said to him, "If you are the Son of God, change this stone into a loaf of bread."

[4]But Jesus told him, "No! The Scriptures say, 'People need more than bread for their life.'"

[5]Then the Devil took him up and revealed to him all the kingdoms of the world in a moment of time. [6]The Devil told him, "I will give you the glory of these kingdoms and authority over them—because they are mine to give to anyone I please. [7]I will give it all to you if you will bow down and worship me."

[8]Jesus replied, "The Scriptures say,
'You must worship the Lord your God;
serve only him.'"

[9]Then the Devil took him to Jerusalem, to the highest point of the Temple, and said, "If you are the Son of God, jump off! [10]For the Scriptures say,
'He orders his angels to protect and guard you.
[11]And they will hold you with their hands
to keep you from striking your foot on a stone.'"

[12]Jesus responded, "The Scriptures also say, 'Do not test the Lord your God.'"

[13]When the Devil had finished tempting Jesus, he left him until the next opportunity came.

## Jesus Rejected at Nazareth

[14]Then Jesus returned to Galilee, filled with the Holy Spirit's power. Soon he became well known throughout the surrounding country. [15]He taught in their synagogues and was praised by everyone.

[16]When he came to the village of Nazareth, his boyhood home, he went as usual to the synagogue on the Sabbath and stood up to read the Scriptures. [17]The scroll containing the messages of Isaiah the prophet was handed to him, and he unrolled the scroll to the place where it says:

[18]"The Spirit of the Lord is upon me,
for he has appointed me to preach Good News to the poor.
He has sent me to proclaim
that captives will be released,
that the blind will see,
that the downtrodden will be freed from their oppressors,
[19]and that the time of the Lord's favour has come."

[20]He rolled up the scroll, handed it back to the attendant, and sat down. Everyone in the synagogue stared at him intently. [21]Then he said, "This Scripture has come true today

**count on it**

**He will take your troubles!**
Have you ever felt so weak that you thought there was no way you could continue? Are there times in your life when you feel so overwhelmed that you are virtually paralysed? God will give you special strength in those times. Imagine your life is a walk along the shore with God. If some days, there is only one set of footprints in the sand it's not because God has left you, but because he is carrying you! "My gracious favour is all you need. My power works best in your weakness."
2 Corinthians 12:9
**Count on it!**

before your very eyes!"

[22]All who were there spoke well of him and were amazed by the gracious words that fell from his lips. "How can this be?" they asked. "Isn't this Joseph's son?"

[23]Then he said, "Probably you will quote me that proverb, 'Physician, heal your-self'—meaning, 'Why don't you do miracles here in your home town like those you did in Capernaum?' [24]But the truth is, no prophet is accepted in his own home town.

[25]"Certainly there were many widows in Israel who needed help in Elijah's time, when there was no rain for three and a half years and hunger stalked the land. [26]Yet Elijah was not sent to any of them. He was sent instead to a widow of Zarephath—a foreigner in the land of Sidon. [27]**Or think of the prophet Elisha, who healed Naaman, a Syrian,**

rather than the many lepers in Israel who needed help."

[28]When they heard this, the people in the synagogue were furious.

[29]Jumping up, they mobbed him and took him to the edge of the hill on which the city was built. They intended to push him over the cliff, [30]but he slipped away through the crowd and left them.

## Jesus Casts Out a Demon

[31]Then Jesus went to Capernaum, a town in Galilee, and taught there in the synagogue every Sabbath day. [32]There, too, the people were amazed at the things he said, because he spoke with authority.

[33]Once when he was in the synagogue, a man possessed by a demon began shouting at Jesus, [34]"Go away! Why are you bothering us, Jesus of Nazareth? Have you come to destroy us? I know who you are—the Holy One sent from God."

[35]Jesus cut him short. "Be silent!" he told the demon. "Come out of the man!" The demon threw the man to the floor as the crowd watched; then it left him without hurting him further.

[36]Amazed, the people exclaimed, "What authority and power this man's words possess! Even evil spirits obey him and flee at his command!" [37]The story of what he had done spread like wildfire throughout the whole region.

## Jesus Heals Many People

[38]After leaving the synagogue that day, Jesus went to Simon's home, where he found Simon's mother-in-law very sick with a high fever. "Please heal her," everyone begged. [39]Standing at her bedside, he spoke to the fever, rebuking it, and immediately her temperature returned to normal. She got up at once and prepared a meal for them.

[40]As the sun went down that evening, people throughout the village brought sick family members to Jesus. No matter what their diseases were, the touch of his hand healed every one. [41]Some were possessed by demons; and the demons came out at his command, shouting, "You are the Son of God." But because they knew he was the Messiah, he stopped them and told them to be silent.

## Jesus Continues to Preach

[42]Early the next morning Jesus went out into the wilderness. The crowds searched everywhere for him, and when they finally found him, they begged him not to leave them. [43]But he replied, "I must preach the Good News of the Kingdom of God in other places,

too, because that is why I was sent." [44]So he continued to travel around, preaching in synagogues throughout Judea.

## The First Disciples

# 5

One day as Jesus was preaching on the shore of the Sea of Galilee, great crowds pressed in on him to listen to the word of God. [2]He noticed two empty boats at the water's edge, for the fishermen had left them and were washing their nets. [3]Stepping into one of the boats, Jesus asked Simon, its owner, to push it out into the water. So he sat in the boat and taught the crowds from there.

[4]When he had finished speaking, he said to Simon, "Now go out where it is deeper and let down your nets, and you will catch many fish."

[5]"Master," Simon replied, "we worked hard all last night and didn't catch a thing. But if you say so, we'll try again." [6]And this time their nets were so full they began to tear! [7]A shout for help brought their partners in the other boat, and soon both boats were filled with fish and on the verge of sinking.

[8]When Simon Peter realized what had happened, he fell to his knees before Jesus and said, "Oh, Lord, please leave me—I'm too much of a sinner to be around you." [9]For he was awestruck by the size of their catch, as were the others with him. [10]His partners, James and John, the sons of Zebedee, were also amazed. **Jesus replied to Simon, "Don't be afraid! From now on you'll be fishing for people!"** [11]**And as soon as they landed, they left everything and followed Jesus.**

## Jesus Heals a Man with Leprosy

[12]In one of the villages, Jesus met a man with an advanced case of leprosy. When the man saw Jesus, he fell to the ground, face down in the dust, begging to be healed. "Lord," he said, "if you want to, you can make me well again."

[13]Jesus reached out and touched the man.

"I want to," he said. "Be healed!" And instantly the leprosy disappeared. [14]Then Jesus instructed him not to tell anyone what had happened. He said, "Go straight to the priest and let him examine you. Take along the offering required in the law of Moses for those who have been healed of leprosy, so everyone will have proof of your healing." [15]Yet despite Jesus'

instructions, the report of his power spread even faster, and vast crowds came to hear him preach and to be healed of their diseases.

[16]But Jesus often withdrew to the wilderness for prayer.

## Jesus Heals a Paralysed Man

[17]One day while Jesus was teaching, some Pharisees and teachers of religious law were sitting nearby. (It seemed that these men showed up from every village in all Galilee and Judea, as well as from Jerusalem.) And the Lord's healing power was strongly with Jesus. [18]Some men came carrying a paralysed man on a sleeping mat. They tried to push through the crowd to Jesus, [19]but they couldn't reach him. So they went up to the roof, took off some tiles, and lowered the sick man down into the crowd, still on his mat, right in front of Jesus. [20]Seeing their faith, Jesus said to the man, "My son, your sins are forgiven."

[21]"Who does this man think he is?" the Pharisees and teachers of religious law said to each other. "This is blasphemy! Who but God can forgive sins?"

[22]Jesus knew what they were thinking, so he asked them,

"Why do you think this is blasphemy? [23]Is it easier to say, 'Your sins are forgiven' or 'Get up and walk'? [24]I will prove that I, the Son of Man, have the authority on earth to forgive sins." Then Jesus turned to the paralysed man and said, "Stand up, take your mat, and go on home, because you are healed!"

[25]And immediately, as everyone watched, the man jumped to his feet, picked up his mat, and went home praising God. [26]Everyone was gripped with great wonder and awe. And they praised God, saying over and over again, "We have seen amazing things today."

## Jesus Calls Levi (Matthew)

[27]Later, as Jesus left the town, he saw a tax collector named Levi sitting at his tax-collection booth. "Come, be my disciple!" Jesus said to him. [28]**So Levi got up, left everything, and followed him.**

[29]Soon Levi held a banquet in his home with Jesus as the guest of honour. Many of Levi's fellow tax collectors and other guests were there. [30]But the Pharisees and their teachers of religious law complained bitterly to Jesus' disciples, "Why do you eat and drink with such scum?"

[31]Jesus answered them, "Healthy people don't need a doctor—sick people do. [32]I have come to call sinners to turn from their sins, not to spend my time with those who think they are already good enough."

## A Discussion about Fasting

[33]The religious leaders complained that Jesus' disciples were feasting instead of fasting. "John the Baptist's disciples always fast and pray," they declared, "and so do the disciples of the Pharisees. Why are yours always feasting?"

[34]Jesus asked, "Do wedding guests fast while celebrating with the groom? [35]Someday he will be taken away from them, and then they will fast."

[36]Then Jesus gave them this illustration: "No one tears a piece of cloth from a new garment and uses it to patch an old garment. For then the new garment would be torn, and the patch wouldn't even match the old garment. [37]And no one puts new wine into old wineskins. The new wine would burst the old skins, spilling the wine and ruining the skins. [38]New wine must be put into new wineskins. [39]But no one who drinks the old wine seems to want the fresh and the new. 'The old is better,' they say."

**CH 5:24-26 WHAT'S IT SAYING?**

**WHAT AM I GOING TO DO ABOUT IT?**

## A Discussion about the Sabbath

# 6

One Sabbath day as Jesus was walking through some cornfields, his disciples broke off heads of wheat, rubbed off

the husks in their hands, and ate the grain. ²But some Pharisees said, "You shouldn't be doing that! It's against the law to work by harvesting corn on the Sabbath."
³Jesus replied, "Haven't you ever read in the Scriptures what King David did when he and his companions were hungry? ⁴He went into the house of God, ate the special bread reserved for the priests alone, and then gave some to his friends. That was breaking the law, too." ⁵And Jesus added, "I, the Son of Man, am master even of the Sabbath."

## Jesus Heals on the Sabbath

⁶On another Sabbath day, a man with a deformed right hand was in the synagogue while Jesus was teaching. ⁷The teachers of religious law and the Pharisees watched closely to see whether Jesus would heal the man on the Sabbath, because they were eager to find some legal charge to bring against him. ⁸But Jesus knew their thoughts. He said to the man with the deformed hand, "Come and stand here where everyone can see." So the man came forward. ⁹Then Jesus said to his critics,
"I have a question for you. Is it legal to do good deeds on the Sabbath, or is it a day for doing harm? Is this a day to save life or to destroy it?" ¹⁰He looked around at them one by one and then said to the man, "Reach out your hand." The man reached out his hand, and it became normal again! ¹¹At this, the enemies of Jesus were wild with rage and began to discuss what to do with him.

## Jesus Chooses the Twelve Apostles

¹²One day soon afterwards Jesus went to a mountain to pray, and he prayed to God all night. ¹³At daybreak he called together all of his disciples and chose twelve of them to be apostles. Here are their names:
¹⁴Simon (he also called him Peter),
Andrew (Peter's brother),
James,
John,
Philip,
Bartholomew,
¹⁵Matthew,
Thomas,
James (son of Alphaeus),
Simon (the Zealot),
¹⁶Judas (son of James),
Judas Iscariot (who later betrayed him).

## Crowds Follow Jesus

¹⁷When they came down the slopes of the mountain, the disciples stood with Jesus on a large, level area, surrounded by many of his followers and by the crowds. There were people from all over Judea and from Jerusalem and from as far

north as the seacoasts of Tyre and Sidon. ¹⁸They had come to hear him and to be healed, and Jesus cast out many evil spirits. ¹⁹Everyone was trying to touch him, because healing power went out from him, and they were all cured.

## The Beatitudes

²⁰Then Jesus turned to his disciples and said,
"God blesses you who are poor,
for the Kingdom of God is given to you.
²¹God blesses you who are hungry now,
for you will be satisfied.
God blesses you who weep now,
for the time will come when you will laugh with joy.
²²God blesses you who are hated and excluded and mocked and cursed
because you are identified with me, the Son of Man.
²³"When that happens, rejoice! Yes, leap for joy! For a great reward awaits you in heaven. And remember, the ancient prophets were also treated that way by your ancestors.

## Sorrows Foretold

²⁴"What sorrows await you who are rich,
for you have your only happiness now.
²⁵What sorrows await you who are satisfied and prosperous now,
for a time of awful hunger is before you.
What sorrows await you who laugh carelessly,
for your laughing will turn to mourning and sorrow.
²⁶What sorrows await you who are praised by the crowds,
for their ancestors also praised false prophets.

## Love for Enemies

²⁷"But if you are willing to listen, I say, love your enemies. Do good to those who hate you. ²⁸Pray for the happiness of those who curse you. Pray for those who hurt you. ²⁹If someone slaps you on one cheek, turn the other cheek. If someone demands your coat, offer your shirt also. ³⁰Give what you have to anyone who asks you for it; and when things are taken away from you, don't try to get them back. ³¹Do for others as you would like them to do for you.
³²"Do you think you deserve credit merely for loving those who love you? Even the sinners do that! ³³And if you do good only to those who do good to you, is that so wonderful? Even sinners do that much! ³⁴And if you lend money only to those who can repay you, what good is that? Even sinners will lend to their own kind for a full return.

³⁵"Love your enemies! Do good to them! Lend to them! And don't be concerned that they might not repay. Then your reward from heaven will be very great, and you will truly be acting as children of the Most High, for he is kind to the unthankful and to those who are wicked. ³⁶You must be compassionate, just as your Father is compassionate.

action

CH 6:32-38 WHAT'S IT SAYING?

WHAT AM I GOING TO DO ABOUT IT?

## Don't Condemn Others

³⁷"Stop judging others, and you will not be judged. Stop criticizing others, or it will all come back on you. If you forgive others, you will be forgiven. ³⁸If you give, you will receive. Your gift will return to you in full measure, pressed down, shaken together to make room for more, and running over. Whatever measure you use in giving—large or small—it will be used to measure what is given back to you."
³⁹Then Jesus gave the following illustration: "What good is it for one blind person to lead another? The first one will fall into a ditch and pull the other down also. ⁴⁰A student is not greater than the teacher. But the student who works hard will become like the teacher.
⁴¹"And why worry about a speck in your friend's eye when you have a log in your own? ⁴²How can you think

of saying,

'Friend, let me help you get rid of that speck in your eye,' when you can't see past the log in your own eye? Hypocrite! First get rid of the log from your own eye; then perhaps you will see well enough to deal with the speck in your friend's eye.

## The Tree and Its Fruit

43"A good tree can't produce bad fruit, and a bad tree can't produce good fruit. 44A tree is identified by the kind of fruit it produces. Figs never grow on thorn bushes or grapes on bramble bushes. 45A good person produces good deeds from a good heart, and an evil person produces evil deeds from an evil heart. Whatever is in your heart determines what you say.

## Building on a Solid Foundation

46"So why do you call me 'Lord,' when you won't obey me? 47I will show you what it's like when someone comes to me, listens to my teaching, and then obeys me. 48It is like a person who builds a house on a strong foundation laid upon the underlying rock. When the floodwaters rise and break against the house, it stands firm because it is well built. 49But anyone who listens and doesn't obey is like a person who builds a house without a foundation. When the floods sweep down against that house, it will crumble into a heap of ruins."

## Faith of the Roman Officer

# 7

When Jesus had finished saying all this, he went back to Capernaum. 2Now the highly valued slave of a Roman officer was sick and near death. 3When the officer heard about Jesus, he sent some respected Jewish leaders to ask him to come and heal his slave. 4So they earnestly begged Jesus to come with them and help the man. "If anyone deserves your help, it is he," they said, 5"for he loves the Jews and even built a synagogue for us."

6So Jesus went with them. But just before they arrived at the house, the officer sent some friends to say, "Lord, don't trouble yourself by coming to my home, for I am not worthy of such an honour. 7I am not even worthy to come and meet you. Just say the word from where you are, and my servant will be healed. 8I know because I am under the authority of my superior officers, and I have authority over my soldiers. I only need to say, 'Go,' and they go, or 'Come,' and they

come. And if I say to my slaves, 'Do this or that,' they do it."

9When Jesus heard this, he was amazed. Turning to the crowd, he said, "I tell you, I haven't seen faith like this in all the land of Israel!" 10And when the officer's friends returned to his house, they found the slave completely healed.

## Jesus Raises a Widow's Son

11Soon afterwards Jesus went with his disciples to the village of Nain, with a great crowd following him. 12A funeral procession was coming out as he approached the village gate. The boy who had died was the only son of a widow, and many mourners from the village were with her. 13When the Lord saw her, his heart overflowed with compassion. "Don't cry!" he said. 14Then he walked over to the coffin and touched it, and the bearers stopped. "Young man," he said, "get up."

15Then the dead boy sat up and began to talk to those around him! And Jesus gave him back to his mother. 16Great fear swept the crowd, and they praised God, saying, "A mighty prophet has risen among us," and "We have seen the hand of God at work today." 17The report of what Jesus had done that day spread all over Judea and even out across its borders.

## Jesus and John the Baptist

18The disciples of John the Baptist told John about everything Jesus was doing. So John called for two of his disciples, 19and he sent them to the Lord to ask him, "Are you the Messiah we've been expecting, or should we keep looking for someone else?"

20John's two disciples found Jesus and said to him, "John the Baptist sent us to ask, 'Are you the Messiah we've been expecting, or should we keep looking for someone else?'"

21At that very time, he cured many people of their various diseases, and he cast out evil spirits and restored sight to the blind.

22Then he told John's disciples, "Go back to John and tell him what you have seen and heard—the blind see, the lame walk, the lepers are cured, the deaf hear, the dead are raised to life, and the Good News is being preached to the poor. 23And tell him, 'God blesses those who are not offended by me.'"

24After they left, Jesus talked to the crowd about John. "Who is this man in the wilderness that you went out to see? Did you find him weak as a reed, moved by every breath of wind? 25Or were you expecting to see a man dressed in expensive clothes? No, people who wear beautiful clothes and live in luxury are found in palaces, not in the wilderness. 26Were you looking for a prophet? Yes, and he is more than a prophet. 27John is the man to whom the Scriptures refer when they

### STAND POINT

**When you feel like cheating**

6:31

Do for others as you would like them to do for you.

---

What are the five best characteristics of a winner?

1
2
3
4
5

# BIG FIVE

say,

'Look, I am sending my messenger before you,
and he will prepare your way before you.'

[28]I tell you, of all who have ever lived, none is greater than John. Yet even the most insignificant person in the Kingdom of God is greater than he is!"

[29]When they heard this, all the people, including the unjust tax collectors, agreed that God's plan was right, for they had been baptized by John. [30]But the Pharisees and experts in religious law had rejected God's plan for them, for they had refused John's baptism.

[31]"How shall I describe this generation?" Jesus asked. "With what will I compare them? [32]They are like a group of children playing a game in the public square. They complain to their friends, 'We played wedding songs, and you weren't happy, so we played funeral songs, but you weren't sad.'

[33]For John the Baptist didn't drink wine and he often fasted, and you say, 'He's demon possessed.'

[34]And I, the Son of Man, feast and drink, and you say, 'He's a glutton and a drunkard, and a friend of the worst sort of sinners!'

**[35]But wisdom is shown to be right by the lives of those who follow it."**

## Jesus Anointed by a Sinful Woman

[36]One of the Pharisees asked Jesus to come to his home for a meal, so Jesus accepted the invitation and sat down to eat. [37]A certain immoral woman heard he was there and brought a beautiful jar filled with expensive perfume. [38]Then she knelt behind him at his feet, weeping. Her tears fell on his feet, and she wiped them off with her hair. Then she kept kissing his feet and putting perfume on them.

[39]When the Pharisee who was the host saw what was happening and who the woman was, he said to himself, "This proves that Jesus is no prophet. If God had really sent him, he would know what kind of woman is touching him. She's a sinner!"

[40]Then Jesus spoke up and answered his thoughts. "Simon," he said to the Pharisee, "I have something to say to you."

"All right, Teacher," Simon replied, "go ahead."

[41]Then Jesus told him this story: "A man loaned money to two people—five hundred pieces of silver to one and fifty pieces to the other. [42]But neither of them could repay him, so he kindly forgave them both, cancelling their debts. Who do you suppose loved him more after that?"

[43]Simon answered, "I suppose the one for whom he cancelled the larger debt."

"That's right," Jesus said. [44]Then he turned to the woman and said to Simon, "Look at this woman kneeling here. When I entered your home, you didn't offer me water to wash the dust from my feet, but she has washed them with her tears and wiped them with her hair. [45]You didn't give me a kiss of greeting, but she has kissed my feet again and again from the time I first came in. [46]You neglected the courtesy of olive oil to anoint my head, but she has anointed my feet with rare perfume. [47]I tell you, her sins—and they are many—have been forgiven, so she has shown me much love. But a person who is forgiven little shows only little love." [48]Then Jesus said to the woman, "Your sins are forgiven."

[49]The men at the table said among themselves, "Who does this man think he is, going around forgiving sins?"

[50]And Jesus said to the woman, "Your faith has saved you; go in peace."

**action**

CH 8:4–15 WHAT'S IT SAYING?

WHAT AM I GOING TO DO ABOUT IT?

## Women Who Followed Jesus

# 8

Not long afterwards Jesus began a tour of the nearby cities and villages to announce the Good News concerning the Kingdom of God. He took his twelve disciples with him, [2]along with some women he had healed and from whom he had cast out evil spirits. Among them were Mary Magdalene, from whom he had cast out seven demons; [3]Joanna, the wife of Chuza, Herod's business manager; Susanna; and many others who were contributing from their own resources to support Jesus and his disciples.

## Story of the Farmer Scattering Seed

[4]One day Jesus told this story to a large crowd that had gathered from many towns to hear him: [5]"A farmer went out to plant some seed. As he scattered it across his field, some seed fell on a footpath, where it was stepped on, and the birds came and ate it. [6]Other seed fell on shallow soil with underlying rock. This seed began to grow, but soon it withered and died for lack of moisture. [7]Other seed fell among thorns that shot up and choked out the tender blades. [8]Still other seed fell on fertile soil. This seed grew and produced a crop one hundred times as much as had been planted." When he had said this, he called out, "Anyone who is willing to hear should listen and understand!"

[9]His disciples asked him what the story meant. [10]He replied, "You have been permitted to understand the secrets of the Kingdom of God. But I am using these stories to conceal everything about it from outsiders, so that the Scriptures might be fulfilled:

'They see what I do,
but they don't really see;
they hear what I say,
but they don't understand.'

[11]"This is the meaning of the story: The seed is God's message. [12]The seed that fell on the hard path represents those who hear the message, but then the Devil comes and steals it away and prevents them from believing and being saved. [13]The rocky soil represents those who hear the message with joy. But like young plants in such soil, their roots don't go very deep. They believe for a while, but they wilt when the hot winds of testing blow. [14]The thorny ground represents those who hear and accept the message, but all too quickly the message is crowded out by the cares and riches and pleasures of this life. And so they never grow into maturity. [15]But the good soil represents honest, good-hearted people who hear God's message, cling to it, and steadily produce a huge harvest.

## Illustration of the Lamp

[16]"No one would light a lamp and then cover it up or put it under a bed. No, lamps are mounted in the open, where they can be seen by those entering the house. [17]For everything that is hidden or secret will eventually be brought to light and made plain to all. [18]So be sure to pay attention to what you hear. To those who are open to my teaching, more understanding will be given. But to those who are not

In 1970, 127 runners ran the New York Marathon. In 2000, over 32,000 did.

listening, even what they think they have will be taken away from them."

## The True Family of Jesus

[19]Once when Jesus' mother and brothers came to see him, they couldn't get to him because of the crowds. [20]Someone told Jesus, "Your mother and your brothers are outside, and they want to see you."

[21]Jesus replied, "My mother and my brothers are all those who hear the message of God and obey it."

## Jesus Calms the Storm

[22]One day Jesus said to his disciples, "Let's cross over to the other side of the lake." So they got into a boat and started out. [23]On the way across, Jesus lay down for a nap, and while he was sleeping the wind began to rise. A fierce storm developed that threatened to swamp them, and they were in real danger.

[24]The disciples woke him up, shouting, "Master, Master, we're going to drown!"

So Jesus rebuked the wind and the raging waves. The storm stopped and all was calm! **[25]Then he asked them, "Where is your faith?" And they were filled with awe and amazement. They said to one another, "Who is this man, that even the winds and waves obey him?"**

**The Bible was originally written in three languages - Hebrew, Aramaic, & Greek.**

## Jesus Heals a Demon-Possessed Man

[26]So they arrived in the land of the Gerasenes, across the lake from Galilee. [27]As Jesus was climbing out of the boat, a man who was possessed by demons came out to meet him. Homeless and naked, he had lived in a cemetery for a long time. [28]As soon as he saw Jesus, he shrieked and fell to the ground before him, screaming, "Why are you bothering me, Jesus, Son of the Most High God? Please, I beg you, don't torture me!" [29]For Jesus had already commanded the evil spirit to come out of him. This spirit had often taken control of the man. Even when he was shackled with chains, he simply broke them and rushed out into the wilderness, completely under the demon's power.

[30]"What is your name?" Jesus asked.

"Legion," he replied—for the man was filled with many demons. [31]The demons kept begging Jesus not to send them into the Bottomless Pit. [32]A large herd of pigs was feeding on the hillside nearby, and the demons pleaded with him to let them enter into the pigs. Jesus gave them permission. [33]So the demons came out of the man and entered the pigs, and the whole herd plunged down the steep hillside into the lake, where they drowned.

[34]When the herdsmen saw it, they fled to the nearby city and the surrounding countryside, spreading the news as they ran. [35]A crowd soon gathered around Jesus, for they wanted to see for themselves what had happened. And they saw the man who had been possessed by demons sitting quietly at Jesus' feet, clothed and sane. And the whole crowd was afraid. [36]Then those who had seen what happened told the others how the demon-possessed man had been healed. [37]And all the people in that region begged Jesus to go away and leave them alone, for a great wave of fear swept over them.

So Jesus returned to the boat and left, crossing back to the other side of the lake. [38]The man who had been demon possessed begged to go, too, but Jesus said, **[39]"No, go back to your family and tell them all the wonderful things God has done for you." So he went all through the city telling about the great thing Jesus had done for him.**

## Jesus Heals in Response to Faith

[40]On the other side of the lake the crowds received Jesus with open arms because they had been waiting for him. [41]And now a man named Jairus, a leader of the local synagogue, came and fell down at Jesus' feet, begging him to come home with him.

[42]His only child was dying, a little girl twelve years old. As Jesus went with him, he was surrounded by the crowds.

[43]And there was a woman in the crowd who had had a haemorrhage for twelve years. She had spent everything she had on doctors and still could find no cure. [44]She came up behind Jesus and touched the fringe of his robe. Immediately, the bleeding stopped.

[45]"Who touched me?" Jesus asked.

Everyone denied it, and Peter said, "Master, this whole crowd is pressing up against you."

[46]But Jesus told him, "No, someone deliberately touched me, for I felt healing power go out from me."

[47]When the woman realized that Jesus knew, she began to tremble and fell to her knees before him. The whole crowd heard her explain why she had touched him and that she had been immediately healed. [48]"Daughter," he said to her, "your faith has made you well. Go in peace."

[49]While he was still speaking to her, a messenger arrived from Jairus's home with the message, "Your little girl is dead. There's no use troubling the Teacher now."

[50]But when Jesus heard what had happened, he said to Jairus, "Don't be afraid. Just trust me, and she will be all right."

[51]When they arrived at the house, Jesus wouldn't let anyone go in with him except Peter, James, John, and the little girl's father and mother. [52]The house was filled with people weeping and wailing, but he said, "Stop the weeping! She isn't dead; she is only asleep."

[53]But the crowd laughed at him because they all knew she had died. [54]Then Jesus took her by the hand and said in a loud voice, "Get up, my child!" [55]And at that moment her life returned, and she immediately stood up! Then Jesus told them to give her something to eat. [56]Her parents were overwhelmed, but Jesus insisted that they not tell anyone what had happened.

## Jesus Sends Out the Twelve Apostles

 9

One day Jesus called together his twelve apostles and gave them power and authority to cast out demons and to heal all diseases.

[2]Then he sent them out to tell everyone about the coming of the Kingdom of God and to heal the sick. [3]"Don't even take along a walking stick," he instructed them, "nor a traveller's bag, nor food, nor money. Not even an extra coat.

[4]When you enter each village, be a guest in only one home. [5]If the people of the village won't receive your message when you enter it, shake off its dust from your feet as you leave. It

is a sign that you have abandoned that village to its fate."

⁶So they began their circuit of the villages, preaching the Good News and healing the sick.

### Herod's Confusion

⁷When reports of Jesus' miracles reached Herod Antipas, he was worried and puzzled because some were saying,

"This is John the Baptist come back to life again." ⁸Others were saying, "It is Elijah or some other ancient prophet risen from the dead."

⁹"I beheaded John," Herod said, "so who is this man about whom I hear such strange stories?" And he tried to see him.

### Jesus Feeds Five Thousand

¹⁰When the apostles returned, they told Jesus everything they had done. Then he slipped quietly away with them towards the town of Bethsaida. ¹¹But the crowds found out where he was going, and they followed him. And he welcomed them, teaching them about the Kingdom of God and curing those who were ill.

¹²Late in the afternoon the twelve disciples came to him and said, "Send the crowds away to the nearby villages and farms, so they can find food and lodging for the night. There is nothing to eat here in this deserted place."

¹³But Jesus said, "You feed them."

"Impossible!" they protested. "We have only five loaves of bread and two fish. Or are you expecting us to go and buy enough food for this whole crowd?" ¹⁴For there were about five thousand men there.

"Just tell them to sit down on the ground in groups of about fifty each," Jesus replied. ¹⁵So the people all sat down. ¹⁶Jesus took the five loaves and two fish, looked up towards heaven, and asked God's blessing on the food. Breaking the loaves into pieces, he kept giving the bread and fish to the disciples to give to the people. ¹⁷They all ate as much as they wanted, and they picked up twelve baskets of leftovers!

### Peter's Declaration about Jesus

¹⁸One day as Jesus was alone, praying, he came over to his disciples and asked them, "Who do people say I am?"

¹⁹"Well," they replied, "some say John the Baptist, some say Elijah, and others say you are one of the other ancient prophets risen from the dead."

²⁰Then he asked them, "Who do you say I am?" Peter replied, **"You are the Messiah sent from God!"**

## Winners stay in the zone!

Great athletes stay in control, they can keep their cool under pressure. You may remember watching an athlete throw a tantrum but, if you watch closely, you will realise the majority of professional sport is played with discipline and control. For the best to win, they need to stay focused and master their emotions. God's Spirit will keep you in his zone and under control. Stay in the zone – in the Spirit!

"But when the Holy Spirit controls our lives, he will produce this kind of fruit in us: love, joy, peace, patience, kindness, goodness, faithfulness, gentleness and self-control." Galatians 5:22-23

## Winners stay focused!

### Jesus Predicts His Death

[21]Jesus warned them not to tell anyone about this. [22]"For I, the Son of Man, must suffer many terrible things," he said. "I will be rejected by the leaders, the leading priests, and the teachers of religious law. I will be killed, but three days later I will be raised from the dead."

[23]Then he said to the crowd, "If any of you wants to be my follower, you must put aside your selfish ambition, shoulder your cross daily, and follow me. [24]If you try to keep your life for yourself, you will lose it. But if you give up your life for me, you will find true life. [25]And how do you benefit if you gain the whole world but lose or forfeit your own soul in the process?

[26]If a person is ashamed of me and my message, I, the Son of Man, will be ashamed of that person when I return in my glory and in the glory of the Father and the holy angels. [27]And I assure you that some of you standing here right now will not die before you see the Kingdom of God."

### The Transfiguration

[28]About eight days later Jesus took Peter, James, and John to a mountain to pray. [29]And as he was praying, the appearance of his face changed, and his clothing became dazzling white.

[30]Then two men, Moses and Elijah, appeared and began talking with Jesus. [31]**They were glorious to see. And they were speaking of how he was about to fulfil God's plan by dying in Jerusalem.**

[32]Peter and the others were very drowsy and had fallen asleep. Now they woke up and saw Jesus' glory and the two men standing with him. [33]As Moses and Elijah were starting to leave, Peter, not even knowing what he was saying, blurted out, "Master, this is wonderful! We will make three shrines—one for you, one for Moses, and one for Elijah." [34]But even as he was saying this, a cloud came over them; and terror gripped them as it covered them.

[35]Then a voice from the cloud said, "This is my Son, my Chosen One. Listen to him." [36]When the voice died away, Jesus was there alone. They didn't tell anyone what they had seen until long after this happened.

### Jesus Heals a Demon-Possessed Boy

[37]The next day, after they had come down the mountain, a huge crowd met Jesus. [38]A man in the crowd called out to him, "Teacher, look at my boy, who is my only son. [39]An evil spirit keeps seizing him, making him scream. It throws him into convulsions so that he foams at the mouth. It is always hitting and injuring him. It hardly ever leaves him alone. [40]I begged your disciples to cast the spirit out, but they couldn't do it."

[41]"You stubborn, faithless people," Jesus said, "how long must I be with you and put up with you? Bring him here." [42]As the boy came forward, the demon knocked him to the ground and threw him into a violent convulsion. But Jesus rebuked the evil spirit and healed the boy. Then he gave him back to his father. [43]**Awe gripped the people as they saw this display of God's power.**

### Jesus Again Predicts His Death

While everyone was marvelling over all the wonderful things he was doing, Jesus said to his disciples, [44]"Listen to me and remember what I say. The Son of Man is going to be betrayed." [45]But they didn't know what he meant. Its significance was hidden from them, so they could not understand it, and they were afraid to ask him about it.

### The Greatest in the Kingdom

[46]Then there was an argument among them as to which of them would be the greatest. [47]But Jesus knew their thoughts, so he brought a little child to his side. [48]**Then he said to them, "Anyone who welcomes a little child like this on my behalf welcomes me, and anyone who welcomes me welcomes my Father who sent me. Whoever is the least among you is the greatest."**

### Using the Name of Jesus

[49]John said to Jesus, "Master, we saw someone using your name to cast out demons. We tried to stop him because he isn't in our group."

[50]But Jesus said, "Don't stop him! Anyone who is not against you is for you."

### Did Jesus really rise from the dead?

Nobody could have stolen the body as it was guarded by soldiers and a heavy boulder. Once risen, he appeared to many eyewitnesses (1 Corinthians 15:4-8) including 500 at once – they couldn't all have been hallucinating. What is most convincing is that many of these same witnesses were later willing to be tortured and die for their belief that Jesus was resurrected; no one withdrew their faith!

## Opposition from Samaritans

⁵¹As the time drew near for his return to heaven, Jesus resolutely set out for Jerusalem. ⁵²He sent messengers ahead to a Samaritan village to prepare for his arrival. ⁵³But they were turned away. The people of the village refused to have anything to do with Jesus because he had resolved to go to Jerusalem. ⁵⁴When James and John heard about it, they said to Jesus, "Lord, should we order down fire from heaven to burn them up?" ⁵⁵But Jesus turned and rebuked them.* ⁵⁶So they went on to another village.

## The Cost of Following Jesus

⁵⁷As they were walking along someone said to Jesus, "I will follow you no matter where you go."

⁵⁸But Jesus replied, "Foxes have dens to live in, and birds have nests, but I, the Son of Man, have no home of my own, not even a place to lay my head."

⁵⁹He said to another person, "Come, be my disciple." The man agreed, but he said, "Lord, first let me return home and bury my father."

⁶⁰Jesus replied, "Let those who are spiritually dead look after their own dead. Your duty is to go and preach the coming of the Kingdom of God."

⁶¹Another said, "Yes, Lord, I will follow you, but first let me say goodbye to my family."

⁶²But Jesus told him, "Anyone who puts a hand to the plough and then looks back is not fit for the Kingdom of God."

## Jesus Sends Out His Disciples

# 10

The Lord now chose seventy-two other disciples and sent them on ahead in pairs to all the towns and villages he planned to visit. ²These were his instructions to them: "The harvest is so great, but the workers are so few. Pray to the Lord who is in charge of the harvest, and ask him to send out more workers for his fields. ³Go now, and remember that I am sending you out as lambs among wolves. ⁴Don't take along any money, or a traveller's bag, or even an extra pair of sandals. And don't stop to greet anyone on the road.

⁵"Whenever you enter a home, give it your blessing. ⁶If those who live there are worthy, the blessing will stand; if they are not, the blessing will return to you. ⁷When you enter a town, don't move around from home to home. Stay in one place, eating and drinking what they provide for you. Don't hesitate to accept hospitality, because those who work deserve their pay.

⁸"If a town welcomes you, eat whatever is set before you ⁹and heal the sick. As you heal them, say, 'The Kingdom of God is near you now.' ¹⁰But if a town refuses to welcome you, go out into its streets and say, ¹¹'We wipe the dust of your town from our feet as a public announcement of your doom. And don't forget the Kingdom of God is near!'

¹²The truth is, even wicked Sodom will be better off than such a town on the judgement day.

¹³"What horrors await you, Korazin and Bethsaida! For if the miracles I did in you had been done in wicked Tyre and Sidon, their people would have sat in deep repentance long ago, clothed in sackcloth and throwing ashes on their heads to show their remorse. ¹⁴Yes, Tyre and Sidon will be better off on the judgement day than you. ¹⁵And you people of Capernaum, will you be exalted to heaven? No, you will be brought down to the place of the dead."

¹⁶Then he said to the disciples, "Anyone who accepts your message is also accepting me. And anyone who rejects you is rejecting me. And anyone who rejects me is rejecting God who sent me."

¹⁷When the seventy-two disciples returned, they joyfully reported to him, "Lord, even the demons obey us when we use your name!"

¹⁸"Yes," he told them, "I saw Satan falling from heaven as a flash of lightning! ¹⁹And I have given you authority over all the power of the enemy, and you can walk among snakes and scorpions and crush them. Nothing will injure you. ²⁰But don't rejoice just because evil spirits obey you; rejoice because your names are registered as citizens of heaven."

## Jesus' Prayer of Thanksgiving

²¹Then Jesus was filled with the joy of the Holy Spirit and said, "O Father, Lord of heaven and earth, thank you for hiding the truth from those who think themselves so wise and clever, and for revealing it to the childlike. Yes, Father, it pleased you to do it this way.

²²"My Father has given me authority over everything. No one really knows the Son except the Father, and no one really knows the Father except the Son and those to whom the Son chooses to reveal him."

²³Then when they were alone, he turned to the disciples and said, "How privileged you are to see what you have seen. ²⁴I tell you, many prophets and kings have longed to see and hear what you have seen and heard, but they could not."

## The Most Important Commandment

²⁵One day an expert in religious law stood up to test Jesus by asking him this question: "Teacher, what must I do to receive eternal life?"

²⁶Jesus replied, "What does the law of Moses say? How do you read it?"

²⁷The man answered, "'You must love the Lord your God with all your heart, all your soul, all your strength, and all your mind.' And, 'Love your neighbour as yourself.'"

²⁸"Right!" Jesus told him. "Do this and you will live!"

²⁹The man wanted to justify his actions, so he asked Jesus,

"And who is my neighbour?"

## Story of the Good Samaritan

³⁰Jesus replied with an illustration: "A Jewish man was travelling on a trip from Jerusalem to Jericho, and he was attacked by bandits. They stripped him of his clothes and money, beat him up, and left him half dead beside the road.

³¹"By chance a Jewish priest came along; but when he saw the man lying there, he crossed to the other side of the road and passed him by. ³²A Temple assistant walked over and looked at him lying there, but he also passed by on the other side.

³³"Then a despised Samaritan came along, and when he saw the man, he felt deep pity. ³⁴Kneeling beside him, the Samaritan soothed his wounds with medicine and bandaged them. Then he put the man on his own

'Put it into Practice' LUKE 11:17–28

It is time to choose the winning team - and the captain of that team is the Lord Jesus Christ. Always training never playing makes sport pretty boring - the same is true in the Christian faith. You have been training - now is the time to play. USE YOUR WEAPONRY. When it is your turn to bat you don't leave your bat in your chair! Well don't forget in the spiritual battle, our offensive weapon is the word of God, the Bible. As we hear and obey the Bible so we experience God's blessing (verse 28). It is not just hearing – it is putting what we hear into action!

9:55 Some manuscripts add And he said, "You don't realize what your hearts are like. ⁵⁶For the Son of Man has not come to destroy people's lives, but to save them."

donkey and took him to an inn, where he took care of him. ³⁵The next day he handed the innkeeper two pieces of silver and told him to take care of the man. 'If his bill runs higher than that,' he said, 'I'll pay the difference the next time I am here.'

³⁶"Now which of these three would you say was a neighbour to the man who was attacked by bandits?" Jesus asked.

³⁷The man replied, "The one who showed him mercy." Then Jesus said, "Yes, now go and do the same."

## Jesus Visits Martha and Mary

³⁸As Jesus and the disciples continued on their way to Jerusalem, they came to a village where a woman named Martha welcomed them into her home. ³⁹Her sister, Mary, sat at the Lord's feet, listening to what he taught. ⁴⁰But Martha was worrying over the big dinner she was preparing. She came to Jesus and said, "Lord, doesn't it seem unfair to you that my sister just sits here while I do all the work? Tell her to come and help me."

⁴¹But the Lord said to her, "My dear Martha, you are so upset over all these details! ⁴²There is really only one thing worth being concerned about. Mary has discovered it—and I won't take it away from her."

## Teaching about Prayer

# 11

Once when Jesus had been out praying, one of his disciples came to him as he finished and said, "Lord, teach us to pray, just as John taught his disciples."

²He said, "This is how you should pray:

"Father, may your name be honoured.
May your Kingdom come soon.
³Give us our food day by day.
⁴And forgive us our sins—
just as we forgive those who have sinned against us.
And don't let us yield to temptation."

⁵Then, teaching them more about prayer, he used this illustration: "Suppose you went to a friend's house at midnight, wanting to borrow three loaves of bread. You would say to him, ⁶'A friend of mine has just arrived for a visit, and I have nothing for him to eat.' ⁷He would call out from his bedroom, 'Don't bother me. The door is locked for the night, and we are all in bed. I can't help you this time.' ⁸But I tell you this—though he won't do it as a friend, if you keep knocking long enough, he will get up and give you what you want so his reputation won't be damaged.

⁹"And so I tell you, keep on asking, and you will be given what you ask for. Keep on looking, and you will find. Keep on knocking, and the door will be opened. ¹⁰For everyone who asks, receives. Everyone who seeks, finds. And the door is opened to everyone who knocks. ¹¹"You fathers—if your children ask for a fish, do you give them a snake instead? ¹²Or if they ask for an egg, do you give them a scorpion? Of course not! ¹³**If you sinful people know how to give good gifts to your children, how much more will your heavenly Father give the Holy Spirit to those who ask him."**

## Jesus and the Prince of Demons

¹⁴One day Jesus cast a demon out of a man who couldn't speak, and the man's voice returned to him. The crowd was amazed, ¹⁵but some said, "No wonder he can cast out demons. He gets his power from Satan, the prince of demons!"

¹⁶Trying to test Jesus, others asked for a miraculous sign from heaven to see if he was from God.

¹⁷He knew their thoughts, so he said, "Any kingdom at war with itself is doomed. A divided home is also doomed. ¹⁸You say I am empowered by the prince of demons. But if Satan is fighting against himself by empowering me to cast out his demons, how can his kingdom survive? ¹⁹And if I am empowered by the prince of demons, what about your own followers? They cast out demons, too, so they will judge you for what you have said. ²⁰But if I am casting out demons by the power of God, then the Kingdom of God has arrived among you. ²¹For when Satan, who is completely armed, guards his palace, it is safe—²²until someone who is stronger attacks and overpowers him, strips him of his weapons, and carries off his belongings.

²³"Anyone who isn't helping me opposes me, and anyone who isn't working with me is actually working against me.

²⁴"When an evil spirit leaves a person, it goes into the desert, searching for rest. But when it finds none, it says, 'I will return to the person I came from.' ²⁵So it returns and finds that its former home is all swept and clean. ²⁶Then the spirit finds seven other spirits more evil than itself, and they all enter the person and live there. And so that person is worse off than before."

²⁷As he was speaking, a woman in the crowd called out, "God bless your mother—the womb from which you came, and the breasts that nursed you!"

²⁸**He replied, "But even more blessed are all who hear the word of God and put it into practice."**

**action**

CH 11:27-28 WHAT'S IT SAYING?

**WHAT AM I GOING TO DO ABOUT IT?**

## The Sign of Jonah

²⁹As the crowd pressed in on Jesus, he said, "These are evil times, and this evil generation keeps asking me to show them a miraculous sign. But the only sign I will give them is the sign of the prophet Jonah. ³⁰What happened to him was a sign to the people of Nineveh that God had sent him. What happens to me will be a sign that God has sent me, the Son of Man, to these people.

³¹"The queen of Sheba will rise up against this generation on judgement day and condemn it, because she came from a distant land to hear the wisdom of Solomon. And now someone greater than Solomon is here—and you refuse to listen to him. ³²The people of Nineveh, too, will rise up against this generation on judgement day and condemn it, because they repented at the preaching of Jonah. And now someone greater than Jonah is here—and you refuse to repent.

## Receiving the Light

³³"No one lights a lamp and then hides it or puts it under a basket. Instead, it is put on a lampstand to give light to all who enter the room. ³⁴Your eye is a lamp for your body. A pure eye lets sunshine into your soul. But an evil eye shuts out the light and plunges you into darkness. ³⁵Make sure that the light you think you have is not really darkness. ³⁶If you are filled with light, with no dark corners, then your

whole life will be radiant, as though a floodlight is shining on you."

## Jesus Criticizes the Religious Leaders

[37]As Jesus was speaking, one of the Pharisees invited him home for a meal. So he went in and took his place at the table. [38]His host was amazed to see that he sat down to eat without first performing the ceremonial washing required by Jewish custom. [39]Then the Lord said to him, "You Pharisees are so careful to clean the outside of the cup and the dish, but inside you are still filthy—full of greed and wickedness! [40]Fools! Didn't God make the inside as well as the outside? [41]So give to the needy what you greedily possess, and you will be clean all over.

[42]But how terrible it will be for you Pharisees! For you are careful to tithe even the tiniest part of your income, but you completely forget about justice and the love of God. You should tithe, yes, but you should not leave undone the more important things.

[43]How terrible it will be for you Pharisees! For how you love the seats of honour in the synagogues and the respectful greetings from everyone as you walk through the markets! [44]Yes, how terrible it will be for you. For you are like hidden graves in a field. People walk over them without knowing the corruption they are stepping on."

[45]"Teacher," said an expert in religious law, "you have insulted us, too, in what you just said."

[46]"Yes," said Jesus, "how terrible it will be for you experts in religious law! For you crush people beneath impossible religious demands, and you never lift a finger to help ease the burden. [47]How terrible it will be for you! For you build tombs for the very prophets your ancestors killed long ago. [48]urderers! You agree with your ancestors that what they did was right. You would have done the same yourselves. [49]This is what God in his wisdom said about you: 'I will send prophets and apostles to them, and they will kill some and persecute the others.'

[50]And you of this generation will be held responsible for the murder of all God's prophets from the creation of the world—[51]from the murder of Abel to the murder of Zechariah, who was killed between the altar and the sanctuary. Yes, it will surely be charged against you.

[52]How terrible it will be for you experts in religious law! For you hide the key to knowledge from the people. You don't enter the Kingdom yourselves, and you prevent others from entering."

[53]As Jesus finished speaking, the Pharisees and teachers of religious law were furious. From that time on they grilled him with many hostile questions, [54]trying to trap him into saying something they could use against him.

## A Warning against Hypocrisy

# 12

Meanwhile, the crowds grew until thousands were milling about and crushing each other. Jesus turned first to his disciples and warned them, "Beware of the yeast of the Pharisees—beware of their hypocrisy. [2]The time is coming when everything will be revealed; all that is secret will be made public. [3]Whatever you have said in the dark will be heard in the light, and what you have whispered behind closed doors will be shouted from the housetops for all to hear!

[4]Dear friends, don't be afraid of those who want to kill you. They can only kill the body; they cannot do any more to you. [5]But I'll tell you whom to fear. Fear God, who has the power to kill people and then throw them into hell.

[6]What is the price of five sparrows? A couple of pennies? Yet God does not forget a single one of them. [7]And the very hairs on your head are all numbered. So don't be afraid; you are more valuable to him than a whole flock of sparrows.

[8]And I assure you of this: If anyone acknowledges me publicly here on earth, I, the Son of Man, will openly acknowledge that person in the presence of God's angels. [9]But if anyone denies me here on earth, I will deny that person before God's angels. [10]Yet those who speak against the Son of Man may be forgiven, but anyone who speaks blasphemies against the Holy Spirit will never be forgiven.

[11]And when you are brought to trial in the synagogues and before rulers and authorities, don't worry about what to say in your defence, [12]for the Holy Spirit will teach you what needs to be said even as you are standing there."

## Story of the Rich Fool

[13]Then someone called from the crowd, "Teacher, please tell my brother to divide our father's estate with me." [14]Jesus replied, "Friend, who made me a judge over you to decide such things as that?" [15]Then he said, "Beware! **Don't be greedy for what you don't have. Real life is not measured by how much we own.**"

[16]And he gave an illustration: "A rich man had a fertile farm that produced fine crops. [17]In fact, his barns were full to overflowing. [18]So he said, 'I know! I'll tear down my barns and build bigger ones. Then I'll have room enough to store everything. [19]And I'll sit back and say to myself: My friend, you have enough stored away for years to come. Now take it easy! Eat, drink, and be merry!'

[20]But God said to him, 'You fool! You will die this very night. Then who will get it all?'

[21]Yes, a person is a fool to store up earthly wealth but not have a rich relationship with God."

## Teaching about Money and Possessions

[22]Then turning to his disciples, Jesus said, "So I tell you, don't worry about everyday life—

count on it

**You don't have to be good to go to God!**

Have you ever felt like you were too messed up to meet with God? Have you ever felt some strange resistance keeping you from praying or reading your Bible? Did you ever feel you had to somehow get your life straight before you could live the Christian life? Don't worry about it! Jesus came to help you in your trouble. He is the great doctor. Go to him with your problems. Not going to him is like waiting until you are cured of a deadly disease before you go to a doctor. Jesus came to help! "Healthy people don't need a doctor - sick people do. I have come to call sinners, not those who think they are already good enough."
Mark 2:17
**Count on it!**

whether you have enough food to eat or clothes to wear. ²³For life consists of far more than food and clothing. ²⁴Look at the ravens. They don't need to plant or harvest or put food in barns because God feeds them. And you are far more valuable to him than any birds! ²⁵Can all your worries add a single moment to your life? Of course not! ²⁶And if worry can't do little things like that, what's the use of worrying over bigger things?

²⁷"Look at the lilies and how they grow. They don't work or make their clothing, yet Solomon in all his glory was not dressed as beautifully as they are. ²⁸And if God cares so wonderfully for flowers that are here today and gone tomorrow, won't he more surely care for you? You have so little faith! ²⁹And don't worry about food—what to eat and drink. Don't worry whether God will provide it for you. ³⁰These things dominate the thoughts of most people, but your Father already knows your needs. ³¹**He will give you all you need from day to day if you make the Kingdom of God your primary concern.**

³²"So don't be afraid, little flock. For it gives your Father great happiness to give you the Kingdom.

³³"Sell what you have and give to those in need. This will store up treasure for you in heaven! And the purses of heaven have no holes in them. Your treasure will be safe—no thief can steal it and no moth can destroy it. ³⁴**Wherever your treasure is, there your heart and thoughts will also be.**

## Be Ready for the Lord's Coming

³⁵"Be dressed for service and well prepared, ³⁶as though you were waiting for your master to return from the wedding feast. Then you will be ready to open the door and let him in the moment he arrives and knocks. ³⁷There will be special favour for those who are ready and waiting for his return. I tell you, he himself will seat them, put on an apron, and serve them as they sit and eat! ³⁸He may come in the middle of the night or just before dawn. But whenever he comes, there will be special favour for his servants who are ready!

³⁹"Know this: A home-owner who knew exactly when a burglar was coming would not permit the house to be broken into. ⁴⁰You must be ready all the time, for the Son of Man will come when least expected."

⁴¹Peter asked, "Lord, is this illustration just for us or for everyone?"

⁴²And the Lord replied, "I'm talking to any faithful, sensible servant to whom the master gives the responsibility of managing his household and feeding his family. ⁴³If the master returns and finds that the servant has done a good job, there will be a reward. ⁴⁴I assure you, the master will put that servant in charge of all he owns. ⁴⁵But if the servant thinks, 'My master won't be back for a while,' and begins oppressing the other servants, partying, and getting drunk——⁴⁶well, the master will return unannounced and unexpected. He will tear the servant apart and banish him with the unfaithful. ⁴⁷The servant will be severely punished, for though he knew his duty, he refused to do it.

⁴⁸"But people who are not aware that they are doing wrong will be punished only lightly. Much is required from those to whom much is given, and much more is required from those to whom much more is given.

## Jesus Causes Division

⁴⁹"I have come to bring fire to the earth, and I wish that my task were already completed! ⁵⁰There is a terrible baptism ahead of me, and I am under a heavy burden until it is accomplished. ⁵¹Do you think I have come to bring peace to the earth? No, I have come to bring strife and division!

⁵²From now on families will be split apart, three in favour of me, and two against—or the other way around. ⁵³There will be a division between father and son, mother and daughter, mother-in-law and daughter-in-law."

⁵⁴Then Jesus turned to the crowd and said, "When you see clouds beginning to form in the west, you say, 'Here comes a shower.' And you are right. ⁵⁵When the south wind blows, you say, 'Today will be a scorcher.' And it is. ⁵⁶You hypocrites! You know how to interpret the appearance of the earth and the sky, but you can't interpret these present times.

⁵⁷"Why can't you decide for yourselves what is right? ⁵⁸If you are on the way to court and you meet your accuser, try to settle the matter before it reaches the judge, or you may be sentenced and handed over to an officer and thrown into jail. ⁵⁹And if that happens, you won't be free again until you have paid the last penny."

## A Call to Repentance

# 13

About this time Jesus was informed that Pilate had murdered some people from Galilee as they were sacrificing at the Temple in Jerusalem. ²"Do you think those Galileans were worse sinners than other people from Galilee?" he asked. "Is that why they suffered? ³Not at all! And you will also perish unless you turn from your evil ways and turn to God. ⁴And what about the eighteen men who died when the Tower of Siloam fell on them? Were they the worst sinners in Jerusalem? ⁵No, and I tell you again that unless you repent, you will also perish."

## Illustration of the Barren Fig Tree

⁶Then Jesus used this illustration: "A man planted a fig tree in his garden and came again and again to see if there was any fruit on it, but he was always disappointed. ⁷Finally, he said to his gardener, 'I've waited three years, and there hasn't been a single fig! Cut it down. It's taking up space we can use for something else.'

⁸"The gardener answered, 'Give it one more chance. Leave it another year, and I'll give it special attention and plenty of fertilizer. ⁹If we get figs next year, fine. If not, you can cut it down.'"

## Jesus Heals on the Sabbath

¹⁰One Sabbath day as Jesus was teaching in a synagogue, ¹¹he saw a woman who had been crippled by an evil spirit. She had been bent double for eighteen years and was unable to stand up straight. ¹²When Jesus saw her, he called her over and said,

"Woman, you are healed of your sickness!" ¹³Then he touched her, and instantly she could stand straight. How she praised and thanked God!

¹⁴But the leader in charge of the synagogue was indignant that Jesus had healed her on the Sabbath day. "There are six days of the week for working," he said to the crowd. "Come on those days to be healed, not on the Sabbath."

¹⁵But the Lord replied, "You hypocrite! You work on the Sabbath day! Don't you untie your ox or your donkey from their stalls on the Sabbath and lead them out for water? ¹⁶Wasn't it necessary for me, even on the Sabbath day, to free this dear woman from the bondage in which Satan has held her for eighteen years?"

¹⁷This shamed his enemies. And all the people rejoiced at the wonderful things he did.

## Illustration of the Mustard Seed

¹⁸Then Jesus said, "What is the Kingdom of God like? How can I illustrate it? ¹⁹It is like a tiny mustard seed planted in a garden; it grows and becomes a tree, and the birds come and find shelter among its branches."

## Illustration of the Yeast

²⁰He also asked, "What else is the Kingdom of God like? ²¹It is like yeast used by a woman making bread. Even though she used a large amount of flour, the yeast permeated every part of the dough."

CH 13:22-28 WHAT'S IT SAYING?

**WHAT AM I GOING TO DO ABOUT IT?**

## The Narrow Door

[22]Jesus went through the towns and villages, teaching as he went, always pressing on towards Jerusalem. [23]Someone asked him, "Lord, will only a few be saved?"

He replied, [24]"The door to heaven is narrow. Work hard to get in, because many will try to enter, [25]but when the head of the house has locked the door, it will be too late. Then you will stand outside knocking and pleading, 'Lord, open the door for us!' But he will reply, 'I do not know you.'

[26]You will say, 'But we ate and drank with you, and you taught in our streets.' [27]And he will reply,

'I tell you, I don't know you. Go away, all you who do evil.'

[28]"And there will be great weeping and gnashing of teeth, for you will see Abraham, Isaac, Jacob, and all the prophets within the Kingdom of God, but you will be thrown out. [29]Then people will come from all over the world to take their places in the Kingdom of God. [30]And note this: Some who are despised now will be greatly honoured then; and some who are greatly honoured now will be despised then."

## Jesus Grieves over Jerusalem

[31]A few minutes later some Pharisees said to him, "Get out of here if you want to live, because Herod Antipas wants to kill you!"

[32]Jesus replied, "Go tell that fox that I will keep on casting out demons and doing miracles of healing today and tomorrow; and the third day I will accomplish my purpose. [33]Yes, today, tomorrow, and the next day I must proceed on my way. For it wouldn't do for a prophet of God to be killed except in Jerusalem!

[34]"O Jerusalem, Jerusalem, the city that kills the prophets and stones God's messengers! How often I have wanted to gather your children together as a hen protects her chicks beneath her wings, but you wouldn't let me. [35]And now look, your house is left to you empty. And you will never see me again until you say,

'Bless the one who comes in the name of the Lord!'"

## Jesus Heals on the Sabbath

# 14

One Sabbath day Jesus was in the home of a leader of the Pharisees. The people were watching him closely, [2]because there was a man there whose arms and legs were swollen. [3]Jesus asked the Pharisees and experts in religious law, "Well, is it permitted in the law to heal people on the Sabbath day, or not?"

[4]When they refused to answer, Jesus touched the sick man and healed him and sent him away. [5]Then he turned to them and asked, "Which of you doesn't work on the Sabbath? If your son or your cow falls into a pit, don't you proceed at once to get him out?" [6]Again they had no answer.

## Jesus Teaches about Humility

[7]When Jesus noticed that all who had come to the dinner were trying to sit near the head of the table, he gave them this advice: [8]"If you are invited to a wedding feast, don't always head for the best seat. What if someone more respected than you has also been invited? [9]The host will say, 'Let this person sit here instead.' Then you will be embarrassed and will have to take whatever seat is left at the foot of the table!

[10]"Do this instead—sit at the foot of the table. Then when your host sees you, he will come and say, 'Friend, we have a better place than this for you!' Then you will be honoured in front of all the other guests. [11]For the proud will be humbled, but the humble will be honoured."

[12]Then he turned to his host. "When you put on a luncheon or a dinner," he said, "don't invite your friends, brothers, relatives, and rich neighbours. For they will repay you by inviting you back. [13]Instead, invite the poor, the crippled, the lame, and the blind. [14]Then at the resurrection of the godly, God will reward you for inviting those who could not repay you."

## Story of the Great Feast

[15]Hearing this, a man sitting at the table with Jesus exclaimed, "What a privilege it would be to have a share in the Kingdom of God!"

[16]Jesus replied with this illustration: "A man prepared a great feast and sent out many invitations. [17]When all was ready, he sent his servant around to notify the guests that it was time for them to come. [18]But they all began making excuses. One said he had just bought a field and wanted to inspect it, so he asked to be

# WHAT DOES IT MEAN?

**Angel:**

It can mean messenger but usually its unique application is to certain heavenly intelligences whom God employs in carrying on his management of the world. These superior beings are very numerous. As to their nature, they are spirits (Heb. 1:14), like the soul of man, but not incorporeal. They are possessed of superhuman intelligence and power (Mark 13:32; 2 Thessalonians. 1:7). It is possible you have met an angel unaware and they will take you to paradise (Luke 16:22).

excused. ¹⁹Another said he had just bought five pair of oxen and wanted to try them out. ²⁰Another had just been married, so he said he couldn't come.

²¹"The servant returned and told his master what they had said. His master was angry and said, 'Go quickly into the streets and alleys of the city and invite the poor, the crippled, the lame, and the blind.' ²²After the servant had done this, he reported, 'There is still room for more.' ²³So his master said, 'Go out into the country lanes and behind the hedges and urge anyone you find to come, so that the house will be full. ²⁴For none of those I invited first will get even the smallest taste of what I had prepared for them.'"

**CH 14:25-30 WHAT'S IT SAYING?**

**WHAT AM I GOING TO DO ABOUT IT?**

## The Cost of Being a Disciple

²⁵Great crowds were following Jesus. He turned around and said to them, ²⁶"If you want to be my follower you must love me more than your own father and mother, wife and children, brothers and sisters—yes, more than your own life. Otherwise, you cannot be my disciple. ²⁷And you cannot be my disciple if you do not carry your own cross and follow me.

²⁸"But don't begin until you count the cost. For who would begin construction of a building without first getting estimates and then checking to see if there is enough money to pay the bills? ²⁹Otherwise, you might complete only the foundation before running out of funds. And then how everyone would laugh at you! ³⁰They would say, 'There's the person who started that building and ran out of money before it was finished!' ³¹Or what king would ever dream of going to war without first sitting down with his counsellors and discussing whether his army of ten thousand is strong enough to defeat the twenty thousand soldiers who are marching against him? ³²If he is not able, then while the enemy is still far away, he will send a delegation to discuss terms of peace. ³³So no one can become my disciple without giving up everything for me.

³⁴"Salt is good for seasoning. But if it loses its flavour, how do you make it salty again? ³⁵Flavourless salt is good neither for the soil nor for fertilizer. It is thrown away. Anyone who is willing to hear should listen and understand!"

## Story of the Lost Sheep

# 15

Tax collectors and other notorious sinners often came to listen to Jesus teach. ²This made the Pharisees and teachers of religious law complain that he was associating with such despicable people—even eating with them!

³So Jesus used this illustration: ⁴"If you had one hundred sheep, and one of them strayed away and was lost in the wilderness, wouldn't you leave the ninety-nine others to go and search for the lost one until you found it? ⁵And then you would joyfully carry it home on your shoulders. ⁶When you arrived, you would call together your friends and neighbours to rejoice with you because your lost sheep was found. ⁷In the same way, heaven will be happier over one lost sinner who returns to God than over ninety-nine others who are righteous and haven't strayed away!

## Story of the Lost Coin

⁸"Or suppose a woman has ten valuable silver coins and loses one. Won't she light a lamp and look in every corner of the house and sweep every nook and cranny until she finds it? ⁹And when she finds it, she will call in her friends and neighbours to rejoice with her because she has found her lost coin. ¹⁰In the same way, there is joy in the presence of God's angels when even one sinner repents."

## Story of the Lost Son

¹¹To illustrate the point further, Jesus told them this story: "A man had two sons. ¹²The younger son told his father, 'I want my share of your estate now, instead of waiting until you die.' So his father agreed to divide his wealth between his sons.

¹³"A few days later this younger son packed all his belongings and took a trip to a distant land, and there he wasted all his money on wild living. ¹⁴About the time his money ran out, a great famine swept over the land, and he began to starve. ¹⁵He persuaded a local farmer to hire him to feed his pigs. ¹⁶The boy became so hungry that even the pods he was feeding the pigs looked good to him. But no one gave him anything. ¹⁷"When he finally came to his senses, he said to himself, 'At home even the hired men have food enough to spare, and here I am, dying of hunger! ¹⁸I will go home to my father and say,

"Father, I have sinned against both heaven and you, ¹⁹and I am no longer worthy of being called your son. Please take me on as a hired man."'

²⁰"So he returned home to his father. And while he was still a long distance away, his father saw him coming. Filled with love and compassion, he ran to his son, embraced him, and kissed him.

**Brain Power:**

The brain is able to learn a new skill, such as walking, talking and jumping. If we practise walking often enough, then the skill becomes automatic. We no longer have to think how to walk. Walking has become a skill controlled by the 'subconscious' part of our brain. This allows us to look about, talk and do other things controlled by the 'conscious' part of the brain, all at the same time.

'We have a Master' LUKE 17:5
Jesus reminds the disciples in very graphic language that we are dependent on God. He is the Master and we are servants. The focus of our lives should not be our lack of faith, but God the object of our faith. The servant coming in from the fields should not have his mind full of his "rights" and his "wants" but of the needs and desires of the Master.

BIBLE HIT

²¹His son said to him, 'Father, I have sinned against both heaven and you, and I am no longer worthy of being called your son.'

²²"But his father said to the servants, 'Quick! Bring the finest robe in the house and put it on him. Get a ring for his finger, and sandals for his feet. ²³And kill the calf we have been fattening in the pen. We must celebrate with a feast, ²⁴for this son of mine was dead and has now returned to life. He was lost, but now he is found.' So the party began.

²⁵"Meanwhile, the older son was in the fields working. When he returned home, he heard music and dancing in the house, ²⁶and he asked one of the servants what was going on. ²⁷"Your brother is back,' he was told, 'and your father has killed the calf we were fattening and has prepared a great feast. We are celebrating because of his safe return.'

²⁸"The older brother was angry and wouldn't go in. His father came out and begged him, ²⁹but he replied, 'All these years I've worked hard for you and never once refused to do a single thing you told me to. And in all that time you never gave me even one young goat for a feast with my friends. ³⁰Yet when this son of yours comes back after squandering your money on prostitutes, you celebrate by killing the finest calf we have.'

³¹"His father said to him, 'Look, dear son, you and I are very close, and everything I have is yours. ³²We had to celebrate this happy day. For your brother was dead and has come back to life! He was lost, but now he is found!'"

## Story of the Shrewd Manager

# 16

Jesus told this story to his disciples: "A rich man hired a manager to handle his affairs, but soon a rumour went around that the manager was thoroughly dishonest. ²So his employer called him in and said, 'What's this I hear about your stealing from me? Get your report in order, because you are going to be dismissed.'

³"The manager thought to himself, 'Now what? I'm finished here, and I don't have the strength to go out and dig ditches, and I'm too proud to beg. ⁴I know just the thing! Then I'll have plenty of friends to take care of me when I leave!'

⁵"So he invited each person who owed money to his employer

to come and discuss the situation. He asked the first one, 'How much do you owe him?' ⁶The man replied, 'I owe him eight hundred measures of olive oil.' So the manager told him, 'Tear up that bill and write another one for four hundred measures.'

⁷"'And how much do you owe my employer?' he asked the next man. 'A thousand measures of wheat,' was the reply. 'Here,' the manager said, 'take your bill and replace it with one for only eight hundred measures.'

⁸"The rich man had to admire the dishonest rascal for being so shrewd. And it is true that the citizens of this world are more shrewd than the godly are. ⁹I tell you, use your worldly resources to benefit others and make friends. In this way, your generosity stores up a reward for you in heaven.

¹⁰"Unless you are faithful in small matters, you won't be faithful in large ones. If you cheat even a little, you won't be honest with greater responsibilities. ¹¹And if you are untrustworthy about worldly wealth, who will trust you with the true riches of heaven? ¹²And if you are not faithful with other people's money, why should you be trusted with money of your own? ¹³No one can serve two masters. For you will hate one and love the other, or be devoted to one and despise the other. You cannot serve both God and money."

¹⁴The Pharisees, who dearly loved their money, naturally scoffed at all this. ¹⁵Then he said to them, "You like to look good in public, but God knows your evil hearts. What this world honours is an abomination in the sight of God.

¹⁶"Until John the Baptist began to preach, the laws of Moses and the messages of the prophets were your guides. But now the Good News of the Kingdom of God is preached, and eager multitudes are forcing their way in. ¹⁷But that doesn't mean that the law has lost its force in even the smallest point. It is stronger and more permanent than heaven and earth.

¹⁸"Anyone who divorces his wife and marries someone else commits adultery, and anyone who marries a divorced woman commits adultery."

## The Rich Man and Lazarus

¹⁹Jesus said, "There was a certain rich man who was splendidly clothed and who lived each day in luxury. ²⁰At his door lay a diseased beggar named Lazarus. ²¹As Lazarus lay there longing for scraps from the rich man's table, the dogs would come and lick his open sores. ²²Finally, the beggar died and was carried by the angels to be with Abraham. The rich man also died and was buried, ²³and his soul went to the place of the dead. There, in torment, he saw Lazarus in the far distance with Abraham.

²⁴"The rich man shouted, 'Father Abraham, have some pity! Send Lazarus over here to dip the tip of his finger in water and cool my tongue, because I am in anguish in these flames.'

²⁵"But Abraham said to him, 'Son, remember that during your lifetime you had everything you wanted, and Lazarus had nothing. So now he is here being comforted, and you are in anguish. ²⁶And besides, there is a great chasm separating us. Anyone who wants to cross over to you from here is stopped at its edge, and no one there can cross over to us.'

²⁷"Then the rich man said, 'Please, Father Abraham, send him to my father's home. ²⁸For I have five brothers, and I want him to warn them about this place of torment so they won't have to come here when they die.'

²⁹"But Abraham said, 'Moses and the prophets have warned them. Your brothers can read their writings any time they want to.'

³⁰"The rich man replied, 'No, Father Abraham! But if someone is sent to them from the dead, then they will turn from their sins.'

³¹"But Abraham said, 'If they won't listen to Moses and the prophets, they won't listen even if someone rises from the dead.'"

## Teachings about Forgiveness and Faith

# 17

One day Jesus said to his disciples, "There will always

be temptations to sin, but how terrible it will be for the person who does the tempting. ²**It would be better to be thrown into the sea with a large millstone tied around the neck than to face the punishment in store for harming one of these little ones.** ³I am warning you! If another believer sins, rebuke him; then if he repents, forgive him. ⁴Even if he wrongs you seven times a day and each time turns again and asks forgiveness, forgive him."

action

**CH 17:1-4 WHAT'S IT SAYING?**

**WHAT AM I GOING TO DO ABOUT IT?**

⁵One day the apostles said to the Lord, "We need more faith; tell us how to get it."

⁶"Even if you had faith as small as a mustard seed," the Lord answered, "you could say to this mulberry tree, 'May God uproot you and throw you into the sea,' and it would obey you!

⁷"When a servant comes in from ploughing or looking after the sheep, he doesn't just sit down and eat. ⁸He must first prepare his master's meal and serve him his supper before eating his own. ⁹And the servant is not even thanked, because he is merely doing what he is supposed to do. ¹⁰In the same way, when you obey me you should say, 'We are not worthy of praise. We are servants who have simply done our duty.'"

## Ten Healed of Leprosy

¹¹As Jesus continued on towards Jerusalem, he reached the border between Galilee and Samaria. ¹²As he entered a village there, ten lepers stood at a distance, ¹³crying out,

"Jesus, Master, have mercy on us!"

¹⁴He looked at them and said, "Go and show yourselves to the priests." And as they went, their leprosy disappeared.

¹⁵One of them, when he saw that he was healed, came back to Jesus, shouting, "Praise God, I'm healed!" ¹⁶He fell face down on the ground at Jesus' feet, thanking him for what he had done. This man was a Samaritan.

¹⁷Jesus asked, "Didn't I heal ten men? Where are the other nine? ¹⁸Does only this foreigner return to give glory to God?" ¹⁹And Jesus said to the man, "Stand up and go. Your faith has made you well."

## The Coming of the Kingdom

²⁰One day the Pharisees asked Jesus, "When will the Kingdom of God come?"

Jesus replied, "The Kingdom of God isn't ushered in with visible signs. ²¹You won't be able to say, 'Here it is!' or 'It's over there!' For the Kingdom of God is among you."

²²Later he talked again about this with his disciples. "The time is coming when you will long to share in the days of the Son of Man, but you won't be able to," he said. ²³"Reports will reach you that the Son of Man has returned and that he is in this place or that. Don't believe such reports or go out to look for him. ²⁴For when the Son of Man returns, you will know it beyond all doubt. It will be as evident as the lightning that flashes across the sky. ²⁵But first the Son of Man must suffer terribly and be rejected by this generation.

²⁶"When the Son of Man returns, the world will be like the people were in Noah's day. ²⁷In those days before the flood, the people enjoyed banquets and parties and weddings right up to the time Noah entered his boat and the flood came to destroy them all.

²⁸"And the world will be as it was in the days of Lot. People went about their daily business—eating and drinking, buying and selling, farming and building— ²⁹until the morning Lot left Sodom. Then fire and burning sulphur rained down from heaven and destroyed them all. ³⁰Yes, it will be 'business as usual' right up to the hour when the Son of Man returns.

³¹On that day a person outside the house must not go into the house to pack. A person in the field must not return to town.

³²Remember what happened to Lot's wife! ³³Whoever clings to this life will lose it, and whoever loses this life will save it. ³⁴That night two people will be asleep in one bed; one will be taken away, and the other will be left. ³⁵Two women will be grinding flour together at the mill; one will be taken, the other left."*

³⁷"Lord, where will this happen?" the disciples asked.

Jesus replied, "Just as the gathering of vultures shows there is a carcass nearby, so these signs indicate that the end is near."

## Story of the Persistent Widow

# 18

**One day Jesus told his disciples a story to illustrate their need for constant prayer and to show them that they must never give up.**

²"There was a judge in a certain city," he said, "who was a godless man with great contempt for everyone. ³A widow of that city came to him repeatedly, appealing for justice against someone who had harmed her. ⁴The judge ignored her for a while, but eventually she wore him out. 'I fear neither God nor man,' he said to himself, ⁵'but this woman is driving me crazy. I'm going to see that she gets justice, because she is wearing me out with her constant requests!'"

⁶Then the Lord said, "Learn a lesson from this evil judge. ⁷Even he rendered a just decision in the end, so don't you think God will surely give justice to his chosen people who plead with him day and night? Will he keep putting them off? ⁸I tell you, he will grant justice to them quickly! But when I, the Son of Man, return, how many will I find who have faith?"

## Story of the Pharisee and Tax Collector

⁹Then Jesus told this story to some who had great self-

**STAND**

**When you need to be pumped up**

**17:5**

One day the apostles said to the Lord, "We need more faith; tell us how to get it."

**POINT**

17:35 Some manuscripts add verse 36, *Two men will be working in the field; one will be taken, the other left.* Compare Matt 24:40.

LUKE

# APRIL M.A.P.

## 1
| S.D. | P.L. | P.G. | S.G. |
|---|---|---|---|
| P. ☐ | F. ☐ | F. ☐ | T. ☐ |
| F. ☐ | W. ☐ | W. ☐ | P. ☐ |
| B. ☐ | P. ☐ | C. ☐ | C. ☐ |

## 2
| S.D. | P.L. | P.G. | S.G. |
|---|---|---|---|
| P. ☐ | F. ☐ | F. ☐ | T. ☐ |
| F. ☐ | W. ☐ | W. ☐ | P. ☐ |
| B. ☐ | P. ☐ | C. ☐ | C. ☐ |

## 3
| S.D. | P.L. | P.G. | S.G. |
|---|---|---|---|
| P. ☐ | F. ☐ | F. ☐ | T. ☐ |
| F. ☐ | W. ☐ | W. ☐ | P. ☐ |
| B. ☐ | P. ☐ | C. ☐ | C. ☐ |

## 4
| S.D. | P.L. | P.G. | S.G. |
|---|---|---|---|
| P. ☐ | F. ☐ | F. ☐ | T. ☐ |
| F. ☐ | W. ☐ | W. ☐ | P. ☐ |
| B. ☐ | P. ☐ | C. ☐ | C. ☐ |

## 9
| S.D. | P.L. | P.G. | S.G. |
|---|---|---|---|
| P. ☐ | F. ☐ | F. ☐ | T. ☐ |
| F. ☐ | W. ☐ | W. ☐ | P. ☐ |
| B. ☐ | P. ☐ | C. ☐ | C. ☐ |

## 10
| S.D. | P.L. | P.G. | S.G. |
|---|---|---|---|
| P. ☐ | F. ☐ | F. ☐ | T. ☐ |
| F. ☐ | W. ☐ | W. ☐ | P. ☐ |
| B. ☐ | P. ☐ | C. ☐ | C. ☐ |

## 11
| S.D. | P.L. | P.G. | S.G. |
|---|---|---|---|
| P. ☐ | F. ☐ | F. ☐ | T. ☐ |
| F. ☐ | W. ☐ | W. ☐ | P. ☐ |
| B. ☐ | P. ☐ | C. ☐ | C. ☐ |

## 12
| S.D. | P.L. | P.G. | S.G. |
|---|---|---|---|
| P. ☐ | F. ☐ | F. ☐ | T. ☐ |
| F. ☐ | W. ☐ | W. ☐ | P. ☐ |
| B. ☐ | P. ☐ | C. ☐ | C. ☐ |

## 17
| S.D. | P.L. | P.G. | S.G. |
|---|---|---|---|
| P. ☐ | F. ☐ | F. ☐ | T. ☐ |
| F. ☐ | W. ☐ | W. ☐ | P. ☐ |
| B. ☐ | P. ☐ | C. ☐ | C. ☐ |

## 18
| S.D. | P.L. | P.G. | S.G. |
|---|---|---|---|
| P. ☐ | F. ☐ | F. ☐ | T. ☐ |
| F. ☐ | W. ☐ | W. ☐ | P. ☐ |
| B. ☐ | P. ☐ | C. ☐ | C. ☐ |

## 19
| S.D. | P.L. | P.G. | S.G. |
|---|---|---|---|
| P. ☐ | F. ☐ | F. ☐ | T. ☐ |
| F. ☐ | W. ☐ | W. ☐ | P. ☐ |
| B. ☐ | P. ☐ | C. ☐ | C. ☐ |

## 20
| S.D. | P.L. | P.G. | S.G. |
|---|---|---|---|
| P. ☐ | F. ☐ | F. ☐ | T. ☐ |
| F. ☐ | W. ☐ | W. ☐ | P. ☐ |
| B. ☐ | P. ☐ | C. ☐ | C. ☐ |

## 25
| S.D. | P.L. | P.G. | S.G. |
|---|---|---|---|
| P. ☐ | F. ☐ | F. ☐ | T. ☐ |
| F. ☐ | W. ☐ | W. ☐ | P. ☐ |
| B. ☐ | P. ☐ | C. ☐ | C. ☐ |

## 26
| S.D. | P.L. | P.G. | S.G. |
|---|---|---|---|
| P. ☐ | F. ☐ | F. ☐ | T. ☐ |
| F. ☐ | W. ☐ | W. ☐ | P. ☐ |
| B. ☐ | P. ☐ | C. ☐ | C. ☐ |

## 27
| S.D. | P.L. | P.G. | S.G. |
|---|---|---|---|
| P. ☐ | F. ☐ | F. ☐ | T. ☐ |
| F. ☐ | W. ☐ | W. ☐ | P. ☐ |
| B. ☐ | P. ☐ | C. ☐ | C. ☐ |

## 28
| S.D. | P.L. | P.G. | S.G. |
|---|---|---|---|
| P. ☐ | F. ☐ | F. ☐ | T. ☐ |
| F. ☐ | W. ☐ | W. ☐ | P. ☐ |
| B. ☐ | P. ☐ | C. ☐ | C. ☐ |

## Spiritual Disciplines

**Prayer**

**Faith Community**

**Bible Reading**

## Prayer List

**Friends**

**World**

**Personal**

**(For designing your MAP - Monthly Action Plan - see introduction pages)**

Who am I....
Where am I going....
How am I going to get there?

nt:sport
MONTHLY ACTION PLAN

**5**

| S.D. | P.L. | P.G. | S.G. |
|------|------|------|------|
| P. ☐ | F. ☐ | F. ☐ | T. ☐ |
| F. ☐ | W. ☐ | W. ☐ | P. ☐ |
| B. ☐ | P. ☐ | C. ☐ | C. ☐ |

**6**

| S.D. | P.L. | P.G. | S.G. |
|------|------|------|------|
| P. ☐ | F. ☐ | F. ☐ | T. ☐ |
| F. ☐ | W. ☐ | W. ☐ | P. ☐ |
| B. ☐ | P. ☐ | C. ☐ | C. ☐ |

**7**

| S.D. | P.L. | P.G. | S.G. |
|------|------|------|------|
| P. ☐ | F. ☐ | F. ☐ | T. ☐ |
| F. ☐ | W. ☐ | W. ☐ | P. ☐ |
| B. ☐ | P. ☐ | C. ☐ | C. ☐ |

**8**

| S.D. | P.L. | P.G. | S.G. |
|------|------|------|------|
| P. ☐ | F. ☐ | F. ☐ | T. ☐ |
| F. ☐ | W. ☐ | W. ☐ | P. ☐ |
| B. ☐ | P. ☐ | C. ☐ | C. ☐ |

**13**

| S.D. | P.L. | P.G. | S.G. |
|------|------|------|------|
| P. ☐ | F. ☐ | F. ☐ | T. ☐ |
| F. ☐ | W. ☐ | W. ☐ | P. ☐ |
| B. ☐ | P. ☐ | C. ☐ | C. ☐ |

**14**

| S.D. | P.L. | P.G. | S.G. |
|------|------|------|------|
| P. ☐ | F. ☐ | F. ☐ | T. ☐ |
| F. ☐ | W. ☐ | W. ☐ | P. ☐ |
| B. ☐ | P. ☐ | C. ☐ | C. ☐ |

**15**

| S.D. | P.L. | P.G. | S.G. |
|------|------|------|------|
| P. ☐ | F. ☐ | F. ☐ | T. ☐ |
| F. ☐ | W. ☐ | W. ☐ | P. ☐ |
| B. ☐ | P. ☐ | C. ☐ | C. ☐ |

**16**

| S.D. | P.L. | P.G. | S.G. |
|------|------|------|------|
| P. ☐ | F. ☐ | F. ☐ | T. ☐ |
| F. ☐ | W. ☐ | W. ☐ | P. ☐ |
| B. ☐ | P. ☐ | C. ☐ | C. ☐ |

**21**

| S.D. | P.L. | P.G. | S.G. |
|------|------|------|------|
| P. ☐ | F. ☐ | F. ☐ | T. ☐ |
| F. ☐ | W. ☐ | W. ☐ | P. ☐ |
| B. ☐ | P. ☐ | C. ☐ | C. ☐ |

**22**

| S.D. | P.L. | P.G. | S.G. |
|------|------|------|------|
| P. ☐ | F. ☐ | F. ☐ | T. ☐ |
| F. ☐ | W. ☐ | W. ☐ | P. ☐ |
| B. ☐ | P. ☐ | C. ☐ | C. ☐ |

**23**

| S.D. | P.L. | P.G. | S.G. |
|------|------|------|------|
| P. ☐ | F. ☐ | F. ☐ | T. ☐ |
| F. ☐ | W. ☐ | W. ☐ | P. ☐ |
| B. ☐ | P. ☐ | C. ☐ | C. ☐ |

**24**

| S.D. | P.L. | P.G. | S.G. |
|------|------|------|------|
| P. ☐ | F. ☐ | F. ☐ | T. ☐ |
| F. ☐ | W. ☐ | W. ☐ | P. ☐ |
| B. ☐ | P. ☐ | C. ☐ | C. ☐ |

**29**

| S.D. | P.L. | P.G. | S.G. |
|------|------|------|------|
| P. ☐ | F. ☐ | F. ☐ | T. ☐ |
| F. ☐ | W. ☐ | W. ☐ | P. ☐ |
| B. ☐ | P. ☐ | C. ☐ | C. ☐ |

**30**

| S.D. | P.L. | P.G. | S.G. |
|------|------|------|------|
| P. ☐ | F. ☐ | F. ☐ | T. ☐ |
| F. ☐ | W. ☐ | W. ☐ | P. ☐ |
| B. ☐ | P. ☐ | C. ☐ | C. ☐ |

**Psalm 139:10**

...even there your hand will guide me, and your strength will support me.

## Personal Goals

**Family**

**Work/School/Social**

**Challenge**

## Sport Goals

**Training**

**Performance**

**Competition Results**

confidence and scorned everyone else: [10]"Two men went to the Temple to pray. One was a Pharisee, and the other was a dishonest tax collector. [11]The proud Pharisee stood by himself and prayed this prayer: 'I thank you, God, that I am not a sinner like everyone else, especially like that tax collector over there! For I never cheat, I don't sin, I don't commit adultery, [12]I fast twice a week, and I give you a tenth of my income.'

[13]"But the tax collector stood at a distance and dared not even lift his eyes to heaven as he prayed. Instead, he beat his chest in sorrow, saying, 'O God, be merciful to me, for I am a sinner.' [14]I tell you, this sinner, not the Pharisee, returned home justified before God. For the proud will be humbled, but the humble will be honoured."

## Jesus Blesses the Children

[15]One day some parents brought their little children to Jesus so he could touch them and bless them, but the disciples told them not to bother him. [16]**Then Jesus called for the children and said to the disciples, "Let the children come to me. Don't stop them! For the Kingdom of God belongs to such as these.** [17]I assure you, anyone who doesn't have their kind of faith will never get into the Kingdom of God."

## When you are losing

### 18:27

"What is impossible from a human perspective is possible with God."

## The Rich Man

[18]Once a religious leader asked Jesus this question: "Good teacher, what should I do to get eternal life?"

[19]"Why do you call me good?" Jesus asked him. "Only God is truly good. [20]But as for your question, you know the commandments: 'Do not commit adultery. Do not murder. Do not steal. Do not testify falsely. Honour your father and mother.'"

[21]The man replied, "I've obeyed all these commandments since I was a child."

[22]"There is still one thing you lack," Jesus said.

"Sell all you have and give the money to the poor, and you will have treasure in heaven. Then come, follow me."

[23]But when the man heard this, he became sad because he was very rich.

[24]Jesus watched him go and then said to his disciples, "How hard it is for rich people to get into the Kingdom of God! [25]It is easier for a camel to go through the eye of a needle than for a rich person to enter the Kingdom of God!"

[26]Those who heard this said, "Then who in the world can be saved?"

[27]He replied, "What is impossible from a human perspective is possible with God."

[28]Peter said, "We have left our homes and followed you."

[29]"Yes," Jesus replied, "and I assure you, everyone who has given up house or wife or brothers or parents or children, for the sake of the Kingdom of God, [30]will be repaid many times over in this life, as well as receiving eternal life in the world to come."

## Jesus Again Predicts His Death

[31]Gathering the twelve disciples around him, Jesus told them, "As you know, we are going to Jerusalem. And when we get there, all the predictions of the ancient prophets concerning the Son of Man will come true. [32]He will be handed over to the Romans to be mocked, treated shamefully, and spit upon. [33]They will whip him and kill him, but on the third day he will rise again."

[34]But they didn't understand a thing he said. Its significance was hidden from them, and they failed to grasp what he was talking about.

## Jesus Heals a Blind Beggar

[35]As they approached Jericho, a blind beggar was sitting beside the road. [36]When he heard the noise of a crowd going past, he asked what was happening. [37]They told him that Jesus of Nazareth was going by. [38]So he began shouting,

"Jesus, Son of David, have mercy on me!" [39]The crowds ahead of Jesus tried to hush the man, but he only shouted louder, "Son of David, have mercy on me!"

[40]When Jesus heard him, he stopped and ordered that the man be brought to him. [41]Then Jesus asked the man, "What do you want me to do for you?"

"Lord," he pleaded, "I want to see!"

[42]And Jesus said, "All right, you can see! Your faith has healed you." [43]Instantly the man could see, and he followed Jesus, praising God. And all who saw it praised God, too.

# count on it

**You do not have to be a Bible scholar to understand faith!**

Jesus loved children and used them often to teach us how to trust. A child that loves a parent puts their entire life in the care of that parent. That is what God wants for you. Like a trusting child, put your whole life (especially your sport) in God's hands and allow God to be your 'Father'. He will not let you down! "Let the children come to me. Don't stop them! For the Kingdom of God belongs to such as these." Mark 10:16 **Count on it!**

## Jesus and Zacchaeus

# 19

Jesus entered Jericho and made his way through the town. [2]There was a man there named Zacchaeus. He was one of the most influential Jews in the Roman tax-collecting business, and he had become very rich. [3]He tried to get a look at Jesus, but he was too short to see over the crowds. [4]So he ran ahead and climbed a sycamore tree beside the road, so he could watch from there.

[5]When Jesus came by, he looked up at Zacchaeus and called him by name. "Zacchaeus!" he said. "Quick, come down! For I must be a guest in your home today." [6]Zacchaeus quickly climbed down and took Jesus to his house in great excitement and joy. [7]But the crowds were displeased.

"He has gone to be the guest of a notorious sinner," they grumbled.

[8]Meanwhile, Zacchaeus stood there and said to the Lord, "I will give half my wealth to the poor, Lord,

and if I have overcharged people on their taxes, I will give them back four times as much!"

⁹Jesus responded, "Salvation has come to this home today, for this man has shown himself to be a son of Abraham. ¹⁰And I, the Son of Man, have come to seek and save those like him who are lost."

## Story of the Ten Servants

¹¹The crowd was listening to everything Jesus said. And because he was nearing Jerusalem, he told a story to correct the impression that the Kingdom of God would begin right away. ¹²He said, "A nobleman was called away to a distant empire to be crowned king and then return. ¹³Before he left, he called together ten servants and gave them a small fortune in silver to invest for him while he was gone. ¹⁴But his people hated him and sent a delegation after him to say they did not want him to be their king.

¹⁵"When he returned, the king called in the servants to whom he had given the money. He wanted to find out what they had done with the money and what their profits were. ¹⁶The first servant reported a tremendous gain—ten times as much as the original amount! ¹⁷"Well done!" the king exclaimed.

'You are a trustworthy servant. You have been faithful with the little I entrusted to you, so you will be governor of ten cities as your reward.'

¹⁸"The next servant also reported a good gain—five times the original amount. ¹⁹"Well done!" the king said. 'You can be governor over five cities.'

²⁰"But the third servant brought back only the original amount of money and said, 'I hid it and kept it safe. ²¹I was afraid because you are a hard man to deal with, taking what isn't yours and harvesting crops you didn't plant.'

²²"You wicked servant!' the king roared. 'Hard, am I? If you knew so much about me and how tough I am, ²³why didn't you deposit the money in the bank so I could at least get some interest on it?' ²⁴Then turning

to the others standing nearby, the king ordered, 'Take the money from this servant, and give it to the one who earned the most.'

²⁵"'But, master,' they said, 'that servant has enough already!'

²⁶"'Yes,' the king replied, 'but to those who use well what they are given, even more will be given. But from those who are unfaithful, even what little they have will be taken away. ²⁷And now about these enemies of mine who didn't want me to be their king—bring them in and execute them right here in my presence.'"

## The Triumphal Entry

²⁸After telling this story, Jesus went on towards Jerusalem, walking ahead of his disciples. ²⁹As they came to the towns of Bethphage and Bethany, on the Mount of Olives, he sent two disciples ahead. ³⁰"Go into that village over there," he told them, "and as you enter it, you will see a colt tied there that has never been ridden. Untie it and bring it here. ³¹If anyone asks what you are doing, just say, 'The Lord needs it.'"

³²So they went and found the colt, just as Jesus had said.

³³And sure enough, as they were untying it, the owners asked them, "Why are you untying our colt?"

³⁴And the disciples simply replied, "The Lord needs it."

³⁵So they brought the colt to Jesus and threw their garments over it for him to ride on.

³⁶Then the crowds spread out their coats on the road ahead of Jesus. ³⁷As they reached the place where the road started down from the Mount of Olives, all of his followers began to shout and sing as they walked along, praising God for all the wonderful miracles they had seen.

³⁸"Bless the King who comes in the name of the Lord! Peace in heaven

and glory in highest heaven!"

³⁹But some of the Pharisees among the crowd said, "Teacher, rebuke your followers for saying things like that!"

⁴⁰He replied, "If they kept quiet, the stones along the road would burst into cheers!"

## Jesus Weeps over Jerusalem

⁴¹But as they came closer to Jerusalem and Jesus saw the city ahead, he began to weep. ⁴²"I wish that even today you would find the way of peace. But now it is too late, and peace is hidden from you. ⁴³Before long your enemies will build ramparts against your walls and encircle you and close in on you. ⁴⁴They will crush

you to the ground, and your children with you. Your enemies will not leave a single stone in place, because you have rejected the opportunity God offered you."

**CH 19:45-48 WHAT'S IT SAYING?**

**WHAT AM I GOING TO DO ABOUT IT?**

## Jesus Clears the Temple

⁴⁵Then Jesus entered the Temple and began to drive out the merchants from their stalls. ⁴⁶He told them, "The Scriptures declare, 'My Temple will be a place of prayer,' but you have turned it into a den of thieves."

⁴⁷After that, he taught daily in the Temple, but the leading priests, the teachers of religious law, and the other leaders of the people began planning how to kill him. ⁴⁸But they could think of nothing, because all the people hung on every word he said.

## The Authority of Jesus Challenged

# 20

One day as Jesus was teaching and preaching the Good News in the Temple, the leading priests and teachers of religious law and other leaders came up to him. ²They demanded, "By whose authority did you drive out the merchants from the Temple? Who gave you such authority?"

³"Let me ask you a question first," he replied. ⁴"Did John's

**STATS**

Olympic badminton rules say that the bird has to have exactly fourteen feathers.

**'Give to Caesar' LUKE 20:20 – 26**

Jerusalem had been conquered by Rome leaving the Jews and their way of life under threat of annihilation. The Pharisees were often walking a tight rope working between the occupying government and the Jews whom they led. Many of the Pharisees had lost sight of their calling and hungered for more power and prestige. Jesus was a threat to their power and they assumed (along with many of his supporters) that he was trying to take back the power and political structure and make himself, by force or subterfuge, a temporal King. The Pharisees were threatened and looking for a way to remove him so they tried to lay a trap for Christ by forcing him to side for either Roman government or not. Jesus avoids the trap and his answer helps Christians understand that they have dual citizenship. They are both to be loyal to their government (unless the civil authority veers from God's direct commandments) and obedient to their supreme authority, God.

baptism come from heaven, or was it merely human?" [5]They talked it over among themselves. "If we say it was from heaven, he will ask why we didn't believe him. [6]But if we say it was merely human, the people will stone us, because they are convinced he was a prophet." [7]Finally they replied, "We don't know." [8]And Jesus responded, "Then I won't answer your question either."

## Story of the Evil Farmers

[9]Now Jesus turned to the people again and told them this story: "A man planted a vineyard, leased it out to tenant farmers, and moved to another country to live for several years. [10]At grape-picking time, he sent one of his servants to collect his share of the crop. But the farmers attacked the servant, beat him up, and sent him back empty-handed. [11]So the owner sent another servant, but the same thing happened; he was beaten up and treated shamefully, and he went away empty-handed. [12]A third man was sent and the same thing happened. He, too, was wounded and chased away.

[13]"What will I do?' the owner asked himself. 'I know! I'll send my cherished son. Surely they will respect him.'

[14]"But when the farmers saw his son, they said to each other, 'Here comes the heir to this estate. Let's kill him and get the estate for ourselves!' [15]So they dragged him out of the vineyard and murdered him.

"What do you suppose the owner of the vineyard will do to those farmers?" Jesus asked. [16]"I'll tell you—he will come and kill them all and lease the vineyard to others."

"But God forbid that such a thing should ever happen," his listeners protested.

[17]Jesus looked at them and said, "Then what do the Scriptures mean?

'The stone rejected by the builders has now become the cornerstone.'

[18]All who stumble over that stone will be broken to pieces, and it will crush anyone on whom it falls."

[19]When the teachers of religious law and the leading priests heard this story, they wanted to arrest Jesus immediately because they realized he was pointing at them—that they were the farmers in the story. But they were afraid there would be a riot if they arrested him.

## Taxes for Caesar

[20]Watching for their opportunity, the leaders sent secret agents pretending to be honest men. They tried to get Jesus to say something that could be reported to the Roman governor so he would arrest Jesus. [21]They said, "Teacher, we know that you speak and teach what is right and are not influenced by what others think. You sincerely teach the ways of God. [22]Now tell us—is it right to pay taxes to the Roman government or not?"

[23]He saw through their trickery and said, [24]"Show me a Roman coin. Whose picture and title are stamped on it?"

"Caesar's," they replied.

[25]"Well then," he said, "give to Caesar what belongs to him. But everything that belongs to God must be given to God." [26]So they failed to trap him in the presence of the people. Instead, they were amazed by his answer, and they were silenced.

## Discussion about Resurrection

[27]Then some Sadducees stepped forward—a group of Jews who say there is no resurrection after death. [28]They posed this question: "Teacher, Moses gave us a law that if a man dies, leaving a wife but no children, his brother should marry the widow and have a child who will be the brother's heir. [29]Well, there were seven brothers. The oldest married and then died without children. [30]His brother married the widow, but he also died. Still no children. [31]And so it went, one after the other, until each of the seven had married her and died, leaving no children. [32]Finally, the woman died, too. [33]So tell us, whose wife will she be in the resurrection? For all seven were married to her!"

[34]Jesus replied, "Marriage is for people here on earth. [35]But that is not the way it will be in the age to come. For those worthy of being raised from the dead won't be married then. [36]And they will never die again. In these respects they are like angels. They are children of God raised up to new life. [37]But now, as to whether the dead will be raised—even Moses proved this when he wrote about the burning bush. Long

## Make the Skill Automatic:

The athlete's performance becomes automatic as the 'subconscious' part of the brain becomes 'programmed'. This allows the athlete's 'conscious' part of the brain to concentrate only on the changing variables. Much of sport should be taught to perfection and with time the skills will be automatic.

after Abraham, Isaac, and Jacob had died, he referred to the Lord as 'the God of Abraham, the God of Isaac, and the God of Jacob.' [38]So he is the God of the living, not the dead. They are all alive to him."

[39]"Well said, Teacher!" remarked some of the teachers of religious law who were standing there. [40]And that ended their questions; no one dared to ask any more.

## Whose Son Is the Messiah?

[41]Then Jesus presented them with a question. "Why is it," he asked, "that the Messiah is said to be the son of David? [42]For David himself wrote in the book of Psalms:

'The LORD said to my Lord,
Sit in honour at my right hand
[43]until I humble your enemies,
making them a footstool under your feet.'

[44]Since David called him Lord, how can he be his son at the same time?"

[45]Then, with the crowds listening, he turned to his disciples and said, [46]"Beware of these teachers of religious law! For they love to parade in flowing robes and to have everyone bow to them as they walk in the marketplaces. And how they love the seats of honour in the synagogues and at banquets. [47]But they shamelessly cheat widows out of their property, and then, to cover up the kind of people they really are, they make long prayers in public. Because of this, their punishment will be the greater."

## The Widow's Offering

# 21

While Jesus was in the Temple, he watched the rich people putting their gifts into the collection box. [2]Then a poor widow came by and dropped in two pennies. [3]"I assure you," he said, "this poor widow has given more than all the rest of them. [4]For they have given a tiny part of their surplus, but she, poor as she is, has given everything she has."

## Jesus Foretells the Future

[5]Some of his disciples began talking about the beautiful stonework of the Temple and the memorial decorations on the walls. But Jesus said, [6]"The time is coming when all these things will be so completely demolished that not one stone will be left on top of another."

[7]"Teacher," they asked, "when will all this take place? And will there be any sign ahead of time?"

[8]He replied, "Don't let anyone mislead you. For many will come in my name, claiming to be the Messiah and saying, 'The time has come!' But don't believe them. [9]And when you hear of wars and insurrections, don't panic. Yes, these things must come, but the end won't follow immediately." [10]Then he added, "Nations and kingdoms will proclaim war against

each other. [11]There will be great earthquakes, and there will be famines and epidemics in many lands, and there will be terrifying things and great miraculous signs in the heavens.

[12]"But before all this occurs, there will be a time of great persecution. You will be dragged into synagogues and prisons, and you will be accused before kings and governors of being my followers. [13]This will be your opportunity to tell them about me. [14]So don't worry about how to answer the charges against you, [15]for I will give you the right words and such wisdom that none of your opponents will be able to reply! [16]Even those closest to you—your parents, brothers, relatives, and friends—will betray you. And some of you will be killed. [17]And everyone will hate you because of your allegiance to me. [18]But not a hair of your head will perish! [19]By standing firm, you will win your souls.

[20]"And when you see Jerusalem surrounded by armies, then you will know that the time of its destruction has arrived. [21]Then those in Judea must flee to the hills. Let those in Jerusalem escape, and those outside the city should not enter it for shelter. [22]For those will be days of God's vengeance, and the prophetic words of the Scriptures will be fulfilled. [23]How terrible it will be for pregnant women and for mothers nursing their babies. For there will be great distress in the land and wrath upon this people. [24]They will be brutally killed by the sword or sent away as captives to all the nations of the world. And Jerusalem will be conquered and trampled down by the Gentiles until the age of the Gentiles comes to an end.

[25]"And there will be strange events in the skies—signs in the sun, moon, and stars. And down here on earth the nations will be in turmoil, perplexed by roaring seas and strange tides. [26]The courage of many people will falter because of the fearful fate they see coming upon the earth, because the stability of the very heavens will be broken up. [27]Then everyone will see the Son of Man arrive on the clouds with power and great glory. [28]So when all these things begin to happen, stand straight and look up, for your salvation is near!"

[29]Then he gave them this illustration: "Notice the fig tree, or any other tree. [30]When the leaves come out, you know without being told that summer is near. [31]Just so, when you see the events I've described taking place, you can be sure that the Kingdom of God is near. [32]I assure you, this generation will not pass from the scene until all these events have taken place. [33]Heaven and earth will disappear, but my words will

remain for ever.

[34]"Watch out! Don't let me find you living in careless ease and drunkenness, and filled with the worries of this life. Don't let that day catch you unaware, [35]as in a trap. For that day will come upon everyone living on the earth. [36]Keep a constant watch. And pray that, if possible, you may escape these horrors and stand before the Son of Man."

[37]Every day Jesus went to the Temple to teach, and each evening he returned to spend the night on the Mount of Olives. [38]The crowds gathered early each morning to hear him.

action

CH 21:12-19 WHAT'S IT SAYING?

WHAT AM I GOING TO DO ABOUT IT?

## Judas Agrees to Betray Jesus

# 22

The Festival of Unleavened Bread, which begins with the Passover celebration, was drawing near. [2]The leading priests and teachers of religious law were actively plotting Jesus' murder. But they wanted to kill him without starting a riot, a possibility they greatly feared.

[3]Then Satan entered into Judas Iscariot, who was one of the twelve disciples, [4]and he went over to the leading

# PERSONAL ASSESSMENTS

## So where am I at Spiritually with the Lord? Am I on God's team?

- ☐ I am so lost I did not even know there was a game being played.
- ☐ I know there is a game going on but I just can't find the stadium.
- ☐ I found the stadium but I am on the outside.
- ☐ I am watching God's team from far away.
- ☐ I am watching God's team up close.
- ☐ I want to be on God's team but am not sure how to join.
- ☐ I am on God's team but I am not making any impact.
- ☐ I am on God's team and playing as hard as I can!
- ☐ I am on God's team but I keep fouling!

priests and captains of the Temple guard to discuss the best way to betray Jesus to them. [5]They were delighted that he was ready to help them, and they promised him a reward. [6]So he began looking for an opportunity to betray Jesus so they could arrest him quietly when the crowds weren't around.

### The Last Supper

[7]Now the Festival of Unleavened Bread arrived, when the Passover lambs were sacrificed. [8]Jesus sent Peter and John ahead and said, "Go and prepare the Passover meal, so we can eat it together."

[9]"Where do you want us to go?" they asked him.

[10]He replied, "As soon as you enter Jerusalem, a man carrying a pitcher of water will meet you. Follow him. At the house he enters, [11]say to the owner, 'The Teacher asks: Where is the guest room where I can eat the Passover meal with my disciples?'

[12]He will take you upstairs to a large room that is already set up. That is the place. Go ahead and prepare our supper there."

[13]They went off to the city and found everything just as Jesus had said, and they prepared the Passover supper there.

[14]Then at the proper time Jesus and the twelve apostles sat down together at the table. [15]Jesus said, "I have looked forward to this hour with deep longing, anxious to eat this Passover meal with you before my suffering begins. [16]For I tell you now that I won't eat it again until it comes to fulfilment in the Kingdom of God."

[17]Then he took a cup of wine, and when he had given thanks for it, he said, "Take this and share it among yourselves. [18]For I will not drink wine again until the Kingdom of God has come."

[19]Then he took a loaf of bread; and when he had thanked God for it, he broke it in pieces and gave it to the disciples, saying,

"This is my body, given for you. Do this in remembrance of me."

[20]After supper he took another cup of wine and said, "This wine is the token of God's new covenant to save you—an agreement sealed with the blood I will pour out for you.

[21]"But here at this table, sitting among us as a friend, is the man who will betray me. [22]For I, the Son of Man, must die since it is part of God's plan. But how terrible it will be for my betrayer!" [23]Then the disciples began to ask each other which of them would ever do such a thing.

[24]And they began to argue among themselves as to who would be the greatest in the coming Kingdom. [25]Jesus told them, "In this world the kings and great men order their people around, and yet they are called 'friends of the people.' [26]But among you, those who are the greatest should take the lowest rank, and the leader should be like a servant. [27]Normally the master sits at the table and is served by his servants. But not here! For I am your servant. [28]You have remained true to me in my time of trial. [29]And just as my Father has granted me a Kingdom, I now grant you the right [30]to eat and drink at my table in that Kingdom. And you will sit on thrones, judging the twelve tribes of Israel.

### Jesus Predicts Peter's Denial

[31]"Simon, Simon, Satan has asked to have all of you, to sift you like wheat. [32]But I have pleaded in prayer for you, Simon, that your faith should not fail. So when you have repented

and turned to me again, strengthen and build up your brothers."

³³Peter said, "Lord, I am ready to go to prison with you, and even to die with you."

³⁴But Jesus said, "Peter, let me tell you something. The cock will not crow tomorrow morning until you have denied three times that you even know me."

³⁵Then Jesus asked them, "When I sent you out to preach the Good News and you did not have money, a traveller's bag, or extra clothing, did you lack anything?"

"No," they replied.

³⁶"But now," he said, "take your money and a traveller's bag. And if you don't have a sword, sell your clothes and buy one! ³⁷For the time has come for this prophecy about me to be fulfilled: 'He was counted among those who were rebels.' Yes, everything written about me by the prophets will come true."

³⁸"Lord," they replied, "we have two swords among us."

"That's enough," he said.

## Jesus Prays on the Mount of Olives

³⁹Then, accompanied by the disciples, Jesus left the upstairs room and went as usual to the Mount of Olives. ⁴⁰There he told them, "Pray that you will not be overcome by temptation."

⁴¹He walked away, about a stone's throw, and knelt down and prayed, ⁴²"Father, if you are willing, please take this cup of suffering away from me. Yet I want your will, not mine."

⁴³Then an angel from heaven appeared and strengthened him.

⁴⁴He prayed more fervently, and he was in such agony of spirit that his sweat fell to the ground like great drops of blood. ⁴⁵At last he stood up again and returned to the disciples, only to find them asleep, exhausted from grief. ⁴⁶"Why are you sleeping?" he asked. "Get up and pray. Otherwise temptation will overpower you."

## Jesus Is Betrayed and Arrested

⁴⁷But even as he said this, a mob approached, led by Judas, one of his twelve disciples. Judas walked over to Jesus and greeted him with a kiss. ⁴⁸But Jesus said, "Judas, how can you betray me, the Son of Man, with a kiss?"

⁴⁹When the other disciples saw what was about to happen, they exclaimed, "Lord, should we fight? We brought the swords!" ⁵⁰And one of them slashed at the high priest's servant and cut off his right ear.

⁵¹But Jesus said, "Don't resist any more." And he touched the place where the man's ear had been and healed him. ⁵²Then Jesus spoke to the leading priests and captains of the Temple guard and the other leaders who headed the mob. "Am I some dangerous criminal," he asked, "that you have come armed with swords and clubs to arrest me? ⁵³Why didn't you arrest me in the Temple? I was there every day. But this is

your moment, the time when the power of darkness reigns."

## Peter Denies Jesus

54So they arrested him and led him to the high priest's residence, and Peter was following far behind. 55The guards lit a fire in the courtyard and sat around it, and Peter joined them there. 56A servant girl noticed him in the firelight and began staring at him. Finally she said, "This man was one of Jesus' followers!"

57Peter denied it. "Woman," he said, "I don't even know the man!"

58After a while someone else looked at him and said, "You must be one of that group!"

"No, man, I'm not!" Peter replied.

59About an hour later someone else insisted, "This must be one of Jesus' disciples because he is a Galilean, too."

60But Peter said, "Man, I don't know what you are talking about." And as soon as he said these words, the cock crowed. 61At that moment the Lord turned and looked at Peter. Then Peter remembered that the Lord had said, "Before the cock crows tomorrow morning, you will deny me three times." 62And Peter left the courtyard, crying bitterly.

63**Now the guards in charge of Jesus began mocking and beating him.** 64**They blindfolded him; then they hit him and asked, "Who hit you that time, you prophet?"** 65**And they threw all sorts of terrible insults at him.**

## Jesus before the Council

66At daybreak all the leaders of the people assembled, including the leading priests and the teachers of religious law. Jesus was led before this high council, 67and they said, "Tell us if you are the Messiah."

But he replied, "If I tell you, you won't believe me. 68And if I ask you a question, you won't answer. 69But the time is soon coming when I, the Son of Man, will be sitting at God's right hand in the place of power."

70They all shouted, "Then you claim you are the Son of God?"

And he replied, "You are right in saying that I am."

71"What need do we have for other witnesses?" they shouted. "We ourselves heard him say it."

## Jesus' Trial before Pilate

# 23

Then the entire council took Jesus over to Pilate, the Roman governor. 2They began at once to state their case: "This man has been leading our people to ruin by telling them not to pay their taxes to the Roman government and by claiming he is the Messiah, a king." 3So Pilate asked him, "Are you the King of the Jews?"

Jesus replied, "Yes, it is as you say."

4Pilate turned to the leading priests and to the crowd and said, "I find nothing wrong with this man!"

5Then they became desperate. "But he is causing riots everywhere he goes, all over Judea, from Galilee to Jerusalem!"

6"Oh, is he a Galilean?" Pilate asked. 7When they answered that he was, Pilate sent him to Herod Antipas, because Galilee was under Herod's jurisdiction, and Herod happened to be in Jerusalem at the time.

8Herod was delighted at the opportunity to see Jesus, because he had heard about him and had been hoping for a long time to see him perform a miracle. 9He asked Jesus question after question, but Jesus refused to answer. 10Meanwhile, the leading priests and the teachers of religious law stood there shouting their accusations.

11Now Herod and his soldiers began mocking and ridiculing Jesus. Then they put a royal robe on him and sent him back to Pilate. 12Herod and Pilate, who had been enemies before, became friends that day.

13Then Pilate called together the leading priests and other religious leaders, along with the people, 14and he announced his verdict. "You brought this man to me, accusing him of leading a revolt. I have examined him thoroughly on this point in your presence and find him innocent. 15Herod came to the same conclusion and sent him back to us. Nothing this man has done calls for the death penalty. 16So I will have him flogged, but then I will release him."*

18Then a mighty roar rose from the crowd, and with one voice they shouted, "Kill him, and release Barabbas to us!" 19(Barabbas was in prison for murder and for taking part in an insurrection in Jerusalem against the government.) 20Pilate argued with them, because he wanted to release Jesus. 21But they shouted, "Crucify him! Crucify him!"

22For the third time he demanded, "Why? What crime has he committed? I have found no reason to sentence him to death. I will therefore flog him and let him go."

23But the crowd shouted louder and louder for Jesus' death, and their voices prevailed. 24So Pilate sentenced Jesus to die as they demanded. 25As they had requested, he released Barabbas, the man in prison for insurrection and murder. But he delivered Jesus over to them to do as they wished.

## The Crucifixion

26As they led Jesus away, Simon of Cyrene, who was coming in from the country just then, was forced to follow Jesus and carry his cross. 27Great crowds trailed along behind, including many grief-stricken women. 28But Jesus turned and said to them, "Daughters of Jerusalem, don't weep for me, but weep for yourselves and for your children. 29For the days are coming when they will say, 'Fortunate indeed are the women who are childless, the wombs that have not borne a child and the breasts that have never nursed.' 30People will beg the mountains to fall on them and the hills to bury them. 31For if these things are done when the tree is green, what will happen when it is dry?"

32Two others, both criminals, were led out to be executed with him. 33Finally, they came to a place called The Skull. All three were crucified there—Jesus on the centre cross, and the two criminals on either side.

34Jesus said, "Father, forgive these people, because they don't know what they are doing." And the soldiers gambled for his clothes by throwing dice.

35The crowd watched, and the leaders laughed and scoffed. "He saved others," they said, "let him save himself if he is really God's Chosen One, the Messiah." 36The soldiers mocked him, too, by offering him a drink of sour wine. 37They called out to him, "If you are the King of the Jews, save yourself!"

38A signboard was nailed to the cross above him with these words: "This is the King of the Jews."

39One of the criminals hanging beside him scoffed, "So you're the Messiah, are you? Prove it by saving yourself—and us, too, while you're at it!"

40But the other criminal protested, "Don't you fear God even when you are dying? 41We deserve to die for our evil deeds, but this man hasn't done anything wrong." 42Then he said, "Jesus, remember me when you come into your Kingdom."

43And Jesus replied, "I assure you, today you will be with me in paradise."

## The Death of Jesus

44By this time it was noon, and darkness fell across the whole land until three o'clock. 45The light from the sun was gone. And suddenly, the thick veil hanging in the Temple was torn apart. 46Then Jesus shouted, "Father, I entrust my spirit into your hands!" And with those words he breathed his last.

47When the captain of the Roman soldiers handling the executions saw what had happened, he praised God and said, "Surely this man was innocent." 48And when the crowd that came to see the crucifixion saw all that had happened, they went home in deep sorrow. 49But Jesus' friends, including the women who had followed him from Galilee, stood at a distance watching.

23:16 Some manuscripts add verse 17, *Now it was necessary for him to release one prisoner to them during the Passover celebration.* Compare Matt 27:15; Mark 15:6; John 18:39.

## The Burial of Jesus

⁵⁰Now there was a good and righteous man named Joseph. He was a member of the Jewish high council, ⁵¹but he had not agreed with the decision and actions of the other religious leaders. He was from the town of Arimathea in Judea, and he had been waiting for the Kingdom of God to come. ⁵²He went to Pilate and asked for Jesus' body. ⁵³Then he took the body down from the cross and wrapped it in a long linen cloth and laid it in a new tomb that had been carved out of rock. ⁵⁴This was done late on Friday afternoon, the day of preparation for the Sabbath.

⁵⁵As his body was taken away, the women from Galilee followed and saw the tomb where they placed his body. ⁵⁶Then they went home and prepared spices and ointments to embalm him. But by the time they were finished it was the Sabbath, so they rested all that day as required by the law.

## The Resurrection

# 24

But very early on Sunday morning the women came to the tomb, taking the spices they had prepared. ²They found that the stone covering the entrance had been rolled aside. ³So they went in, but they couldn't find the body of the Lord Jesus. ⁴They were puzzled, trying to think what could have happened to it. Suddenly, two men appeared to them, clothed in dazzling robes. ⁵**The women were terrified and bowed low before them. Then the men asked, "Why are you looking in a tomb for someone who is alive?** ⁶He isn't here! He has risen from the dead! Don't you remember what he told you back in Galilee, ⁷that the Son of Man must be betrayed into the hands of sinful men and be crucified, and that he would rise again the third day?"

⁸Then they remembered that he had said this. ⁹So they rushed back to tell his eleven disciples—and everyone else—what had happened. ¹⁰The women who went to the tomb were Mary Magdalene, Joanna, Mary the mother of James, and several others. They told the apostles what had happened, ¹¹but the story sounded like nonsense, so they didn't believe it. ¹²However, Peter ran to the tomb to look. Stooping, he peered in and saw the empty linen wrappings; then he went home again, wondering what had happened.

## The Walk to Emmaus

¹³That same day two of Jesus' followers were walking to the village of Emmaus, eleven kilometres out of Jerusalem. ¹⁴As they walked along they were talking about everything that had happened. ¹⁵Suddenly, Jesus himself came along and joined them and began walking beside them. ¹⁶But they didn't know who he was, because God kept them from recognizing him.

¹⁷"You seem to be in a deep discussion about something," he said. "What are you so concerned about?"

They stopped short, sadness written across their faces. ¹⁸Then one of them, Cleopas, replied, "You must be the only person in Jerusalem who hasn't heard about all the things that have happened there the last few days."

¹⁹"What things?" Jesus asked.

"The things that happened to Jesus, the man from Nazareth," they said. "He was a prophet who did wonderful miracles. He was a mighty teacher, highly regarded by both God and all the people.

²⁰But our leading priests and other religious leaders arrested him and handed him over to be condemned to death, and they crucified him. ²¹We had thought he was the Messiah who had come to rescue Israel. That all happened three days ago. ²²Then some women from our group of his followers were at his tomb early this morning, and they came back with an amazing report. ²³**They said his body was missing, and they had seen angels who told them Jesus is alive!** ²⁴Some of our men ran out to see, and sure enough, Jesus' body was gone, just as the women had said."

²⁵Then Jesus said to them, "You are such foolish people! You find it so hard to believe all that the prophets wrote in the Scriptures. ²⁶Wasn't it clearly predicted by the prophets that the Messiah would have to suffer all these things before entering his time of glory?" ²⁷Then Jesus quoted passages from the writings of Moses and all the prophets, explaining what all the Scriptures said about himself.

²⁸By this time they were nearing Emmaus and the end of their journey. Jesus would have gone on, ²⁹but they begged him to stay the night with them, since it was getting late. So he went home with them. ³⁰As they sat down to eat, he took a small loaf of bread, asked God's blessing on it, broke it, then gave it to them. ³¹Suddenly, their eyes were opened, and they recognized him. And at that moment he disappeared! ³²They said to each other, "Didn't our hearts feel

strangely warm as he talked with us on the road and explained the Scriptures to us?" ³³And within the hour they were on their way back to Jerusalem, where the eleven disciples and the other followers of Jesus were gathered. When they arrived, they were greeted with the report, ³⁴"The Lord has really risen! He appeared to Peter!"

## Jesus Appears to the Disciples

³⁵Then the two from Emmaus told their story of how Jesus had appeared to them as they were walking along the road and how they had recognized him as he was breaking the bread. ³⁶And just as they were telling about it, Jesus himself was suddenly standing there among them. He said, "Peace be with you."

³⁷But the whole group was terribly frightened, thinking they were seeing a ghost. ³⁸"Why are you frightened?" he asked. "Why do you doubt who I am? ³⁹Look at my hands. Look at my feet. You can see that it's really me. Touch me and make sure that I am not a ghost, because ghosts don't have bodies, as you see that I do!" ⁴⁰As he spoke, he held out his hands for them to see, and he showed them his feet.

⁴¹Still they stood there doubting, filled with joy and wonder. Then he asked them, "Do you have anything here to eat?"

⁴²They gave him a piece of broiled fish, ⁴³and he ate it as they watched.

⁴⁴Then he said, "When I was with you before, I told you that everything written about me by Moses and the prophets and in the Psalms must all come true." ⁴⁵Then he opened their minds to understand these many Scriptures. ⁴⁶And he said, "Yes, it was written long ago that the Messiah must suffer and die and rise again from the dead on the third day. ⁴⁷**With my authority, take this message of repentance to all the nations, beginning in Jerusalem: 'There is forgiveness of sins for all who turn to me.' ⁴⁸You are witnesses of all these things.**

⁴⁹"And now I will send the Holy Spirit, just as my Father promised. But stay here in the city until the Holy Spirit comes and fills you with power from heaven."

## The Ascension

⁵⁰Then Jesus led them to Bethany, and lifting his hands to heaven, he blessed them. ⁵¹While he was blessing them, he left them and was taken up to heaven. ⁵²They worshipped him and then returned to Jerusalem filled with great joy. ⁵³And they spent all of their time in the Temple, praising God.

Like an old team-mate personally recounting past experiences with a famous and historic athlete, John recounts Jesus' life and ministry. John was there and he wants others to know about his hero Jesus. With a unique flavour and personal touch, the last Gospel was written long after the first three. John the author and namesake of the book, referring to himself as the 'Disciple whom Jesus loved', was nicknamed 'Son of Thunder' by Jesus himself. John had seen quite a lot of history, originally following John the Baptist with his brother James, he had lived closely and followed Jesus throughout his ministry. The youthful John had a perceptive knack for recognising and enjoying Jesus. He out-lived his friends and fellow disciples many of whom were executed for their faith. He watched their precious city of Jerusalem destroyed by the Romans. John himself had been exiled to the Island of Patmos. Finally, advanced in years, it was time for John to write his powerful account of Jesus' life.

Writing both for Jews and Gentiles, John emphasises how Jesus was God and Saviour. One of his key words is 'believe'. It is packed with fantastic detail, several other witnesses and loads of miracles. You are taken into the world of the disciple as he recalls the last days of Jesus' life, crucifixion and resurrection. Lastly, John gives an intimate account of Jesus' response to Peter who had denied him earlier. We must act on the same directive that Peter was given by Jesus, 'Follow me!'

# John

# abundant life
## MORE THAN A LIFE STYLE

My purpose is to give life

in all its fulness

JOHN 10:10

# JOHN

## Christ, the Eternal Word

# 1

In the beginning the Word already existed. He was with God, and he was God. [2]He was in the beginning with God. [3]He created everything there is. Nothing exists that he didn't make. [4]Life itself was in him, and this life gives light to everyone. [5]The light shines through the darkness, and the darkness can never extinguish it.

[6]God sent John the Baptist [7]to tell everyone about the light so that everyone might believe because of his testimony.

[8]John himself was not the light; he was only a witness to the light. [9]The one who is the true light, who gives light to everyone, was going to come into the world.

[10]But although the world was made through him, the world didn't recognize him when he came. [11]Even in his own land and among his own people, he was not accepted. [12]But to all who believed him and accepted him, he gave the right to become children of God.

[13]They are reborn! This is not a physical birth resulting from human passion or plan—this rebirth comes from God.

[14]So the Word became human and lived here on earth among us. He was full of unfailing love and faithfulness. And we have seen his glory, the glory of the only Son of the Father.

[15]John pointed him out to the people. He shouted to the crowds,

"This is the one I was talking about when I said, 'Someone is coming who is far greater than I am, for he existed long before I did.'"

[16]We have all benefited from the rich blessings he brought to us—one gracious blessing after another. [17]For the law was given through Moses; God's unfailing love and faithfulness came through Jesus Christ. [18]No one has ever seen God. But his only Son, who is himself God, is near to the Father's heart; he has told us about him.

## The Testimony of John the Baptist

[19]This was the testimony of John when the Jewish leaders sent priests and Temple assistants from Jerusalem to ask John whether he claimed to be the Messiah. [20]He flatly denied it. "I am not the Messiah," he said.

[21]"Well then, who are you?" they asked. "Are you Elijah?"

"No," he replied.

"Are you the Prophet?"

"No."

[22]"Then who are you? Tell us, so we can give an answer to those who sent us. What do you have to say about yourself?"

[23]John replied in the words of Isaiah:

"I am a voice shouting in the wilderness,
'Prepare a straight pathway for the Lord's coming!'"

[24]Then those who were sent by the Pharisees [25]asked him, "If you aren't the Messiah or Elijah or the Prophet, what right do you have to baptize?"

[26]John told them, "I baptize with water, but right here in the crowd is someone you do not know, [27]who will soon begin his ministry. I am not even worthy to be his slave." [28]This incident took place at Bethany, a village east of the River Jordan, where John was baptizing.

On February 6, 1971 the first golf ball was hit on the moon by Alan Shepard.

## Jesus, the Lamb of God

[29]The next day John saw Jesus coming towards him and said, "Look! There is the Lamb of God who takes away the sin of the world! [30]He is the one I was talking about when I said, 'Soon a man is coming who is far greater than I am, for he existed long before I did.' [31]I didn't know he was the one, but I have been baptizing with water in order to point him out to Israel."

[32]Then John said, "I saw the Holy Spirit descending like a dove from heaven and resting upon him. [33]I didn't know he was the one, but when God sent me to baptize with water, he told me, 'When you see the Holy Spirit descending and resting upon someone, he is the one you are looking for. He is the one who baptizes with the Holy Spirit.' [34]I saw this happen to Jesus, so I testify that he is the Son of God."

## The First Disciples

[35]The following day, John was again standing with two of his disciples. [36]As Jesus walked by, John looked at him and then declared, "Look! There is the Lamb of God!"

[37]Then John's two disciples turned and followed Jesus.

[38]Jesus looked around and saw them following. "What do you want?" he asked them.

They replied, "Rabbi" (which means Teacher), "where are you staying?"

[39]"Come and see," he said. It was about four o'clock in the afternoon when they went with him to the place, and they stayed there the rest of the day.

[40]Andrew, Simon Peter's brother, was one of these men who had heard what John said and then followed Jesus. [41]The first thing Andrew did was to find his brother, Simon, and tell him,

"We have found the Messiah" (which means the Christ).

[42]Then Andrew brought Simon to meet Jesus. Looking intently at Simon, Jesus said, "You are Simon, the son of John—but you will be called Cephas" (which means Peter).

[43]The next day Jesus decided to go to Galilee. He found Philip and said to him, "Come, be my disciple." [44]Philip was from Bethsaida, Andrew and Peter's home town.

[45]Philip went off to look for Nathanael and told him, "We have found the very person Moses and the prophets wrote about! His name is Jesus, the son of Joseph from Nazareth."

[46]"Nazareth!" exclaimed Nathanael. "Can anything good come from there?"

"Just come and see for yourself," Philip said.

[47]As they approached, Jesus said, "Here comes an honest man—a true son of Israel."

[48]"How do you know about me?" Nathanael asked.

And Jesus replied, "I could see you under the fig tree before Philip found you."

[49]Nathanael replied, "Teacher, you are the Son of God—the King of Israel!"

[50]Jesus asked him, "Do you believe all this just because I told you I had seen you under the fig tree? You will see greater things than this." [51]Then he said, "The truth is, you will all see heaven open and the angels of God going up and down upon the Son of Man."

## The Wedding at Cana

# 2

The next day Jesus' mother was a guest at a wedding celebration in the village of Cana in Galilee. [2]Jesus and his disciples were also invited to the celebration. [3]The wine supply ran out during the festivities, so Jesus' mother spoke to him about the problem. "They have no more wine," she told him.

[4]"How does that concern you and me?" Jesus asked.

"My time has not yet come."

[5]But his mother told the servants, "Do whatever he tells you."

## Chewing Gum & Walking:

Have you ever just got it really, really wrong? It is when both parts of our brain try to control the same skill, at the same instant that the wires get all crossed up and the 'programme' is corrupted. As it is very difficult to think about two different things at exactly the same time, the brain will rapidly try to switch between both. That is why practice will help you reduce crossed wires as some skills become automatic.

[6]Six stone waterpots were standing there; they were used for Jewish ceremonial purposes and held seventy-five to a hundred litres each. [7]Jesus told the servants, "Fill the jars with water." When the jars had been filled to the brim, [8]he said, "Dip some out and take it to the master of ceremonies." So they followed his instructions.

[9]When the master of ceremonies tasted the water that was now wine, not knowing where it had come from (though, of course, the servants knew), he called the bridegroom over. [10]"Usually a host serves the best wine first," he said. "Then, when everyone is full and doesn't care, he brings out the less expensive wines. But you have kept the best until now!"

[11]This miraculous sign at Cana in Galilee was Jesus' first display of his glory. And his disciples believed in him.

[12]After the wedding he went to Capernaum for a few days with his mother, his brothers, and his disciples.

### Jesus Clears the Temple

[13]It was time for the annual Passover celebration, and Jesus went to Jerusalem. [14]In the Temple area he saw merchants selling cattle, sheep, and doves for sacrifices; and he saw money changers behind their counters. [15]Jesus made a whip from some ropes and chased them all out of the Temple. He drove out the sheep and oxen, scattered the money changers' coins over the floor, and turned over their tables. [16]Then, going over to the people who sold doves, he told them, "Get these things out of here. Don't turn my Father's house into a marketplace!"

[17]**Then his disciples remembered this prophecy from the Scriptures:**
**"Passion for God's house burns within me."**

[18]"What right do you have to do these things?" the Jewish leaders demanded. "If you have this authority from God, show us a miraculous sign to prove it."

[19]"All right," Jesus replied. "Destroy this temple, and in three days I will raise it up."

[20]"What!" they exclaimed. "It took forty-six years to build this Temple, and you can do it in three days?"

[21]But by "this temple," Jesus meant his body.

[22]After he was raised from the dead, the disciples remembered that he had said this. And they believed both Jesus and the Scriptures.

[23]Because of the miraculous signs he did in Jerusalem at the Passover celebration, many people were convinced that he was indeed the Messiah. [24]But Jesus didn't trust them, because he knew what people were really like. [25]No one needed to tell him about human nature.

### Jesus and Nicodemus

## 3

After dark one evening, a Jewish religious leader named Nicodemus, a Pharisee, [2]came to speak with Jesus. "Teacher," he said, "we all know that God has sent you to teach us. Your miraculous signs are proof enough that God is with you."

[3]Jesus replied, "I assure you, unless you are born again, you can never see the Kingdom of God."

[4]"What do you mean?" exclaimed Nicodemus. "How can an old man go back into his mother's womb and be born again?"

[5]Jesus replied, "The truth is, no one can enter the Kingdom of God without being born of water and the Spirit. [6]Humans can reproduce only human life, but the Holy Spirit gives new life from heaven. [7]So don't be surprised at my statement that you must be born again. [8]Just as you can hear the wind but can't tell where it comes from or where it is going, so you can't explain how people are born of the Spirit."

[9]"What do you mean?" Nicodemus asked.

[10]Jesus replied, "You are a respected Jewish teacher, and yet you don't understand these things? [11]I assure you, I am telling you what we know and have seen, and yet you won't believe us. [12]But if you don't even believe me when I tell you about things that happen here on earth, how can you possibly believe if I tell you what is going on in heaven? [13]For only I, the Son of Man, have come to earth and will return to heaven again.

[14]And as Moses lifted up the bronze snake on a pole in the wilderness, so I, the Son of Man, must be lifted up on a pole, [15]so that everyone who believes in me will have eternal life.

[16]"For God so loved the world that he gave his only Son, so that everyone who believes in him will not perish but have eternal life. [17]God did not send his Son into the world to condemn it, but to save it.

[18]"There is no judgement awaiting those who trust him. But those who do not trust him have already been judged for not believing in the only Son of God. [19]Their judgement is based on this fact: The light from heaven came into the world, but they loved the darkness more than the light, for their actions were evil. [20]They hate the light because they want to sin in the darkness. They stay away from the light for fear their sins will be exposed and they will be punished. [21]But those who do what is right come to the light gladly, so everyone can see that they are doing what God wants."

### John the Baptist Exalts Jesus

[22]Afterwards Jesus and his disciples left Jerusalem, but they stayed in Judea for a while and baptized there. [23]At this time John the Baptist was baptizing at Aenon, near Salim, because there was plenty of water there and people kept coming to him for baptism. [24]This was before John was put into prison.

[25]At that time a certain Jew began an argument with John's disciples over ceremonial cleansing. [26]John's disciples came to him and said, "Teacher, the man you met on the other side of the River Jordan, the one you said was the Messiah, is also baptizing people. And everybody is going over there instead of coming here to us."

[27]John replied, "God in heaven appoints each person's work. [28]You yourselves know how plainly I told you that I am not the Messiah. I am here to prepare the way for him—that is all. [29]The bride will go where the bridegroom is. A bridegroom's friend rejoices with him. I am the bridegroom's friend, and I am filled with joy at his success. [30]He must become greater and greater, and I must become less and less.

³¹"He has come from above and is greater than anyone else. I am of the earth, and my understanding is limited to the things of earth, but he has come from heaven. ³²He tells what he has seen and heard, but how few believe what he tells them! ³³Those who believe him discover that God is true. ³⁴For he is sent by God. He speaks God's words, for God's Spirit is upon him without measure or limit. ³⁵The Father loves his Son, and he has given him authority over everything. ³⁶And all who believe in God's Son have eternal life. Those who don't obey the Son will never experience eternal life, but the wrath of God remains upon them."

Be joyful always! This is a tough habit! To have that deep down in your gut happiness (joy) even when you've blown it or lost a match. How can you do it? By knowing no matter what your circumstances, God totally loves you. "Always be joyful. Keep on praying. No matter what happens, always be thankful, for this is God's will for you who belong to Christ Jesus."

1 Thessalonians 5:16-18

**action**

**CH 3:10-21 WHAT'S IT SAYING?**

**WHAT AM I GOING TO DO ABOUT IT?**

**Jesus and the Samaritan Woman**

**4**

Jesus learned that the Pharisees had heard, "Jesus is baptizing and making more disciples than John" ²(though Jesus himself didn't baptize them—his disciples did). ³So he left Judea to return to Galilee. ⁴He had to go through Samaria on the way. ⁵Eventually he came to the Samaritan village of Sychar, near the parcel of ground that Jacob gave to his son Joseph. ⁶Jacob's well was there; and Jesus, tired from the long walk, sat wearily beside the well about midday. ⁷Soon a Samaritan woman came to draw water, and Jesus said to her, "Please give me a drink." ⁸He was alone at the time because his disciples had gone into the village to buy some food.

⁹The woman was surprised, for Jews refuse to have anything to do with Samaritans. She said to Jesus, "You are a Jew, and I am a Samaritan woman. Why are you asking me for a drink?"

¹⁰Jesus replied, "If you only knew the gift God has for you and who I am, you would ask me, and I would give you living water."

¹¹"But sir, you don't have a rope or a bucket," she said, "and this is a very deep well. Where would you get this living water? ¹²And besides, are you greater than our ancestor Jacob who gave us this well? How can you offer better water than he and his sons and his cattle enjoyed?"

¹³Jesus replied, "People soon become thirsty again after drinking this water. ¹⁴**But the water I give them takes away thirst altogether. It becomes a perpetual spring within them, giving them eternal life.**"

¹⁵"Please, sir," the woman said, "give me some of that water! Then I'll never be thirsty again, and I won't have to come here to haul water."

¹⁶"Go and get your husband," Jesus told her.

¹⁷"I don't have a husband," the woman replied. Jesus said, "You're right! You don't have a husband— ¹⁸for you have had five husbands, and you aren't even married to the man you're living with now."

¹⁹"Sir," the woman said, "you must be a prophet. ²⁰So tell me, why is it that you Jews insist that Jerusalem is the only place of worship, while we Samaritans claim it is here at Mount Gerizim, where our ancestors worshipped?"

²¹Jesus replied, "Believe me, the time is coming when it will no longer matter whether you worship the Father here or in Jerusalem. ²²You Samaritans know so little about the one you worship, while we Jews know all about him, for salvation comes through the Jews. ²³But the time is coming and is already here when true worshippers will worship the Father in spirit and in truth. The Father is looking for anyone who will worship him that way. ²⁴For God is Spirit, so those who worship him must worship in spirit and in truth."

²⁵The woman said, "I know the Messiah will come—the one who is called Christ. When he comes, he will explain everything to us."

²⁶Then Jesus told her, "I am the Messiah!"

²⁷Just then his disciples arrived. They were astonished to find him talking to a woman, but none of them asked him why he was doing it or what they had been discussing. ²⁸The woman left her water jar beside the well and went back to the village and told everyone, ²⁹"Come and meet a man who told me everything I ever did! Can this be the Messiah?" ³⁰So the people came streaming from the village to see him.

³¹Meanwhile, the disciples were urging Jesus to eat. ³²"No," he said, "I have food you don't know about."

³³"Who brought it to him?" the disciples asked each other.

³⁴Then Jesus explained: "My nourishment comes from doing the will of God, who sent me, and from finishing his work. ³⁵Do you think the work of harvesting will not begin until the summer ends four months from now? Look around you! Vast fields are ripening all around us and are ready now for the harvest. ³⁶The harvesters are paid good wages, and the fruit they harvest is people brought to eternal life. What joy awaits both the planter and the harvester alike! ³⁷You know the saying, 'One person plants and someone else harvests.'

**I am the only Christian on the team. I don't really feel like I'm making a difference. Am I?**
You are making a massive impact by simply praying for the your team-mates! Don't be fooled into an idea that you are not being effective. Be super positive and live out your faith. Both positive and negative attitudes are highly contagious. Negativism can spread through a team like a disease. Carefully guard what you think and say. Start an epidemic of enthusiasm on your team by being optimistic and positive.

**Pray, play and say!** Keep asking God for opportunities to reflect and share Jesus.

And it's true. [38]I sent you to harvest where you didn't plant; others had already done the work, and you will gather the harvest."

## Many Samaritans Believe

[39]Many Samaritans from the village believed in Jesus because the woman had said, "He told me everything I ever did!" [40]When they came out to see him, they begged him to stay at their village. So he stayed for two days, [41]long enough for many of them to hear his message and believe. [42]Then they said to the woman, "Now we believe because we have heard him ourselves, not just because of what you told us. He is indeed the Saviour of the world."

## Jesus Heals an Official's Son

[43]At the end of the two days' stay, Jesus went on into Galilee. [44]He had previously said, "A prophet is honoured everywhere except in his own country." [45]The Galileans welcomed him, for they had been in Jerusalem at the Passover celebration and had seen all his miraculous signs.

[46]In the course of his journey through Galilee, he arrived at the town of Cana, where he had turned the water into wine. There was a government official in the city of Capernaum whose son was very sick. [47]When he heard that Jesus had come from Judea and was travelling in Galilee, he went over to Cana. He found Jesus and begged him to come to Capernaum with him to heal his son, who was about to die. [48]Jesus asked, "Must I do miraculous signs and wonders before you people will believe in me?"

[49]The official pleaded, "Lord, please come now before my little boy dies."

[50]Then Jesus told him, "Go back home. Your son will live!" And the man believed Jesus' word and started home.

[51]While he was on his way, some of his servants met him with the news that his son was alive and well. [52]He asked them when the boy had begun to feel better, and they replied, "Yesterday afternoon at one o'clock his fever suddenly disappeared!"

[53]Then the father realized it was the same time that Jesus had told him, "Your son will live." And the officer and his entire household believed in Jesus. [54]This was Jesus' second miraculous sign in Galilee after coming from Judea.

**CH 4:19-24 WHAT'S IT SAYING?**

**WHAT AM I GOING TO DO ABOUT IT?**

## Jesus Heals a Lame Man

# 5

Afterwards Jesus returned to Jerusalem for one of the Jewish holy days. [2]Inside the city, near the Sheep Gate, was the pool of Bethesda, with five covered porches. [3]Crowds of sick people—blind, lame, or paralysed—lay on the porches.*

[5]One of the men lying there had been sick for thirty-eight years. [6]**When Jesus saw him and knew how long he had been ill, he asked him, "Would you like to get well?"**

[7]"I can't, sir," the sick man said, "for I have no one to help me into the pool when the water is stirred up. While I am trying to get there, someone else always gets in ahead of me."

[8]Jesus told him, "Stand up, pick up your sleeping mat, and walk!"

[9]Instantly, the man was healed! He rolled up the mat and began walking! But this miracle happened on the Sabbath day. [10]So the Jewish leaders objected. They said to the man who was cured,

"You can't work on the Sabbath! It's illegal to carry that sleeping mat!"

[11]He replied, "The man who healed me said to me, 'Pick up your sleeping mat and walk.'"

[12]"Who said such a thing as that?" they demanded. [13]The man didn't know, for Jesus had disappeared into the crowd. [14]But afterwards Jesus found him in the Temple and told him, "Now you are well; so stop sinning, or something even worse may happen to you."

[15]Then the man went to find the Jewish leaders and told them it was Jesus who had healed him.

## Jesus Claims to Be the Son of God

[16]So the Jewish leaders began harassing Jesus for breaking the Sabbath rules. [17]But Jesus replied, "My Father never stops working, so why should I?" [18]So the Jewish leaders tried all the more to kill him. In addition to disobeying the Sabbath rules, he had spoken of God as his Father, thereby making himself equal with God.

[19]Jesus replied, "I assure you, the Son can do nothing by himself. He does only what he sees the Father doing. Whatever the Father does, the Son also does. [20]For the Father loves the Son and tells him everything he is doing, and the Son will do far greater things than healing this man. You will be astonished at what he

**5:3** Some manuscripts add *waiting for a certain movement of the water,* *for an angel of the Lord came from time to time and stirred up the water. And the first person to step in after the water was stirred was healed of whatever disease he had.*

does. ²¹He will even raise from the dead anyone he wants to, just as the Father does. ²²And the Father leaves all judgement to his Son, ²³so that everyone will honour the Son, just as they honour the Father. But if you refuse to honour the Son, then you are certainly not honouring the Father who sent him. ²⁴"I assure you, those who listen to my message and believe in God who sent me have eternal life. They will never be condemned for their sins, but they have already passed from death into life.

²⁵"And I assure you that the time is coming, in fact it is here, when the dead will hear my voice—the voice of the Son of God. And those who listen will live. ²⁶The Father has life in himself, and he has granted his Son to have life in himself. ²⁷And he has given him authority to judge all mankind because he is the Son of Man. ²⁸Don't be so surprised! Indeed, the time is coming when all the dead in their graves will hear the voice of God's Son, ²⁹and they will rise again. Those who have done good will rise to eternal life, and those who have continued in evil will rise to judgement. ³⁰But I do nothing without consulting the Father. I judge as I am told. And my judgement is absolutely just, because it is according to the will of God who sent me; it is not merely my own.

## Witnesses to Jesus

³¹"If I were to testify on my own behalf, my testimony would not be valid. ³²But someone else is also testifying about me, and I can assure you that everything he says about me is true. ³³In fact, you sent messengers to listen to John the Baptist, and he preached the truth. ³⁴But the best testimony about me is not from a man, though I have reminded you about John's testimony so you might be saved. ³⁵John shone brightly for a while, and you benefited and rejoiced. ³⁶But I have a greater witness than John—my teachings and my miracles. They have been assigned to me by the Father, and they testify that the Father has sent me. ³⁷And the Father himself has also testified about me. You have never heard his voice or seen him face to face, ³⁸and you do not have his message in your hearts, because you do not believe me—the one he sent to you.

³⁹"**You search the Scriptures because you believe they give you eternal life. But the Scriptures point to me!** ⁴⁰Yet you refuse to come to me so that I can give you this eternal life.

⁴¹"Your approval or disapproval means nothing to me, ⁴²because I know you don't have God's love within you. ⁴³For I have come to you representing my Father, and you refuse to welcome me, even though you readily accept others who represent only themselves.

⁴⁴No wonder you can't believe! For you gladly honour each other, but you don't care about the honour that comes from God alone.

⁴⁵"Yet it is not I who will accuse you of this before the Father. Moses will accuse you! Yes, Moses, on whom you set your hopes. ⁴⁶But if you had believed Moses, you would have believed me because he wrote about me. ⁴⁷And since you don't believe what he wrote, how will you believe what I say?"

## Jesus Feeds Five Thousand

**6**

After this, Jesus crossed over the Sea of Galilee, also known as the Sea of Tiberias. ²And a huge crowd kept following him wherever he went, because they saw his miracles as he healed the sick. ³Then Jesus went up into the hills and sat down with his disciples around him. ⁴(It was nearly time for the annual Passover celebration.) ⁵Jesus soon saw a great crowd of people climbing the hill, looking for him. Turning to Philip, he asked, "Philip, where can we buy bread to feed all these people?"

⁶He was testing Philip, for he already knew what he was going to do.

⁷Philip replied, "It would take a small fortune to feed them!"

⁸Then Andrew, Simon Peter's brother, spoke up. ⁹"There's a young boy here with five barley loaves and two fish. But what good is that with this huge crowd?"

¹⁰"Tell everyone to sit down," Jesus ordered. So all of them—the men alone numbered five thousand—

**STAND POINT**

**When you feel unfulfilled**

6:35

"I am the bread of life. No one who comes to me will ever be hungry again. Those who believe in me will never thirst".

sat down on the grassy slopes. ¹¹Then Jesus took the loaves, gave thanks to God, and passed them out to the people. Afterwards he did the same with the fish. And they all ate until they were full.

¹²"Now gather the leftovers," Jesus told his disciples, "so that nothing is wasted." ¹³**There were only five barley loaves to start with, but twelve baskets were filled with the pieces of bread the people did not eat!**

¹⁴When the people saw this miraculous sign, they exclaimed, "Surely, he is the Prophet we have been expecting!" ¹⁵Jesus saw that they were ready to take him by force and make him king, so he went higher into the hills alone.

## Jesus Walks on Water

¹⁶That evening his disciples went down to the shore to wait for him. ¹⁷But as darkness fell and Jesus still hadn't come back, they got into the boat and headed out across the lake towards Capernaum. ¹⁸Soon a gale swept down upon them as they rowed, and the sea grew very rough. ¹⁹They were five or six kilometres out when suddenly they saw Jesus walking

What are your five favourite books?

1
2
3
4
5

BIG FIVE

on the water towards the boat. They were terrified, [20]but he called out to them, "I am here! Don't be afraid." [21]Then they were eager to let him in, and immediately the boat arrived at their destination!

## Jesus, the Bread of Life

[22]The next morning, back across the lake, crowds began gathering on the shore, waiting to see Jesus. For they knew that he and his disciples had come over together and that the disciples had gone off in their boat, leaving him behind. [23]Several boats from Tiberias landed near the place where the Lord had blessed the bread and the people had eaten. [24]When the crowd saw that Jesus wasn't there, nor his disciples, they got into the boats and went across to Capernaum to look for him. [25]When they arrived and found him, they asked, "Teacher, how did you get here?"

[26]Jesus replied, "The truth is, you want to be with me because I fed you, not because you saw the miraculous sign. [27]**But you shouldn't be so concerned about perishable things like food. Spend your energy seeking the eternal life that I, the Son of Man, can give you. For God the Father has sent me for that very purpose.**"

[28]They replied, "What does God want us to do?"

[29]Jesus told them, "This is what God wants you to do: Believe in the one he has sent."

[30]They replied, "You must show us a miraculous sign if you want us to believe in you. What will you do for us? [31]After all, our ancestors ate manna while they journeyed through the wilderness! As the Scriptures say, 'Moses gave them bread from heaven to eat.'"

[32]Jesus said, "I assure you, Moses didn't give them bread from heaven. My Father did. And now he offers you the true bread from heaven. [33]The true bread of God is the one who comes down from heaven and gives life to the world."

[34]"Sir," they said, "give us that bread every day of our lives."

[35]Jesus replied, "I am the bread of life. No one who comes to me will ever be hungry again. Those who believe in me will never thirst. [36]But you haven't believed in me even though you have seen me. [37]However, those the Father has given me will come to me, and I will never reject them. [38]For I have come down from heaven to do the will of God who sent me, not to do what I want. [39]And this is the will of God, that I should not lose even one of all those he has given me, but that I should raise them to eternal life at the last day. [40]For it is my Father's will that all who see his Son and believe in him should have eternal life—that I should raise them at the last day."

[41]Then the people began to murmur in disagreement because he had said, "I am the bread from heaven." [42]They said, "This is Jesus, the son of Joseph. We know his father and mother. How can he say, 'I came down from heaven'?"

[43]But Jesus replied, "Don't complain about what I said. [44]For people can't come to me unless the Father who sent me draws them to me, and at the last day I will raise them from the dead. [45]As it is written in the Scriptures, 'They will all be taught by God.' Everyone who hears and learns from the Father comes to me. [46](Not that anyone has ever seen the Father; only I, who was sent from God, have seen him.)

[47]"I assure you, anyone who believes in me already has eternal life. [48]Yes, I am the bread of life! [49]Your ancestors ate manna in the wilderness, but they all died. [50]However, the bread from heaven gives eternal life to everyone who eats it. [51]I am the living bread that came down out of heaven. Anyone who eats this bread will live for ever; this bread is my flesh, offered so the world may live."

[52]Then the people began arguing with each other about what he meant. "How can this man give us his flesh to eat?" they asked.

[53]So Jesus said again, "I assure you, unless you eat the flesh of the Son of Man and drink his blood, you cannot have eternal life within you. [54]But those who eat my flesh and drink my blood have eternal life, and I will raise them at the last day. [55]For my flesh is the true food, and my blood is the true drink. [56]All who eat my flesh and drink my blood remain in me, and I in them. [57]I live by the power of the living Father who sent me; in the same way, those who partake of me will live because of me. [58]I am the true bread from heaven. Anyone who eats this bread will live for ever and not die as your ancestors did, even though they ate the manna."

[59]He said these things while he was teaching in the synagogue in Capernaum.

## Many Disciples Desert Jesus

[60]Even his disciples said, "This is very hard to understand. How can anyone accept it?"

[61]Jesus knew within himself that his disciples were complaining, so he said to them, "Does this offend you? [62]Then what will you think if you see me, the Son of Man, return to heaven again? [63]It is the Spirit who gives eternal life. Human effort accomplishes nothing. And the very words I have spoken to you are spirit and life. [64]But some of you don't believe me." (For Jesus knew from the beginning who didn't believe, and he knew who would betray him.) [65]Then he said, "That is what I meant when I said that people can't come to me unless the Father brings them to me."

[66]At this point many of his disciples turned away and deserted him. [67]Then Jesus turned to the Twelve and asked, "Are you going to leave, too?"

[68]Simon Peter replied, "Lord, to whom would we go? You alone have the words that give eternal life. [69]We believe them, and we know you are the Holy One of God."

## Winners keep a balanced perspective!

Having God at the centre of your life puts everything in a true perspective. Great athletes don't fall apart when they lose, unless their life is out of balance. The French philosopher said, "There is a God-shaped void in the heart of every man." We would certainly never call sport our "god", but when we put too much emphasis on anything, or rather not enough emphasis on God, in our lives we become lop-sided, we create mini-god substitutes. Winning and losing a match can be dangerously over-emphasised. Keep God at the centre of your life, spend your life in pursuit of pleasing him and your perspective will be perfect!

'Try to find out what is pleasing to the Lord.' Ephesians 5:10

Winners see the big picture!

⁷⁰Then Jesus said, "I chose the twelve of you, but one is a devil." ⁷¹He was speaking of Judas, son of Simon Iscariot, one of the Twelve, who would betray him.

## Jesus and His Brothers

# 7

After this, Jesus stayed in Galilee, going from village to village. He wanted to stay out of Judea where the Jewish leaders were plotting his death. ²But soon it was time for the Festival of Shelters, ³and Jesus' brothers urged him to go to Judea for the celebration. "Go where your followers can see your miracles!" they scoffed. ⁴"You can't become a public figure if you hide

# WHAT
# DOES
# IT
# MEAN?

## Adultery

An adulterer was a man or woman who had sex with a married or an engaged person. Intercourse between unmarried people is fornication. Adultery and fornication were regarded as great social wrongs, as well as a great sin. It has been inferred from John 8:1-11 that this sin became very common during the age preceding the destruction of Jerusalem.

like this! If you can do such wonderful things, prove it to the world!" ⁵For even his brothers didn't believe in him.

⁶Jesus replied, "Now is not the right time for me to go. But you can go any time, and it will make no difference. ⁷The world can't hate you, but it does hate me because I accuse it of sin and evil. ⁸You go on. I am not yet ready to go to this festival, because my time has not yet come." ⁹So Jesus remained in Galilee.

## Jesus Teaches Openly at the Temple

¹⁰But after his brothers had left for the festival, Jesus also went, though secretly, staying out of public view. ¹¹The Jewish leaders tried to find him at the festival and kept asking if anyone had seen him. ¹²There was a lot of discussion about him among the crowds. Some said, "He's a wonderful man," while others said, "He's nothing but a fraud, deceiving the people." ¹³But no one had the courage to speak favourably about him in public, for they were afraid of getting into trouble with the Jewish leaders.

¹⁴Then, midway through the festival, Jesus went up to the Temple and began to teach. ¹⁵The Jewish leaders were surprised when they heard him. "How does he know so much when he hasn't studied everything we've studied?" they asked.

¹⁶So Jesus told them, "I'm not teaching my own ideas, but those of God who sent me. ¹⁷Anyone who wants to do the will of God will know whether my teaching is from God or is merely my own. ¹⁸Those who present their own ideas are looking for praise for themselves, but those who seek to honour the one who sent them are good and genuine. ¹⁹None of you obeys the law of Moses! In fact, you are trying to kill me."

²⁰The crowd replied, "You're demon possessed! Who's trying to kill you?"

²¹Jesus replied, "I worked on the Sabbath by healing a man, and you were offended. ²²But you work on the Sabbath, too, when you obey Moses' law of circumcision. (Actually, this tradition of circumcision is older than the law of Moses; it goes back to Abraham.) ²³For if the correct time for circumcising your son falls on the Sabbath, you go ahead and do it, so as not to break the law of Moses. So why should I be condemned for making a man completely well on the Sabbath? ²⁴Think this through and you will see that I am right."

## Is Jesus the Messiah?

²⁵Some of the people who lived there in Jerusalem said among themselves, "Isn't this the man they are trying

# profiles

## John:

At the last supper we see a beautiful picture of closeness, a relaxed manner that John had with Jesus. Peter asks John to ask Jesus who is the betrayer. We see John hanging out with Christ in an intimate easy-going way. John was originally with his (probably older) brother James, a disciple of John the Baptist. It appears but is unclear that Jesus' mother Mary is his aunt. We know that Jesus had a special close circle of disciples and an even closer ring that accompanied Jesus, which included John. There are insights in John's writings that reveal he knew the master's heart. John had a knack for recognising Jesus when no one else did (John 21:7) and was with Jesus at his death when Jesus charged him to take care of his mother Mary. Jesus also nicknamed John and his brother 'the sons of thunder', perhaps after they wanted to blast with lightning a village that spurned Jesus (Luke 9:54). John wrote five books of the New Testament, The Gospel of John, the three Letters of John and Revelation. If Jesus was in the room with you now, could you enjoy the same closeness that John enjoyed or would the relationship be stiff and formal? I hope it would be close because he is here with you and wants to be close to you.

to kill? [26]But here he is, speaking in public, and they say nothing to him. Can it be that our leaders know that he really is the Messiah? [27]But how could he be? For we know where this man comes from. When the Messiah comes, he will simply appear; no one will know where he comes from." [28]While Jesus was teaching in the Temple, he called out, "Yes, you know me, and you know where I come from. But I represent one you don't know, and he is true. [29]I know him because I have come from him, and he sent me to you." [30]Then the leaders tried to arrest him; but no one laid a hand on him, because his time had not yet come.

[31]Many among the crowds at the Temple believed in him. "After all," they said, "would you expect the Messiah to do more miraculous signs than this man has done?"

[32]When the Pharisees heard that the crowds were murmuring such things, they and the leading priests sent Temple guards to arrest Jesus. [33]But Jesus told them, "I will be here a little longer. Then I will return to the one who sent me. [34]You will search for me but not find me. And you won't be able to come where I am."

[35]The Jewish leaders were puzzled by this statement. "Where is he planning to go?" they asked. "Maybe he is thinking of leaving the country and going to the Jews in other lands, or maybe even to the Gentiles! [36]What does he mean when he says, 'You will search for me but not find me,' and 'You won't be able to come where I am'?"

## Jesus Promises Living Water

[37]On the last day, the climax of the festival, Jesus stood and shouted to the crowds, "If you are thirsty, come to me! [38]If you believe in me, come and drink! For the Scriptures declare that rivers of living water will flow out from within."

[39](When he said "living water," he was speaking of the Spirit, who would be given to everyone believing in him. But the Spirit had not yet been given, because Jesus had not yet entered into his glory.)

## Division and Unbelief

[40]When the crowds heard him say this, some of them declared, "This man surely is the Prophet." [41]Others said, "He is the Messiah." Still others said, "But he can't be! Will the Messiah come from Galilee? [42]For the Scriptures clearly state that the Messiah will be born of the royal line of David, in Bethlehem, the village where King David was born." [43]So the crowd was divided in their opinion about him. [44]And some wanted him arrested, but no one touched him.

[45]The Temple guards who had been sent to arrest him returned to the leading priests and Pharisees. "Why didn't you bring him in?" they demanded.

[46]"We have never heard anyone talk like this!" the guards responded.

Poland's Stella Walsh (Stanislawa Walasiewicz) won the women's 100-metre race at the 1932 Olympics in Los Angeles, becoming the first woman to break the 12-second barrier. When she was killed in 1980 as an innocent victim in a robbery attempt, an autopsy declared her to be a male.

[47]"Have you been led astray, too?" the Pharisees mocked. [48]"Is there a single one of us rulers or Pharisees who believes in him? [49]These ignorant crowds do, but what do they know about it? A curse on them anyway!"

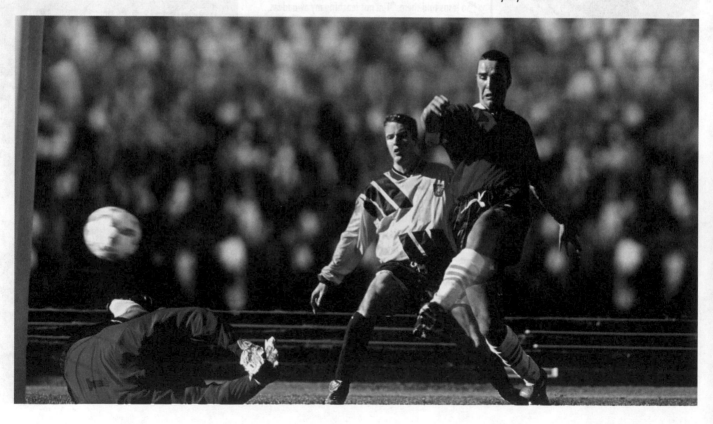

⁵⁰Nicodemus, the leader who had met with Jesus earlier, then spoke up. ⁵¹"Is it legal to convict a man before he is given a hearing?" he asked.

⁵²They replied, "Are you from Galilee, too? Search the Scriptures and see for yourself—no prophet ever comes from Galilee!"

[The most ancient Greek manuscripts do not include John 7:53-8:11]

⁵³Then the meeting broke up and everybody went home.

**CH 8:31-47 WHAT'S IT SAYING?**

**WHAT AM I GOING TO DO ABOUT IT?**

## A Woman Caught in Adultery

# 8

Jesus returned to the Mount of Olives, ²but early the next morning he was back again at the Temple. A crowd soon gathered, and he sat down and taught them. ³As he was speaking, the teachers of religious law and Pharisees brought a woman they had caught in the act of adultery. They put her in front of the crowd.

⁴"Teacher," they said to Jesus, "this woman was caught in the very act of adultery. ⁵The law of Moses says to stone her. What do you say?"

⁶They were trying to trap him into saying something they could use against him, but Jesus stooped down and wrote in the dust with his finger. ⁷They kept demanding an answer, so he stood up again and said, "All right, stone her. But let those who have never sinned throw the first stones!" ⁸Then he stooped down again and wrote in the dust.

⁹When the accusers heard this, they slipped away one by one, beginning with the oldest, until only Jesus was left in the middle of the crowd with the woman. ¹⁰Then Jesus stood up again and said to her, "Where are your accusers? Didn't even one of them condemn you?"

¹¹"No, Lord," she said.

And Jesus said, "Neither do I. Go and sin no more."

## Jesus, the Light of the World

¹²**Jesus said to the people, "I am the light of the world. If you follow me, you won't be stumbling through the darkness, because you will have the light that leads to life."**

¹³The Pharisees replied, "You are making false claims about yourself!"

¹⁴Jesus told them, "These claims are valid even though I make them about myself. For I know where I came from and where I am going, but you don't know this about me. ¹⁵You judge me with all your human limitations, but I am not judging anyone. ¹⁶And if I did, my judgement would be correct in every respect because I am not alone—I have with me the Father who sent me. ¹⁷Your own law says that if two people agree about something, their witness is accepted as fact. ¹⁸I am one witness, and my Father who sent me is the other."

¹⁹"Where is your father?" they asked.

Jesus answered, "Since you don't know who I am, you don't know who my Father is. If you knew me, then you would know my Father, too." ²⁰Jesus made these statements while he was teaching in the section of the Temple known as the Treasury. But he was not arrested, because his time had not yet come.

## The Unbelieving People Warned

²¹Later Jesus said to them again, "I am going away. You will search for me and die in your sin. You cannot come where I am going."

²²The Jewish leaders asked, "Is he planning to commit suicide? What does he mean, 'You cannot come where I am going'?"

²³Then he said to them, "You are from below; I am from above. You are of this world; I am not. ²⁴That is why I said that you will die in your sins; for unless you believe that I am who I say I am, you will die in your sins."

²⁵"Tell us who you are," they demanded.

Jesus replied, "I am the one I have always claimed to be. ²⁶I have much to say about you and much to condemn, but I won't. For I say only what I have heard from the one who sent me, and he is true." ²⁷But they still didn't understand that he was talking to them about his Father.

²⁸So Jesus said, "When you have lifted up the Son of Man on the cross, then you will realize that I am he and that I do nothing on my own, but I speak what the Father taught me. ²⁹And the one who sent me is with me—he has not deserted me. For I always do those things that are pleasing to him." ³⁰Then many who heard him say these things believed in him.

## Jesus and Abraham

³¹Jesus said to the people who believed in him, "You are truly my disciples if you keep obeying my teachings. ³²And you will know the truth, and the truth will set you free."

³³"But we are descendants of Abraham," they said.

"We have never been slaves to anyone on earth. What do you mean, 'set free'?"

³⁴Jesus replied, "I assure you that everyone who sins is a slave of sin. ³⁵A slave is not a permanent member of the family, but a son is part of the family for ever. ³⁶So if the Son sets you free, you will indeed be free. ³⁷Yes, I realize that you are descendants of Abraham. And yet some of you are trying to kill me because my message does not find a place in your hearts. ³⁸I am telling you what I saw when I was with my Father. But you are following the advice of your father."

³⁹"Our father is Abraham," they declared.

"No," Jesus replied, "for if you were children of Abraham, you would follow his good example. ⁴⁰I told you the truth I heard from God, but you are trying to kill me. Abraham wouldn't do a thing like that. ⁴¹No, you are obeying your real father when you act that way."

They replied, "We were not born out of wedlock! Our true Father is God himself."

⁴²Jesus told them, "If God were your Father, you would love me, because I have come to you from God. I am not here on my own, but he sent me. ⁴³Why can't you understand what I am saying? It is because you are unable to do so! ⁴⁴For you are the children of your father the Devil, and you love to do the evil things he does. He was a murderer from the beginning and has always hated the truth. There is no truth in him. When he lies, it is consistent with his character; for he is a liar and the father of lies. ⁴⁵So when I tell the truth, you just naturally don't believe me! ⁴⁶Which of you can truthfully accuse me of sin? And since I am telling you the truth, why don't you believe me? ⁴⁷Anyone whose Father is God listens gladly to the words of God. Since you don't, it proves you

aren't God's children."

⁴⁸The people retorted, "You Samaritan devil! Didn't we say all along that you were possessed by a demon?"

⁴⁹"No," Jesus said, "I have no demon in me. For I honour my Father—and you dishonour me. ⁵⁰And though I have no wish to glorify myself, God wants to glorify me. Let him be the judge. ⁵¹I assure you, anyone who obeys my teaching will never die!"

⁵²The people said, "Now we know you are possessed by a demon. Even Abraham and the prophets died, but you say that those who obey your teaching will never die! ⁵³Are you greater than our father Abraham, who died? Are you greater than the prophets, who died? Who do you think you are?"

⁵⁴Jesus answered, "If I am merely boasting about myself, it doesn't count. But it is my Father who says these glorious things about me. You say, 'He is our God,' ⁵⁵but you do not even know him. I know him. If I said otherwise, I would be as great a liar as you! But it is true—I know him and obey him. ⁵⁶Your ancestor Abraham rejoiced as he looked forward to my coming. He saw it and was glad."

⁵⁷The people said, "You aren't even fifty years old. How can you say you have seen Abraham?"

⁵⁸Jesus answered, "The truth is, I existed before Abraham was even born!" ⁵⁹At that point they picked up stones to kill him. But Jesus hid himself from them and left the Temple.

## Jesus Heals a Man Born Blind

# 9

As Jesus was walking along, he saw a man who had been blind from birth. ²"Teacher," his disciples asked him, "why was this man born blind? Was it a result of his own sins or those of his parents?"

³"It was not because of his sins or his parents' sins," Jesus answered. "He was born blind so the power of God could be seen in him. ⁴All of us must quickly carry out the tasks assigned us by the one who sent me, because there is little time left before the night falls and all work comes to an end. ⁵But while I am still here in the world, I am the light of the world."

⁶Then he spat on the ground, made mud with the saliva, and smoothed the mud over the blind man's eyes. ⁷He told him, "Go and wash in the pool of Siloam" (Siloam means Sent). So the man went and washed, and came back seeing!

⁸His neighbours and others who knew him as a blind beggar asked each other, "Is this the same man—that beggar?" ⁹Some said he was, and others said, "No, but he surely looks like him!"

And the beggar kept saying, "I am the same man!"

¹⁰They asked, "Who healed you? What happened?"

¹¹He told them, "The man they call Jesus made mud and

## count on it

### Try Hard!

You do not have to try hard to get God to love you - he loved you so that you would try hard! How much does God love you? Spread out your hands as wide as you can. That much! God sent his son to the cross that, in the bloody sacrifice of Jesus, you would be forgiven! In that love respond in gratitude. Try hard! "He is so rich in kindness that he purchased our freedom through the blood of his Son, and our sins are forgiven." Ephesians 1:7

**Count on it!**

smoothed it over my eyes and told me, 'Go to the pool of Siloam and wash off the mud.' I went and washed, and now I can see!"

¹²"Where is he now?" they asked.

"I don't know," he replied.

¹³Then they took the man to the Pharisees. ¹⁴Now as it happened, Jesus had healed the man on a Sabbath. ¹⁵The Pharisees asked the man all about it. So he told them, "He smoothed the mud over my eyes, and when it was washed away, I could see!"

¹⁶Some of the Pharisees said, "This man Jesus is not from God, for he is working on the Sabbath." Others said, "But how could an ordinary sinner do such miraculous signs?" So there was a deep division of opinion among them.

¹⁷Then the Pharisees once again questioned the man who had been blind and demanded, "This man who

opened your eyes—who do you say he is?"

The man replied, "I think he must be a prophet."

¹⁸The Jewish leaders wouldn't believe he had been blind, so they called in his parents. ¹⁹They asked them, "Is this your son? Was he born blind? If so, how can he see?"

²⁰His parents replied, "We know this is our son and that he was born blind, ²¹but we don't know how he can see or who healed him. He is old enough to speak for himself. Ask him."

²²They said this because they were afraid of the Jewish leaders, who had announced that anyone saying Jesus was the Messiah would be expelled from the synagogue. ²³That's why they said, "He is old enough to speak for himself. Ask him."

²⁴So for the second time they called in the man who had been blind and told him, "Give glory to God by telling the truth, because we know Jesus is a sinner."

²⁵"I don't know whether he is a sinner," the man replied. "But I know this: I was blind, and now I can see!"

²⁶"But what did he do?" they asked. "How did he heal you?"

²⁷"Look!" the man exclaimed. "I told you once. Didn't you listen? Why do you want to hear it again? Do you want to become his disciples, too?"

²⁸Then they cursed him and said, "You are his disciple, but we are disciples of Moses. ²⁹We know God spoke to Moses, but as for this man, we don't know anything about him."

³⁰"Why, that's very strange!" the man replied.

"He healed my eyes, and yet you don't know anything about him! ³¹Well, God doesn't listen to sinners, but he is ready to hear those who worship him and do his will. ³²Never since the world began has anyone been able to open the eyes of someone born blind. ³³If this man were not from God, he couldn't do it."

³⁴"You were born in sin!" they answered. "Are you trying to teach us?" And they threw him out of the synagogue.

## Spiritual Blindness

³⁵When Jesus heard what had happened, he found the man and said, "Do you believe in the Son of Man?"

³⁶The man answered, "Who is he, sir? I want to believe in him."

³⁷"You have seen him," Jesus said, "and he is speaking to you!"

³⁸"Yes, Lord," the man said, "I believe!" And he worshipped Jesus.

³⁹**Then Jesus told him, "I have come to judge the world. I have come to give**

JOHN – CHAPTER 10:10

Pro athletes can be the most open to following Christ. They have realised what most athletes dream of, getting to the top. They achieved their dream and climbed the ladder to success. So why are they so open to the gospel? Because the ladder is on the wrong wall! For this reason, they grasp the fact that sporting accomplishments do not make you ultimately happy. There is an emptiness in the heart of every person that can only be filled up by God, through Jesus your Lord and Saviour. Everyone wants to have life to the max. Having Jesus in your life – 'life to the full' - is the only way to fulfilment.

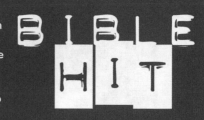
**BIBLE HIT**

sight to the blind and to show those who think they see that they are blind."

⁴⁰The Pharisees who were standing there heard him and asked,

"Are you saying we are blind?"

⁴¹"If you were blind, you wouldn't be guilty," Jesus replied. "But you remain guilty because you claim you can see.

**action**

**CH 10:1-10 WHAT'S IT SAYING?**

**WHAT AM I GOING TO DO ABOUT IT?**

## The Good Shepherd and His Sheep

# 10

"I assure you, anyone who sneaks over the wall of a sheepfold, rather than going through the gate, must surely be a thief and a robber! ²For a shepherd enters through the gate. ³The gatekeeper opens the gate for him, and the sheep hear his voice and come to him. He calls his own sheep by name and leads them out. ⁴After he has gathered his own flock, he walks ahead of them, and they follow him because they recognize his voice. ⁵They won't follow a stranger; they will run from him because they don't recognize his voice."

⁶Those who heard Jesus use this illustration didn't understand what he meant, ⁷so he explained it to them. "I assure you, I am the gate for the sheep," he said. ⁸"All others who came before me were thieves and robbers. But the true sheep did not listen to them. ⁹Yes, I am the gate. Those who come in through me will be saved. Wherever they go, they will find green pastures. ¹⁰**The thief's purpose is to steal and kill and destroy. My purpose is to give life in all its fullness.**

¹¹"I am the good shepherd. The good shepherd lays down his life for the sheep. ¹²A hired hand will run when he sees a wolf coming. He will leave the sheep because they aren't his and he isn't their shepherd. And so the wolf attacks them and scatters the flock. ¹³The hired hand runs away because he is merely hired and has no real concern for the sheep.

¹⁴"I am the good shepherd; I know my own sheep, and they know me, ¹⁵just as my Father knows me and I know the Father. And I lay down my life for the sheep. ¹⁶I have other sheep, too, that are not in this sheepfold. I must bring them also, and they will listen to my voice; and there will be one flock with one shepherd. ¹⁷"The Father loves me because I lay down my life that I may have it back again. ¹⁸No one can take my life from me. I lay down my life voluntarily. For I have the right to lay it down when I want to and also the power to take it again. For my Father has given me this command."

¹⁹When he said these things, the people were again divided in their opinions about him. ²⁰Some of them said, "He has a demon, or he's crazy. Why listen to a man like that?"

²¹Others said, "This doesn't sound like a man possessed by a demon! Can a demon open the eyes of the blind?"

## Jesus Claims to Be the Son of God

²²It was now winter, and Jesus was in Jerusalem at the time of Hanukkah. ²³He was at the Temple, walking through the section known as Solomon's Colonnade. ²⁴The Jewish leaders surrounded him and asked, "How long are you going to keep us in suspense? If you are the Messiah, tell us plainly."

²⁵Jesus replied, "I have already told you, and you don't believe me. The proof is what I do in the name of my Father. ²⁶But you don't believe me because you are not part of my flock. ²⁷My sheep recognize my voice; I know them, and they follow me. ²⁸I give them eternal life, and they will never perish. No one will snatch them away from me, ²⁹for my Father has given them to me, and he is more powerful than anyone else. So no one can take them from me. ³⁰The Father and I are one."

³¹Once again the Jewish leaders picked up stones to kill him. ³²Jesus said, "At my Father's direction I have done many things to help the people. For which one of these good deeds are you killing me?"

³³They replied, "Not for any good work, but for blasphemy, because you, a mere man, have made yourself God."

³⁴Jesus replied, "It is written in your own law that God said to certain leaders of the people, 'I say, you are gods!' ³⁵And you know that the Scriptures cannot be altered. So if those people, who received God's message, were called 'gods,'

**STAND POINT**

**When you want to know God**

**11:27**

"I have always believed you are the Messiah, the Son of God, the one who has come into the world from God."

KNOW it

**BIBLE HIT** 'This will not end in death' JOHN – CHAPTER 11

Jesus had many friends besides his disciples including the sisters and brother, Mary, Martha and Lazarus, with whom he often stayed. When their brother fell deathly ill the sisters sent word immediately to Jesus to come and help. Jesus was preaching nearby, across the Jordan River, and could have been with them shortly. But it was not God's timing and Jesus knew the story was not to end in the death of Lazarus, but strengthen the faith of many of Jesus' followers. Though Lazarus died and Jesus' delay seemed to be the actions of an insincere, heartless friend, it turned into a marvellous miracle as Jesus raised Lazarus from the dead. God's timing is always perfect. Wait and trust in that perfect timing.

[36]why do you call it blasphemy when the Holy One who was sent into the world by the Father says, 'I am the Son of God'? [37]Don't believe me unless I carry out my Father's work. [38]But if I do his work, believe in what I have done, even if you don't believe me. Then you will realize that the Father is in me, and I am in the Father." [39]Once again they tried to arrest him, but he got away and left them. [40]He went beyond the River Jordan to stay near the place where John was first baptizing. [41]And many followed him.

"John didn't do miracles," they remarked to one another, "but all his predictions about this man have come true."

[42]And many believed in him there.

## The Death of Lazarus

# 11

A man named Lazarus was sick. He lived in Bethany with his sisters, Mary and Martha. [2]This is the Mary who poured the expensive perfume on the Lord's feet and wiped them with her hair. Her brother, Lazarus, was sick. [3]So the two sisters sent a message to Jesus telling him, "Lord, the one you love is very sick." [4]But when Jesus heard about it he said, "Lazarus's sickness will not end in death. No, it is for the glory of God. I, the Son of God, will receive glory from this." [5]Although Jesus loved Martha, Mary, and Lazarus, [6]he stayed where he was for the next two days and did not go to them. [7]Finally after two days, he said to his disciples, "Let's go to Judea again."

[8]But his disciples objected. "Teacher," they said, "only a few days ago the Jewish leaders in Judea were trying to kill you. Are you going there again?" [9]Jesus replied, "There are twelve hours of daylight every day. As long as it is light, people can walk safely. They can see because they have the light of this world. [10]Only at night is there danger of stumbling because there is no light."

[11]Then he said, "Our friend Lazarus has fallen asleep, but now I will go and wake him up." [12]The disciples said, "Lord, if he is sleeping, that means he is getting better!" [13]They thought Jesus meant Lazarus was having a good night's rest, but Jesus meant Lazarus had died.

[14]Then he told them plainly, "Lazarus is dead. [15]And for your sake, I am glad I wasn't there, because this will give you another opportunity to believe in me. Come, let's go and see him."

[16]Thomas, nicknamed the Twin, said to his fellow disciples, "Let's go, too—and die with Jesus."

[17]When Jesus arrived at Bethany, he was told that Lazarus had already been in his grave for four days. [18]Bethany was only about three kilometres down the road from Jerusalem, [19]and many of the people had come to pay their respects and console Martha and Mary on their loss. [20]When Martha got word that Jesus was coming, she went to meet him. But Mary stayed at home. [21]Martha said to Jesus, "Lord, if you had been here, my brother would not have died. [22]But even now I know that God will give you whatever you ask."

[23]Jesus told her, "Your brother will rise again."

[24]"Yes," Martha said, "when everyone else rises, on resurrection day."

[25]**Jesus told her, "I am the resurrection and the life. Those who believe in me, even though they die like everyone else, will live again.** [26]They are given eternal life for believing in me and will never perish. Do you believe this, Martha?"

[27]"Yes, Lord," she told him. "I have always believed you are the Messiah, the Son of God, the one who has come into the world from God." [28]Then she left him and returned to Mary. She called Mary aside from the mourners and told her, "The Teacher is here and wants to see you." [29]So Mary immediately went to him.

[30]Now Jesus had stayed outside the village, at the place where Martha met him. [31]When the people who were at the house trying to console Mary saw her leave so hastily, they assumed she was going to Lazarus's grave to weep. So they followed her there.

[32]When Mary arrived and saw Jesus, she fell down at his feet and said, "Lord, if you had been here, my brother would not have died."

[33]When Jesus saw her weeping and saw the other people wailing with her, he was moved with indignation and was deeply troubled. [34]"Where have you put him?" he asked them. They told him, "Lord, come and see." [35]Then Jesus wept. [36]The people who were standing nearby said, "See how much he loved him." [37]But some said, "This man healed a blind man. Why couldn't he keep Lazarus from dying?"

## Progressively challenge yourself:

Progressively challenge yourself: Where you have hesitation, lack of control, loss of confidence or a feeling of tenseness, then in training find a simpler shot and when you have perfected it move toward a more challenging position, distance or target.

'Access'
You need to be part of the team if you want to get legitimate access to the pitch of an important match. You get access to God and a home in heaven, through trusting in Jesus. Jesus explains he is the only way to God. With Jesus you have admission, you are on his team and part of his game plan.

## Jesus Raises Lazarus from the Dead

[38] And again Jesus was deeply troubled. Then they came to the grave. It was a cave with a stone rolled across its entrance. [39] "Roll the stone aside," Jesus told them.

But Martha, the dead man's sister, said, "Lord, by now the smell will be terrible because he has been dead for four days." [40] Jesus responded, "Didn't I tell you that you will see God's glory if you believe?" [41] So they rolled the stone aside. Then Jesus looked up to heaven and said, "Father, thank you for hearing me. [42] You always hear me, but I said it out loud for the sake of all these people standing here, so they will believe you sent me." [43] Then Jesus shouted, "Lazarus, come out!"

**Bible**

## The shortest verse is John 11:35 "Then Jesus wept."

[44] And Lazarus came out, bound in graveclothes, his face wrapped in a headcloth. Jesus told them, "Unwrap him and let him go!"

## The Plot to Kill Jesus

[45] Many of the people who were with Mary believed in Jesus when they saw this happen. [46] But some went to the Pharisees and told them what Jesus had done. [47] Then the leading priests and Pharisees called the high council together to discuss the situation. "What are we going to do?" they asked each other. "This man certainly performs many miraculous signs.

[48] If we leave him alone, the whole nation will follow him, and then the Roman army will come and destroy both our Temple and our nation."

[49] And one of them, Caiaphas, who was high priest that year, said, "How can you be so stupid? [50] Why should the whole nation be destroyed? Let this one man die for the people."

[51] This prophecy that Jesus should die for the entire nation came from Caiaphas in his position as high priest. He didn't think of it himself; he was inspired to say it. [52] It was a prediction that Jesus' death would be not for Israel only, but for the gathering together of all the children of God scattered around the world.

[53] So from that time on the Jewish leaders began to plot Jesus' death. [54] As a result, Jesus stopped his public ministry among the people and left Jerusalem. He went to a place near the wilderness, to the village of Ephraim, and stayed there with his disciples.

[55] It was now almost time for the celebration of Passover, and many people from the country arrived in Jerusalem several days early so they could go through the cleansing ceremony before the Passover began. [56] They wanted to see Jesus, and as they talked in the Temple, they asked each other, "What do you think? Will he come for the Passover?" [57] Meanwhile, the leading priests and Pharisees had publicly announced that anyone seeing Jesus must report him immediately so they could arrest him.

## Jesus Anointed at Bethany

# 12

Six days before the Passover ceremonies began, Jesus arrived in Bethany, the home of Lazarus—the man he had raised from the dead. [2] A dinner was prepared in Jesus' honour. Martha served, and Lazarus sat at the table with him. [3] Then Mary took more than three hundred grams of expensive perfume made from essence of nard, and she anointed Jesus' feet with it and wiped his feet with her hair. And the house was filled with fragrance.

[4] But Judas Iscariot, one of his disciples—the one who would betray him—said, [5] "That perfume was worth a small fortune. It should have been sold and the money given to the poor." [6] Not that he cared for the poor—he was a thief who was in charge of the disciples' funds, and he often took some for his own use.

[7] Jesus replied, "Leave her alone. She did it in preparation for my burial. [8] You will always have the poor among you, but I will not be here with you much longer."

[9] When all the people heard of Jesus' arrival, they flocked to see him and also to see Lazarus, the man Jesus had raised from the dead. [10] Then the leading priests decided to kill Lazarus, too, [11] for it was because of him that many of the people had deserted them and believed in Jesus.

**action**

### CH 12:23-36 WHAT'S IT SAYING?

### WHAT AM I GOING TO DO ABOUT IT?

## The Triumphal Entry

[12] The next day, the news that Jesus was on the way to Jerusalem swept through the city. A huge crowd of Passover visitors [13] took palm branches and went down the road to meet him. They shouted,

"Praise God!
Bless the one who comes in the name of the Lord!

Hail to the King of Israel!"
[14]Jesus found a young donkey and sat on it, fulfilling the prophecy that said:
[15]"Don't be afraid, people of Israel.
Look, your King is coming,
sitting on a donkey's colt."
[16]His disciples didn't realize at the time that this was a fulfilment of prophecy. But after Jesus entered into his glory, they remembered that these Scriptures had come true before their eyes.
[17]Those in the crowd who had seen Jesus call Lazarus back to life were telling others all about it. [18]That was the main reason so many went out to meet him—because they had heard about this mighty miracle.
[19]Then the Pharisees said to each other, "We've lost. Look, the whole world has gone after him!"

## Jesus Predicts His Death

[20]Some Greeks who had come to Jerusalem to attend the Passover [21]paid a visit to Philip, who was from Bethsaida in Galilee. They said, "Sir, we want to meet Jesus."
[22]Philip told Andrew about it, and they went together to ask Jesus.
[23]Jesus replied, "The time has come for the Son of Man to enter into his glory. [24]The truth is, a kernel of wheat must be planted in the soil. Unless it dies it will be

The first ancient Olympic games, held in Olympia, Greece, from 776 BC through 393 AD, were part of a religious festival that honoured Zeus.

alone—a single seed. But its death will produce many new kernels—a plentiful harvest of new lives. [25]Those who love their life in this world will lose it. Those who despise their life in this world will keep it for eternal life. [26]All those who want to be my disciples must come and follow me, because my servants must be where I am. And if they follow me, the Father will honour them. [27]Now my soul is deeply troubled. Should I pray, 'Father, save me from what lies ahead'? But that is the very reason why I came! [28]Father, bring glory to your name."
Then a voice spoke from heaven, saying, "I have already brought it glory, and I will do it again." [29]When the crowd heard the voice, some thought it was thunder, while others declared an angel had spoken to him.
[30]Then Jesus told them, "The voice was for your benefit, not mine. [31]The time of judgement for the world has come, when the prince of this world will be cast out. [32]And when I am lifted up on the cross, I will draw everyone to myself."
[33]He said this to indicate how he was going to die.
[34]"Die?" asked the crowd. "We understood from Scripture that the Messiah would live for ever. Why are you saying the

# MAY M.A.P.

## 1
| S.D. | P.L. | P.G. | S.G. |
|------|------|------|------|
| P. ☐ | F. ☐ | F. ☐ | T. ☐ |
| F. ☐ | W. ☐ | W. ☐ | P. ☐ |
| B. ☐ | P. ☐ | C. ☐ | C. ☐ |

## 2
| S.D. | P.L. | P.G. | S.G. |
|------|------|------|------|
| P. ☐ | F. ☐ | F. ☐ | T. ☐ |
| F. ☐ | W. ☐ | W. ☐ | P. ☐ |
| B. ☐ | P. ☐ | C. ☐ | C. ☐ |

## 3
| S.D. | P.L. | P.G. | S.G. |
|------|------|------|------|
| P. ☐ | F. ☐ | F. ☐ | T. ☐ |
| F. ☐ | W. ☐ | W. ☐ | P. ☐ |
| B. ☐ | P. ☐ | C. ☐ | C. ☐ |

## 4
| S.D. | P.L. | P.G. | S.G. |
|------|------|------|------|
| P. ☐ | F. ☐ | F. ☐ | T. ☐ |
| F. ☐ | W. ☐ | W. ☐ | P. ☐ |
| B. ☐ | P. ☐ | C. ☐ | C. ☐ |

## 9
| S.D. | P.L. | P.G. | S.G. |
|------|------|------|------|
| P. ☐ | F. ☐ | F. ☐ | T. ☐ |
| F. ☐ | W. ☐ | W. ☐ | P. ☐ |
| B. ☐ | P. ☐ | C. ☐ | C. ☐ |

## 10
| S.D. | P.L. | P.G. | S.G. |
|------|------|------|------|
| P. ☐ | F. ☐ | F. ☐ | T. ☐ |
| F. ☐ | W. ☐ | W. ☐ | P. ☐ |
| B. ☐ | P. ☐ | C. ☐ | C. ☐ |

## 11
| S.D. | P.L. | P.G. | S.G. |
|------|------|------|------|
| P. ☐ | F. ☐ | F. ☐ | T. ☐ |
| F. ☐ | W. ☐ | W. ☐ | P. ☐ |
| B. ☐ | P. ☐ | C. ☐ | C. ☐ |

## 12
| S.D. | P.L. | P.G. | S.G. |
|------|------|------|------|
| P. ☐ | F. ☐ | F. ☐ | T. ☐ |
| F. ☐ | W. ☐ | W. ☐ | P. ☐ |
| B. ☐ | P. ☐ | C. ☐ | C. ☐ |

## 17
| S.D. | P.L. | P.G. | S.G. |
|------|------|------|------|
| P. ☐ | F. ☐ | F. ☐ | T. ☐ |
| F. ☐ | W. ☐ | W. ☐ | P. ☐ |
| B. ☐ | P. ☐ | C. ☐ | C. ☐ |

## 18
| S.D. | P.L. | P.G. | S.G. |
|------|------|------|------|
| P. ☐ | F. ☐ | F. ☐ | T. ☐ |
| F. ☐ | W. ☐ | W. ☐ | P. ☐ |
| B. ☐ | P. ☐ | C. ☐ | C. ☐ |

## 19
| S.D. | P.L. | P.G. | S.G. |
|------|------|------|------|
| P. ☐ | F. ☐ | F. ☐ | T. ☐ |
| F. ☐ | W. ☐ | W. ☐ | P. ☐ |
| B. ☐ | P. ☐ | C. ☐ | C. ☐ |

## 20
| S.D. | P.L. | P.G. | S.G. |
|------|------|------|------|
| P. ☐ | F. ☐ | F. ☐ | T. ☐ |
| F. ☐ | W. ☐ | W. ☐ | P. ☐ |
| B. ☐ | P. ☐ | C. ☐ | C. ☐ |

## 25
| S.D. | P.L. | P.G. | S.G. |
|------|------|------|------|
| P. ☐ | F. ☐ | F. ☐ | T. ☐ |
| F. ☐ | W. ☐ | W. ☐ | P. ☐ |
| B. ☐ | P. ☐ | C. ☐ | C. ☐ |

## 26
| S.D. | P.L. | P.G. | S.G. |
|------|------|------|------|
| P. ☐ | F. ☐ | F. ☐ | T. ☐ |
| F. ☐ | W. ☐ | W. ☐ | P. ☐ |
| B. ☐ | P. ☐ | C. ☐ | C. ☐ |

## 27
| S.D. | P.L. | P.G. | S.G. |
|------|------|------|------|
| P. ☐ | F. ☐ | F. ☐ | T. ☐ |
| F. ☐ | W. ☐ | W. ☐ | P. ☐ |
| B. ☐ | P. ☐ | C. ☐ | C. ☐ |

## 28
| S.D. | P.L. | P.G. | S.G. |
|------|------|------|------|
| P. ☐ | F. ☐ | F. ☐ | T. ☐ |
| F. ☐ | W. ☐ | W. ☐ | P. ☐ |
| B. ☐ | P. ☐ | C. ☐ | C. ☐ |

## Spiritual Disciplines

**Prayer**

**Faith Community**

**Bible Reading**

## Prayer List

**Friends**

**World**

**Personal**

**(For designing your MAP - Monthly Action Plan - see introduction pages)**

Who am I....
Where am I going....
How am I going to get there?

# nt:sport
## MONTHLY ACTION PLAN

### 5

| S.D. | P.L. | P.G. | S.G. |
|---|---|---|---|
| P. ☐ | F. ☐ | F. ☐ | T. ☐ |
| F. ☐ | W. ☐ | W. ☐ | P. ☐ |
| B. ☐ | P. ☐ | C. ☐ | C. ☐ |

### 6

| S.D. | P.L. | P.G. | S.G. |
|---|---|---|---|
| P. ☐ | F. ☐ | F. ☐ | T. ☐ |
| F. ☐ | W. ☐ | W. ☐ | P. ☐ |
| B. ☐ | P. ☐ | C. ☐ | C. ☐ |

### 7

| S.D. | P.L. | P.G. | S.G. |
|---|---|---|---|
| P. ☐ | F. ☐ | F. ☐ | T. ☐ |
| F. ☐ | W. ☐ | W. ☐ | P. ☐ |
| B. ☐ | P. ☐ | C. ☐ | C. ☐ |

### 8

| S.D. | P.L. | P.G. | S.G. |
|---|---|---|---|
| P. ☐ | F. ☐ | F. ☐ | T. ☐ |
| F. ☐ | W. ☐ | W. ☐ | P. ☐ |
| B. ☐ | P. ☐ | C. ☐ | C. ☐ |

### 13

| S.D. | P.L. | P.G. | S.G. |
|---|---|---|---|
| P. ☐ | F. ☐ | F. ☐ | T. ☐ |
| F. ☐ | W. ☐ | W. ☐ | P. ☐ |
| B. ☐ | P. ☐ | C. ☐ | C. ☐ |

### 14

| S.D. | P.L. | P.G. | S.G. |
|---|---|---|---|
| P. ☐ | F. ☐ | F. ☐ | T. ☐ |
| F. ☐ | W. ☐ | W. ☐ | P. ☐ |
| B. ☐ | P. ☐ | C. ☐ | C. ☐ |

### 15

| S.D. | P.L. | P.G. | S.G. |
|---|---|---|---|
| P. ☐ | F. ☐ | F. ☐ | T. ☐ |
| F. ☐ | W. ☐ | W. ☐ | P. ☐ |
| B. ☐ | P. ☐ | C. ☐ | C. ☐ |

### 16

| S.D. | P.L. | P.G. | S.G. |
|---|---|---|---|
| P. ☐ | F. ☐ | F. ☐ | T. ☐ |
| F. ☐ | W. ☐ | W. ☐ | P. ☐ |
| B. ☐ | P. ☐ | C. ☐ | C. ☐ |

### 21

| S.D. | P.L. | P.G. | S.G. |
|---|---|---|---|
| P. ☐ | F. ☐ | F. ☐ | T. ☐ |
| F. ☐ | W. ☐ | W. ☐ | P. ☐ |
| B. ☐ | P. ☐ | C. ☐ | C. ☐ |

### 22

| S.D. | P.L. | P.G. | S.G. |
|---|---|---|---|
| P. ☐ | F. ☐ | F. ☐ | T. ☐ |
| F. ☐ | W. ☐ | W. ☐ | P. ☐ |
| B. ☐ | P. ☐ | C. ☐ | C. ☐ |

### 23

| S.D. | P.L. | P.G. | S.G. |
|---|---|---|---|
| P. ☐ | F. ☐ | F. ☐ | T. ☐ |
| F. ☐ | W. ☐ | W. ☐ | P. ☐ |
| B. ☐ | P. ☐ | C. ☐ | C. ☐ |

### 24

| S.D. | P.L. | P.G. | S.G. |
|---|---|---|---|
| P. ☐ | F. ☐ | F. ☐ | T. ☐ |
| F. ☐ | W. ☐ | W. ☐ | P. ☐ |
| B. ☐ | P. ☐ | C. ☐ | C. ☐ |

### 29

| S.D. | P.L. | P.G. | S.G. |
|---|---|---|---|
| P. ☐ | F. ☐ | F. ☐ | T. ☐ |
| F. ☐ | W. ☐ | W. ☐ | P. ☐ |
| B. ☐ | P. ☐ | C. ☐ | C. ☐ |

### 30

| S.D. | P.L. | P.G. | S.G. |
|---|---|---|---|
| P. ☐ | F. ☐ | F. ☐ | T. ☐ |
| F. ☐ | W. ☐ | W. ☐ | P. ☐ |
| B. ☐ | P. ☐ | C. ☐ | C. ☐ |

### 31

| S.D. | P.L. | P.G. | S.G. |
|---|---|---|---|
| P. ☐ | F. ☐ | F. ☐ | T. ☐ |
| F. ☐ | W. ☐ | W. ☐ | P. ☐ |
| B. ☐ | P. ☐ | C. ☐ | C. ☐ |

**Proverbs 1:5**

Let those who are wise listen to these proverbs and become even wiser. And let those who understand receive guidance.

## Personal Goals

**Family**

**Work/School/Social**

**Challenge**

## Sport Goals

**Training**

**Performance**

**Competition Results**

Son of Man will die? Who is this Son of Man you are talking about?"

<sup>35</sup>Jesus replied, "My light will shine out for you just a little while longer. Walk in it while you can, so you will not stumble when the darkness falls. If you walk in the darkness, you cannot see where you are going. <sup>36</sup>Believe in the light while there is still time; then you will become children of the light." After saying these things, Jesus went away and was hidden from them.

## The Unbelief of the People

<sup>37</sup>But despite all the miraculous signs he had done, most of the people did not believe in him. <sup>38</sup>This is exactly what Isaiah the prophet had predicted:

"Lord, who has believed our message?
To whom will the Lord reveal his saving power?"

<sup>39</sup>But the people couldn't believe, for as Isaiah also said,
<sup>40</sup>"The Lord has blinded their eyes
and hardened their hearts—
so their eyes cannot see,
and their hearts cannot understand,
and they cannot turn to me
and let me heal them."

<sup>41</sup>Isaiah was referring to Jesus when he made this prediction, because he was given a vision of the Messiah's glory. <sup>42</sup>Many people, including some of the Jewish leaders, believed in him. But they wouldn't admit it to anyone because of their fear that the Pharisees would expel them from the synagogue. <sup>43</sup>For they loved human praise more than the praise of God. <sup>44</sup>Jesus shouted to the crowds, "If you trust me, you are really trusting God who sent me. <sup>45</sup>For when you see me, you are seeing the one who sent me. <sup>46</sup>I have come as a light to shine in this dark world, so that all who put their trust in me will no longer remain in the darkness. <sup>47</sup>If anyone hears me and doesn't obey me, I am not his judge—for I have come to save the world and not to judge it. <sup>48</sup>But all who reject me and my message will be judged at the day of judgement by the truth I have spoken. <sup>49</sup>I don't speak on my own authority. The Father who sent me gave me his own instructions as to what I should say. <sup>50</sup>And I know his instructions lead to eternal life; so I say whatever the Father tells me to say!"

## Jesus Washes His Disciples' Feet

# 13

Before the Passover celebration, Jesus knew that his hour had come to leave this world and return to his Father. He now showed the disciples the full extent of his love. <sup>2</sup>It was time for supper, and the Devil had already enticed Judas, son of Simon Iscariot, to carry out his plan to betray Jesus. <sup>3</sup>Jesus knew that the Father had given him authority over everything and that he had come from God and would return

to God. <sup>4</sup>So he got up from the table, took off his robe, wrapped a towel around his waist, <sup>5</sup>and poured water into a basin. Then he began to wash the disciples' feet and to wipe them with the towel he had around him. <sup>6</sup>When he came to Simon Peter, Peter said to him, "Lord, why are you going to wash my feet?"

<sup>7</sup>Jesus replied, "You don't understand now why I am doing it; someday you will."

<sup>8</sup>"No," Peter protested, "you will never wash my feet!"

Jesus replied, "But if I don't wash you, you won't belong to me."

<sup>9</sup>Simon Peter exclaimed, "Then wash my hands and head as well, Lord, not just my feet!"

<sup>10</sup>Jesus replied, "A person who has bathed all over does not need to wash, except for the feet, to be entirely clean. And you are clean, but that isn't true of everyone here."

<sup>11</sup>For Jesus knew who would betray him. That is what he meant when he said, "Not all of you are clean."

<sup>12</sup>After washing their feet, he put on his robe again and sat down and asked, "Do you understand what I was doing? <sup>13</sup>You call me 'Teacher' and 'Lord,' and you are right, because it is true. <sup>14</sup>And since I, the Lord and Teacher, have washed your feet, you ought to wash each other's feet. <sup>15</sup>I have given you an example to follow. Do as I have done to you. <sup>16</sup>How true it is that a servant is not greater than the master. Nor are messengers more important than the one who sends them. <sup>17</sup>You know these things-now do them! That is the path of blessing.

# WHAT DOES IT MEAN?

### Adoption

Adoption is the giving of the family name and place and privileges of an offspring to someone who is not a descendant by birth. Spiritually it is an act of God's goodness by which he brings people into the number of his family, and makes them share in all the blessings and inheritance he has provided for them. See: 1 Pet. 1:14; 2 John 4; Rom. 8:15-21; Gal. 5:1.

## Jesus Predicts His Betrayal

<sup>18</sup>"I am not saying these things to all of you; I know so well each one of you I chose. The Scriptures declare, 'The one who shares my food has turned against me,' and this will soon come true. <sup>19</sup>I tell you this now, so that when it happens you will believe I am the Messiah. <sup>20</sup>Truly, anyone who welcomes my messenger is welcoming me, and anyone who welcomes me is welcoming the Father who sent me."

<sup>21</sup>Now Jesus was in great anguish of spirit, and he exclaimed,

"The truth is, one of you will betray me!"

<sup>22</sup>The disciples looked at each other, wondering whom he could mean. <sup>23</sup>One of Jesus' disciples, the one Jesus loved, was sitting next to Jesus at the table. <sup>24</sup>Simon Peter motioned to him to ask who would do this terrible thing. <sup>25</sup>Leaning towards Jesus, he asked, "Lord, who is it?"

<sup>26</sup>Jesus said, "It is the one to whom I give the bread dipped in the sauce." And when he had dipped it, he gave it to Judas, son of Simon Iscariot. <sup>27</sup>As soon as Judas had eaten the bread, Satan entered into him. Then Jesus told him, "Hurry. Do it now." <sup>28</sup>None of the others at the table knew what Jesus meant. <sup>29</sup>Since Judas was their treasurer, some thought Jesus was telling him to go and pay for the food or to give some money to the poor. <sup>30</sup>So Judas left at once, going out into the night.

## Jesus Predicts Peter's Denial

<sup>31</sup>As soon as Judas left the room, Jesus said, "The time has come for me, the Son of Man, to enter into my glory, and God will receive glory because of all that happens to me. <sup>32</sup>And God will bring me into my glory very soon. <sup>33</sup>Dear children, how brief are these moments before I must go away and leave you!

Then, though you search for me, you cannot come to me—just as I told the Jewish leaders. ³⁴So now I am giving you a new commandment: Love each other. Just as I have loved you, you should love each other. ³⁵**Your love for one another will prove to the world that you are my disciples.**"

³⁶Simon Peter said, "Lord, where are you going?" And Jesus replied, "You can't go with me now, but you will follow me later."

³⁷"But why can't I come now, Lord?" he asked. "I am ready to die for you."

³⁸Jesus answered, "Die for me? No, before the cock crows tomorrow morning, you will deny three times that you even know me.

## Jesus, the Way to the Father

# 14

"Don't be troubled. You trust God, now trust in me. ²There are many rooms in my Father's home, and I am going to prepare a place for you. If this were not so, I would tell you plainly. ³When everything is ready, I will come and get you, so that you will always be with me where I am. ⁴And you know where I am going and how to get there."

⁵"No, we don't know, Lord," Thomas said. "We haven't any idea where you are going, so how can we know the way?"

⁶Jesus told him, "I am the way, the truth, and the life. No one can come to the Father except through me. ⁷If you had known who I am, then you would have known who my Father is. From now on you know him and have seen him!"

⁸Philip said, "Lord, show us the Father and we will be satisfied."

⁹Jesus replied, "Philip, don't you even yet know who I am, even after all the time I have been with you? Anyone who has seen me has seen the Father! So why are you asking to see him?

¹⁰Don't you believe that I am in the Father and the Father is in me? The words I say are not my own, but my Father who lives in me does his work through me. ¹¹Just believe that I am in the Father and the Father is in me. Or at least believe because of what you have seen me do.

¹²"The truth is, anyone who believes in me will do the same works I have done, and even greater works, because I am going to be with the Father. ¹³You can ask for anything in my name, and I will do it, because the work of the Son brings glory to the Father. ¹⁴Yes, ask anything in my name, and I will do it!

## Jesus Promises the Holy Spirit

¹⁵"If you love me, obey my commandments. ¹⁶And I will ask the Father, and he will give you another Counsellor, who will never leave you. ¹⁷He is the Holy Spirit, who leads into all truth. The world at large cannot receive him, because it isn't looking for him and doesn't recognize him. But you do, because he lives with you now and later will be in you. ¹⁸No, I will not abandon you as orphans—I will come to you. ¹⁹In just a little while the world will not see me again, but you will. For I will live again, and you will, too. ²⁰When I am raised to life again, you will know that I am in my Father, and you are in me, and I am in you. ²¹Those who obey my commandments are the ones who love me. And because they love me, my Father will love them, and I will love them. And I will reveal myself to each one of them."

²²Judas (not Judas Iscariot, but the other disciple with that name) said to him, "Lord, why are you going to reveal yourself only to us and not to the world at large?"

²³Jesus replied, "All those who love me will do what I say. My Father will love them, and we will come to them and live with them. ²⁴Anyone who doesn't love me will not do what I say. And remember, my words are not my own. This message is from the Father who sent me. ²⁵I am telling you these things now while I am still with you. ²⁶But when the Father sends the Counsellor as my representative—and by the Counsellor I mean the Holy Spirit—he will teach you

**When people say all religions lead to God**

**John 14:6**

Jesus told him, "I am the way, the truth, and the life. No one can come to the Father except through me."

everything and will remind you of everything I myself have told you.

²⁷"I am leaving you with a gift—peace of mind and heart. And the peace I give isn't like the peace the world gives. So don't be troubled or afraid. ²⁸Remember what I told you: I am going away, but I will come back to you again. If you really love me, you will be very happy for me, because now I can go to the Father, who is greater than I am. ²⁹I have told you these things before they happen so that you will believe when they do happen.

³⁰"I don't have much more time to talk to you, because the prince of this world approaches. He has no power over me, ³¹but I will do what the Father requires of me, so that the world will know that I love the Father. Come, let's be going.

## Jesus, the True Vine

# 15

"I am the true vine, and my Father is the gardener. ²He cuts off every branch that doesn't produce fruit, and he prunes the branches that do bear fruit so they will produce even more. ³You have already been pruned for greater fruitfulness by the message I have given you. ⁴Remain in me, and I will remain in you. For a branch cannot produce fruit if it is severed from the vine, and you cannot be fruitful apart from me.

⁵"Yes, I am the vine; you are the branches. Those who remain

## When you lose your form:

If a skill slump occurs, then switch your practice routine to include specific skill training to your troubled area and performance sequence. This suggested solution to the problem may help some athletes, but not all. Some people may require different techniques to solve their particular problem.

in me, and I in them, will produce much fruit. For apart from me you can do nothing. ⁶Anyone who parts from me is thrown away like a useless branch and withers. Such branches are gathered into a pile to be burned. ⁷But if you stay joined to me and my words remain in you, you may ask any request you like, and it will be granted! ⁸My true disciples produce much fruit. This brings great glory to my Father.

⁹"I have loved you even as the Father has loved me. Remain in my love. ¹⁰When you obey me, you remain in my love, just as I obey my Father and remain in his love. ¹¹I have told you this so that you will be filled with my joy. Yes, your joy will overflow! ¹²I command you to love each other in the same way that I love you. ¹³And here is how to measure it—the greatest love is shown when people lay down their lives for their friends. ¹⁴You are my friends if you obey me. ¹⁵I no longer call you servants, because a master doesn't confide in his servants. Now you are my friends, since I have told you everything the Father told me. ¹⁶You didn't choose me. I chose you. I appointed you to go and produce fruit that will last, so that the Father will give you whatever you ask for, using my name. ¹⁷I command you to love each other.

## The World's Hatred

¹⁸"When the world hates you, remember it hated me before it hated you. ¹⁹The world would love you if you belonged to it, but you don't. I chose you to come out of the world, and so it hates you. ²⁰Do you remember what I told you? 'A servant is not greater than the master.' Since they persecuted me, naturally they will persecute you. And if they had listened to me, they would listen to you! ²¹The people of the world will hate you because you belong to me, for they don't know God who sent me. ²²They would not be guilty if I had not come and spoken to them. But now they have no excuse for their sin.

²³Anyone who hates me hates my Father, too. ²⁴If I hadn't done such miraculous signs among them that no one else could do, they would not be counted guilty. But as it is, they saw all that I did and yet hated both of us—me and my Father. ²⁵This has fulfilled what the Scriptures said: 'They hated me without cause.'

²⁶"But I will send you the Counsellor—the Spirit of truth. He will come to you from the Father and will tell you all about me. ²⁷And you must also tell others about me because you have been with me from the beginning.

# 16

"I have told you these things so that you won't fall away. ²For you will be expelled from the synagogues, and the time is coming when those who kill you will think they are doing God a service. ³This is because they have never known the Father or me. ⁴Yes, I'm telling you these things now, so that when they happen, you will remember I warned you. I didn't tell you earlier because I was going to be with you for a while longer.

## The Work of the Holy Spirit

⁵"But now I am going away to the one who sent me, and none of you has asked me where I am going. ⁶Instead, you are very sad. ⁷But it is actually best for you that I go away, because if I don't, the Counsellor won't come. If I do go away, he will come because I will send him to you. ⁸And when he comes, he will convince the world of its sin, and of God's righteousness, and of the coming judgement. ⁹The world's sin is unbelief in me. ¹⁰Righteousness is available because I go to the Father, and you will see me no more. ¹¹Judgement will come because the prince of this world has already been judged.

¹²"Oh, there is so much more I want to tell you, but you can't bear it now. ¹³When the Spirit of truth comes, he will guide you into all truth. He will not be presenting his own ideas; he will be telling you what he has heard. He will tell you about the future. ¹⁴He will bring me glory by revealing to you whatever he receives from me. ¹⁵All that the Father has is mine; this is what I mean when I say that the Spirit will reveal to you whatever he receives from me.

## Sadness Will Be Turned to Joy

¹⁶"In just a little while I will be gone, and you won't see me any more. Then, just a little while after that,

you will see me again."

¹⁷The disciples asked each other, "What does he mean when he says, 'You won't see me, and then you will see me'? And what does he mean when he says, 'I am going to the Father'? ¹⁸And what does he mean by 'a little while'? We don't understand."

¹⁹Jesus realized they wanted to ask him, so he said, "Are you asking yourselves what I meant? I said in just a little while I will be gone, and you won't see me any more. Then, just a little while after that, you will see me again. ²⁰Truly, you will weep and mourn over what is going to happen to me, but the world will rejoice. You will grieve, but your grief will suddenly turn to wonderful joy when you see me again. ²¹It will be like a woman experiencing the pains of labour. When her child is born, her anguish gives place to joy because she has brought a new person into the world. ²²You have sorrow now, but I will see you again; then you will rejoice, and no one can rob you of that joy. ²³At that time you won't need to ask me for anything. The truth is, you can go directly to the Father and ask him, and he will grant your request because you use my name. ²⁴You haven't done this before. Ask, using my name, and you will receive, and you will have abundant joy.

²⁵"I have spoken of these matters in parables, but the time will come when this will not be necessary, and I will tell you plainly all about the Father. ²⁶Then you will ask in my name. I'm not saying I will ask the Father on your behalf, ²⁷for the Father himself loves you dearly because you love me and believe that I came from God. ²⁸**Yes, I came from the Father into the world, and I will leave the world and return to the Father."**

²⁹Then his disciples said, "At last you are speaking plainly and not in parables. ³⁰Now we understand that you know everything and don't need anyone to tell you anything. From this we believe that you came from God."

³¹Jesus asked, "Do you finally believe? ³²But the time is coming—in fact, it is already here—when you will be scattered, each one going his own way, leaving me alone. Yet I am not alone because the Father is

## Is looking at pornography wrong?

Yes, and very dangerous. Like trying to drink salt water to quench your thirst, sexually explicit images will not satisfy your sexual desires. Your mind fills with unrealistic and unhealthy images that distort a healthy sexual relationship, which God intended for marriage.

With the Internet, this is a modern landmine. Create ways to block these sites and work hard to control your thoughts. Resist temptation to look at pornography and pray for strength.

with me. [33]I have told you all this so that you may have peace in me. Here on earth you will have many trials and sorrows. But take heart, because I have overcome the world."

Bible FACTS

**When Jesus was crucified a sign was posted on the cross. The exact phrase is slightly different in each of the four gospels. "This is Jesus, the King of the Jews". (Matt. 27:37)**

## The Prayer of Jesus

# 17

When Jesus had finished saying all these things, he looked up to heaven and said, "Father, the time has come. Glorify your Son so he can give glory back to you. [2]For you have given him authority over everyone in all the earth. He gives eternal life to each one you have given him. [3]And this is the way to have eternal life—to know you, the only true God, and Jesus Christ, the one you sent to earth. [4]I brought glory to you here on earth by doing everything you told me to do. [5]And now, Father, bring me into the glory we shared before the world began.

[6]"I have told these men about you. They were in the world, but then you gave them to me. Actually, they were always yours, and you gave them to me; and they have kept your word. [7]Now they know that everything I have is a gift from you, [8]for I have passed on to them the words you gave me; and they accepted them and know that I came from you, and they believe you sent me.

[9]"My prayer is not for the world, but for those you have given me, because they belong to you. [10]And all of them, since they are mine, belong to you; and you have given them back to me, so they are my glory! [11]Now I am departing from the world; I am leaving them behind and coming to you. Holy Father, keep them and care for them—all those you have given

me—so that they will be united just as we are. [12]During my time here, I have kept them safe. I guarded them so that not one was lost, except the one heading for destruction, as the Scriptures foretold.

[13]"And now I am coming to you. I have told them many things while I was with them so they would be filled with my joy. [14]I have given them your word. And the world hates them because they do not belong to the world, just as I do not. [15]I'm not asking you to take them out of the world, but to keep them safe from the evil one. [16]They are not part of this world any more than I am. [17]Make them pure and holy by teaching them your words of truth. [18]As you sent me into the world, I am sending them into the world. [19]And I give myself entirely to you so they also might be entirely yours.

[20]"I am praying not only for these disciples but also for all who will ever believe in me because of their testimony. [21]My prayer for all of them is that they will be one, just as you and I are one, Father—that just as you are in me and I am in you, so they will be in us, and the world will believe you sent me. [22]I have given them the glory you gave me, so that they may be one, as we are— [23]I in them and you in me, all being perfected into one. Then the world will know that you sent me and will understand that you love them as much as you love me. [24]Father, I want these whom you've given me to be with me, so they can see my glory. You gave me the glory because you loved me even before the world began!

[25]"O righteous Father, the world doesn't know you, but I do; and these disciples know you sent me. [26]And I have revealed you to them and will keep on revealing you. I will do this so that your love for me may be in them and I in them."

## Jesus Is Betrayed and Arrested

# 18

After saying these things, Jesus crossed the Kidron Valley with his disciples and entered a grove of olive trees. [2]Judas, the betrayer, knew this place, because Jesus had gone there many times with his disciples. [3]The leading priests and Pharisees had given Judas a battalion of Roman soldiers and Temple guards to accompany him. Now with blazing torches, lanterns, and weapons, they arrived at the olive grove. [4]Jesus fully realized all that was going to happen to him. Stepping forward to meet them, he asked, "Whom are you looking for?"

[5]"Jesus of Nazareth," they replied.

"I am he," Jesus said. Judas was standing there with them when Jesus identified himself. [6]And as he said, "I am he," they all fell backwards to the ground!

[7]Once more he asked them, "Whom are you searching for?" And again they replied, "Jesus of Nazareth."

[8]"I told you that I am he," Jesus said. "And since I am the one you want, let these others go." [9]He did this to fulfil his own statement: "I have not lost a single one of those you gave me."

[10]Then Simon Peter drew a sword and slashed off the right ear of Malchus, the high priest's servant. [11]But Jesus said to Peter, "Put your sword back into its sheath. Shall I not drink from the cup the Father has given me?"

## Annas Questions Jesus

[12]So the soldiers, their commanding officer, and the Temple guards arrested Jesus and tied him up. [13]First they took him to Annas, the father-in-law of Caiaphas, the high priest that year. [14]Caiaphas was the one who had told the other Jewish leaders, "Better that one should die for all."

## Peter's First Denial

[15]Simon Peter followed along behind, as did another of the disciples. That other disciple was acquainted with the high priest, so he was allowed to enter the courtyard with Jesus. [16]Peter stood outside the gate. Then the other disciple spoke to the woman watching at the gate, and she let Peter in. [17]The woman asked Peter, "Aren't you one of Jesus' disciples?"

"No," he said, "I am not."

[18]The guards and the household servants were standing around a charcoal fire they had made because it was cold. And Peter stood there with them, warming himself.

## The High Priest Questions Jesus

[19]Inside, the high priest began asking Jesus about his followers and what he had been teaching them. [20]Jesus replied, "What I teach is widely known, because I have preached regularly in the synagogues and the Temple. I have been heard by people everywhere, and I teach nothing in private that I have not said in public. [21]Why are you asking me this question? Ask those who heard me. They know what I said."

[22]One of the Temple guards standing there struck Jesus on the face. "Is that the way to answer the high priest?" he demanded.

[23]Jesus replied, "If I said anything wrong, you must give evidence for it. Should you hit a man for telling the truth?" [24]Then Annas bound Jesus and sent him to Caiaphas, the high priest.

## Peter's Second and Third Denials

[25]Meanwhile, as Simon Peter was standing by the fire, they

asked him again, "Aren't you one of his disciples?"

"I am not," he said.

²⁶But one of the household servants of the high priest, a relative of the man whose ear Peter had cut off, asked, "Didn't I see you out there in the olive grove with Jesus?" ²⁷Again Peter denied it. And immediately a cock crowed.

## Jesus' Trial before Pilate

²⁸Jesus' trial before Caiaphas ended in the early hours of the morning. Then he was taken to the headquarters of the Roman governor. His accusers didn't go in themselves because it would defile them, and they wouldn't be allowed to celebrate the Passover feast. ²⁹So Pilate, the governor, went out to them and asked, "What is your charge against this man?"

³⁰"We wouldn't have handed him over to you if he weren't a criminal!" they retorted.

³¹"Then take him away and judge him by your own laws," Pilate told them.

"Only the Romans are permitted to execute someone," the Jewish leaders replied. ³²This fulfilled Jesus' prediction about the way he would die.

³³Then Pilate went back inside and called for Jesus to be brought to him. "Are you the King of the Jews?" he asked him.

³⁴Jesus replied, "Is this your own question, or did others tell you about me?"

³⁵"Am I a Jew?" Pilate asked. "Your own people and their leading priests brought you here. Why? What have you done?"

³⁶**Then Jesus answered, "I am not an earthly king. If I were, my followers would have fought when I was arrested by the Jewish leaders. But my Kingdom is not of this world."**

³⁷Pilate replied, "You are a king then?"

"You say that I am a king, and you are right," Jesus said. "I was born for that purpose. And I came to bring truth to the world. All who love the truth recognize that what I say is true."

³⁸"What is truth?" Pilate asked. Then he went out again to the people and told them, "He is not guilty of any crime.

³⁹But you have a custom of asking me to release someone from prison each year at Passover. So if you want me to, I'll release the King of the Jews."

⁴⁰But they shouted back, "No! Not this man, but Barabbas!" (Barabbas was a criminal.)

## Jesus Sentenced to Death

# 19

Then Pilate had Jesus flogged with a lead-tipped whip.

²The soldiers made a crown of long, sharp thorns and put it on his head, and they put a royal purple robe on him. ³"Hail! King of the Jews!" they mocked, and they hit him with their fists.

⁴Pilate went outside again and said to the people, "I am going to bring him out to you now, but understand clearly that I find him not guilty." ⁵Then Jesus came out wearing the crown of thorns and the purple robe. And Pilate said, "Here is the man!"

⁶When they saw him, the leading priests and Temple guards began shouting, "Crucify! Crucify!"

"You crucify him," Pilate said. "I find him not guilty."

⁷The Jewish leaders replied, "By our laws he ought to die because he called himself the Son of God."

⁸When Pilate heard this, he was more frightened than ever. ⁹He took Jesus back into the headquarters again and asked him, "Where are you from?" But Jesus gave no answer. ¹⁰"You won't talk to me?" Pilate demanded. "Don't you realize that I have the power to release you or to crucify you?"

¹¹Then Jesus said, "You would have no power over me at all unless it were given to you from above. So the one who brought me to you has the greater sin."

¹²Then Pilate tried to release him, but the Jewish leaders told him, "If you release this man, you are not a friend of Caesar. Anyone who declares himself a king is a rebel against Caesar."

¹³When they said this, Pilate brought Jesus out to them again. Then Pilate sat down on the judgement seat on the platform that is called the Stone Pavement (in Hebrew, Gabbatha).

¹⁴It was now about noon of the day of preparation for the Passover. And Pilate said to the people, "Here is your king!"

¹⁵"Away with him," they yelled. "Away with him—crucify him!"

"What? Crucify your king?" Pilate asked.

"We have no king but Caesar," the leading priests shouted back.

¹⁶Then Pilate gave Jesus to them to be crucified.

## The Crucifixion

So they took Jesus and led him away. ¹⁷Carrying the cross by himself, Jesus went to the place called Skull Hill (in Hebrew, *Golgotha*). ¹⁸There they crucified him. There were two others crucified with him, one on either side, with Jesus between them. ¹⁹And Pilate posted a sign over him that read, "Jesus of Nazareth, the King of the Jews."

²⁰The place where Jesus was crucified was near the city; and the sign was written in Hebrew, Latin, and Greek, so that many people could read it.

²¹Then the leading priests said to Pilate, "Change it from 'The King of the Jews' to 'He said, I am King of the Jews.'"

²²Pilate replied, "What I have written, I have written. It stays exactly as it is."

²³When the soldiers had crucified Jesus, they divided his clothes among the four of them. They also took his robe, but it was seamless, woven in one piece from the top. ²⁴So they said, "Let's not tear it but throw dice to see who gets it." This fulfilled the Scripture that says, "They divided my clothes among themselves and threw dice for my robe." So that is what they did.

²⁵Standing near the cross were Jesus' mother, and his mother's sister, Mary (the wife of Clopas), and Mary Magdalene.

²⁶When Jesus saw his mother standing there beside the disciple he loved, he said to her, "Woman, he is your son." ²⁷And he said to this disciple, "She is your mother." And from then on this disciple took her into his home.

CH 19:28-35 WHAT'S IT SAYING?

WHAT AM I GOING TO DO ABOUT IT?

## The Death of Jesus

²⁸Jesus knew that everything was now finished, and to fulfil the Scriptures he said, "I am thirsty." ²⁹A jar of sour wine was sitting there, so they soaked a sponge in it, put it on a hyssop branch, and held it up to his

lips. ³⁰When Jesus had tasted it, he said, "It is finished!" Then he bowed his head and gave up his spirit.

³¹The Jewish leaders didn't want the victims hanging there the next day, which was the Sabbath (and a very special Sabbath at that, because it was the Passover), so they asked Pilate to hasten their deaths by ordering that their legs be broken. Then their bodies could be taken down. ³²So the soldiers came and broke the legs of the two men crucified with Jesus. ³³But when they came to Jesus, they saw that he was dead

already, so they didn't break his legs. ³⁴One of the soldiers, however, pierced his side with a spear, and blood and water flowed out. ³⁵This report is from an eyewitness giving an accurate account; it is presented so that you also can believe. ³⁶These things happened in fulfilment of the Scriptures that say, "Not one of his bones will be broken," ³⁷and "They will look on him whom they pierced."

## The Burial of Jesus

³⁸Afterwards Joseph of Arimathea, who had been a

secret disciple of Jesus (because he feared the Jewish leaders), asked Pilate for permission to take Jesus' body down. When Pilate gave him permission, he came and took the body away. ³⁹Nicodemus, the man who had come to Jesus at night, also came, bringing about thirty-three kilograms of embalming ointment made from myrrh and aloes. ⁴⁰Together they wrapped Jesus' body in a long linen cloth with the spices, as is the Jewish custom of burial.

⁴¹The place of crucifixion was near a garden, where there was a new tomb, never used before. ⁴²And so, because it was the day of preparation before the Passover and since the tomb was close at hand, they laid Jesus there.

## PERSONAL ASSESSMENTS

### TEAM POSITION  On a scale from 1 to 10

**Besides playing on the Team:**

- [ ] I like to 'take charge' on a team.
- [ ] I know how to build the team's spirit even when we are losing.
- [ ] I can help other team members to better their skill.
- [ ] I see when a team-mate is down and know how to encourage them.
- [ ] I want to include others to get involved on the team.
- [ ] I want to help the team succeed.
- [ ] I enjoy planning strategy and team plays.
- [ ] I enjoy organising the team and helping them achieve success.
- [ ] I enjoy teaching the techniques and developing others' skills.
- [ ] I really enjoy hanging around my team-mates and having them to my house.
- [ ] I enjoy creating and equipping the team.

## The Resurrection

# 20

Early on Sunday morning, while it was still dark, Mary Magdalene came to the tomb and found that the stone had been rolled away from the entrance. ²She ran and found Simon Peter and the other disciple, the one whom Jesus loved. She said, "They have taken the Lord's body out of the tomb, and I don't know where they have put him!"

³Peter and the other disciple ran to the tomb to see. ⁴The other disciple outran Peter and got there first.

⁵He stooped and looked in and saw the linen cloth lying there, but he didn't go in. ⁶Then Simon Peter arrived and went inside. He also noticed the linen wrappings lying there, ⁷while the cloth that had covered Jesus' head was folded up and lying to the side. ⁸Then the other disciple also went in, and he saw and believed—⁹for until then they hadn't realized that the Scriptures said he would rise from the dead. ¹⁰Then they went home.

## Jesus Appears to Mary Magdalene

¹¹Mary was standing outside the tomb crying, and as she wept, she stooped and looked in. ¹²She saw two white-robed angels sitting at the head and foot of the place where the body of Jesus had been lying. ¹³"Why are you crying?" the angels asked her.

"Because they have taken away my Lord," she replied, "and I don't know where they have put him."

¹⁴She glanced over her shoulder and saw someone standing behind her. It was Jesus, but she didn't recognize him. ¹⁵"Why are you crying?" Jesus asked her. "Who are you looking for?" She thought he was the gardener. "Sir," she said, "if you have taken him away, tell me where you have put him, and I will go and get him."

¹⁶"Mary!" Jesus said.

She turned towards him and exclaimed, "Teacher!"

¹⁷"Don't cling to me," Jesus said, "for I haven't yet ascended to the Father. But go and find my brothers and tell them that I am ascending to my Father and your Father, my God and your God."

¹⁸Mary Magdalene found the disciples and told them, "I have seen the Lord!" Then she gave them his message.

## Jesus Appears to His Disciples

¹⁹That evening, on the first day of the week, the disciples were meeting behind locked doors because they were afraid of the Jewish leaders. Suddenly, Jesus was standing there among them! "Peace be with you," he said. ²⁰As he spoke, he held out his hands for them to see, and he showed them his side. They were filled with joy when they saw their Lord! ²¹He spoke to them again and said, "Peace be with you. As the

## count on it

### You don't have to be good to go to God!

Have you ever felt like you were too messed up to meet with God? Have you ever felt some strange resistance keeping you from praying or reading your Bible? Did you ever feel you had to somehow get your life straight before you could live the Christian life? Don't worry about it! Jesus came to help you in your trouble. He is the great doctor. Go to him with your problems. Not going to him is like waiting until you are cured of a deadly disease before you go to a doctor. Jesus came to help! "Healthy people don't need a doctor - sick people do. I have come to call sinners, not those who think they are already good enough."

Mark 2:17

**Count on it!**

Father has sent me, so I send you." ²²Then he breathed on them and said to them, "Receive the Holy Spirit. ²³If you forgive anyone's sins, they are forgiven. If you refuse to forgive them, they are unforgiven."

## Jesus Appears to Thomas

²⁴One of the disciples, Thomas (nicknamed the Twin), was not with the others when Jesus came. ²⁵They told him,

"We have seen the Lord!" But he replied, "I won't believe it unless I see the nail wounds in his hands,

put my fingers into them, and place my hand into the wound in his side."

²⁶Eight days later the disciples were together again, and this time Thomas was with them. The doors were locked; but suddenly, as before, Jesus was standing among them. He said, "Peace be with you." ²⁷Then he said to Thomas, "Put your finger here and see my hands. Put your hand into the wound in my side. Don't be faithless any longer. Believe!"

²⁸"My Lord and my God!" Thomas exclaimed.

²⁹**Then Jesus told him, "You believe because you have seen me. Blessed are those who haven't seen me and believe anyway."**

## Purpose of the Book

³⁰Jesus' disciples saw him do many other miraculous signs besides the ones recorded in this book. ³¹But these are written so that you may believe that Jesus is the Messiah, the Son of God, and that by believing in him you will have life.

## Jesus Appears to Seven Disciples

# 21

Later Jesus appeared again to the disciples beside the Sea of Galilee. This is how it happened. ²Several of the disciples were there—Simon Peter, Thomas (nicknamed the Twin), Nathanael from Cana in Galilee, the sons of Zebedee, and two other disciples.

³Simon Peter said, "I'm going fishing."

"We'll come, too," they all said. So they went out in the boat, but they caught nothing all night.

⁴At dawn the disciples saw Jesus standing on the beach, but they couldn't see who he was. ⁵He called out, "Friends, have you caught any fish?"

"No," they replied.

⁶Then he said, "Throw out your net on the right-hand side of the boat, and you'll get plenty of fish!" So they did, and they couldn't draw in the net because there were so many fish in it.

⁷Then the disciple whom Jesus loved said to Peter, "It is the Lord!" When Simon Peter heard that it was the Lord, he put on his tunic (for he had stripped for work), jumped into the water, and swam ashore. ⁸The others stayed with the boat and pulled the loaded net to the shore, for they were only about ninety metres from shore. ⁹When they got there, they saw that a charcoal fire was burning and fish were frying over it, and there was bread.

[10]"Bring some of the fish you've just caught," Jesus said. [11]So Simon Peter went aboard and dragged the net to the shore. There were [153] large fish, and yet the net hadn't torn.

[12]"Now come and have some breakfast!" Jesus said. And no one dared ask him if he really was the Lord because they were sure of it. [13]Then Jesus served them the bread and the fish. [14]This was the third time Jesus had appeared to his disciples since he had been raised from the dead.

## Jesus Challenges Peter

[15]After breakfast Jesus said to Simon Peter, "Simon son of John, do you love me more than these?"

"Yes, Lord," Peter replied, "you know I love you."

"Then feed my lambs," Jesus told him.

[16]Jesus repeated the question: "Simon son of John, do you love me?"

"Yes, Lord," Peter said, "you know I love you."

"Then take care of my sheep," Jesus said.

[17]Once more he asked him, "Simon son of John, do you love me?"

Peter was grieved that Jesus asked the question a third time. He said, "Lord, you know everything. You know I love you."

Jesus said, "Then feed my sheep. [18]The truth is, when you were young, you were able to do as you liked and go wherever you wanted to. But when you are old, you will stretch out your hands, and others will direct you and take you where you don't want to go." [19]Jesus said this to let him know what kind of death he would die to glorify God. Then Jesus told him, "Follow me."

[20]Peter turned around and saw the disciple Jesus loved following them—the one who had leaned over to Jesus during supper and asked, "Lord, who among us will betray you?" [21]Peter asked Jesus, "What about him, Lord?"

[22]Jesus replied, "If I want him to remain alive until I return, what is that to you? You follow me."

[23]So the rumour spread among the community of believers that that disciple wouldn't die. But that isn't what Jesus said at all. He only said, "If I want him to remain alive until I return, what is that to you?"

## Conclusion

[24]This is that disciple who saw these events and recorded them here. And we all know that his account of these things is accurate.

[25]**And I suppose that if all the other things Jesus did were written down, the whole world could not contain the books.**

# Joining the Team

'I am the way, the truth and the life. No one can come to the Father except through me.'
John 14:6

At some point in your life you decided to get involved in sport. Your mother or father may have been sporty, your brothers, sisters, and friends may be been sporty, and you may have gone to an athletic school. However, being around sport does not make you an athlete. You may have had athletic attributes for example 'good balance', 'a keen eye', or 'an aggressive attitude'. But until you join a team, you are not really a sports person; you are more like a fan. At a certain point in your life, you made the transition from fan to participant. You signed up, tried out and were chosen for some sort of organised sport.

A few legendary sports stars grew up in remote areas of the world. As children they heard vague echoes of the sport and team they would one day compete for in distant lands. But someone noticed them and introduced them to the foreign world and seemingly strange activities they would soon outrival. Other sports stars were almost bred for sport, they gave the impression of coming out of the womb with a racquet in their hand. Some great pros are pedigrees from second or third generation

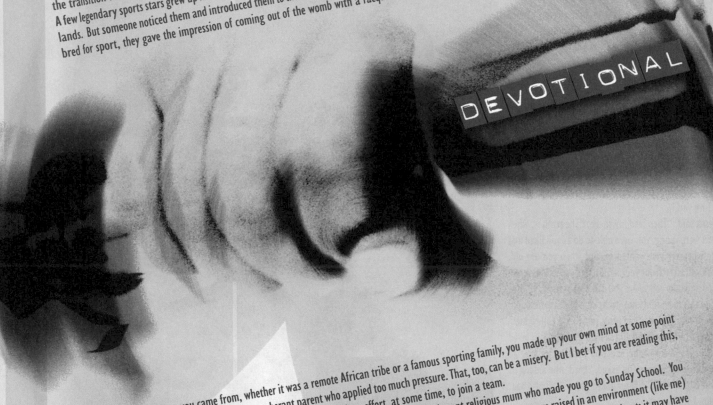

sporting heroes. Regardless of where you came from, whether it was a remote African tribe or a famous sporting family, you made up your own mind at some point to join a team. Or you may have been pushed by an over-exuberant parent who applied too much pressure. That, too, can be a misery. But I bet if you are reading this, you are probably old enough to make decisions for yourself. You made a conscious effort, at some time, to join a team.

The idea of being picked for a team is not too far off the Christian life. You may have had an over-exuberant religious mum who made you go to Sunday School. You may have had religious family or friends. Perhaps you went to a religious school or live in a 'Christian' country. Or maybe you were raised in an environment (like me) remote from most things Christian. You may have peeked over the fence into that strange religious world and wondered what those people were all about; it may have seemed so foreign, so strange. You dreaded thinking about entering that religious world and the changes that may occur in your life. Yet something drew you, or is now drawing you to God. Until you make the decision for yourself (your mum, friend, husband or wife cannot make that decision) you will merely be a spectator on the sidelines. Until you say,

'Yes I want to be on God's Team (Team Jesus)', the best you can be is just a religious fan. This book is a challenge to sign up, and to compete on Jesus' team, to build the 'inner life' and participate with Christ.

## Reflection
Where am I in my Christian life? A spectator, an ardent fan, or a participant?

## Prayer
Help me, Almighty God, to participate in the spiritual life.

'Come follow me'
Jesus

Nicked from: A Sporting Guide to Eternity, Steve Connor,
Christian Focus Publications - ISBN 1-85792-746-X

# Acts

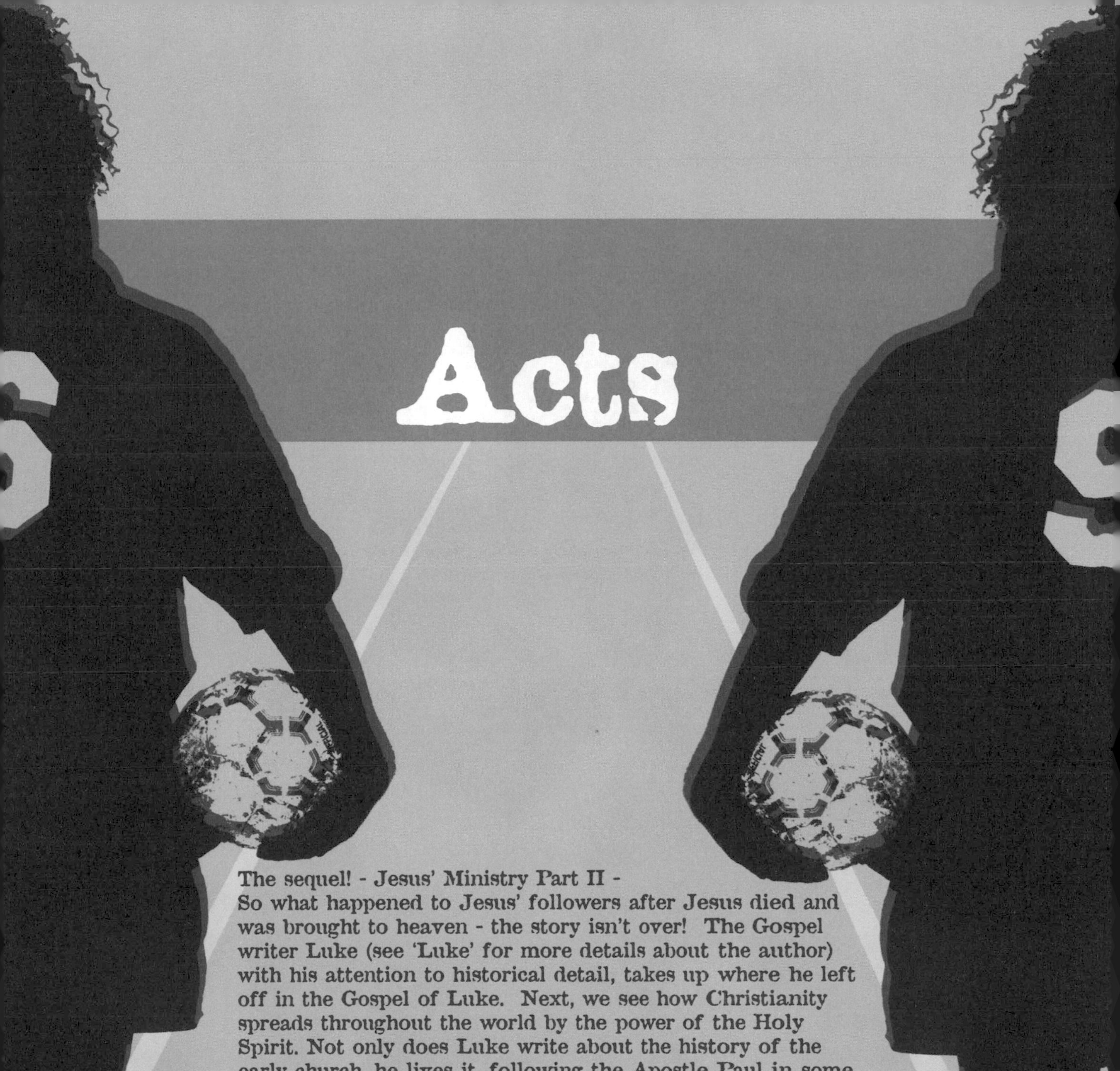

The sequel! - Jesus' Ministry Part II -
So what happened to Jesus' followers after Jesus died and
was brought to heaven - the story isn't over!  The Gospel
writer Luke (see 'Luke' for more details about the author)
with his attention to historical detail, takes up where he left
off in the Gospel of Luke.  Next, we see how Christianity
spreads throughout the world by the power of the Holy
Spirit. Not only does Luke write about the history of the
early church, he lives it, following the Apostle Paul in some
dangerous and exciting assignments!  Read on.

Luke records:
• Jesus' resurrection
• His ascension to Heaven
• The obedience of the Apostles
• The coming of the Holy Spirit
• The progress of Jesus' followers encouraging the church.
• The persecution of Jesus' followers including Stephen's execution.
• The dispersal of Jesus' followers.
• The spread of the good news and the impact it has on new areas.
• The dramatic conversion of Paul.
• Lastly we read of Paul's courage and commitment to spread Christ's
  message further throughout the world.

· UNITY · POWER ·
# GOD'S TEAM

# ACTS

## The Promise of the Holy Spirit

# 1

Dear Theophilus:

In my first book I told you about everything Jesus began to do and teach [2]until the day he ascended to heaven after giving his chosen apostles further instructions from the Holy Spirit. [3]**During the forty days after his crucifixion, he appeared to the apostles from time to time and proved to them in many ways that he was actually alive. On these occasions he talked to them about the Kingdom of God.**

[4]In one of these meetings as he was eating a meal with them, he told them, "Do not leave Jerusalem until the Father sends you what he promised. Remember, I have told you about this before. [5]John baptized with water, but in just a few days you will be baptized with the Holy Spirit."

## The Ascension of Jesus

[6]When the apostles were with Jesus, they kept asking him, "Lord, are you going to free Israel now and restore our kingdom?"

[7]"The Father sets those dates," he replied, "and they are not for you to know. [8]But when the Holy Spirit has come upon you, you will receive power and will tell people about me everywhere—in Jerusalem, throughout Judea, in Samaria, and to the ends of the earth."

[9]It was not long after he said this that he was taken up into the sky while they were watching, and he disappeared into a cloud. [10]As they were straining their eyes to see him, two white-robed men suddenly stood there among them. [11]They said, "Men of Galilee, why are you standing here staring at the sky? Jesus has been taken away from you into heaven. And someday, just as you saw him go, he will return!"

## Matthias Replaces Judas

[12]The apostles were at the Mount of Olives when this happened, so they walked the kilometre back to Jerusalem. [13]Then they went to the upstairs room of the house where they were staying. Here is the list of those who were present:

Peter,
John,
James,
Andrew,
Philip,
Thomas,
Bartholomew,
Matthew,
James (son of Alphaeus),
Simon (the Zealot),
and Judas (son of James).

**Esther (Old Testament) is the only book in the Bible that does not contain the word "God".**

[14]They all met together continually for prayer, along with Mary the mother of Jesus, several other women, and the brothers of Jesus.

[15]During this time, on a day when about 120 believers were present, Peter stood up and addressed them as follows:

[16]"Brothers, it was necessary for the Scriptures to be fulfilled concerning Judas, who guided the Temple police to arrest Jesus. This was predicted long ago by the Holy Spirit, speaking through King David. [17]Judas was one of us, chosen to share in the ministry with us."

[18](Judas bought a field with the money he received for his treachery, and falling there, he burst open, spilling out his intestines. [19]The news of his death spread rapidly among all the people of Jerusalem, and they gave the place the Aramaic name Akeldama, which means "Field of Blood.")

[20]Peter continued, "This was predicted in the book of Psalms, where it says, 'Let his home become desolate, with no one living in it.' And again, 'Let his position be given to someone else.'

[21]"So now we must choose another man to take Judas's place. It must be someone who has been with us all the time that we were with the Lord Jesus—[22]from the time he was baptized by John until the day he was taken from us into heaven. Whoever is chosen will join us as a witness of Jesus' resurrection."

[23]So they nominated two men: Joseph called Barsabbas (also known as Justus) and Matthias. [24]Then they all prayed for the right man to be chosen. "O Lord," they said, "you know every heart. Show us which of these men you have chosen [25]as an apostle to replace Judas the traitor in this ministry, for he has deserted us and gone where he belongs."

[26]Then they cast lots, and in this way Matthias was chosen and became an apostle with the other eleven.

## The Holy Spirit Comes

# 2

On the day of Pentecost, seven weeks after Jesus' resurrection, the believers were meeting together in one place. [2]Suddenly, there was a sound from heaven like the roaring of a mighty windstorm in the skies above them, and it filled the house where they were meeting. [3]Then, what looked like flames or tongues of fire appeared and settled on each of them. [4]And everyone present was filled with the Holy Spirit and began speaking in other languages, as the Holy Spirit gave them this ability.

[5]Godly Jews from many nations were living in Jerusalem at that time. [6]When they heard this sound, they came running to see what it was all about, and they were bewildered to hear their own languages being spoken by the believers. [7]They were beside themselves with wonder. "How can this be?" they exclaimed. "These people are all from Galilee, [8]and yet we hear them speaking the languages of the lands where we were born! [9]Here we are—Parthians, Medes, Elamites, people from Mesopotamia, Judea, Cappadocia, Pontus, the province of Asia, [10]Phrygia, Pamphylia, Egypt, and the areas of Libya towards Cyrene, visitors from Rome (both Jews and converts to Judaism), [11]Cretans, and Arabians. And we all hear these people speaking in our own languages about the wonderful things God has done!" [12]They stood there amazed

### When you need real power

### 1:8

But when the Holy Spirit has come upon you, you will receive power and will tell people about me everywhere—in Jerusalem, throughout Judea, in Samaria, and to the ends of the earth.

You will go the distance: Know that as a Christian you will live forever, your existence will never stop - you have been born into a life that will never die. We may be in the land of the dying, but we are going to the land of the living. "For you have been born again. Your new life did not come from your earthly parents because the life they gave you will end in death. But this new life will last forever because it comes from the eternal, living word of God."

1 Peter 1:23

and perplexed. "What can this mean?" they asked each other. [13]But others in the crowd were mocking. "They're drunk, that's all!" they said.

## Peter Preaches to a Crowd

[14]Then Peter stepped forward with the eleven other apostles and shouted to the crowd, "Listen carefully, all of you, fellow Jews and residents of Jerusalem! Make no mistake about this. [15]Some of you are saying these people are drunk. It isn't true! It's much too early for that. People don't get drunk by nine o'clock in the morning. [16]No, what you see this morning was predicted centuries ago by the prophet Joel:

[17]In the last days, God said,
I will pour out my Spirit upon all people.

Your sons and daughters will prophesy,
your young men will see visions,
and your old men will dream dreams.
[18]In those days I will pour out my Spirit
upon all my servants, men and women alike,
and they will prophesy.
[19]And I will cause wonders in the heavens above
and signs on the earth below—
blood and fire and clouds of smoke.
[20]The sun will be turned into darkness,
and the moon will turn blood-red,
before that great and glorious day of the Lord arrives.
[21]And anyone who calls on the name of the Lord

will be saved.'
[22]"People of Israel, listen! God publicly endorsed Jesus of Nazareth by doing wonderful miracles, wonders, and signs through him, as you well know. [23]But you followed God's prearranged plan. With the help of lawless Gentiles, you nailed him to the cross and murdered him. [24]However, God released him from the horrors of death and raised him back to life again, for death could not keep him in its grip. [25]King David said this about him:

'I know the Lord is always with me.
I will not be shaken, for he is right beside me.
[26]No wonder my heart is filled with joy,
and my mouth shouts his praises!
My body rests in hope.
[27]For you will not leave my soul among the dead
or allow your Holy One to rot in the grave.
[28]You have shown me the way of life,
and you will give me wonderful joy in your presence.'

[29]"Dear brothers, think about this! David wasn't referring to himself when he spoke these words I have quoted, for he died and was buried, and his tomb is still here among us. [30]But he was a prophet, and he knew God had promised with an oath that one of David's own descendants would sit on David's throne as the Messiah. [31]David was looking into the future and predicting the Messiah's resurrection. He was saying that the Messiah would not be left among the dead and that his body would not rot in the grave.

[32]This prophecy was speaking of Jesus, whom God raised from the dead, and we all are witnesses of this. [33]Now he sits on the throne of highest honour in heaven, at God's right hand. And the Father, as he had promised, gave him the Holy Spirit to pour out upon us, just as you see and hear today. [34]For David himself never ascended into heaven, yet he said,

'The LORD said to my Lord,
Sit in honour at my right hand
[35]until I humble your enemies,
making them a footstool under your feet.'

[36]So let it be clearly known by everyone in Israel that God has made this Jesus whom you crucified to be both Lord and Messiah!"

[37]Peter's words convicted them deeply, and they said to him and to the other apostles, "Brothers, what should we do?"

[38]Peter replied, "Each of you must turn from your sins and turn to God, and be baptized in the name of Jesus Christ for the forgiveness of your sins. Then you will receive the gift of the Holy Spirit. [39]This promise is to you and to your children, and even to the Gentiles— all who have been called by the Lord our God." [40]Then

Peter continued preaching for a long time, strongly urging all his listeners, "Save yourselves from this generation that has gone astray!"

[41]Those who believed what Peter said were baptized and added to the church—about three thousand in all. [42]They joined with the other believers and devoted themselves to the apostles' teaching and fellowship, sharing in the Lord's Supper and in prayer.

**action**

**CH 2:37-40 WHAT'S IT SAYING?**

**WHAT AM I GOING TO DO ABOUT IT?**

## The Believers Meet Together

[43]A deep sense of awe came over them all, and the apostles performed many miraculous signs and wonders. [44]And all the believers met together constantly and shared everything they had. [45]They sold their possessions and shared the proceeds with those in need. [46]They worshipped together at the Temple each day, met in homes for the Lord's Supper, and shared their meals with great joy and generosity—[47]all the while praising God and enjoying the goodwill of all the people. And each day the Lord added to their group those who were being saved.

## Peter Heals a Crippled Beggar

**3**

Peter and John went to the Temple one afternoon to take part in the three o'clock prayer service. [2]As they approached the Temple, a man lame from birth was being carried in. Each day he was put beside the Temple gate, the one called the Beautiful Gate, so he could beg from the people going into the Temple. [3]When he saw Peter and John about to enter, he asked them for some money.

[4]Peter and John looked at him intently, and Peter said, "Look at us!" [5]The lame man looked at them eagerly, expecting a gift. [6]But Peter said, "I don't have any money for you. But I'll give you what I have. In the name of Jesus Christ of Nazareth, get up and walk!" [7]Then Peter took the lame man by the right hand and helped him up. And as he did, the man's feet and anklebones were healed and strengthened. [8]He jumped up, stood on his feet, and began to walk! Then, walking, leaping, and praising God, he went into the Temple with them.

[9]All the people saw him walking and heard him praising God. [10]When they realized he was the lame beggar they had seen so often at the Beautiful Gate, they were absolutely astounded! [11]They all rushed out to Solomon's Colonnade, where he was holding tightly to Peter and John. Everyone stood there in awe of the wonderful thing that had happened.

## Peter Preaches in the Temple

[12]Peter saw his opportunity and addressed the crowd. "People of Israel," he said, "what is so astounding about this? And why look at us as though we had made this man walk by our own power and godliness? [13]For it is the God of Abraham, the God of Isaac, the God of Jacob, the God of all our ancestors who has brought

glory to his servant Jesus by doing this. This is the same Jesus whom you handed over and rejected before Pilate, despite Pilate's decision to release him. [14]You rejected this holy, righteous one and instead demanded the release of a murderer.

[15]You killed the author of life, but God raised him to life. And we are witnesses of this fact!

[16]The name of Jesus has healed this man—and you know how lame he was before. Faith in Jesus' name has caused this healing before your very eyes.

[17]Friends, I realize that what you did to Jesus was done in ignorance; and the same can be said of your leaders. [18]But God was fulfilling what all the prophets had declared about the Messiah beforehand—that he must suffer all these things. [19]Now turn from your sins and turn to God, so you can be cleansed of your sins. [20]Then wonderful times of refreshment will come from the presence of the Lord, and he will send Jesus your Messiah to you again. [21]For he must remain in heaven until the time for the final restoration of all things, as God promised long ago through his prophets. [22]Moses said, 'The Lord your God will raise up a Prophet like me from among your own people. Listen carefully to everything he tells you.' [23]Then Moses said, 'Anyone who will not listen to that Prophet will be cut off from God's people and utterly destroyed.'

[24]"Starting with Samuel, every prophet spoke about what is happening today. [25]You are the children of those prophets, and you are included in the covenant God promised to your ancestors. For God said to Abraham, 'Through your descendants all the families on earth will be blessed.' [26]When God raised up his servant, he sent him first to you people of Israel, to bless you by turning each of you back from your sinful ways."

## Peter and John before the Council

**4**

While Peter and John were speaking to the people, the leading priests, the captain of the Temple guard, and some of the Sadducees came over to them. [2]They were very disturbed that Peter and John were claiming, on the authority of Jesus, that there is a resurrection of the dead. [3]They arrested them and, since it was already evening, jailed them until morning. [4]**But many of the people who heard their message believed it, so that the number of believers totalled about five thousand men, not counting women and children.**

[5]The next day the council of all the rulers and elders and teachers of religious law met in Jerusalem. [6]Annas the high priest was there, along with Caiaphas, John, Alexander, and other relatives of the high priest. [7]They brought in the two disciples and demanded, "By what power, or in whose name,

**STATS**

The 'huddle' in American football was formed due to a deaf football player who used sign language to communicate and his team didn't want the opposition to see the signals he used and in turn huddled around him.

## Walk the Walk:

Be willing to "lead by example". Be an example, and model the desired behaviour and performance you want the rest of your team to exhibit. Do not expect your team-mates to do something you can't do in front of them.

have you done this?"

[8]Then Peter, filled with the Holy Spirit, said to them, "Leaders and elders of our nation, [9]are we being questioned because we've done a good deed for a crippled man? Do you want to know how he was healed? [10]Let me clearly state to you and to all the people of Israel that he was healed in the name and power of Jesus Christ from Nazareth, the man you crucified, but whom God raised from the dead. [11]For Jesus is the one referred to in the Scriptures, where it says,

'The stone that you builders rejected
has now become the cornerstone.'

[12]There is salvation in no one else! There is no other name in all of heaven for people to call on to save them."

[13]The members of the council were amazed when they saw the boldness of Peter and John, for they could see that they were ordinary men who had had no special training. They also recognized them as men who had been with Jesus. [14]But since the man who had been healed was standing right there among them, the council had nothing to say. [15]So they sent Peter and John out of the council chamber and conferred among themselves.

[16]"What should we do with these men?" they asked each other. "We can't deny they have done a miraculous sign, and everybody in Jerusalem knows about it.

[17]But perhaps we can stop them from spreading their propaganda. We'll warn them not to speak to anyone in Jesus' name again." [18]So they called the apostles back in and told them never again to speak or teach about Jesus.

## STAND POINT

### When you need an example of teamwork

**4:32**

All the believers were of one heart and mind, and they felt that what they owned was not their own; they shared everything they had.

[19]But Peter and John replied, "Do you think God wants us to obey you rather than him? [20]We cannot stop telling about the wonderful things we have seen and heard."

[21]The council then threatened them further, but they finally let them go because they didn't know how to punish them without starting a riot. For everyone was praising God [22]for this miraculous sign—the healing of a man who had been lame for more than forty years.

action

**CH 4:13-15 WHAT'S IT SAYING?**

**WHAT AM I GOING TO DO ABOUT IT?**

### The Believers Pray for Courage

[23]As soon as they were freed, Peter and John found the other believers and told them what the leading priests and elders had said. [24]Then all the believers were

united as they lifted their voices in prayer: "O Sovereign Lord, Creator of heaven and earth, the sea, and everything in them—[25]you spoke long ago by the Holy Spirit through our ancestor King David, your servant, saying,

'Why did the nations rage?
Why did the people waste their time with futile plans?
[26]The kings of the earth prepared for battle;
the rulers gathered together
against the Lord
and against his Messiah.'

[27]"That is what has happened here in this city! For Herod Antipas, Pontius Pilate the governor, the Gentiles, and the people of Israel were all united against Jesus, your holy servant, whom you anointed. [28]In fact, everything they did occurred according to your eternal will and plan. [29]And now, O Lord, hear their threats, and give your servants great boldness in their preaching. [30]Send your healing power; may miraculous signs and wonders be done through the name of your holy servant Jesus."

[31]After this prayer, the building where they were meeting shook, and they were all filled with the Holy Spirit. And they preached God's message with boldness.

### The Believers Share Their Possessions

[32]All the believers were of one heart and mind, and they felt that what they owned was not their own; they shared everything they had. [33]And the apostles gave powerful witness to the resurrection of the Lord Jesus, and God's great favour was upon them all.

[34]There was no poverty among them, because people who owned land or houses sold them [35]and brought the money to the apostles to give to others in need.

[36]For instance, there was Joseph, the one the apostles nicknamed Barnabas (which means "Son of Encouragement"). He was from the tribe of Levi and came from the island of Cyprus.

[37]He sold a field he owned and brought the money to the apostles for those in need.

# WHAT

# DOES IT MEAN?

### Amen

This Hebrew word means firm 'rock solid', and hence also faithful (Rev. 3:14). It is found singly and sometimes doubly at the end of prayers. In the early churches it was common for the general audience to say "Amen" at the close of the prayer (1 Cor. 14:16). The promises of God are Amen 'rock solid'; i.e. they are all true and definite (2 Cor. 1:20).

### Ananias and Sapphira

# 5

There was also a man named Ananias who, with his wife, Sapphira, sold some property. ²He brought part of the money to the apostles, but he claimed it was the full amount. His wife had agreed to this deception. ³Then Peter said, "Ananias, why has Satan filled your heart? You lied to the Holy Spirit, and you kept some of the money for yourself. ⁴The property was yours to sell or not sell, as you wished. And after selling it, the money was yours to give away. How could you do a thing like this? You weren't lying to us but to God." ⁵As soon as Ananias heard these words, he fell to the floor and died. Everyone who heard about it was

terrified. ⁶Then some young men wrapped him in a sheet and took him out and buried him.

⁷About three hours later his wife came in, not knowing what had happened. ⁸Peter asked her, "Was this the price you and your husband received for your land?"

"Yes," she replied, "that was the price."

⁹And Peter said, "How could the two of you even think of doing a thing like this—conspiring together to test the Spirit of the Lord? Just outside that door are the young men who buried your husband, and they will carry you out, too."

¹⁰Instantly, she fell to the floor and died. When the young men came in and saw that she was dead, they carried her out and buried her beside her husband. ¹¹Great fear gripped the entire church and all others who heard what had happened.

### CH 5:1-11 WHAT'S IT SAYING?

### WHAT AM I GOING TO DO ABOUT IT?

### The Apostles Heal Many

¹²Meanwhile, the apostles were performing many miraculous signs and wonders among the people. And the believers were meeting regularly at the Temple in the area known as Solomon's Colonnade.

¹³No one else dared to join them, though everyone had high regard for them. ¹⁴And more and more people believed and were brought to the Lord—crowds of both men and women.

# profiles

### Paul:

When you open your life to Jesus, you change. Perhaps nobody has ever changed so quickly or dramatically as Paul. Like an athlete he was single-minded, focused and intense by nature, in fact in his letters he used sport to illustrate his teaching. Paul, originally called Saul, was a well-trained Jewish Pharisee who saw followers of Jesus as a threat to the Jewish religion. His passion and intensity and energy were turned towards crushing the Christian movement. He was part of the stoning of Stephen, a devout follower of Christ, and was heading to the town of Damascus about 160 miles north of the capital, Jerusalem, when Jesus struck him down and he was overnight transformed into a follower of Christ. His zeal for Christ was immediate and he always carried the knowledge that he at one point had persecuted and killed his Saviour's followers. In time he became a zealous strategic Christian with a passion for telling the good news of Jesus and encouraging Christian communities to do the same. Besides Christ himself, no one has affected the world more than Paul. What will it be like when we get to heaven and see Stephen and Paul arm in arm praising God?

### Can I really control my sex drive?

Yes you can! This may be your longest and toughest challenge. For every encouragement you will have to keep your life pure and follow God's plan for sex, you will have countless negative messages lying to you, telling you just to follow your urges. Remember, Jesus was tempted and he defeated temptation. Ask God for help! He will give you power and will pick you up if you fall. God has a history of restoring his fallen people to himself. The biggest mistake you can make is when you fail and then withdraw from God. Instead run to God, apologise and commit yourself to staying on the right path.

Scripture says next to nothing about masturbation (this may be more of a guy issue), but it is very strong on keeping your thoughts pure and under control. 'God wants you to be holy, so you should keep clear of sexual sin. Then each of you will control your body and live in holiness and honour' 1 Thessalonians 4:4.

¹⁵As a result of the apostles' work, sick people were brought out into the streets on beds and mats so that Peter's shadow might fall across some of them as he went by. ¹⁶Crowds came in from the villages around Jerusalem, bringing their sick and those possessed by evil spirits, and they were all healed.

### The Apostles Meet Opposition

¹⁷The high priest and his friends, who were Sadducees, reacted with violent jealousy. ¹⁸They arrested the apostles and put them in the jail. ¹⁹But an angel of the Lord came at night, opened the gates of the jail, and brought them out. Then he told them, ²⁰"Go to the Temple and give the people this message of life!" ²¹So the apostles entered the Temple about daybreak and immediately began teaching.

When the high priest and his officials arrived, they convened the high council, along with all the elders of Israel. Then they sent for the apostles to be brought for trial. ²²But when the Temple guards went to the jail, the men were gone. So they returned to the council and reported, ²³"The jail was locked, with the guards standing outside, but when we opened the gates, no one was there!"

²⁴When the captain of the Temple guard and the leading priests heard this, they were perplexed, wondering where it would all end.

²⁵Then someone arrived with the news that the men they had jailed were out in the Temple, teaching the people.

²⁶The captain went with his Temple guards and arrested them, but without violence, for they were afraid the people would kill them if they treated the apostles roughly. ²⁷Then they brought the apostles in before the council. ²⁸"Didn't we tell you never again to teach in this man's name?" the high priest demanded. "Instead, you have filled all Jerusalem with your teaching about Jesus, and you intend to blame us for his death!"

²⁹But Peter and the apostles replied, "We must obey God rather than human authority. ³⁰The God of our ancestors raised Jesus from the dead after you killed him by crucifying him. ³¹Then God put him in the place of honour at his right hand as Prince and Saviour. He did this to give the people of Israel an opportunity to turn from their sins and turn to God so their sins would be forgiven.

³²We are witnesses of these things and so is the Holy Spirit, who is given by God to those who obey him."

³³At this, the high council was furious and decided to kill them. ³⁴But one member had a different perspective. He was a Pharisee named Gamaliel, who was an expert on religious law and was very popular with the people. He stood up and ordered that the apostles be sent outside the council chamber for a while. ³⁵Then he addressed his colleagues as follows: "Men of Israel, take care what you are planning to do to these men! ³⁶Some time ago there was that fellow Theudas, who pretended to be someone great. About four hundred others joined him, but he was killed, and his followers went their various ways. The whole movement came to nothing. ³⁷After him, at the time of the census, there was Judas of Galilee. He got some people to follow him, but he was killed, too, and all his followers were scattered.

³⁸So my advice is, leave these men alone. If they are teaching and doing these things merely on their own, it will soon be overthrown. ³⁹But if it is of God, you will not be able to stop them. You may even find yourselves fighting against God."

⁴⁰The council accepted his advice. They called in the apostles and had them flogged. Then they ordered them never again to speak in the name of Jesus, and they let them go. ⁴¹The apostles left the high council rejoicing that God had counted them worthy to suffer dishonour for the name of Jesus. ⁴²And every day, in the Temple and in their homes, they continued to teach and preach this message: "The Messiah you are looking for is Jesus."

### Seven Men Chosen to Serve

**6**

But as the believers rapidly multiplied, there were rumblings of discontent. Those who spoke Greek complained against those who spoke Hebrew, saying that their widows were being discriminated against in the daily distribution of food. ²So the Twelve called a meeting of all the believers.

"We apostles should spend our time preaching and teaching the word of God, not administering a food programme," they said.

³"Now look around among yourselves, brothers, and select seven men who are well respected and are full of the Holy Spirit and wisdom. We will put them in charge of this business. ⁴Then we can spend our time in prayer and preaching and teaching the word."

⁵This idea pleased the whole group, and they chose the following: Stephen (a man full of faith and the Holy Spirit), Philip, Procorus, Nicanor, Timon, Parmenas, and Nicolas of Antioch (a Gentile convert to the Jewish faith, who had now become a Christian). ⁶These seven were presented to the apostles, who prayed for them as they laid their hands on them.

⁷God's message was preached in ever-widening circles. The number of believers greatly increased in Jerusalem, and many of the Jewish priests were converted, too.

### Stephen Is Arrested

⁸Stephen, a man full of God's grace and power, performed amazing miracles and signs among the people. ⁹But one day some men from the Synagogue of Freed Slaves, as it was called, started to debate with him. They were Jews from Cyrene, Alexandria, Cilicia, and the province of Asia. ¹⁰None of them was able to stand against the wisdom and Spirit by which Stephen spoke.

¹¹So they persuaded some men to lie about Stephen, saying, "We heard him blaspheme Moses, and even God." ¹²Naturally, this roused the crowds, the elders, and the teachers of religious law. So they arrested Stephen and brought him before the high council.

[13]The lying witnesses said, "This man is always speaking against the Temple and against the law of Moses. [14]We have heard him say that this Jesus of Nazareth will destroy the Temple and change the customs Moses handed down to us." [15]At this point everyone in the council stared at Stephen because his face became as bright as an angel's.

## Stephen Addresses the Council

# 7

Then the high priest asked Stephen, "Are these accusations true?"

[2]This was Stephen's reply: "Brothers and honourable fathers, listen to me. Our glorious God appeared to our ancestor Abraham in Mesopotamia before he moved to Haran. [3]God told him, 'Leave your native land and your relatives, and come to the land that I will show you.' [4]So Abraham left the land of the Chaldeans and lived in Haran until his father died. Then God brought him here to the land where you now live. [5]But God gave him no inheritance here, not even one square metre of land. God did promise, however, that eventually the whole country would belong to Abraham and his descendants—though he had no children yet. [6]But God also told him that his descendants would live in a foreign country where they would be mistreated as slaves for four hundred years. [7]'But I will punish the nation that enslaves them,' God told him, 'and in the end they will come out and worship me in this place.' [8]God also gave Abraham the covenant of circumcision at that time. And so Isaac, Abraham's son, was circumcised when he was eight days old. Isaac became the father of Jacob, and Jacob was the father of the twelve patriarchs of the Jewish nation.

[9]"These sons of Jacob were very jealous of their brother Joseph, and they sold him to be a slave in Egypt. But God was with him [10]and delivered him from his anguish. And God gave him favour before Pharaoh, king of Egypt. God also gave Joseph unusual wisdom, so that Pharaoh appointed him governor over all of Egypt and put him in charge of all the affairs of the palace.

[11]"But a famine came upon Egypt and Canaan. There was great misery for our ancestors, as they ran out of food.

[12]Jacob heard that there was still corn in Egypt, so he sent his sons to buy some. [13]The second time they went, Joseph revealed his identity to his brothers, and they were introduced to Pharaoh. [14]Then Joseph sent for his father, Jacob, and all his relatives to come to Egypt, seventy-five persons in all. [15]So Jacob went to Egypt. He died there, as did all his sons. [16]All of them were taken to Shechem and buried in the tomb Abraham had bought from the sons of Hamor in Shechem.

[17]"As the time drew near when God would fulfil his promise to Abraham, the number of our people in Egypt greatly increased. [18]But then a new king came to the throne of Egypt who knew nothing about Joseph. [19]This king plotted against our people and forced parents to abandon their newborn babies so they would die.

[20]"At that time Moses was born—a beautiful child in God's eyes. His parents cared for him at home for three months. [21]When at last they had to abandon him, Pharaoh's daughter found him and raised him as her own son. [22]Moses was taught all the wisdom of the Egyptians, and he became mighty in both speech and action.

[23]"One day when he was forty years old, he decided to visit his relatives, the people of Israel. [24]During this visit, he saw an Egyptian mistreating a man of Israel. So Moses came to his defence and avenged him, killing the Egyptian. [25]Moses assumed his brothers would realize that God had sent him to rescue them, but they didn't.

[26]"The next day he visited them again and saw two men of Israel fighting. He tried to be a peacemaker. 'Men,' he said, 'you are brothers. Why are you hurting each other?'

[27]"But the man in the wrong pushed Moses aside and told him to mind his own business. 'Who made you a ruler and judge over us?' he asked. [28]'Are you going to kill me as you killed that Egyptian yesterday?' [29]When Moses heard that, he fled the country and lived as a foreigner in the land of Midian, where his two sons were born.

[30]"Forty years later, in the desert near Mount Sinai, an angel appeared to Moses in the flame of a burning bush. [31]Moses saw it and wondered what it was. As he went to see, the voice of the Lord called out to him, [32]'I am the God of your ancestors—the God of Abraham, Isaac, and Jacob.' Moses shook with terror and dared not look.

[33]"And the Lord said to him, 'Take off your sandals, for you are standing on holy ground. [34]You can be sure that I have seen the misery of my people in Egypt. I have heard their cries. So I have come to rescue them. Now go, for I will send you to Egypt.' [35]And so God sent back the same man his people had previously rejected by demanding, 'Who made you a ruler and judge over us?' Through the angel who appeared to him in the burning bush, Moses was sent to be their ruler and saviour.

[36]And by means of many miraculous signs and wonders, he led them out of Egypt, through the Red Sea, and back and forth through the wilderness for forty years.

[37]"Moses himself told the people of Israel, 'God will raise up a Prophet like me from among your own people.' [38]Moses was with the assembly of God's people in the wilderness. He was the mediator between the people of Israel and the angel who gave him life-giving words on Mount Sinai to pass on to us.

[39]"But our ancestors rejected Moses and wanted to return to Egypt. [40]They told Aaron, 'Make us some gods who can lead us, for we don't know what has become of this Moses, who brought us out of Egypt.' [41]So they made an idol shaped like a calf, and they sacrificed to it and rejoiced in this thing they had made. [42]Then God turned away from them and gave them up to serve the sun, moon, and stars as their gods! In the book of the prophets it is written,

'Was it to me you were bringing sacrifices
during those forty years in the wilderness, Israel?
[43]No, your real interest was in your pagan gods—
the shrine of Molech,
the star god Rephan,
and the images you made to worship them.
So I will send you into captivity
far away in Babylon.'

[44]"Our ancestors carried the Tabernacle with them through the wilderness. It was constructed in exact accordance with the plan shown to Moses by God. [45]Years later, when Joshua led the battles against the Gentile nations that God drove out of this land, the Tabernacle was taken with them into their new territory. And it was used there until the time of King David.

[46]"David found favour with God and asked for the privilege

**STAND POINT**

**When you need to forgive someone**
**7:59-60**

And as they stoned him, Stephen prayed, "Lord Jesus, receive my spirit." And he fell to his knees, shouting, "Lord, don't charge them with this sin!" And with that, he died.

of building a permanent Temple for the God of Jacob. ⁴⁷But it was Solomon who actually built it. ⁴⁸However, the Most High doesn't live in temples made by human hands. As the prophet says,

⁴⁹**Heaven is my throne,
and the earth is my footstool.
Could you ever build me a temple as good
as that?'**
asks the Lord.
**'Could you build a dwelling place for me?**
⁵⁰Didn't I make everything in heaven and earth?'**

⁵¹'You stubborn people! You are heathen at heart and deaf to the truth. Must you forever resist the Holy Spirit? But your ancestors did, and so do you! ⁵²Name one prophet your ancestors didn't persecute! They even killed the ones who predicted the coming of the Righteous One—the Messiah whom you betrayed and murdered. ⁵³You deliberately disobeyed God's law, though you received it from the hands of angels.'

⁵⁴The Jewish leaders were infuriated by Stephen's accusation, and they shook their fists in rage. ⁵⁵But Stephen, full of the Holy Spirit, gazed steadily upwards into heaven and saw the glory of God, and he saw Jesus standing in the place of honour at God's right hand. ⁵⁶And he told them, "Look, I see the heavens opened and the Son of Man standing in the place of honour at God's right hand!"

⁵⁷Then they put their hands over their ears, and drowning out his voice with their shouts, they rushed at him. ⁵⁸They dragged him out of the city and began to stone him. The official witnesses took off their coats and laid them at the feet of a young man named Saul.

⁵⁹And as they stoned him, Stephen prayed, "Lord Jesus, receive my spirit." ⁶⁰And he fell to his knees, shouting, "Lord, don't charge them with this sin!" And with that, he died.

# 8

Saul was one of the official witnesses at the killing of Stephen.

## Persecution Scatters the Believers

A great wave of persecution began that day, sweeping over the church in Jerusalem, and all the believers except the apostles fled into Judea and Samaria. ²(Some godly men came and buried Stephen with loud weeping.) ³Saul was going everywhere to devastate the church. He went from house to house, dragging out both men and women to throw them into jail.

## Philip Preaches in Samaria

⁴**But the believers who had fled Jerusalem went everywhere preaching the Good News**

about Jesus. ⁵**Philip, for example, went to the city of Samaria and told the people there about the Messiah.**

⁶Crowds listened intently to what he had to say because of the miracles he did. ⁷Many evil spirits were cast out, screaming as they left their victims. And many who had been paralysed or lame were healed. ⁸So there was great joy in that city.

⁹A man named Simon had been a sorcerer there for many years, claiming to be someone great. ¹⁰The Samaritan people, from the least to the greatest, often spoke of him as "the Great One—the Power of God." ¹¹He was very influential because of the magic he performed. ¹²But now the people believed Philip's message of Good News concerning the Kingdom of God and the name of Jesus Christ. As a result, many men and women were baptized. ¹³Then Simon himself believed and was baptized. He began following Philip wherever he went, and he was amazed by the great miracles and signs Philip performed.

¹⁴When the apostles back in Jerusalem heard that the people of Samaria had accepted God's message, they sent Peter and John there. ¹⁵As soon as they arrived, they prayed for these new Christians to receive the Holy Spirit. ¹⁶The Holy Spirit had not yet come upon any of them, for they had only been baptized in the name of the Lord Jesus. ¹⁷Then Peter and John laid their hands upon these believers, and they received the Holy Spirit.

¹⁸When Simon saw that the Holy Spirit was given when the apostles placed their hands upon people's heads, he offered money to buy this power. ¹⁹"Let me have this power, too," he exclaimed, "so that when I lay my hands on people, they will receive the Holy Spirit!" ²⁰But Peter replied, "May your money perish with you

for thinking God's gift can be bought! ²¹You can have no part in this, for your heart is not right before God. ²²Turn from your wickedness and pray to the Lord. Perhaps he will forgive your evil thoughts, ²³for I can see that you are full of bitterness and held captive by sin."

²⁴"Pray to the Lord for me," Simon exclaimed, "that these terrible things won't happen to me!"

²⁵After testifying and preaching the word of the Lord in Samaria, Peter and John returned to Jerusalem. And they stopped in many Samaritan villages along the way to preach the Good News to them, too.

**action**

**CH 8:18-24 WHAT'S IT SAYING?**

**WHAT AM I GOING TO DO ABOUT IT?**

## Philip and the Ethiopian Eunuch

²⁶As for Philip, an angel of the Lord said to him, "Go south down the desert road that runs from Jerusalem to Gaza." ²⁷So he did, and he met the treasurer of Ethiopia, a eunuch of great authority under the queen of Ethiopia. The eunuch had gone to Jerusalem to worship, ²⁸and he was now returning. Seated in his carriage, he was reading aloud from the book of the prophet Isaiah.

²⁹The Holy Spirit said to Philip, "Go over and walk along beside the carriage."

³⁰Philip ran over and heard the man reading from the

**STATS**

The first Wimbledon Tennis Competition took place in 1877 solely as an amateur competition. Men's singles was the only event that took place. There were 22 competitors and Spencer Gore won the championship.

prophet Isaiah; so he asked, "Do you understand what you are reading?"

³¹The man replied, "How can I, when there is no one to instruct me?" And he begged Philip to come up into the carriage and sit with him. ³²The passage of Scripture he had been reading was this:
"He was led as a sheep to the slaughter.
And as a lamb is silent before the shearers,
he did not open his mouth.
³³He was humiliated and received no justice.
Who can speak of his descendants?
For his life was taken from the earth."

³⁴The eunuch asked Philip, "Was Isaiah talking about himself or someone else?" ³⁵So Philip began with this same Scripture and then used many others to tell him the Good News about Jesus.

³⁶As they rode along, they came to some water, and the eunuch said, "Look! There's some water! Why can't I be baptized?"* ³⁸He ordered the carriage to stop, and they went down into the water, and Philip baptized him.

³⁹When they came up out of the water, the Spirit of the Lord caught Philip away. The eunuch never saw him again but went on his way rejoicing. ⁴⁰Meanwhile, Philip found himself farther north at the city of Azotus! He preached the Good News there and in every city along the way until he came to Caesarea.

## Saul's Conversion

**9**

Meanwhile, Saul was uttering threats with every breath. He was eager to destroy the Lord's followers, so he went to the high priest. ²He requested letters addressed to the synagogues in Damascus, asking their cooperation in the arrest of any followers of the Way he found there. He wanted to bring them—both men and women—back to Jerusalem in chains.

³As he was nearing Damascus on this mission, a brilliant light from heaven suddenly beamed down upon him! ⁴He fell to the ground and heard a voice saying to him, "Saul! Saul! Why are you persecuting me?"

⁵"Who are you, sir?" Saul asked.
And the voice replied, "I am Jesus, the one you are persecuting!
⁶Now get up and go into the city, and you will be told what you are to do."

⁷The men with Saul stood speechless with surprise, for they heard the sound of someone's voice, but they saw no one! ⁸As Saul picked himself up off the ground,

## count on it

**You do not have to be a Bible scholar to understand faith!**
Jesus loved children and used them often to teach us how to trust. A child that loves a parent puts their entire life in the care of that parent. That is what God wants for you. Like a trusting child, put your whole life (especially your sport) in God's hands and allow God to be your 'Father'. He will not let you down! "Let the children come to me. Don't stop them! For the Kingdom of God belongs to such as these." Mark 10:14
**Count on it!**

he found that he was blind. ⁹So his companions led him by the hand to Damascus. He remained there blind for three days. And all that time he went without food and water.

¹⁰Now there was a believer in Damascus named Ananias. The Lord spoke to him in a vision, calling, "Ananias!"

"Yes, Lord!" he replied.

¹¹The Lord said, "Go over to Straight Street, to the house of Judas. When you arrive, ask for Saul of Tarsus. He is praying to me right now. ¹²I have shown him a vision of a man named Ananias coming in and laying his hands on him so that he can see again."

¹³"But Lord," exclaimed Ananias,
"I've heard about the terrible things this man has done to the believers in Jerusalem! ¹⁴And we hear that he is authorized by the leading priests to arrest every believer in Damascus."

¹⁵But the Lord said, "Go and do what I say. For Saul is

my chosen instrument to take my message to the Gentiles and to kings, as well as to the people of Israel. ¹⁶And I will show him how much he must suffer for me."

¹⁷So Ananias went and found Saul. He laid his hands on him and said, "Brother Saul, the Lord Jesus, who appeared to you on the road, has sent me so that you may get your sight back and be filled with the Holy Spirit." ¹⁸Instantly something like scales fell from Saul's eyes, and he regained his sight. Then he got up and was baptized. ¹⁹Afterwards he ate some food and was strengthened.

## Saul in Damascus and Jerusalem

Saul stayed with the believers in Damascus for a few days. **²⁰And immediately he began preaching about Jesus in the synagogues, saying, "He is indeed the Son of God!"**

**²¹All who heard him were amazed. "Isn't this the same man who persecuted Jesus' followers with such devastation in Jerusalem?" they asked. "And we understand that he came here to arrest them and take them in chains to the leading priests."**

²²Saul's preaching became more and more powerful, and the Jews in Damascus couldn't refute his proofs that Jesus was indeed the Messiah. ²³After a while the Jewish leaders decided to kill him. ²⁴But Saul was told about their plot, and that they were watching for him day and night at the city gate so they could murder him. ²⁵So during the night, some of the other believers let him down in a large basket through an opening in the city wall.

²⁶When Saul arrived in Jerusalem, he tried to meet with the believers, but they were all afraid of him. They thought he was only pretending to be a believer! ²⁷Then Barnabas brought him to the apostles and told them how Saul had seen the Lord on the way to Damascus. Barnabas also told them what the Lord had said to Saul and how he boldly preached in the name of Jesus in Damascus. ²⁸Then the apostles accepted Saul, and after that he was constantly with them in Jerusalem, preaching boldly in the name of the Lord. ²⁹He debated with some Greek-speaking Jews, but they plotted to murder him. ³⁰When the believers heard about it, however, they took him to Caesarea and sent him on to his home town of Tarsus.

³¹The church then had peace throughout Judea, Galilee, and Samaria, and it grew in strength and numbers. The believers were walking in the fear of the Lord and in the comfort of the Holy Spirit.

## Peter Heals Aeneas and Raises Dorcas

³²Peter travelled from place to place to visit the believers, and in his travels he came to the Lord's people in the town

8:36 Some manuscripts add verse 37, "You can," Philip answered, "if you believe with all your heart." And the eunuch replied, "I believe that Jesus Christ is the Son of God."

of Lydda. [33]There he met a man named Aeneas, who had been paralysed and bedridden for eight years. [34]Peter said to him, "Aeneas, Jesus Christ heals you! Get up and make your bed!" And he was healed instantly. [35]Then the whole population of Lydda and Sharon turned to the Lord when they saw Aeneas walking around. [36]There was a believer in Joppa named Tabitha (which in Greek is Dorcas). She was always doing kind things for others and helping the poor. [37]About this time she became ill and died. Her friends prepared her for burial and laid her in an upstairs room. [38]But they had heard that Peter was nearby at Lydda, so they sent two men to beg him, "Please come as soon as possible!"

[39]So Peter returned with them; and as soon as he arrived, they took him to the upstairs room. The room was filled with widows who were weeping and showing him the coats and other garments Dorcas had made for them. [40]But Peter asked them all to leave the room; then he knelt and prayed. Turning to the body he said, "Get up, Tabitha." And she opened her eyes! When she saw Peter, she sat up! [41]He gave her his hand and helped her up. Then he called in the widows and all the believers, and he showed them that she was alive. [42]The news raced through the whole town, and many believed in the Lord. [43]And Peter stayed a long time in Joppa, living with Simon, a leatherworker.

## Cornelius Calls for Peter

# 10

In Caesarea there lived a Roman army officer named Cornelius, who was a captain of the Italian Regiment. [2]He was a devout man who feared the God of Israel, as did his entire household. He gave generously to charity and was a man who regularly prayed to God.

[3]One afternoon about three o'clock, he had a vision in which he saw an angel of God coming towards him. "Cornelius!" the angel said.

[4]Cornelius stared at him in terror. "What is it, sir?" he asked the angel.

And the angel replied, "Your prayers and gifts to the poor have not gone unnoticed by God! [5]Now send some men down to Joppa to find a man named Simon Peter. [6]He is staying with Simon, a leatherworker who lives near the shore. Ask him to come and visit you."

[7]As soon as the angel was gone, Cornelius called two of his household servants and a devout soldier, one of his personal attendants. [8]He told them what had happened and sent them off to Joppa.

## Peter Visits Cornelius

[9]The next day as Cornelius's messengers were nearing the city, Peter went up to the flat roof to pray. It was about midday, [10]and he was hungry. But while lunch was being prepared, he fell into a trance. [11]He saw the sky open, and something like a large sheet was let down by its four corners. [12]In the sheet were all sorts of animals, reptiles, and birds. [13]Then a voice said to him, "Get up, Peter; kill and eat them."

[14]"Never, Lord," Peter declared. "I have never in all my life eaten anything forbidden by our Jewish laws."

[15]The voice spoke again, "If God says something is acceptable, don't say it isn't." [16]The same vision was repeated three times. Then the sheet was pulled up again to heaven.

[17]Peter was very perplexed. What could the vision mean? Just then the men sent by Cornelius found the house and stood outside at the gate. [18]They asked if this was the place where Simon Peter was staying. [19]Meanwhile, as Peter was puzzling over the vision, the Holy Spirit said to him, "Three men have come looking for you. [20]Go down and go with them without hesitation. All is well, for I have sent them."

[21]So Peter went down and said, "I'm the man you are looking for. Why have you come?"

[22]They said, "We were sent by Cornelius, a Roman officer. He is a devout man who fears the God of Israel and is well respected by all the Jews. A holy angel instructed him to send for you so you can go to his house and give him a message." [23]So Peter invited the men to be his guests for the night. The next day he went with them, accompanied by some other believers from Joppa.

[24]They arrived in Caesarea the following day. Cornelius was waiting for him and had called together his relatives and close friends to meet Peter. [25]As Peter entered his home, Cornelius fell to the floor before him in worship. [26]But Peter pulled him up and said, "Stand up! I'm a human being like you!"

[27]So Cornelius got up, and they talked together and went inside where the others were assembled. [28]Peter told them, "You know it is against the Jewish laws for me to come into a Gentile home like this. But God has shown me that I should never think of anyone as impure. [29]So I came as soon as I was sent for. Now tell me why you sent for me."

[30]Cornelius replied, "Four days ago I was praying in my house at three o'clock in the afternoon. Suddenly, a man in dazzling clothes was standing in front of me. [31]He told me, 'Cornelius, your prayers have been heard, and your gifts to the poor have been noticed by God! [32]Now send some men to Joppa and summon Simon Peter. He is staying in the home of Simon, a leatherworker who lives near the shore.' [33]So I sent for you at once, and it was good of you to come. Now here we are, waiting before God to hear the message the Lord has given you."

## The Gentiles Hear the Good News

[34]Then Peter replied, "I see very clearly that God doesn't show partiality. [35]In every nation he accepts those who fear him and do what is right. [36]I'm sure you have heard about the Good News for the people of Israel—that there is peace with God through Jesus Christ, who is Lord of all.

[37]You know what happened all through Judea, beginning in Galilee after John the Baptist began preaching. [38]And no doubt you know that God anointed Jesus of Nazareth with the Holy Spirit and with power. Then Jesus went around doing good and healing all who were oppressed by the Devil, for God was with him.

[39]"And we apostles are witnesses of all he did throughout Israel and in Jerusalem. They put him to death by crucifying him, [40]but God raised him to life three days later. Then God allowed him to appear, [41]not to the general public, but to us whom God had chosen

**BIBLE HIT 'Doing Good' Acts 10:38**
Are you doing good? Jesus always did 'good'. Goodness is the character of God. We can also see glimpses of goodness coming out in people since we are made in God's image. What are some 'good' role models you can follow and try to be like? What good can you do today?

your best
isn't good
enough

His is

sport

## TIPS

# When you are being trained ask yourself:

What's the general skill principle on which you are focusing?
What are your objectives?
What are your greatest strengths and weaknesses?

beforehand to be his witnesses. We were those who ate and drank with him after he rose from the dead. [42]And he ordered us to preach everywhere and to testify that Jesus is ordained of God to be the judge of all—the living and the dead. [43]He is the one all the prophets testified about, saying that everyone who believes in him will have their sins forgiven through his name."

## The Gentiles Receive the Holy Spirit

[44]Even as Peter was saying these things, the Holy Spirit fell upon all who had heard the message. [45]The Jewish believers who came with Peter were amazed that the gift of the Holy Spirit had been poured out upon the Gentiles, too. [46]And there could be no doubt about it, for they heard them speaking in tongues and praising God.

Then Peter asked, [47]"Can anyone object to their being baptized, now that they have received the Holy Spirit just as we did?" [48]So he gave orders for them to be baptized in the name of Jesus Christ. Afterwards Cornelius asked him to stay with them for several days.

## Peter Explains His Actions

# 11

Soon the news reached the apostles and other believers in Judea that the Gentiles had received the word of God. [2]But when Peter arrived back in Jerusalem, some of the Jewish believers criticized him. [3]"You entered the home of Gentiles and even ate with them!" they said.

[4]Then Peter told them exactly what had happened. [5]"One day in Joppa," he said, "while I was praying, I went into a trance and saw a vision. Something like a large sheet was let down by its four corners from the sky. And it came right down to me. [6]When I looked inside the sheet, I saw all sorts of small animals, wild animals, reptiles, and birds that we are not allowed to eat. [7]And I heard a voice say, 'Get up, Peter; kill and eat them.'

[8]"'Never, Lord,' I replied. 'I have never eaten anything forbidden by our Jewish laws.'

[9]"But the voice from heaven came again, 'If God says something is acceptable, don't say it isn't.'

[10]"This happened three times before the sheet and all it contained was pulled back up to heaven. [11]Just then three men who had been sent from Caesarea arrived at the house where I was staying. [12]The Holy Spirit told me to go with them and not to worry about their being Gentiles. These six brothers here accompanied me, and we soon arrived at the home of the man who had sent for us.

[13]He told us how an angel had appeared to him in his home and had told him, 'Send messengers to Joppa to find Simon Peter. [14]He will tell you how you and all your household will be saved!'

[15]"Well, I began telling them the Good News, but just as I was getting started, the Holy Spirit fell on them, just as he fell on us at the beginning. [16]Then I thought of the Lord's words when he said, 'John baptized with water, but you will be baptized with the Holy Spirit.' [17]And since God gave these Gentiles the same gift he gave us when we believed in the Lord Jesus Christ, who was I to argue?"

[18]When the others heard this, all their objections were answered and they began praising God. They said, "God has also given the Gentiles the privilege of turning from sin and receiving eternal life."

## The Church in Antioch of Syria

[19]Meanwhile, the believers who had fled from Jerusalem during the persecution after Stephen's death travelled as far as Phoenicia, Cyprus, and Antioch of Syria. They preached the Good News, but only to Jews. [20]However, some of the believers who went to Antioch from Cyprus and Cyrene began preaching to Gentiles about the Lord Jesus. [21]The power of the Lord was upon them, and large numbers of these Gentiles believed and turned to the Lord.

[22]When the church at Jerusalem heard what had happened, they sent Barnabas to Antioch. [23]When he arrived and saw this proof of God's favour, he was filled with joy, and he encouraged the believers to stay true to the Lord. [24]Barnabas was a good man, full of the Holy Spirit and strong in faith. And large numbers of people were brought to the Lord.

[25]Then Barnabas went on to Tarsus to find Saul. [26]When he found him, he brought him back to Antioch. Both of them stayed there with the church for a full year, teaching great numbers of people. (It was there at Antioch that the believers were first called Christians.)

[27]During this time, some prophets travelled from Jerusalem to Antioch. [28]One of them named Agabus stood up in one of the meetings to predict by the Spirit that a great famine was coming upon the entire Roman world. (This was fulfilled during the reign of Claudius.) [29]So the believers in Antioch decided to send relief to the brothers and sisters in Judea, everyone giving as much as they could. [30]This they did, entrusting their gifts to Barnabas and Saul to take to the elders of the church in Jerusalem.

## James Is Killed and Peter Is Imprisoned

# 12

About that time King Herod Agrippa began to persecute some believers in the church. [2]He had the apostle James (John's brother) killed with a sword. [3]When Herod saw how much this pleased the Jewish leaders, he arrested Peter during the Passover celebration [4]and imprisoned him, placing him under the guard of four squads of four soldiers each. Herod's intention was to bring Peter out for public trial after the Passover.

[5]But while Peter was in prison, the church prayed very earnestly for him.

## Peter's Miraculous Escape from Prison

[6]The night before Peter was to be placed on trial, he was asleep, chained between two soldiers, with others standing guard at the prison gate. [7]Suddenly, there was a bright light in the cell, and an angel of the Lord stood before Peter. The angel tapped him on the side to awaken him and said, "Quick! Get up!" And the chains fell off his wrists. [8]Then the angel

told him, "Get dressed and put on your sandals." And he did. "Now put on your coat and follow me," the angel ordered.

[9]So Peter left the cell, following the angel. But all the time he thought it was a vision. He didn't realize it was really happening. [10]They passed the first and second guard posts and came to the iron gate to the street, and this opened to them all by itself. So they passed through and started walking down the street, and then the angel suddenly left him.

[11]Peter finally realized what had happened. "It's really true!" he said to himself. "The Lord has sent his angel and saved me from Herod and from what the Jews were hoping to do to me!"

[12]After a little thought, he went to the home of Mary, the mother of John Mark, where many were gathered for prayer. [13]He knocked at the door in the gate, and a servant girl named Rhoda came to open it. [14]When she recognized Peter's voice, she was so overjoyed that, instead of opening the door, she ran back inside and told everyone, "Peter is standing at the door!"

[15]"You're out of your mind," they said. When she insisted, they decided, "It must be his angel."

[16]Meanwhile, Peter continued knocking. When they finally went out and opened the door, they were amazed. [17]He motioned for them to quieten down and told them what had happened and how the Lord had led him out of jail. "Tell James and the other brothers what happened," he said. And then he went to another place.

[18]At dawn, there was a great commotion among the soldiers about what had happened to Peter. [19]Herod Agrippa ordered a thorough search for him. When he couldn't be found, Herod interrogated the guards and sentenced them to death. Afterwards Herod left Judea to stay in Caesarea for a while.

## The Death of Herod Agrippa

[20]Now Herod was very angry with the people of Tyre and Sidon. So they sent a delegation to make peace with him because their cities were dependent upon Herod's country for their food. They made friends with Blastus, Herod's personal assistant, [21]and an appointment with Herod was granted. When the day arrived, Herod put on his royal robes, sat on his throne, and made a speech to them.
[22]The people gave him a great ovation, shouting, "It is the voice of a god, not of a man!"

[23]Instantly, an angel of the Lord struck Herod with a sickness, because he accepted the people's worship instead of giving the glory to God. So he was consumed with worms and died. [24]But God's Good News was spreading rapidly, and there were many new believers.

[25]When Barnabas and Saul had finished their mission in Jerusalem, they returned to Antioch, taking John Mark with them.

## Barnabas and Saul Are Sent Out

# 13

Among the prophets and teachers of the church at Antioch of Syria were Barnabas, Simeon (called "the black man"), Lucius (from Cyrene), Manaen (the childhood companion of King Herod Antipas), and Saul. [2]One day as these men were worshipping the Lord and fasting, the Holy Spirit said, "Dedicate Barnabas and Saul for the special work I have for them." [3]So after more fasting and prayer, the men laid their hands on them and sent them on their way.

## Paul's First Missionary Journey

[4]Sent out by the Holy Spirit, Saul and Barnabas went down to the seaport of Seleucia and then sailed for the island of Cyprus. [5]There, in the town of Salamis, they went to the Jewish synagogues and preached the word of God. (John Mark went with them as their assistant.)

[6]Afterwards they preached from town to town across the entire island until finally they reached Paphos, where they met a Jewish sorcerer, a false prophet named Bar-Jesus. [7]He had attached himself to the governor, Sergius Paulus, a man of considerable insight and understanding. The governor invited Barnabas and Saul to visit him, for he wanted to hear the word of God. [8]But Elymas, the sorcerer (as his name means in Greek), interfered and urged the governor to pay no attention to what Saul and Barnabas said. He was trying to turn the governor away from the Christian faith.

[9]Then Saul, also known as Paul, filled with the Holy Spirit, looked the sorcerer in the eye and said, [10]"You son of the Devil, full of every sort of trickery and villainy, enemy of all that is good, will you never stop perverting the true ways of the Lord? [11]And now the Lord has laid his hand of punishment upon you, and you will be stricken awhile with blindness." Instantly mist and darkness fell upon him, and he began wandering around begging for someone to take his hand and lead him. [12]When the governor saw what had happened, he believed and was astonished at what he learned about the Lord.

## Paul Preaches in Antioch of Pisidia

[13]Now Paul and those with him left Paphos by ship for Pamphylia, landing at the port town of Perga. There

# WHAT DOES IT MEAN?

## Justification

A legal term for God's judicial act, by which he pardons all the sins of those who believe in Christ, and accounts, recognises, and treats them as righteous in the eye of the law, i.e. as conformed to all its demands. In addition to the pardon of sin, justification declares that all the claims of the law are satisfied in respect of the justified (Rom. 5:1-10). The act of faith which thus secures our justification secures also at the same time our sanctification; and thus the doctrine of justification by faith does not lead to licentiousness (Rom. 6:2-7).

John Mark left them and returned to Jerusalem. [14]But Barnabas and Paul travelled inland to Antioch of Pisidia.
On the Sabbath they went to the synagogue for the services. [15]After the usual readings from the books of Moses and from the Prophets, those in charge of the service sent them this message: "Brothers, if you have any word of encouragement for us, come and give it!"

**Individual Sports:**

Though your sport may mean that you perform on your own, like golf or cycling, it is usually easier and more challenging to train with others.

¹⁶So Paul stood, lifted his hand to quieten them, and started speaking. "People of Israel," he said, "and you devout Gentiles who fear the God of Israel, listen to me.

¹⁷"The God of this nation of Israel chose our ancestors and made them prosper in Egypt. Then he powerfully led them out of their slavery. ¹⁸He put up with them through forty years of wandering around in the wilderness. ¹⁹Then he destroyed seven nations in Canaan and gave their land to Israel as an inheritance. ²⁰All this took about 450 years. After that, judges ruled until the time of Samuel the prophet. ²¹Then the people begged for a king, and God gave them Saul son of Kish, a man of the tribe of Benjamin, who reigned for forty years. ²²But God removed him from the kingship and replaced him with David, a man about whom God said, 'David son of Jesse is a man after my own heart, for he will do everything I want him to.'

²³"And it is one of King David's descendants, Jesus, who is God's promised Saviour of Israel! ²⁴But before he came, John the Baptist preached the need for everyone in Israel to turn from sin and turn to God and be baptized. ²⁵As John was finishing his ministry he asked, 'Do you think I am the Messiah? No! But he is coming soon—and I am not even worthy to be his slave.'

²⁶"Brothers—you sons of Abraham, and also all of you devout Gentiles who fear the God of Israel—this salvation is for us! ²⁷The people in Jerusalem and their leaders fulfilled prophecy by condemning Jesus to death. They didn't recognize him or realize that he is the one the prophets had written about, though they hear the prophets' words read every Sabbath. ²⁸They found no just cause to execute him, but they asked Pilate to have him killed anyway.

²⁹"When they had fulfilled all the prophecies concerning his death, they took him down from the cross and placed him in a tomb. ³⁰But God raised him from the dead! ³¹And he appeared over a period of many days to those who had gone with him from Galilee to Jerusalem—these are his witnesses to the people of Israel.

³²"**And now Barnabas and I are here to bring you this Good News. God's promise to our ancestors has come true in our own time, ³³in that God raised Jesus. This is what the second psalm is talking about when it says concerning Jesus,**

**'You are my Son.**
**Today I have become your Father.'**

³⁴For God had promised to raise him from the dead, never again to die. This is stated in the Scripture that says, 'I will give you the sacred blessings I promised to David.' ³⁵Another psalm explains more fully, saying, 'You will not allow your Holy One to rot in the grave.' ³⁶Now this is not a reference to David, for after David had served his generation according to the will of God, he died and was buried, and his body decayed. ³⁷No, it was a reference to someone else—someone whom God raised and whose body did not decay.

³⁸"Brothers, listen! In this man Jesus there is forgiveness for your sins. ³⁹Everyone who believes in him is freed from all guilt and declared right with God—something the Jewish law could never do. ⁴⁰Be careful! Don't let the prophets' words apply to you. For they said,

⁴¹"Look, you mockers,
be amazed and die!
For I am doing something in your own day,
something you wouldn't believe
even if someone told you about it.'"

⁴²As Paul and Barnabas left the synagogue that day, the people asked them to return again and speak about these things the next week. ⁴³Many Jews and godly converts to Judaism who worshipped at the synagogue followed Paul and Barnabas, and the two men urged them, "By God's grace, remain faithful."

## Paul Turns to the Gentiles

⁴⁴The following week almost the entire city turned out to

## Winners know they are loved!

You never have to worry about earning God's love by playing well! Fortunately, you do not have to change, grow and be good to be loved by God! Rather, you are "loved by God, so that you will change, grow and be good!" Perhaps you should read the last sentence again, especially if you are a rugby player! This is quite a hard concept for someone whose whole life has been governed by the teaching that one succeeds by one's own determination! The freedom of knowing you are radically loved by God will give you the security to live life to the full.

"God saved you by his special favour when you believed. And you can't take credit for this; it is a gift from God. Salvation is not a reward for the good things we have done, so none of us can boast about it." Ephesians 2:8-9

## Winners are freed by love!

hear them preach the word of the Lord. ⁴⁵But when the Jewish leaders saw the crowds, they were jealous; so they slandered Paul and argued against whatever he said.

⁴⁶Then Paul and Barnabas spoke out boldly and declared, "It was necessary that this Good News from God be given first to you Jews. But since you have rejected it and judged yourselves unworthy of eternal life—well, we will offer it to Gentiles.

⁴⁷For this is as the Lord commanded us when he said,
'I have made you a light to the Gentiles,
to bring salvation to the farthest corners of the earth.'"

⁴⁸When the Gentiles heard this, they were very glad and thanked the Lord for his message; and all who were appointed to eternal life became believers. ⁴⁹So the Lord's message spread throughout that region.

⁵⁰Then the Jewish leaders stirred up the influential religious women and the leaders of the city, and they incited a mob against Paul and Barnabas and ran them out of town. ⁵¹But they shook off the dust of their feet against them and went to the city of Iconium. ⁵²And the believers were filled with joy and with the Holy Spirit.

## Paul and Barnabas in Iconium

# 14

In Iconium, Paul and Barnabas went together to the synagogue and preached with such power that a great number of both Jews and Gentiles believed. ²But the Jews who spurned God's message stirred up distrust among the Gentiles against Paul and Barnabas, saying all sorts of evil things about them. ³The apostles stayed there a long time, preaching boldly about the grace of the Lord. The Lord proved their message was true by giving them power to do miraculous signs and wonders. ⁴But the people of the city were divided in their opinion about them. Some sided with the Jews, and some with the apostles.

⁵A mob of Gentiles and Jews, along with their leaders, decided to attack and stone them. ⁶When the apostles learned of it, they fled for their lives. They went to the region of Lycaonia, to the cities of Lystra and Derbe and the surrounding area, ⁷and they preached the Good News there.

## Paul and Barnabas in Lystra and Derbe

⁸While they were at Lystra, Paul and Barnabas came upon a man with crippled feet. He had been that way from birth, so he had never walked. ⁹He was listening

as Paul preached, and Paul noticed him and realized he had faith to be healed. [10]So Paul called to him in a loud voice, "Stand up!" And the man jumped to his feet and started walking.

[11]When the listening crowd saw what Paul had done, they shouted in their local dialect, "These men are gods in human bodies!" [12]They decided that Barnabas was the Greek god Zeus and that Paul, because he was the chief speaker, was Hermes. [13]The temple of Zeus was located on the outskirts of the city. The priest of the temple and the crowd brought oxen and wreaths of flowers, and they prepared to sacrifice to the apostles at the city gates. [14]But when Barnabas and Paul heard what was happening, they tore their clothing in dismay and ran out among the people, shouting, [15]"Friends, why are you doing this? We are merely human beings like yourselves! We have come to bring you the Good News that you should turn from these worthless things to the living God, who made heaven and earth, the sea, and everything in them. [16]In earlier days he permitted all the nations to go their own ways, [17]but he never left himself without a witness. There were always his reminders, such as sending you rain and good crops and giving you food and joyful hearts." [18]But even so, Paul and Barnabas could scarcely restrain the people from sacrificing to them.

[19]Now some Jews arrived from Antioch and Iconium and turned the crowds into a murderous mob. They stoned Paul and dragged him out of the city, apparently dead. [20]But as the believers stood around him, he got up and went back into the city. The next day he left with Barnabas for Derbe.

## Paul and Barnabas Return to Antioch of Syria

[21]After preaching the Good News in Derbe and making many disciples, Paul and Barnabas returned again to Lystra, Iconium, and Antioch of Pisidia, [22]where they strengthened the believers. They encouraged them to continue in the faith, reminding them that they must enter into the Kingdom of God through many tribulations.

[23]Paul and Barnabas also appointed elders in every church and prayed for them with fasting, turning them over to the care of the Lord, in whom they had come to trust. [24]Then they travelled back through Pisidia to Pamphylia. [25]They preached again in Perga, then went on to Attalia.

[26]Finally, they returned by ship to Antioch of Syria, where their journey had begun and where they had been committed to the grace of God for the work they

## count on it

### God will speak!

The Christian life is not easy! There will be times when you are laughed at, when you will want to lash out against an opponent and when you are unfairly treated by a coach. But Jesus does promise that when you need to defend yourself and you seek God's power he will give you the right way to respond. Let God represent you! "Don't worry about what to say in your defence. Just say what God tells you to. Then it is not you who will be speaking, but the Holy Spirit." Mark 13:11
**Count on it!**

had now completed. [27]Upon arriving in Antioch, they called the church together and reported about their trip, telling all that God had done and how he had opened the door of faith to the Gentiles, too. [28]And they stayed there with the believers in Antioch for a long time.

## The Council at Jerusalem

# 15

While Paul and Barnabas were at Antioch of Syria, some men from Judea arrived and began to teach the Christians: "Unless you keep the ancient Jewish custom of circumcision taught by Moses, you cannot be saved." [2]Paul and Barnabas, disagreeing with them, argued forcefully and at length. Finally, Paul and Barnabas were sent to Jerusalem, accompanied by some local believers, to talk to the apostles and elders

about this question. [3]The church sent the delegates to Jerusalem, and they stopped along the way in Phoenicia and Samaria to visit the believers. They told them—much to everyone's joy—that the Gentiles, too, were being converted. [4]When they arrived in Jerusalem, Paul and Barnabas were welcomed by the whole church, including the apostles and elders. They reported on what God had been doing through their ministry. [5]But then some of the men who had been Pharisees before their conversion stood up and declared that all Gentile converts must be circumcised and be required to follow the law of Moses.

[6]So the apostles and church elders got together to decide this question. [7]At the meeting, after a long discussion, Peter stood and addressed them as follows: "Brothers, you all know that God chose me from among you some time ago to preach to the Gentiles so that they could hear the Good News and believe. [8]God, who knows people's hearts, confirmed that he accepts Gentiles by giving them the Holy Spirit, just as he gave him to us. [9]He made no distinction between us and them, for he also cleansed their hearts through faith. [10]Why are you now questioning God's way by burdening the Gentile believers with a yoke that neither we nor our ancestors were able to bear? [11]We believe that we are all saved the same way, by the special favour of the Lord Jesus."

[12]There was no further discussion, and everyone listened as Barnabas and Paul told about the miraculous signs and wonders God had done through them among the Gentiles.

[13]When they had finished, James stood and said, "Brothers, listen to me. [14]Peter has told you about the time God first visited the Gentiles to take from them a people for himself. [15]And this conversion of Gentiles agrees with what the prophets predicted. For instance, it is written:

[16]'Afterwards I will return,
and I will restore the fallen kingdom of David.
From the ruins I will rebuild it,

## STAND POINT

### When you need an example of boldness

**18:9-10**

One night the Lord spoke to Paul in a vision and told him, "Don't be afraid! Speak out! Don't be silent! For I am with you, and no one will harm you because many people here in this city belong to me."

# JUNE M.A.P.

## 1
| S.D. | P.L. | P.G. | S.G. |
|---|---|---|---|
| P. ☐ | F. ☐ | F. ☐ | T. ☐ |
| F. ☐ | W. ☐ | W. ☐ | P. ☐ |
| B. ☐ | P. ☐ | C. ☐ | C. ☐ |

## 2
| S.D. | P.L. | P.G. | S.G. |
|---|---|---|---|
| P. ☐ | F. ☐ | F. ☐ | T. ☐ |
| F. ☐ | W. ☐ | W. ☐ | P. ☐ |
| B. ☐ | P. ☐ | C. ☐ | C. ☐ |

## 3
| S.D. | P.L. | P.G. | S.G. |
|---|---|---|---|
| P. ☐ | F. ☐ | F. ☐ | T. ☐ |
| F. ☐ | W. ☐ | W. ☐ | P. ☐ |
| B. ☐ | P. ☐ | C. ☐ | C. ☐ |

## 4
| S.D. | P.L. | P.G. | S.G. |
|---|---|---|---|
| P. ☐ | F. ☐ | F. ☐ | T. ☐ |
| F. ☐ | W. ☐ | W. ☐ | P. ☐ |
| B. ☐ | P. ☐ | C. ☐ | C. ☐ |

## 9
| S.D. | P.L. | P.G. | S.G. |
|---|---|---|---|
| P. ☐ | F. ☐ | F. ☐ | T. ☐ |
| F. ☐ | W. ☐ | W. ☐ | P. ☐ |
| B. ☐ | P. ☐ | C. ☐ | C. ☐ |

## 10
| S.D. | P.L. | P.G. | S.G. |
|---|---|---|---|
| P. ☐ | F. ☐ | F. ☐ | T. ☐ |
| F. ☐ | W. ☐ | W. ☐ | P. ☐ |
| B. ☐ | P. ☐ | C. ☐ | C. ☐ |

## 11
| S.D. | P.L. | P.G. | S.G. |
|---|---|---|---|
| P. ☐ | F. ☐ | F. ☐ | T. ☐ |
| F. ☐ | W. ☐ | W. ☐ | P. ☐ |
| B. ☐ | P. ☐ | C. ☐ | C. ☐ |

## 12
| S.D. | P.L. | P.G. | S.G. |
|---|---|---|---|
| P. ☐ | F. ☐ | F. ☐ | T. ☐ |
| F. ☐ | W. ☐ | W. ☐ | P. ☐ |
| B. ☐ | P. ☐ | C. ☐ | C. ☐ |

## 17
| S.D. | P.L. | P.G. | S.G. |
|---|---|---|---|
| P. ☐ | F. ☐ | F. ☐ | T. ☐ |
| F. ☐ | W. ☐ | W. ☐ | P. ☐ |
| B. ☐ | P. ☐ | C. ☐ | C. ☐ |

## 18
| S.D. | P.L. | P.G. | S.G. |
|---|---|---|---|
| P. ☐ | F. ☐ | F. ☐ | T. ☐ |
| F. ☐ | W. ☐ | W. ☐ | P. ☐ |
| B. ☐ | P. ☐ | C. ☐ | C. ☐ |

## 19
| S.D. | P.L. | P.G. | S.G. |
|---|---|---|---|
| P. ☐ | F. ☐ | F. ☐ | T. ☐ |
| F. ☐ | W. ☐ | W. ☐ | P. ☐ |
| B. ☐ | P. ☐ | C. ☐ | C. ☐ |

## 20
| S.D. | P.L. | P.G. | S.G. |
|---|---|---|---|
| P. ☐ | F. ☐ | F. ☐ | T. ☐ |
| F. ☐ | W. ☐ | W. ☐ | P. ☐ |
| B. ☐ | P. ☐ | C. ☐ | C. ☐ |

## 25
| S.D. | P.L. | P.G. | S.G. |
|---|---|---|---|
| P. ☐ | F. ☐ | F. ☐ | T. ☐ |
| F. ☐ | W. ☐ | W. ☐ | P. ☐ |
| B. ☐ | P. ☐ | C. ☐ | C. ☐ |

## 26
| S.D. | P.L. | P.G. | S.G. |
|---|---|---|---|
| P. ☐ | F. ☐ | F. ☐ | T. ☐ |
| F. ☐ | W. ☐ | W. ☐ | P. ☐ |
| B. ☐ | P. ☐ | C. ☐ | C. ☐ |

## 27
| S.D. | P.L. | P.G. | S.G. |
|---|---|---|---|
| P. ☐ | F. ☐ | F. ☐ | T. ☐ |
| F. ☐ | W. ☐ | W. ☐ | P. ☐ |
| B. ☐ | P. ☐ | C. ☐ | C. ☐ |

## 28
| S.D. | P.L. | P.G. | S.G. |
|---|---|---|---|
| P. ☐ | F. ☐ | F. ☐ | T. ☐ |
| F. ☐ | W. ☐ | W. ☐ | P. ☐ |
| B. ☐ | P. ☐ | C. ☐ | C. ☐ |

## Spiritual Disciplines

**Prayer**

**Faith Community**

**Bible Reading**

## Prayer List

**Friends**

**World**

**Personal**

Who am I....
Where am I going....
How am I going to get there?

# nt:sport
## MONTHLY ACTION PLAN

### 5
| S.D. | P.L. | P.G. | S.G. |
|------|------|------|------|
| P. ☐ | F. ☐ | F. ☐ | T. ☐ |
| F. ☐ | W. ☐ | W. ☐ | P. ☐ |
| B. ☐ | P. ☐ | C. ☐ | C. ☐ |

### 6
| S.D. | P.L. | P.G. | S.G. |
|------|------|------|------|
| P. ☐ | F. ☐ | F. ☐ | T. ☐ |
| F. ☐ | W. ☐ | W. ☐ | P. ☐ |
| B. ☐ | P. ☐ | C. ☐ | C. ☐ |

### 7
| S.D. | P.L. | P.G. | S.G. |
|------|------|------|------|
| P. ☐ | F. ☐ | F. ☐ | T. ☐ |
| F. ☐ | W. ☐ | W. ☐ | P. ☐ |
| B. ☐ | P. ☐ | C. ☐ | C. ☐ |

### 8
| S.D. | P.L. | P.G. | S.G. |
|------|------|------|------|
| P. ☐ | F. ☐ | F. ☐ | T. ☐ |
| F. ☐ | W. ☐ | W. ☐ | P. ☐ |
| B. ☐ | P. ☐ | C. ☐ | C. ☐ |

### 13
| S.D. | P.L. | P.G. | S.G. |
|------|------|------|------|
| P. ☐ | F. ☐ | F. ☐ | T. ☐ |
| F. ☐ | W. ☐ | W. ☐ | P. ☐ |
| B. ☐ | P. ☐ | C. ☐ | C. ☐ |

### 14
| S.D. | P.L. | P.G. | S.G. |
|------|------|------|------|
| P. ☐ | F. ☐ | F. ☐ | T. ☐ |
| F. ☐ | W. ☐ | W. ☐ | P. ☐ |
| B. ☐ | P. ☐ | C. ☐ | C. ☐ |

### 15
| S.D. | P.L. | P.G. | S.G. |
|------|------|------|------|
| P. ☐ | F. ☐ | F. ☐ | T. ☐ |
| F. ☐ | W. ☐ | W. ☐ | P. ☐ |
| B. ☐ | P. ☐ | C. ☐ | C. ☐ |

### 16
| S.D. | P.L. | P.G. | S.G. |
|------|------|------|------|
| P. ☐ | F. ☐ | F. ☐ | T. ☐ |
| F. ☐ | W. ☐ | W. ☐ | P. ☐ |
| B. ☐ | P. ☐ | C. ☐ | C. ☐ |

### 21
| S.D. | P.L. | P.G. | S.G. |
|------|------|------|------|
| P. ☐ | F. ☐ | F. ☐ | T. ☐ |
| F. ☐ | W. ☐ | W. ☐ | P. ☐ |
| B. ☐ | P. ☐ | C. ☐ | C. ☐ |

### 22
| S.D. | P.L. | P.G. | S.G. |
|------|------|------|------|
| P. ☐ | F. ☐ | F. ☐ | T. ☐ |
| F. ☐ | W. ☐ | W. ☐ | P. ☐ |
| B. ☐ | P. ☐ | C. ☐ | C. ☐ |

### 23
| S.D. | P.L. | P.G. | S.G. |
|------|------|------|------|
| P. ☐ | F. ☐ | F. ☐ | T. ☐ |
| F. ☐ | W. ☐ | W. ☐ | P. ☐ |
| B. ☐ | P. ☐ | C. ☐ | C. ☐ |

### 24
| S.D. | P.L. | P.G. | S.G. |
|------|------|------|------|
| P. ☐ | F. ☐ | F. ☐ | T. ☐ |
| F. ☐ | W. ☐ | W. ☐ | P. ☐ |
| B. ☐ | P. ☐ | C. ☐ | C. ☐ |

### 29
| S.D. | P.L. | P.G. | S.G. |
|------|------|------|------|
| P. ☐ | F. ☐ | F. ☐ | T. ☐ |
| F. ☐ | W. ☐ | W. ☐ | P. ☐ |
| B. ☐ | P. ☐ | C. ☐ | C. ☐ |

### 30
| S.D. | P.L. | P.G. | S.G. |
|------|------|------|------|
| P. ☐ | F. ☐ | F. ☐ | T. ☐ |
| F. ☐ | W. ☐ | W. ☐ | P. ☐ |
| B. ☐ | P. ☐ | C. ☐ | C. ☐ |

**Proverbs 3:6**

Seek his will in all you do, and he will direct your paths.

## Personal Goals

**Family**

**Work/School/Social**

**Challenge**

## Sport Goals

**Training**

**Performance**

**Competition Results**

(For designing your MAP - Monthly Action Plan - see introduction pages)

## FUTURE CHARACTER TRAITS

**When I die, if ten different types of people were to say something true and nice at my funeral I would like them to say, 'I was...'**

- Friend:
- Team-mate:
- Coach:
- Minister:
- Teacher:
- Boss:
- Work colleague:
- Someone that worked for me:
- Spouse:
- Son:
- Daughter:
- God:

Consider Jesus: Parable of the Talents, Matthew 25: 14 – 30

and I will restore it,
[17] so that the rest of humanity might find the Lord, including the Gentiles—
all those I have called to be mine.
This is what the Lord says,
[18] he who made these things known long ago.'
[19] And so my judgement is that we should stop troubling the Gentiles who turn to God, [20] except that we should write to them and tell them to abstain from eating meat sacrificed to idols, from sexual immorality, and from consuming blood or eating the meat of strangled animals. [21] For these laws of Moses have been preached in Jewish synagogues in every city on every Sabbath for many generations."

### The Letter for Gentile Believers

[22] Then the apostles and elders and the whole church in Jerusalem chose delegates, and they sent them to Antioch of Syria with Paul and Barnabas to report on this decision. The men chosen were two of the church leaders—Judas (also called Barsabbas) and Silas. [23] This is the letter they took along with them:

"This letter is from the apostles and elders, your brothers in Jerusalem. It is written to the Gentile believers in Antioch, Syria, and Cilicia. Greetings! [24] "We understand that some men from here have troubled you and upset you with their teaching, but they had no such instructions from us. [25] So it seemed good to us, having unanimously agreed on our decision, to send you these official representatives, along with our beloved Barnabas and Paul, [26] who have risked their lives for the sake of our Lord Jesus Christ. [27] So we are sending Judas and Silas to tell you what we have decided concerning your question.

[28] "For it seemed good to the Holy Spirit and to us to lay no greater burden on you than these requirements: [29] You must abstain from eating food offered to idols, from consuming blood or eating the meat of strangled animals, and from sexual immorality. If you do this, you will do well. Farewell."

[30] The four messengers went at once to Antioch, where they called a general meeting of the Christians and delivered the letter. [31] And there was great joy throughout the church that day as they read this encouraging message.

[32] Then Judas and Silas, both being prophets, spoke extensively to the Christians, encouraging and strengthening their faith. [33] They stayed for a while, and then Judas and Silas were sent back to Jerusalem, with the blessings of the Christians, to those who had sent them.* [35] Paul and Barnabas stayed in Antioch to assist many others who were teaching and preaching the word of the Lord there.

15:33 Some manuscripts add verse 34, *But Silas decided to stay there.*

## Paul and Barnabas Separate

³⁶After some time Paul said to Barnabas, "Let's return to each city where we previously preached the word of the Lord, to see how the new believers are getting along." ³⁷Barnabas agreed and wanted to take along John Mark. ³⁸But Paul disagreed strongly, since John Mark had deserted them in Pamphylia and had not shared in their work. ³⁹Their disagreement over this was so sharp that they separated. Barnabas took John Mark with him and sailed for Cyprus. ⁴⁰Paul chose Silas, and the believers sent them off, entrusting them to the Lord's grace. ⁴¹So they travelled throughout Syria and Cilicia to strengthen the churches there.

## Paul's Second Missionary Journey

# 16

Paul and Silas went first to Derbe and then on to Lystra. There they met Timothy, a young disciple whose mother was a Jewish believer, but whose father was a Greek. ²Timothy was well thought of by the believers in Lystra and Iconium, ³so Paul wanted him to join them on their journey. In deference to the Jews of the area, he arranged for Timothy to be circumcised before they left, for everyone knew that his father was a Greek. ⁴Then they went from town to town, explaining the decision regarding the commandments that were to be obeyed, as decided by the apostles and elders in Jerusalem. ⁵So the churches were strengthened in their faith and grew daily in numbers.

## A Call from Macedonia

⁶Next Paul and Silas travelled through the area of Phrygia and Galatia, because the Holy Spirit had told them not to go into the province of Asia at that time. ⁷Then coming to the borders of Mysia, they headed for the province of Bithynia, but again the Spirit of Jesus did not let them go. ⁸So instead, they went on through Mysia to the city of Troas.

⁹That night Paul had a vision. He saw a man from Macedonia in northern Greece, pleading with him, "Come over here and help us." ¹⁰So we decided to leave for Macedonia at once, for we could only conclude that God was calling us to preach the Good News there.

## Lydia of Philippi Believes in Jesus

¹¹We boarded a boat at Troas and sailed straight across to the island of Samothrace, and the next day we landed at Neapolis. ¹²From there we reached Philippi, a major city of the district of Macedonia and a Roman colony; we stayed there several days.

¹³On the Sabbath we went a little way outside the city to a river-bank, where we supposed that some people met for prayer, and we sat down to speak with some women who had come together. ¹⁴One of them was Lydia from Thyatira, a merchant of expensive purple cloth. She was a worshipper of God. As she listened to us, the Lord opened her heart, and she accepted what Paul was saying. ¹⁵She was baptized along with other members of her household, and she asked us to be her guests.

"If you agree that I am faithful to the Lord," she said, "come and stay at my home." And she urged us until we did.

action

CH 16:22-40 WHAT'S IT SAYING?

WHAT AM I GOING TO DO ABOUT IT?

## Paul and Silas in Prison

¹⁶One day as we were going down to the place of prayer, we met a demon-possessed slave girl. She was a fortune-teller who earned a lot of money for her masters. ¹⁷She followed along behind us shouting, "These men are servants of the Most High God, and they have come to tell you how to be saved."

¹⁸This went on day after day until Paul got so exasperated that he turned and spoke to the demon within her. "I command you in the name of Jesus Christ to come out of her," he said. And instantly it left her.

¹⁹Her masters' hopes of wealth were now shattered, so they grabbed Paul and Silas and dragged them before the authorities at the marketplace. ²⁰"The whole city is in an uproar because of these Jews!" they shouted. ²¹"They are teaching the people to do things that are against Roman customs."

²²A mob quickly formed against Paul and Silas, and the city officials ordered them stripped and beaten with wooden rods. ²³They were severely beaten, and then they were thrown into prison. The jailer was ordered to make sure they didn't escape. ²⁴So he took no chances but put them into the inner dungeon and clamped their feet in the stocks.

²⁵Around midnight, Paul and Silas were praying and singing hymns to God, and the other prisoners were listening. ²⁶Suddenly, there was a great earthquake, and the prison was shaken to its foundations. All the doors flew open, and the chains of every prisoner fell off! ²⁷The jailer woke up to see the prison doors wide open. He assumed the prisoners had escaped, so he drew his sword to kill himself. ²⁸But Paul shouted to him, "Don't do it! We are all here!"

²⁹Trembling with fear, the jailer called for lights and ran to the dungeon and fell down before Paul and Silas. ³⁰He brought them out and asked, "Sirs, what must I do to be saved?"

³¹They replied, "Believe on the Lord Jesus and you will be saved, along with your entire household." ³²Then they shared the word of the Lord with him and all who lived in his household. ³³That same hour the jailer washed their wounds, and he and everyone in his household were immediately baptized.

³⁴Then he brought them into his house and set a meal before them. He and his entire household rejoiced because they all believed in God.

³⁵The next morning the city officials sent the police to tell the jailer, "Let those men go!" ³⁶So the jailer told Paul, "You and Silas are free to leave. Go in peace."

³⁷But Paul replied, "They have publicly beaten us without trial and jailed us—and we are Roman citizens. So now they want us to leave secretly? Certainly not! Let them come themselves to release us!"

³⁸When the police made their report, the city officials were alarmed to learn that Paul and Silas were Roman citizens. ³⁹They came to the jail and apologized to them. Then they brought them out and begged them to leave the city. ⁴⁰Paul and Silas then returned to the home of Lydia, where they met with the believers and encouraged them once more before leaving town.

## Paul Preaches in Thessalonica

# 17

Now Paul and Silas travelled through the towns of Amphipolis and Apollonia and came to Thessalonica, where there was a

Jewish synagogue. [2]As was Paul's custom, he went to the synagogue service, and for three Sabbaths in a row he interpreted the Scriptures to the people. [3]He was explaining and proving the prophecies about the sufferings of the Messiah and his rising from the dead. He said, "This Jesus I'm telling you about is the Messiah." [4]Some who listened were persuaded and became converts, including a large number of godly Greek men and also many important women of the city.

[5]But the Jewish leaders were jealous, so they gathered some worthless fellows from the streets to form a mob and start a riot. They attacked the home of Jason, searching for Paul and Silas so they could drag them out to the crowd. [6]Not finding them there, they dragged out Jason and some of the other believers instead and took them before the city council. "Paul and Silas have turned the rest of the world upside down, and now they are here disturbing our city," they shouted. [7]"And Jason has let them into his home. They are all guilty of treason against Caesar, for they profess allegiance to another king, Jesus."

[8]The people of the city, as well as the city officials, were thrown into turmoil by these reports. [9]But the officials released Jason and the other believers after they were bailed out.

## action

CH 17:10–12 WHAT'S IT SAYING?

WHAT AM I GOING TO DO ABOUT IT?

## count on it

**Have you ever felt thirsty?**
Wouldn't that suggest you need to get re-hydrated? Have you ever felt hungry? Wouldn't that suggest that you need some nutrition? Have you ever felt lonely? Wouldn't that suggest you need companionship? Have you ever felt lonely in a crowd? Wouldn't that suggest that you needed companionship with someone other than another person? God will be there for you! "I will never fail you, I will never forsake you."
Hebrews 13:5
**Count on it!**

## Paul and Silas in Berea

[10]That very night the believers sent Paul and Silas to Berea. When they arrived there, they went to the synagogue. [11]And the people of Berea were more open-minded than those in Thessalonica, and they listened eagerly to Paul's message. They searched the Scriptures day after day to check up on Paul and Silas, to see if they were really teaching the truth. [12]As a result, many Jews believed, as did some of the prominent Greek women and many men.

[13]But when some Jews in Thessalonica learned that Paul was preaching the word of God in Berea, they went there and stirred up trouble. [14]The believers acted at once, sending Paul on to the coast, while Silas and Timothy remained behind. [15]Those escorting Paul went with him to Athens; then they returned to Berea with a message for Silas and Timothy to hurry and join him.

## Paul Preaches in Athens

[16]While Paul was waiting for them in Athens, he was deeply troubled by all the idols he saw everywhere in the city.

[17]He went to the synagogue to debate with the Jews and the God-fearing Gentiles, and he spoke daily in the public square to all who happened to be there.

[18]He also had a debate with some of the Epicurean and Stoic philosophers. When he told them about Jesus and his resurrection, they said, "This babbler has picked up some strange ideas." Others said, "He's pushing some foreign religion."

[19]Then they took him to the Council of Philosophers. "Come and tell us more about this new religion," they said. [20]"You are saying some rather startling things, and we want to know what it's all about." [21](It should be explained that all the Athenians as well as the foreigners in Athens seemed to spend all their time discussing the latest ideas.)

[22]So Paul, standing before the Council, addressed them as follows: "Men of Athens, I notice that you are very religious,

[23]for as I was walking along I saw your many altars. And one of them had this inscription on it—'To an Unknown God.' You have been worshipping him without knowing who he is, and now I wish to tell you about him.

[24]"He is the God who made the world and everything in it. Since he is Lord of heaven and earth, he doesn't live in man-made temples, [25]and human hands can't serve his needs—for he has no needs. He himself gives life and breath to everything, and he satisfies every need there is. [26]From one man he created all the nations throughout the whole earth. He decided beforehand which should rise and fall, and he determined their boundaries.

[27]"His purpose in all of this was that the nations should seek after God and perhaps feel their way towards him and find him—though he is not far from any one of us. [28]For in him we live and move and exist. As one of your own poets says, 'We are his offspring.' [29]And since this is true, we shouldn't think of God as an idol designed by craftsmen from gold or silver or stone. [30]God overlooked people's former ignorance about these things, but now he commands everyone everywhere to turn away from idols and turn to him. [31]For he has set a day for judging the world with justice by the man he has appointed, and he proved to everyone who this is by raising him from the dead."

[32]When they heard Paul speak of the resurrection of a person who had been dead, some laughed, but others

said, "We want to hear more about this later." [33]That ended Paul's discussion with them, [34]but some joined him and became believers. Among them were Dionysius, a member of the Council, a woman named Damaris, and others.

## Paul Meets Priscilla and Aquila in Corinth

# 18

Then Paul left Athens and went to Corinth. [2]There he became acquainted with a Jew named Aquila, born in Pontus, who had recently arrived from Italy with his wife, Priscilla. They had been expelled from Italy as a result of Claudius Caesar's order to deport all Jews from Rome. [3]Paul lived and worked with them, for they were tentmakers just as he was.

[4]Each Sabbath found Paul at the synagogue, trying to convince the Jews and Greeks alike. [5]And after Silas and Timothy came down from Macedonia, Paul spent his full time preaching and testifying to the Jews, telling them, "The Messiah you are looking for is Jesus." [6]But when the Jews opposed him and insulted him, Paul shook the dust from his robe and said, "Your blood be upon your own heads—I am innocent. From now on I will go to the Gentiles."

[7]After that he stayed with Titius Justus, a Gentile who worshipped God and lived next door to the synagogue. [8]Crispus, the leader of the synagogue, and all his household believed in the Lord. Many others in Corinth also became believers and were baptized.

[9]One night the Lord spoke to Paul in a vision and told him,

"Don't be afraid! Speak out! Don't be silent! [10]For I am with you, and no one will harm you because many people here in this city belong to me." [11]So Paul stayed there for the next year and a half, teaching the word of God.

[12]But when Gallio became governor of Achaia, some Jews rose in concerted action against Paul and brought him before the governor for judgement. [13]They accused Paul of "persuading people to worship God in ways that are contrary to the law."

[14]But just as Paul started to make his defence, Gallio turned to Paul's accusers and said, "Listen, you Jews, if this were a case involving some wrongdoing or a serious crime, I would be obliged to listen to you. [15]But since it is merely a question of words and names and your Jewish laws, you take care of it. I refuse to judge such matters." [16]And he drove them out of the courtroom. [17]The mob had grabbed Sosthenes, the leader of the synagogue, and had beaten him right there in the courtroom. But Gallio paid no attention.

## Paul Returns to Antioch of Syria

[18]Paul stayed in Corinth for some time after that and then said goodbye to the brothers and sisters and sailed for the coast of Syria, taking Priscilla and Aquila with him. (Earlier, at Cenchrea, Paul had shaved his head according to Jewish custom, for he had taken a vow.) [19]When they arrived at the port of Ephesus, Paul left the others behind. But while he was there, he went to the synagogue to debate with the Jews. [20]They asked him to stay longer, but he declined. [21]So he left, saying, "I will come back later, God willing." Then he set sail from Ephesus.

[22]The next stop was at the port of Caesarea. From there he went up and visited the church at Jerusalem and then went back to Antioch.

[23]After spending some time in Antioch, Paul went back to Galatia and Phrygia, visiting all the believers, encouraging them and helping them to grow in the Lord.

## Apollos Instructed at Ephesus

[24]Meanwhile, a Jew named Apollos, an eloquent speaker who knew the Scriptures well, had just arrived in Ephesus from Alexandria in Egypt. [25]He had been taught the way of the Lord and talked to others with great enthusiasm and accuracy about Jesus. However, he knew only about John's baptism. [26]When Priscilla and Aquila heard him preaching boldly in the synagogue, they took him aside and explained the way

of God more accurately.

[27]Apollos had been thinking about going to Achaia, and the brothers and sisters in Ephesus encouraged him in this. They wrote to the believers in Achaia, asking them to welcome him. When he arrived there, he proved to be of great benefit to those who, by God's grace, had believed. [28]He refuted all the Jews with powerful arguments in public debate. Using the Scriptures, he explained to them, "The Messiah you are looking for is Jesus."

## Paul's Third Missionary Journey

# 19

While Apollos was in Corinth, Paul travelled through the interior provinces. Finally, he came to Ephesus, where he found several believers. [2]"Did you receive the Holy Spirit when you believed?" he asked them.

"No," they replied, "we don't know what you mean. We haven't even heard that there is a Holy Spirit."

[3]"Then what baptism did you experience?" he asked.

And they replied, "The baptism of John."

[4]Paul said, "John's baptism was to demonstrate a desire to turn from sin and turn to God. John himself told the people to believe in Jesus, the one John said would come later." [5]As soon as they heard this, they were baptized in the name of the Lord Jesus. [6]Then when Paul laid his hands on them, the Holy Spirit came on them, and they spoke in other tongues and prophesied. [7]There were about twelve men in all.

## Paul Ministers in Ephesus

[8]Then Paul went to the synagogue and preached boldly for the next three months, arguing persuasively about the Kingdom of God. [9]But some rejected his message and publicly spoke against the Way, so Paul left the synagogue and took the believers with him. Then he began preaching daily at the lecture hall of Tyrannus. [10]This went on for the next two years, so that people throughout the province of Asia—both Jews and Greeks—heard the Lord's message.

[11]God gave Paul the power to do unusual miracles, [12]so that even when handkerchiefs or cloths that had touched his skin were placed on sick people, they were healed of their diseases, and any evil spirits within them came out.

### Will reading my Bible help me in my sport?

Yes, definitely. God's book will help you in every area of your life. God's coaching manual – the Bible – may not help us technically with our game, nor will it give us six principles for effective concentration, but if we live our lives by its rules, we will enormously increase our chances of maximising performance. So to play our sport for Jesus, means maintaining a central place in our lives for Jesus' book. Serious athletes neglect training at their peril; serious Christians neglect the Bible at their peril.

[13]A team of Jews who were travelling from town to town casting out evil spirits tried to use the name of the Lord Jesus. The incantation they used was this: "I command you by Jesus, whom Paul preaches, to come out!" [14]Seven sons of Sceva, a leading priest, were doing this. [15]But when they tried it on a man possessed by an evil spirit, the spirit replied, "I know Jesus, and I know Paul. But who are you?" [16]And he leaped on them and attacked them with such violence that they fled from the house, naked and badly injured.

[17]The story of what happened spread quickly all through Ephesus, to Jews and Greeks alike. A solemn fear descended on the city, and the name of the Lord Jesus was greatly honoured. [18]Many who became believers confessed their sinful practices. [19]A number of them who had been practising magic brought their incantation books and burned them at a public bonfire. The value of the books was several million pounds. [20]So the message about the Lord spread widely and had a powerful effect.

action

**CH 19:19-20 WHAT'S IT SAYING?**

**WHAT AM I GOING TO DO ABOUT IT?**

## The Riot in Ephesus

[21]Afterwards Paul felt impelled by the Holy Spirit to go over to Macedonia and Achaia before returning to Jerusalem. "And after that," he said, "I must go on to Rome!" [22]He sent his two assistants, Timothy and Erastus, on ahead to Macedonia while he stayed awhile longer in the province of Asia.

[23]But about that time, serious trouble developed in Ephesus concerning the Way. [24]It began with Demetrius, a silversmith who had a large business manufacturing silver shrines of the Greek goddess Artemis. He kept many craftsmen busy. [25]He called the craftsmen together, along with others employed in related trades, and addressed them as follows: "Gentlemen, you know that our wealth comes from this business.

[26]As you have seen and heard, this man Paul has persuaded many people that handmade gods aren't gods at all. And this is happening not only here in Ephesus but throughout the entire province! [27]Of course, I'm not just talking about the loss of public respect for our business. I'm also concerned that the temple of the great goddess Artemis will lose its influence and that Artemis—this magnificent goddess worshipped throughout the province of Asia and all around the world—will be robbed of her prestige!"

[28]At this their anger boiled, and they began shouting, "Great is Artemis of the Ephesians!" [29]A crowd began to gather, and soon the city was filled with confusion. Everyone rushed to the amphitheatre, dragging along Gaius and Aristarchus, who were Paul's travelling companions from Macedonia. [30]Paul wanted to go in, but the believers wouldn't let him. [31]Some of the officials of the province, friends of Paul, also sent a message to him, begging him not to risk his life by entering the amphitheatre.

[32]Inside, the people were all shouting, some one thing and some another. Everything was in confusion. In fact, most of them didn't even know why they were there. [33]Alexander was thrust forward by some of the Jews, who encouraged him to explain the situation. He motioned for silence and tried to speak in defence. [34]But when the crowd realized he was a Jew, they started shouting again and kept it up for two hours: "Great is Artemis of the Ephesians! Great is Artemis of the Ephesians!"

[35]At last the mayor was able to quieten them down enough to speak. "Citizens of Ephesus," he said. "Everyone knows that Ephesus is the official guardian of the temple of the great Artemis, whose image fell down to us from heaven. [36]Since this is an indisputable fact, you shouldn't be disturbed, no matter what is said. Don't do anything rash. [37]You have brought these men here, but they have stolen nothing from the temple and have not spoken against our goddess. [38]If Demetrius and the craftsmen have a case against

them, the courts are in session and the judges can take the case at once. Let them go through legal channels. [39]And if there are complaints about other matters, they can be settled in a legal assembly. [40]I am afraid we are in danger of being charged with rioting by the Roman government, since there is no cause for all this commotion. And if Rome demands an expla-nation, we won't know what to say." [41]Then he dismissed them, and they dispersed.

## Paul Goes to Macedonia and Greece

# 20

When it was all over, Paul sent for the believers and encouraged them. Then he said goodbye and left for Macedonia.

[2]Along the way, he encouraged the believers in all the towns he passed through. Then he travelled down to Greece, [3]where he stayed for three months. He was preparing to sail back to Syria when he discovered a plot by some Jews against his life, so he decided to return through Macedonia.

[4]Several men were travelling with him. They were Sopater of Berea, the son of Pyrrhus; Aristarchus and Secundus, from Thessalonica; Gaius, from Derbe; Timothy; and Tychicus and Trophimus, who were from the province of Asia. [5]They went ahead and waited for us at Troas. [6]As soon as the Passover season ended, we boarded a ship at Philippi in Macedonia and five days later arrived in Troas, where we stayed a week.

## Paul's Final Visit to Troas

[7]On the first day of the week, we gathered to observe the Lord's Supper. Paul was preaching; and since he was leaving the next day, he talked until midnight. [8]The upstairs room where we met was lit with many flickering lamps. [9]As Paul spoke on and on, a young man named Eutychus, sitting on the windowsill, became very drowsy. Finally, he sank into a deep sleep and fell three storeys to his death below. [10]Paul went down, bent over him, and took him into his arms. "Don't worry," he said, "he's alive!" [11]Then they all went back upstairs and ate the Lord's Supper together. And Paul continued talking to them until dawn; then he left. [12]Meanwhile, the young man was taken home unhurt, and everyone was greatly relieved.

## Paul Meets the Ephesian Elders

[13]Paul went by land to Assos, where he had arranged

for us to join him, and we went on ahead by ship. ¹⁴He joined us there and we sailed together to Mitylene. ¹⁵The next day we passed the island of Kios. The following day, we crossed to the island of Samos. And a day later we arrived at Miletus.

¹⁶Paul had decided against stopping at Ephesus this time because he didn't want to spend further time in the province of Asia. He was hurrying to get to Jerusalem, if possible, for the Festival of Pentecost. ¹⁷But when we landed at Miletus, he sent a message to the elders of the church at Ephesus, asking them to come down to meet him.

¹⁸When they arrived he declared, "You know that from the day I set foot in the province of Asia until now ¹⁹I have done the Lord's work humbly—yes, and with tears. I have endured the trials that came to me from the plots of the Jews. ²⁰Yet I never shrank from telling you the truth, either publicly or in your homes. ²¹I have had one message for Jews and Gentiles alike—the necessity of turning from sin and turning to God, and of faith in our Lord Jesus.

²²"And now I am going to Jerusalem, drawn there irresistibly by the Holy Spirit, not knowing what awaits me, ²³except that the Holy Spirit has told me in city after city that jail and suffering lie ahead. ²⁴But my life is worth nothing unless I use it for doing the work assigned me by the Lord Jesus—the work of telling others the Good News about God's wonderful kindness and love.

²⁵"And now I know that none of you to whom I have preached the Kingdom will ever see me again. ²⁶Let me say plainly that I have been faithful. No one's damnation can be blamed on me, ²⁷for I didn't shrink from declaring all that God wants for you.

²⁸"And now beware! Be sure that you feed and shepherd God's flock—his church, purchased with his blood—over whom the Holy Spirit has appointed you as elders.

### The longest book chapter in the Bible is Psalm 119 the shortest is Psalm 117.

²⁹I know full well that false teachers, like vicious wolves, will come in among you after I leave, not sparing the flock. ³⁰Even some of you will distort the truth in order to draw a following. ³¹Watch out! Remember the three years I was with you—my constant watch and care over you night and day, and my many tears for you.

³²"And now I entrust you to God and the word of his grace—his message that is able to build you up and give you an inheritance with all those he has set apart for himself.

³³"I have never coveted anyone's money or fine clothing.

³⁴You know that these hands of mine have worked to pay my own way, and I have even supplied the needs of those who were with me.

³⁵And I have been a constant example of how you can help the poor by working hard. You should remember the words of the Lord Jesus:

'It is more blessed to give than to receive.'"

³⁶When he had finished speaking, he knelt and prayed with them.

³⁷They wept aloud as they embraced him in farewell, ³⁸sad most of all because he had said that they would never see him again. Then they accompanied him down to the ship.

## Paul's Journey to Jerusalem

# 21

After saying farewell to the Ephesian elders, we sailed straight to the island of Cos. The next day we reached Rhodes and then went to Patara. ²There we boarded a ship sailing for the Syrian province of Phoenicia. ³We sighted the island of Cyprus, passed it on our left, and landed at the harbour of Tyre, in Syria, where the ship was to unload. ⁴We went ashore, found the local believers, and stayed with them a week. These disciples prophesied through the Holy Spirit that Paul should not go on to Jerusalem. ⁵When we returned to the ship at the end of the week, the entire congregation, including wives and children, came down to the shore with us. There we knelt, prayed, ⁶and said our farewells. Then we went aboard, and they returned home.

⁷The next stop after leaving Tyre was Ptolemais, where we greeted the brothers and sisters but stayed only one day. ⁸Then we went on to Caesarea and stayed at the home of Philip the Evangelist, one of the seven men who had been chosen to distribute food. ⁹He had four unmarried daughters who had the gift of prophecy.

¹⁰During our stay of several days, a man named Agabus, who also had the gift of prophecy, arrived from Judea. ¹¹When he visited us, he took Paul's belt and bound his own feet and hands with it. Then he said, "The Holy Spirit declares, 'So shall the owner of this belt be bound by the Jewish leaders in Jerusalem and turned over to the Romans.'"

¹²When we heard this, we who were travelling with him, as well as the local believers, begged Paul not to go on to Jerusalem.

¹³But he said, "Why all this weeping? You are breaking my heart! For I am ready not only to be jailed at Jerusalem but also to die for the sake of the Lord Jesus." ¹⁴When it was clear that we couldn't persuade him, we gave up and said, "The will of the Lord be done."

## Get Good Coaching!

The brain is able to learn a new skill, such as walking. If we practise walking often enough, then the skill becomes automatic. We no longer have to think how to walk. Walking has become a skill controlled by the 'subconscious' part of our brain. This allows us to look about, talk and do other things controlled by the 'conscious' part of the brain, all at the same time. Like a computer, the 'conscious' part of the brain learns what is required, writes the programme code and then stores it in the 'subconscious' for instant execution when required. So if you are taught poor technique it will take more time to root it out and retrain properly.

## Paul Arrives at Jerusalem

¹⁵Shortly afterwards we packed our things and left for Jerusalem. ¹⁶Some believers from Caesarea accompanied us, and they took us to the home of Mnason, a man originally from Cyprus and one of the early disciples. ¹⁷All the brothers and sisters in Jerusalem welcomed us warmly.

¹⁸The next day Paul went in with us to meet with James, and all the elders of the Jerusalem church were present. ¹⁹After greetings were exchanged, Paul gave a detailed account of the things God had accomplished among the Gentiles through his ministry.

²⁰After hearing this, they praised God. But then they said, "You know, dear brother, how many thousands of Jews have also believed, and they all take the law of Moses very seriously. ²¹Our Jewish Christians here at Jerusalem have been told that you are teaching all the Jews living in the Gentile world to turn their backs on the laws of Moses. They say that you teach people not to circumcise their children or follow other Jewish customs. ²²Now what can be done? For they will certainly hear that you have come.

²³"Here's our suggestion. We have four men here who have taken a vow and are preparing to shave their heads. ²⁴Go with them to the Temple and join them in the purification ceremony, and pay for them to have their heads shaved. Then everyone will know that the rumours are all false and that you yourself observe the Jewish laws.

²⁵"As for the Gentile Christians, all we ask of them is what we already told them in a letter: They should not eat food offered to idols, nor consume blood, nor eat meat from strangled animals, and they should stay away from all sexual immorality."

## Paul Is Arrested

²⁶So Paul agreed to their request, and the next day he went through the purification ritual with the men and went to the Temple. Then he publicly announced the date when their vows would end and sacrifices would be offered for each of them.

²⁷The seven days were almost ended when some Jews from the province of Asia saw Paul in the Temple and roused a mob against him. They grabbed him, ²⁸yelling, "Men of Israel! Help! This is the man who teaches against our people and tells everybody to disobey the Jewish laws. He speaks against the Temple—and he even defiles it by bringing Gentiles in!" ²⁹(For earlier that day they had seen him in the city with Trophimus, a Gentile from Ephesus, and they assumed Paul had taken him into the Temple.)

³⁰The whole population of the city was rocked by these accusations, and a great riot followed. Paul was dragged out of the Temple, and immediately the gates were closed behind him. ³¹As they were trying to kill him, word reached the commander of the Roman regiment that all Jerusalem was in an uproar. ³²He immediately called out his soldiers and officers and ran down among the crowd. When the mob saw the commander and the troops coming, they stopped beating Paul. ³³The commander arrested him and ordered him bound with two chains. Then he asked the crowd who he was and what he had done. ³⁴Some shouted one thing and some another. He couldn't find out the truth in all the uproar and confusion, so he ordered Paul to be taken to the fortress. ³⁵As they reached the stairs, the mob grew so violent the soldiers had to lift Paul onto their shoulders to protect him. ³⁶And the crowd followed behind shouting, "Kill him, kill him!"

## Paul Speaks to the Crowd

³⁷As Paul was about to be taken inside, he said to the commander, "May I have a word with you?"

"Do you know Greek?" the commander asked, surprised. ³⁸"Aren't you the Egyptian who led a rebellion some time ago and took four thousand members of the Assassins out into the desert?"

³⁹"No," Paul replied, "I am a Jew from Tarsus in Cilicia, which is an important city. Please, let me talk to these people." ⁴⁰The commander agreed, so Paul stood on the stairs and motioned to the people to be quiet. Soon a deep silence enveloped the crowd, and he addressed them in their own language, Aramaic.

# 22

"Brothers and esteemed fathers," Paul said, "listen to me as I offer my defence." ²When they heard him speaking in their own language, the silence was even greater.

³"I am a Jew, born in Tarsus, a city in Cilicia, and I was brought up and educated here in Jerusalem under Gamaliel. At his feet I learned to follow our Jewish laws and customs very carefully. I became very zealous to honour God in everything I did, just as all of you are today. ⁴And I persecuted the followers of the Way,

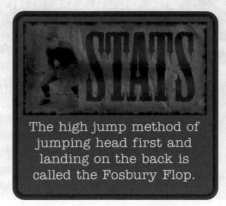

The high jump method of jumping head first and landing on the back is called the Fosbury Flop.

hounding some to death, binding and delivering both men and women to prison. ⁵The high priest and the whole council of leaders can testify that this is so. For I received letters from them to our Jewish brothers in Damascus, authorizing me to bring the Christians from there to Jerusalem, in chains, to be punished.

⁶"As I was on the road, nearing Damascus, about midday a very bright light from heaven suddenly shone around me. ⁷I fell to the ground and heard a voice saying to me, 'Saul, Saul, why are you persecuting me?'

⁸"'Who are you, sir?' I asked. And he replied, 'I am Jesus of Nazareth, the one you are persecuting.' ⁹The people with me saw the light but didn't hear the voice.

¹⁰"I said, 'What shall I do, Lord?' And the Lord told me, 'Get up and go into Damascus, and there you will be told all that you are to do.'

¹¹"I was blinded by the intense light and had to be led into Damascus by my companions. ¹²A man named Ananias lived there. He was a godly man in his devotion to the law, and he was well thought of by all the Jews of Damascus. ¹³He came to me and stood beside me and said, 'Brother Saul, receive your sight.' And that very hour I could see him!

¹⁴"Then he told me, 'The God of our ancestors has chosen you to know his will and to see the Righteous One and hear him speak. **¹⁵You are to take his message everywhere, telling the whole world what you have seen and heard.**

¹⁶And now, why delay? Get up and be baptized, and have your sins washed away, calling on the name of the Lord.'

¹⁷"One day after I returned to Jerusalem, I was praying in the Temple, and I fell into a trance. ¹⁸I saw a vision of Jesus saying to me, 'Hurry! Leave Jerusalem, for the people here won't believe you when you give them your testimony about me.'

¹⁹"'But Lord,' I argued, 'they certainly know that I imprisoned and beat those in every synagogue who believed on you. ²⁰And when your witness Stephen was killed, I was standing there agreeing. I kept the coats they laid aside as they stoned him.'

²¹"But the Lord said to me, 'Leave Jerusalem, for I will send you far away to the Gentiles!'"

²²The crowd listened until Paul came to that word; then with one voice they shouted, "Away with such a fellow! Kill him! He isn't fit to live!" ²³They yelled, threw off their coats, and tossed handfuls of dust into the air.

## Paul Reveals His Roman Citizenship

²⁴The commander brought Paul inside and ordered him lashed with whips to make him confess his crime. He wanted to find out why the crowd had become so furious. ²⁵As they tied Paul down to lash him, Paul said to the officer standing there, "Is it legal for you to whip a Roman citizen who hasn't even been tried?"

²⁶The officer went to the commander and asked, "What are you doing? This man is a Roman citizen!"

²⁷So the commander went over and asked Paul, "Tell me, are you a Roman citizen?"

"Yes, I certainly am," Paul replied.

²⁸"I am, too," the commander muttered, "and it cost me a lot!"

"But I am a citizen by birth!"

²⁹The soldiers who were about to interrogate Paul quickly withdrew when they heard he was a Roman citizen, and the commander was frightened because he had ordered him bound and whipped.

## Paul before the High Council

³⁰The next day the commander freed Paul from his chains and ordered the leading priests into session with the Jewish high council. He had Paul brought in before them to try to find out what the trouble was all about.

## 23

Gazing intently at the high council, Paul began: "Brothers, I have always lived before God in all good conscience!"

²Instantly Ananias the high priest commanded those close to Paul to slap him on the mouth. ³But Paul said to him, "God will slap you, you whitewashed wall! What kind of judge are you to break the law yourself by ordering me struck like that?"

⁴Those standing near Paul said to him, "Is that the way to talk to God's high priest?"

⁵"I'm sorry, brothers. I didn't realize he was the high priest," Paul replied, "for the Scriptures say, 'Do not speak evil of anyone who rules over you.'"

⁶Paul realized that some members of the high council were Sadducees and some were Pharisees, so he shouted, "Brothers, I am a Pharisee, as were all my ancestors! And I am on trial because my hope is in the resurrection of the dead!"

⁷This divided the council—the Pharisees against the Sadducees—⁸for the Sadducees say there is no resurrection or angels or spirits, but the Pharisees believe in all of these. ⁹So a great clamour arose. Some of the teachers of religious law who were Pharisees jumped up to argue that Paul was all right. "We see nothing wrong with him," they shouted. "Perhaps a spirit or an angel spoke to him." ¹⁰The shouting grew louder and louder, and the men were tugging at Paul from both sides, pulling him this way and that. Finally, the commander, fearing they would tear him apart, ordered his soldiers to take him away from them and bring him back to the fortress.

¹¹That night the Lord appeared to Paul and said, "Be encouraged, Paul. Just as you have told the people about me here in Jerusalem, you must preach the Good News in Rome."

## The Plan to Kill Paul

[12]The next morning a group of Jews got together and bound themselves with an oath neither to eat nor drink until they had killed Paul. [13]There were more than forty of them. [14]They went to the leading priests and other leaders and told them what they had done. "We have bound ourselves under oath neither to eat nor drink until we have killed Paul. [15]You and the high council should tell the commander to bring Paul back to the council again," they requested. "Pretend you want to examine his case more fully. We will kill him on the way."

[16]But Paul's nephew heard of their plan and went to the fortress and told Paul. [17]Paul called one of the officers and said, "Take this young man to the commander. He has something important to tell him."

[18]So the officer did, explaining, "Paul, the prisoner, called me over and asked me to bring this young man to you because he has something to tell you."

[19]The commander took him by the arm, led him aside, and asked,

"What is it you want to tell me?"

[20]Paul's nephew told him, "Some Jews are going to ask you to bring Paul before the Jewish high council tomorrow, pretending they want to get some more information. [21]But don't do it! There are more than forty men hiding along the way ready to ambush him and kill him. They have vowed not to eat or drink until they kill him. They are ready, expecting you to agree to their request."

[22]"Don't let a soul know you told me this," the commander warned the young man as he sent him away.

## Paul Is Sent to Caesarea

[23]Then the commander called two of his officers and ordered, "Get two hundred soldiers ready to leave for Caesarea at nine o'clock tonight. Also take two hundred spearmen and seventy horsemen. [24]Provide horses for Paul to ride, and get him safely to Governor Felix." [25]Then he wrote this letter to the governor:

[26]"From Claudius Lysias, to his Excellency, Governor Felix. Greetings! [27]This man was seized by some Jews, and they were about to kill him when I arrived with the troops. When I learned that he was a Roman citizen, I removed him to safety. [28]Then I took him to their high council to try to find out what he had done.

[29]I soon discovered it was something regarding their religious law—certainly nothing worthy of imprisonment or death. [30]But when I was informed of a plot to kill him, I immediately sent him on to you. I have told his accusers to bring their charges before you."

[31]So that night, as ordered, the soldiers took Paul as far as Antipatris. [32]They returned to the fortress the next morning, while the horsemen took him on to Caesarea. [33]When they arrived in Caesarea, they presented Paul and the letter to Governor Felix. [34]He read it and then asked Paul what province he was from. "Cilicia," Paul answered.

[35]"I will hear your case myself when your accusers arrive," the governor told him. Then the governor ordered him kept in the prison at Herod's headquarters.

## Paul Appears before Felix

# 24

Five days later Ananias, the high priest, arrived with some of the Jewish leaders and the lawyer Tertullus, to press charges against Paul. [2]When Paul was called in, Tertullus laid charges against Paul in the following address to the governor:

"Your Excellency, you have given peace to us Jews and have enacted reforms for us. [3]And for all of this we are very grateful to you. [4]But lest I bore you, kindly give me your attention for only a moment as I briefly outline our case against this man. [5]For we have found him to be a troublemaker, a man who is constantly inciting the Jews throughout the world to riots and rebellions against the Roman government. He is a ringleader of the sect known as the Nazarenes. [6]Moreover he was trying to defile the Temple when we arrested him.* [8]You can find out the truth of our accusations by examining him yourself." [9]Then the other Jews chimed in, declaring that everything Tertullus said was true.

[10]Now it was Paul's turn. The governor motioned for him to rise and speak. Paul said, "I know, sir, that you have been a judge of Jewish affairs for many years, and this gives me confidence as I make my defence. [11]You can quickly discover that it was no more than twelve days ago that I arrived in Jerusalem to worship at the Temple. [12]I didn't argue with anyone in the Temple, nor did I incite a riot in any synagogue or on the streets of the city. [13]These men certainly cannot prove the things they accuse me of doing.

[14]But I admit that I follow the Way, which they call a sect. I worship the God of our ancestors, and I firmly believe the Jewish law and everything written in the books of prophecy.

[15]I have hope in God, just as these men do, that he will raise both the righteous and the ungodly. [16]Because of this, I always try to maintain a clear conscience before God and everyone else.

[17]After several years away, I returned to Jerusalem with money to aid my people and to offer sacrifices to God. [18]My accusers saw me in the Temple as I was completing a purification ritual. There was no crowd around me and no rioting. [19]But some Jews from the province of Asia were there—and they ought to be here to bring charges if they have anything against me! [20]Ask these men here what wrongdoing the Jewish high council found in me, [21]except for one thing I said when I shouted out, 'I am on trial before you today because I believe in the resurrection of the dead!'"

[22]Felix, who was quite familiar with the Way, adjourned the hearing and said, "Wait until Lysias, the garrison commander, arrives. Then I will decide the case." [23]He ordered an officer to keep Paul in custody but to give him some freedom and allow his friends to visit him and take care of his needs.

[24]A few days later Felix came with his wife, Drusilla, who was Jewish. Sending for Paul, they listened as he told them about faith in Christ Jesus. [25]As he reasoned with them about righteousness and self-control and the judgement to come, Felix was terrified. "Go away for now," he replied. "When it is more convenient, I'll call for you again." [26]He also hoped that Paul would bribe him, so he sent for him quite often and talked with him.

---

**'Cringe Factor' Acts 24:25**

Felix, was curious to find out more of Paul's faith. As Paul spoke about living a righteous life, self-control and the judgement to come, Felix was terrified. Many will feel awkward and guilty when you speak about the reality of life. Don't be afraid, speak plainly about faith in Christ, a little cringing by your friends now may save them an eternity of cringing later.

---

24:6 Some manuscripts add *We would have judged him by our law,* [7]*but Lysias, the commander of the garrison, came and violently took him away from us,* [8]*commanding his accusers to come before you.*

27 Two years went by in this way; then Felix was succeeded by Porcius Festus. And because Felix wanted to gain favour with the Jewish leaders, he left Paul in prison.

## Paul Appears before Festus

# 25

Three days after Festus arrived in Caesarea to take over his new responsibilities, he left for Jerusalem, ²where the leading priests and other Jewish leaders met with him and made their accusations against Paul. ³They asked Festus as a favour to transfer Paul to Jerusalem. (Their plan was to waylay and kill him.) ⁴But Festus replied that Paul was at Caesarea and he himself would be returning there soon. ⁵So he said, "Those of you in authority can return with me. If Paul has done anything wrong, you can make your accusations."

⁶Eight or ten days later he returned to Caesarea, and on the following day Paul's trial began. ⁷On Paul's arrival in court, the Jewish leaders from Jerusalem gathered around and made many serious accusations they couldn't prove. ⁸Paul denied the charges. "I am not guilty," he said. "I have committed no crime against the Jewish laws or the Temple or the Roman government."

⁹Then Festus, wanting to please the Jews, asked him, "Are you willing to go to Jerusalem and stand trial before me there?"

¹⁰But Paul replied, "No! This is the official Roman court, so I ought to be tried right here. You know very well I am not guilty. ¹¹If I have done something worthy of death, I don't refuse to die. But if I am innocent, neither you nor anyone else has a right to turn me over to these men to kill me. I appeal to Caesar!"

¹²Festus conferred with his advisers and then replied, "Very well! You have appealed to Caesar, and to Caesar you shall go!"

¹³A few days later King Agrippa arrived with his sister, Bernice, to pay their respects to Festus. ¹⁴During their stay of several days, Festus discussed Paul's case with the king. "There is a prisoner here," he told him, "whose case was left for me by Felix. ¹⁵When I was in Jerusalem, the leading priests and other Jewish leaders pressed charges against him and asked me to sentence him. ¹⁶Of course, I quickly pointed out to them that Roman law does not convict people without a trial. They are given an opportunity to defend themselves face to face with their accusers.

¹⁷"When they came here for the trial, I called the case the very next day and ordered Paul brought in. ¹⁸But the accusations made against him weren't at all what I expected. ¹⁹It was something about their religion and about someone called Jesus who died, but whom Paul insists is alive. ²⁰I was perplexed as to how to conduct an investigation of this kind, and I asked him whether he would be willing to stand trial on these charges in Jerusalem. ²¹But Paul appealed to the emperor. So I ordered him back to jail until I could arrange to send him to Caesar."

²²"I'd like to hear the man myself," Agrippa said. And Festus replied, "You shall—tomorrow!"

## Paul Speaks to Agrippa

²³So the next day Agrippa and Bernice arrived at the auditorium with great pomp, accompanied by military officers and prominent men of the city. Festus ordered that Paul be brought in. ²⁴Then Festus said, "King Agrippa and all present, this is the man whose death is demanded both by the local Jews and by those in Jerusalem. ²⁵But in my opinion he has done nothing worthy of death. However, he appealed his case to the emperor, and I decided to send him. ²⁶But what shall I write the emperor? For there is no real charge against him. So I have brought him before all of you, and especially you, King Agrippa, so that after we examine him, I might have something to write. ²⁷For it doesn't seem reasonable to send a prisoner to the emperor without specifying the charges against him!"

# 26

Then Agrippa said to Paul, "You may speak in your defence."

So Paul, with a gesture of his hand, started his defence: ²"I am fortunate, King Agrippa, that you are the one hearing my defence against all these accusations made by the Jewish leaders, ³for I know you are an expert on Jewish customs and controversies. Now please listen to me patiently!

⁴"As the Jewish leaders are well aware, I was given a thorough Jewish training from my earliest childhood among my own people and in Jerusalem. ⁵If they would admit it, they know that I have been a member of the Pharisees, the strictest sect of our religion. ⁶Now I am on trial because I am looking forward to the fulfilment of God's promise made to our ancestors. ⁷In fact, that is why the twelve tribes of Israel worship God night and day, and they share the same hope I have. Yet, O

king, they say it is wrong for me to have this hope! ⁸Why does it seem incredible to any of you that God can raise the dead?

⁹"I used to believe that I ought to do everything I could to oppose the followers of Jesus of Nazareth. ¹⁰Authorized by the leading priests, I caused many of the believers in Jerusalem to be sent to prison. And I cast my vote against them when they were condemned to death. ¹¹Many times I had them whipped in the synagogues to try to get them to curse Christ. I was so violently opposed to them that I even hounded them in distant cities of foreign lands.

¹²"One day I was on such a mission to Damascus, armed with the authority and commission of the leading priests. ¹³About midday, Your Majesty, a light from heaven brighter than the sun shone down on me and my companions. ¹⁴We all fell down, and I heard a voice saying to me in Aramaic, 'Saul, Saul, why are you persecuting me? It is hard for you to fight against my will.'

¹⁵"'Who are you, sir?' I asked.

"And the Lord replied, 'I am Jesus, the one you are persecuting. ¹⁶Now stand up! For I have appeared to you to appoint you as my servant and my witness. You are to tell the world about this experience and about other times I will appear to you. ¹⁷And I will protect you from both your own people and the Gentiles. Yes, I am going to send you to the Gentiles, ¹⁸to open their eyes so they may turn from darkness to light, and from the power of Satan to God. Then they will receive forgiveness for their sins and be given a place among God's people, who are set apart by faith in me.'

¹⁹"And so, O King Agrippa, I was not disobedient to that vision from heaven. ²⁰I preached first to those in Damascus, then in Jerusalem and throughout all Judea, and also to the Gentiles, that all must turn from their sins and turn to God—and prove they have changed by the good things they do. ²¹Some Jews arrested me in the Temple for preaching this, and they tried to kill me. ²²But God protected me so that I am still alive today to tell these facts to everyone, from the least to the greatest. I teach nothing except what the prophets and Moses said would happen—²³that the Messiah would suffer and be the first to rise from the dead as a light to Jews and Gentiles alike."

²⁴Suddenly, Festus shouted, "Paul, you are insane. Too much study has made you crazy!"

²⁵But Paul replied, "I am not insane, Most Excellent Festus. I am speaking the sober truth. ²⁶And King Agrippa knows about these things. I speak frankly, for I am sure these events are all familiar to him, for they were not done in a corner! ²⁷King Agrippa, do you believe the prophets? I know you do—"

²⁸**Agrippa interrupted him. "Do you think you can make me a Christian so quickly?"**

<sup>29</sup>**Paul replied, "Whether quickly or not, I pray to God that both you and everyone here in this audience might become the same as I am, except for these chains."**

<sup>30</sup>Then the king, the governor, Bernice, and all the others stood and left. <sup>31</sup>As they talked it over they agreed, "This man hasn't done anything worthy of death or imprisonment." <sup>32</sup>And Agrippa said to Festus, "He could be set free if he hadn't appealed to Caesar!"

## Paul Sails for Rome

# 27

When the time came, we set sail for Italy. Paul and several other prisoners were placed in the custody of an army officer named Julius, a captain of the Imperial Regiment. <sup>2</sup>And Aristarchus, a Macedonian from Thessalonica, was also with us. We left on a boat whose home port was Adramyttium; it was scheduled to make several stops at ports along the coast of the province of Asia.

<sup>3</sup>The next day when we docked at Sidon, Julius was very kind to Paul and let him go ashore to visit with friends so they could provide for his needs. <sup>4</sup>Putting out to sea from there, we encountered headwinds that made it difficult to keep the ship on course, so we sailed north of Cyprus between the island and the mainland. <sup>5</sup>We passed along the coast of the provinces of Cilicia and Pamphylia, landing at Myra, in the province of Lycia.

<sup>6</sup>There the officer found an Egyptian ship from Alexandria that was bound for Italy, and he put us on board.

<sup>7</sup>We had several days of rough sailing, and after great difficulty we finally neared Cnidus. But the wind was against us, so we sailed down to the leeward side of Crete, past the cape of Salmone. <sup>8</sup>We struggled along the coast with great difficulty and finally arrived at Fair Havens, near the city of Lasea. <sup>9</sup>We had lost a lot of time. The weather was becoming dangerous for long voyages by then because it was so late in the autumn, and Paul spoke to the ship's officers about it. <sup>10</sup>"Sirs," he said, "I believe there is trouble ahead if we go on—shipwreck, loss of cargo, injuries, and danger to our lives." <sup>11</sup>But the officer in charge of the prisoners listened more to the ship's captain and the owner than to Paul. <sup>12</sup>And since Fair Havens was an exposed harbour—a poor place to spend the winter—most of the crew wanted to go to Phoenix, farther up the coast of Crete, and spend the winter there. Phoenix was a good harbour with only a south-west and north-west exposure.

## The Storm at Sea

<sup>13</sup>When a light wind began blowing from the south, the sailors thought they could make it. So they pulled up anchor and sailed along close to shore. <sup>14</sup>But the weather changed abruptly, and a wind of typhoon strength (a "northeaster," they called it) caught the ship and blew it out to sea. <sup>15</sup>They couldn't turn the ship into the wind, so they gave up and let it run before the gale. <sup>16</sup>We sailed behind a small island named Cauda, where with great difficulty we hoisted aboard the lifeboat that was being towed behind us. <sup>17</sup>Then we passed ropes under the ship to strengthen the hull. The sailors were afraid of being driven across to the sandbars of Syrtis off the African coast, so they lowered the sea anchor and were thus driven before the wind.

<sup>18</sup>The next day, as gale-force winds continued to batter the ship, the crew began throwing the cargo overboard. <sup>19</sup>The following day they even threw out the ship's equipment and anything else they could lay their hands on. <sup>20</sup>The terrible storm raged unabated for many days, blotting out the sun and the stars, until at last all hope was gone.

<sup>21</sup>No one had eaten for a long time. Finally, Paul called the crew together and said, "Men, you should have listened to me in the first place and not left Fair Havens. You would have avoided all this injury and loss. <sup>22</sup>But take courage! None of you will lose your lives, even though the ship will go down. <sup>23</sup>For last night an angel of the God to whom I belong and whom I serve stood beside me, <sup>24</sup>and he said, 'Don't be afraid, Paul, for you will surely stand trial before Caesar! What's more, God in his goodness has granted safety to everyone sailing with you.' <sup>25</sup>So take courage! For I believe God. It will be just as he said. <sup>26</sup>But we will be shipwrecked on an island."

## The Shipwreck

<sup>27</sup>About midnight on the fourteenth night of the storm, as we were being driven across the Sea of Adria, the sailors sensed land was near. <sup>28</sup>They took soundings and found the water was only 37 metres deep. A little later they sounded again and found only 27 metres. <sup>29</sup>At this rate they were afraid we would soon be driven against the rocks along the shore, so they threw out four anchors from the stern and prayed for daylight. <sup>30</sup>Then the sailors tried to abandon the ship; they lowered the lifeboat as though they were going to put out anchors from the prow. <sup>31</sup>But Paul said to the commanding officer and the soldiers, "You will all die unless the sailors stay aboard." <sup>32</sup>So the soldiers cut the ropes and let the boat fall off.

<sup>33</sup>As the darkness gave way to the early morning light, Paul begged everyone to eat. "You haven't touched food for two weeks," he said. <sup>34</sup>"Please eat something now for your own good. For not a hair of your heads will perish."

<sup>35</sup>Then he took some bread, gave thanks to God before them all, and broke off a piece and ate it. <sup>36</sup>Then everyone was encouraged, <sup>37</sup>and all 276 of us began eating—for that is the number we had aboard. <sup>38</sup>After eating, the crew lightened the ship further by throwing the cargo of wheat overboard.

<sup>39</sup>When morning dawned, they didn't recognize the coastline, but they saw a bay with a beach and wondered if they could get between the rocks and get the ship safely to shore. <sup>40</sup>So they cut off the anchors and left them in the sea. Then they lowered the rudders, raised the foresail, and headed towards shore. <sup>41</sup>But the ship hit a shoal and ran aground. The bow of the ship stuck fast, while the stern was repeatedly smashed by the force of the waves and began to break apart.

<sup>42</sup>The soldiers wanted to kill the prisoners to make sure they didn't swim ashore and escape. <sup>43</sup>But the commanding officer wanted to spare Paul, so he didn't let them carry out their plan. Then he ordered all who could swim to jump overboard first and make for land, <sup>44</sup>and he told the others to try to follow on planks and debris from the broken ship. So everyone escaped safely ashore!

## Paul on the Island of Malta

# 28

Once we were safe on shore, we learned that we were on the island of Malta. <sup>2</sup>The people of the island were very kind to us. It was cold and rainy, so they built a fire on the shore to welcome us and warm us.

<sup>3</sup>As Paul gathered an armful of sticks and was laying them on the fire, a poisonous snake, driven out by the heat, fastened itself onto his hand. <sup>4</sup>The people of the island saw it hanging there and said to each other, "A murderer, no doubt! Though he escaped the sea, justice will not permit him to live." <sup>5</sup>But Paul shook off the snake into the fire and was unharmed. <sup>6</sup>The people waited for him to swell up or suddenly drop dead. But when they had waited a long time and saw no harm come to him, they changed their minds and decided he was a god.

<sup>7</sup>Near the shore where we landed was an estate belonging to Publius, the chief official of the island. He welcomed us courteously and fed us for three days. <sup>8</sup>As it happened, Publius's father was ill with fever and dysentery. Paul went in and prayed for him, and

laying his hands on him, he healed him. ⁹Then all the other sick people on the island came and were cured. ¹⁰As a result we were showered with honours, and when the time came to sail, people put on board all sorts of things we would need for the trip.

## Paul Arrives at Rome

¹¹It was three months after the shipwreck that we set sail on another ship that had wintered at the island—an Alexandrian ship with the twin gods as its figurehead. ¹²Our first stop was Syracuse, where we stayed three days. ¹³From there we sailed across to Rhegium. A day later a south wind began blowing, so the following day we sailed up the coast to Puteoli. ¹⁴There we found some believers, who invited us to stay with them seven days. And so we came to Rome. ¹⁵The brothers and sisters in Rome had heard we were coming, and they came to meet us at the Forum on the Appian Way. Others joined us at The Three Taverns. When Paul saw them, he thanked God and took courage.

¹⁶When we arrived in Rome, Paul was permitted to have his own private lodging, though he was guarded by a soldier.

**action**

**CH 28:11-16 WHAT'S IT SAYING?**

**WHAT AM I GOING TO DO ABOUT IT?**

## Paul Preaches at Rome under Guard

¹⁷Three days after Paul's arrival, he called together the local Jewish leaders. He said to them, "Brothers, I was arrested in Jerusalem and handed over to the Roman government, even though I had done nothing against our people or the customs of our ancestors. ¹⁸The Romans tried me and wanted to release me, for they found no cause for the death sentence. ¹⁹But when the Jewish leaders protested against the decision, I felt it necessary to appeal to Caesar, even though I had no desire to press charges against my own people. ²⁰I asked you to come here today so we could get acquainted and so I could tell you that I am bound with this chain because I believe that the hope of Israel—the Messiah—has already come."

²¹They replied, "We have heard nothing against you. We have had no letters from Judea or reports from anyone who has arrived here. ²²But we want to hear what you believe, for the only thing we know about these Christians is that they are denounced everywhere."

²³So a time was set, and on that day a large number of people came to Paul's house. He told them about the Kingdom of God and taught them about Jesus from the Scriptures—from the five books of Moses and the books of the prophets. He began lecturing in the morning and went on into the evening. ²⁴Some believed and some didn't. ²⁵But after they had argued back and forth among themselves, they left with this final word from Paul: "The Holy Spirit was right when he said to our ancestors through Isaiah the prophet,

²⁶'Go and say to my people,
You will hear my words,
but you will not understand;
you will see what I do,
but you will not perceive its meaning.
²⁷For the hearts of these people are hardened,
and their ears cannot hear,
and they have closed their eyes—
so their eyes cannot see,
and their ears cannot hear,
and their hearts cannot understand,
and they cannot turn to me
and let me heal them.'

²⁸So I want you to realize that this salvation from God is also available to the Gentiles, and they will accept it."

³⁰For the next two years, Paul lived in his own rented house. He welcomed all who visited him, ³¹proclaiming the Kingdom of God with all boldness and teaching about the Lord Jesus Christ. And no one tried to stop him.

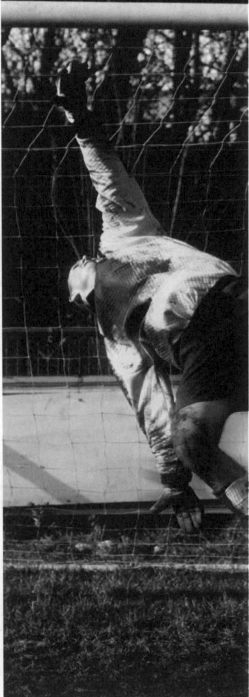

28:28 Some manuscripts add verse 29, *And when he had said these words, the Jews departed, greatly disagreeing with each other.*

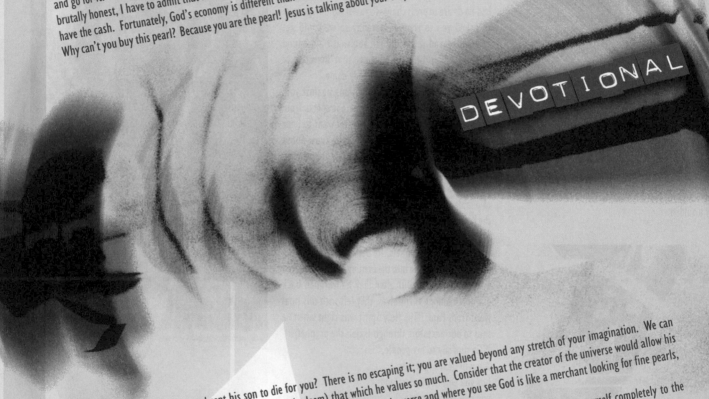

## Commitment

'Again, the Kingdom of Heaven is like a pearl merchant on the lookout for choice pearls. When he discovered a pearl of great value, he sold everything he owned and bought it.' Matthew 13:45-46

Jesus keeps trying to explain how his Father lavishes his love on us! Even though I understand grace, my first impulse is to try to buy my way to heaven. At the first glance I treat the parable of the pearl like I was taught to treat life — to be self-sufficient. In the world of sport we were taught that if we had a dream to play for a certain team, or run a certain distance, we should set a goal for ourselves and go for it. 'Sell out' for the dream. When you find that great goal — go for it! So I equate my goal setting to my spiritual life and 'sell out' for God! But if I am brutally honest, I have to admit that I don't have much to sell! I fail too often; I can't really afford the pearl. We will never be able to afford the pearl — we just don't have the cash. Fortunately, God's economy is different than ours.

Why can't you buy this pearl? Because you are the pearl! Jesus is talking about you. Do you understand your value in God's eyes? Do you see that you are so important to God that he 'lavished his love on you' and sent his son to die for you? There is no escaping it; you are valued beyond any stretch of your imagination. We can scarcely comprehend that God would sacrifice his son to purchase (redeem) that which he values so much. Consider that the creator of the universe would allow his son to be beaten and cursed by his creation so that you could be redeemed! Look back at the verse and where you see God is like a merchant looking for fine pearls, replace pearls with your name. It becomes clear you are valued beyond what you can imagine. Understanding God's commitment to you and the value placed on your life should bring you to your knees in gratitude, ready to give yourself completely to the purchaser.

## Reflection

'Sell out' for the Lord, because he gave his life for you.

## Prayer

Lord, I have heard so many times that you died on the cross for me; help me to appreciate its meaning.

'He is so rich in kindness that he purchased our freedom through the blood of his Son. He has showered his kindness on us, along with all wisdom and understanding.'

Ephesians 1:7-8

Nicked from: A Sporting Guide to Eternity, Steve Connor,
Christian Focus Publications - ISBN 1-85792-746-X

# Romans

Including 'Romans' the next 13 Books of your Bible are written by this passionate follower of Christ, the Apostle Paul.

Christianity was spreading around the known world. The spread was systematic, but also because Christians were fleeing from harassment and execution by Jewish leaders in Jerusalem. After Paul's conversion (see Acts: 9 for the dramatic account) his single-minded dedication to the eradication of Christianity changes to that of establishing Christianity. Paul becomes a major advocate for planting faith communities, 'the church', around the known world.

Paul knew that he needed to clearly explain the 'why's of Christianity. Following Jesus can be hard to explain, many questions need to be answered and made clear. Many people in Paul's time were trying to warp the truth of Jesus, and hurt this very important movement of God. In 'Romans', Paul writes a systematic explanation about man's relationship to God through Jesus, to the followers of Christ in Rome. Many famous writings were coming out of the most powerful capital of its time, but nothing changed the world like this letter, which made its way into the small Christian community, in the city of Rome.

# It's a gift
## FIND it

For the wages of sin is death, but the free gift of God is eternal life through Jesus Christ our Lord

ROMANS 6:23

# ROMANS

## Greetings from Paul

# 1

This letter is from Paul, Jesus Christ's slave, chosen by God to be an apostle and sent out to preach his Good News. [2]This Good News was promised long ago by God through his prophets in the holy Scriptures. [3]It is the Good News about his Son, Jesus, who came as a man, born into King David's royal family line. [4]And Jesus Christ our Lord was shown to be the Son of God when God powerfully raised him from the dead by means of the Holy Spirit. [5]Through Christ, God has given us the privilege and authority to tell Gentiles everywhere what God has done for them, so that they will believe and obey him, bringing glory to his name. [6]You are among those who have been called to belong to Jesus Christ, [7]dear friends in Rome. God loves you dearly, and he has called you to be his very own people. May grace and peace be yours from God our Father and the Lord Jesus Christ.

## God's Good News

[8]Let me say first of all that your faith in God is becoming known throughout the world. How I thank God through Jesus Christ for each one of you. [9]God knows how often I pray for you. Day and night I bring you and your needs in prayer to God, whom I serve with all my heart by telling others the Good News about his Son.

[10]One of the things I always pray for is the opportunity, God willing, to come at last to see you. [11]For I long to visit you so I can share a spiritual blessing with you that will help you grow strong in the Lord. [12]I'm eager to encourage you in your faith, but I also want to be encouraged by yours. In this way, each of us will be a blessing to the other.

[13]I want you to know, dear brothers and sisters, that I planned many times to visit you, but I was prevented until now. I want to work among you and see good results, just as I have done among other Gentiles. [14]For I have a great sense of obligation to people in our culture and to people in other cultures, to the educated and uneducated alike. [15]So I am eager to come to you in Rome, too, to preach God's Good News.

[16]For I am not ashamed of this Good News about Christ. It is the power of God at work, saving everyone who believes—Jews first and also Gentiles. [17]This Good News tells us how God makes us right in his sight. This is accomplished from start to finish by faith. As

What are five things you would like to do in your life?

1
2
3
4
5

BIG FIVE

the Scriptures say, "It is through faith that a righteous person has life."

## God's Anger at Sin

[18]But God shows his anger from heaven against all sinful, wicked people who push the truth away from themselves. [19]For the truth about God is known to them instinctively. God has put this knowledge in their hearts. [20]From the time the world was created, people have seen the earth and sky and all that God made. They can clearly see his invisible qualities—his eternal power and divine nature. So they have no excuse whatsoever for not knowing God.

[21]Yes, they knew God, but they wouldn't worship him as God or even give him thanks. And they began to think up foolish ideas of what God was like. The result was that their minds became dark and confused. [22]Claiming to be wise, they became utter fools instead. [23]And instead of worshipping the glorious, ever-living God, they worshipped idols made to look like mere people, or birds and animals and snakes.

[24]So God let them go ahead and do whatever shameful things their hearts desired. As a result, they did vile and degrading things with each other's bodies. [25]Instead of believing what they knew was the truth about God, they deliberately chose to believe lies. So they worshipped the things God made but not the Creator himself, who is to be praised for ever. Amen. [26]That is why God abandoned them to their shameful desires. Even the women turned against the natural way to have sex and instead indulged in sex with each other. [27]And the men, instead of having normal sexual relationships with women, burned with lust for each other. Men did shameful things with other men and, as a result, suffered within themselves the penalty they so richly deserved.

[28]When they refused to acknowledge God, he abandoned them to their evil minds and let them do things that should never be done.

Hang out with encouraging believers. As a sportsperson you know the value of training with a team. In a group of like-minded athletes competing for the same results, you will be pushed harder and be encouraged more than you can be on your own. These same qualities are what God wants for his faith communities (His church). "And let us not neglect our meeting together, as some people do, but encourage and warn each other, especially now that the day of his coming back again is drawing near."
Hebrews 10:25

POWER HABITS

ROMANS

<sup>29</sup>Their lives became full of every kind of wickedness, sin, greed, hate, envy, murder, fighting, deception, malicious behaviour, and gossip. <sup>30</sup>They are backstabbers, haters of God, insolent, proud, and boastful. They are forever inventing new ways of sinning and are disobedient to their parents. <sup>31</sup>They refuse to understand, break their promises, and are heartless and unforgiving. <sup>32</sup>They are fully aware of God's death penalty for those who do these things, yet they go right ahead and do them anyway. And, worse yet, they encourage others to do them, too.

## God's Judgement of Sin

## 2

You may be saying, "What terrible people you have been talking about!" But you are just as bad, and you have no excuse! When you say they are wicked and should be punished, you are condemning yourself, for you do these very same things. <sup>2</sup>And we know that God, in his justice, will punish anyone who does such things. <sup>3</sup>Do you think that God will judge and condemn others for doing them and not judge you when you do them, too? <sup>4</sup>Don't you realize how kind, tolerant, and patient God is with you? Or don't you care? Can't you see how kind he has been in giving you time to turn from your sin?

<sup>5</sup>But no, you won't listen. So you are storing up terrible punishment for yourself because of your stubbornness in refusing to turn from your sin. For there is going to come a day of judgement when God, the just judge of all the world, <sup>6</sup>will judge all people according to what they have done. <sup>7</sup>He will give eternal life to those who persist in doing what is

Soviet gymnast Larissa Latynina holds the record for the most Olympic medals ever won. Competing in three Olympics, between 1956 and 1964, she won 18 medals.

good, seeking after the glory and honour and immortality that God offers. <sup>8</sup>But he will pour out his anger and wrath on those who live for themselves, who refuse to obey the truth and practise evil deeds. <sup>9</sup>There will be trouble and calamity for everyone who keeps on sinning—for the Jew first and also for the Gentile. <sup>10</sup>But there will be glory and honour and peace from God for all who do good—for the Jew first and also for the Gentile. <sup>11</sup>For God does not show favouritism.

<sup>12</sup>God will punish the Gentiles when they sin, even though they never had God's written law. And he will punish the Jews when they sin, for they do have the law. <sup>13</sup>For it is not merely knowing the law that brings

God's approval. Those who obey the law will be declared right in God's sight. <sup>14</sup>Even when Gentiles, who do not have God's written law, instinctively follow what the law says, they show that in their hearts they know right from wrong. <sup>15</sup>They demonstrate that God's law is written within them, for their own consciences either accuse them or tell them they are doing what is right. <sup>16</sup>The day will surely come when God, by Jesus Christ, will judge everyone's secret life. This is my message.

## The Jews and the Law

<sup>17</sup>If you are a Jew, you are relying on God's law for your special relationship with him. You boast that all is well between yourself and God. <sup>18</sup>Yes, you know what he wants; you know right from wrong because you have been taught his law. <sup>19</sup>You are convinced that you are a guide for the blind and a beacon light for people who are lost in darkness without God. <sup>20</sup>You think you can instruct the ignorant and teach children the ways of God. For you are certain that in God's law you have complete knowledge and truth.

<sup>21</sup>Well then, if you teach others, why don't you teach yourself? You tell others not to steal, but do you steal? <sup>22</sup>You say it is wrong to commit adultery, but do you do it? You condemn idolatry, but do you steal from pagan temples? <sup>23</sup>You are so proud of knowing the law, but you dishonour God by breaking it. <sup>24</sup>No wonder the Scriptures say, "The world blasphemes the name of God because of you."

<sup>25</sup>The Jewish ceremony of circumcision is worth

### I have done some pretty bad things. Will God really forgive me?

The Bible is full of God's special people who have messed up and have been restored to God's love. Consider for a moment King David. David had it all: a tough warrior, good looks, riches, fame, and God's love and favour. Yet, in a heartbeat David fell and messed-up. He had an affair with Bathsheba, and she became pregnant. David tried to cover it up and, when that failed, he then had Bathsheba's husband, Uriah, killed in battle (2 Samuel 11). No matter what David did, God still loved him greatly. David was confronted with his sin, he paid a deep price for his sin, and he repented of the mistakes he made. God said this of David, " David, son of Jesse, is a man after my own heart." (Acts 13:22).

No matter what we do, how badly we mess up, God still loves us. He tells us, 'No matter how deep the stain of your sins, I can remove it. I can make you as clean as freshly fallen snow…if you will only obey me and let me help you…" (Isaiah 1:18-20).

The choice is yours. Today you have the opportunity to turn it around and have your sins washed away by following God. He loves you as much as he loved David. In fact, he sent his Son, Jesus, to the cross to pay the price for your sin. If you take the time to ask for forgiveness, turn away from those sins and ask God to come into your life, he will wash away those sins forever. (see John 3:16) That is a promise you can count on.

## Cooling Down:

Cooling down is defined as performing a group of light exercises immediately after an activity to provide the body with a period of adjustment from exercise to rest. The cool-down period is valuable for athletes who want to maintain or enhance their flexibility. As tissue temperatures rise, stiffness decreases and extensibility increases. Because tissue temperatures will be highest immediately after a workout and during the cool-down phase, stretching is thought to be both safer and more productive.

something only if you obey God's law. But if you don't obey God's law, you are no better off than an uncircumcised Gentile. ²⁶And if the Gentiles obey God's law, won't God give them all the rights and honours of being his own people? ²⁷In fact, uncircumcised Gentiles who keep God's law will be much better off than you Jews who are circumcised and know so much about God's law but don't obey it.

²⁸For you are not a true Jew just because you were born of Jewish parents or because you have gone through the Jewish ceremony of circumcision. ²⁹No, a true Jew is one whose heart is right with God. And true circumcision is not a cutting of the body but a change of heart produced by God's Spirit. Whoever has that kind of change seeks praise from God, not from people.

## God Remains Faithful

# 3

Then what's the advantage of being a Jew? Is there any value in the Jewish ceremony of circumcision? ²Yes, being a Jew has many advantages. First of all, the Jews were entrusted with the whole revelation of God. ³True, some of them were unfaithful; but just because they broke their promises, does that mean God will break his promises? ⁴Of course not! Though everyone else in the world is a liar, God is true. As the Scriptures say, "He will be proved right in what he says, and he will win his case in court."

⁵"But," some say, "our sins serve a good purpose, for people will see God's goodness when he declares us sinners to be innocent. Isn't it unfair, then, for God to punish us?" (That is actually the way some people talk.) ⁶Of course not! If God is not just, how is he qualified to judge the world? ⁷"But," some might still argue, "how can God judge and condemn me as a sinner if my dishonesty highlights his truthfulness and

brings him more glory?" ⁸If you follow that kind of thinking, however, you might as well say that the more we sin the better it is! Those who say such things deserve to be condemned, yet some slander me by saying this is what I preach!

## All People Are Sinners

⁹Well then, are we Jews better than others? No, not at all, for we have already shown that all people, whether Jews or Gentiles, are under the power of sin. ¹⁰As the Scriptures say,

"No one is good—
not even one.
¹¹No one has real understanding;
no one is seeking God.
¹²All have turned away from God;
all have gone wrong.
No one does good,
not even one."
¹³"Their talk is foul, like the stench from an open grave. Their speech is filled with lies."
"The poison of a deadly snake drips from their lips."
¹⁴"Their mouths are full of cursing and bitterness."
¹⁵"They are quick to commit murder.
¹⁶Wherever they go, destruction and misery follow them.
¹⁷They do not know what true peace is."

**The King James Old Testament consists of 592,439 words consisting of 2,728,100 letters**

¹⁸"They have no fear of God to restrain them."

¹⁹Obviously, the law applies to those to whom it was given, for its purpose is to keep people from having excuses and to bring the entire world into judgement before God. ²⁰For no one can ever be made right in God's sight by doing what his law commands. For the more we know God's law, the clearer it becomes that we aren't obeying it.

## action

**CH 3:21-31 WHAT'S IT SAYING?**

**WHAT AM I GOING TO DO ABOUT IT?**

## Christ Took Our Punishment

²¹But now God has shown us a different way of being right in his sight—not by obeying the law but by the way promised

in the Scriptures long ago. [22]We are made right in God's sight when we trust in Jesus Christ to take away our sins. And we all can be saved in this same way, no matter who we are or what we have done.

[23]**For all have sinned; all fall short of God's glorious standard.** [24]Yet now God in his gracious kindness declares us not guilty. He has done this through Christ Jesus, who has freed us by taking away our sins. [25]For God sent Jesus to take the punishment for our sins and to satisfy God's anger against us. We are made right with God when we believe that Jesus shed his blood, sacrificing his life for us. God was being entirely fair and just when he did not punish those who sinned in former times.

[26]And he is entirely fair and just in this present time when he declares sinners to be right in his sight because they believe in Jesus.

[27]Can we boast, then, that we have done anything to be accepted by God? No, because our acquittal is not based on our good deeds. It is based on our faith. [28]So we are made right with God through faith and not by obeying the law. [29]After all, God is not the God of the Jews only, is he? Isn't he also the God of the Gentiles? Of course he is. [30]There is only one God, and there is only one way of being accepted by him. He makes people right with himself only by faith, whether they are Jews or Gentiles. [31]Well then, if we emphasize faith, does this mean that we can forget about the law? Of course not! In fact, only when we have faith do we truly fulfil the law.

## When you face tough competition

### 5:3-5

We can rejoice, too, when we run into problems and trials, for we know that they are good for us—they help us learn to endure. And endurance develops strength of character in us, and character strengthens our confident expectation of salvation. And this expectation will not disappoint us. For we know how dearly God loves us, because he has given us the Holy Spirit to fill our hearts with his love.

## The Faith of Abraham

# 4

Abraham was, humanly speaking, the founder of our Jewish nation. What were his experiences concerning this question of being saved by faith? [2]Was it because of his good deeds that God accepted him? If so, he would have had something to boast about. But from God's point of view Abraham had no basis at all for pride. [3]For the Scriptures tell us, "Abraham believed God, so God declared him to be righteous."

[4]When people work, their wages are not a gift. Workers earn what they receive. [5]But people are declared righteous because of their faith, not because of their work.

[6]King David spoke of this, describing the happiness of an undeserving sinner who is declared to be righteous:

[7]"Oh, what joy for those whose disobedience is forgiven, whose sins are put out of sight.

[8]Yes, what joy for those whose sin is no longer counted against them by the Lord."

[9]Now then, is this blessing only for the Jews, or is it for Gentiles, too? Well, what about Abraham? We have been saying he was declared righteous by God because of his faith. [10]But how did his faith help him? Was he declared righteous only after he had been circumcised, or was it before he was circumcised? The answer is that God accepted him first, and then he was circumcised later!

[11]The circumcision ceremony was a sign that Abraham already had faith and that God had already accepted him and declared him to be righteous—even before he was circumcised. So Abraham is the spiritual father of those who have faith but have not been circumcised. They are made right with God by faith. [12]And Abraham is also the spiritual father of those who have been circumcised, but only if they have the same kind of faith Abraham had before he was circumcised.

[13]It is clear, then, that God's promise to give the whole earth to Abraham and his descendants was not based on obedience to God's law, but on the new relationship with God that comes by faith. [14]So if you claim that God's promise is for those who obey God's law and think they are "good enough" in God's sight, then you are saying that faith is useless. And in that case, the promise is also meaningless. [15]But the law brings punishment on those who try to obey it. (The only way to avoid breaking the law is to have no law to break!)

[16]So that's why faith is the key! God's promise is given to us as a free gift. And we are certain to receive it, whether or not we follow Jewish customs, if we have faith like Abraham's. For Abraham is the father of all who believe. [17]That is what the Scriptures mean when God told him, "I have made you the father of many nations." This happened because Abraham believed in the God who brings the dead back to life and who brings into existence what didn't exist before.

[18]When God promised Abraham that he would become the father of many nations, Abraham believed him. God had also said, "Your descendants will be as numerous as the stars," even though such a promise seemed utterly impossible! [19]And Abraham's faith did not weaken, even though he knew that he was too old to be a father at the age of one hundred and that Sarah, his wife, had never been able to have children. [20]Abraham never wavered in believing God's promise. In fact, his faith grew stronger, and in this he brought glory to God. [21]He was absolutely convinced that God was able to do anything he promised. [22]And because of Abraham's faith, God declared him to be righteous. [23]Now this wonderful truth—that God declared him to be righteous—wasn't just for Abraham's benefit. [24]It was for us, too, assuring us that God will also declare us to be righteous if we believe in God, who brought Jesus our Lord back from the dead. [25]He was handed over to die because of our sins, and he was raised from the dead to make us right with God.

## Faith Brings Joy

# 5

Therefore, since we have been made right in God's sight by faith, we have peace with God because of what Jesus Christ our Lord has done for us. [2]Because of our faith, Christ has brought us into this place of highest privilege where we now stand, and we confidently and joyfully look forward to sharing God's glory.

[3]We can rejoice, too, when we run into problems and trials, for we know that they are good for us—they help us learn to endure. [4]And endurance develops strength of character in us, and character strengthens our confident expectation of salvation. [5]And this expectation will not disappoint us. For we know how dearly God loves us, because he has given us the Holy Spirit to fill our hearts with his love.

[6]When we were utterly helpless, Christ came at just the right time and died for us sinners. [7]Now, no one is

likely to die for a good person, though someone might be willing to die for a person who is especially good. [8]But God showed his great love for us by sending Christ to die for us while we were still sinners. [9]And since we have been made right in God's sight by the blood of Christ, he will certainly save us from God's judgement. [10]For since we were restored to friendship with God by the death of his Son while we were still his enemies, we will certainly be delivered from eternal punishment by his life. [11]So now we can rejoice in our wonderful new relationship with God—all because of what our Lord Jesus Christ has done for us in making us friends of God.

## Adam and Christ Contrasted

[12]**When Adam sinned, sin entered the entire human race. Adam's sin brought death, so death spread to everyone, for everyone sinned.** [13]Yes, people sinned even before the law was given. And though there was no law to break, since it had not yet been given, [14]they all died anyway—even though they did not disobey an explicit commandment of God, as Adam did. What a contrast between Adam and Christ, who was yet to come! [15]And what a difference between our sin and God's generous gift of forgiveness. For this one man, Adam, brought death to many through his sin. But this other man, Jesus Christ, brought forgiveness to many through God's bountiful gift. [16]And the result of God's gracious gift is very different from the result of that one man's sin. For Adam's sin led to condemnation, but we have the free gift of being accepted by God, even though we are guilty of many sins. [17]The sin of this one man, Adam, caused death to rule over us, but all who receive God's wonderful, gracious gift of righteousness will live in triumph over sin and death through this one man, Jesus Christ. [18]Yes, Adam's one sin brought condemnation upon

everyone, but Christ's one act of righteousness makes all people right in God's sight and gives them life. [19]Because one person disobeyed God, many people became sinners. But because one other person obeyed God, many people will be made right in God's sight. [20]God's law was given so that all people could see how sinful they were. But as people sinned more and more, God's wonderful kindness became more abundant. [21]So just as sin ruled over all people and brought them to death, now God's wonderful kindness rules instead, giving us right standing with God and resulting in eternal life through Jesus Christ our Lord.

## Sin's Power Is Broken

### 6

Well then, should we keep on sinning so that God can show us more and more kindness and forgiveness? [2]Of course not! Since we have died to sin, how can we continue to live in it? [3]Or have you forgotten that when we became Christians and were baptized to become one with Christ Jesus, we died with him? [4]For we died and were buried with Christ by baptism. And just as Christ was raised from the dead by the glorious power of the Father, now we also may live new lives. [5]Since we have been united with him in his death, we will also be raised as he was. [6]Our old sinful selves were crucified with Christ so that sin might lose its power in our lives. We are no longer slaves to sin. [7]For when we died with Christ we were set free from the power of sin. [8]And since we died with Christ, we know we will also share his new life. [9]We are sure of this because Christ rose from the dead, and he will never die again. Death no longer has any power over him. [10]He died once to defeat sin, and now he lives for the glory of God. [11]So you should consider yourselves dead to sin and able to live for the glory of God through Christ Jesus.

[12]Do not let sin control the way you live; do not give in to its lustful desires. [13]Do not let any part of your body become a tool of wickedness, to be used for sinning. Instead, give yourselves completely to God since you have been given new life. And use your whole body as a tool to do what is right for the glory of God. [14]Sin is no longer your master, for you are no longer subject to the law, which enslaves you to sin. Instead, you are free by God's grace.

**CH 6:15-23 WHAT'S IT SAYING?**

**WHAT AM I GOING TO δO ABOUT IT?**

### Freedom to Obey God

[15]So since God's grace has set us free from the law, does this

'Miracles' Romans 5:8

The Lord God is the God of miracles. The Playbook for Life, the Bible, is full of examples. Time and again God has shown his true character by touching a person's life with a miracle. Perhaps the greatest miracle of all is God's love for us. Paul writes, 'But God showed his great love for us by sending Christ to die for us while we were still sinners.' It is a miracle that God sent his only Son to die on the cross for our sins. It is a miracle that God loves us just the way we are and that we don't have to change before we can receive his love. Eventually everyone that Christ healed physically died, but the coolest thing is, those that Christ healed spiritually live forever! Grab on to a miracle. Grab on to Jesus!

mean we can go on sinning? Of course not! [16]Don't you realize that whatever you choose to obey becomes your master? You can choose sin, which leads to death, or you can choose to obey God and receive his approval. [17]Thank God! Once you were slaves of sin, but now you have obeyed with all your heart the new teaching God has given you. [18]Now you are free from sin, your old master, and you have become slaves to your new master, righteousness.

[19]I speak this way, using the illustration of slaves and masters, because it is easy to understand. Before, you let yourselves be slaves of impurity and lawlessness. Now you must choose to be slaves of righteousness so that you will become holy. [20]In those days, when you were slaves of sin, you weren't concerned with doing what was right. [21]And what was the result? It was not good, since now you are ashamed of the things you used to do, things that end in eternal doom. [22]But now you are free from the power of sin and have become slaves of God. Now you do those things that lead to holiness and result in eternal life. [23]**For the wages of sin is death, but the free gift of God is eternal life through Christ Jesus our Lord.**

Bible FACTS

## The Old Testament has 929 chapters, the New Testament 260.

## No Longer Bound to the Law

# 7

Now, dear brothers and sisters—you who are familiar with the law—don't you know that the law applies only to a person who is still living? [2]Let me illustrate. When a woman marries, the law binds her to her husband as long as he is alive. But if he dies, the laws of marriage no longer apply to her. [3]So while her husband is alive, she would be committing adultery if

the law that showed me my sin. I would never have known that coveting is wrong if the law had not said, "Do not covet." [8]But sin took advantage of this law and aroused all kinds of forbidden desires within me! If there were no law, sin would not have that power. [9]I felt fine when I did not understand what the law demanded. But when I learned the truth, I realized I had broken the law and was a sinner, doomed to die. [10]So the good law, which was supposed to show me the way of life, instead gave me the death penalty. [11]Sin took advantage of the law and fooled me; it took the good law and used it to make me guilty of death. [12]But still, the law itself is holy and right and good.

[13]But how can that be? Did the law, which is good, cause my doom? Of course not! Sin used what was good to bring about my condemnation. So we can see how terrible sin really is. It uses God's good commandment for its own evil purposes.

### Struggling with Sin

[14]The law is good, then. The trouble is not with the law but with me, because I am sold into slavery, with

'Peace' Romans 8:6

Most professional athletes are presumed to live a 'wild and crazy life'. But most 'pro's' just want a little peace. Peace is a gift from God and the rightful legacy of all believers, but far too many do not enjoy it. The peace of God flows from a full, unhindered fellowship with God who is our peace. Allow the Holy Spirit to fill you and keep you in the 'zone', in peace.

BIBLE HIT

STAND POINT

### When you are facing death

### 8:38

I am convinced that nothing can ever separate us from his love. Death can't, and life can't. The angels can't, and the demons can't. Our fears for today, our worries about tomorrow, and even the powers of hell can't keep God's love away.

she married another man. But if her husband dies, she is free from that law and does not commit adultery when she remarries.

[4]So this is the point: The law no longer holds you in its power, because you died to its power when you died with Christ on the cross. And now you are united with the one who was raised from the dead. As a result, you can produce good fruit, that is, good deeds for God. [5]When we were controlled by our old nature, sinful desires were at work within us, and the law aroused these evil desires that produced sinful deeds, resulting in death. [6]But now we have been released from the law, for we died with Christ, and we are no longer captive to its power. Now we can really serve God, not in the old way by obeying the letter of the law, but in the new way, by the Spirit.

### God's Law Reveals Our Sin

[7]Well then, am I suggesting that the law of God is evil? Of course not! The law is not sinful, but it was

sin as my master. [15]I don't understand myself at all, for I really want to do what is right, but I don't do it. Instead, I do the very thing I hate. [16]I know perfectly well that what I am doing is wrong, and my bad conscience shows that I agree that the law is good. [17]But I can't help myself, because it is sin inside me that makes me do these evil things.

[18]I know I am rotten through and through so far as my old sinful nature is concerned. No matter which way I turn, I can't make myself do right. I want to, but I can't. [19]When I want to do good, I don't. And when I try not to do wrong, I do it anyway. [20]But if I am doing what I don't want to do, I am not really the one doing it; the sin within me is doing it.

[21]It seems to be a fact of life that when I want to do what is right, I inevitably do what is wrong. [22]I love God's law with all my heart. [23]But there is another law at work within me that is at war with my mind. This law wins the fight and makes me a slave to the sin that is still within me. [24]Oh, what a miserable

person I am! Who will free me from this life that is dominated by sin? [25]Thank God! The answer is in Jesus Christ our Lord. So you see how it is: In my mind I really want to obey God's law, but because of my sinful nature I am a slave to sin.

## Life in the Spirit

# 8

So now there is no condemnation for those who belong to Christ Jesus. [2]For the power of the life-giving Spirit has freed you through Christ Jesus from the power of sin that leads to death. [3]The law of Moses could not save us, because of our sinful nature. But God put into effect a different plan to save us. He sent his own Son in a human body like ours, except that ours are sinful. God destroyed sin's control over us by giving his Son as a sacrifice for our sins. [4]He did this so that the requirement of the law would be fully accomplished for us who no longer follow our sinful nature but instead follow the Spirit.

[5]Those who are dominated by the sinful nature think about sinful things, but those who are controlled by the Holy Spirit think about things that please the Spirit. [6]If your sinful nature controls your mind, there is death. But if the Holy Spirit controls your mind, there is life and peace. [7]For the sinful nature is always hostile to God. It never did obey God's laws, and it never will. [8]That's why those who are still under the control of their sinful nature can never please God.

[9]**But you are not controlled by your sinful nature. You are controlled by the Spirit if you have the Spirit of God living in you. (And remember that those who do not have the Spirit of Christ living in them are not Christians at all.)** [10]Since Christ lives within you, even though your body will die because of sin, your spirit is alive because you have been made right with God. [11]The Spirit of God, who raised Jesus from the dead, lives in you. And just as he raised Christ from the dead, he will give life to

## Mistakes:

When an athlete makes a mistake that costs the team a game, they feel it more than anyone. The last thing in the world they need is someone yelling at them that they goofed up. They already got that feedback. Even if the mistake is made in a training session, they are probably feeling frustrated. As a player and coach pick the right time to correct and the right time to encourage.

# profiles

## Joshua:

Exodus 33:1, 'Inside the Tent of Meeting, the Lord would speak to Moses face to face, as a man speaks to a friend. Afterward Moses would return to the camp, but the young man who assisted him, Joshua son of Nun, stayed behind in the Tent of Meeting.'

Joshua would take the baton from the hugest character of the Old Testament and run a faultless race. Moses took the Israelites out of Egypt but was not allowed to enter the 'Promised Land'. But the sign of success is a great successor and he had that in Joshua. Joshua was trained for greatness and his commitment to obedience kept him on a successful path. Two of many key ingredients that Joshua had for successful leadership were the desire to stay close to God and the knowledge that no one (not even Moses) was indispensable. We see from Exodus 33 that Joshua stayed in the Tent of Meeting in God's presence and he watched God deal harshly with Moses when he veered from God's rule and consequently was not allowed to cross the Jordan River and enter the land promised to his people. Joshua crossed instead and took on the responsibility of the great leader. You in some way will be called into leadership. Don't get arrogant and think the world will not go on without you. Stay close to God and listen to his guidance.

your mortal body by this same Spirit living within you.

[12]So, dear brothers and sisters, you have no obligation whatsoever to do what your sinful nature urges you to do. [13]For if you keep on following it, you will perish. But if through the power of the Holy Spirit you turn from it and its evil deeds, you will live. [14]For all who are led by the Spirit of God are children of God.

[15]So you should not be like cowering, fearful slaves. You should behave instead like God's very own children, adopted into his family—calling him "Father, dear Father." [16]For his Holy Spirit speaks to us deep in our hearts and tells us that we are God's children. [17]And since we are his children, we will share his treasures—for everything God gives to his Son, Christ, is ours, too. But if we are to share his glory, we must also share his suffering.

## The Future Glory

[18]Yet what we suffer now is nothing compared to the glory he will give us later. [19]For all creation is waiting eagerly for that future day when God will reveal who his children really are. [20]Against its will, everything on earth was subjected to God's curse. [21]All creation anticipates the day when it will join God's children in glorious freedom from death and decay. [22]For we know that all creation has been groaning as in the pains of childbirth right up to the present time. [23]And even we Christians, although we have the Holy Spirit within us as a foretaste of future glory, also groan to be released from pain and suffering. We, too, wait anxiously for that day when God will give us our full rights as his children, including the new bodies he has promised us. [24]Now that we are saved, we eagerly look forward to this freedom. For if you already have something, you don't need to hope for it. [25]But if we look forward to something we don't have yet, we must wait patiently and confidently.

[26]And the Holy Spirit helps us in our distress. For we don't even know what we should pray for, nor how we should pray. But the Holy Spirit prays for us with groanings that cannot be expressed in words. [27]And the Father who knows all hearts knows what the Spirit is saying, for the Spirit pleads for us believers in harmony with God's own will. [28]And we know that God causes everything to work together for the good of those who love God and are called according to his purpose for them. [29]For God knew his people in advance, and he chose them to become like his Son, so that his Son would be the first-born, with many brothers and sisters. [30]And having chosen them, he called them to come to him. And he gave them right

standing with himself, and he promised them his glory.

## Nothing Can Separate Us from God's Love

[31]**What can we say about such wonderful things as these? If God is for us, who can ever be against us?** [32]Since God did not spare even his own Son but gave him up for us all, won't God, who gave us Christ, also give us everything else?

[33]Who dares accuse us whom God has chosen for his own? Will God? No! He is the one who has given us right standing with himself. [34]Who then will condemn us? Will Christ Jesus? No, for he is the one who died for us and was raised to life for us and is sitting at the place of highest honour next to God, pleading for us. [35]Can anything ever separate us from Christ's love? Does it mean he no longer loves us if we have trouble or calamity, or are persecuted, or are hungry or cold or in danger or threatened with death? [36](Even the Scriptures say, "For your sake we are killed every day; we are being slaughtered like sheep.") [37]No, despite all these things, overwhelming victory is ours through Christ, who loved us.

[38]And I am convinced that nothing can ever separate us from his love. Death can't, and life can't. The angels can't, and the demons can't. Our fears for today, our worries about tomorrow, and even the powers of hell can't keep God's love away. [39]Whether we are high above the sky or in the deepest ocean, nothing in all creation will ever be able to separate us from the love of God that is revealed in Christ Jesus our Lord.

## God's Selection of Israel

# 9

In the presence of Christ, I speak with utter truthfulness—I do not lie—and my conscience and the Holy Spirit confirm that what I am saying is true. [2]My heart is filled with bitter sorrow and unending grief [3]for my people, my Jewish brothers and sisters. I would be willing to be forever cursed—cut off from Christ!—if that would save them. [4]They are the people of Israel, chosen to be God's special children. God revealed his glory to them. He made covenants with them and gave his law to them. They have the privilege of worshipping him and receiving his wonderful promises. [5]Their ancestors were great people of God, and Christ himself was a Jew as far as his human nature is concerned. And he is God, who rules over everything and is worthy of eternal praise! Amen.

# WHAT DOES IT MEAN?

### Fellowship

We have fellowship with God and other believers. Fellowship with God and one another consists of enjoying God's encouragement, love, joy, interests, sufferings and spiritual growth (Rom. 12:4, 13; Heb. 13:16). Fellowship among Christians does not mean being in proximity to other Christians, but to mutually participate in God's Kingdom.

⁶Well then, has God failed to fulfil his promise to the Jews? No, for not everyone born into a Jewish family is truly a Jew! ⁷Just the fact that they are descendants of Abraham doesn't make them truly Abraham's children. For the Scriptures say, "Isaac is the son through whom your descendants will be counted," though Abraham had other children, too. ⁸This means that Abraham's physical descendants are not necessarily children of God. It is the children of the promise who are considered to be Abraham's children. ⁹For God had promised, "Next year I will return, and Sarah will have a son."

¹⁰This son was our ancestor Isaac. When he grew up, he married Rebekah, who gave birth to twins. ¹¹But before they were born, before they had done anything good or bad, she received a message from God. (This message proves that God chooses according to his own plan, ¹²not according to our good or bad works.) She was told, "The descendants of your older son will serve the descendants of your younger son." ¹³In the words of the Scriptures, "I loved Jacob, but I rejected Esau."

¹⁴What can we say? Was God being unfair? Of course not! ¹⁵For God said to Moses,
"I will show mercy to anyone I choose,
and I will show compassion to anyone I choose."

¹⁶So receiving God's promise is not up to us. We can't get it by choosing it or working hard for it. God will show mercy to anyone he chooses.

¹⁷For the Scriptures say that God told Pharaoh, "I have appointed you for the very purpose of displaying my power in you, and so that my fame might spread throughout the earth." ¹⁸So you see, God shows mercy to some just because he wants to, and he chooses to make some people refuse to listen.

¹⁹Well then, you might say, "Why does God blame people for not listening? Haven't they simply done what he made them do?"

²⁰No, don't say that. Who are you, a mere human being, to criticize God? Should the thing that was created say to the one who made it, "Why have you made me like this?" ²¹When a potter makes jars out of clay, doesn't he have a right to use the same lump of clay to make one jar for decoration and another to throw garbage into? ²²God has every right to exercise his judgement and his power, but he also has the right to be very patient with those who are the objects of his judgement and are fit only for destruction. ²³He also has the right to pour out the riches of his glory upon those he prepared to be the objects of his mercy——²⁴even upon us, whom he selected, both from the Jews and from the Gentiles.

²⁵Concerning the Gentiles, God says in the prophecy of Hosea,
"Those who were not my people,
I will now call my people.
And I will love those
whom I did not love before."
²⁶And,
"Once they were told,
'You are not my people.'
But now he will say,
'You are children of the living God.'"

²⁷Concerning Israel, Isaiah the prophet cried out,
"Though the people of Israel are as numerous as the sand on the seashore,
only a small number will be saved.
²⁸For the Lord will carry out his sentence upon the earth quickly and with finality."
²⁹And Isaiah said in another place,
"If the Lord Almighty
had not spared a few of us,
we would have been wiped out
as completely as Sodom and Gomorrah."

**STATS**

Fans of the Spanish soccer team, 'ONDA', are paid to attend games at the local stadium.

### Israel's Unbelief

³⁰Well then, what shall we say about these things? Just this: The Gentiles have been made right with God by faith, even though they were not seeking him. ³¹But the Jews, who tried so hard to get right with God by keeping the law, never succeeded.

³²Why not? Because they were trying to get right with God by keeping the law and being good instead of by depending on faith. They stumbled over the great rock in their path. ³³God warned them of this in the Scriptures when he said,

"I am placing a stone in Jerusalem that
causes people to stumble,
and a rock that makes them fall.
But anyone who believes in him
will not be disappointed."

# 10

Dear brothers and sisters, the longing of my heart and my prayer to God is that the Jewish people might be saved. [2]I know what enthusiasm they have for God, but it is misdirected zeal.

[3]For they don't understand God's way of making people right with himself. Instead, they are clinging to their own way of getting right with God by trying to keep the law. They won't go along with God's way. [4]For Christ has accomplished the whole purpose of the law. All who believe in him are made right with God.

**CH 10:5-15 WHAT'S IT SAYING?**

**WHAT AM I GOING TO DO ABOUT IT?**

## Salvation Is for Everyone

[5]For Moses wrote that the law's way of making a person right with God requires obedience to all of its commands. [6]But the way of getting right with God through faith says,
"You don't need to go to heaven" (to find Christ and bring him down to help you). [7]And it says, "You don't need to go to the place of the dead" (to bring Christ back to life again). [8]Salvation that comes from trusting Christ—which is the message we preach—is already within easy reach. In fact, the Scriptures say, "The message is close at hand; it is on your lips and in your heart." [9]For if you confess with your mouth that Jesus is Lord and believe in your heart that God raised him from the dead, you will be saved. [10]**For it is by believing in your heart that you are made right with God, and it is by confessing with your mouth that you are saved.** [11]As the Scriptures tell us, "Anyone who believes in him will not be disappointed." [12]Jew and Gentile are the same in this respect. They all have the same Lord, who generously gives his riches to all who ask for them. [13]For "Anyone who calls on the name of the Lord will be saved."

[14]But how can they call on him to save them unless they believe in him? And how can they believe in him if they have never heard about him? And how can they hear about him unless someone tells them? [15]And how will anyone go and tell them without being sent? That is what the Scriptures mean when they say, "How beautiful are the feet of those who bring good news!" [16]But not everyone welcomes the Good News, for Isaiah the prophet said, "Lord, who has believed our message?" [17]Yet faith comes from listening to this message of good news—the Good News about Christ. [18]But what about the Jews? Have they actually heard the message? Yes, they have:
"The message of God's creation has gone out to everyone,
and its words to all the world."
[19]But did the people of Israel really understand? Yes, they did, for even in the time of Moses, God had said,
"I will rouse your jealousy by blessing other nations.
I will make you angry by blessing the foolish Gentiles."
[20]And later Isaiah spoke boldly for God:
"I was found by people
who were not looking for me.
I showed myself to those

Fishing is the biggest
participant sport in the
world.

who were not asking for me."
[21]But regarding Israel, God said,
"All day long I opened my arms to them,
but they kept disobeying me and arguing with me."

## God's Mercy on Israel

# 11

I ask, then, has God rejected his people, the Jews? Of course not! Remember that I myself am a Jew, a descendant of Abraham and a member of the tribe of Benjamin.

[2]No, God has not rejected his own people, whom he chose from the very beginning. Do you remember what the Scriptures say about this? Elijah the prophet complained to God about the people of Israel and said, [3]"Lord, they have killed your prophets and torn down your altars. I alone am left, and now they are trying to kill me, too."

[4]And do you remember God's reply? He said, "You are not the only one left. I have seven thousand others who have never bowed down to Baal!"

[5]It is the same today, for not all the Jews have turned away from God. A few are being saved as a result of God's kindness in choosing them. [6]And if they are saved by God's kindness, then it is not by their good works. For in that case, God's wonderful kindness would not be what it really is—free and undeserved. [7]So this is the situation: Most of the Jews have not found the favour of God they are looking for so earnestly. A few have—the ones God has chosen—but the rest were made unresponsive. [8]As the Scriptures say,
"God has put them into a deep sleep.
To this very day he has shut their eyes so they do not see,
and closed their ears so they do not hear."
[9]David spoke of this same thing when he said,
"Let their bountiful table become a snare,
a trap that makes them think all is well.
Let their blessings cause them to stumble.
[10]Let their eyes go blind so they cannot see,
and let their backs grow weaker and weaker."
[11]Did God's people stumble and fall beyond recovery? Of course not! His purpose was to make his salvation available to the Gentiles, and then the Jews would be jealous and want it for themselves. [12]Now if the Gentiles were enriched because the Jews turned down God's offer of salvation, think how much greater a blessing the world will share when the Jews finally accept it.

[13]I am saying all of this especially for you Gentiles. God has appointed me as the apostle to the Gentiles. I lay great stress on this, [14]for I want to find a way to make the Jews want what you Gentiles have, and in that way I might save some of them. [15]For since the Jews' rejection meant that God offered salvation to the rest of the world, how much more wonderful their acceptance will be. It will be life for those who were dead! [16]And since Abraham and the other patriarchs were holy, their children will also be holy. For if the roots of the tree are holy, the branches will be, too.

[17]But some of these branches from Abraham's tree, some of the Jews, have been broken off. And you Gentiles, who were branches from a wild olive tree, were grafted in. So now you also receive the blessing God has promised Abraham and his children, sharing in God's rich nourishment of his special olive tree.

[18]But you must be careful not to brag about being grafted in to replace the branches that were broken off. Remember, you are just a branch, not the root.

[19]"Well," you may say, "those branches were broken off to make room for me." [20]Yes, but remember—those branches, the Jews, were broken off because they didn't believe God, and you are there because you do believe. Don't think highly of yourself, but fear what could happen. [21]For if God did not spare the branches he put there in the first place, he won't spare you either.

[22]Notice how God is both kind and severe. He is severe to those who disobeyed, but kind to you as you continue to trust in his kindness. But if you stop trusting, you also will be cut off. [23]And if the Jews turn from their unbelief, God will graft them back into the tree again. He has the power to do it. [24]For if God was willing to take you who were, by nature, branches from a wild olive tree and graft you into his own good tree—a very unusual thing to do—he will be far more eager to graft the Jews back into the tree where they belong.

**The longest word in the Bible is Maher-shalal-hash-baz: Isaiah 8:1.**

### God's Mercy Is for Everyone

[25]I want you to understand this mystery, dear brothers and sisters, so that you will not feel proud and start bragging. Some of the Jews have hard hearts, but this will last only until the complete number of Gentiles comes to Christ. [26]And so all Israel will be saved. Do you remember what the prophets said about this?

"A Deliverer will come from Jerusalem,
and he will turn Israel from all ungodliness.

[27]And then I will keep my covenant with them
and take away their sins."

[28]Many of the Jews are now enemies of the Good News. But this has been to your benefit, for God has given his gifts to you Gentiles. Yet the Jews are still his chosen people because of his promises to Abraham, Isaac, and Jacob. [29]For God's gifts and his call can never be withdrawn. [30]Once, you Gentiles were rebels against God, but when the Jews refused his mercy, God was merciful to you instead. [31]And now, in the same way, the Jews are the rebels, and God's mercy has come to you. But someday they, too, will share in God's mercy. [32]For God has imprisoned all people in their own disobedience so he could have mercy on everyone.

[33]Oh, what a wonderful God we have! How great are his riches and wisdom and knowledge! How impossible it is for us to understand his decisions and his methods! [34]For who can know what the Lord is thinking? Who knows enough to be his counsellor? [35]And who could ever give him so much that he would have to pay it back? [36]For everything comes from him; everything exists by his power and is intended for his glory. To him be glory evermore. Amen.

**CH 12:3-11 WHAT'S IT SAYING?**

**WHAT AM I GOING TO DO ABOUT IT?**

### A Living Sacrifice to God

**12**

And so, dear brothers and sisters, I plead with you to give your bodies to God. Let them be a living and holy sacrifice—the kind he will accept. When you think of what he has done for you, is this too much to ask? [2]Don't copy the behaviour and customs of this world, but let God transform you into a new person by changing the way you think. Then you will know what God wants you to do, and you will know how good and pleasing and perfect his will really is.

**I feel like the only Christian athlete on the planet. Sometimes I am worn down, what do you suggest?**

Be encouraged, you are not the only Christian athlete on the planet, though it may feel like it at times! For this very reason, the Bible encourages Christians to get together and build each other up, for encouragement, training and living. There are several Christian sports web sites around with stories of other athletes that have the same challenges you have. If you are fortunate enough to have a Christian sports camp near you, try to go. Go to the website addresses in the resource section of your **nt:sport**. Lastly, encourage others - it is contagious.

# JULY M.A.P.

## 1
| S.D. | P.L. | P.G. | S.G. |
|---|---|---|---|
| P. ☐ | F. ☐ | F. ☐ | T. ☐ |
| F. ☐ | W. ☐ | W. ☐ | P. ☐ |
| B. ☐ | P. ☐ | C. ☐ | C. ☐ |

## 2
| S.D. | P.L. | P.G. | S.G. |
|---|---|---|---|
| P. ☐ | F. ☐ | F. ☐ | T. ☐ |
| F. ☐ | W. ☐ | W. ☐ | P. ☐ |
| B. ☐ | P. ☐ | C. ☐ | C. ☐ |

## 3
| S.D. | P.L. | P.G. | S.G. |
|---|---|---|---|
| P. ☐ | F. ☐ | F. ☐ | T. ☐ |
| F. ☐ | W. ☐ | W. ☐ | P. ☐ |
| B. ☐ | P. ☐ | C. ☐ | C. ☐ |

## 4
| S.D. | P.L. | P.G. | S.G. |
|---|---|---|---|
| P. ☐ | F. ☐ | F. ☐ | T. ☐ |
| F. ☐ | W. ☐ | W. ☐ | P. ☐ |
| B. ☐ | P. ☐ | C. ☐ | C. ☐ |

## 9
| S.D. | P.L. | P.G. | S.G. |
|---|---|---|---|
| P. ☐ | F. ☐ | F. ☐ | T. ☐ |
| F. ☐ | W. ☐ | W. ☐ | P. ☐ |
| B. ☐ | P. ☐ | C. ☐ | C. ☐ |

## 10
| S.D. | P.L. | P.G. | S.G. |
|---|---|---|---|
| P. ☐ | F. ☐ | F. ☐ | T. ☐ |
| F. ☐ | W. ☐ | W. ☐ | P. ☐ |
| B. ☐ | P. ☐ | C. ☐ | C. ☐ |

## 11
| S.D. | P.L. | P.G. | S.G. |
|---|---|---|---|
| P. ☐ | F. ☐ | F. ☐ | T. ☐ |
| F. ☐ | W. ☐ | W. ☐ | P. ☐ |
| B. ☐ | P. ☐ | C. ☐ | C. ☐ |

## 12
| S.D. | P.L. | P.G. | S.G. |
|---|---|---|---|
| P. ☐ | F. ☐ | F. ☐ | T. ☐ |
| F. ☐ | W. ☐ | W. ☐ | P. ☐ |
| B. ☐ | P. ☐ | C. ☐ | C. ☐ |

## 17
| S.D. | P.L. | P.G. | S.G. |
|---|---|---|---|
| P. ☐ | F. ☐ | F. ☐ | T. ☐ |
| F. ☐ | W. ☐ | W. ☐ | P. ☐ |
| B. ☐ | P. ☐ | C. ☐ | C. ☐ |

## 18
| S.D. | P.L. | P.G. | S.G. |
|---|---|---|---|
| P. ☐ | F. ☐ | F. ☐ | T. ☐ |
| F. ☐ | W. ☐ | W. ☐ | P. ☐ |
| B. ☐ | P. ☐ | C. ☐ | C. ☐ |

## 19
| S.D. | P.L. | P.G. | S.G. |
|---|---|---|---|
| P. ☐ | F. ☐ | F. ☐ | T. ☐ |
| F. ☐ | W. ☐ | W. ☐ | P. ☐ |
| B. ☐ | P. ☐ | C. ☐ | C. ☐ |

## 20
| S.D. | P.L. | P.G. | S.G. |
|---|---|---|---|
| P. ☐ | F. ☐ | F. ☐ | T. ☐ |
| F. ☐ | W. ☐ | W. ☐ | P. ☐ |
| B. ☐ | P. ☐ | C. ☐ | C. ☐ |

## 25
| S.D. | P.L. | P.G. | S.G. |
|---|---|---|---|
| P. ☐ | F. ☐ | F. ☐ | T. ☐ |
| F. ☐ | W. ☐ | W. ☐ | P. ☐ |
| B. ☐ | P. ☐ | C. ☐ | C. ☐ |

## 26
| S.D. | P.L. | P.G. | S.G. |
|---|---|---|---|
| P. ☐ | F. ☐ | F. ☐ | T. ☐ |
| F. ☐ | W. ☐ | W. ☐ | P. ☐ |
| B. ☐ | P. ☐ | C. ☐ | C. ☐ |

## 27
| S.D. | P.L. | P.G. | S.G. |
|---|---|---|---|
| P. ☐ | F. ☐ | F. ☐ | T. ☐ |
| F. ☐ | W. ☐ | W. ☐ | P. ☐ |
| B. ☐ | P. ☐ | C. ☐ | C. ☐ |

## 28
| S.D. | P.L. | P.G. | S.G. |
|---|---|---|---|
| P. ☐ | F. ☐ | F. ☐ | T. ☐ |
| F. ☐ | W. ☐ | W. ☐ | P. ☐ |
| B. ☐ | P. ☐ | C. ☐ | C. ☐ |

## Spiritual Disciplines

**Prayer**

**Faith Community**

**Bible Reading**

## Prayer List

**Friends**

**World**

**Personal**

(For designing your MAP - Monthly Action Plan - see introduction pages)

Who am I....
Where am I going....
How am I going to get there?

# nt:sport
# MONTHLY ACTION PLAN

## 5
| S.D. | P.L. | P.G. | S.G. |
|------|------|------|------|
| P. ☐ | F. ☐ | F. ☐ | T. ☐ |
| F. ☐ | W. ☐ | W. ☐ | P. ☐ |
| B. ☐ | P. ☐ | C. ☐ | C. ☐ |

## 6
| S.D. | P.L. | P.G. | S.G. |
|------|------|------|------|
| P. ☐ | F. ☐ | F. ☐ | T. ☐ |
| F. ☐ | W. ☐ | W. ☐ | P. ☐ |
| B. ☐ | P. ☐ | C. ☐ | C. ☐ |

## 7
| S.D. | P.L. | P.G. | S.G. |
|------|------|------|------|
| P. ☐ | F. ☐ | F. ☐ | T. ☐ |
| F. ☐ | W. ☐ | W. ☐ | P. ☐ |
| B. ☐ | P. ☐ | C. ☐ | C. ☐ |

## 8
| S.D. | P.L. | P.G. | S.G. |
|------|------|------|------|
| P. ☐ | F. ☐ | F. ☐ | T. ☐ |
| F. ☐ | W. ☐ | W. ☐ | P. ☐ |
| B. ☐ | P. ☐ | C. ☐ | C. ☐ |

## 13
| S.D. | P.L. | P.G. | S.G. |
|------|------|------|------|
| P. ☐ | F. ☐ | F. ☐ | T. ☐ |
| F. ☐ | W. ☐ | W. ☐ | P. ☐ |
| B. ☐ | P. ☐ | C. ☐ | C. ☐ |

## 14
| S.D. | P.L. | P.G. | S.G. |
|------|------|------|------|
| P. ☐ | F. ☐ | F. ☐ | T. ☐ |
| F. ☐ | W. ☐ | W. ☐ | P. ☐ |
| B. ☐ | P. ☐ | C. ☐ | C. ☐ |

## 15
| S.D. | P.L. | P.G. | S.G. |
|------|------|------|------|
| P. ☐ | F. ☐ | F. ☐ | T. ☐ |
| F. ☐ | W. ☐ | W. ☐ | P. ☐ |
| B. ☐ | P. ☐ | C. ☐ | C. ☐ |

## 16
| S.D. | P.L. | P.G. | S.G. |
|------|------|------|------|
| P. ☐ | F. ☐ | F. ☐ | T. ☐ |
| F. ☐ | W. ☐ | W. ☐ | P. ☐ |
| B. ☐ | P. ☐ | C. ☐ | C. ☐ |

## 21
| S.D. | P.L. | P.G. | S.G. |
|------|------|------|------|
| P. ☐ | F. ☐ | F. ☐ | T. ☐ |
| F. ☐ | W. ☐ | W. ☐ | P. ☐ |
| B. ☐ | P. ☐ | C. ☐ | C. ☐ |

## 22
| S.D. | P.L. | P.G. | S.G. |
|------|------|------|------|
| P. ☐ | F. ☐ | F. ☐ | T. ☐ |
| F. ☐ | W. ☐ | W. ☐ | P. ☐ |
| B. ☐ | P. ☐ | C. ☐ | C. ☐ |

## 23
| S.D. | P.L. | P.G. | S.G. |
|------|------|------|------|
| P. ☐ | F. ☐ | F. ☐ | T. ☐ |
| F. ☐ | W. ☐ | W. ☐ | P. ☐ |
| B. ☐ | P. ☐ | C. ☐ | C. ☐ |

## 24
| S.D. | P.L. | P.G. | S.G. |
|------|------|------|------|
| P. ☐ | F. ☐ | F. ☐ | T. ☐ |
| F. ☐ | W. ☐ | W. ☐ | P. ☐ |
| B. ☐ | P. ☐ | C. ☐ | C. ☐ |

## 29
| S.D. | P.L. | P.G. | S.G. |
|------|------|------|------|
| P. ☐ | F. ☐ | F. ☐ | T. ☐ |
| F. ☐ | W. ☐ | W. ☐ | P. ☐ |
| B. ☐ | P. ☐ | C. ☐ | C. ☐ |

## 30
| S.D. | P.L. | P.G. | S.G. |
|------|------|------|------|
| P. ☐ | F. ☐ | F. ☐ | T. ☐ |
| F. ☐ | W. ☐ | W. ☐ | P. ☐ |
| B. ☐ | P. ☐ | C. ☐ | C. ☐ |

## 31
| S.D. | P.L. | P.G. | S.G. |
|------|------|------|------|
| P. ☐ | F. ☐ | F. ☐ | T. ☐ |
| F. ☐ | W. ☐ | W. ☐ | P. ☐ |
| B. ☐ | P. ☐ | C. ☐ | C. ☐ |

**Proverbs 8:17**

"I love all who love me. Those who search for me will surely find me."

## Personal Goals

**Family**

**Work/School/Social**

**Challenge**

## Sport Goals

**Training**

**Performance**

**Competition Results**

## STAND POINT

### When you need motivation

#### 12:1

And so, dear brothers and sisters,* I plead with you to give your bodies to God. Let them be a living and holy sacrifice—the kind he will accept. When you think of what he has done for you, is this too much to ask?

³As God's messenger, I give each of you this warning: Be honest in your estimate of yourselves, measuring your value by how much faith God has given you. ⁴Just as our bodies have many parts and each part has a special function, ⁵so it is with Christ's body. We are all parts of his one body, and each of us has different work to do. And since we are all one body in Christ, we belong to each other, and each of us needs all the others.

⁶God has given each of us the ability to do certain things well. So if God has given you the ability to prophesy, speak out when you have faith that God is speaking through you. ⁷If your gift is that of serving others, serve them well. If you are a teacher, do a good job of teaching. ⁸If your gift is to encourage others, do it! If you have money, share it generously. If God has given you leadership ability, take the responsibility seriously. And if you have a gift for showing kindness to others, do it gladly. ⁹Don't just pretend that you love others. Really love them. Hate what is wrong. Stand on the side of the good. ¹⁰Love each other with genuine affection, and take delight in honouring each other. ¹¹Never be lazy in your work, but serve the Lord enthusiastically. ¹²Be glad for all God is planning for you. Be patient in trouble, and always be prayerful. ¹³When God's children are in need, be the one to help them out. And get into the habit of inviting guests home for dinner or, if they need lodging, for the night.

¹⁴If people persecute you because you are a Christian, don't curse them; pray that God will bless them. ¹⁵When others are happy, be happy with them. If they are sad, share their sorrow. ¹⁶Live in harmony with each other. Don't try to act important, but enjoy the company of ordinary people. And don't think you know it all!

¹⁷Never pay back evil for evil to anyone. Do things in such a way that everyone can see you are honourable. ¹⁸Do your part to live in peace with everyone, as much as possible.

¹⁹Dear friends, never avenge yourselves. Leave that to God. For it is written,

"I will take vengeance;
I will repay those who deserve it,"

says the Lord.

²⁰Instead, do what the Scriptures say:

"If your enemies are hungry, feed them.
If they are thirsty, give them something to drink,
and they will be ashamed of what they have done to you."

²¹Don't let evil get the best of you, but conquer evil by doing good.

## Respect for Authority

## 13

Obey the government, for God is the one who put it there. **All governments have been placed in power by God.** ²So those who refuse to obey the laws of the land are refusing to obey God, and punishment will follow. ³For the authorities do not frighten people who are doing right, but they frighten those who do wrong. So do what they say, and you will get along well. ⁴The authorities are sent by God to help you. But if you are doing something wrong, of course you should be afraid, for you will be punished. The authorities are established by God for that very purpose, to punish those who do wrong. ⁵So you must obey the government for two reasons: to keep from being punished and to keep a clear conscience.

⁶Pay your taxes, too, for these same reasons. For government workers need to be paid so they can keep on doing the work God intended them to do. ⁷Give to everyone what you owe them: Pay your taxes and import duties, and give respect and honour to all to whom it is due.

---

## Winners know humility!

'I don't want my kids to compete because they may get embarrassed.' Many leaders and parents want to shelter their kids from humiliation. These attitudes, generated out of genuine love for kids can be very unhealthy. We all have to learn to live with embarrassment and humility. Everyone in sport will eventually 'goof-up' and be embarrassed and humbled. It is indeed a shame when a youngster (or anyone) is unduly humiliated. Yet humility is also a great virtue. This is nothing to shy away from. Humility comes before honour (Proverbs 15:33). A Dominican monk once wrote, "He who learns to laugh at himself will never cease to be entertained." Many sporting experiences are not glorious but they do teach us not to take ourselves too seriously! Sport often reveals shortcomings and facing up to these can be a valuable lesson. "Be honest in your estimate of yourselves, measuring your value by how much faith God has given you." Romans 12:3

Winners can laugh at themselves!

## Love Fulfils God's Requirements

[8]Pay all your debts, except the debt of love for others. You can never finish paying that! If you love your neighbour, you will fulfil all the requirements of God's law. [9]For the commandments against adultery and murder and stealing and coveting—and any other commandment—are all summed up in this one commandment: "Love your neighbour as yourself." [10]Love does no wrong to anyone, so love satisfies all of God's requirements.

[11]Another reason for right living is that you know how late it is; time is running out. Wake up, for the coming of our salvation is nearer now than when we first believed. [12]The night is almost gone; the day of salvation will soon be here. So don't live in darkness. Get rid of your evil deeds. Shed them like dirty clothes. Clothe yourselves with the armour of right living, as those who live in the light. [13]We should be decent and true in everything we do, so that everyone can approve of our behaviour. Don't participate in wild parties and getting drunk, or in adultery and immoral living, or in fighting and jealousy. [14]But let the Lord Jesus Christ take control of you, and don't think of ways to indulge your evil desires.

**action**

**CH 14:1-9 WHAT'S IT SAYING?**

**WHAT AM I GOING TO DO ABOUT IT?**

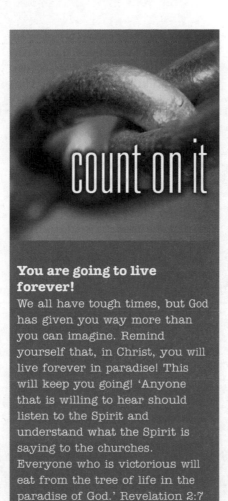

## count on it

### You are going to live forever!

We all have tough times, but God has given you way more than you can imagine. Remind yourself that, in Christ, you will live forever in paradise! This will keep you going! 'Anyone that is willing to hear should listen to the Spirit and understand what the Spirit is saying to the churches. Everyone who is victorious will eat from the tree of life in the paradise of God.' Revelation 2:7 **Count on it!**

## The Danger of Criticism

# 14

Accept Christians who are weak in faith, and don't argue with them about what they think is right or wrong. [2]For instance, one person believes it is all right to eat anything. But another believer who has a sensitive conscience will eat only vegetables. [3]Those who think it is all right to eat anything must not look down on those who won't. And those who won't eat certain foods must not condemn those who do, for God has accepted them. [4]Who are you to condemn God's servants? They are responsible to the Lord, so let him tell them whether they are right or wrong. The Lord's power will help them do as they should. [5]In the same way, some think one day is more holy than another day, while others think every day is alike. Each person should have a personal conviction about this matter. [6]Those who have a special day for worshipping the Lord are trying to honour him. Those who eat all kinds of food do so to honour the Lord, since they give thanks to God before eating. And those who won't eat everything also want to please the Lord and give thanks to God. [7]For we are not our own masters when we live or when we die. [8]While we live, we live to please the Lord. And when we die, we go to be with the Lord. So in life and in death, we belong to the Lord. [9]Christ died and rose again for this very purpose, so that he might be Lord of those who are alive and of those who have died.

[10]So why do you condemn another Christian? Why do you look down on another Christian? Remember, each of us will stand personally before the judgement seat of God. [11]For the Scriptures say,

"'As surely as I live,' says the Lord,
'every knee will bow to me
and every tongue will confess allegiance to God.'"

[12]Yes, each of us will have to give a personal account to God. [13]So don't condemn each other any more. Decide instead to live in such a way that you will not put an obstacle in another Christian's path.

[14]I know and am perfectly sure on the authority of the Lord Jesus that no food, in and of itself, is wrong to eat. But if someone believes it is wrong, then for that person it is wrong. [15]And if another Christian is distressed by what you eat, you are not acting in love if you eat it. Don't let your eating ruin someone for whom Christ died. [16]Then you will not be condemned for doing something you know is all right. [17]For the Kingdom of God is not a matter of what we eat or drink, but of living a life of goodness and peace and joy in the Holy Spirit. [18]If you serve Christ with this attitude, you will please God. And other people will approve of you, too. [19]**So then, let us aim for harmony in the church and try to build each other up.** [20]Don't tear apart the work of God over what you eat. Remember, there is nothing wrong with these things in themselves. But it is wrong to eat anything if it makes another person stumble. [21]Don't eat meat or drink wine or do anything else if it might cause another Christian to stumble. [22]You may have the faith to believe that there is nothing wrong with what you are doing, but keep it between yourself and God. Blessed are those who do not condemn themselves by doing something they know is all right. [23]But if people have doubts about whether they should eat something, they shouldn't eat it. They would be condemned for not acting in faith before God. If you do anything you believe is not right, you are sinning.

## Living to Please Others

# 15

We may know that these things make no difference, but we cannot just go ahead and do them to please ourselves. We must be considerate of the doubts and fears of those who think these things are wrong. [2]We should please others. If we do what helps them, we will build them up in the Lord. [3]For even Christ didn't please himself. As the Scriptures say, "Those who insult you are also insulting me." [4]Such things were written in the Scriptures long ago to teach us. They give us hope and encouragement as we wait patiently for God's promises.

[5]May God, who gives this patience and encouragement, help you live in complete harmony with each other—each with the attitude of Christ Jesus towards the other. [6]Then all of you can join together with one voice, giving praise and glory to God, the Father of our Lord Jesus Christ.

[7]So accept each other just as Christ has accepted you; then God will be glorified. [8]Remember that Christ came as a servant to the Jews to show that God is true to the promises he made to their ancestors. [9]And he came so the Gentiles might also give glory to God for his mercies to them. That is what the psalmist meant when he wrote:

"I will praise you among the Gentiles;
I will sing praises to your name."

[10]And in another place it is written,

"Rejoice, O you Gentiles,
along with his people, the Jews."

[11]And yet again,

"Praise the Lord, all you Gentiles;
praise him, all you people of the earth."

[12]And the prophet Isaiah said,

"The heir to David's throne will come,
and he will rule over the Gentiles.
They will place their hopes on him."

[13]So I pray that God, who gives you hope, will keep you happy and full of peace as you believe in him. May you overflow with hope through the power of the Holy Spirit.

## Paul's Reason for Writing

[14]I am fully convinced, dear brothers and sisters, that you are full of goodness. You know these things so well that you are able to teach others all about them. [15]Even so, I have been bold enough to emphasize some of these points, knowing that all you need is this reminder from me. For I am, by God's grace, [16]a special messenger from Christ Jesus to you Gentiles. I bring you the Good News and offer you up as a fragrant sacrifice to God so that you might be pure and pleasing to him by the Holy Spirit. [17]So it is right for me to be enthusiastic about all Christ Jesus has done through me in

my service to God. [18]I dare not boast of anything else. I have brought the Gentiles to God by my message and by the way I lived before them. [19]I have won them over by the miracles done through me as signs from God—all by the power of God's Spirit. In this way, I have fully presented the Good News of Christ all the way from Jerusalem right over into Illyricum.

[20]**My ambition has always been to preach the Good News where the name of Christ has never been heard, rather than where a church has already been started by someone else.** [21]I have been following the plan spoken of in the Scriptures, where it says,

"Those who have never been told about him will see, and those who have never heard of him will understand."

[22]In fact, my visit to you has been delayed so long because I have been preaching in these places.

## Paul's Travel Plans

[23]But now I have finished my work in these regions, and after all these long years of waiting, I am eager to visit you.

[24]I am planning to go to Spain, and when I do, I will

count on it

**Perfection:**
We can never make ourselves completely perfect on our own. But we are made perfect through Jesus Christ. When you have faith in Christ you are complete.
"For by that one offering, he perfected forever all those whom he is making holy."
Hebrews 10:14
**Count on it!**

stop off in Rome. And after I have enjoyed your fellowship for a little while, you can send me on my way again.

[25]But before I come, I must go down to Jerusalem to take a gift to the Christians there. [26]For you see, the believers in Greece have eagerly taken up an offering for the Christians in Jerusalem, who are going through such hard times. [27]They were very glad to do this because they feel they owe a real debt to them. Since the Gentiles received the wonderful spiritual blessings of the Good News from the Jewish Christians, they feel the least they can do in return is help them financially. [28]As soon as I have delivered this money and completed this good deed of theirs, I will come to see you on my way to Spain. [29]And I am sure that when I come, Christ will give me a great blessing for you.

[30]Dear brothers and sisters, I urge you in the name of our Lord Jesus Christ to join me in my struggle by praying to God for me. Do this because of your love for me, given to you by the Holy Spirit. [31]Pray that I will be rescued from those in Judea who refuse to obey God. Pray also that the Christians there will be willing to accept the donation I am bringing them. [32]Then, by the will of God, I will be able to come to you with a happy heart, and we will be an encouragement to each other.

[33]And now may God, who gives us his peace, be with you all. Amen.

## Paul Greets His Friends

# 16

Our sister Phoebe, a deacon in the church in Cenchrea, will be coming to see you soon. [2]Receive her in the Lord, as one who is worthy of high honour. Help her in every way you can, for she has helped many in their needs, including me.

[3]Greet Priscilla and Aquila. They have been co-workers in my ministry for Christ Jesus. [4]In fact, they risked their lives for me. I am not the only one who is thankful to them; so are all the Gentile churches. [5]Please give my greetings to the church that meets in their home. Greet my dear friend Epenetus. He was the very first person to become a Christian in the province of Asia. [6]Give my greetings to Mary, who has worked so hard for your benefit. [7]Then there are Andronicus and Junia, my relatives, who were in prison with me. They are respected among the apostles and became Christians before I did. Please give them my greetings. [8]Say hello to Ampliatus, whom I love as one of the Lord's own

children, ⁹and Urbanus, our co-worker in Christ, and beloved Stachys.

¹⁰Give my greetings to Apelles, a good man whom Christ approves. And give my best regards to the members of the household of Aristobulus. ¹¹Greet Herodion, my relative. Greet the Christians in the household of Narcissus. ¹²Say hello to Tryphena and Tryphosa, the Lord's workers, and to dear Persis, who has worked so hard for the Lord. ¹³Greet Rufus, whom the Lord picked out to be his very own; and also his dear mother, who has been a mother to me.

¹⁴And please give my greetings to Asyncritus, Phlegon, Hermes, Patrobas, Hermas, and the brothers and sisters who are with them. ¹⁵Give my greetings to Philologus, Julia, Nereus and his sister, and to Olympas and all the other believers who are with them. ¹⁶Greet each other in Christian love. All the churches of Christ send you their greetings.

## Paul's Final Instructions

¹⁷And now I make one more appeal, my dear brothers and sisters. Watch out for people who cause divisions and upset people's faith by teaching things that are contrary to what you have been taught. Stay away from them. ¹⁸Such people are not serving Christ our Lord; they are serving their own personal interests. By smooth talk and glowing words they deceive innocent people. ¹⁹But everyone knows that you are obedient to the Lord. This makes me very happy. I want you to see clearly what is right and to stay innocent of any wrong. ²⁰The God of peace will soon crush Satan under your feet. May the grace of our Lord Jesus Christ be with you.

²¹Timothy, my fellow worker, and Lucius, Jason, and Sosipater, my relatives, send you their good wishes. ²²I, Tertius, the one who is writing this letter for Paul, send my greetings, too, as a Christian brother.

²³Gaius says hello to you. I am his guest, and the church meets here in his home. Erastus, the city treasurer, sends you his greetings, and so does Quartus, a Christian brother.* ²⁵God is able to make you strong, just as the Good News says. It is the message about Jesus Christ and his plan for you Gentiles, a plan kept secret from the beginning of time. ²⁶But now as the prophets foretold and as the eternal God has commanded, this message is made known to all Gentiles everywhere, so that they might believe and obey Christ. ²⁷**To God, who alone is wise, be the glory for ever through Jesus Christ. Amen.**

## PERSONAL ASSESSMENTS

### TRAINING ASSESSMENT:

#### Pick a sport you want to focus on and see where you need to emphasise:

| | |
|---|---|
| My sport needs a lot of power. | 1 2 3 4 5 6 7 8 9 10 |
| I work hard on developing strength and power: | 1 2 3 4 5 6 7 8 9 10 |
| My own strength and power for my age is: | 1 2 3 4 5 6 7 8 9 10 |
| In my sport muscular endurance is: | 1 2 3 4 5 6 7 8 9 10 |
| In my sport aerobic fitness is: | 1 2 3 4 5 6 7 8 9 10 |
| In my training I place a lot of emphasis on aerobic fitness: | 1 2 3 4 5 6 7 8 9 10 |
| I rate my level of aerobic fitness (for your age): | 1 2 3 4 5 6 7 8 9 10 |
| I am maintaining a balanced life style. | 1 2 3 4 5 6 7 8 9 10 |
| I have an effective training routine and plan. | 1 2 3 4 5 6 7 8 9 10 |
| I understand that if I want to achieve a certain level of skill and performance I will have to work at it. | 1 2 3 4 5 6 7 8 9 10 |

### They say that a goal not written down is merely a wish:

#### Write down five goals you have after responding to this assessment.

1 _____

2 _____

3 _____

4 _____

5 _____

16:23 Some manuscripts add verse 24, *May the grace of our Lord Jesus Christ be with you all. Amen.* Still others add this sentence after verse 27.

# He's the Boss

'Look! Here I stand at the door and knock. If you hear me calling and open the door, I will come in, and we will share a meal as friends.' Revelation 3:20

Feel your pulse beat and your blood course through you body. Grasp the fact that you not only encompass blood, bone and tissue. You also house a sophisticated psyche, a complex computer and a multiplicity of different systems: circulatory, digestive, nervous, respiratory, endocrine, immune, reproductive, lymphatic, and urinary systems. Your body has huge potential.

Another item you contain within your body is a throne. You have the capacity to host the Creator of the Universe in the core of your being, the capacity to be in the companionship of God Almighty.

A rugby player from Keble College, Oxford was the first to show me the famous portrait, 'The Light of the World', by Holman Hunt. It is a beautiful mid-nineteenth century paining of Jesus knocking at a door carrying a lantern. It was inspired by several scriptures including Revelation 3:20. The door symbolizes the entrance to a person's heart or life. The painting took three years to make and when completed was at first misunderstood. The critics laughed at Hunt and mocked that after

DEVOTIONAL

three years of detailed work he forgot to paint a handle for the door! A friend, John Ruskin, boldly defended Hunt's symbolic 'Pre-Raphaelite' art in a letter to the London Times. In my words, the door handle is on the inside, Christ will not crash your party or force himself into a place he is not wanted. You have to invite him in. When Jesus was crucified on the cross, the Temple in Israel had a thick (probably wool) curtain that separated a small exclusive part of the building. It separated the holy area from the 'Holy of Holies', which hosted the presence of God. On Christ's death the curtain was torn from top to bottom, symbolizing that God would not be contained in a room, but now dwells inside all who ask, inside all who are chosen. But when inviting a king into your life, be careful; he will demand centre stage, he will want to sit on the throne. Head coaches want what's best for their team, and they call the shots, so their team is unified and performs well. God wants to lead you so you will perform the best in life that you can.

## Reflection
I want Christ to be my Saviour but do I want him to be my Lord?

## Prayer
Father in heaven, give me the courage to answer your Son's calling: 'Come follow me.'

'If anyone loves me, he will obey my teaching. My Father will love him, and we will come to him and make our home with him.'
Jesus

Nicked from: A Sporting Guide to Eternity, Steve Connor, Christian Focus Publications - ISBN 1-85792-746-X

Paul's first letter to the Corinthians is an honest, strong, loving and nurturing response to a church full of problems.

Imagine a great coach sees your potential, recruits you, trains you and keeps encouraging you, long after your sports career is established. The Apostle Paul in many ways is like a spiritual coach, in many of his letters he is encouraging his 'recruits' to follow and be transformed by Christ. God is speaking through Paul to instruct believers to live a life worthy of Christ. In this book, Paul is writing to people that he knows and loves. He spent a lot of time in Corinth, a very strategic city, and helped establish and care for a young Christian community.

But though the church was started by a great man of God, the movement at Corinth had plenty of problems. We can detect frustration by Paul and shock that the church has turned a blind eye to some clear offences to God. Corinth was a very immoral community. Not unlike the world we live today. The lessons are as fresh and applicable today as they were in Paul's time.

The book ends with a positive look at the gifts that each believer has and how best to use them to further the cause of Christ. One of the most famous chapters in the Bible is 1 Corinthians 13. Here Paul, emphasises Jesus' teaching about loving and the priority it must have in our lives.

# 1 Corinthians

# Adversity
## EXPECT IT

# 1 CORINTHIANS

## Greetings from Paul

# 1

This letter is from Paul, chosen by the will of God to be an apostle of Christ Jesus, and from our brother Sosthenes.

²We are writing to the church of God in Corinth, you who have been called by God to be his own holy people. He made you holy by means of Christ Jesus, just as he did all Christians everywhere—whoever calls upon the name of Jesus Christ, our Lord and theirs.

³May God our Father and the Lord Jesus Christ give you his grace and peace.

## Paul Gives Thanks to God

⁴I can never stop thanking God for all the generous gifts he has given you, now that you belong to Christ Jesus. ⁵He has enriched your church with the gifts of eloquence and every kind of knowledge. ⁶This shows that what I told you about Christ is true. ⁷Now you have every spiritual gift you need as you eagerly wait for the return of our Lord Jesus Christ. ⁸He will keep you strong right up to the end, and he will keep you free from all blame on the great day when our Lord Jesus Christ returns.

⁹God will surely do this for you, for he always does just what he says, and he is the one who invited you into this wonderful friendship with his Son, Jesus Christ our Lord.

## Divisions in the Church

¹⁰Now, dear brothers and sisters, I appeal to you by the authority of the Lord Jesus Christ to stop arguing among yourselves. Let there be real harmony so there won't be divisions in the church. I plead with you to be of one mind, united in thought and purpose. ¹¹For some members of Chloe's household have told me about your arguments, dear brothers and sisters. ¹²Some of you are saying, "I am a follower of Paul." Others are saying, "I follow Apollos," or "I follow Peter," or "I follow only Christ." ¹³Can Christ be divided into pieces?

Was I, Paul, crucified for you? Were any of you baptized in the name of Paul? ¹⁴I thank God that I did not baptize any of you except Crispus and Gaius, ¹⁵for now no one can say they were baptized in my name. ¹⁶(Oh yes, I also baptized the household of Stephanas. I don't remember baptizing anyone else.) ¹⁷For Christ didn't send me to baptize, but to preach the Good News—and not with clever speeches and high-sounding ideas, for fear that the cross of Christ would lose its power.

## The Wisdom of God

¹⁸I know very well how foolish the message of the cross sounds to those who are on the road to destruction. But we who are being saved recognize this message as the very power of God. ¹⁹As the Scriptures say,

"I will destroy human wisdom
and discard their most brilliant ideas."

²⁰So where does this leave the philosophers, the scholars, and the world's brilliant debaters? God has made them all look foolish and has shown their wisdom to be useless nonsense.

²¹Since God in his wisdom saw to it that the world would never find him through human wisdom, he has used our foolish preaching to save all who believe. ²²God's way seems foolish to the Jews because they want a sign from heaven to prove it is true. And it is foolish to the Greeks because they believe only what agrees with their own wisdom. ²³So when we preach that Christ was crucified, the Jews are offended, and the Gentiles say it's all nonsense. ²⁴But to those called by God to salvation, both Jews and Gentiles, Christ is the mighty power of God and the wonderful wisdom of God. ²⁵**This "foolish" plan of God is far wiser than the wisest of human plans, and God's weakness is far stronger than the greatest of human strength.**

²⁶Remember, dear brothers and sisters, that few of you were wise in the world's eyes, or powerful, or wealthy when God called you. ²⁷Instead, God deliberately chose things the world considers foolish in order to shame those who think they are wise. And he chose those who are powerless to shame those who are powerful. ²⁸God chose things despised by the world, things counted as nothing at all, and used them to bring to nothing what the world considers important, ²⁹so that no one can ever boast in the presence of God.

³⁰God alone made it possible for you to be in Christ Jesus. For our benefit God made Christ to be wisdom itself. He is the one who made us acceptable to God. He made us pure and holy, and he gave himself to purchase our freedom. ³¹As the Scriptures say,

"The person who wishes to boast
should boast only of what the Lord has done."

Want what God wants! God knows you better than even your mama! He designed you, has a purpose for you and wants the best for you. Father knows best! "And we can be confident that he will listen to us whenever we ask him for anything in line with his will. And if we make our requests, we can be sure that he will give us what we ask for."

1 John 5:14-15

## Paul Preaches Wisdom

# 2

Dear brothers and sisters, when I first came to you I didn't use lofty words and brilliant ideas to tell you God's message. ²For I decided to concentrate only on Jesus Christ and his death on the cross. ³I came to you in weakness—timid and trembling. ⁴And my message and my preaching were very plain. I did not use wise and persuasive speeches, but the Holy Spirit was powerful among you. ⁵I did this so that you might trust the power of God rather than human wisdom.

⁶Yet when I am among mature Christians, I do speak with words of wisdom, but not the kind of wisdom that belongs to this world, and not the kind that appeals to the rulers of this world, who are being brought to nothing. ⁷No, the wisdom we speak of is the secret wisdom of God, which was hidden in former times, though he made it for our benefit before the world began. ⁸But the rulers of this world have not understood it; if they had, they would never have crucified our glorious Lord. ⁹That is what the Scriptures mean when they say,

## STAND POINT

### When you are jealous

**2:9**

"No eye has seen, no ear has heard, and no mind has imagined what God has prepared for those who love him."

"No eye has seen, no ear has heard, and no mind has imagined what God has prepared for those who love him." [10]But we know these things because God has revealed them to us by his Spirit, and his Spirit searches out everything and shows us even God's deep secrets. [11]No one can know what anyone else is really thinking except that person alone, and no one can know God's thoughts except God's own Spirit. [12]And God has actually given us his Spirit (not the world's spirit) so we can know the wonderful things God has freely given us.

[13]When we tell you this, we do not use words of human wisdom. We speak words given to us by the Spirit, using the Spirit's words to explain spiritual truths. [14]**But people who aren't Christians can't understand these truths from God's Spirit. It all sounds foolish to them because only those who have the Spirit can understand what the Spirit means.** [15]We who have the Spirit understand these things, but others can't understand us at all. [16]How could they? For,

"Who can know what the Lord is thinking?
Who can give him counsel?"
But we can understand these things, for we have the mind of Christ.

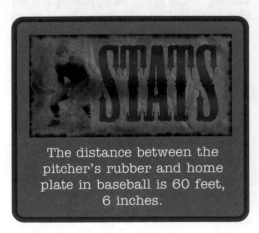

The distance between the pitcher's rubber and home plate in baseball is 60 feet, 6 inches.

## action

**CH 2:14-15 WHAT'S IT SAYING?**

**WHAT AM I GOING TO DO ABOUT IT?**

## Paul and Apollos, Servants of Christ

# 3

Dear brothers and sisters, when I was with you I couldn't talk to you as I would to mature Christians. I had to talk as though you belonged to this world or as though you were infants in the Christian life. [2]I had to feed you with milk and not with solid food, because you couldn't handle anything stronger. And you still aren't ready, [3]for you are still controlled by your own sinful desires. You are jealous of one another and quarrel with each other. Doesn't that prove you are controlled by your own desires? You are acting like people who don't belong to the Lord. [4]When one of you says, "I am a follower of Paul," and another says, "I prefer Apollos," aren't you acting like those who are not Christians?

[5]Who is Apollos, and who is Paul, that we should be the cause of such quarrels? Why, we're only servants. Through us God caused you to believe. Each of us did the work the Lord gave us. [6]My job was to plant the seed in your hearts, and Apollos watered it, but it was God, not we, who made it grow. [7]The ones who do the planting or watering aren't important, but God is important because he is the one who makes the seed grow. [8]The one who plants and the one who waters work as a team with the same purpose. Yet they will be rewarded individually, according to their own hard work. [9]We work together as partners who belong to God. You are God's field, God's building—not ours. [10]Because of God's special favour to me, I have laid the foundation like an expert builder. Now others are building on it. But whoever is building on this foundation must be very careful. [11]For no one can lay any other foundation than the one we already have—Jesus Christ. [12]Now anyone who builds on that foundation may use gold, silver, jewels, wood, hay, or straw. [13]But there is going to come a time of testing at the judgement day to see what kind of work each builder has done. Everyone's work will be put through the fire to see whether or not it keeps its value. [14]If the work survives the fire, that builder will receive a reward. [15]But if the work is burned up, the builder will suffer great loss. The builders themselves will be saved, but like someone escaping through a wall of flames.

[16]**Don't you realize that all of you together are the temple of God and that the Spirit of God lives in you? [17]God will bring ruin upon anyone who ruins this temple. For God's temple is holy, and you Christians are that temple.**

[18]Stop fooling yourselves. If you think you are wise by this world's standards, you will have to become a fool so you can become wise by God's standards. [19]For the wisdom of this world is foolishness to God. As the Scriptures say,

"God catches those who think they are wise in their own cleverness."
[20]And again,
"The Lord knows the thoughts of the wise, that they are worthless."

[21]So don't take pride in following a particular leader. Everything belongs to you: [22]Paul and Apollos and Peter; the whole world and life and death; the present and the future. Everything belongs to you, [23]and you belong to Christ, and Christ belongs to God.

## Paul and the Corinthians

# 4

So look at Apollos and me as mere servants of Christ who have been put in charge of explaining God's secrets. [2]Now, a person who is put in charge as a manager must be faithful. [3]What about me? Have I

# WHAT

# DOES IT MEAN?

**Apostle**

It is, generally agreed as designating the body of disciples to whom he entrusted his church and the spreading of his gospel, The Twelve, as they are called (Matt. 10:1-5; Mark 3:14; 6:7; Luke 6:13; 9:1). We have four lists of the apostles, one by each of the synoptic evangelists (Matt. 10:2-4; Mark 3:16; Luke 6:14), and one in the Acts (1:13). Our Lord gave them the "keys of the kingdom", and by the gift of his Spirit fitted them to be the founders and governors of his church (John 14:16, 17, 26; 15:26, 27; 16:7-15). Another qualification was the authority of working miracles (Mark 16:20; Acts 2:43; 1 Cor. 12:8-11).

been faithful? Well, it matters very little what you or anyone else thinks. I don't even trust my own judgement on this point. ⁴My conscience is clear, but that isn't what matters. It is the Lord himself who

will examine me and decide.

⁵So be careful not to jump to conclusions before the Lord returns as to whether or not someone is faithful. **When the Lord comes, he will bring our deepest secrets to light and will reveal our private motives. And then God will give to everyone whatever praise is due.** ⁶Dear brothers and sisters, I have used Apollos and myself to illustrate what I've been saying. If you pay attention to the Scriptures, you won't brag about one of your leaders at the expense of another. ⁷What makes you better than anyone else? What do you have that God hasn't given you? And if all you have is from God, why boast as though you have accomplished something on your own?

⁸You think you already have everything you need! You are already rich! Without us you have become kings! I wish you really were on your thrones already, for then we would be reigning with you!

⁹But sometimes I think God has put us apostles on display, like prisoners of war at the end of a victor's parade, condemned to die. We have become a spectacle to the entire world—to people and angels alike. ¹⁰Our dedication to Christ makes us look like fools, but you are so wise! We are weak, but you are so powerful! You are well thought of, but we are laughed at. ¹¹To this very hour we go hungry and thirsty, without enough clothes to keep us warm. We have endured many beatings, and we have no homes of our own. ¹²We have worked wearily with our own hands to earn our living. We bless those who curse us. We are patient with those who abuse us. ¹³We respond gently when evil things are said about us. Yet we are treated like the world's waste, like everybody's rubbish—right up to the present moment.

¹⁴I am not writing these things to shame you, but to warn you as my beloved children. ¹⁵For even if you had ten thousand others to teach you about Christ, you have only one spiritual father. For I became your father in Christ Jesus when I preached the Good News to you. ¹⁶So I ask you to follow my example and do as I do.

¹⁷That is the very reason I am sending Timothy—to help you do this. For he is my beloved and trustworthy child in the Lord. He will remind you of what I teach about Christ Jesus in all the churches wherever I go. ¹⁸I know that some of you have become arrogant, thinking I will never visit you again. ¹⁹But I will come—and soon—if the Lord will let me, and then I'll find out whether these arrogant people are just big talkers or whether they really have God's power.

²⁰For the Kingdom of God is not just fancy talk; it is living by God's power. ²¹Which do you choose? Should I come with punishment and scolding, or should I come with quiet love and gentleness?

## Paul Condemns Spiritual Pride

# 5

I can hardly believe the report about the sexual immorality going on among you, something so evil that even the pagans don't do it. I am told that you have a man in your church who is living in sin with his father's wife. ²And you are so proud of yourselves! Why aren't you mourning in sorrow and shame? And why haven't you removed this man from your fellowship?

³Even though I am not there with you in person, I am with you in the Spirit. Concerning the one who has done this, I have already passed judgement ⁴in the name of the Lord Jesus. You are to call a meeting of the church, and I will be there in spirit, and the power of the Lord Jesus will be with

**The Bible contains 66 books written by over 40 different authors with one central theme.**

you as you meet. ⁵Then you must cast this man out of the church and into Satan's hands, so that his sinful nature will be destroyed and he himself will be saved when the Lord returns.

⁶**How terrible that you should boast about your spirituality, and yet you let this sort of thing go on. Don't you realize that if even one person is allowed to go on sinning, soon all will be affected?** ⁷Remove this wicked person from among you so that you can stay pure. Christ, our Passover Lamb, has been sacrificed for us. ⁸So let us celebrate the festival, not by eating the old bread of wickedness and evil, but by eating the new bread of purity and truth.

⁹When I wrote to you before, I told you not to associate with people who indulge in sexual sin. ¹⁰But I wasn't talking about unbelievers who indulge in sexual sin, or who are greedy or are swindlers or idol worshippers. You would have to leave this world to avoid people like that. ¹¹What I meant was that

you are not to associate with anyone who claims to be a Christian yet indulges in sexual sin, or is greedy, or worships idols, or is abusive, or a drunkard, or a swindler. Don't even eat with such people.

[12]It isn't my responsibility to judge outsiders, but it certainly is your job to judge those inside the church who are sinning in these ways. [13]God will judge those on the outside; but as the Scriptures say, "You must remove the evil person from among you."

### CH 5:9-12 WHAT'S IT SAYING?

### WHAT AM I GOING TO DO ABOUT IT?

## Avoiding Lawsuits with Christians

# 6

When you have something against another Christian, why do you file a lawsuit and ask a secular court to decide the matter, instead of taking it to other Christians to decide who is right? [2]Don't you know that someday we Christians are going to judge the world? And since you are going to judge the world, can't you decide these little things among yourselves? [3]Don't you realize that we Christians will judge angels? So you should surely be able to resolve ordinary disagreements here on earth. [4]If you have legal disputes about such matters, why do you go to outside judges who are not respected by the church? [5]I am saying this to shame you. Isn't there anyone in all the church who is wise enough to decide these arguments? [6]But instead, one Christian sues another—right in front of unbelievers!

[7]To have such lawsuits at all is a real defeat for you. Why not just accept the injustice and leave it at that? Why not let yourselves be cheated? [8]But instead, you yourselves are the ones who do wrong and cheat even your own Christian brothers and sisters.

## Avoiding Sexual Sin

[9]Don't you know that those who do wrong will have no share in the Kingdom of God? Don't fool yourselves. Those who indulge in sexual sin, who are idol worshippers, adulterers, male prostitutes, homosexuals, [10]thieves, greedy people, drunkards, abusers, and swindlers—none of these will have a share in the Kingdom of God. [11]There was a time when some of you were just like that, but now your sins have been washed away, and you have been set apart for God. You have been made right with God because of what the Lord Jesus Christ and the Spirit of our God have done for you.

[12]You may say, "I am allowed to do anything." But I reply, "Not everything is good for you." And even though "I am allowed to do anything," I must not become a slave to anything. [13]You say, "Food is for the stomach, and the stomach is for food." This is true, though someday God will do away with both of them. But our bodies were not made for sexual immorality. They were made for the Lord, and the Lord cares about our bodies. [14]And God will raise our bodies from the

dead by his marvellous power, just as he raised our Lord from the dead. [15]Don't you realize that your bodies are actually parts of Christ? Should a man take his body, which belongs to Christ, and join it to a prostitute? Never! [16]And don't you know that if a man joins himself to a prostitute, he becomes one body with her? For the Scriptures say, "The two are united into one." [17]But the person who is joined to the Lord becomes one spirit with him.

[18]Run away from sexual sin! No other sin so clearly affects the body as this one does. For sexual immorality is a sin against your own body. [19]Or don't you know that your body is the temple of the Holy Spirit, who lives in you and was given to you by God? You do not

The modern Olympic Games were held in the first time in 1896 at Athens and were then followed by the 1900 Paris games. The winter games were added in 1924.

belong to yourself, [20]for God bought you with a high price. So you must honour God with your body.

**action**

**CH 6:18-20 WHAT'S IT SAYING?**

**WHAT AM I GOING TO DO ABOUT IT?**

## Instruction on Marriage

# 7

Now about the questions you asked in your letter. Yes, it is good to live a celibate life. [2]But because there is so much

**How can sport really be a ministry? Shouldn't I give up my sport and go into missionary work if I am serious about Christ?**

A famous cricketer, C.T. Studd said, 'Some want to live within the sound of church or chapel bell, I want to run a rescue shop within a yard of hell.'

Everything you do should be given up to God. What does it mean to 'give up everything'? Does it, for instance, mean that all of us who love sports should quit playing? It has often been understood in this way, especially if it involves Sunday sport. Surely what Jesus is getting at is 'a real disciple must give Christ full control over his whole life, with everything he is and all that he possesses including his wealth and his talents'. We, who are passionate about our sport and our Lord, must be prepared to pray, 'Lord, I will only continue in sport if you want me to'. There is no point, absolutely no point, in the Christian doing anything that is outside God's will and purpose. Let us get to the point where we put everything into God's hands. He will lead us, some maybe to be missionaries and others to wholehearted discipleship within the culture-shaping arena of sport. Perhaps in a way we will all then be missionaries. Who best to reach a team-mate for Christ than a fellow team-mate?

sexual immorality, each man should have his own wife, and each woman should have her own husband.

³The husband should not deprive his wife of sexual intimacy, which is her right as a married woman, nor should the wife deprive her husband. ⁴The wife gives authority over her body to her husband, and the husband also gives authority over his body to his wife. ⁵So do not deprive each other of sexual relations. The only exception to this rule would be the agreement of both husband and wife to refrain from sexual intimacy for a limited time, so they can give themselves more completely to prayer. Afterwards they should come together again so that Satan won't be able to tempt them because of their lack of self-control. ⁶This is only my suggestion. It's not meant to be an absolute rule. ⁷I wish everyone could get along without marrying, just as I do. But we are not all the same. God gives some the gift of marriage, and to others he gives the gift of singleness.

⁸Now I say to those who aren't married and to widows—it's better to stay unmarried, just as I am. ⁹But if they can't control themselves, they should go ahead and marry. It's better to marry than to burn with lust.

¹⁰Now, for those who are married I have a command that comes not from me, but from the Lord. A wife must not leave her husband. ¹¹But if she does leave him, let her remain single or else go back to him. And the husband must not leave his wife.

because of you. And you husbands must remember that your wives might be converted because of you. ¹⁷You must accept whatever situation the Lord has put you in, and continue on as you were when God first called you. This is my rule for all the churches. ¹⁸For instance, a man who was circumcised before he became a believer should not try to reverse it. And the man who was uncircumcised when he became a believer should not be circumcised now. ¹⁹For it makes no difference whether or not a man has been circumcised. The important thing is to keep God's commandments.

²⁰You should continue on as you were when God called you. ²¹Are you a slave? Don't let that worry you—but if you get a chance to be free, take it. ²²And remember, if you were a slave when the Lord called you, the Lord has now set you free from the awful power of sin. And if you were free when the Lord called you, you are now a slave of Christ. ²³God purchased you at a high price. Don't be enslaved by the world. ²⁴So, dear brothers and sisters, whatever situation you were in when you became a believer, stay there in your new relationship with God.

²⁵Now, about the young women who are not yet married. I do not have a command from the Lord for them. But the Lord in his kindness has given me

without becoming attached to them, for this world and all it contains will pass away. ³²In everything you do, I want you to be free from the concerns of this life. An unmarried man can spend his time doing the Lord's work and thinking how to please him. ³³But a married man can't do that so well. He has to think about his earthly responsibilities and how to please his wife. ³⁴His interests are divided. In the same way, a woman who is no longer married or has never been married can be more devoted to the Lord in body and in spirit, while the married woman must be concerned about her earthly responsibilities and how to please her husband.

³⁵I am saying this for your benefit, not to place restrictions on you. **I want you to do whatever will help you serve the Lord best, with as few distractions as possible.** ³⁶But if a man thinks he ought to marry his fiancée because he has trouble controlling his passions and time is passing, it is all right; it is not a sin. Let them marry. ³⁷But if he has decided firmly not to marry and there is no urgency and he can control his passion, he does well not to marry. ³⁸So the person who marries does well, and the person who doesn't marry does even better.

³⁹A wife is married to her husband as long as he lives.

# I Don't Get it:

When you do not know the answer to a question, admit it. Asking questions shows you are interested in improving, don't waste the coach's time or yours by pretending you understand when you don't.

¹²Now, I will speak to the rest of you, though I do not have a direct command from the Lord. If a Christian man has a wife who is an unbeliever and she is willing to continue living with him, he must not leave her. ¹³And if a Christian woman has a husband who is an unbeliever, and he is willing to continue living with her, she must not leave him. ¹⁴For the Christian wife brings holiness to her marriage, and the Christian husband brings holiness to his marriage. Otherwise, your children would not have a godly influence, but now they are set apart for him. ¹⁵(But if the husband or wife who isn't a Christian insists on leaving, let them go. In such cases the Christian husband or wife is not required to stay with them, for God wants his children to live in peace.) ¹⁶You wives must remember that your husbands might be converted

wisdom that can be trusted, and I will share it with you. ²⁶Because of the present crisis, I think it is best to remain just as you are. ²⁷If you have a wife, do not end the marriage. If you do not have a wife, do not get married. ²⁸But if you do get married, it is not a sin. And if a young woman gets married, it is not a sin. However, I am trying to spare you the extra problems that come with marriage.

²⁹Now let me say this, dear brothers and sisters: The time that remains is very short, so husbands should not let marriage be their major concern. ³⁰Happiness or sadness or wealth should not keep anyone from doing God's work. ³¹Those in frequent contact with the things of the world should make good use of them

If her husband dies, she is free to marry whomever she wishes, but this must be a marriage acceptable to the Lord. ⁴⁰But in my opinion it will be better for her if she doesn't marry again, and I think I am giving you counsel from God's Spirit when I say this.

## Food Sacrificed to Idols

# 8

Now let's talk about food that has been sacrificed to idols. You think that everyone should agree with your perfect knowledge. While knowledge may make us feel important, it is love that really builds up the church. ²Anyone who claims to know all the answers doesn't

really know very much. ³But the person who loves God is the one God knows and cares for.

⁴So now, what about it? Should we eat meat that has been sacrificed to idols? Well, we all know that an idol is not really a god and that there is only one God and no other. ⁵According to some people, there are many so-called gods and many lords, both in heaven and on earth. ⁶But we know that there is only one God, the Father, who created everything, and we exist for him. And there is only one Lord, Jesus Christ, through whom God made everything and through whom we have been given life.

⁷However, not all Christians realize this. Some are accustomed to thinking of idols as being real, so when they eat food that has been offered to idols, they think of it as the worship of real gods, and their weak consciences are violated. ⁸It's true that we can't win God's approval by what we eat. We don't miss out on anything if we don't eat it, and we don't gain anything if we do. ⁹But you must be careful with this freedom of yours. Do not cause a brother or sister with a weaker conscience to stumble.

¹⁰You see, this is what can happen: Weak Christians who think it is wrong to eat this food will see you eating in the temple of an idol. You know there's nothing wrong with it, but they will be encouraged to violate their conscience by eating food that has been dedicated to the idol. ¹¹So because of your superior knowledge, a weak Christian, for whom Christ died, will be destroyed.

¹²And you are sinning against Christ when you sin against other Christians by encouraging them to do something they believe is wrong. ¹³If what I eat is going to make another Christian sin, I will never eat meat again as long as I live—for I don't want to make another Christian stumble.

**CH 8:7-13 WHAT'S IT SAYING?**

**WHAT AM I GOING TO DO ABOUT IT?**

## Paul Gives Up His Rights

**9**

Do I not have as much freedom as anyone else? Am I not an apostle? Haven't I seen Jesus our Lord with my own eyes? Isn't it because of my hard work that you are in the Lord? ²Even if others think I am not an apostle, I certainly am to you, for you are living proof that I am the Lord's apostle.

³This is my answer to those who question my authority as an apostle. ⁴Don't we have the right to live in your homes and share your meals? ⁵Don't we have the right to bring a Christian wife along with us as the other disciples and the Lord's brothers and Peter do? ⁶Or is it only Barnabas and I who have to work to support ourselves? ⁷What soldier has to pay his own expenses? And have you ever heard of a farmer who harvests his crop and doesn't have the right to eat some of it? What shepherd takes care of a flock of sheep and isn't allowed to drink some of the milk? ⁸And this isn't merely human opinion. Doesn't God's law say the same thing? ⁹For the law of Moses says, "Do not keep an ox from eating as it treads out the grain." Do you suppose God was thinking only about oxen when he said this? ¹⁰Wasn't he also speaking to us? Of course he was. Just as farm workers who plough fields and thresh the grain expect a share of the harvest, Christian workers should be paid by those they serve.

¹¹We have planted good spiritual seed among you. Is it too much to ask, in return, for mere food and clothing? ¹²If you support others who preach to you, shouldn't we have an even greater right to be supported? Yet we have never used this right. We would rather put up with anything than put an obstacle in the way of the Good News about Christ.

¹³Don't you know that those who work in the Temple get their meals from the food brought to the Temple as offerings? And those who serve at the altar get a share of the sacrificial offerings. ¹⁴In the same way, the Lord gave orders that those who preach the Good News should be supported by those who benefit from it. ¹⁵Yet I have never used any of these rights. And I am not writing this to suggest that I would like to start now. In fact, I would rather die than lose my distinction of preaching without charge. ¹⁶For preaching the Good News is not something I can boast about. I am compelled by God to do it. How terrible for me if I didn't do it!

¹⁷If I were doing this of my own free will, then I would deserve payment. But God has chosen me and given me this sacred trust, and I have no choice. ¹⁸What then is my pay? It is the satisfaction I get from preaching the Good News without expense to anyone, never demanding my rights as a preacher.

## Winners have fun!

God loves to watch his creation enjoying life! Some people think God's job is finding people that are having a good time and then saying, 'stop doing that!' The truth is our life is the most fun when we stay on God's path. A great pro once said, 'I do not want to cheat, because I want to feel good about myself.' Trying to keep on God's 'path' is not easy, but it is the best, and the wrong turns are no fun at all!

"Whoever abandons the right path will be severely punished; whoever hates correction will die." Proverbs 15:10

Winners stay on the path!

## When you are tempted to cheat

### 10:13

But remember that the temptations that come into your life are no different from what others experience. And God is faithful. He will keep the temptation from becoming so strong that you can't stand up against it. When you are tempted, he will show you a way out so that you will not give in to it.

¹⁹This means I am not bound to obey people just because they pay me, yet I have become a servant of everyone so that I can bring them to Christ. ²⁰When I am with the Jews, I become one of them so that I can bring them to Christ. When I am with those who follow the Jewish laws, I do the same, even though I am not subject to the law, so that I can bring them to Christ. ²¹When I am with the Gentiles who do not have the Jewish law, I fit in with them as much as I can. In this way, I gain their confidence and bring them to Christ. But I do not discard the law of God; I obey the law of Christ. **²²When I am with those who are oppressed, I share their oppression so that I might bring them to Christ. Yes, I try to find common ground with everyone so that I might bring them to Christ. ²³I do all this to spread the Good News, and in doing so I enjoy its blessings.**

²⁴Remember that in a race everyone runs, but only one person gets the prize. You also must run in such a way that you will win. ²⁵All athletes practise strict self-control. They do it to win a prize that will fade away, but we do it for an eternal prize. ²⁶So I run straight to the goal with purpose in every step. I am not like a boxer who misses his punches. ²⁷I discipline my body like an athlete, training it to do what it should. Otherwise, I fear that after preaching to others I myself might be disqualified.

## Warnings against Idolatry

# 10

I don't want you to forget, dear brothers and sisters, what

happened to our ancestors in the wilderness long ago. God guided all of them by sending a cloud that moved along ahead of them, and he brought them all safely through the waters of the sea on dry ground.

²As followers of Moses, they were all baptized in the cloud and the sea. ³And all of them ate the same miraculous food, ⁴and all of them drank the same miraculous water. For they all drank from the miraculous rock that travelled with them, and that rock was Christ. ⁵Yet after all this, God was not pleased with most of them, and he destroyed them in the wilderness.

⁶These events happened as a warning to us, so that we would not crave evil things as they did ⁷or worship idols as some of them did. For the Scriptures say, "The people celebrated with feasting and drinking, and they indulged themselves in pagan revelry."

⁸And we must not engage in sexual immorality as some of them did, causing 23,000 of them to die in one day. ⁹Nor should we put Christ to the test, as some of them did and then died from snakebites. ¹⁰And don't grumble as some of them did, for that is why God sent his angel of death to destroy them. ¹¹All these events happened to them as examples for us. They were written down to warn us, who live at the time when this age is drawing to a close.

¹²If you think you are standing strong, be careful, for you, too, may fall into the same sin. ¹³But remember that the temptations that come into your life are no different from what others experience. And God is faithful. He will keep the temptation from becoming so strong that you can't stand up against it. When you are tempted, he will show you a way out so that you will not give in to it.

¹⁴So, my dear friends, flee from the worship of idols. ¹⁵You are reasonable people. Decide for yourselves if what I am about to say is true. ¹⁶When we bless the cup at the Lord's Table, aren't we sharing in the benefits of the blood of Christ? And when we break the loaf of bread, aren't we sharing in the benefits of the body of Christ? ¹⁷And we all eat from one loaf, showing that we are one body. ¹⁸And think about the nation of Israel; all who eat the sacrifices are united by that act.

¹⁹What am I trying to say? Am I saying that the idols to whom the pagans bring sacrifices are real gods and that these sacrifices are of some value? ²⁰No, not at all. What I am saying is that these sacrifices are offered to demons, not to God. And I don't want any of you to be partners with demons.

²¹You cannot drink from the cup of the Lord and from

the cup of demons, too. You cannot eat at the Lord's Table and at the table of demons, too. ²²What? Do you dare to rouse the Lord's jealousy as Israel did? Do you think we are stronger than he is?

²³You say, "I am allowed to do anything"—but not everything is helpful. You say, "I am allowed to do anything"—but not everything is beneficial. ²⁴Don't think only of your own good. Think of other Christians and what is best for them.

**action**

**CH 10:22–24 WHAT'S IT SAYING?**

**WHAT AM I GOING TO DO ABOUT IT?**

²⁵Here's what you should do. You may eat any meat that is sold in the marketplace. Don't ask whether or not it was offered to idols, and then your conscience won't be bothered. ²⁶For "the earth is the Lord's, and everything in it."

²⁷If someone who isn't a Christian asks you home for dinner, go ahead; accept the invitation if you want to. Eat whatever is offered to you and don't ask any questions about it. Your conscience should not be bothered by this. ²⁸But suppose someone warns you that this meat has been offered to an idol. Don't eat it, out of consideration for the conscience of the one who told you. ²⁹It might not be a matter of conscience for you, but it is for the other person.

Subterfuge and conspiracy:
Herod, Pilate and the
Jewish Council:

**profiles**

Herod Antipas inherited his power and kingdom along with three other half brothers from his father Herod the Great. His 1/4 empire was the region of Galilee north of Jerusalem (approx 40 miles) where Jesus spent his boyhood and early ministry. Herod who had a partial Jewish upbringing, was shamed by John the Baptist for marrying his brother's wife. Herod, though he liked John, eventually had him beheaded. When he heard of Jesus, he immediately thought that it was John coming back to haunt him. Herod, like many others from the outer regions, was in the Holy City to celebrate Passover when he briefly encountered Jesus.

Pilate was a Roman Governor and a corrupt career politician. His rule over Jerusalem, which could be fragile powder keg of a city, was tenuous. He was a weak man who would make judgments not by a code of ethics but by what was expedient for himself. Pilate was obviously intimidated by the Jewish council and tried to placate them and simultaneously intimidate them.

Jewish Council
The Jews in Jerusalem were under authority by the occupying power (like many other regions) of Rome. The Jewish council had limited power and could not execute anyone without the express authority of Rome. They saw Jesus as a threat to their power and way of life yet they could not crucify Jesus unless they had it approved by Pilate who represented Rome. So Jesus went from the Jewish Council to Pilate to Herod and back to Pilate. He was never found guilty of anything but through the pressure put on Pilate he was handed over for execution.

Now, why should my freedom be limited by what someone else thinks? ³⁰If I can thank God for the food and enjoy it, why should I be condemned for eating it? ³¹**Whatever you eat or drink or whatever you do, you must do all for the glory of God.** ³²Don't give offence to Jews or Gentiles or the church of God. ³³That is the plan I follow, too. I try to please everyone in everything I do. I don't just do what I like or what is best for me, but what is best for them so they may be saved.

# 11

And you should follow my example, just as I follow Christ's.

## Instructions for Public Worship

²I am so glad, dear friends, that you always keep me in your thoughts and you are following the Christian teaching I passed on to you. ³But there is one thing I want you to know: A man is responsible to Christ, a woman is responsible to her husband, and Christ is responsible to God. ⁴A man dishonours Christ if he covers his head while praying or prophesying. ⁵But a woman dishonours her husband if she prays or prophesies without a covering on her head, for this is the same as shaving her head. ⁶Yes, if she refuses to wear a head covering, she should cut off all her hair. And since it is shameful for a woman to have her hair cut or her head shaved, then she should wear a covering. ⁷A man should not wear anything on his head when worshipping, for man is God's glory, made in God's own image, but woman is the glory of man.

⁸For the first man didn't come from woman, but the first woman came from man. ⁹And man was not made for woman's benefit, but woman was made for man. ¹⁰So a woman should wear a covering on her head as a sign of authority because the angels are watching.

¹¹But in relationships among the Lord's people, women are not independent of men, and men are not independent of women. ¹²For although the first woman came from man, all men have been born from women ever since, and everything comes from God.

¹³What do you think about this? Is it right for a woman to pray to God in public without covering her head? ¹⁴Isn't it obvious that it's disgraceful for a man to have long hair? ¹⁵And isn't it obvious that long hair is a woman's pride and joy? For it has been given to her as a covering. ¹⁶But if anyone wants to argue about this, all I can say is that we have no other custom than this, and all the churches of God feel the same way about it.

## Order at the Lord's Supper

¹⁷But now when I mention this next issue, I cannot praise you. For it sounds as if more harm than good is done when

you meet together. [18]First of all, I hear that there are divisions among you when you meet as a church, and to some extent I believe it. [19]But, of course, there must be divisions among you so that those of you who are right will be recognized! [20]It's not the Lord's Supper you are concerned about when you come together. [21]For I am told that some of you hurry to eat your own meal without sharing with others. As a result, some go hungry while others get drunk. [22]What? Is this really true? Don't you have your own homes for eating and drinking? Or do you really want to disgrace the church of God and shame the poor? What am I supposed to say about these things? Do you want me to praise you? Well, I certainly do not!

[23]For this is what the Lord himself said, and I pass it on to you just as I received it. On the night when he was betrayed, the Lord Jesus took a loaf of bread, [24]and when he had given thanks, he broke it and said, **"This is my body, which is given for you. Do this in remembrance of me." [25]In the same way, he took the cup of wine after supper, saying, "This cup is the new covenant between God and you, sealed by the shedding of my blood. Do this in remembrance of me as often as you drink it."**

[26]For every time you eat this bread and drink this cup, you are announcing the Lord's death until he comes again.

[27]So if anyone eats this bread or drinks this cup of the Lord unworthily, that person is guilty of sinning against the body and the blood of the Lord. [28]That is why you should examine yourself before eating the bread and drinking from the cup. [29]For if you eat the bread or drink the cup unworthily, not honouring the body of Christ, you are eating and drinking God's judgement upon yourself. [30]That is why many of you are weak and sick and some have even died.

[31]But if we examine ourselves, we will not be examined by God and judged in this way. [32]But when we are judged and disciplined by the Lord, we will not be condemned with the world. [33]So, dear brothers and sisters, when you gather for the Lord's Supper, wait for each other. [34]If you are really hungry, eat at home so you won't bring judgement upon yourselves when you meet together.

I'll give you instructions about the other matters after I arrive.

## Spiritual Gifts

# 12

And now, dear brothers and sisters, I will write about the special abilities the Holy Spirit gives to each of us, for I must correct your misunderstandings about them.

Bible FACTS

**The entire Bible was written over a 1500 year span.**

²You know that when you were still pagans you were led astray and swept along in worshipping speechless idols. ³So I want you to know how to discern what is truly from God: No one speaking by the Spirit of God can curse Jesus, and no one is able to say, "Jesus is Lord," except by the Holy Spirit.

⁴Now there are different kinds of spiritual gifts, but it is the same Holy Spirit who is the source of them all. ⁵There are different kinds of service in the church, but it is the same Lord we are serving. ⁶There are different ways God works in our lives, but it is the same God who does the work through all of us. ⁷**A spiritual gift is given to each of us as a means of helping the entire church.**

⁸To one person the Spirit gives the ability to give wise advice; to another he gives the gift of special knowledge. ⁹The Spirit gives special faith to another, and to someone else he gives the power to heal the sick. ¹⁰He gives one person the power to perform miracles, and to another the ability to prophesy. He gives someone else the ability to know whether it is really the Spirit of God or another spirit that is speaking. Still another person is given the ability to speak in unknown languages, and another is given the ability to interpret what is being said. ¹¹It is the one and only Holy Spirit who distributes these gifts. He alone decides which gift each person should have.

## One Body with Many Parts

¹²The human body has many parts, but the many parts make up only one body. So it is with the body of Christ. ¹³Some of us are Jews, some are Gentiles, some are slaves, and some are free. But we have all been baptized into Christ's body by one Spirit, and we have all received the same Spirit.

¹⁴Yes, the body has many different parts, not just one part. ¹⁵If the foot says, "I am not a part of the body because I am not a hand," that does not make it any less a part of the body. ¹⁶And if the ear says, "I am not part of the body because I am only an ear and not an eye," would that make it any less a part of the body? ¹⁷Suppose the whole body were an eye—then how would you hear? Or if your whole body were just one big ear, how could you smell anything?

¹⁸But God made our bodies with many parts, and he has put each part just where he wants it. ¹⁹What a strange thing a body would be if it had only one part! ²⁰Yes, there are many parts, but only one body. ²¹The eye can never say to the hand, "I don't need you." The head can't say to the feet, "I don't need you." ²²In fact, some of the parts that seem weakest and least important are really the most necessary. ²³And

## count on it

### Do you want to be cool?

Cool under pressure. There are many that just have that touch, a gift that keeps them in the zone and focused. God does not promise that he will give you every physical gift in the world. He doesn't promise that you will get faster or taller - he is not some genie in a bottle. But he does promise peace under pressure. "I am leaving you with a gift - peace of mind and heart. And the peace I give isn't the like the peace the world gives. So don't be troubled or afraid." John 14:27

**Count on it!**

the parts we regard as less honourable are those we clothe with the greatest care. So we carefully protect from the eyes of others those parts that should not be seen, ²⁴while other parts do not require this special care. So God has put the body together in such a way that extra honour and care are given to those parts that have less dignity. ²⁵This makes for harmony among the members, so that all the members care for each other equally. ²⁶If one part suffers, all the parts suffer with it, and if one part is honoured, all the parts are glad.

²⁷Now all of you together are Christ's body, and each one of you is a separate and necessary part of it. ²⁸Here is a list of some of the members that God has placed in the body of Christ:

first are apostles,

second are prophets,

third are teachers,

then those who do miracles,

those who have the gift of healing,

those who can help others,

those who can get others to work together,

those who speak in unknown languages.

²⁹Is everyone an apostle? Of course not. Is everyone a prophet? No. Are all teachers? Does everyone have the power to do miracles? ³⁰Does everyone have the gift of healing? Of course not. Does God give all of us the ability to speak in unknown languages? Can everyone interpret unknown languages? No! ³¹And in any event, you should desire the most helpful gifts.

## action

### CH 12:12-31 WHAT'S IT SAYING?

### WHAT AM I GOING TO do ABOUT IT?

## Love Is the Greatest

First, however, let me tell you about something else that is better than any of them!

# 13

If I could speak in any language in heaven or on earth but didn't love others, I would only be making meaningless noise like a loud gong or a clanging cymbal. ²If I had the gift of prophecy, and if I knew all the mysteries of the future and knew everything about everything, but didn't love others, what good would I be? And if I had the gift of faith so that I could speak to a mountain and make it move, without love I would be no good to anybody. ³If I gave everything I have to the poor and even sacrificed my body, I could boast about it; but if I didn't love others, I would be of no value whatsoever. ⁴Love is patient and kind. Love is not jealous or boastful or proud ⁵or rude. Love does not demand its own way. Love is not irritable, and it keeps no record of when it has been wronged. ⁶It is never glad about injustice but rejoices whenever the truth wins out. ⁷Love never gives up, never loses faith, is always hopeful, and endures through every circumstance.

⁸Love will last for ever, but prophecy and speaking in unknown languages and special knowledge will all disappear.

⁹Now we know only a little, and even the gift of prophecy reveals little! ¹⁰But when the end comes, these special gifts will all disappear. ¹¹It's like this: When I was a child, I spoke and thought and reasoned as a child does. But when I grew up, I put away childish things. ¹²Now we see things imperfectly as in a poor mirror, but then we will see everything with perfect clarity. All that I know now is partial and incomplete, but then I will know everything completely, just as God knows me now. ¹³There are three things that will endure—faith, hope, and love—and the greatest of these is love.

## The Gifts of Tongues and Prophecy

## 14

Let love be your highest goal, but also desire the special abilities the Spirit gives, especially the gift of prophecy. ²For if your gift is the ability to speak in tongues, you will be talking to God but not to people, since they won't be able to understand you. You will be speaking by the power of the Spirit, but it will all be mysterious. ³But one who prophesies is helping others grow in the Lord, encouraging and comforting them. ⁴A person

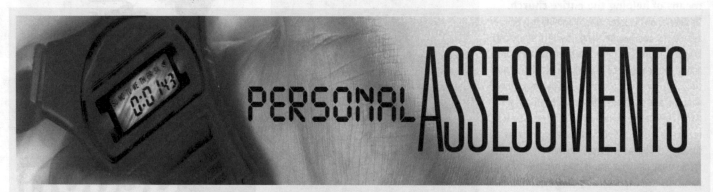

## WHEN I BLOW IT!

Answer this assessment with True or False:

When I blow it (a sin, veering from God's way - not a mistake like a spelling error) I generally:

☐ Ignore it and hope it goes away.

☐ Blame others.

☐ Wallow in self pity and feel sorry for myself.

☐ Take pride in being a screw up.

☐ Learn from it.

☐ Become overwhelmed by guilt.

☐ Feel bad but in time move on.

☐ Ask forgiveness when it concerns others.

☐ Ask God to forgive me.

*"For God can use sorrow in our lives to help us turn away from sin and seek salvation. We will never regret that kind of sorrow. But sorrow without repentance is the kind that results in death."* 2 Corinthians 7: 10

who speaks in tongues is strengthened personally in the Lord, but one who speaks a word of prophecy strengthens the entire church.

[5] I wish you all had the gift of speaking in tongues, but even more I wish you were all able to prophesy. For prophecy is a greater and more useful gift than speaking in tongues, unless someone interprets what you are saying so that the whole church can get some good out of it.

[6] Dear brothers and sisters, if I should come to you talking in an unknown language, how would that help you? But if I bring you some revelation or some special knowledge or some prophecy or some teaching—that is what will help you. [7] Even musical instruments like the flute or the harp, though they are lifeless, are examples of the need for speaking in plain language. For no one will recognize the melody unless the notes are played clearly. [8] And if the bugler doesn't sound a clear call, how will the soldiers know they are being called to battle? [9] And it's the same for you. If you talk to people in a language they don't understand, how will they know what you mean? You might as well be talking to an empty room.

[10] There are so many different languages in the world, and all are excellent for those who understand them, [11] but to me they mean nothing. I will not understand people who speak those languages, and they will not understand me. [12] **Since you are so eager to have spiritual gifts, ask God for those that will be of real help to the whole church.**

[13] So anyone who has the gift of speaking in tongues should pray also for the gift of interpretation in order to tell people plainly what has been said. [14] For if I pray in tongues, my spirit is praying, but I don't understand what I am saying.

[15] Well then, what shall I do? I will do both. I will pray in the spirit, and I will pray in words I understand. I will sing in the spirit, and I will sing in words I understand. [16] For if you praise God only in the spirit, how can those who don't understand you praise God along with you? How can they join you in giving thanks when they don't understand what you are saying? [17] You will be giving thanks very nicely, no doubt, but it doesn't help the other people present.

[18] I thank God that I speak in tongues more than all of you. [19] But in a church meeting I would much rather speak five understandable words that will help others than ten thousand words in an unknown language.

[20] Dear brothers and sisters, don't be childish in your understanding of these things. Be innocent as babies when it comes to evil, but be mature and wise in understanding matters of this kind. [21] It is written in the Scriptures,

"I will speak to my own people

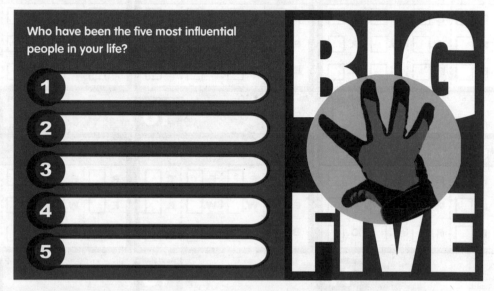

Who have been the five most influential people in your life?

1
2
3
4
5

BIG FIVE

through unknown languages
and through the lips of foreigners.
But even then, they will not listen to me,"
says the Lord.

[22] So you see that speaking in tongues is a sign, not for believers, but for unbelievers; prophecy, however, is for the benefit of believers, not unbelievers. [23] Even so, if unbelievers or people who don't understand these things come into your meeting and hear everyone talking in an unknown language, they will think you are crazy. [24] But if all of you are prophesying, and unbelievers or people who don't understand these things come into your meeting, they will be convicted

The Olympic Games were held in St. Louis, MO. in 1904, the first time that the games were held in the United States.

of sin, and they will be condemned by what you say. [25] As they listen, their secret thoughts will be laid bare, and they will fall down on their knees and worship God, declaring, "God is really here among you."

## A Call to Orderly Worship

[26] Well, my brothers and sisters, let's summarize what I am saying. When you meet, one will sing, another will teach, another will share some special revelation God has given, one will speak in an unknown language, while another will interpret what is said. But everything that is done must be useful to all and build them up in the Lord. [27] No more than two or three should speak in an unknown language. They must speak one at a time, and someone must be ready to interpret what they are saying. [28] But if no one is present who can interpret, they must be silent in your church meeting and speak in tongues to God privately.

[29] Let two or three prophesy, and let the others evaluate what is said. [30] But if someone is prophesying and another person receives a revelation from the Lord, the one who is speaking must stop. [31] In this way, all who prophesy will have a turn to speak, one after the other, so that everyone will learn and be encouraged. [32] Remember that people who prophesy are in control of their spirit and can wait their turn. [33] For God is not a God of disorder but of peace, as in all the other churches. [34] Women should be silent during the church meetings. It is not proper for them to speak. They should be submissive, just as the law says. [35] If they have any questions to ask, let them ask their husbands at home, for it is improper for women to speak in church meetings.

[36] Do you think that the knowledge of God's word begins and ends with you Corinthians? Well, you are mistaken! [37] If you claim to be a prophet or think you are very spiritual, you

# AUGUST M.A.P.

| **1** | | | | **2** | | | | **3** | | | | **4** | | | |
|---|---|---|---|---|---|---|---|---|---|---|---|---|---|---|---|
| S.D. | P.L. | P.G. | S.G. | S.D. | P.L. | P.G. | S.G. | S.D. | P.L. | P.G. | S.G. | S.D. | P.L. | P.G. | S.G. |
| P. ☐ | F. ☐ | F. ☐ | T. ☐ | P. ☐ | F. ☐ | F. ☐ | T. ☐ | P. ☐ | F. ☐ | F. ☐ | T. ☐ | P. ☐ | F. ☐ | F. ☐ | T. ☐ |
| F. ☐ | W. ☐ | W. ☐ | P. ☐ | F. ☐ | W. ☐ | W. ☐ | P. ☐ | F. ☐ | W. ☐ | W. ☐ | P. ☐ | F. ☐ | W. ☐ | W. ☐ | P. ☐ |
| B. ☐ | P. ☐ | C. ☐ | C. ☐ | B. ☐ | P. ☐ | C. ☐ | C. ☐ | B. ☐ | P. ☐ | C. ☐ | C. ☐ | B. ☐ | P. ☐ | C. ☐ | C. ☐ |

| **9** | | | | **10** | | | | **11** | | | | **12** | | | |
|---|---|---|---|---|---|---|---|---|---|---|---|---|---|---|---|
| S.D. | P.L. | P.G. | S.G. | S.D. | P.L. | P.G. | S.G. | S.D. | P.L. | P.G. | S.G. | S.D. | P.L. | P.G. | S.G. |
| P. ☐ | F. ☐ | F. ☐ | T. ☐ | P. ☐ | F. ☐ | F. ☐ | T. ☐ | P. ☐ | F. ☐ | F. ☐ | T. ☐ | P. ☐ | F. ☐ | F. ☐ | T. ☐ |
| F. ☐ | W. ☐ | W. ☐ | P. ☐ | F. ☐ | W. ☐ | W. ☐ | P. ☐ | F. ☐ | W. ☐ | W. ☐ | P. ☐ | F. ☐ | W. ☐ | W. ☐ | P. ☐ |
| B. ☐ | P. ☐ | C. ☐ | C. ☐ | B. ☐ | P. ☐ | C. ☐ | C. ☐ | B. ☐ | P. ☐ | C. ☐ | C. ☐ | B. ☐ | P. ☐ | C. ☐ | C. ☐ |

| **17** | | | | **18** | | | | **19** | | | | **20** | | | |
|---|---|---|---|---|---|---|---|---|---|---|---|---|---|---|---|
| S.D. | P.L. | P.G. | S.G. | S.D. | P.L. | P.G. | S.G. | S.D. | P.L. | P.G. | S.G. | S.D. | P.L. | P.G. | S.G. |
| P. ☐ | F. ☐ | F. ☐ | T. ☐ | P. ☐ | F. ☐ | F. ☐ | T. ☐ | P. ☐ | F. ☐ | F. ☐ | T. ☐ | P. ☐ | F. ☐ | F. ☐ | T. ☐ |
| F. ☐ | W. ☐ | W. ☐ | P. ☐ | F. ☐ | W. ☐ | W. ☐ | P. ☐ | F. ☐ | W. ☐ | W. ☐ | P. ☐ | F. ☐ | W. ☐ | W. ☐ | P. ☐ |
| B. ☐ | P. ☐ | C. ☐ | C. ☐ | B. ☐ | P. ☐ | C. ☐ | C. ☐ | B. ☐ | P. ☐ | C. ☐ | C. ☐ | B. ☐ | P. ☐ | C. ☐ | C. ☐ |

| **25** | | | | **26** | | | | **27** | | | | **28** | | | |
|---|---|---|---|---|---|---|---|---|---|---|---|---|---|---|---|
| S.D. | P.L. | P.G. | S.G. | S.D. | P.L. | P.G. | S.G. | S.D. | P.L. | P.G. | S.G. | S.D. | P.L. | P.G. | S.G. |
| P. ☐ | F. ☐ | F. ☐ | T. ☐ | P. ☐ | F. ☐ | F. ☐ | T. ☐ | P. ☐ | F. ☐ | F. ☐ | T. ☐ | P. ☐ | F. ☐ | F. ☐ | T. ☐ |
| F. ☐ | W. ☐ | W. ☐ | P. ☐ | F. ☐ | W. ☐ | W. ☐ | P. ☐ | F. ☐ | W. ☐ | W. ☐ | P. ☐ | F. ☐ | W. ☐ | W. ☐ | P. ☐ |
| B. ☐ | P. ☐ | C. ☐ | C. ☐ | B. ☐ | P. ☐ | C. ☐ | C. ☐ | B. ☐ | P. ☐ | C. ☐ | C. ☐ | B. ☐ | P. ☐ | C. ☐ | C. ☐ |

## Spiritual Disciplines

**Prayer**

**Faith Community**

**Bible Reading**

## Prayer List

**Friends**

**World**

**Personal**

Who am I....
Where am I going....
How am I going to get there?

# MONTHLY ACTION PLAN

## 5

| S.D. | P.L. | P.G. | S.G. |
|------|------|------|------|
| P. ☐ | F. ☐ | F. ☐ | T. ☐ |
| F. ☐ | W. ☐ | W. ☐ | P. ☐ |
| B. ☐ | P. ☐ | C. ☐ | C. ☐ |

## 6

| S.D. | P.L. | P.G. | S.G. |
|------|------|------|------|
| P. ☐ | F. ☐ | F. ☐ | T. ☐ |
| F. ☐ | W. ☐ | W. ☐ | P. ☐ |
| B. ☐ | P. ☐ | C. ☐ | C. ☐ |

## 7

| S.D. | P.L. | P.G. | S.G. |
|------|------|------|------|
| P. ☐ | F. ☐ | F. ☐ | T. ☐ |
| F. ☐ | W. ☐ | W. ☐ | P. ☐ |
| B. ☐ | P. ☐ | C. ☐ | C. ☐ |

## 8

| S.D. | P.L. | P.G. | S.G. |
|------|------|------|------|
| P. ☐ | F. ☐ | F. ☐ | T. ☐ |
| F. ☐ | W. ☐ | W. ☐ | P. ☐ |
| B. ☐ | P. ☐ | C. ☐ | C. ☐ |

## 13

| S.D. | P.L. | P.G. | S.G. |
|------|------|------|------|
| P. ☐ | F. ☐ | F. ☐ | T. ☐ |
| F. ☐ | W. ☐ | W. ☐ | P. ☐ |
| B. ☐ | P. ☐ | C. ☐ | C. ☐ |

## 14

| S.D. | P.L. | P.G. | S.G. |
|------|------|------|------|
| P. ☐ | F. ☐ | F. ☐ | T. ☐ |
| F. ☐ | W. ☐ | W. ☐ | P. ☐ |
| B. ☐ | P. ☐ | C. ☐ | C. ☐ |

## 15

| S.D. | P.L. | P.G. | S.G. |
|------|------|------|------|
| P. ☐ | F. ☐ | F. ☐ | T. ☐ |
| F. ☐ | W. ☐ | W. ☐ | P. ☐ |
| B. ☐ | P. ☐ | C. ☐ | C. ☐ |

## 16

| S.D. | P.L. | P.G. | S.G. |
|------|------|------|------|
| P. ☐ | F. ☐ | F. ☐ | T. ☐ |
| F. ☐ | W. ☐ | W. ☐ | P. ☐ |
| B. ☐ | P. ☐ | C. ☐ | C. ☐ |

## 21

| S.D. | P.L. | P.G. | S.G. |
|------|------|------|------|
| P. ☐ | F. ☐ | F. ☐ | T. ☐ |
| F. ☐ | W. ☐ | W. ☐ | P. ☐ |
| B. ☐ | P. ☐ | C. ☐ | C. ☐ |

## 22

| S.D. | P.L. | P.G. | S.G. |
|------|------|------|------|
| P. ☐ | F. ☐ | F. ☐ | T. ☐ |
| F. ☐ | W. ☐ | W. ☐ | P. ☐ |
| B. ☐ | P. ☐ | C. ☐ | C. ☐ |

## 23

| S.D. | P.L. | P.G. | S.G. |
|------|------|------|------|
| P. ☐ | F. ☐ | F. ☐ | T. ☐ |
| F. ☐ | W. ☐ | W. ☐ | P. ☐ |
| B. ☐ | P. ☐ | C. ☐ | C. ☐ |

## 24

| S.D. | P.L. | P.G. | S.G. |
|------|------|------|------|
| P. ☐ | F. ☐ | F. ☐ | T. ☐ |
| F. ☐ | W. ☐ | W. ☐ | P. ☐ |
| B. ☐ | P. ☐ | C. ☐ | C. ☐ |

## 29

| S.D. | P.L. | P.G. | S.G. |
|------|------|------|------|
| P. ☐ | F. ☐ | F. ☐ | T. ☐ |
| F. ☐ | W. ☐ | W. ☐ | P. ☐ |
| B. ☐ | P. ☐ | C. ☐ | C. ☐ |

## 30

| S.D. | P.L. | P.G. | S.G. |
|------|------|------|------|
| P. ☐ | F. ☐ | F. ☐ | T. ☐ |
| F. ☐ | W. ☐ | W. ☐ | P. ☐ |
| B. ☐ | P. ☐ | C. ☐ | C. ☐ |

## 31

| S.D. | P.L. | P.G. | S.G. |
|------|------|------|------|
| P. ☐ | F. ☐ | F. ☐ | T. ☐ |
| F. ☐ | W. ☐ | W. ☐ | P. ☐ |
| B. ☐ | P. ☐ | C. ☐ | C. ☐ |

**Proverbs 11:3**

Good people are guided by their honesty; treacherous people are destroyed by their dishonesty.

## Personal Goals

**Family**

**Work/School/Social**

**Challenge**

## Sport Goals

**Training**

**Performance**

**Competition Results**

## Making Adjustments:

A great skill in sport is the ability to 'adjust to change'. Players should be able to apply individual tactics flexibly, adapting their technical and tactical skills to each new situation quickly and correctly. The same tactical flexibility is required for each position-group and also for the team as a whole.

should recognize that what I am saying is a command from the Lord himself. ³⁸But if you do not recognize this, you will not be recognized.

³⁹So, dear brothers and sisters, be eager to prophesy, and don't forbid speaking in tongues. ⁴⁰But be sure that everything is done properly and in order.

## The Resurrection of Christ

# 15

Now let me remind you, dear brothers and sisters, of the Good News I preached to you before. You welcomed it then and still do now, for your faith is built on this wonderful message. ²And it is this Good News that saves you if you firmly believe it—unless, of course, you believed something that was never true in the first place.

³I passed on to you what was most important and what had also been passed on to me—that Christ died for our sins, just as the Scriptures said. ⁴He was buried, and he was raised from the dead on the third day, as the Scriptures said. ⁵He was seen by Peter and then by the twelve apostles. ⁶After that, he was seen by more than five hundred of his followers at one time, most of whom are still alive, though some have died by now. ⁷Then he was seen by James and later by all the apostles. ⁸Last of all, I saw him, too, long after the others, as though I had been born at the wrong time. ⁹For I am the least of all the apostles, and I am not worthy to be called an apostle after the way I persecuted the church of God. ¹⁰But whatever I am now, it is all because God poured out his special favour on me—and not without results. For I have worked harder than all the other apostles, yet it was not I but God who was working through me by his grace. ¹¹So it makes no difference whether I preach or they preach. The important thing is that you believed what we preached to you.

## The Resurrection of the Dead

¹²But tell me this—since we preach that Christ rose from the dead, why are some of you saying there will be no resurrection of the dead? ¹³For if there is no resurrection of the dead, then Christ has not been raised either. ¹⁴And if Christ was not raised, then all our preaching is useless, and your trust in God is useless. ¹⁵And we apostles would all be

lying about God, for we have said that God raised Christ from the grave, but that can't be true if there is no resurrection of the dead. ¹⁶If there is no resurrection of the dead, then Christ has not been raised. ¹⁷And if Christ has not been raised, then your faith is useless, and you are still under condemnation for your sins. ¹⁸In that case, all who have died believing in Christ have perished! ¹⁹And if we have hope in Christ only for this life, we are the most miserable people in the world.

²⁰But the fact is that Christ has been raised from the dead. He has become the first of a great harvest of those who will be raised to life again.

²¹So you see, just as death came into the world through a man, Adam, now the resurrection from the dead has begun through another man, Christ. ²²**Everyone dies because all of us are related to Adam, the first man. But all who are related to Christ, the other man, will be given new life.** ²³But there is an order to this resurrection: Christ was raised first; then when Christ comes back, all his people will be raised.

²⁴After that the end will come, when he will turn the Kingdom over to God the Father, having put down all enemies of every kind. ²⁵For Christ must reign until he humbles all his enemies beneath his feet. ²⁶And the last enemy to be destroyed is death.

²⁷For the Scriptures say, "God has given him authority over all things." (Of course, when it says "authority over all things," it does not include God himself, who gave Christ his authority.) ²⁸Then, when he has conquered all things, the Son will present himself to God, so that God, who gave his Son authority over all things, will be utterly supreme over everything everywhere.

²⁹If the dead will not be raised, then what point is there in people being baptized for those who are dead? Why do it unless the dead will someday rise again? ³⁰And why should we ourselves be continually risking our lives, facing death hour by hour? ³¹For I swear, dear brothers and sisters, I face death daily. This is as certain as my pride in what the Lord Jesus Christ has done in you. ³²And what value was there in fighting

wild beasts—those men of Ephesus—if there will be no resurrection from the dead? If there is no resurrection,

"Let's feast and get drunk,
for tomorrow we die!"

³³Don't be fooled by those who say such things, for "bad company corrupts good character." ³⁴Come to your senses and stop sinning. For to your shame I say that some of you don't even know God.

## The Resurrection Body

³⁵But someone may ask, "How will the dead be raised? What kind of bodies will they have?" ³⁶What a foolish question! When you put a seed into the ground, it doesn't grow into a plant unless it dies first. ³⁷And what you put in the ground is not the plant that will grow, but only a dry little seed of wheat or whatever it is you are planting. ³⁸Then God gives it a new body—just the kind he wants it to have. A different kind of plant grows from each kind of seed. ³⁹And just as there are different kinds of seeds and plants, so also there are different kinds of flesh—whether of humans, animals, birds, or fish.

⁴⁰There are bodies in the heavens, and there are bodies on earth. The glory of the heavenly bodies is different from the beauty of the earthly bodies. ⁴¹The sun has one kind of glory, while the moon and stars each have another kind. And even the stars differ from each other in their beauty and brightness.

⁴²It is the same way for the resurrection of the dead. Our earthly bodies, which die and decay, will be different when they are resurrected, for they will never die. ⁴³Our bodies now disappoint us, but when they are raised, they will be full of glory. They are weak now, but when they are raised, they will be full of power. ⁴⁴They are natural human bodies now, but when they are raised, they will be spiritual bodies. For just as there are natural bodies, so also there are spiritual bodies.

⁴⁵The Scriptures tell us, "The first man, Adam, became a living person." But the last Adam—that is, Christ—is a life-giving Spirit. ⁴⁶What came first was the natural body, then the spiritual body comes later.

⁴⁷Adam, the first man, was made from the dust of the earth, while Christ, the second man, came from heaven. ⁴⁸Every human being has an earthly body just like Adam's, but our heavenly bodies will be just like Christ's. ⁴⁹Just as we are now like Adam, the man of the earth, so we will someday be like Christ, the man from heaven.

⁵⁰What I am saying, dear brothers and sisters, is that flesh and blood cannot inherit the Kingdom of God. These perishable bodies of ours are not able to live for ever.

⁵¹But let me tell you a wonderful secret God has revealed to us. Not all of us will die, but we will all be transformed. ⁵²It will happen in a moment, in the blinking of an eye, when the last trumpet is blown. For when the trumpet sounds, the Christians who have died will be raised with transformed bodies. And then we who are living will be transformed so that we will never die. ⁵³For our perishable earthly bodies must be transformed into heavenly bodies that will never die.

⁵⁴When this happens—when our perishable earthly bodies have been transformed into heavenly bodies that will never die—then at last the Scriptures will come true:

"Death is swallowed up in victory.
⁵⁵O death, where is your victory?
O death, where is your sting?"

⁵⁶For sin is the sting that results in death, and the law gives sin its power. ⁵⁷How we thank God, who gives us victory over sin and death through Jesus Christ our Lord!

⁵⁸So, my dear brothers and sisters, be strong and steady, always enthusiastic about the Lord's work, for you know that nothing you do for the Lord is ever useless.

## The Collection for Jerusalem

# 16

Now about the money being collected for the Christians in Jerusalem: You should follow the same procedures I gave to the churches in Galatia. ²On every Lord's Day, each of you should put aside some amount of money in relation to what you have earned and save it for this offering. Don't wait until I get there and then try to collect it all at once. ³When I come I will write letters of recommendation for the messengers you choose to deliver your gift to Jerusalem. ⁴And if it seems appropriate for me also to go along, then we can travel together.

## Paul's Final Instructions

⁵I am coming to visit you after I have been to Macedonia, for I am planning to travel through Macedonia. ⁶It could be that I will stay awhile with you, perhaps all winter, and then you can send me on my way to the next destination. ⁷This time I don't want to make just a short visit and then go right on. I

want to come and stay awhile, if the Lord will let me. ⁸In the meantime, I will be staying here at Ephesus until the Festival of Pentecost, ⁹for there is a wide-open door for a great work here, and many people are responding. But there are many who oppose me. ¹⁰When Timothy comes, treat him with respect. He is doing the Lord's work, just as I am. ¹¹Don't let anyone despise him. Send him on his way with your blessings when he returns to me. I am looking forward to seeing him soon, along with the other brothers.

¹²Now about our brother Apollos—I urged him to join the other brothers when they visit you, but he was not willing to come right now. He will be seeing you later, when the time is right.

¹³**Be on guard. Stand true to what you believe. Be courageous. Be strong. ¹⁴And everything you do must be done with love.**

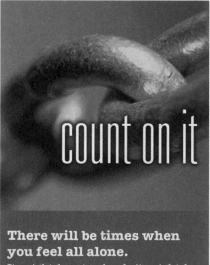

## count on it

**There will be times when you feel all alone.**

It might be at school, it might be at work or when you are on the road. It could be when you take that shot in a championship game. But if you love Christ you will never walk alone! "I will never fail you, I will never forsake you." Hebrews 13:5
**Count on it!**

¹⁵You know that Stephanas and his household were the first to become Christians in Greece, and they are spending their lives in service to other Christians. I urge you, dear brothers and sisters, ¹⁶to respect them fully and others like them who serve with such real devotion. ¹⁷I am so glad that Stephanas, Fortunatus, and Achaicus have come here. They have been making up for the help you weren't here to give me. ¹⁸They have been a wonderful encouragement to me, as they have been to you, too. You must give proper honour to all who serve so well.

## action

**CH 16:13-18 WHAT'S IT SAYING?**

**WHAT AM I GOING TO DO ABOUT IT?**

## Paul's Final Greetings

¹⁹The churches here in the province of Asia greet you heartily in the Lord, along with Aquila and Priscilla and all the others who gather in their home for church meetings. ²⁰All the brothers and sisters here have asked me to greet you for them. Greet each other in Christian love.

²¹Here is my greeting, which I write with my own hand—PAUL.

²²If anyone does not love the Lord, that person is cursed. Our Lord, come!

²³May the grace of the Lord Jesus be with you.

²⁴My love to all of you in Christ Jesus.

After his first letter Paul was curious to know the true response of the people of Corinth and wondered how well it had been received. He sent one of his top workers, Timothy to find out. 2 Corinthians is a response to his scouting. In this letter, through the influence of the Holy Spirit, Paul provides encouragement, guidance and strong leadership.

Paul tirelessly invested a lot of time and energy in the people of this city, living there off-and-on, supporting his ministry, originally by making tents, a major business of the day. The Corinthian church was a lighthouse in a very powerful, wealthy but immoral, seaport. Paul established, encouraged and nurtured the Corinthian faith community for years.

The book expresses his joy that the church is moving forward and his first letter seems to have been taken in the right attitude and spirit. Paul reveals more of his amazing history and the pain and privilege he has gone through for the cause of Christ. This is another personal and warm letter to a church that needs a lot of leadership, love and encouragement to progress in the cause of Christ.

# 2 Corinthians

# It's a gift
## LIVE it

For the wages
of sin is death,
but the free
gift of God
is eternal life
through Jesus
Christ
our Lord

ROMANS 6:23

# 2 CORINTHIANS

## Greetings from Paul

# 1

This letter is from Paul, appointed by God to be an apostle of Christ Jesus, and from our dear brother Timothy.

We are writing to God's church in Corinth and to all the Christians throughout Greece.

[2]May God our Father and the Lord Jesus Christ give you his grace and peace.

## God Offers Comfort to All

[3]All praise to the God and Father of our Lord Jesus Christ. He is the source of every mercy and the God who comforts us. [4]**He comforts us in all our troubles so that we can comfort others. When others are troubled, we will be able to give them the same comfort God has given us.** [5]You can be sure that the more we suffer for Christ, the more God will shower us with his comfort through Christ. [6]So when we are weighed down with troubles, it is for your benefit and salvation! For when God comforts us, it is so that we, in turn, can be an encouragement to you. Then you can patiently endure the same things we suffer. [7]We are confident that as you share in suffering, you will also share God's comfort.

[8]I think you ought to know, dear brothers and sisters, about the trouble we went through in the province of Asia. We were crushed and completely overwhelmed, and we thought we would never live through it. [9]In fact, we expected to die. But as a result, we learned not to rely on ourselves, but on God who can raise the dead. [10]And he did deliver us from mortal danger. And we are confident that he will continue to deliver us. [11]He will rescue us because you are helping by praying

for us. As a result, many will give thanks to God because so many people's prayers for our safety have been answered.

### CH 1:8-11 WHAT'S IT SAYING?

### WHAT AM I GOING TO DO ABOUT IT?

## Paul's Change of Plans

[12]We can say with confidence and a clear conscience that we have been honest and sincere in all our dealings. We have depended on God's grace, not on our own earthly wisdom. That is how we have acted towards everyone, and especially towards you. [13]My letters have been straightforward, and there is nothing written between the lines and nothing you can't understand. I hope someday you will fully understand us, [14]even if you don't fully understand us now. Then on the day when our Lord Jesus comes back again, you will be proud of us in the same way we are proud of you.

[15]Since I was so sure of your understanding and trust, I wanted to give you a double blessing. [16]I wanted to stop and see you on my way to Macedonia and again on my return trip. Then you could send me on my way to Judea.

[17]You may be asking why I changed my plan. Hadn't I made up my mind yet? Or am I like people of the world who say yes when they really mean no? [18]As

surely as God is true, I am not that sort of person. My yes means yes [19]because Jesus Christ, the Son of God, never wavers between yes and no. He is the one whom Timothy, Silas, and I preached to you, and he is the divine Yes—God's affirmation. [20]For all of God's promises have been fulfilled in him. That is why we say "Amen" when we give glory to God through Christ. [21]It is God who gives us, along with you, the ability to stand firm for Christ. He has commissioned us, [22]and he has identified us as his own by placing the Holy Spirit in our hearts as the first instalment of everything he will give us.

[23]Now I call upon God as my witness that I am telling the truth. The reason I didn't return to Corinth was to spare you from a severe rebuke. [24]But that does not mean we want to tell you exactly how to put your faith into practice. We want to work together with you so you will be full of joy as you stand firm in your faith.

# 2

So I said to myself, "No, I won't do it. I won't make them unhappy with another painful visit." [2]For if I cause you pain and make you sad, who is going to make me glad? [3]That is why I wrote as I did in my last letter, so that when I do come, I will not be made sad by the very ones who ought to give me the greatest joy. Surely you know that my happiness depends on your happiness.

[4]How painful it was to write that letter! Heartbroken, I cried over it. I didn't want to hurt you, but I wanted you to know how very much I love you.

## Forgiveness for the Sinner

[5]I am not overstating it when I say that the man who caused all the trouble hurt your entire church more than he hurt me. [6]He was punished enough when most of you were united in your judgement against him. [7]Now it is time to forgive him and comfort him. Otherwise he may become so discouraged that he won't be able to recover. [8]Now show him that you still love him.

[9]I wrote to you as I did to find out how far you would go in obeying me. [10]When you forgive this man, I forgive him, too. And when I forgive him (for whatever is to be forgiven), I do so with Christ's authority for your benefit, [11]so that Satan will not outsmart us. For we are very familiar with his evil schemes.

## Ministers of the New Covenant

[12]Well, when I came to the city of Troas to preach the Good News of Christ, the Lord gave me tremendous opportunities. [13]But I couldn't rest because my dear brother Titus hadn't yet arrived with a report from you. So I said goodbye and went on to Macedonia to find him.

[14]But thanks be to God, who made us his captives and leads

**STATS**

There are 1,929,770,126,028,800 different colour combinations possible on a Rubik's Cube.

Change! We all have things that need to be put right. You may look at parts of scripture and think: no way!...I can't do what God wants me to do! I will be a failure! Don't worry God knows you can't and does not want you to change alone! He wants to help you change. He will help you if you are courageous enough to let him help you! "Humanly speaking, it is impossible. But with God everything is possible". Matthew 19:26

us along in Christ's triumphal procession. Now wherever we go he uses us to tell others about the Lord and to spread the Good News like a sweet perfume. ¹⁵Our lives are a fragrance presented by Christ to God. But this fragrance is perceived differently by those being saved and by those perishing. ¹⁶To those who are perishing we are a fearful smell of death and doom. But to those who are being saved we are a life-giving perfume. And who is adequate for such a task as this? ¹⁷You see, we are not like those hawkers—and there are many of them—who preach just to make money. We preach God's message with sincerity and with Christ's authority. And we know that the God who sent us is watching us.

# 3

Are we beginning again to tell you how good we are? Some people need to bring letters of recommendation with them or ask you to write letters of recommendation for them. ²But the only letter of recommendation we need is you yourselves! Your lives are a letter written in our hearts, and everyone can read it and recognize our good work among you. ³Clearly, you are a letter from Christ prepared by us. It is written not

## STAND POINT

### When you need an example of boldness

4:9

We are hunted down, but God never abandons us. We get knocked down, but we get up again and keep going.

with pen and ink, but with the Spirit of the living God. It is carved not on stone, but on human hearts. ⁴We are confident of all this because of our great trust in God through Christ. ⁵It is not that we think we can do anything of lasting value by ourselves. Our only power and success come from God. ⁶He is the one who has enabled us to represent his new covenant. This is a covenant, not of written laws, but of the Spirit. The old way ends in death; in the new way, the Holy Spirit gives life.

## The Glory of the New Covenant

⁷That old system of law etched in stone led to death, yet it began with such glory that the people of Israel could not bear to look at Moses' face. For his face shone with the glory of God, even though the brightness was already fading away. ⁸Shouldn't we expect far greater glory when the Holy Spirit is giving life? ⁹If the old covenant, which brings condemnation, was glorious, how much more glorious is the new covenant, which makes us right with God! ¹⁰In fact, that first glory was not glorious at all compared with the overwhelming glory of the new covenant. ¹¹So if the old covenant, which has been set aside, was full of glory, then the new covenant, which remains for ever, has far greater glory. ¹²Since this new covenant gives us such confidence, we can be very bold. ¹³We are not like Moses, who put a veil over his face so the people of Israel would not see the glory fading away. ¹⁴But the people's minds were hardened, and even to this day whenever the old covenant is being read, a veil covers their minds so they cannot understand the truth. And this veil can be removed only by believing in Christ. ¹⁵Yes, even today when they read Moses'

writings, their hearts are covered with that veil, and they do not understand. ¹⁶But whenever anyone turns to the Lord, then the veil is taken away. ¹⁷Now, the Lord is the Spirit, and wherever the Spirit of the Lord is, he gives freedom. ¹⁸And all of us have had that veil removed so that we can be mirrors that brightly reflect the glory of the Lord. And as the Spirit of the Lord works within us, we become more and more like him and reflect his glory even more.

## Treasure in Perishable Containers

# 4

And so, since God in his mercy has given us this wonderful ministry, we never give up. ²We reject all shameful and underhand methods. We do not try to trick anyone, and we do not distort the word of God. We tell the truth before God, and all who are honest know that. ³If the Good News we preach is veiled from anyone, it is a sign that they are perishing. ⁴Satan, the god of this evil world, has blinded the minds of those who don't believe, so they are unable to see the glorious light of the Good News that is shining upon them. They don't understand the message we preach about the glory of Christ, who is the exact likeness of God. ⁵We don't go around preaching about ourselves; we preach Christ Jesus, the Lord. All we say about ourselves is that we are your servants because of what Jesus has done for us. ⁶For God, who said, "Let there be light in the darkness," has made us understand that this light is the brightness of the glory of God that is seen in the face of Jesus Christ. ⁷But this precious treasure—this light and power that now shine within us—is held in perishable containers, that is, in our weak bodies. So everyone can see that our glorious power is from God and is not our own. ⁸We are pressed on every side by troubles, but we are not crushed and broken. We are perplexed, but we don't give up and quit. ⁹We are hunted down, but God never abandons us. We get knocked down, but we get up again and keep going. ¹⁰Through suffering, these bodies of ours constantly share in the death of Jesus so that the life of Jesus may also be seen in our bodies. ¹¹Yes, we live under constant danger of death because we serve Jesus, so that the life of Jesus will be obvious in our dying bodies. ¹²So we live in the face of death, but it has resulted in eternal life for you.

[13]But we continue to preach because we have the same kind of faith the psalmist had when he said, "I believed in God, and so I speak." [14]We know that the same God who raised our Lord Jesus will also raise us with Jesus and present us to himself along with you. [15]All of these things are for your benefit. And as God's grace brings more and more people to Christ, there will be great thanksgiving, and God will receive more and more glory.

[16]That is why we never give up. Though our bodies are dying, our spirits are being renewed every day. [17]For our present troubles are quite small and won't last very long. Yet they produce for us an immeasurably great glory that will last for ever! [18]So we don't look at the troubles we can see right now; rather, we look forward to what we have not yet seen. For the troubles we see will soon be over, but the joys to come will last for ever.

## New Bodies

# 5

For we know that when this earthly tent we live in is taken down—when we die and leave these bodies—we will have a home in heaven, an eternal body made for us by God himself and not by human hands. [2]We grow weary in our present bodies, and we long for the day when we will put on our heavenly bodies like new clothing. [3]For we will not be spirits without bodies, but we will put on new heavenly bodies. [4]Our dying bodies make us groan and sigh, but it's not that we want to die and have no bodies at all. We want to slip into our new bodies so that these dying bodies will be swallowed up by everlasting life. [5]God himself has prepared us for this, and as a guarantee he has given us his Holy Spirit.

[6]So we are always confident, even though we know that as long as we live in these bodies we are not at home with the Lord. [7]That is why we live by believing and not by seeing. [8]Yes, we are fully confident, and we would rather be away

## The Bible contains 1,189 chapters and over 31,000 verses.

from these bodies, for then we will be at home with the Lord. [9]So our aim is to please him always, whether we are here in this body or away from this body. [10]For we must all stand before Christ to be judged. We will each receive whatever we deserve for the good or evil we have done in our bodies.

### We Are God's Ambassadors

[11]It is because we know this solemn fear of the Lord that we work so hard to persuade others. God knows we are sincere, and I hope you know this, too. [12]Are we trying to pat ourselves on the back again? No, we are giving you a reason to be proud of us, so you can answer those who brag about having a spectacular ministry rather than having a sincere heart before God. [13]If it seems that we are crazy, it is to bring glory to God. And if we are in our right minds, it is for your benefit. [14]Whatever we do, it is because Christ's love controls us. Since we believe that Christ died for everyone, we also believe that we have all died to the old life we used to live. [15]He died for everyone so that those who receive his new life will no longer live to please themselves. Instead, they will live to please Christ, who died and was raised for them.

[16]So we have stopped evaluating others by what the world thinks about them. Once I mistakenly thought of Christ that way, as though he were merely a human being. How differently I think about him now! [17]What this means is that those who become Christians become new persons. They are not the same any more, for the old life is gone. A new life has begun!

# count on it

### No Fear!

Some people are terrified by the fear of failure. 'If I can't win - I will not run!' Others can compete with reckless abandon knowing: "The Lord is my helper, so I will not be afraid. What can mere mortals do to me?" Hebrews 13:6
**Count on it!**

[18] All this newness of life is from God, who brought us back to himself through what Christ did. And God has given us the task of reconciling people to him. [19] For God was in Christ, reconciling the world to himself, no longer counting people's sins against them. This is the wonderful message he has given us to tell others. [20] We are Christ's ambassadors, and God is using us to speak to you. We urge you, as though Christ himself were here pleading with you, "Be reconciled to God!" [21] **For God made Christ, who never sinned, to be the offering for our sin, so that we could be made right with God through Christ.**

# 6

As God's partners, we beg you not to reject this marvellous message of God's great kindness. [2] For God says,
"At just the right time, I heard you.
On the day of salvation, I helped you."
Indeed, God is ready to help you right now. Today is the day of salvation.

## Paul's Hardships

[3] We try to live in such a way that no one will be hindered from finding the Lord by the way we act, and so no one can find fault with our ministry. [4] In everything we do we try to show that we are true ministers of God. We patiently endure troubles and hardships and calamities of every kind. [5] We

have been beaten, been put in jail, faced angry mobs, worked to exhaustion, endured sleepless nights, and gone without food. [6] We have proved ourselves by our purity, our understanding, our patience, our kindness, our sincere love, and the power of the Holy Spirit. [7] We have faithfully preached the truth. God's power has been working in us. We have righteousness as our weapon, both to attack and to defend ourselves. [8] We serve God whether people honour us or despise us, whether they slander us or praise us. We are honest, but they call us impostors. [9] We are well known, but we are treated as unknown. We live close to death, but here we are, still alive. We have been beaten within an inch of our lives. [10] Our hearts ache, but we always have joy. We are poor, but we give spiritual riches to others. We own nothing, and yet we have everything. [11] Oh, dear Corinthian friends! We have spoken honestly with you. Our hearts are open to you. [12] If there is a problem between us, it is not because of a lack of love on our part, but because you have withheld your love from us. [13] I am talking now as I would to my own children. Open your hearts to us!

### action

**CH 6:3-13 WHAT'S IT SAYING?**

**WHAT AM I GOING TO DO ABOUT IT?**

## The Temple of the Living God

[14] Don't team up with those who are unbelievers. How can goodness be a partner with wickedness? How can light live with darkness? [15] What harmony can there be between Christ and the Devil? How can a believer be a partner with an unbeliever? [16] And what union can there be between God's temple and idols? For we are the temple of the living God. As God said:
"I will live in them
and walk among them.
I will be their God,
and they will be my people.
[17] Therefore, come out from them
and separate yourselves from them, says the Lord.
Don't touch their filthy things,
and I will welcome you.
[18] And I will be your Father,
and you will be my sons and daughters,
says the Lord Almighty."

# 7

Because we have these promises, dear friends, let us cleanse ourselves from everything that can defile our body or spirit. And let us work towards complete purity because we fear God.

## Paul's Joy at the Church's Repentance

[2] Please open your hearts to us. We have not done wrong to anyone. We have not led anyone astray. We have not taken advantage of anyone. [3] I'm not saying this to condemn you, for I said before that you are in our hearts for ever. We live or die together with you. [4] I have the highest confidence in you, and my pride in you is great. You have greatly encouraged me; you have made me happy despite all our troubles.

[5] When we arrived in Macedonia there was no rest for us. Outside there was conflict from every direction, and inside there was fear. [6] But God, who encourages those who are discouraged, encouraged us by the arrival of Titus. [7] His presence was a joy, but so was the news he brought of the encouragement he received from you. When he told me how much you were looking forward to my visit, and how sorry you were about what had happened, and how loyal your love is for me, I was filled with joy!

[8] I am no longer sorry that I sent that letter to you, though I was sorry for a time, for I know that it was painful to you for a little while. [9] Now I am glad I sent it, not because it hurt you, but because the pain caused you to have remorse and change your ways. It was the kind of sorrow God wants his people to have, so you were not harmed by us in any way. [10] **For God**

can use sorrow in our lives to help us turn away from sin and seek salvation. We will never regret that kind of sorrow. But sorrow without repentance is the kind that results in death.

[11]Just see what this godly sorrow produced in you! Such earnestness, such concern to clear yourselves, such indignation, such alarm, such longing to see me, such zeal, and such a readiness to punish the wrongdoer. You showed that you have done everything you could to make things right. [12]My purpose was not to write about who did the wrong or who was wronged. I wrote to you so that in the sight of God you could show how much you really do care for us. [13]We have been encouraged by this.

In addition to our own encouragement, we were especially delighted to see how happy Titus was at the way you welcomed him and set his mind at ease. [14]I had told him how proud I was of you—and you didn't disappoint me. I have always told you the truth, and now my boasting to Titus has also proved true! [15]Now he cares for you more than ever when he remembers the way you listened to him and welcomed him with such respect and deep concern. [16]I am very happy now because I have complete confidence in you.

## A Call to Generous Giving

# 8

Now I want to tell you, dear brothers and sisters, what God in his kindness has done for the churches in Macedonia. [2]Though they have been going through much trouble and hard times, their wonderful joy and deep poverty have overflowed in rich generosity. [3]For I can testify that they gave not only what they could afford but far more. And they did it of their own free will. [4]They begged us again and again for the gracious privilege of sharing in the gift for the Christians in Jerusalem. [5]Best of all, they went beyond our highest hopes, for their first action was to dedicate themselves to the Lord and to us for whatever directions God might give them.

[6]So we have urged Titus, who encouraged your giving in the first place, to return to you and encourage you to complete your share in this ministry of giving. [7]Since you excel in so many ways—you have so much faith, such gifted speakers, such knowledge, such enthusiasm, and such love for us—now I want you to excel also in this gracious ministry of giving. [8]I am not saying you must do it, even though the other churches are eager to do it. This is one way to prove your love is real.

[9]You know how full of love and kindness our Lord Jesus Christ was. Though he was very rich, yet for your sakes he became poor, so that by his poverty he could make you rich.

[10]I suggest that you finish what you started a year ago, for you were the first to propose this idea, and you were the first to begin doing something about it. [11]Now you should carry this project through to completion just as enthusiastically as you began it. Give whatever you can according to what you have. [12]If you are really eager to give, it isn't important how much you are able to give. God wants you to give what you have, not what you don't have. [13]Of course, I don't mean you should give so much that you suffer from having too little. I only mean that there should be some equality. [14]Right now you have plenty and can help them. Then at some other time they can share with you when you need it. In this way, everyone's needs will be met. [15]Do you remember what the Scriptures say about this?

"Those who gathered a lot had nothing left over, and those who gathered only a little had enough."

## Titus and His Companions

[16]I am thankful to God that he has given Titus the same enthusiasm for you that I have. [17]He welcomed our request

---

### BIG FIVE

Who are the top five most influential people in history?

1.
2.
3.
4.
5.

---

**Bible Hit: 'Good Fit' 2 Corinthians 6:14**

You would never run a Marathon in shoes two sizes too small. Paul is using Jesus' illustration to point out that we should not hang around or associate with people or organisations that will compromise our friendship with Christ. This is especially relevant to dating and choosing a spouse. Jesus, a master carpenter, used a metaphor that was contemporary to his day (Matt. 11:30). Master carpenters fitted yokes to animals that would plough the farm fields. It was important to get a comfortable fit or a valuable animal could be rendered useless, many yokes were doubles so you had a 'team' of animals. Jesus said, 'my yoke fits perfectly, my burden is light.' This does not mean that you should stay away from those that do not follow Jesus; in fact we are to be an influence on those that do not know him. But all your closest friends, the ones that influence you should be going the in the same direction, a good fit, following Jesus.

that he visit you again. In fact, he himself was eager to go and see you. [18]We are also sending another brother with Titus. He is highly praised in all the churches as a preacher of the Good News. [19]He was appointed by the churches to accompany us as we take the offering to Jerusalem—a service that glorifies the Lord and shows our eagerness to help. [20]By travelling together we will guard against any suspicion, for we are anxious that no one should find fault with the way we are handling this generous gift.

[21]We are careful to be honourable before the Lord, but we also want everyone else to know we are honourable.

[22]And we are also sending with them another brother who has been thoroughly tested and has shown how earnest he is on many occasions. He is now even more enthusiastic because of his increased confidence in you. [23]If anyone asks about Titus, say that he is my partner who works with me to help you. And these brothers are representatives of the churches. They are splendid examples of those who bring glory to Christ. [24]So show them your love, and prove to all the churches that our boasting about you is justified.

## The Collection for Christians in Jerusalem

### 9

I really don't need to write to you about this gift for the Christians in Jerusalem. [2]For I know how eager you are to help, and I have been boasting to our friends in Macedonia that you Christians in Greece were ready to send an offering a year ago. In fact, it was your enthusiasm that stirred up many of them to begin helping. [3]But I am sending these brothers just to be sure that you really are ready, as I told them you would be, with your money all collected. I don't want it to turn out that I was wrong in my boasting about you. [4]I would be humiliated—and so would you—if some Macedonian Christians came with me, only to find that you still weren't ready after all I had told them! [5]So I thought I should send these brothers ahead of me to make sure the gift you promised is ready. But I want it to be a willing gift, not one given under pressure.

[6]Remember this—a farmer who plants only a few seeds will get a small crop. But the one who plants generously will get

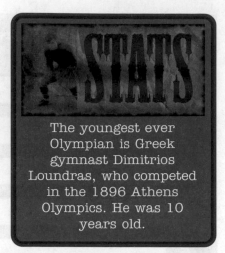

The youngest ever Olympian is Greek gymnast Dimitrios Loundras, who competed in the 1896 Athens Olympics. He was 10 years old.

a generous crop. [7]You must each make up your own mind as to how much you should give. **Don't give reluctantly or in response to pressure. For God loves the person who gives cheerfully.**

[8]And God will generously provide all you need. Then you will always have everything you need and plenty left over to share with others. [9]As the Scriptures say,

"Godly people give generously to the poor.
Their good deeds will never be forgotten."

[10]For God is the one who gives seed to the farmer and then bread to eat. In the same way, he will give you many opportunities to do good, and he will produce a great harvest of generosity in you.

[11]Yes, you will be enriched so that you can give even more generously. And when we take your gifts to those who need them, they will break out in thanksgiving to God. [12]So two good things will happen—the needs of the Christians in Jerusalem will be met, and they will joyfully express their thanksgiving to God. [13]You will be glorifying God through your generous gifts. For your generosity to them will prove that you are obedient to the Good News of Christ.

[14]And they will pray for you with deep affection because of the wonderful grace of God shown through you.

[15]Thank God for his Son—a gift too wonderful for words!

## Paul Defends His Authority

### 10

Now I, Paul, plead with you. I plead with the gentleness and kindness that Christ himself would use, even though some of you say I am bold in my letters but timid in person. [2]I hope it won't be necessary, but when I come I may have to be very bold with those who think we act from purely human motives. [3]We are human, but we don't wage war with human plans and methods.

[4]We use God's mighty weapons, not mere worldly weapons, to knock down the Devil's strongholds. [5]With these weapons we break down every proud argument that keeps people from knowing God. With these weapons we conquer their rebellious ideas, and we teach them to obey Christ. [6]And we will punish those who remained disobedient after the rest of you became loyal and obedient.

[7]The trouble with you is that you make your decisions on the basis of appearance. You must recognize that we belong to Christ just as much as those who proudly declare that they belong to Christ.

[8]I may seem to be boasting too much about the authority given to us by the Lord. But this authority is to build you up, not to tear you down. And I will not be put to shame by having my work among you destroyed.

[9]Now this is not just an attempt to frighten you by my letters.

[10]For some say, "Don't worry about Paul. His letters are demanding and forceful, but in person he is weak, and his speeches are really bad!" [11]The ones who say this must realize that we will be just as demanding and forceful in person as we are in our letters.

[12]Oh, don't worry; I wouldn't dare say that I am as wonderful as these other men who tell you how important they are! But they are only comparing themselves with each other, and measuring themselves by themselves. What foolishness!

[13]But we will not boast of authority we do not have. Our goal is to stay within the boundaries of God's

**I have real trouble not swearing - I hear it so much on my team.**

The language you hear can be a bad influence on you. Asking politely for your team-mates to use positive language because you desire to honour God, usually creates a stir on the team and will help you to stand up for what you believe. What the Bible repeats over and over is this; if your heart is good, good things will flow out of it! We are commanded to make a difference in this world (to be salt and light) so we cannot shy away from what we are called to influence. But we are to ask for protection and strap on God's protection. Go read Galatians, chapter 6.

## How to Run Farther, Faster & Smarter:

One of the most important aspects of running is to land more on the whole foot rather than landing on the heel with the sole of the foot angled upward. This is one of the most frequently occurring errors that lead to injury – and to slower speeds.

plan for us, and this plan includes our working there with you. [14]We are not going too far when we claim authority over you, for we were the first to travel all the way to you with the Good News of Christ. [15]Nor do we claim credit for the work someone else has done. Instead, we hope that your faith will grow and that our work among you will be greatly enlarged. [16]Then we will be able to go and preach the Good News in other places that are far beyond you, where no one else is working. Then there will be no question about being in someone else's territory.

[17]**As the Scriptures say,**
**"The person who wishes to boast should boast only of what the Lord has done."**

[18]When people boast about themselves, it doesn't count for much. But when the Lord commends someone, that's different!

## Paul and the False Apostles

# 11

I hope you will be patient with me as I keep on talking like a fool. Please bear with me. [2]I am jealous for you with the jealousy of God himself. For I promised you as a pure bride to one husband, Christ. [3]But I fear that somehow you will be led away from your pure and simple devotion to Christ, just as Eve was deceived by the serpent. [4]You seem to believe whatever anyone tells you, even if they preach about a different Jesus from the one we preach, or a different Spirit from the one you received, or a different kind of gospel from the one you believed. [5]But I don't think I am inferior to these "super apostles." [6]I may not be a trained speaker, but I know what I am talking about. I think you realize this by now, for we have proved it again and again.

[7]Did I do wrong when I humbled myself and honoured you by preaching God's Good News to you without expecting anything in return? [8]I "robbed" other churches by accepting their contributions so I could serve you at no cost. [9]And when I was with you and didn't have enough to live on, I did not ask you to

help me, for the brothers who came from Macedonia brought me another gift. I have never yet asked you for any support, and I never will. [10]As surely as the truth of Christ is in me, I will never stop boasting about this all over Greece. [11]Why? Because I don't love you? God knows I do.

[12]But I will continue doing this to cut the ground out from under the feet of those who boast that their work is just like ours. [13]These people are false apostles. They have fooled you by disguising themselves as apostles of Christ. [14]But I am not surprised! Even Satan can disguise himself as an angel of light.

[15]So it is no wonder his servants can also do it by pretending to be godly ministers. In the end they will get every bit of punishment their wicked deeds deserve.

## Paul's Many Trials

[16]Once again, don't think that I have lost my wits as I talk like this. But even if you do, listen to me, as you would to a foolish person, while I also boast a little. [17]Such bragging is not something the Lord wants, but I am acting like a fool. [18]And since others boast about their human achievements, I will, too. [19]After all, you, who think you are so wise, enjoy listening to fools! [20]You put up with it when they make you their slaves, take everything you have, take advantage of you, put on airs, and slap you in the face. [21]I'm ashamed to say that we were not strong enough to do that!

But whatever they dare to boast about—I'm talking like a fool again—I can boast about it, too. [22]They say they are Hebrews, do they? So am I. And they say they are Israelites? So am I. And they are descendants of Abraham? So am I. [23]They say they serve Christ? I know I sound like a madman, but I have served him far more! I have worked harder, been put in jail more often, been whipped times without number, and faced death again and again. [24]Five different times the Jews gave me thirty-nine lashes. [25]Three times I was beaten with rods. Once I was stoned. Three times I was shipwrecked. Once I spent a whole night and a day adrift at sea. [26]I have travelled many weary miles. I have faced danger from flooded rivers and from robbers. I have faced danger from my own people,

the Jews, as well as from the Gentiles. I have faced danger in the cities, in the deserts, and on the stormy seas. And I have faced danger from men who claim to be Christians but are not. [27]I have lived with weariness and pain and sleepless nights. Often I have been hungry and thirsty and have gone without food. Often I have shivered with cold, without enough clothing to keep me warm.

[28]Then, besides all this, I have the daily burden of how the churches are getting along. [29]Who is weak without my feeling that weakness? Who is led astray, and I do not burn with anger?

## STAND POINT

### When you feel like bragging
**11:30**

If I must boast, I would rather boast about the things that show how weak I am.

[30]If I must boast, I would rather boast about the things that show how weak I am. [31]God, the Father of our Lord Jesus, who is to be praised for ever, knows I tell the truth. [32]When I was in Damascus, the governor under King Aretas kept guards at the city gates to catch me. [33]But I was lowered in a basket through a window in the city wall, and that's how I got away!

## Paul's Vision and His Thorn in the Flesh

# 12

This boasting is all so foolish, but let me go on. Let me tell about the visions and revelations I received from the Lord. [2]I was caught up into the third heaven fourteen years ago. [3]Whether my body was there or just my spirit, I don't know; only God knows. [4]But I do know that I was caught up into

# WHAT

# DOES IT MEAN?

## Antichrist

Being against Christ, or an opposition Christ or a rival Christ. The word is used only by the apostle John. (1 John 2:18, 22; 4:3; 2 John 1:7), and it has been applied to the "beast from the sea" (Rev. 13:1; 17:1-18).

paradise and heard things so astounding that they cannot be told. [5]That experience is something worth boasting about, but I am not going to do it. I am going to boast only about my weaknesses. [6]I have plenty to boast about and would be no fool in doing it, because I would be telling the truth. But I won't do it. I don't want anyone to think more highly of me than what they can actually see in my life and my message, [7]even though I have received wonderful revelations from God. But to keep me from getting puffed up, I was given a thorn in my flesh, a messenger from Satan to torment me and keep me from getting proud.

[8]Three different times I begged the Lord to take it away. [9]Each time he said, "My gracious favour is all you need. **My power works best in your weakness."** So now I am glad to boast about my weaknesses, so

**CH 12:8-10 WHAT'S IT SAYING?**

**WHAT AM I GOING TO DO ABOUT IT?**

## Paul's Concern for the Corinthians

[11]You have made me act like a fool—boasting like this. You ought to be writing commendations for me, for I am not at all inferior to these "super apostles," even though I am nothing at all. [12]When I was with you, I certainly gave you every proof that I am truly an apostle, sent to you by God himself. For I patiently did many signs and wonders and miracles among you. [13]The only thing I didn't do, which I do in the other churches, was to become a burden to you. Please forgive me for this wrong!

[14]Now I am coming to you for the third time, and I will not be a burden to you. I don't want what you have; I want you. And anyway, little children don't pay for their parents' food. It's the other way around; parents supply food for their children. [15]I will gladly spend myself and all I have for your spiritual good, even though it seems that the more I love you, the

less you love me.

[16]Some of you admit I was not a burden to you. But they still think I was sneaky and took advantage of you by trickery. [17]But how? Did any of the men I sent to you take advantage of you? [18]When I urged Titus to visit you and sent our other brother with him, did Titus take advantage of you? No, of course not! For we both have the same Spirit and walk in each other's steps, doing things the same way.

[19]Perhaps you think we are saying all this just to defend ourselves. That isn't it at all. We tell you this as Christ's servants, and we know that God is listening. Everything we do, dear friends, is for your benefit. [20]For I am afraid that when I come to visit you I won't like what I find, and then you won't like my response. I am afraid that I will find quarrelling, jealousy, outbursts of anger, selfishness, backstabbing, gossip, conceit, and disorderly behaviour. [21]Yes, I am afraid that when I come, God will humble me again because

**The Bible was divided into chapters 800 years ago (by Stephen Langton, not the original writers).**

of you. And I will have to grieve because many of you who sinned earlier have not repented of your impurity, sexual immorality, and eagerness for lustful pleasure.

## Paul's Final Advice

# 13

This is the third time I am coming to visit you. As the Scriptures say, "The facts of every case must be established by the testimony of two or three witnesses." [2]I have already warned those who had been sinning when I was there on my second visit. Now I again warn them and all others, just as I did before, that this next time I will not spare them.

[3]I will give you all the proof you want that Christ speaks through me. Christ is not weak in his dealings with you; he is a mighty power among you. [4]Although he died on the cross in weakness, he now lives by the mighty power of God. We, too, are weak, but we live

that the power of Christ may work through me. [10]Since I know it is all for Christ's good, I am quite content with my weaknesses and with insults, hardships, persecutions, and calamities. For when I am weak, then I am strong.

in him and have God's power—the power we use in dealing with you.

⁵Examine yourselves to see if your faith is really genuine. Test yourselves. If you cannot tell that Jesus Christ is among you, it means you have failed the test. ⁶I hope you recognize that we have passed the test and are approved by God.

⁷We pray to God that you will not do anything wrong. We pray this, not to show that our ministry to you has been successful, but because we want you to do right even if we ourselves seem to have failed. ⁸Our responsibility is never to oppose the truth, but to stand for the truth at all times. ⁹We are glad to be weak, if you are really strong. What we pray for is your restoration to maturity.

¹⁰I am writing this to you before I come, hoping that I won't need to deal harshly with you when I do come. **For I want to use the authority the Lord has given me to build you up, not to tear you down.**

## Paul's Final Greetings

¹¹Dear brothers and sisters, I close my letter with these last words: Rejoice. Change your ways. Encourage each other. Live in harmony and peace. Then the God of love and peace will be with you.

¹²Greet each other in Christian love. All the Christians here send you their greetings.

¹³May the grace of our Lord Jesus Christ, the love of God, and the fellowship of the Holy Spirit be with you all.

'So Noah did everything exactly as God had commanded him.'

What a claim to fame!  This is what you want the minister to say at your funeral.  It is not where you start in your faith that is important but where you finish.  God gave Noah a huge challenge, build a boat in the middle of dry land and fill it full of every type of male and female animal.  It must have seemed crazy, but God had a plan and Noah was obedient.

The world was so evil that God had decided to create a flood that would destroy the evil. The perfect world had been quickly destroyed by Adam's rebellion and disobedience. Noah and his family listened to God and obeyed his commands, Noah's obedience in the face of a seemingly obscure command and a huge task which took one hundred and twenty years to materialize, was a model in obedience and persistence.  Noah was faithful to the vision and, in his enduring obedience, survived the devastating flood and he and the other survivors went on to repopulate the world.

What task has God given you that seems insurmountable and crazy to the world?  Follow Noah's example and be obedient to God and carry out the tasks he sets you.

Read more of Noah in the Old Testament in the first book of the Bible, Genesis, starting in Chapter 6.

Bible Hit: 'He's Alive' 2 Corinthians 3:3.
Paul's reference to the living God is significant. How much spirit can a dead god have? Is our God alive in your life? Christians should be a living walking billboard for how awesome the Christian life is.  Is God writing a message across your heart?

# Can I impress God?

'For all have sinned; all fall short of God's glorious standard. Yet now God in his gracious kindness declares us not guilty. He has done this through Jesus Christ, who has freed us by taking away our sins.' Romans 3:23-4

An NFL Coach once barked at me,
'Remember you're only around here until someone comes along who is a little stronger, faster or cheaper than you! Then you are gone!'
The sober reality of professional sports is that you have to fight your way up the ranking and you only remain there until someone more talented, cheaper, healthier or younger than you pushes you out. To compare being picked for God's Team as 'earning you salvation' or impressing God with your skills as a Christian is poor theology. You cannot climb the ladder to attain anything in God's economy; this idea is not only dangerous, it is also stupid. We do not go up the ranks to meet God; he came down the ranks to meet us. We do not 'sign on' to God's team by impressing him with our skill; he offers us a free ticket.
I once heard an amateur golfer desperately trying to impress a certain professional golfer with his play. The amateur was embarrassing himself with his delusional golf

skills before a seasoned professional. I believe he thought the pro would not befriend him unless he was a good golfer. The pro was polite but unimpressed with his goodness.
The Apostle Paul 'zealously' tried to impress God with his actions before his conversion. He saw Christ's followers as a threat to his cause as a Jewish leader, and even helped kill a guy because he followed Jesus. But God was not impressed; he was actually rather unimpressed with Paul. (God does not like it when his people are killed.) Later Paul understood the futility in trying to show off before God. The reformed man was inspired by God to write a part of the Bible to address this very issue: trying to earn or impress your way into heaven. Here are a few small excerpts by Paul from one of his many letters in the Bible: 'For all have sinned; all fall short of God's glorious standard.' Romans 3:23; 'For the wages of sin is death, but the free gift of God is eternal life, through Christ Jesus our Lord.' Romans 6:23
There is nothing we can do to earn our way onto God's Team. It is a 'free gift'. Our actions and lifestyle may be impressive in comparison to some. If we compare ourselves to Hitler or the hypocrite that goes to church, we look pretty good. But when we try to make it onto God's Team by the standard of a righteous life we 'fall short'. The good news is it is a free gift. You are chosen for the team because God loves you. He values you. He even likes you and desires you to spend time with him. But you do not make the team because of your skills as a player or as a person.

### Reflection
If God loves me just as I am, why do I recoil from His love? Can I relax before God?

### Prayer
Lord in heaven, help me to respond to your unconditional love, help me to embrace that love.

'Nothing you can do can make God love you more.
Nothing you can do can make God love you less.'
Mark Burlingame

Nicked from: A Sporting Guide to Eternity, Steve Connor,
Christian Focus Publications - ISBN 1-85792-746-X

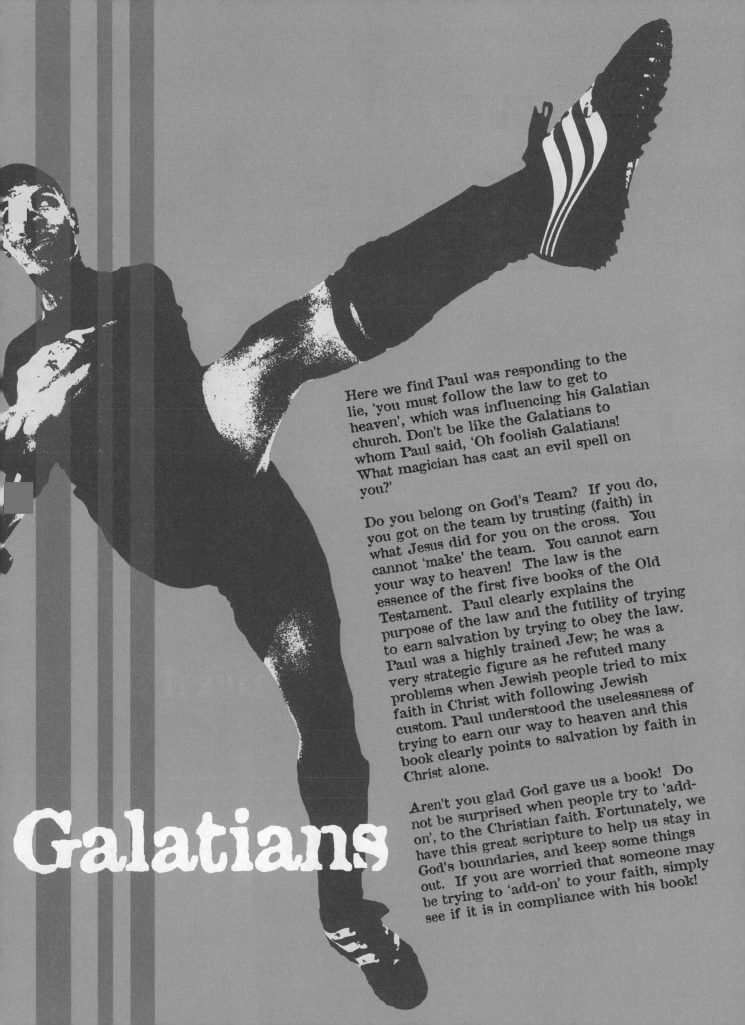

Here we find Paul was responding to the lie, 'you must follow the law to get to heaven', which was influencing his Galatian church. Don't be like the Galatians to whom Paul said, 'Oh foolish Galatians! What magician has cast an evil spell on you?'

Do you belong on God's Team? If you do, you got on the team by trusting (faith) in what Jesus did for you on the cross. You cannot earn 'make' the team. You cannot earn your way to heaven! The law is the essence of the first five books of the Old Testament. Paul clearly explains the purpose of the law and the futility of trying to earn salvation by trying to obey the law. Paul was a highly trained Jew; he was a very strategic figure as he refuted many problems when Jewish people tried to mix faith in Christ with following Jewish custom. Paul understood the uselessness of trying to earn our way to heaven and this book clearly points to salvation by faith in Christ alone.

Aren't you glad God gave us a book! Do not be surprised when people try to 'add-on', to the Christian faith. Fortunately, we have this great scripture to help us stay in God's boundaries, and keep some things out. If you are worried that someone may be trying to 'add-on' to your faith, simply see if it is in compliance with his book!

# Galatians

# In all we do
# this one's
# for You

**live it**

# GALATIANS

## Greetings from Paul

# 1

This letter is from Paul, an apostle. I was not appointed by any group or by human authority. My call is from Jesus Christ himself and from God the Father, who raised Jesus from the dead.

[2]All the brothers and sisters here join me in sending greetings to the churches of Galatia.

[3]May grace and peace be yours from God our Father and from the Lord Jesus Christ. [4]He died for our sins, just as God our Father planned, in order to rescue us from this evil world in which we live. [5]That is why all glory belongs to God through all the ages of eternity. Amen.

## There Is Only One Good News

[6]I am shocked that you are turning away so soon from God, who in his love and mercy called you to share the eternal life he gives through Christ. You are already following a different way [7]that pretends to be the Good News but is not the Good News at all. You are being fooled by those who twist and change the truth concerning Christ.

[8]Let God's curse fall on anyone, including myself, who preaches any other message than the one we told you about. Even if an angel comes from heaven and preaches any other message, let him be forever cursed. [9]I will say it again: If anyone preaches any other gospel than the one you welcomed, let God's curse fall upon that person.

[10]Obviously, I'm not trying to be a people pleaser! No, I am trying to please God. If I were still trying to please people, I would not be Christ's servant.

Who are your five favourite sports people of all time?

1
2
3
4
5

BIG FIVE

## Paul's Message Comes from Christ

[11]Dear brothers and sisters, I solemnly assure you that the Good News of salvation which I preach is not based on mere human reasoning or logic. [12]For my message came by a direct revelation from Jesus Christ himself. No one else taught me.

[13]**You know what I was like when I followed the Jewish religion—how I violently persecuted the Christians. I did my best to get rid of them.** [14]I was one of the most religious Jews of my own age, and I tried as hard as possible to follow all the old traditions of my religion.

[15]But then something happened! For it pleased God in his kindness to choose me and call me, even before I was born! What undeserved mercy! [16]Then he revealed his Son to me so that I could proclaim the Good News about Jesus to the Gentiles. When all this happened to me, I did not rush out to consult with anyone else; [17]nor did I go up to Jerusalem to consult with those

who were apostles before I was. No, I went away into Arabia and later returned to the city of Damascus. [18]It was not until three years later that I finally went to Jerusalem for a visit with Peter and stayed there with him for fifteen days. [19]And the only other apostle I met at that time was James, our Lord's brother.

[20]You must believe what I am saying, for I declare before God that I am not lying. [21]Then after this visit, I went north into the provinces of Syria and Cilicia. [22]And still the Christians in the churches in Judea didn't know me personally. [23]All they knew was that people were saying, "The one who used to persecute us now preaches the very faith he tried to destroy!" [24]And they gave glory to God because of me.

## The Apostles Accept Paul

# 2

Then fourteen years later I went back to Jerusalem again, this time with Barnabas; and Titus came along, too. [2]I went there because God revealed to me that I should go. While I

## Winners have hope!

Long before the 'fish'-sign, followers of Christ used an 'anchor' as a symbol of their faith in Christ. In the up and down world of sport what can be more valuable than an anchor. Many athletes live in fear of losing their place on their team or even losing their careers. You can see the fear in their face, it says, 'what is going to happen to me when my career is over?' Though it can be deeply disappointing when their career comes to an end, many Christian professional athletes know they have an anchor to God which will keep them safe and secure. No matter what level you play at, disappointment is part of sport, but instead of trying to find your happiness in short term success, Christianity offers permanent joy knowing we will spend 'forever' with God!

"This confidence is like a strong and trustworthy anchor for our souls." Hebrews 6:19

Winners

Winners hang onto the big picture!

was there I talked privately with the leaders of the church. I wanted them to understand what I had been preaching to the Gentiles. I wanted to make sure they did not disagree, or my ministry would have been useless. [3]And they did agree. They did not even demand that my companion Titus be circumcised, though he was a Gentile.

[4]Even that question wouldn't have come up except for some so-called Christians there—false ones, really—who came to spy on us and see our freedom in Christ Jesus. They wanted to force us, like slaves, to follow their Jewish regulations. [5]But we refused to listen to them for a single moment. We wanted to preserve the truth of the Good News for you.

[6]And the leaders of the church who were there had nothing to add to what I was preaching. (By the way, their reputation as great leaders made no difference to me, for God has no favourites.) [7]They saw that God had given me the responsibility of preaching the Good News to the Gentiles, just as he had given Peter the responsibility of preaching to the Jews. [8]For the same God who worked through Peter for the benefit of the Jews worked through me for the benefit of the Gentiles. [9]In fact, James, Peter, and John, who were known as pillars of the church, recognized the gift God had given me, and they accepted Barnabas and me as their co-workers. They encouraged us to keep preaching to the Gentiles, while they continued their work with the Jews. [10]The only thing they suggested was that we remember to help the poor, and I have certainly been eager to do that.

## Paul Confronts Peter

[11]But when Peter came to Antioch, I had to oppose him publicly, speaking strongly against what he was doing, for it was very wrong. [12]When he first arrived, he ate with the Gentile Christians, who don't bother with circumcision. But afterwards, when some Jewish friends of James came, Peter wouldn't eat with the Gentiles any more because he was afraid of what these legalists would say. [13]Then the other Jewish Christians followed Peter's hypocrisy, and even Barnabas was

Bible FACTS

**The Old Testament was divided into verses in 1448 for ease of use. The New Testament was divided into verses in 1551 for ease of use.**

influenced to join them in their hypocrisy.

[14]When I saw that they were not following the truth of the Good News, I said to Peter in front of all the others, "Since you, a Jew by birth, have discarded the Jewish laws and are living like a Gentile, why are you trying to make these Gentiles obey the Jewish laws you abandoned? [15]You and I are Jews by birth, not 'sinners' like the Gentiles. [16]And yet we Jewish Christians know that we become right with God, not by doing what the law commands, but by faith in Jesus Christ. So we have believed in Christ Jesus, that we might be accepted by God because of our faith in Christ—and not because we have obeyed the law. For no one will ever be saved by obeying the law."

[17]But what if we seek to be made right with God through faith in Christ and then find out that we are still sinners? Has Christ led us into sin? Of course not! [18]Rather, I make myself guilty if I rebuild the old system I already tore down. [19]For when I tried to keep the law, I realized I could never earn God's approval. So I died to the law so that I might live for God. I have been crucified with Christ. [20]I myself no longer live, but Christ lives in me. So I live my life in this earthly body by trusting in the Son of God, who loved me and

gave himself for me. [21]I am not one of those who treats the grace of God as meaningless. For if we could be saved by keeping the law, then there was no need for Christ to die.

action

**CH 3:1-5 WHAT'S IT SAYING?**

**WHAT AM I GOING TO DO ABOUT IT?**

## The Law and Faith in Christ

# 3

Oh, foolish Galatians! What magician has cast an evil spell on you? For you used to see the meaning of Jesus

BIBLE HIT

'Fruit is good for you.' Galatians 6

I will endeavor to exhibit a Christian behaviour in my sport.

LOVE: I will show genuine concern for team-mates and ask them how they are doing and mean it.

JOY: I will remind myself how God has given me eternal life.

PEACE: I will prepare harder for competitions and know that I have done all that I have done to be prepared with the talent God has given me.

PATIENCE: I will remember that teammates may not respond the same way I do.

KINDNESS: I will encourage team-mates and competitors.

GOODNESS: I will assert a positive atmosphere in the locker-room.

GENTLENESS: I will be gracious when I win and lose.

SELF-CONTROL: I will remember that God has given me great power and I will keep that power within his boundaries.

TIPS

## Warm-up is Essential:

A warm-up consisting of exercises performed immediately before an activity to increase circulation and heart rate is an essential part of a good conditioning programme.

Christ's death as clearly as though I had shown you a signboard with a picture of Christ dying on the cross. [2]Let me ask you this one question: Did you receive the Holy Spirit by keeping the law? Of course not, for the Holy Spirit came upon you only after you believed the message you heard about Christ. [3]Have you lost your senses? After starting your Christian lives in the Spirit, why are you now trying to become perfect by your own human effort? [4]You have suffered so much for the Good News. Surely it was not in vain, was it? Are you now going to just throw it all away?

[5]I ask you again, does God give you the Holy Spirit and work miracles among you because you obey the law of Moses? Of course not! It is because you believe the message you heard about Christ.

[6]In the same way, "Abraham believed God, so God declared him righteous because of his faith." [7]The real children of Abraham, then, are all those who put their faith in God.

[8]What's more, the Scriptures looked forward to this time when God would accept the Gentiles, too, on the basis of their faith. God promised this good news to Abraham long ago when he said, "All nations will be blessed through you." [9]And so it is: All who put their faith in Christ share the same blessing Abraham received because of his faith.

[10]But those who depend on the law to make them right with God are under his curse, for the Scriptures say, "Cursed is everyone who does not observe and obey all these commands that are written in God's Book of the Law." [11]Consequently, it is clear that no one can ever be right with God by trying to keep the law. For the Scriptures say, "It is through faith that a righteous person has life." [12]How different from this way of faith is the way of law, which says, "If you wish to find life by obeying the law, you must obey all of its commands."

[13]But Christ has rescued us from the curse pronounced by the law. When he was hung on the cross, he took upon himself the curse for our wrongdoing. For it is written in the Scriptures, "Cursed is everyone who is hung on a tree." [14]Through the work of Christ Jesus, God has blessed the Gentiles with the same blessing he promised to Abraham, and we Christians receive the promised Holy Spirit through faith.

## The Law and God's Promises

[15]Dear brothers and sisters, here's an example from everyday life. Just as no one can set aside or amend an irrevocable agreement, so it is in this case. [16]God gave the promise to Abraham and his child. And notice that it doesn't say the

**STATS**

Until 1967 it wasn't illegal for Olympic athletes to use drugs to enhance their performance during competition.

# PERSONAL ASSESSMENTS

## SPIRITUAL MATURITY

True or False

- I really want to spend time with God.     T/F

- I really want to know more about how to become a stronger Christian.     T/F

- I really believe prayer makes a difference     T/F

- I really want to encourage others to grow in their faith in Jesus Christ.     T/F

- I really want to go to heaven when I die.     T/F

- I really am grateful for the sacrifices God has made for me by sending his son to be the sacrifice that takes away my sin and separation with God.     T/F

- Out of gratitude I really want to obey and serve God.     T/F

promise was to his children, as if it meant many descendants. But the promise was to his child—and that, of course, means Christ.

[17]This is what I am trying to say: The agreement God made with Abraham could not be cancelled 430 years later when God gave the law to Moses. God would be breaking his promise. [18]For if the inheritance could be received only by keeping the law, then it would not be the result of accepting God's promise. But God gave it to Abraham as a promise.

[19]Well then, why was the law given? It was given to show people how guilty they are. But this system of law was to last only until the coming of the child to whom God's promise was made. And there is this further difference. God gave his laws to angels to give to Moses, who was the mediator between God and the people. [20]Now a mediator is needed if two people enter into an agreement, but God acted on his own when he made his promise to Abraham.

[21]Well then, is there a conflict between God's law and God's promises? Absolutely not! If the law could have given us new life, we could have been made right with God by obeying it. [22]But the Scriptures have declared that we are all prisoners of sin, so the only way to receive God's promise is to believe in Jesus Christ.

[23]Until faith in Christ was shown to us as the way of becoming right with God, we were guarded by the law. We were kept in protective custody, so to speak, until we could put our faith in the coming Saviour.

### God's Children through Faith

[24]**Let me put it another way. The law was our guardian and teacher to lead us until Christ came. So now, through faith in Christ, we are made right with God.** [25]But now that faith in Christ has come, we no longer need the law as our guardian. [26]So you are all children of God through faith in Christ Jesus. [27]And all who have been united with Christ in baptism have been made like him. [28]There is no longer Jew or Gentile, slave or free, male or female. For you are all Christians—you are one in Christ Jesus.

[29]And now that you belong to Christ, you are the true children of Abraham. You are his heirs, and now all the promises God gave to him belong to you.

## 4

Think of it this way. If a father dies and leaves great wealth for his young children, those children are not much better off than slaves until they grow up, even though they actually own everything their father had. [2]They have to obey their guardians until they reach whatever age their father set.

[3]And that's the way it was with us before Christ came. We were slaves to the spiritual powers of this world.

Until the 1870s, baseball was played without the use of gloves.

⁴But when the right time came, God sent his Son, born of a woman, subject to the law. ⁵God sent him to buy freedom for us who were slaves to the law, so that he could adopt us as his very own children. ⁶And because you Gentiles have become his children, God has sent the Spirit of his Son into your hearts, and now you can call God your dear Father.

⁷Now you are no longer a slave but God's own child. And since you are his child, everything he has belongs to you.

## Paul's Concern for the Galatians

⁸Before you Gentiles knew God, you were slaves to so-called gods that do not even exist. ⁹And now that you have found God (or should I say, now that God has found you), why do you want to go back again and become slaves once more to the weak and useless spiritual powers of this world? ¹⁰You are trying to find favour with God by what you do or don't do on certain days or months or seasons or years. ¹¹I fear for you. I am afraid that all my hard work for you was worth nothing. ¹²Dear brothers and sisters, I plead with you to live as I do in freedom from these things, for I have become like you Gentiles were—free from the law. You did not mistreat me when I first preached to you. ¹³Surely you remember that I was sick when I first brought you the Good News of Christ. ¹⁴But even though my sickness was revolting to you, you did not reject me and turn me away. No, you took me in and cared for me as though I were an angel from God or even Christ Jesus himself. ¹⁵Where is that joyful spirit we felt together then? In those days, I know you would gladly have taken out your own eyes and given them to me if it had been possible. ¹⁶Have I now become your enemy because I am telling you the truth?

¹⁷Those false teachers who are so anxious to win your favour are not doing it for your good. They are trying to shut you off from me so that you will pay more attention to them. ¹⁸Now it's wonderful if you are eager to do good, and especially when I am not with you. ¹⁹But oh, my dear children! I feel as if I am going through labour pains for you again, and they will continue until Christ is fully developed in your lives. ²⁰How I wish I were there with you right now, so that I could be more gentle with you. But at this distance I frankly don't know what else to do.

## Abraham's Two Children

²¹Listen to me, you who want to live under the law. Do you know what the law really says? ²²The Scriptures say that Abraham had two sons, one from his slave-wife and one from his freeborn wife. ²³The son of the slave-wife was born in a human attempt to bring about the fulfilment of God's promise. But the son of the freeborn wife was born as God's own fulfilment of his promise.

²⁴Now these two women serve as an illustration of God's two covenants. Hagar, the slave-wife, represents Mount Sinai where people first became enslaved to the law. ²⁵And now Jerusalem is just like Mount Sinai in Arabia, because she and her children live in slavery. ²⁶But Sarah, the free woman, represents the heavenly Jerusalem. And she is our mother. ²⁷That is what Isaiah meant when he prophesied,

"Rejoice, O childless woman!
Break forth into loud and joyful song,
even though you never gave birth to a child.
For the woman who could bear no children
now has more than all the other women!"

²⁸And you, dear brothers and sisters, are children of the promise, just like Isaac. ²⁹And we who are born of the Holy Spirit are persecuted by those who want us to keep the law, just as Isaac, the child of promise, was persecuted by Ishmael, the son of the slave-wife. ³⁰But what do the Scriptures say about that? "Get rid of the slave and her son, for the son of the slave woman will not share the family inheritance with the free woman's son."

³¹So, dear brothers and sisters, we are not children of the slave woman, obligated to the law. We are children of the free woman, acceptable to God because of our faith.

## Freedom in Christ

# 5

So Christ has really set us free. **Now make sure that you stay free, and don't get tied up again in slavery to the law.**

²Listen! I, Paul, tell you this: If you are counting on circumcision to make you right with God, then Christ cannot help you. ³I'll say it again. If you are trying to find favour with God by being circumcised, you must obey all of the regulations in the whole law of Moses. ⁴For if you are trying to make yourselves right with God by keeping the law, you have been cut off from Christ! You have fallen away from God's grace.

⁵But we who live by the Spirit eagerly wait to receive everything promised to us who are right with God through faith. ⁶For when we place our faith in Christ Jesus, it makes no difference to God whether we are circumcised or not circumcised. What is important is faith expressing itself in love.

⁷You were getting along so well. Who has interfered with you to hold you back from following the truth? ⁸It certainly isn't God, for he is the one who called you to freedom. ⁹But it takes only one wrong person among you to infect all the others—a little yeast spreads quickly through the whole batch of dough! ¹⁰I am trusting the Lord to bring you back to believing as I do about these things. God will judge that person, whoever it is, who has been troubling and confusing you.

¹¹Dear brothers and sisters, if I were still preaching that you must be circumcised—as some say I do—why would the Jews persecute me? The fact that I am still being persecuted proves that I am still preaching salvation through the cross

# WHAT DOES IT MEAN?

### Noah's Ark

Noah's ark, a building of gopher-wood, and covered with pitch, 300 cubits long, 50 cubits broad, and 30 cubits high (Gen. 6:14-16); an oblong floating house of three stories, with a door in the side and a window in the roof. It was 100 years in building (Gen. 5:32; 7:6). It was intended to preserve certain persons and animals from the deluge which God was about to bring over the earth.

of Christ alone.

[12]I only wish that those troublemakers who want to mutilate you by circumcision would mutilate themselves. [13]For you have been called to live in freedom—not freedom to satisfy your sinful nature, but freedom to serve one another in love. [14]For the whole law can be summed up in this one command: "Love your neighbour as yourself." [15]But if instead of showing love among yourselves you are always biting and devouring one another, watch out! Beware of destroying one another.

## Living by the Spirit's Power

[16]So I advise you to live according to your new life in the Holy Spirit. Then you won't be doing what your sinful nature craves. [17]The old sinful nature loves to do evil, which is the exact opposite from what the Holy Spirit wants. And the Spirit gives us desires that are opposite from what the sinful nature desires. These two forces are constantly fighting each other, and your choices are never free from this conflict. [18]But when you are directed by the Holy Spirit, you are no longer subject to the law.

[19]When you follow the desires of your sinful nature, your lives will produce these evil results: sexual immorality, impure thoughts, eagerness for lustful pleasure, [20]idolatry, participation in demonic activities, hostility, quarrelling, jealousy, outbursts of anger, selfish ambition, divisions, the feeling that everyone is wrong except those in your own little group, [21]envy, drunkenness, wild parties, and other kinds of sin. Let me tell you again, as I have before, that anyone living that sort of life will not inherit the Kingdom of God. [22]But when the Holy Spirit controls our lives, he will produce this kind of fruit in us: love, joy, peace, patience, kindness, goodness, faithfulness, [23]gentleness, and self-control. Here there is no conflict with the law.

[24]**Those who belong to Christ Jesus have nailed the passions and desires of their sinful nature to his cross and crucified them there.** [25]If we are living now by the Holy Spirit, let us follow the

**When you want to give up**

6:9

So don't get tired of doing what is good. Don't get discouraged and give up, for we will reap a harvest of blessing at the appropriate time.

Holy Spirit's leading in every part of our lives. [26]Let us not become conceited, or irritate one another, or be jealous of one another.

### CH 5:16-26 WHAT'S IT SAYING?

### WHAT AM I GOING TO DO ABOUT IT?

## We Reap What We Sow

# 6

Dear brothers and sisters, if another Christian is overcome by some sin, you who are godly should gently and humbly help that person back onto the right path. And be careful not to fall into the same temptation yourself. [2]Share each other's troubles and problems, and in this way obey the law of Christ. [3]If you think you are too important to help someone in need, you are only fooling yourself. You are really a nobody. [4]Be sure to do what you should, for then you will enjoy the personal satisfaction of having done your work well, and you won't need to compare yourself with anyone else. [5]For we are each responsible for our own conduct.

[6]Those who are taught the word of God should help their teachers by paying them.

[7]Don't be misled. Remember that you can't ignore God and get away with it. You will always reap what you sow! [8]Those who live only to satisfy their own sinful

desires will harvest the consequences of decay and death. But those who live to please the Spirit will harvest everlasting life from the Spirit. [9]So don't get tired of doing what is good. Don't get discouraged and give up, for we will reap a harvest of blessing at the appropriate time. [10]Whenever we have the opportunity, we should do good to everyone, especially to our Christian brothers and sisters.

## Paul's Final Advice

[11]Notice what large letters I use as I write these closing words in my own hand-writing. [12]Those who are trying to force you to be circumcised are doing it for just one reason. They don't want to be persecuted for teaching that the cross of Christ alone can save. [13]And even those who advocate circumcision don't really keep the whole law. They only want you to be circumcised so they can brag about it and claim you as their disciples.

[14]**As for me, God forbid that I should boast about anything except the cross of our Lord Jesus Christ.** Because of that cross, my interest in this world died long ago, and the world's interest in me is also long dead. [15]It doesn't make any difference now whether we have been circumcised or not. What counts is whether we really have been changed into new and different people. [16]May God's mercy and peace be upon all those who live by this principle. They are the new people of God. [17]From now on, don't let anyone trouble me with these things. For I bear on my body the scars that show I belong to Jesus.

[18]My dear brothers and sisters, may the grace of our Lord Jesus Christ be with you all. Amen.

**What The Bible Says About Itself:** "All scripture is inspired by God and is useful to teach us what is true, and to make us realize what is wrong in our lives. It straightens us out and teaches us to do what is right." (2 Timothy 3:16)

Lock and load! We are a united team and we have battle to fight. Paul ends his letter to the Ephesian church (which was based on the beautiful Mediterranean coast of modern day Turkey) with an order to, 'strap it up', and get ready for battle; to 'put on God's full armour'! Ephesians was written for the readers to get a glimpse of the majestic works of God and take action in everyday life, with a Godly attitude and purpose for living. Paul most likely, was writing this book from a Roman prison or house arrest.

In the first three chapters we have a privileged view of God's grand character and his purpose for our life ('I pray that you will begin to understand the incredible greatness of his power for us who believe in him.'). This understanding of God fires us up to live a life worthy of our inheritance in his family. The last three chapters are to be lived out in response to the first three.

As you see the excitement and joy that pours out of Paul, remember that his circumstances do not dictate his attitude; he is suffering and in prison for his faith.

# Ephesians

Game Plan
USEFUL INFORMATION
ETERNAL LIFE
SIN
ETERNAL LIFE
SIN
Copyright © The Book People Ltd 1998
For the wages of sin is death,
but the free gift of God is eternal life
through Christ Jesus our Lord
Romans 6:23
sport

# EPHESIANS

## Greetings from Paul

# 1

This letter is from Paul, chosen by God to be an apostle of Christ Jesus.

It is written to God's holy people in Ephesus, who are faithful followers of Christ Jesus.

[2]May grace and peace be yours, sent to you from God our Father and Jesus Christ our Lord.

## Spiritual Blessings

[3]How we praise God, the Father of our Lord Jesus Christ, who has blessed us with every spiritual blessing in the heavenly realms because we belong to Christ. [4]Long ago, even before he made the world, God loved us and chose us in Christ to be holy and without fault in his eyes. [5]His unchanging plan has always been to adopt us into his own family by bringing us to himself through Jesus Christ. And this gave him great pleasure. [6]So we praise God for the wonderful kindness he has poured out on us because we belong to his dearly loved Son. [7]He is so rich in kindness that he purchased our freedom through the blood of his Son, and our sins are forgiven. [8]He has showered his kindness on us, along with all wisdom and understanding.

[9]God's secret plan has now been revealed to us; it is a plan centred on Christ, designed long ago according to his good pleasure. [10]And this is his plan: At the right time he will bring everything together under the

## STATS

Forrest Towns beat a prize cavalry horse, trained as a running jumper, in the 120-yard hurdles, using only five hurdles to give the horse's longer stride a fair chance.

authority of Christ—everything in heaven and on earth. [11]Furthermore, because of Christ, we have

received an inheritance from God, for he chose us from the beginning, and all things happen just as he decided long ago. [12]God's purpose was that we who were the first to trust in Christ should praise our glorious God. [13]And now you also have heard the truth, the Good News that God saves you. And when you believed in Christ, he identified you as his own by giving you the Holy Spirit, whom he promised long ago. [14]The Spirit is God's guarantee that he will give us everything he promised and that he has purchased us to be his own people. This is just one more reason for us to praise our glorious God.

## Paul's Prayer for Spiritual Wisdom

[15]Ever since I first heard of your strong faith in the Lord Jesus and your love for Christians everywhere, [16]I have never stopped thanking God for you. I pray for

Eat up! Consider the word of God as your spiritual food. Would you not eat for a couple days before you ran in a Marathon? Would you let a child go without food and stunt their growth? So why starve spiritually? Get in there and eat some more! It's pure power! "You must crave pure spiritual milk so that you can grow into the fullness of your salvation. Cry out for this nourishment as a baby cries for milk."

1 Peter 2:2

you constantly, [17]asking God, the glorious Father of our Lord Jesus Christ, to give you spiritual wisdom and understanding, so that you might grow in your knowledge of God. [18]I pray that your hearts will be flooded with light so that you can understand the wonderful future he has promised to those he called. I want you to realize what a rich and glorious inheritance he has given to his people.

[19]I pray that you will begin to understand the incredible greatness of his power for us who believe him. This is the same mighty power [20]that raised Christ from the dead and seated him in the place of honour at God's right hand in the heavenly realms.

[21]Now he is far above any ruler or authority or power or leader or anything else in this world or in the world to come. [22]And God has put all things under the authority of Christ, and he gave him this authority for the benefit of the church. [23]And the church is his body;

it is filled by Christ, who fills everything everywhere with his presence.

## Made Alive with Christ

# 2

Once you were dead, doomed for ever because of your many sins. [2]You used to live just like the rest of the world, full of sin, obeying Satan, the mighty prince of the power of the air. He is the spirit at work in the hearts of those who refuse to obey God. [3]All of us used to live that way, following the passions and desires of our evil nature. We were born with an evil nature, and we were under God's anger just like everyone else.

[4]**But God is so rich in mercy, and he loved us so very much,** [5]that even while we were dead because of our sins, he gave us life when he raised Christ from the dead.

(It is only by God's special favour that you have been saved!) [6]For he raised us from the dead along with Christ, and we are seated with him in the heavenly realms—all because we are one with Christ Jesus. [7]And so God can always point to us as examples of the incredible wealth of his favour and kindness towards us, as shown in all he has done for us through Christ Jesus.

[8]God saved you by his special favour when you believed. And you can't take credit for this; it is a gift from God. [9]Salvation is not a reward for the good things we have done, so none of us can boast about it. [10]For we are God's masterpiece. He has created us anew in Christ Jesus, so that we can do the good things he planned for us long ago.

## Oneness and Peace in Christ

[11]Don't forget that you Gentiles used to be outsiders by birth. You were called "the uncircumcised ones" by the Jews, who were proud of their circumcision, even though it affected only

their bodies and not their hearts. [12]In those days you were living apart from Christ. You were excluded from God's people, Israel, and you did not know the promises God had made to them. You lived in this world without God and without hope. [13]But now you belong to Christ Jesus. Though you once were far away from God, now you have been brought near to him because of the blood of Christ.

[14]For Christ himself has made peace between us Jews and you Gentiles by making us all one people. He has broken down the wall of hostility that used to separate us. [15]By his death he ended the whole system of Jewish law that excluded the Gentiles. His purpose was to make peace between Jews and Gentiles by creating in himself one new person from the two groups. [16]Together as one body, Christ reconciled both groups to God by means of his death, and our hostility towards each other was put to death. [17]He has brought this Good News of peace to you Gentiles who were far away from him, and to us Jews who were near. [18]Now all of us, both Jews and Gentiles, may come to the Father through the same Holy Spirit because of what Christ has done for us.

## A Temple for the Lord

[19]So now you Gentiles are no longer strangers and foreigners. You are citizens along with all of God's holy people. You are members of God's family. [20]We are his house, built on the foundation of the apostles and the prophets. And the cornerstone is Christ Jesus himself. [21]We who believe are carefully joined together, becoming a holy temple for the Lord. [22]Through him you Gentiles are also joined together as part of this dwelling where God lives by his Spirit.

**In reading the Bible, it soon becomes apparent that certain numbers occur more frequently than we would expect. FORTY is the number of testing. Jesus was tempted in the wilderness FORTY days and nights. Israel wandered in the wilderness FORTY years. During the flood of Noah, the rain fell FORTY days and nights.**

**CH 2:19-22 WHAT'S IT SAYING?**

**WHAT AM I GOING TO DO ABOUT IT?**

## God's Secret Plan Revealed

**3**

I, Paul, am a prisoner of Christ Jesus because of my preaching to you Gentiles. [2]As you already know, God has given me this special ministry of announcing his favour to you Gentiles.

[3]As I briefly mentioned earlier in this letter, God himself revealed his secret plan to me. [4]As you read what I have written, you will understand what I know about this plan regarding Christ.

[5]God did not reveal it to previous generations, but now he has revealed it by the Holy Spirit to his holy apostles and prophets.

[6]And this is the secret plan: The Gentiles have an equal share with the Jews in all the riches inherited by God's children. Both groups have believed the Good News, and both are part of the same body and enjoy together the promise of blessings through Christ Jesus. [7]By God's special favour and mighty power, I have been given the wonderful privilege of serving him by spreading this Good News.

[8]Just think! Though I did nothing to deserve it, and though I am the least deserving Christian there is, I was chosen for this special joy of telling the Gentiles

about the endless treasures available to them in Christ. [9]I was chosen to explain to everyone this plan that God, the Creator of all things, had kept secret from the beginning.

[10]God's purpose was to show his wisdom in all its rich variety to all the rulers and authorities in the heavenly realms. They will see this when Jews and Gentiles are joined together in his church. [11]This was his plan from all eternity, and it has now been carried out through Christ Jesus our Lord.

[12]Because of Christ and our faith in him, we can now come fearlessly into God's presence, assured of his glad welcome. [13]So please don't despair because of what they are doing to me here. It is for you that I am suffering, so you should feel honoured and encouraged.

## Paul's Prayer for Spiritual Empowering

[14]When I think of the wisdom and scope of God's plan, I fall to my knees and pray to the Father, [15]the Creator of everything in heaven and on earth. [16]I pray that from his glorious, unlimited resources he will give you mighty inner strength through his Holy Spirit. [17]And I pray that Christ will be more and more at home in your hearts as you trust in him. May your roots go down deep into the soil of God's marvellous love. [18]And may you have the power to understand, as all God's people should, how wide, how long, how high, and how deep his love really is. [19]May you experience the love of Christ, though it is so great you will never fully understand it. Then you will be filled with the fullness of life and power that comes from God.

[20]**Now glory be to God! By his mighty power at work within us, he is able to accomplish infinitely more than we**

**When you are planning your future**

**3:20**

Now glory be to God! By his mighty power at work within us, he is able to accomplish infinitely more than we would ever dare to ask or hope.

would ever dare to ask or hope. [21]May he be given glory in the church and in Christ Jesus for ever and ever through endless ages. Amen.

[14]Then we will no longer be like children, forever changing our minds about what we believe because someone has told us something different or because someone has cleverly lied to us and made the lie sound

impurity and greed.
[20]But that isn't what you were taught when you learned about Christ. [21]Since you have heard all about him and have learned the truth that is in Jesus, [22]throw off your old evil nature and

### Sport dominates my life. Should I quit it?

You will fight with idols (things that become more important than God) all your life. Sport dominating your life may be the first of many challenges you struggle through. Whenever you have an idol, you have to deal with it severely. Jesus uses hyperbole (overstatement) to demonstrate our immediate need to deal with the problem: 'if your eye causes you to sin, pluck it out!' Dealing with an idol in our lives is hard. Sometimes we should stop the activity that becomes an idol, but sometimes we should fight hard to put it in its proper order in our life. Many parents make children more important than God, but they do not 'quit' being a parent. Instead you work out how to make God number one in your heart. Can you do the same with your sport?

## Unity in the Body

## 4

Therefore I, a prisoner for serving the Lord, beg you to lead a life worthy of your calling, for you have been called by God. [2]Be humble and gentle. Be patient with each other, making allowance for each other's faults because of your love. [3]Always keep yourselves united in the Holy Spirit, and bind yourselves together with peace.

[4]We are all one body, we have the same Spirit, and we have all been called to the same glorious future. [5]There is only one Lord, one faith, one baptism, [6]and there is only one God and Father, who is over us all and in us all and living through us all. [7]However, he has given each one of us a special gift according to the generosity of Christ. [8]That is why the Scriptures say,

"When he ascended to the heights,
he led a crowd of captives
and gave gifts to his people."

[9]Notice that it says "he ascended." This means that Christ first came down to the lowly world in which we live. [10]The same one who came down is the one who ascended higher than all the heavens, so that his rule might fill the entire universe.

[11]He is the one who gave these gifts to the church: the apostles, the prophets, the evangelists, and the pastors and teachers. [12]Their responsibility is to equip God's people to do his work and build up the church, the body of Christ, [13]until we come to such unity in our faith and knowledge of God's Son that we will be mature and full grown in the Lord, measuring up to the full stature of Christ.

like the truth. [15]Instead, we will hold to the truth in love, becoming more and more in every way like Christ, who is the head of his body, the church. [16]Under his direction, the whole body is fitted together perfectly. As each part does its own special work, it helps the other parts grow, so that the whole body is healthy and growing and full of love.

### Living as Children of Light

[17]With the Lord's authority let me say this: Live no longer as the ungodly do, for they are hopelessly confused. [18]Their closed minds are full of darkness; they are far away from the life of God because they have shut their minds and hardened their hearts against him. [19]They don't care any more about right and wrong, and they have given themselves over to immoral ways. Their lives are filled with all kinds of

your former way of life, which is rotten through and through, full of lust and deception. [23]Instead, there must be a spiritual renewal of your thoughts and attitudes. [24]You must display a new nature because you are a new person, created in God's likeness—righteous, holy, and true.

[25]So put away all falsehood and "tell your neighbour the truth" because we belong to each other. [26]And "don't sin by letting anger gain control over you." Don't let the sun go down while you are still angry, [27]for anger gives a mighty foothold to the Devil.

[28]If you are a thief, stop stealing. Begin using your hands for honest work, and then give generously to others in need. [29]Don't use foul or abusive language. Let everything you say be good and helpful, so that your words will be an encouragement to those who hear them.

[30]And do not bring sorrow to God's Holy Spirit by the way

Who are your five favourite Bible heroes?

1
2
3
4
5

BIG FIVE

# SEPTEMBER M.A.P.

## 1
| S.D. | P.L. | P.G. | S.G. |
|------|------|------|------|
| P. ☐ | F. ☐ | F. ☐ | T. ☐ |
| F. ☐ | W. ☐ | W. ☐ | P. ☐ |
| B. ☐ | P. ☐ | C. ☐ | C. ☐ |

## 2
| S.D. | P.L. | P.G. | S.G. |
|------|------|------|------|
| P. ☐ | F. ☐ | F. ☐ | T. ☐ |
| F. ☐ | W. ☐ | W. ☐ | P. ☐ |
| B. ☐ | P. ☐ | C. ☐ | C. ☐ |

## 3
| S.D. | P.L. | P.G. | S.G. |
|------|------|------|------|
| P. ☐ | F. ☐ | F. ☐ | T. ☐ |
| F. ☐ | W. ☐ | W. ☐ | P. ☐ |
| B. ☐ | P. ☐ | C. ☐ | C. ☐ |

## 4
| S.D. | P.L. | P.G. | S.G. |
|------|------|------|------|
| P. ☐ | F. ☐ | F. ☐ | T. ☐ |
| F. ☐ | W. ☐ | W. ☐ | P. ☐ |
| B. ☐ | P. ☐ | C. ☐ | C. ☐ |

## 9
| S.D. | P.L. | P.G. | S.G. |
|------|------|------|------|
| P. ☐ | F. ☐ | F. ☐ | T. ☐ |
| F. ☐ | W. ☐ | W. ☐ | P. ☐ |
| B. ☐ | P. ☐ | C. ☐ | C. ☐ |

## 10
| S.D. | P.L. | P.G. | S.G. |
|------|------|------|------|
| P. ☐ | F. ☐ | F. ☐ | T. ☐ |
| F. ☐ | W. ☐ | W. ☐ | P. ☐ |
| B. ☐ | P. ☐ | C. ☐ | C. ☐ |

## 11
| S.D. | P.L. | P.G. | S.G. |
|------|------|------|------|
| P. ☐ | F. ☐ | F. ☐ | T. ☐ |
| F. ☐ | W. ☐ | W. ☐ | P. ☐ |
| B. ☐ | P. ☐ | C. ☐ | C. ☐ |

## 12
| S.D. | P.L. | P.G. | S.G. |
|------|------|------|------|
| P. ☐ | F. ☐ | F. ☐ | T. ☐ |
| F. ☐ | W. ☐ | W. ☐ | P. ☐ |
| B. ☐ | P. ☐ | C. ☐ | C. ☐ |

## 17
| S.D. | P.L. | P.G. | S.G. |
|------|------|------|------|
| P. ☐ | F. ☐ | F. ☐ | T. ☐ |
| F. ☐ | W. ☐ | W. ☐ | P. ☐ |
| B. ☐ | P. ☐ | C. ☐ | C. ☐ |

## 18
| S.D. | P.L. | P.G. | S.G. |
|------|------|------|------|
| P. ☐ | F. ☐ | F. ☐ | T. ☐ |
| F. ☐ | W. ☐ | W. ☐ | P. ☐ |
| B. ☐ | P. ☐ | C. ☐ | C. ☐ |

## 19
| S.D. | P.L. | P.G. | S.G. |
|------|------|------|------|
| P. ☐ | F. ☐ | F. ☐ | T. ☐ |
| F. ☐ | W. ☐ | W. ☐ | P. ☐ |
| B. ☐ | P. ☐ | C. ☐ | C. ☐ |

## 20
| S.D. | P.L. | P.G. | S.G. |
|------|------|------|------|
| P. ☐ | F. ☐ | F. ☐ | T. ☐ |
| F. ☐ | W. ☐ | W. ☐ | P. ☐ |
| B. ☐ | P. ☐ | C. ☐ | C. ☐ |

## 25
| S.D. | P.L. | P.G. | S.G. |
|------|------|------|------|
| P. ☐ | F. ☐ | F. ☐ | T. ☐ |
| F. ☐ | W. ☐ | W. ☐ | P. ☐ |
| B. ☐ | P. ☐ | C. ☐ | C. ☐ |

## 26
| S.D. | P.L. | P.G. | S.G. |
|------|------|------|------|
| P. ☐ | F. ☐ | F. ☐ | T. ☐ |
| F. ☐ | W. ☐ | W. ☐ | P. ☐ |
| B. ☐ | P. ☐ | C. ☐ | C. ☐ |

## 27
| S.D. | P.L. | P.G. | S.G. |
|------|------|------|------|
| P. ☐ | F. ☐ | F. ☐ | T. ☐ |
| F. ☐ | W. ☐ | W. ☐ | P. ☐ |
| B. ☐ | P. ☐ | C. ☐ | C. ☐ |

## 28
| S.D. | P.L. | P.G. | S.G. |
|------|------|------|------|
| P. ☐ | F. ☐ | F. ☐ | T. ☐ |
| F. ☐ | W. ☐ | W. ☐ | P. ☐ |
| B. ☐ | P. ☐ | C. ☐ | C. ☐ |

## Spiritual Disciplines

**Prayer**

**Faith Community**

**Bible Reading**

## Prayer List

**Friends**

**World**

**Personal**

Who am I....
Where am I going....
How am I going to get there?

nt:sport
MONTHLY ACTION PLAN

## 5

| S.D. | P.L. | P.G. | S.G. |
|------|------|------|------|
| P. ☐ | F. ☐ | F. ☐ | T. ☐ |
| F. ☐ | W. ☐ | W. ☐ | P. ☐ |
| B. ☐ | P. ☐ | C. ☐ | C. ☐ |

## 6

| S.D. | P.L. | P.G. | S.G. |
|------|------|------|------|
| P. ☐ | F. ☐ | F. ☐ | T. ☐ |
| F. ☐ | W. ☐ | W. ☐ | P. ☐ |
| B. ☐ | P. ☐ | C. ☐ | C. ☐ |

## 7

| S.D. | P.L. | P.G. | S.G. |
|------|------|------|------|
| P. ☐ | F. ☐ | F. ☐ | T. ☐ |
| F. ☐ | W. ☐ | W. ☐ | P. ☐ |
| B. ☐ | P. ☐ | C. ☐ | C. ☐ |

## 8

| S.D. | P.L. | P.G. | S.G. |
|------|------|------|------|
| P. ☐ | F. ☐ | F. ☐ | T. ☐ |
| F. ☐ | W. ☐ | W. ☐ | P. ☐ |
| B. ☐ | P. ☐ | C. ☐ | C. ☐ |

## 13

| S.D. | P.L. | P.G. | S.G. |
|------|------|------|------|
| P. ☐ | F. ☐ | F. ☐ | T. ☐ |
| F. ☐ | W. ☐ | W. ☐ | P. ☐ |
| B. ☐ | P. ☐ | C. ☐ | C. ☐ |

## 14

| S.D. | P.L. | P.G. | S.G. |
|------|------|------|------|
| P. ☐ | F. ☐ | F. ☐ | T. ☐ |
| F. ☐ | W. ☐ | W. ☐ | P. ☐ |
| B. ☐ | P. ☐ | C. ☐ | C. ☐ |

## 15

| S.D. | P.L. | P.G. | S.G. |
|------|------|------|------|
| P. ☐ | F. ☐ | F. ☐ | T. ☐ |
| F. ☐ | W. ☐ | W. ☐ | P. ☐ |
| B. ☐ | P. ☐ | C. ☐ | C. ☐ |

## 16

| S.D. | P.L. | P.G. | S.G. |
|------|------|------|------|
| P. ☐ | F. ☐ | F. ☐ | T. ☐ |
| F. ☐ | W. ☐ | W. ☐ | P. ☐ |
| B. ☐ | P. ☐ | C. ☐ | C. ☐ |

## 21

| S.D. | P.L. | P.G. | S.G. |
|------|------|------|------|
| P. ☐ | F. ☐ | F. ☐ | T. ☐ |
| F. ☐ | W. ☐ | W. ☐ | P. ☐ |
| B. ☐ | P. ☐ | C. ☐ | C. ☐ |

## 22

| S.D. | P.L. | P.G. | S.G. |
|------|------|------|------|
| P. ☐ | F. ☐ | F. ☐ | T. ☐ |
| F. ☐ | W. ☐ | W. ☐ | P. ☐ |
| B. ☐ | P. ☐ | C. ☐ | C. ☐ |

## 23

| S.D. | P.L. | P.G. | S.G. |
|------|------|------|------|
| P. ☐ | F. ☐ | F. ☐ | T. ☐ |
| F. ☐ | W. ☐ | W. ☐ | P. ☐ |
| B. ☐ | P. ☐ | C. ☐ | C. ☐ |

## 24

| S.D. | P.L. | P.G. | S.G. |
|------|------|------|------|
| P. ☐ | F. ☐ | F. ☐ | T. ☐ |
| F. ☐ | W. ☐ | W. ☐ | P. ☐ |
| B. ☐ | P. ☐ | C. ☐ | C. ☐ |

## 29

| S.D. | P.L. | P.G. | S.G. |
|------|------|------|------|
| P. ☐ | F. ☐ | F. ☐ | T. ☐ |
| F. ☐ | W. ☐ | W. ☐ | P. ☐ |
| B. ☐ | P. ☐ | C. ☐ | C. ☐ |

## 30

| S.D. | P.L. | P.G. | S.G. |
|------|------|------|------|
| P. ☐ | F. ☐ | F. ☐ | T. ☐ |
| F. ☐ | W. ☐ | W. ☐ | P. ☐ |
| B. ☐ | P. ☐ | C. ☐ | C. ☐ |

**Proverbs 16:9**

We can make our plans, but the Lord determines our steps.

## Personal Goals

**Family**

**Work/School/Social**

**Challenge**

## Sport Goals

**Training**

**Performance**

**Competition Results**

(For designing your MAP - Monthly Action Plan - see introduction pages)

you live. Remember, he is the one who has identified you as his own, guaranteeing that you will be saved on the day of redemption. [31]Get rid of all bitterness, rage, anger, harsh words, and slander, as well as all types of malicious behaviour. [32]Instead, be kind to each other, tender-hearted, forgiving one another, just as God through Christ has forgiven you.

## Living in the Light

# 5

Follow God's example in everything you do, because you are his dear children. [2]Live a life filled with love for others, following the example of Christ, who loved you and gave himself as a sacrifice to take away your sins. And God was pleased, because that sacrifice was like sweet perfume to him. [3]Let there be no sexual immorality, impurity, or greed among you. Such sins have no place among God's people. [4]Obscene stories, foolish talk, and coarse jokes—these are not for you. Instead, let there be thankfulness to God. [5]You can be sure that no immoral, impure, or greedy person will inherit the Kingdom of Christ and of God. For a greedy person is really an idolater who worships the things of this world. [6]Don't be fooled by those who try to excuse these sins, for the terrible anger of God comes upon all those who disobey him. [7]Don't participate in the things these people do. [8]For though your hearts were once full of darkness, now you are full of light from the Lord, and your behaviour should show it! [9]For this light within you produces only what is good and right and true.

[10]Try to find out what is pleasing to the Lord. [11]Take no part in the worthless deeds of evil and darkness; instead, rebuke and expose them. [12]It is shameful even to talk about the things that ungodly people do in secret. [13]But when the light shines on them, it becomes clear how evil these things are. [14]And where your light shines, it will expose their evil deeds. This is why it is said,

"Awake, O sleeper,
rise up from the dead,
and Christ will give you light."

## Living by the Spirit's Power

[15]So be careful how you live, not as fools but as those who are wise. [16]**Make the most of every opportunity for doing good in these evil days.** [17]Don't act thoughtlessly, but try to understand what the Lord wants you to do. [18]Don't be drunk with wine, because that will ruin your life. Instead, let the Holy Spirit fill and control you. [19]Then you will sing psalms and hymns and spiritual songs among yourselves, making music to the Lord in your hearts. [20]And you will always give thanks for everything to God the Father in the name of our Lord Jesus Christ.

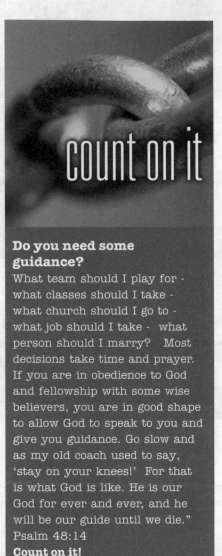

## count on it

### Do you need some guidance?

What team should I play for - what classes should I take - what church should I go to - what job should I take - what person should I marry? Most decisions take time and prayer. If you are in obedience to God and fellowship with some wise believers, you are in good shape to allow God to speak to you and give you guidance. Go slow and as my old coach used to say, 'stay on your knees!' For that is what God is like. He is our God for ever and ever, and he will be our guide until we die."
Psalm 48:14
**Count on it!**

## Spirit-Guided Relationships: Wives and Husbands

[21]And further, you will submit to one another out of reverence for Christ. [22]You wives will submit to your husbands as you do to the Lord. [23]For a husband is the head of his wife as Christ is the head of his body, the church; he gave his life to be her Saviour. [24]As the church submits to Christ, so you wives must submit to your husbands in everything.

[25]And you husbands must love your wives with the same love Christ showed the church. He gave up his life for her [26]to make her holy and clean, washed by baptism and God's word. [27]He did this to present her to himself as a glorious church without a spot or wrinkle or any other blemish. Instead, she will be holy and without fault. [28]In the same way, husbands ought to love their wives as they love their own bodies. For a man is

actually loving himself when he loves his wife. [29]No one hates his own body but lovingly cares for it, just as Christ cares for his body, which is the church. [30]And we are his body.

[31]As the Scriptures say, "A man leaves his father and mother and is joined to his wife, and the two are united into one."

[32]This is a great mystery, but it is an illustration of the way Christ and the church are one. [33]So again I say, each man must love his wife as he loves himself, and the wife must respect her husband.

## Children and Parents

# 6

Children, obey your parents because you belong to the Lord, for this is the right thing to do. [2]"Honour your father and mother." This is the first of the Ten Commandments that ends with a promise. [3]And this is the promise: If you honour your father and mother, "you will live a long life, full of blessing."

[4]And now a word to you fathers. Don't make your children angry by the way you treat them. Rather, bring them up with the discipline and instruction approved by the Lord.

## Slaves and Masters

[5]Slaves, obey your earthly masters with deep respect and fear. Serve them sincerely as you would serve Christ. [6]Work hard, but not just to please your masters when they are watching. As slaves of Christ, do the will of God with all your heart. [7]Work with enthusiasm, as though you were working for the Lord rather than for people. [8]Remember that the Lord will reward each one of us for the good we do, whether we are slaves or free.

[9]And in the same way, you masters must treat your slaves right. Don't threaten them; remember, you both have the same Master in heaven, and he has no favourites.

STATS

Athletic star Jesse Owens beat a racehorse over a 100-yard course in 1936.

## The Whole Armour of God

[10]A final word: Be strong with the Lord's mighty power. [11]Put on all of God's armour so that you will be able to stand firm against all strategies and tricks of the Devil. [12]For we are not fighting against people made of flesh and blood, but against the evil rulers and authorities of the unseen world, against those mighty powers of darkness who rule this world, and against wicked spirits in the heavenly realms.

[13]Use every piece of God's armour to resist the enemy in the time of evil, so that after the battle you will still be standing firm. [14]Stand your ground, putting on the sturdy belt of truth and the body armour of God's righteousness. [15]For shoes, put on the peace that comes from the Good News, so that you will be fully prepared. [16]In every battle you will need faith as your shield to stop the fiery arrows aimed at you by Satan. [17]Put on salvation as your helmet, and take the sword of the Spirit, which is the word of God. [18]Pray at all times and on every occasion in the power of the Holy Spirit. Stay alert and be persistent in your prayers for all Christians everywhere.

[19]And pray for me, too. Ask God to give me the right words as I boldly explain God's secret plan that the Good News is for the Gentiles, too. [20]I am in chains now for preaching this message as God's ambassador. But pray that I will keep on speaking boldly for him, as I should.

## Final Greetings

[21]Tychicus, a much loved brother and faithful helper in the Lord's work, will tell you all about how I am getting along. [22]I am sending him to you for just this purpose. He will let you know how we are, and he will encourage you. [23]May God give you peace, dear brothers and sisters, and love with faith, from God the Father and the Lord Jesus Christ. [24]May God's grace be upon all who love our Lord Jesus Christ with an undying love.

**The first Bible translated into English was started by John Wycliffe in 1382 and completed in 1388.**

# Run for the Prize?

'Remember that in a race everyone runs, but only one person gets the prize. You also must run in such a way that you will win. All athletes practise strict self-control. They do it to win a prize that will fade away, but we do it for an eternal prize.'
I Corinthians 9:24-25

Here Paul is drawing on his knowledge and understanding of Greek culture in the great city of Corinth. At the time when Paul was writing, the population was estimated to have been about 650,000 people. Over 400,000 were slaves. Competing in the city's games would have been seen as an escape from the oppressive world of slavery. To win a wreath (medal) in the biannual Isthmian Games, the second largest games in Greece, could mean physical emancipation. Performing well in sport could offer you freedom. Paul would have understood the cultural power sport had on the psyche of even the most casual fan in Greece. The apostle Paul was committed. Paul had a coach's heart: 'strive', 'beat your body', 'look forward', 'Press-on' — these were all major themes in his letters. It was noted by the historian and gospel writer Luke, that Paul was once nearly beaten to death and driven out of a city. Paul, never to be discouraged, got right back up when

DEVOTIONAL

he had recovered and went back into the city that very night. He was focused and purpose-driven. If he were a coach he would expect and the get the best from you. He hated a half-hearted, 'aimless' effort.

Paul takes everyday illustrations and puts them into eternal perspective. Is your goal high enough? Most of us have a yearning for glory, a passion to win. There is an innate longing set in the heart of man to achieve; unfortunately, we often do not aim at eternal achievement, but merely earthly success, which will not satisfy. Paul understood these 'noble desires' couldn't be satisfied with a wooden wreath or a gold medal. Paul gives us the answer; 'Run for the prize that will not perish' live your life with a higher purpose, for a crown that will last forever. The better the sports person you are, the easier it should be to understand that your earthly prizes will not completely satisfy. I know some of you are reading this and saying to yourselves, 'Ah Steve, you do not know my goals. If only I could win that prize, play for that team or break that record then I would be happy, then I could sit back and rest on my laurels (trophy).'

I really hope you realise your dream and you make that team or win that prize, then you will understand that although winning is great, the euphoria does not last. It is easier to explain these concepts to champions, than to those who think, 'if only'. Go for the crown that will last forever.

## Reflection
Do I keep chasing after things in life that will not make me happy for long?

## Prayer
Lord, there is a yearning in my heart, help me to satisfy it.

'He is no fool who gives what he cannot keep to gain what he could never lose.'
Jim Elliot

Nicked from: A Sporting Guide to Eternity, Steve Connor, Christian Focus Publications - ISBN 1-85792-746-X

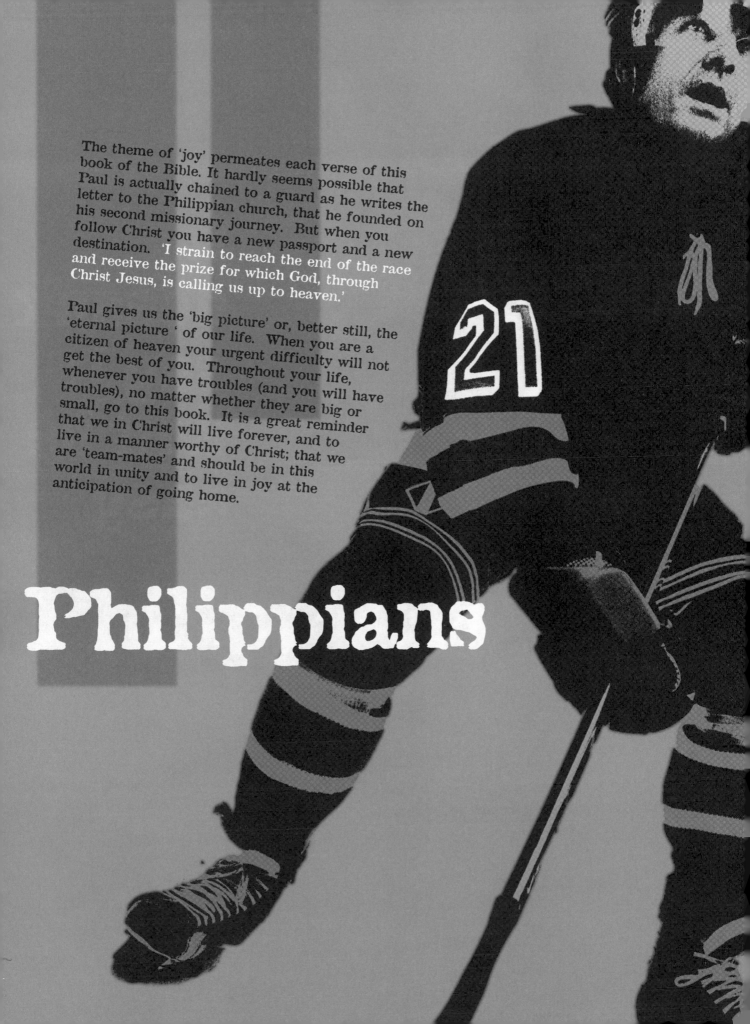

The theme of 'joy' permeates each verse of this book of the Bible. It hardly seems possible that Paul is actually chained to a guard as he writes the letter to the Philippian church, that he founded on his second missionary journey. But when you follow Christ you have a new passport and a new destination. 'I strain to reach the end of the race and receive the prize for which God, through Christ Jesus, is calling us up to heaven.'

Paul gives us the 'big picture' or, better still, the 'eternal picture ' of our life. When you are a citizen of heaven your urgent difficulty will not get the best of you. Throughout your life, whenever you have troubles (and you will have troubles), no matter whether they are big or small, go to this book. It is a great reminder that we in Christ will live forever, and to live in a manner worthy of Christ; that we are 'team-mates' and should be in this world in unity and to live in joy at the anticipation of going home.

# Philippians

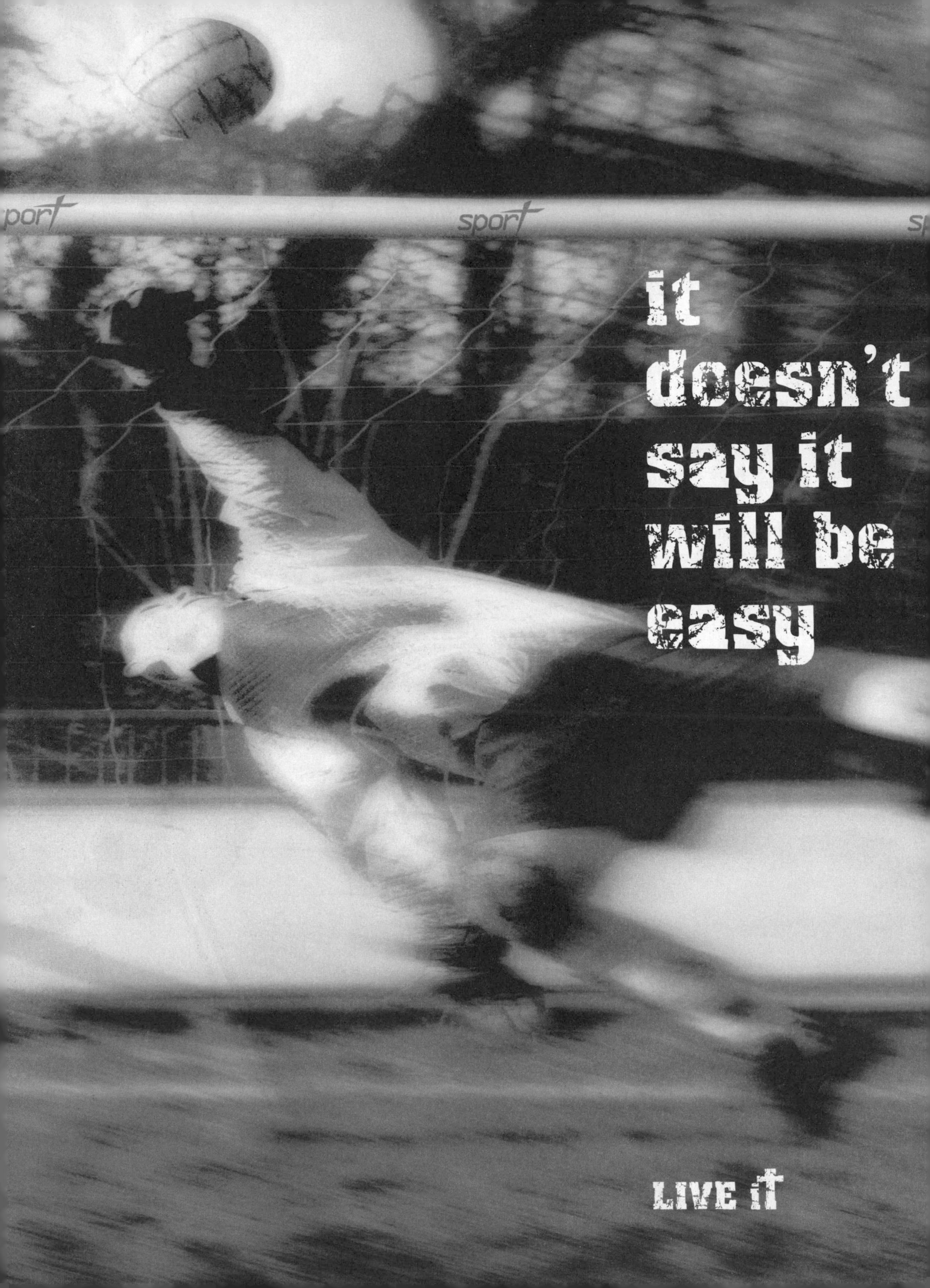

it
doesn't
say it
will be
easy

LIVE it

# PHILIPPIANS

## Greetings from Paul

**1**

This letter is from Paul and Timothy, slaves of Christ Jesus.

It is written to all of God's people in Philippi, who believe in Christ Jesus, and to the elders and deacons. [2]May God our Father and the Lord Jesus Christ give you grace and peace.

## Paul's Thanksgiving and Prayer

[3]Every time I think of you, I give thanks to my God. [4]I always pray for you, and I make my requests with a heart full of joy [5]because you have been my partners in spreading the Good News about Christ from the time you first heard it until now. [6]And I am sure that God, who began the good work within you, will continue his work until it is finally finished on that day when Christ Jesus comes back again.

[7]It is right that I should feel as I do about all of you, for you have a very special place in my heart. We have shared together the blessings of God, both when I was in prison and when I was out, defending the truth and telling others the Good News. [8]God knows how much I love you and long for you with the tender compassion of Christ Jesus. [9]**I pray that your love for each other will overflow more and more, and that you will keep on growing in your knowledge and understanding.** [10]For I want you to understand what really matters, so that you may live pure and blameless lives until Christ returns. [11]May you always be filled with the fruit of your salvation—those good things that are produced in your life by Jesus Christ—for this will bring much glory and praise to God.

## Paul's Joy That Christ Is Preached

[12]And I want you to know, dear brothers and sisters, that everything that has happened to me here has helped to spread the Good News. [13]For everyone here, including all the soldiers in the palace guard, knows that I am in chains because of Christ. [14]And because of my imprisonment, many of the Christians here have gained confidence and become more bold in telling others about Christ.

[15]Some are preaching out of jealousy and rivalry. But others preach about Christ with pure motives. [16]They preach because they love me, for they know the Lord brought me here to defend the Good News. [17]Those others do not have pure motives as they preach about Christ. They preach with selfish ambition, not sincerely, intending to make my chains more painful to me. [18]But whether or not their motives are pure, the fact remains that the message about Christ is being preached, so I rejoice. And I will continue to rejoice.

[19]For I know that as you pray for me and as the Spirit of Jesus Christ helps me, this will all turn out for my deliverance.

## Paul's Life for Christ

[20]For I live in eager expectation and hope that I will never do anything that causes me shame, but that I will always be bold for Christ, as I have been in the past, and that my life will always honour Christ, whether I live or I die. [21]For to me, living is for Christ, and dying is even better. [22]Yet if I live, that means fruitful service for Christ. I really don't know which is better. [23]I'm torn between two desires: Sometimes I want to live, and sometimes I long to go and be with Christ. That would be far better for me, [24]but it is better for you that I live.

[25]I am convinced of this, so I will continue with you so that you will grow and experience the joy of your faith. [26]Then when I return to you, you will have even more reason to boast about what Christ Jesus has done for me.

## Live as Citizens of Heaven

[27]But whatever happens to me, you must live in a manner worthy of the Good News about Christ, as citizens of heaven. Then, whether I come and see you again or only hear about you, I will know that you are standing side by side, fighting together for the Good News. [28]Don't be intimidated by your enemies. This will be a sign to them that they are going to be destroyed, but that you are going to be saved, even by God himself. [29]For you have been given not only the privilege of trusting in Christ but also the privilege of suffering for him. [30]We are in this fight together. You have seen me suffer for him in the past, and you know that I am still in the midst of this great struggle.

## Unity through Humility

**2**

Is there any encouragement from belonging to Christ? Any comfort from his love? Any fellowship together in the Spirit? Are your hearts tender and sympathetic? [2]Then make me truly happy by agreeing

**STAND POINT**

**When you need the 'Big Picture'**
**1:23**

I'm torn between two desires: Sometimes I want to live, and sometimes I long to go and be with Christ. That would be far better for me.

**WHAT DOES IT MEAN?**

**Armour**
is employed in the Bible to denote military equipment, both offensive and defensive. Reference is made by Paul (Eph. 6:14-17) that Christians are in battle and need the whole body protected. You would not go into a major competition without the proper kit, how much more do we have to strap on God's kit for offence and defence. Note, there is no armour for the back, but only for the front; NEVER RETREAT.

## About 50 Bibles are sold every minute.

wholeheartedly with each other, loving one another, and working together with one heart and purpose.
[3]Don't be selfish; don't live to make a good impression on others. Be humble, thinking of others as better than yourself.
[4]Don't think only about your own affairs, but be interested in others, too, and what they are doing.

CH 2:5-11 WHAT'S IT SAYING?

WHAT AM I GOING TO DO ABOUT IT?

## Christ's Humility and Exaltation

[5]Your attitude should be the same that Christ Jesus had.
[6]Though he was God, he did not demand and cling to his rights as God. [7]He made himself nothing; he took the humble position of a slave and appeared in human form. [8]And in human form he obediently humbled himself even further by dying a criminal's death on a cross. [9]Because of this, God

raised him up to the heights of heaven and gave him a name that is above every other name, [10]so that at the name of Jesus every knee will bow, in heaven and on earth and under the earth, [11]and every tongue will confess that Jesus Christ is Lord, to the glory of God the Father.

## Shine Brightly for Christ

[12]Dearest friends, you were always so careful to follow my instructions when I was with you. And now that I am away you must be even more careful to put into action God's saving work in your lives, obeying God with deep reverence and fear. [13]For God is working in you, giving you the desire to obey him and the power to do what pleases him.

[14]In everything you do, stay away from complaining and arguing, [15]so that no one can speak a word of blame against you. You are to live clean, innocent lives as children of God in a dark world full of crooked and perverse people. Let your lives shine brightly before them. [16]Hold tightly to the word of life, so that when Christ returns, I will be proud that I did not lose the

race and that my work was not useless. [17]But even if my life is to be poured out like a drink offering to complete the sacrifice of your faithful service (that is, if I am to die for you), I will rejoice, and I want to share my joy with all of you. [18]And you should be happy about this and rejoice with me.

## Paul Commends Timothy

[19]If the Lord Jesus is willing, I hope to send Timothy to you soon. Then when he comes back, he can cheer me up by telling me how you are getting along. [20]I have

## The Priceless Gain of Knowing Christ

# 3

Whatever happens, dear brothers and sisters, may the Lord give you joy. I never get tired of telling you this. I am doing this for your own good.

[2]Watch out for those dogs, those wicked men and their evil deeds, those mutilators who say you must be circumcised to be saved.

in his death, [11]so that, somehow, I can experience the resurrection from the dead!

## Pressing towards the Goal

[12]I don't mean to say that I have already achieved these things or that I have already reached perfection! But I keep working towards that day when I will finally be all that Christ Jesus saved me for and wants me to be. [13]No, dear brothers and sisters, I am still not all I should be, but I am focusing all my energies on this one thing: Forgetting the past and looking forward to what lies ahead, [14]I strain to reach the end of the

'The secret of living' Philippians 4:12-13

Most superstars realise that all their achievements do not satisfy for long. Are you content, only when you are playing well, when your team is winning - when life is going great? Then the rest of your life will be pretty boring and miserable. The Bible does not promise that your life will be easy or that every time you compete you will win. What the scripture does say is that you will find fulfillment and satisfaction in Christ, and he will give you strength to enjoy life through the good and bad times.

no one else like Timothy, who genuinely cares about your welfare. [21]All the others care only for themselves and not for what matters to Jesus Christ. [22]But you know how Timothy has proved himself. Like a son with his father, he has helped me in preaching the Good News. [23]I hope to send him to you just as soon as I find out what is going to happen to me here. [24]And I have confidence from the Lord that I myself will come to see you soon.

## Paul Commends Epaphroditus

[25]Meanwhile, I thought I should send Epaphroditus back to you. He is a true brother, a faithful worker, and a courageous soldier. And he was your messenger to help me in my need. [26]Now I am sending him home again, for he has been longing to see you, and he was very distressed that you heard he was ill. [27]And he surely was ill; in fact, he almost died. But God had mercy on him—and also on me, so that I would not have such unbearable sorrow.

[28]So I am all the more anxious to send him back to you, for I know you will be glad to see him, and that will lighten all my cares. [29]Welcome him with Christian love and with great joy, and be sure to honour people like him. [30]For he risked his life for the work of Christ, and he was at the point of death while trying to do for me the things you couldn't do because you were far away.

[3]For we who worship God in the Spirit are the only ones who are truly circumcised. We put no confidence in human effort. Instead, we boast about what Christ Jesus has done for us.

[4]Yet I could have confidence in myself if anyone could. If others have reason for confidence in their own efforts, I have even more! [5]For I was circumcised when I was eight days old, having been born into a pure-blooded Jewish family that is a branch of the tribe of Benjamin. So I am a real Jew if there ever was one! What's more, I was a member of the Pharisees, who demand the strictest obedience to the Jewish law. [6]And zealous? Yes, in fact, I harshly persecuted the church. And I obeyed the Jewish law so carefully that I was never accused of any fault.

[7]I once thought all these things were so very important, but now I consider them worthless because of what Christ has done. [8]Yes, everything else is worthless when compared with the priceless gain of knowing Christ Jesus my Lord. **I have discarded everything else, counting it all as rubbish, so that I may have Christ** [9]and become one with him. I no longer count on my own goodness or my ability to obey God's law, but I trust Christ to save me. For God's way of making us right with himself depends on faith. [10]As a result, I can really know Christ and experience the mighty power that raised him from the dead. I can learn what it means to suffer with him, sharing

race and receive the prize for which God, through Christ Jesus, is calling us up to heaven.

[15]I hope all of you who are mature Christians will agree on these things. If you disagree on some point, I believe God will make it plain to you. [16]But we must be sure to obey the truth we have learned already.

[17]Dear brothers and sisters, pattern your lives after mine, and learn from those who follow our example. [18]For I have told you often before, and I say it again with tears in my eyes, that there are many whose conduct shows they are really enemies of the cross of Christ. [19]Their future is eternal destruction. Their god is their appetite, they brag about shameful things, and all they think about is this life here on earth. [20]**But we are citizens of heaven, where the Lord Jesus Christ lives. And we are eagerly waiting for him to return as our Saviour.** [21]He will take these weak mortal bodies of ours and change them into glorious bodies like his own, using the same mighty power that he will use to conquer everything, everywhere.

# 4

Dear brothers and sisters, I love you and long to see you, for you are my joy and the reward for my work. So please stay true to the Lord, my dear friends.

## Paul's Final Thoughts

[2]And now I want to plead with those two women, Euodia and

# profiles

## Abraham:

Imagine walking up a mountain with your one pure precious son knowing that you are to show obedience to God by sacrificing him. Another model of persistence and obedience, Abraham was promised that, through him, his descendants would create a great nation and all the people on earth would be blessed through him. He was rich, given a huge amount of land but could have no offspring. He disobeyed God and had a child with his wife's servant. But God made good his promise and when Abraham and his wife were very old they had a true heir - Isaac. But God tested Abraham and it was a cruel test. 'Show your love for me by sacrificing your only son.' Climbing the mountain Isaac, carrying the wood for the sacrifice, asked 'but where is the sacrifice?' Abraham said 'God will provide.' Abraham was willing but at the last he did not have to sacrifice his son. It was a cruel test - a fact God knew all too well. Fifteen hundred years later God did provide the sacrifice as he sent his own son up the hill carrying a wooden cross and fulfilled Abraham's promise to Isaac by allowing his own son, a descendant, to die and take away the sin of the world.

For more on Abraham, start in Chapter 11 of Genesis in the Old Testament.

Syntyche. Please, because you belong to the Lord, settle your disagreement. [3]And I ask you, my true teammate, to help these women, for they worked hard with me in telling others the Good News. And they worked with Clement and the rest of my co-workers, whose names are written in the Book of Life.

[4]Always be full of joy in the Lord. I say it again—rejoice!

[5]Let everyone see that you are considerate in all you do. Remember, the Lord is coming soon.

[6]Don't worry about anything; instead, pray about everything. Tell God what you need, and thank him for all he has done. [7]If you do this, you will experience God's peace, which is far more wonderful than the human mind can understand. His peace will guard your hearts and minds as you live in Christ Jesus.

## action

**CH 6:14-18 WHAT'S IT SAYING?**

**WHAT AM I GOING TO DO ABOUT IT?**

[8]And now, dear brothers and sisters, let me say one more thing as I close this letter. Fix your thoughts on what is true and honourable and right. Think about things that are pure and lovely and admirable. Think about things that are excellent and worthy of praise. [9]Keep putting into practice all you learned from me and heard from me and saw me doing, and the God of peace will be with you.

## Paul's Thanks for Their Gifts

[10]How grateful I am, and how I praise the Lord that you are concerned about me again. I know you have always been concerned for me, but for a while you didn't have the chance to help me. [11]Not that I was ever in need, for I have learned how to get along happily whether I have much or little. [12]I know how to live on almost nothing or with everything. I have learned the secret of living in every situation, whether it is with a full stomach or empty, with plenty or little. [13]For I can do everything with the help of Christ who gives me the strength I need. [14]But even so, you have done well to share with me in my present difficulty. [15]As you know, you Philippians were the only ones who gave me financial help when I brought you the Good News and then travelled on from Macedonia. No other church did this. [16]Even when I was in Thessalonica you sent help more than once. [17]I don't say this because I want a gift from you. What I want is for you to receive a well-earned reward because of your kindness. [18]At the moment I have all I need—more than I need! I am generously supplied with the gifts you sent me with Epaphroditus. They are a sweet-smelling sacrifice that is acceptable to God and pleases him. [19]And this same God who takes care of me will supply all your needs from his glorious riches, which have been given to us in Christ Jesus. [20]Now glory be to God our Father for ever and ever. Amen.

## Paul's Final Greetings

[21]Give my greetings to all the Christians there. The brothers who are with me here send you their greetings. [22]And all the other Christians send their greetings, too, especially those who work in Caesar's palace.

[23]May the grace of the Lord Jesus Christ be with your spirit.

### STATS

Before they were allowed to compete in the state of Indiana, USA, boxers and pro-wrestlers in 1954 had to swear under oath they were not communists.

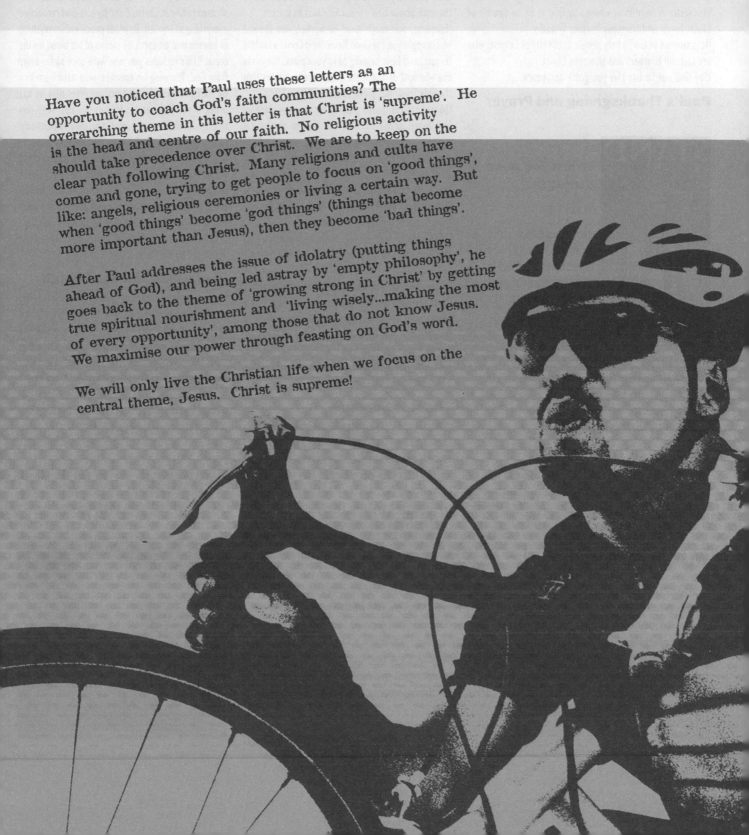

# Colossians

Have you noticed that Paul uses these letters as an opportunity to coach God's faith communities? The overarching theme in this letter is that Christ is 'supreme'. He is the head and centre of our faith. No religious activity should take precedence over Christ. We are to keep on the clear path following Christ. Many religions and cults have come and gone, trying to get people to focus on 'good things', like: angels, religious ceremonies or living a certain way. But when 'good things' become 'god things' (things that become more important than Jesus), then they become 'bad things'.

After Paul addresses the issue of idolatry (putting things ahead of God), and being led astray by 'empty philosophy', he goes back to the theme of 'growing strong in Christ' by getting true spiritual nourishment and 'living wisely...making the most of every opportunity', among those that do not know Jesus. We maximise our power through feasting on God's word.

We will only live the Christian life when we focus on the central theme, Jesus. Christ is supreme!

# COLOSSIANS

## Greetings from Paul

# 1

This letter is from Paul, chosen by God to be an apostle of Christ Jesus, and from our brother Timothy.
[2]It is written to God's holy people in the city of Colosse, who are faithful brothers and sisters in Christ.
May God our Father give you grace and peace.

## Paul's Thanksgiving and Prayer

### When you need strength

### 1:11-12

We also pray that you will be strengthened with his glorious power so that you will have all the patience and endurance you need. May you be filled with joy, always thanking the Father, who has enabled you to share the inheritance that belongs to God's holy people, who live in the light.

[3]We always pray for you, and we give thanks to God the Father of our Lord Jesus Christ, [4]for we have heard that you trust in Christ Jesus and that you love all of God's people.

[5]You do this because you are looking forward to the joys of heaven—as you have been ever since you first heard the truth of the Good News. [6]This same Good News that came to you is going out all over the world. It is changing lives everywhere, just as it changed yours that very first day you heard and understood the truth about God's great kindness to sinners.
[7]Epaphras, our much loved co-worker, was the one who brought you the Good News. He is Christ's faithful servant, and he is helping us in your place. [8]He is the one who told us about the great love for others that the Holy Spirit has given you.

[9]So we have continued praying for you ever since we first heard about you. We ask God to give you a complete understanding of what he wants to do in your lives, and we ask him to make you wise with spiritual wisdom. [10]Then the way you live will always honour and please the Lord, and you will continually do good, kind things for others. All the while, you will learn to know God better and better.
[11]We also pray that you will be strengthened with his glorious power so that you will have all the patience and endurance you need. May you be filled with joy, [12]always thanking the Father, who has enabled you to share the inheritance that belongs to God's holy people, who live in the light. [13]For he has rescued us from the one who rules in the kingdom of darkness, and he has brought us into the Kingdom of his dear Son. [14]God has purchased our freedom with his blood and has forgiven all our sins.

## Christ Is Supreme

[15]Christ is the visible image of the invisible God. He existed before God made anything at all and is supreme over all creation. [16]Christ is the one through whom God created everything in heaven and earth. He made the things we can see and the things we can't see—kings, kingdoms, rulers, and authorities.

Everything has been created through him and for him. [17]He existed before everything else began, and he holds all creation together.

[18]Christ is the head of the church, which is his body. He is the first of all who will rise from the dead, so he is first in everything. [19]For God in all his fullness was pleased to live in Christ, [20]and by him God reconciled everything to himself. He made peace with everything in heaven and on earth by means of his blood on the cross. [21]This includes you who were once so far away from God. You were his enemies, separated from him by your evil thoughts and actions, [22]yet now he has brought you back as his friends. He has done this through his death on the cross in his own human body. As a result, he has brought you into the very presence of God, and you are holy and blameless as you stand before him without a single fault. [23]But you must continue to believe this truth and stand in it firmly. Don't drift away from the assurance you received when you heard the Good News. The Good News has been preached all over the world, and I, Paul, have been appointed by God to proclaim it.

## Paul's Work for the Church

[24]I am glad when I suffer for you in my body, for I am completing what remains of Christ's sufferings for his body, the church. [25]God has given me the responsibility of serving his church by proclaiming his message in all its fullness to you Gentiles. [26]This message was kept secret for centuries and generations past, but now it has been revealed to his own holy people. [27]For it has pleased God to tell his people that the riches and glory of Christ are for you Gentiles, too. For this is the secret: Christ lives in you, and this is your assurance that you will share in his glory.

[28]So everywhere we go, we tell everyone about Christ. We warn them and teach them with all the wisdom God has given us, for we want to present them to

## Winners keep learning!

Competition will push you to be better! Sport has many virtues that can help a person develop in mind, body and soul. You certainly have to be aware of the pitfalls involved in sport, but enjoy the benefits! Sport creates great opportunities to learn and live out God's principles, which develop our Christian character. Winners will never stop learning new skills, life principles and how to approach and respond respectively to others. 'It is not what the boy does with the ball…but what the ball does to the boy.' "Cry out for insight and understanding. Search for them as you would for lost money or hidden treasure." Proverbs 2:3-4

Winners want to know!

Snowboarding made its recent Olympic entrance in the 1998 Winter Games in Nagano, Japan.

God, perfect in their relationship to Christ. [29]I work very hard at this, as I depend on Christ's mighty power that works within me.

# 2

I want you to know how much I have agonized for you and for the church at Laodicea, and for many other friends who have never known me personally. [2]My goal is that they will be encouraged and knit together by strong ties of love. I want them to have full confidence because they have complete understanding of God's secret plan, which is Christ himself. [3]In him lie hidden all the treasures of wisdom and knowledge.

[4]I am telling you this so that no one will be able to deceive you with persuasive arguments. [5]For though I am far away from you, my heart is with you. And I am very happy because you are living as you should and because of your strong faith in Christ.

## Freedom from Rules and New Life in Christ

[6]And now, just as you accepted Christ Jesus as your Lord, you must continue to live in obedience to him. **[7]Let your roots grow down into him and draw up nourishment from him, so you will grow in faith, strong and vigorous in the truth you were taught. Let your lives overflow with thanksgiving for all he has done.**

[8]Don't let anyone lead you astray with empty philosophy and high-sounding nonsense that come from human thinking and from the evil powers of this world, and not from Christ. [9]For in Christ the fullness of God lives in a human body, [10]and you are complete through your union with Christ. He is the Lord over every ruler and authority in the universe.

[11]When you came to Christ, you were "circumcised," but not by a physical procedure. It was a spiritual procedure—the cutting away of your sinful nature. [12]For you were buried with Christ when you were baptized. And with him you were raised to a new life because you trusted the mighty power of God, who raised Christ from the dead.

[13]You were dead because of your sins and because your sinful nature was not yet cut away. Then God made you alive with Christ. He forgave all our sins. [14]He cancelled the record that contained the charges against us. He took it and destroyed it by nailing it to Christ's cross. [15]In this way, God disarmed the evil rulers and authorities. He shamed them publicly by his victory over them on the cross of Christ.

[16]So don't let anyone condemn you for what you eat or drink, or for not celebrating certain holy days or new-moon ceremonies or Sabbaths. [17]For these rules were only shadows of the real thing, Christ himself. [18]Don't let anyone condemn you by insisting on self-denial. And don't let anyone say you must worship angels, even though they say they have had visions about this. These people claim to be so humble, but their sinful minds have made them proud. [19]But they are not connected to Christ, the head of the body. For we are joined together in his body by his strong sinews, and we grow only as we get our nourishment and strength from God.

[20]You have died with Christ, and he has set you free from the evil powers of this world. So why do you keep on following rules of the world, such as, [21]"Don't handle, don't eat, don't touch." [22]Such rules are mere human teaching about things that are gone as soon as we use them. [23]These rules may seem wise because they require strong devotion, humility, and severe bodily discipline. But they have no effect when it comes to conquering a person's evil thoughts and desires.

## CH 2:13-15 WHAT'S IT SAYING?

## WHAT AM I GOING TO DO ABOUT IT?

Who would be the five best teams to play for?

1
2
3
4
5

## Living the New Life

# 3

Since you have been raised to new life with Christ, set your sights on the realities of heaven, where Christ sits at God's right hand in the place of honour and power. [2]Let heaven fill your thoughts. Do not think only about things down here on earth. [3]For you died when Christ died, and your real life is hidden with Christ in God. [4]And when Christ, who is your real life, is revealed to the whole world, you will share in all his glory.

[5]So put to death the sinful, earthly things lurking within you. Have nothing to do with sexual sin, impurity, lust, and shameful desires. Don't be greedy for the good things of this life, for that is idolatry. [6]God's terrible anger will come upon those who do such things. [7]You used to do them when your life was still part of this world. [8]But now is the time to get rid of anger, rage, malicious behaviour, slander, and dirty language.

[9]Don't lie to each other, for you have stripped off your old evil nature and all its wicked deeds. [10]In its place you have clothed yourselves with a brand-new nature that is continually being renewed as you learn more and more about Christ, who created this new nature within you. [11]In this new life, it doesn't matter if you are a Jew or a Gentile, circumcised or uncircumcised, barbaric, uncivilized, slave, or free. Christ is all that matters, and he lives in all of us.

[12]Since God chose you to be the holy people whom he loves, you must clothe yourselves with tender-hearted mercy, kindness, humility, gentleness, and patience. [13]You must make allowance for each other's faults and forgive the person who offends you. Remember, the Lord forgave you, so you must forgive others. [14]And the most important piece of clothing you must wear is love. Love is what binds us all together in perfect harmony. [15]And let the peace that comes from Christ rule in your hearts. For as members of one body you are all called to live in peace. And always be thankful.

[16]**Let the words of Christ, in all their richness, live in your hearts and make you wise. Use his words to teach and counsel each other. Sing psalms and hymns and spiritual songs to God with thankful hearts.** [17]And whatever you do or say, let it be as a representative of the Lord Jesus, all the while giving thanks through him to God the Father.

## Instructions for Christian Households

[18]You wives must submit to your husbands, as is fitting for those who belong to the Lord. [19]And you husbands must love your wives and never treat them harshly.

[20]You children must always obey your parents, for this is what pleases the Lord. [21]Fathers, don't aggravate your children. If you do, they will become discouraged and quit trying.

[22]You slaves must obey your earthly masters in everything you do. Try to please them all the time, not just when they are watching you. Obey them willingly because of your reverent fear of the Lord. [23]Work hard and cheerfully at whatever you do, as though you were working for the Lord rather than for people. [24]Remember that the Lord will give you an inheritance as your reward, and the Master you are serving is Christ. [25]But if you do what is wrong, you will be paid back for the wrong you have done. For God has no favourites who can get away with evil.

## count on it

### God will supply!

Some days I wish Philippians 4:19 read 'my God shall supply all your wants! But it says 'needs'. Sometimes what I want is not the thing I most need. Some people will always be richer than you are, some people will always be more skilful than you and some less. But God is rich, it is all his! And out of his wisdom, he will take good care of you. "And this same God who takes care of me will supply all your needs from his glorious riches, which have been given to us in Christ Jesus." Philippians 4:19
**Count on it!**

# 4

You slave owners must be just and fair to your slaves. Remember that you also have a Master—in heaven.

## An Encouragement for Prayer

[2]Devote yourselves to prayer with an alert mind and a thankful heart. [3]Don't forget to pray for us, too, that God will give us many opportunities to preach about his secret plan—that Christ is also for you Gentiles. That is why I am here in chains. [4]Pray that I will proclaim this message as clearly as I should.

[5]Live wisely among those who are not Christians, and make the most of every opportunity. [6]Let your conversation be gracious and effective so that you will have the right answer for everyone.

## Paul's Final Instructions and Greetings

[7]Tychicus, a much loved brother, will tell you how I am getting along. He is a faithful helper who serves the Lord with me. [8]I have sent him on this special trip to let you know how we are doing and to encourage you. [9]I am also sending Onesimus, a faithful and much loved brother, one of your own people. He and Tychicus will give you all the latest news.

[10]Aristarchus, who is in prison with me, sends you his greetings, and so does Mark, Barnabas's cousin. And as you were instructed before, make Mark welcome if he comes your way. [11]Jesus (the one we call Justus) also sends his greetings. These are the only Jewish Christians among my co-workers; they are working with me here for the Kingdom of God. And what a comfort they have been!

[12]Epaphras, from your city, a servant of Christ Jesus, sends you his greetings. He always prays earnestly for you, asking God to make you strong and perfect, fully confident of the whole will of God. [13]I can assure you that he has agonized for you and also for the Christians in Laodicea and Hierapolis.

[14]Dear Doctor Luke sends his greetings, and so does Demas. [15]Please give my greetings to our Christian brothers and sisters at Laodicea, and to Nympha and those who meet in her house.

[16]After you have read this letter, pass it on to the church at Laodicea so they can read it, too. And you should read the letter I wrote to them. [17]And say to Archippus, "Be sure to carry out the work the Lord gave you."

[18]Here is my greeting in my own handwriting—PAUL. Remember my chains.

May the grace of God be with you.

**Work hard and cheerfully at whatever you do, as though you were working for the Lord rather than for people.**

COLOSSIANS 3:23

# an audience of ONE

# Training

'Those who belong to Christ have nailed the passions and desires of their sinful nature to his cross and crucified them there. If we are living now by the Holy Spirit, let us follow the Holy Spirit's leading in every part of our lives.' Galatians 5:24-25

Again we see Paul using a sporting metaphor, 'keep in step'. In Athletics (Track and Field) training, many sprinters and middle distance runners work out together. A common training technique is an Indian line. One runner leads and another half dozen sprinters follow in a straight line keeping in pace with the leaders. After 300 metres or so the last in the line sprints to the front and sets the new pace. You are caught up in the competition; you do not want to slow down and open-up a gap in the line. It is motivating and fun, you dig deep, push further and challenge each other.

God has you in spiritual training; the Spirit is always pushing you on, challenging you. If you have ever run in a pack you understand the energy of corporate power. Running with others pushes and carries you in a way that you can't get on your own. You are compelled. You are running (spiritually) faster and longer than you have before. The same is true in the life controlled by the Spirit; you feel the pace and the power of God. You are running (spiritually) faster and longer than you have before.

DEVOTIONAL

You can almost hear Christ challenging you, and advancing your spiritual power, 'Come on, live for me'. Keeping in step with the Spirit is pure pleasure; you have purpose, direction and encouragement. You know you're in sync with the Lord, you have kept a short account of sin and you are seeking to be obedient. Life in sync with the Spirit is never stagnant. You are being stretched; you are aiming for things that you rarely thought of. The presence of God in your life is as necessary as the oxygen in your lungs (if not more so). You now hunger and thirst for righteousness. Keep the pace - press on!

## Reflection
Keep in step, push yourself, you know that God will not run ahead of you and leave you in the dust. Enjoy the progress of the spiritual race.

## Prayer
Lord Jesus, thank you that you will help me, guide me and push me. Thank you that I will never take this trip of life on my own.

'Dance then wherever you may be;
I am the Lord of the Dance said he,
And I'll lead you all, wherever you may be,
And I'll lead you all in the dance, said he.'
Sydney Carter

Nicked from: A Sporting Guide to Eternity, Steve Connor,
Christian Focus Publications - ISBN 1-85792-746-X

# 1 Thessalonians

To better understand the drama and relationship that Paul had with the Thessalonians, read Acts Chapter 17. Here again we find Paul going to a strategic city of influence and commerce to start and build up a faith community for the cause of Christ. Thessalonica was a bustling Greek seaport full of international business and a variety of religions. Paul, true to his pattern, based himself at the local synagogue and preached that the fulfilment of the Old Testament was found in Jesus Christ.

We realise from Acts that Paul was only in Thessalonica about three weeks but in that short time established a youthful church. 1 Thessalonians and 2 Thessalonians are letters to the church to encourage, shape, and strengthen the truth about the Jesus they are following. Paul stirred up a lot of trouble in his short time there but the church members blossomed. Paul's mission was to win, build and mobilise followers of Christ around the world. His message was a joy to many but it invoked fury in others. But Paul lived for an audience of one and was motivated to please God, not men. The Thessalonian church had many troubles but Paul kept them focused and on course, emphasising the fact that we will be with Christ again. Jesus is coming back.

# 1 THESSALONIANS

## Greetings from Paul

# 1

This letter is from Paul, Silas, and Timothy.
It is written to the church in Thessalonica, you who belong to God the Father and the Lord Jesus Christ.
May his grace and peace be yours.

action

**CH 1:2-4 WHAT'S IT SAYING?**

**WHAT AM I GOING TO DO ABOUT IT?**

## The Faith of the Thessalonian Believers

[2]We always thank God for all of you and pray for you constantly. [3]As we talk to our God and Father about you, we think of your faithful work, your loving deeds, and your continual anticipation of the return of our Lord Jesus Christ.

[4]We know that God loves you, dear brothers and sisters, and that he chose you to be his own people. [5]For when we brought you the Good News, it was not only with words but also with power, for the Holy Spirit gave you full assurance that what we said was true. And you know that the way we lived among you was further proof of the truth of our message. [6]So you received the message with joy from the Holy Spirit in spite of the severe suffering it brought you. In this way, you imitated both us and the Lord. [7]As a result, you yourselves became an example to all the Christians in Greece. [8]And now the word of the Lord is ringing out from you to people everywhere, even beyond Greece, for wherever we go we find people telling us about your faith in God. We don't need to tell them about it, [9]for they themselves keep talking about the wonderful welcome you gave us and how you turned away from idols to serve the true and living God. [10]**And they speak of how you are looking forward to the coming of God's Son from heaven—Jesus, whom God raised from the dead. He is the one who has rescued us from the terrors of the coming judgement.**

## Paul Remembers His Visit

# 2

You yourselves know, dear brothers and sisters, that our visit to you was not a failure. [2]You know how badly we had been treated at Philippi just before we came to you and how much we suffered there. Yet our God gave us the courage to declare his Good News to you boldly, even though we were surrounded by many who opposed us. [3]So you can see that we were not preaching with any deceit or impure purposes or trickery. [4]For we speak as messengers who have been approved by God to be entrusted with the Good News. Our purpose is to please God, not people. He is the one who examines the motives of our hearts. [5]Never once did we try to win you with flattery, as you very well know. And God is our witness that we were not just pretending to be your friends so you would give us money! [6]As for praise, we have never asked for it from you or anyone else. [7]As apostles of Christ we certainly had a right to make some demands of you, but we were as gentle among you as a mother feeding and caring for her own children. [8]We loved you so much that we gave you not only God's Good News but our own lives, too.

[9]Don't you remember, dear brothers and sisters, how hard we worked among you? Night and day we toiled to earn a living so that our expenses would not be a burden to anyone there as we preached God's Good News among you. [10]You yourselves are our witnesses—and so is God—that we were pure and honest and faultless towards all of you believers. [11]And you know that we treated each of you as a father treats his own children. [12]We pleaded with you, encouraged you, and urged you to live your lives in a way that God would consider worthy. For he called you into his Kingdom to share his glory.

[13]And we will never stop thanking God that when we preached his message to you, you didn't think of the words we spoke as being just our own. You accepted what we said as the very word of God—which, of course, it was. And this word continues to work in you who believe.

[14]And then, dear brothers and sisters, you suffered persecution from your own countrymen. In this way, you imitated the believers in God's churches in Judea who, because of their belief in Christ Jesus, suffered from their own people, the Jews.

[15]For some of the Jews had killed their own prophets, and some even killed the Lord Jesus. Now they have persecuted us and driven us out. They displease God and oppose everyone [16]by trying to keep us from preaching the Good News to the Gentiles, for fear some might be saved. By doing this, they continue to pile up their sins. But the anger of God has caught up with them at last.

## TIPS

## Warm-ups Reduce Injuries:

Warm-up exercises provide an athlete with time to adjust from rest to exercise. These exercises are designed to improve performance and reduce the chance of injury by preparing the athlete mentally as well as physically for his or her sport. Physiologically, a warm-up elevates body temperature and increases blood flow.

## Timothy's Good Report about the Church

[17]Dear brothers and sisters, after we were separated from you for a little while (though our hearts never left you), we tried very hard to come back because of our intense longing to see you again. [18]We wanted very much to come, and I, Paul, tried again and again, but Satan prevented us. [19]After all, what gives us hope and joy, and what is our proud reward and crown? It is you! Yes, you will bring us much joy as we stand together before our Lord Jesus when he comes back again. [20]For you are our pride and joy.

# 3

Finally, when we could stand it no longer, we decided that I should stay alone in Athens, [2]and we sent Timothy to visit you. He is our co-worker for God and our brother in proclaiming the Good News of Christ. We sent him to strengthen you, to encourage you in your faith, [3]and to keep you from becoming disturbed by the troubles you were going through. But, of course, you know that such troubles are going to happen to us Christians. [4]Even while we were with you, we warned you that troubles would soon come—and they did, as you well know.

[5]That is why, when I could bear it no longer, I sent Timothy to find out whether your faith was still strong. I was afraid that the Tempter had got the best of you and that all our work had been useless. [6]Now Timothy has just returned, bringing the good news that your faith and love are as strong as ever. He reports that you remember our visit with joy and that you want to see us just as much as we want to see you. [7]So we have been greatly comforted, dear brothers and sisters, in all of our own crushing troubles and suffering, because you have remained strong in your faith. [8]It gives us new life, knowing you remain strong in the Lord.

[9]How we thank God for you! Because of you we have great joy in the presence of God. [10]Night and day we pray earnestly for you, asking God to let us see you again to fill up anything that may still be missing in your faith.

[11]May God himself, our Father, and our Lord Jesus make it possible for us to come to you very soon. [12]**And may the Lord make your love grow and overflow to each other and to everyone else, just as our love overflows towards you.** [13]As a result, Christ will make your hearts strong, blameless, and holy when you stand before God our Father on that day when our Lord Jesus comes with all those who belong to him.

## Live to Please God

# 4

Finally, dear brothers and sisters, we urge you in the name of the Lord Jesus to live in a way that pleases God, as we have taught you. You are doing this already, and we encourage you to do so more and more. [2]For you remember what we taught you in the name of the Lord Jesus. [3]**God wants you to be holy, so you should keep clear of all sexual sin.** [4]Then each of you will control your body and live in holiness and honour—[5]not in lustful passion as the pagans do, in their ignorance of God and his ways. [6]Never cheat a Christian brother in this matter by taking his wife, for the Lord avenges all such sins, as we have solemnly warned you before. [7]God has called us to be holy, not to live impure lives. [8]Anyone who refuses to live by these rules is not disobeying human rules but is rejecting God, who gives his Holy Spirit to you.

[9]But I don't need to write to you about the Christian love that should be shown among God's people. For God himself has taught you to love one another. [10]Indeed, your love is already strong towards all the Christians in all of Macedonia. Even so, dear brothers and sisters, we beg you to love them more and more. [11]This should be your ambition: to live a quiet life, minding your own business and working with your hands, just as we commanded you before. [12]As a result, people who are not Christians will respect the way you live, and you will not need to depend on others to meet your financial needs.

## The Hope of the Resurrection

[13]And now, brothers and sisters, I want you to know what will happen to the Christians who have died so you will not be full of sorrow like people who have no hope. [14]For since we believe that Jesus died and was raised to life again, we also believe that when Jesus comes, God will bring back with Jesus all the Christians who have died.

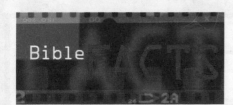

**Dogs are mentioned 14 times in the Bible, and lions 55 times, but domestic cats are not mentioned at all.**

# profiles

**Joseph:**
What would you be like if you were spoiled by your father and hated by your brothers, sold into slavery to a strange land, falsely accused of rape and sent to prison where you were forgotten by those you helped? Would you be bitter towards God or continue to be faithful? Joseph's response transformed his injustices into success. His attitude continued to be faithful to God and he eventually rose to be the leader of a great and foreign nation - Egypt. He was never bitter and helped to rescue his family from starvation and death.

We all have setbacks and discouragements. We can wallow in self-pity and render ourselves paralysed in bitterness or we can follow Joseph's example and press on knowing that God loves us deeply and will use us in those dark times. Joseph gave us a secret to his freedom from bitterness in his two sons Manasseh and Ephraim, which translate as forgiveness and fruitfulness. How not to be bitter? Forgive and be fruitful for God. For more information about Joseph, start in the first book of the Old Testament (Genesis) at chapter 37.

# OCTOBER M.A.P.

## 1
| S.D. | P.L. | P.G. | S.G. |
| --- | --- | --- | --- |
| P. ☐ | F. ☐ | F. ☐ | T. ☐ |
| F. ☐ | W. ☐ | W. ☐ | P. ☐ |
| B. ☐ | P. ☐ | C. ☐ | C. ☐ |

## 2
| S.D. | P.L. | P.G. | S.G. |
| --- | --- | --- | --- |
| P. ☐ | F. ☐ | F. ☐ | T. ☐ |
| F. ☐ | W. ☐ | W. ☐ | P. ☐ |
| B. ☐ | P. ☐ | C. ☐ | C. ☐ |

## 3
| S.D. | P.L. | P.G. | S.G. |
| --- | --- | --- | --- |
| P. ☐ | F. ☐ | F. ☐ | T. ☐ |
| F. ☐ | W. ☐ | W. ☐ | P. ☐ |
| B. ☐ | P. ☐ | C. ☐ | C. ☐ |

## 4
| S.D. | P.L. | P.G. | S.G. |
| --- | --- | --- | --- |
| P. ☐ | F. ☐ | F. ☐ | T. ☐ |
| F. ☐ | W. ☐ | W. ☐ | P. ☐ |
| B. ☐ | P. ☐ | C. ☐ | C. ☐ |

## 9
| S.D. | P.L. | P.G. | S.G. |
| --- | --- | --- | --- |
| P. ☐ | F. ☐ | F. ☐ | T. ☐ |
| F. ☐ | W. ☐ | W. ☐ | P. ☐ |
| B. ☐ | P. ☐ | C. ☐ | C. ☐ |

## 10
| S.D. | P.L. | P.G. | S.G. |
| --- | --- | --- | --- |
| P. ☐ | F. ☐ | F. ☐ | T. ☐ |
| F. ☐ | W. ☐ | W. ☐ | P. ☐ |
| B. ☐ | P. ☐ | C. ☐ | C. ☐ |

## 11
| S.D. | P.L. | P.G. | S.G. |
| --- | --- | --- | --- |
| P. ☐ | F. ☐ | F. ☐ | T. ☐ |
| F. ☐ | W. ☐ | W. ☐ | P. ☐ |
| B. ☐ | P. ☐ | C. ☐ | C. ☐ |

## 12
| S.D. | P.L. | P.G. | S.G. |
| --- | --- | --- | --- |
| P. ☐ | F. ☐ | F. ☐ | T. ☐ |
| F. ☐ | W. ☐ | W. ☐ | P. ☐ |
| B. ☐ | P. ☐ | C. ☐ | C. ☐ |

## 17
| S.D. | P.L. | P.G. | S.G. |
| --- | --- | --- | --- |
| P. ☐ | F. ☐ | F. ☐ | T. ☐ |
| F. ☐ | W. ☐ | W. ☐ | P. ☐ |
| B. ☐ | P. ☐ | C. ☐ | C. ☐ |

## 18
| S.D. | P.L. | P.G. | S.G. |
| --- | --- | --- | --- |
| P. ☐ | F. ☐ | F. ☐ | T. ☐ |
| F. ☐ | W. ☐ | W. ☐ | P. ☐ |
| B. ☐ | P. ☐ | C. ☐ | C. ☐ |

## 19
| S.D. | P.L. | P.G. | S.G. |
| --- | --- | --- | --- |
| P. ☐ | F. ☐ | F. ☐ | T. ☐ |
| F. ☐ | W. ☐ | W. ☐ | P. ☐ |
| B. ☐ | P. ☐ | C. ☐ | C. ☐ |

## 20
| S.D. | P.L. | P.G. | S.G. |
| --- | --- | --- | --- |
| P. ☐ | F. ☐ | F. ☐ | T. ☐ |
| F. ☐ | W. ☐ | W. ☐ | P. ☐ |
| B. ☐ | P. ☐ | C. ☐ | C. ☐ |

## 25
| S.D. | P.L. | P.G. | S.G. |
| --- | --- | --- | --- |
| P. ☐ | F. ☐ | F. ☐ | T. ☐ |
| F. ☐ | W. ☐ | W. ☐ | P. ☐ |
| B. ☐ | P. ☐ | C. ☐ | C. ☐ |

## 26
| S.D. | P.L. | P.G. | S.G. |
| --- | --- | --- | --- |
| P. ☐ | F. ☐ | F. ☐ | T. ☐ |
| F. ☐ | W. ☐ | W. ☐ | P. ☐ |
| B. ☐ | P. ☐ | C. ☐ | C. ☐ |

## 27
| S.D. | P.L. | P.G. | S.G. |
| --- | --- | --- | --- |
| P. ☐ | F. ☐ | F. ☐ | T. ☐ |
| F. ☐ | W. ☐ | W. ☐ | P. ☐ |
| B. ☐ | P. ☐ | C. ☐ | C. ☐ |

## 28
| S.D. | P.L. | P.G. | S.G. |
| --- | --- | --- | --- |
| P. ☐ | F. ☐ | F. ☐ | T. ☐ |
| F. ☐ | W. ☐ | W. ☐ | P. ☐ |
| B. ☐ | P. ☐ | C. ☐ | C. ☐ |

## Spiritual Disciplines

**Prayer**

**Faith Community**

**Bible Reading**

## Prayer List

**Friends**

**World**

**Personal**

# Who am I....
## Where am I going....
### How am I going to get there?

# nt:sport
# MONTHLY ACTION PLAN

**5**

| S.D. | P.L. | P.G. | S.G. |
|------|------|------|------|
| P. ☐ | F. ☐ | F. ☐ | T. ☐ |
| F. ☐ | W. ☐ | W. ☐ | P. ☐ |
| B. ☐ | P. ☐ | C. ☐ | C. ☐ |

**6**

| S.D. | P.L. | P.G. | S.G. |
|------|------|------|------|
| P. ☐ | F. ☐ | F. ☐ | T. ☐ |
| F. ☐ | W. ☐ | W. ☐ | P. ☐ |
| B. ☐ | P. ☐ | C. ☐ | C. ☐ |

**7**

| S.D. | P.L. | P.G. | S.G. |
|------|------|------|------|
| P. ☐ | F. ☐ | F. ☐ | T. ☐ |
| F. ☐ | W. ☐ | W. ☐ | P. ☐ |
| B. ☐ | P. ☐ | C. ☐ | C. ☐ |

**8**

| S.D. | P.L. | P.G. | S.G. |
|------|------|------|------|
| P. ☐ | F. ☐ | F. ☐ | T. ☐ |
| F. ☐ | W. ☐ | W. ☐ | P. ☐ |
| B. ☐ | P. ☐ | C. ☐ | C. ☐ |

**13**

| S.D. | P.L. | P.G. | S.G. |
|------|------|------|------|
| P. ☐ | F. ☐ | F. ☐ | T. ☐ |
| F. ☐ | W. ☐ | W. ☐ | P. ☐ |
| B. ☐ | P. ☐ | C. ☐ | C. ☐ |

**14**

| S.D. | P.L. | P.G. | S.G. |
|------|------|------|------|
| P. ☐ | F. ☐ | F. ☐ | T. ☐ |
| F. ☐ | W. ☐ | W. ☐ | P. ☐ |
| B. ☐ | P. ☐ | C. ☐ | C. ☐ |

**15**

| S.D. | P.L. | P.G. | S.G. |
|------|------|------|------|
| P. ☐ | F. ☐ | F. ☐ | T. ☐ |
| F. ☐ | W. ☐ | W. ☐ | P. ☐ |
| B. ☐ | P. ☐ | C. ☐ | C. ☐ |

**16**

| S.D. | P.L. | P.G. | S.G. |
|------|------|------|------|
| P. ☐ | F. ☐ | F. ☐ | T. ☐ |
| F. ☐ | W. ☐ | W. ☐ | P. ☐ |
| B. ☐ | P. ☐ | C. ☐ | C. ☐ |

**21**

| S.D. | P.L. | P.G. | S.G. |
|------|------|------|------|
| P. ☐ | F. ☐ | F. ☐ | T. ☐ |
| F. ☐ | W. ☐ | W. ☐ | P. ☐ |
| B. ☐ | P. ☐ | C. ☐ | C. ☐ |

**22**

| S.D. | P.L. | P.G. | S.G. |
|------|------|------|------|
| P. ☐ | F. ☐ | F. ☐ | T. ☐ |
| F. ☐ | W. ☐ | W. ☐ | P. ☐ |
| B. ☐ | P. ☐ | C. ☐ | C. ☐ |

**23**

| S.D. | P.L. | P.G. | S.G. |
|------|------|------|------|
| P. ☐ | F. ☐ | F. ☐ | T. ☐ |
| F. ☐ | W. ☐ | W. ☐ | P. ☐ |
| B. ☐ | P. ☐ | C. ☐ | C. ☐ |

**24**

| S.D. | P.L. | P.G. | S.G. |
|------|------|------|------|
| P. ☐ | F. ☐ | F. ☐ | T. ☐ |
| F. ☐ | W. ☐ | W. ☐ | P. ☐ |
| B. ☐ | P. ☐ | C. ☐ | C. ☐ |

**29**

| S.D. | P.L. | P.G. | S.G. |
|------|------|------|------|
| P. ☐ | F. ☐ | F. ☐ | T. ☐ |
| F. ☐ | W. ☐ | W. ☐ | P. ☐ |
| B. ☐ | P. ☐ | C. ☐ | C. ☐ |

**30**

| S.D. | P.L. | P.G. | S.G. |
|------|------|------|------|
| P. ☐ | F. ☐ | F. ☐ | T. ☐ |
| F. ☐ | W. ☐ | W. ☐ | P. ☐ |
| B. ☐ | P. ☐ | C. ☐ | C. ☐ |

**31**

| S.D. | P.L. | P.G. | S.G. |
|------|------|------|------|
| P. ☐ | F. ☐ | F. ☐ | T. ☐ |
| F. ☐ | W. ☐ | W. ☐ | P. ☐ |
| B. ☐ | P. ☐ | C. ☐ | C. ☐ |

**Proverbs 16:32**

It is better to be patient than powerful; it is better to have self-control than to conquer a city.

## Personal Goals

**Family**

**Work/School/Social**

**Challenge**

## Sport Goals

**Training**

**Performance**

**Competition Results**

**(For designing your MAP - Monthly Action Plan - see introduction pages)**

Keep alert & under-control. Don't disrespect your opponent's ability to whip you! Understand that Satan wants to destroy you! Like a keen competitor he probably had a reason for playing where he did, so don't blindly ignore moves that appear stupid or attractive. "Be careful! Watch out for attacks from the Devil, your great enemy."

1 Peter 5:8

**STAND POINT**

**Team-work**

**5:11**

So encourage each other and build each other up, just as you are already doing.

---

[15]I can tell you this directly from the Lord: We who are still living when the Lord returns will not rise to meet him ahead of those who are in their graves. [16]For the Lord himself will come down from heaven with a commanding shout, with the call of the archangel, and with the trumpet call of God. First, all the Christians who have died will rise from their graves. [17]Then, together with them, we who are still alive and remain on the earth will be caught up in the clouds to meet the Lord in the air and remain with him for ever.

[18]So comfort and encourage each other with these words.

# 5

I really don't need to write to you about how and when all this will happen, dear brothers and sisters. [2]**For you know quite well that the day of the Lord will come unexpectedly, like a thief in the night.** [3]When people are saying, "All is well; everything is peaceful and secure," then disaster will fall upon them as suddenly as a woman's birth pains begin when her child is about to be born. And there will be no escape.

[4]But you aren't in the dark about these things, dear brothers and sisters, and you won't be surprised when the day of the Lord comes like a thief. [5]For you are all children of the light and of the day; we don't belong to darkness and night. [6]So be on your guard, not asleep like the others. Stay alert and be sober. [7]Night is the time for sleep and the time when people get drunk. [8]But let us who live in the light think clearly, protected by the body armour of faith and love, and wearing as our helmet the confidence of our salvation. [9]For God decided to save us through our Lord Jesus Christ, not to pour out his anger on us. [10]He died for us so that we can live with him for ever, whether we are dead or alive at the time of his return. [11]So encourage each other and build each other up, just as you are already doing.

## Paul's Final Advice

[12]Dear brothers and sisters, honour those who are your leaders in the Lord's work. They work hard among you and warn you against all that is wrong. [13]Think highly of them and give them your wholehearted love because of their work. And remember to live peaceably with each other.

[14]Brothers and sisters, we urge you to warn those who are lazy. Encourage those who are timid. Take tender care of those who are weak. Be patient with everyone. [15]See that no one pays back evil for evil, but always try to do good to each other and to everyone else. [16]Always be joyful. [17]Keep on praying. [18]No matter what happens, always be thankful, for this is God's will for you who belong to Christ Jesus.

[19]Do not stifle the Holy Spirit. [20]Do not scoff at prophecies, [21]but test everything that is said. Hold on to what is good. [22]Keep away from every kind of evil.

**action**

**CH 5:16-22 WHAT'S IT SAYING?**

**WHAT AM I GOING TO DO ABOUT IT?**

## Paul's Final Greetings

[23]Now may the God of peace make you holy in every way, and may your whole spirit and soul and body be kept blameless until that day when our Lord Jesus Christ comes again. [24]God, who calls you, is faithful; he will do this.

[25]Dear brothers and sisters, pray for us.

[26]Greet all the brothers and sisters in Christian love.

[27]I command you in the name of the Lord to read this letter to all the brothers and sisters.

[28]And may the grace of our Lord Jesus Christ be with all of you.

**STATS**

Romanian Nadia Comaneci achieved the first ever perfect score of 10 in Olympic gymnastics at the 1976 Montreal Olympics. She won 3 gold medals.

Tough times create a dependence on God. The Thessalonian church began in a whirlwind of tough times. Paul had only been in the great city for three weeks when it was clear he had to move on or what he had established would be destroyed by jealous Greeks afraid to embrace the truth of Christ. Though Paul moved on, he was desperate that the church would take root and grow strong. He prayed constantly for the young church and kept reminding them that Christ was going to return. 2 Thessalonians is a response to a message he received after sending out his first letter. Here he clears up some confusion on Jesus' second coming, commends them for their 'flourishing faith' and 'love for each other'.

Though Paul's time in Thessalonia was uncommonly short, it is obvious from this letter that he has developed close and intimate friendships with the church; he never forgot about them. Paul was inspired and delighted that they maintained a genuine love and maturity in God in the midst of trying times. Follow Paul's example and keep praying for team-mates and friends. Encourage other believers and when you need encouragement remember this letter is not just for some ancient Greeks hanging out in the Aegean Sea but also, supernaturally, God knew that it would be a letter for you - today. Be encouraged: Jesus is coming back!

# 2 Thessalonians

# 2 THESSALONIANS

## Greetings from Paul

# 1

This letter is from Paul, Silas, and Timothy.

It is written to the church in Thessalonica, you who belong to God our Father and the Lord Jesus Christ.

[2]May God our Father and the Lord Jesus Christ give you grace and peace.

## Encouragement during Persecution

[3]Dear brothers and sisters, we always thank God for you, as

is right, for we are thankful that your faith is flourishing and you are all growing in love for each other. [4]**We proudly tell God's other churches about your**

endurance and faithfulness in all the persecutions and hardships you are suffering. [5]But God will use this persecution to show his justice. For he will make you worthy of his Kingdom, for which you are suffering, [6]and in his justice he will punish those who persecute you. [7]And God will provide rest for you who are being persecuted and also for us when the Lord Jesus appears from heaven. He will come with his mighty angels, [8]in flaming fire, bringing judgement on those who don't know God and on those who refuse to obey the Good News of our Lord Jesus. [9]They will be punished with everlasting destruction, forever separated from the Lord and from his glorious power [10]when he comes to receive glory and praise from his holy people. And you will be among those praising him on that day, for you believed what we testified about him.

[11]And so we keep on praying for you, that our God will

make you worthy of the life to which he called you. And we pray that God, by his power, will fulfil all your good intentions and faithful deeds. [12]Then everyone will give honour to the name of our Lord Jesus because of you, and you will be honoured along with him. This is all made possible because of the undeserved favour of our God and Lord, Jesus Christ.

## Events prior to the Lord's Second Coming

# 2

And now, brothers and sisters, let us tell you about the coming again of our Lord Jesus Christ and how we will be gathered together to meet him. [2]Please don't be so easily shaken and troubled by those who say that the day of the Lord has already begun. Even if they claim to have had a vision, a revelation, or a letter supposedly from us, don't believe them. [3]Don't be fooled by what they say.

For that day will not come until there is a great rebellion against God and the man of lawlessness is revealed—the one who brings destruction. [4]He will exalt himself and defy every god there is and tear down every object of adoration and worship. He will

position himself in the temple of God, claiming that he himself is God. [5]Don't you remember that I told you this when I was with you? [6]And you know what is holding him back, for he can be revealed only when his time comes.

[7]For this lawlessness is already at work secretly, and it will remain secret until the one who is holding it back steps out of the way. [8]Then the man of lawlessness will be revealed, whom the Lord Jesus will consume with the breath of his mouth and destroy by the splendour of his coming. [9]This evil man will come to do the work of Satan with counterfeit power and signs and miracles.

[10]He will use every kind of wicked deception to fool those who are on their way to destruction because they refuse to believe the truth that would save them. [11]So God will send great deception upon them, and they will believe all these lies. [12]Then they will be

condemned for not believing the truth and for enjoying the evil they do.

## Believers Should Stand Firm

[13]As for us, we always thank God for you, dear brothers and sisters loved by the Lord. We are thankful that God chose you to be among the first to experience salvation, a salvation that came through the Spirit who makes you holy and by your belief in the truth.

[14]He called you to salvation when we told you the Good News; now you can share in the glory of our Lord Jesus Christ.

[15]With all these things in mind, dear brothers and sisters, stand firm and keep a strong grip on everything we taught you both in person and by letter.

[16]May our Lord Jesus Christ and God our Father, who loved us and in his special favour gave us everlasting comfort and good hope, [17]comfort your hearts and give you strength in every good thing you do and say.

## Paul's Request for Prayer

# 3

Finally, dear brothers and sisters, I ask you to pray for us. Pray first that the Lord's message will spread

**Some days I feel close to God and some days far away. What is wrong?**

Knowing that God loves you unconditionally whether you feel close to him or not helps your consistency. Pray and read your Bible every day, whether you feel like it or not! Remember that we don't underpin our faith by how we 'feel' but with the truth of God's Word.

**STAND POINT**

**When you need to encourage your team-mates.**

2:16-17

May our Lord Jesus Christ and God our Father, who loved us and in his special favour gave us everlasting comfort and good hope, comfort your hearts and give you strength in every good thing you do and say.

'Prayer & Protection' 2 Thessalonians 3:1-2

If God answered every one of your prayers this week, how many new Christians would there be in this world? No, not how many 'wee aunties' would get their hips replaced, but how many new converts would be saved from an eternity apart from God? We are to pray that God's message would spread and take hold of the hearts of men. We are also charged to pray for protection; there is a very real evil that wants to keep us from our duty to pray and read the scriptures. Pray that you and your friends and loved ones will be strong and invite God to protect you from evil.

rapidly and be honoured wherever it goes, just as when it came to you. [2]Pray, too, that we will be saved from wicked and evil people, for not everyone believes in the Lord. [3]But the Lord is faithful; he will make you strong and guard you from the evil one. [4]And we are confident in the Lord that you are practising the things we commanded you, and that you always will. **[5]May the Lord bring you into an ever deeper understanding of the love of God and the endurance that comes from Christ.**

## An Exhortation to Proper Living

[6]And now, dear brothers and sisters, we give you this command with the authority of our Lord Jesus Christ: Stay away from any Christian who lives in idleness and doesn't follow the tradition of hard work we gave you. [7]For you know that you ought to follow our example. We were never lazy when we were with you. [8]We never accepted food from anyone without paying for it. We worked hard day and night so that we would not be a burden to any of you. [9]It wasn't that we didn't have the right to ask you to feed us, but we wanted to give you an example to follow. [10]Even while we were with you, we gave you this rule: "Whoever does not work should not eat."

[11]Yet we hear that some of you are living idle lives, refusing to work and wasting time meddling in other people's business.

[12]In the name of the Lord Jesus Christ, we appeal to such people—no, we command them: Settle down and get to work. Earn your own living. [13]And I say to the rest of you, dear brothers and sisters, never get tired of doing good.

[14]Take note of those who refuse to obey what we say in this letter. Stay away from them so they will be ashamed. [15]Don't think of them as enemies, but speak to them as you would to a Christian who needs to be warned.

## Paul's Final Greetings

[16]May the Lord of peace himself always give you his peace no matter what happens. The Lord be with you all.

[17]Now here is my greeting, which I write with my own hand— PAUL. I do this at the end of all my letters to prove that they really are from me.

[18]May the grace of our Lord Jesus Christ be with you all.

# fight well

"Fight well
in the Lord's battles.
Cling tightly to your faith in
Christ, and always keep your
concience clear."

1TIMOTHY 1:18-19

The Bible is timeless and the principles that Paul sets forth in the next three books are invaluable to young leaders that want to make an impact for the cause of Christ. Paul is just out of prison and is concerned for the orderly worship and ministry of the Churches, particularly in Ephesus. Paul encourages Timothy to live in faithfulness and to maintain the truth in the midst of false teaching about Christ and his followers. He goes on to give invaluable training on how to maintain and build a faith community.

## Coaching the Coaches - 1 Timothy, 2 Timothy, Titus

A good coach can make your sporting career fantastic and a bad coach can make it miserable and even put you off sport forever. Paul was aware of that and put a lot of time, prayer and energy into developing the coaches who would take his teams (faith communities) to the next level. Paul's purpose was to create healthy home-grown churches that could survive and flourish without him being there. He needed leaders that would build on the work that he had started and he found two such leaders in Timothy and Titus.

Timothy and Titus were both dear to Paul, they had the privilege of living and learning from the great evangelist and they both experienced many of his adventures and ministry. In the letters to Timothy and Titus we feel Paul's urgency and responsibility to develop and strengthen these younger future leaders, as well as how to organise a community of followers of Jesus Christ.

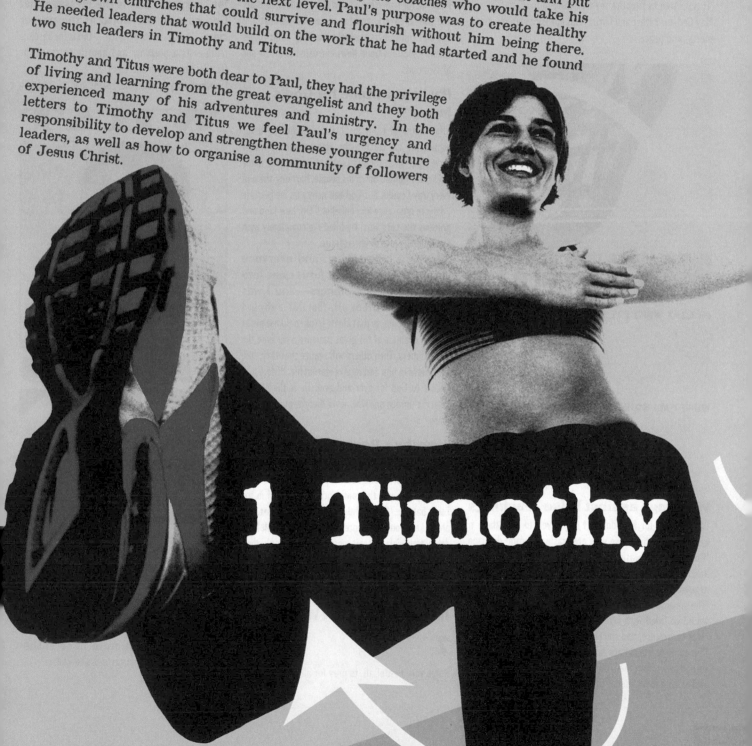

# 1 Timothy

# 1 TIMOTHY

## Greetings from Paul

# 1

This letter is from Paul, an apostle of Christ Jesus, appointed by the command of God our Saviour and by Christ Jesus our hope.

[2]It is written to Timothy, my true child in the faith.

May God our Father and Christ Jesus our Lord give you grace, mercy, and peace.

**CH 1:3–7 WHAT'S IT SAYING?**

**WHAT AM I GOING TO DO ABOUT IT?**

## Warnings against False Teachings

[3]When I left for Macedonia, I urged you to stay there in Ephesus and stop those who are teaching wrong doctrine. [4]Don't let people waste time in endless speculation over myths and spiritual pedigrees. For these things only cause arguments; they don't help people live a life of faith in God. [5]The purpose of my instruction is that all the Christians there would be filled with love that comes from a pure heart, a clear conscience, and sincere faith.

[6]But some teachers have missed this whole point. They have turned away from these things and spend their time arguing and talking foolishness. [7]They want to be known as teachers of the law of Moses, but they don't know what they are talking about, even though they seem so confident. [8]We know these laws are good when they are used as God intended. [9]But they were not made for people who do what is right. They are for people who are disobedient and rebellious, who are ungodly and sinful, who consider nothing sacred and defile what is holy, who murder their father or mother or other people. [10]These laws are for people who are sexually immoral, for homosexuals and slave traders, for liars and oath breakers, and for those who do anything else that contradicts the right teaching [11]that comes from the glorious Good News entrusted to me by our blessed God.

## Paul's Gratitude for God's Mercy

[12]How thankful I am to Christ Jesus our Lord for considering me trustworthy and appointing me to serve him, [13]even though I used to scoff at the name of Christ. I hunted down his people, harming them in every way I could. But God had mercy on me because I did it in ignorance and unbelief. [14]Oh, how kind and gracious the Lord was! He filled me completely with faith and the love of Christ Jesus.

[15]**This is a true saying, and everyone should believe it: Christ Jesus came into the world to save sinners—and I was the worst of them all.** [16]But that is why God had mercy on me, so that Christ Jesus could use me as a prime example of his great patience with even the worst sinners. Then others will realize that they, too, can believe in him and receive eternal life. [17]Glory and honour to God for ever and ever. He is the eternal King, the unseen one who never dies; he alone is God. Amen.

## Timothy's Responsibility

[18]Timothy, my son, here are my instructions for you, based on the prophetic words spoken about you earlier. May they give you the confidence to fight well in the Lord's battles. [19]Cling tightly to your faith in Christ, and always keep your conscience clear. For some people have deliberately violated their consciences; as a result, their faith has been shipwrecked. [20]Hymenaeus and Alexander are two examples of this. I turned them over to Satan so they would learn not to blaspheme God.

## Instructions about Worship

# 2

I urge you, first of all, to pray for all people. As you make your requests, plead for God's mercy upon them, and give thanks. [2]Pray this way for kings and all others who are in authority, so that we can live in peace and quietness, in godliness and dignity. [3]This is good and pleases God our Saviour, [4]for he wants everyone to be saved and to understand the truth.

[5]For there is only one God and one Mediator who can reconcile God and people. He is the man Christ Jesus. [6]**He gave his life to purchase freedom for everyone. This is the message that God gave to the world at the proper time.** [7]And I have been chosen—this is the absolute truth—as a preacher and apostle to teach the Gentiles about faith and truth.

[8]So wherever you assemble, I want men to pray with

## WHAT DOES IT MEAN?

### Assurance

The resurrection of Jesus (Acts 17:31) is the "assurance" or promise God has given that his revelation is true and worthy of acceptance. The "full confidence in God's secret plan" (Col. 2:2) is a rock solid assurance of the truth of the declarations of Scripture. This rock solid conviction of hope is the assurance of a man's salvation through Christ.

holy hands lifted up to God, free from anger and controversy. ⁹And I want women to be modest in their appearance. They should wear decent and appropriate clothing and not draw attention to themselves by the way they arrange their hair or by wearing gold or pearls or expensive clothes. ¹⁰For women who claim to be devoted to God should make themselves attractive by the good things they do. ¹¹Women should listen and learn quietly and submissively. ¹²I do not let women teach men or have authority over them. Let them listen quietly. ¹³For God made Adam first, and afterwards he made Eve. ¹⁴And it was the woman, not Adam, who was deceived by Satan, and sin was the result. ¹⁵But women will be saved through childbearing and by continuing to live in faith, love, holiness, and modesty.

## Leaders in the Church

# 3

It is a true saying that if someone wants to be an elder, he desires an honourable responsibility. ²For an elder must be a man whose life cannot be spoken against. He must be faithful to his wife. He must exhibit self-control, live wisely, and have a good reputation. He must enjoy having guests in his home and must be able to teach. ³He must not be a heavy drinker or be violent. He must be gentle, peace loving, and not one who loves money. ⁴He must manage his own family well, with children who respect and obey him. ⁵For if a man cannot manage his own household, how can he take care of God's church?

⁶An elder must not be a new Christian, because he might be proud of being chosen so soon, and the Devil will use that pride to make him fall. ⁷Also, people outside the church must speak well of him so that he will not fall into the Devil's trap and be disgraced.

⁸In the same way, deacons must be people who are respected and have integrity. They must not be heavy drinkers and must not be greedy for money. ⁹They must be committed to the revealed truths of the Christian faith and must live with a clear conscience.

**What are your five favourite Bible verses?**

1
2
3
4
5

**BIG FIVE**

¹⁰Before they are appointed as deacons, they should be given other responsibilities in the church as a test of their character and ability. If they do well, then they may serve as deacons.

¹¹In the same way, their wives must be respected and must not speak evil of others. They must exercise self-control and be faithful in everything they do.

¹²A deacon must be faithful to his wife, and he must manage his children and household well. ¹³Those who do well as deacons will be rewarded with respect from others and will have increased confidence in their faith in Christ Jesus.

## The Truths of Our Faith

¹⁴I am writing these things to you now, even though I hope to be with you soon, ¹⁵so that if I can't come for a while, you will know how people must conduct themselves in the household of God. This is the church of the living God, which is the pillar and support of the truth.

¹⁶Without question, this is the great mystery of our faith:

Christ appeared in the flesh
and was shown to be righteous by the Spirit.
He was seen by angels

and was announced to the nations.
He was believed on in the world
and was taken up into heaven.

## Warnings against False Teachers

# 4

Now the Holy Spirit tells us clearly that in the last times some will turn away from what we believe; they will follow lying spirits and teachings that come from demons. ²These teachers are hypocrites and liars. They pretend to be religious, but their consciences are dead.

³They will say it is wrong to be married and wrong to eat certain foods. But God created those foods to be eaten with thanksgiving by people who know and believe the truth. ⁴Since everything God created is good, we should not reject any of it. We may receive it gladly, with thankful hearts. ⁵For we know it is made holy by the word of God and prayer.

## A Good Servant of Christ Jesus

⁶If you explain this to the brothers and sisters, you will be doing your duty as a worthy servant of Christ Jesus, one who is fed by the message of faith and the true teaching you have followed. ⁷Do not waste time arguing over godless ideas and

**TIPS**

## Put In Extra Time:

Don't just rely on your training times. Evidence suggests that the most significant contributing factor to a dancer, gymnast, or martial artist improving his or her flexibility takes place when the individual stretches during his or her own time!

## Bible FACTS

**SEVEN is the number of completeness in the old created order. There are seven days of creation and in Revelation this number occurs 54 times.**

old wives' tales. Spend your time and energy in training yourself for spiritual fitness. [8]**Physical exercise has some value, but spiritual exercise is much more important, for it promises a reward in both this life and the next.** [9]This is true, and everyone should accept it. [10]We work hard and suffer much in order that people will believe the truth, for our hope is in the living God, who is the Saviour of all people, and particularly of those who believe.

[11]Teach these things and insist that everyone learn them. [12]Don't let anyone think less of you because you are young. Be an example to all believers in what you teach, in the way you live, in your love, your faith, and your purity. [13]Until I get there, focus on reading the Scriptures to the church, encouraging the believers, and teaching them. [14]Do not neglect the spiritual gift you received through the prophecies spoken to you when the elders of the church laid their hands on you. [15]Give your complete attention to these matters. Throw yourself into your tasks so that everyone will see your progress. [16]Keep a close watch on yourself and on your teaching. Stay true to what is right, and God will save you and those who hear you.

## STAND POINT

### When you are negotiating a contract

**6:9**

People who long to be rich fall into temptation and are trapped by many foolish and harmful desires that plunge them into ruin and destruction.

# 5

Never speak harshly to an older man, but appeal to him respectfully as though he were your own father. Talk to the younger men as you would to your own brothers. [2]Treat the older women as you would your mother, and treat the younger women with all purity as your own sisters.

### action

**CH 5:1-12 WHAT'S IT SAYING?**

**WHAT AM I GOING TO DO ABOUT IT?**

## Advice about Widows, Elders, and Slaves

[3]The church should care for any widow who has no one else to care for her. [4]But if she has children or grandchildren, their first responsibility is to show godliness at home and repay their parents by taking care of them. This is something that pleases God very much.

[5]But a woman who is a true widow, one who is truly alone in this world, has placed her hope in God. Night and day she asks God for help and spends much time in prayer. [6]But the widow who lives only for pleasure is spiritually dead. [7]Give these instructions to the church so that the widows you support will not be criticized.

[8]But those who won't care for their own relatives, especially those living in the same household, have denied what we believe. Such people are worse than unbelievers.

[9]A widow who is put on the list for support must be a woman who is at least sixty years old and was faithful to her husband.

[10]She must be well respected by everyone because of the good she has done. Has she brought up her children well? Has she been kind to strangers? Has she served other Christians humbly? Has she helped those who are in trouble? Has she always been ready to do good? [11]The younger widows should not be on the list, because their physical desires will overpower their devotion to Christ and they will want to remarry. [12]Then they would be guilty of breaking their previous pledge. [13]Besides, they are likely to become lazy and spend their time gossiping from house to house, getting into other people's business and saying things they shouldn't. [14]So I advise these younger widows to marry again, have children, and take care of their own homes. Then the enemy will not be able to say anything against them. [15]For I am afraid that some of them have already gone astray and now follow Satan.

[16]If a Christian woman has relatives who are widows, she must take care of them and not put the responsibility on the church. Then the church can care for widows who are truly alone.

[17]Elders who do their work well should be paid well, especially those who work hard at both preaching and teaching. [18]For the Scripture says, "Do not keep an ox from eating as it treads out the grain." And in another place, "Those who work deserve their pay!"

[19]Do not listen to complaints against an elder unless there are two or three witnesses to accuse him. [20]Anyone who sins should be rebuked in front of the whole church so that others will have a proper fear of God.

[21]I solemnly command you in the presence of God and Christ Jesus and the holy angels to obey these instructions without taking sides or showing special favour to anyone. [22]Never be in a hurry about appointing an elder. Do not participate in the sins of others. Keep yourself pure.

[23]Don't drink only water. You ought to drink a little wine for the sake of your stomach because you are sick so often.

[24]Remember that some people lead sinful lives, and everyone knows they will be judged. But there are others whose sin will not be revealed until later. [25]In the same way, everyone knows how much good some people do, but there are others whose good deeds won't be known until later.

# 6

Christians who are slaves should give their masters full respect so that the name of God and his teaching will not be shamed.

²If your master is a Christian, that is no excuse for being disrespectful. You should work all the harder because you are helping another believer by your efforts.

## False Teaching and True Riches

Teach these truths, Timothy, and encourage everyone to obey them. ³Some false teachers may deny these things, but these are the sound, wholesome teachings of the Lord Jesus Christ, and they are the foundation for a godly life. ⁴Anyone who teaches anything different is both conceited and ignorant. Such a person has an unhealthy desire to quibble over the meaning of words. This stirs up arguments ending in jealousy, fighting, slander, and evil suspicions.

⁵These people always cause trouble. Their minds are corrupt, and they don't tell the truth. To them religion is just a way to get rich.

⁶Yet true religion with contentment is great wealth. ⁷After all, we didn't bring anything with us when we came into the world, and we certainly cannot carry anything with us when we die. ⁸So if we have enough food and clothing, let us be content. ⁹But people who long to be rich fall into temptation and are trapped by many foolish and harmful desires that plunge them into ruin and destruction. ¹⁰For the love of money is at the root of all kinds of evil. And some people, craving money, have wandered from the faith and pierced themselves with many sorrows.

## Paul's Final Instructions

¹¹But you, Timothy, belong to God; so run from all these evil things, and follow what is right and good. Pursue a godly life, along with faith, love, perseverance, and gentleness. ¹²**Fight the good fight for what we believe. Hold tightly to the eternal life that God has given you, which you have confessed so well before many witnesses.** ¹³And I command you before God, who gives life to all, and before Christ Jesus, who gave a good testimony before Pontius Pilate, ¹⁴that you obey his commands with all purity. Then no one can find fault with you from now until our Lord Jesus Christ returns. ¹⁵For at the right time Christ will be revealed from heaven by the blessed and only almighty God, the King of kings and Lord of lords. ¹⁶He alone can never die, and he lives in light so brilliant that no human can approach him. No one has ever seen him, nor ever will. To him be honour and power for ever. Amen.

¹⁷Tell those who are rich in this world not to be proud and not to trust in their money, which will soon be gone. But their trust should be in the living God, who richly gives us all we need for our enjoyment. ¹⁸Tell them to use their money to do good. They should be rich in good works and should give generously to those in need, always being ready to share with others whatever God has given them. ¹⁹By doing this they will be storing up their treasure as a good foundation for the future so that they may take hold of real life.

²⁰Timothy, guard what God has entrusted to you. Avoid godless, foolish discussions with those who oppose you with their so-called knowledge. ²¹Some people have wandered from the faith by following such foolishness.

May God's grace be with you all.

# PERSONAL ASSESSMENTS

## WHAT DO I REALLY LIKE TO DO?

On a scale from one to ten.

- I'd rather watch TV than talk with a friend. [ ]

- I'd rather watch than participate in sport. [ ]

- I love training and working hard for a goal. [ ]

- I like new adventures more than routine. [ ]

- I do not worry about what others think of me. [ ]

- I prefer team sports more than individual sports. [ ]

- I am good at learning new skills and techniques. [ ]

- I listen to my coach. [ ]

# Beauty

'Then God looked over all he had made, and he saw that it was excellent in every way.' Genesis 1:31

Sport can express or reflect certain qualities and virtues that are godly. God gave us an intrinsic desire to appreciate. In sport we have a lot to admire. This may be a faint echo of our Maker: 'And God saw that it was good'. I believe sport is art. Art can be good and bad — good when we ascribe the qualities properly, bad when we worship the activity rather than the creator. From the Christian perspective an athlete can imitate and radiate God's qualities. The origin of beauty starts with God, it's what he does. You need not be a Christian to express these qualities, but a Christian can better understand the origin of these virtues and channel the appreciation accordingly. The sports world is a tool to reach people for Christ but it is so much more; even the execution and admiration of sport is a means to glorify the Maker. On the second day of her gymnastic class, our younger daughter warmed up with cartwheels. She had watched her older sister at home and did her best. The cartwheels were executed poorly in comparison with the more experienced girls, but she was so beautiful in her earnest heartfelt attempt to complete the work. I knew she was trying, and it was beautiful. If an Olympic gymnast came in, her skill would pale by comparison, but her beauty would still shine. As I contemplated this, I

started to look at the others girls through God's eye, and attempted to see the scene from his vantage point — the beauty was amazing. The laughter became musical, the interaction between girls was merriment, the mistakes were comical and the skill was profound. I felt as if all my senses were enhanced and I could not wait to share it with my wife. The hour and a half flew by and I wanted to look at everything this way. God gave us so many things to appreciate, enjoy and attribute to his glory.

## Reflection
God is the origin of beauty; find it in your sport.

## Prayer
Father, thank you that my canvas to glorify your beauty is in sport.

'And wherever, in anything God has made, in the glory of it,
be it sky or flower or human face, we see the glory of God.'
George MacDonald

Nicked from: A Sporting Guide to Eternity, Steve Connor,
Christian Focus Publications - ISBN 1-85792-746-X

# 2 Timothy

This is a passionate letter of encouragement and instruction to someone that is more of an offspring than just a colleague. This letter was probably written about a year or so after the first letter, and from Rome, where Paul was for now in prison, and was sent to Timothy by the hands of Tychicus. In it he urges Timothy to come to him before winter, and to bring Mark with him! He was predicting that 'the time of my death is near', and he wanted his 'son' Timothy to remain faithful to the things he was taught.  In 2 Timothy see great insight into Paul's missionary method for reaching the world for Christ. You have heard me teach many things that have been confirmed by many reliable witnesses. Teach these great truths to trustworthy people who are able to pass them on to others.' 2 Timothy 2:2

## Coaching the Coaches - 1 Timothy, 2 Timothy, Titus
A good coach can make your sporting career fantastic and a bad coach can make it miserable and even put you off sport forever.  Paul was aware of that and put a lot of time, prayer and energy into developing the coaches who would take his teams (faith communities) to the next level. Paul's purpose was to create healthy home-grown churches that could survive and flourish without him being there.  He needed leaders that would build on the work that he had started and he found two such leaders in Timothy and Titus.

Timothy and Titus were both dear to Paul, they had the privilege of living and learning from the great evangelist and they both experienced many of his adventures and ministry.  In the letters to Timothy and Titus we feel Paul's urgency and responsibility to develop and strengthen these younger future leaders, as well as how to organise a community of followers of Jesus Christ.

157

# 2 TIMOTHY

## Greetings from Paul

# 1

This letter is from Paul, an apostle of Christ Jesus by God's will, sent out to tell others about the life he has promised through faith in Christ Jesus.
²It is written to Timothy, my dear son.
May God our Father and Christ Jesus our Lord give you grace, mercy, and peace.

## Encouragement to Be Faithful

³Timothy, I thank God for you. He is the God I serve with a clear conscience, just as my ancestors did. Night and day I constantly remember you in my prayers. ⁴I long to see you again, for I remember your tears as we parted. And I will be filled with joy when we are together again.
⁵I know that you sincerely trust the Lord, for you have the faith of your mother, Eunice, and your grandmother, Lois. ⁶This is why I remind you to fan into flames the spiritual gift God gave you when I laid my hands on you. ⁷**For God has not given us a spirit of fear and timidity, but of power, love, and self-discipline.** ⁸So you must never be ashamed to tell others about our Lord. And don't be ashamed of me, either, even though I'm in prison for Christ. With the strength God gives you, be ready to suffer with me for the proclamation of the Good News.
⁹It is God who saved us and chose us to live a holy life. He did this not because we deserved it, but because that was his plan long before the world began—to show his love and kindness to us through Christ Jesus. ¹⁰And now he has made all of this plain to us by the coming of Christ Jesus, our Saviour, who broke the power of death and showed us the way to everlasting life through the Good News. ¹¹And God chose me to be a preacher, an apostle, and a teacher of this Good News.

¹²And that is why I am suffering here in prison. But I am not ashamed of it, for I know the one in whom I trust, and I am sure that he is able to guard what I have entrusted to him until the day of his return. ¹³Hold on to the pattern of right teaching you learned from me. And remember to live in the faith and love that you have in Christ Jesus. ¹⁴With the help of the Holy Spirit who lives within us, carefully guard what has been entrusted to you.
¹⁵As you know, all the Christians who came here from the province of Asia have deserted me; even Phygelus and Hermogenes are gone. ¹⁶May the Lord show special kindness to Onesiphorus and all his family because he often visited and encouraged me. He was never

## Winners work together!

Winners are more interested in the well-being of the team than themselves. One of the most beautiful things to see is a team coordinating their efforts towards a common goal, alternately subordinating and asserting themselves to achieve real harmony in action. Top sports people learn how to work well with others. When you are competing you have a common focus and purpose. The church is also a team (not a building) of fellow believers with a common purpose, to further the cause of Christ.
"Don't be selfish; don't live to make a good impression on others. Be humble, thinking of others as better than yourself. Don't think only about your own affairs, but be interested in others, too, and what they are doing." **Philippians 2:3-4**

Winners create unity!

ashamed of me because I was in prison. ¹⁷When he came to Rome, he searched everywhere until he found me. ¹⁸May the Lord show him special kindness on the day of Christ's return. And you know how much he helped me at Ephesus.

action

CH 2:14-18 WHAT'S IT SAYING?

WHAT AM I GOING TO DO ABOUT IT?

## A Good Soldier of Christ Jesus

# 2

Timothy, my dear son, be strong with the special favour God gives you in Christ Jesus. ²You have heard me teach many things that have been confirmed by many reliable witnesses. Teach these great truths to trustworthy people who are able to pass them on to others.

³Endure suffering along with me, as a good soldier of Christ Jesus. ⁴And as Christ's soldier, do not let yourself become tied up in the affairs of this life, for then you cannot satisfy the one who has enlisted you in his army. ⁵**Follow the Lord's rules for doing his work, just as an athlete either follows the rules or is disqualified and wins no prize.** ⁶Hardworking farmers are the first to enjoy the fruit of their labour. ⁷Think about what I

am saying. The Lord will give you understanding in all these things.

⁸Never forget that Jesus Christ was a man born into King David's family and that he was raised from the dead. This is the Good News I preach. ⁹And because I preach this Good News, I am suffering and have been chained like a criminal. But the word of God cannot be chained. ¹⁰I am willing to endure anything if it will bring salvation and eternal glory in Christ Jesus to those God has chosen.

¹¹This is a true saying:
If we die with him,
we will also live with him.
¹²If we endure hardship,
we will reign with him.
If we deny him,
he will deny us.
¹³If we are unfaithful,
he remains faithful,
for he cannot deny himself.

## An Approved Worker

¹⁴Remind everyone of these things, and command them in God's name to stop fighting over words. Such arguments are useless, and they can ruin those who hear them. ¹⁵Work hard so God can approve you. Be a good worker, one who does not need to be ashamed and who correctly explains the word of truth. ¹⁶Avoid godless, foolish discussions that lead to more and more ungodliness. ¹⁷This kind of talk spreads like cancer. Hymenaeus and Philetus are examples of this. ¹⁸They have left the path of truth, preaching the lie that the resurrection of the dead has already occurred; and they have undermined the faith of some.

¹⁹But God's truth stands firm like a foundation stone with this inscription: "The Lord knows those who are

## STAND POINT

**When you are frustrated with a teammate.**

2:24

The Lord's servants must not quarrel but must be kind to everyone. They must be able to teach effectively and be patient with difficult people.

his," and "Those who claim they belong to the Lord must turn away from all wickedness."

²⁰In a wealthy home some utensils are made of gold and silver, and some are made of wood and clay. The expensive utensils are used for special occasions, and the cheap ones are for everyday use.

²¹If you keep yourself pure, you will be a utensil God can use for his purpose. Your life will be clean, and you will be ready for the Master to use you for every good work.

²²Run from anything that stimulates youthful lust. Follow anything that makes you want to do right. Pursue faith and love and peace, and enjoy the companionship of those who call on the Lord with pure hearts. ²³Again I say, don't get involved in foolish, ignorant arguments that only start fights. ²⁴The Lord's servants must not quarrel but must be kind to everyone. They must be able to teach effectively and be patient with difficult people. ²⁵They should gently teach those who oppose the truth. Perhaps God will change those people's hearts, and they will believe the truth. ²⁶Then they will come

Let God speak to you. Make a conscious effort to allow the word of God to occupy your thoughts. Think about it night and day. Speak it to yourself. Ask yourself the meaning of what you read. Ask God to tell you the meaning. Meditating on the word is like talking to God. It is during these times that the Holy Spirit will drop godly thoughts into your heart. 'With all my heart I want your blessings. Be merciful just as you promised. I pondered the direction of my life, and I turned to follow your statutes.'
Psalm 119:58-59

POWER HABITS

to their senses and escape from the Devil's trap. For they have been held captive by him to do whatever he wants.

## The Dangers of the Last Days

# 3

You should also know this, Timothy, that in the last days there will be very difficult times. ²For people will love only themselves and their money. They will be boastful and proud, scoffing at God, disobedient to their parents, and ungrateful. They will consider nothing sacred. ³They will be unloving and unforgiving; they will slander others and have no self-control; they will be cruel and have no interest in what is good. ⁴They will betray their friends, be reckless, be puffed up with pride, and love pleasure rather than God. ⁵They will act as if they are religious, but they will reject the power that could make them godly. You must stay away from people like that.

⁶They are the kind who work their way into people's homes and win the confidence of vulnerable women who are burdened with the guilt of sin and controlled by many desires. ⁷Such women are forever following new teachings, but they never understand the truth. ⁸And these teachers fight the truth just as Jannes and Jambres fought against Moses. Their minds are depraved, and their faith is counterfeit. ⁹But they won't get away with this for long. Someday everyone will recognize what fools they are, just as happened with Jannes and Jambres.

## Paul's Charge to Timothy

¹⁰But you know what I teach, Timothy, and how I live, and what my purpose in life is. You know my faith and how long I have suffered. You know my love and my patient endurance. ¹¹You know how much persecution and suffering I have endured. You know all about how I was persecuted in Antioch, Iconium, and Lystra—but the Lord delivered me from all of it. ¹²Yes, and everyone who wants to live a godly life in Christ Jesus will suffer persecution. ¹³But evil people and impostors will flourish. They will go on deceiving others, and they themselves will be deceived.

¹⁴But you must remain faithful to the things you have been taught. You know they are true, for you know you can trust those who taught you. ¹⁵You have been taught the holy Scriptures from childhood, and they have given you the wisdom to receive the salvation that comes by trusting in Christ Jesus. ¹⁶All Scripture is inspired by God and is useful to teach us what is true and to make us realize what is wrong in our lives. It straightens us out and teaches us to do what is right. ¹⁷It is God's way of preparing us in every way, fully equipped for every good thing God wants us to do.

## count on it

### The Ten Commandments

Then God instructed the people as follows:

"I am the LORD your God, who rescued you from slavery in Egypt.

- Do not worship any other gods besides me.
- Do not make idols of any kind.
- Do not misuse the name of the LORD your God.
- Remember to observe the Sabbath day by keeping it holy.
- Honour your father and your mother. Then you will live a long, full life in the land the LORD your God will give you.
- Do not murder.
- Do not commit adultery.
- Do not steal.
- Do not testify falsely against your neighbour.
- Do not covet anything your neighbour owns."

From Exodus 20:1-17

**Count on it!**

# 4

And so I solemnly urge you before God and before Christ Jesus—who will someday judge the living and the dead when he appears to set up his Kingdom: ²Preach the word of God. Be persistent, whether the time is favourable or not. Patiently correct, rebuke, and encourage your people with good teaching.

³**For a time is coming when people will**

no longer listen to right teaching. They will follow their own desires and will look for teachers who will tell them whatever they want to hear. ⁴They will reject the truth and follow strange myths.

⁵But you should keep a clear mind in every situation. Don't be afraid of suffering for the Lord. Work at bringing others to Christ. Complete the ministry God has given you.

## Paul's Final Words

⁶As for me, my life has already been poured out as an offering to God. The time of my death is near. ⁷I have fought a good fight, I have finished the race, and I have remained faithful. ⁸And now the prize awaits me—the crown of righteousness that the Lord, the righteous Judge, will give me on that great day of his return. And the prize is not just for me but for all who eagerly look forward to his glorious return.

⁹Please come as soon as you can. ¹⁰Demas has deserted me because he loves the things of this life and has gone to Thessalonica. Crescens has gone to Galatia, and Titus has gone to Dalmatia. ¹¹Only Luke is with me. Bring Mark with you when you come, for he will be helpful to me. ¹²I sent Tychicus to Ephesus. ¹³When you come, be sure to bring the coat I left with Carpus at Troas. Also bring my books, and especially my papers.

¹⁴Alexander the coppersmith has done me much harm, but the Lord will judge him for what he has done. ¹⁵Be careful of him, for he fought against everything we said.

¹⁶The first time I was brought before the judge, no one was with me. Everyone had abandoned me. I hope it will not be counted against them. ¹⁷But the Lord stood with me and gave me strength, that I might preach the Good News in all its fullness for all the Gentiles to hear. And he saved me from certain death. ¹⁸Yes, and the Lord will deliver me from every evil attack and will bring me safely to his heavenly Kingdom. To God be the glory for ever and ever. Amen.

## Paul's Final Greetings

¹⁹Give my greetings to Priscilla and Aquila and those living at the household of Onesiphorus. ²⁰Erastus stayed at Corinth, and I left Trophimus sick at Miletus. ²¹Hurry so you can get here before winter. Eubulus sends you greetings, and so do Pudens, Linus, Claudia, and all the brothers and sisters.

²²May the Lord be with your spirit. Grace be with you all.

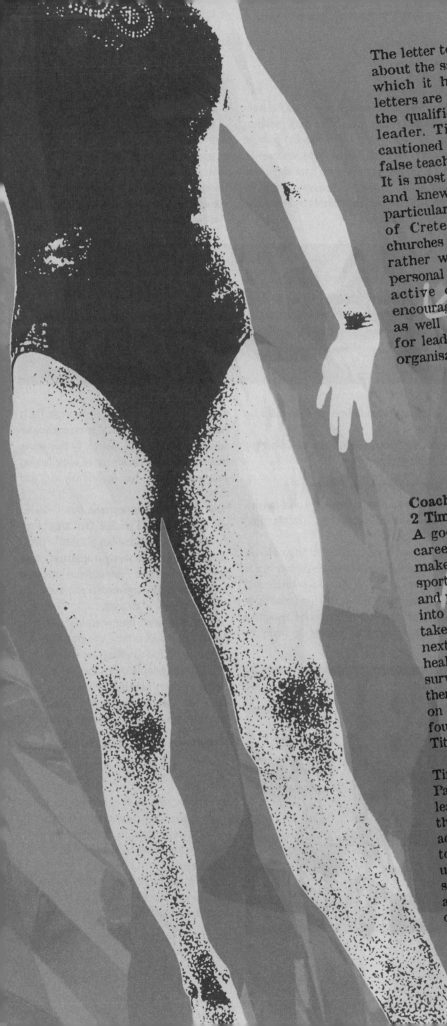

The letter to Titus, was probably written about the same time as 1 Timothy, with which it has many similarities. Both letters are mainly engaged in describing the qualifications required in a church leader. Timothy and Titus are both cautioned against the same widespread false teachings (concerning good works). It is most obvious that Paul loved Titus and knew he had been thrown into a particularly hard ministry on the island of Crete. Paul does not just build churches and leave them floundering, but rather we see long-term concern and personal alliance in maintaining a healthy active church. Here Paul provides encouragement and leadership to Titus as well as giving the world the criteria for leadership and a foundation for the organisation of the church.

# Titus

### Coaching the Coaches - 1 Timothy, 2 Timothy, Titus

A good coach can make your sporting career fantastic and a bad coach can make it miserable and even put you off sport forever. Paul was aware of that and put a lot of time, prayer and energy into developing the coaches who would take his teams (faith communities) to the next level. Paul's purpose was to create healthy home grown churches that could survive and flourish without him being there. He needed leaders that would build on the work that he had started and he found two such leaders in Timothy and Titus.

Timothy and Titus were both dear to Paul, they had the privilege of living and learning from the great evangelist and they both experienced many of his adventures and ministry. In the letters to Timothy and Titus we feel Paul's urgency and responsibility to develop and strengthen these younger future leaders, as well as, how to organise a community of followers of Jesus Christ.

# TITUS

## Greetings from Paul

# 1

This letter is from Paul, a slave of God and an apostle of Jesus Christ. I have been sent to bring faith to those God has chosen and to teach them to know the truth that shows them how to live godly lives. [2]This truth gives them the confidence of eternal life, which God promised them before the world began—and he cannot lie. [3]And now at the right time he has revealed this Good News, and we announce it to everyone. It is by the command of God our Saviour that I have been trusted to do this work for him.

must enjoy having guests in his home and must love all that is good. He must live wisely and be fair. He must live a devout and disciplined life. [9]He must have a strong and steadfast belief in the trustworthy message he was taught; then he will be able to encourage others with right teaching and show those who oppose it where they are wrong.

[10]For there are many who rebel against right teaching;

'You are a messenger' 1 Thessalonians 2:4

The time will come when you are asked to stand tall and be a leader at a Bible study, sports camp or church event. It may simply be a brief opportunity to share your faith with a friend or team-mate. Don't be shy. If you are a Christian, God will use you and sanction you as a messenger for his cause. Remember, you are not speaking on your own behalf but as an ambassador for Christ.

## STAND POINT

### When you are tempted to look at pornography

#### 1:15

Everything is pure to those whose hearts are pure. But nothing is pure to those who are corrupt and unbelieving, because their minds and consciences are defiled.

[4]This letter is written to Titus, my true child in the faith that we share.

May God the Father and Christ Jesus our Saviour give you grace and peace.

## Titus's Work in Crete

[5]I left you on the island of Crete so you could complete our work there and appoint elders in each town as I instructed you.

[6]An elder must be well thought of for his good life. He must be faithful to his wife, and his children must be believers who are not wild or rebellious. [7]An elder must live a blameless life because he is God's minister. He must not be arrogant or quick-tempered; he must not be a heavy drinker, violent, or greedy for money. [8]He

they engage in useless talk and deceive people. This is especially true of those who insist on circumcision for salvation. [11]They must be silenced. By their wrong teaching, they have already turned whole families away from the truth. Such teachers only want your money.

[12]One of their own men, a prophet from Crete, has said about them, "The people of Crete are all liars; they are cruel animals and lazy gluttons." [13]This is true. So rebuke them as sternly as necessary to make them strong in the faith. [14]They must stop listening to Jewish myths and the commands of people who have turned their backs on the truth.

[15]Everything is pure to those whose hearts are pure. But nothing is pure to those who are corrupt and unbelieving, because their minds and consciences are defiled. [16]**Such people claim they know God, but they deny him by the way they live. They are despicable and disobedient, worthless for doing anything good.**

## Promote Right Teaching

# 2

But as for you, promote the kind of living that reflects right teaching. [2]Teach the older men to exercise self-control, to be worthy of respect, and to live wisely. They must have strong faith and be filled with love and patience.

[3]Similarly, teach the older women to live in a way that is appropriate for someone serving the Lord. They must not go around speaking evil of others and must not

What are the five most brutal conditioning workouts?

1.
2.
3.
4.
5.

## BIG FIVE

be heavy drinkers. Instead, they should teach others what is good. ⁴These older women must train the younger women to love their husbands and their children, ⁵to live wisely and be pure, to take care of their homes, to do good, and to be submissive to their husbands. Then they will not bring shame on the word of God.

⁶In the same way, encourage the young men to live wisely in all they do. ⁷And you yourself must be an example to them by doing good deeds of every kind. Let everything you do reflect the integrity and seriousness of your teaching. ⁸Let your teaching be so correct that it can't be criticized. Then those who want to argue will be ashamed because they won't have anything bad to say about us.

⁹Slaves must obey their masters and do their best to please them. They must not talk back ¹⁰or steal, but they must show themselves to be entirely trustworthy and good. Then they will make the teaching about God our Saviour attractive in every way.

¹¹For the grace of God has been revealed, bringing salvation to all people. ¹²And we are instructed to turn from godless living and sinful pleasures. We should live in this evil world with self-control, right conduct, and devotion to God, ¹³while we look forward to that wonderful event when the glory of our great God and Saviour, Jesus Christ, will be revealed. ¹⁴He gave his life to free us from every kind of sin, to cleanse us, and to make us his very own people, totally committed to doing what is right. ¹⁵You must teach these things and encourage your people to do them, correcting them when necessary. You have the authority to do this, so don't let anyone ignore you or disregard what you say.

## Do What Is Good

# 3

Remind your people to submit to the government and its officers. They should be obedient, always ready to do what is good. ²They must not speak evil of anyone, and they must avoid quarrelling. Instead, they should be gentle and show true humility to everyone.

³Once we, too, were foolish and disobedient. We were misled by others and became slaves to many wicked desires and evil pleasures. Our lives were full of evil and envy. We hated others, and they hated us.

⁴But then God our Saviour showed us his kindness and love. ⁵He saved us, not because of the good things we did, but because of his mercy. He washed away our sins and gave us a new life through the Holy Spirit.

⁶He generously poured out the Spirit upon us because of what Jesus Christ our Saviour did. ⁷He declared us not guilty because of his great kindness. And now we know that we will inherit eternal life. ⁸These things I have told you are all true. I want you to insist on them so that everyone who trusts in God will be careful to do good deeds all the time. These things are good and beneficial for everyone.

CH 3:1-2 WHAT'S IT SAYING?

WHAT AM I GOING TO ∂O ABOUT IT?

## Paul's Final Remarks and Greetings

⁹Do not get involved in foolish discussions about spiritual pedigrees or in quarrels and fights about obedience to Jewish laws. These kinds of things are useless and a waste of time. ¹⁰If anyone is causing divisions among you, give a first and second warning. After that, have nothing more to do with that person. ¹¹For people like that have turned away from the truth. They are sinning, and they condemn themselves.

¹²I am planning to send either Artemas or Tychicus to you. As soon as one of them arrives, do your best to meet me at Nicopolis as quickly as you can, for I have decided to stay there for the winter. ¹³Do everything you can to help Zenas the lawyer and Apollos with their trip. See that they are given everything they need.

¹⁴For our people should not have unproductive lives. They must learn to do good by helping others who have urgent needs.

¹⁵Everybody here sends greetings. Please give my greetings to all of the believers who love us. May God's grace be with you all.

# WHAT DOES IT MEAN?

### Faith

"Faith in Jesus Christ is a saving grace, whereby we rest upon him alone to receive our salvation, as offered to us in the gospel." The object of saving faith is the whole revealed word of God. Its primary concept is trust. When a thing is true, it is therefore worthy of trust. Faith in Christ is full assurance of truth, in accordance with the evidence on which it rests. Faith is the result of teaching (Rom. 10:14-17) and knowledge illuminated by the Holy Spirit. Faith in Christ secures for the believer freedom from condemnation, or justification before God. (John 14:19; Rom. 6:4-10; Eph. 4:15,16, etc).

On and
Off the
pitch

live it

They say sport is the great 'evener', which can break down barriers of race, status, wealth and privilege. But once you leave the pitch many of these barriers rise up again. In this very private letter, Paul explains to the slave owner Philemon, in a most tactful way, that those in Christ are all the same, and that there are no walls separating Christians regardless of social status. This book is also a great lesson on how we should forgive and welcome back those who have hurt us.

Philemon was a faithful man and generous worker for the cause of Christ. He was part of the Colossian church, a convert and 'dear friend' of the Apostle Paul. Paul is writing to him pleading that he 'take back' a runaway slave, Onesimus, and not only forgive him but embrace him as a new fellow believer and brother in Christ. Onesimus had fled to Rome where he met Paul and gave his heart to Christ, but now he willingly returned to Philemon his master. We as Christians also serve a master. Our destiny and joy are both found in turning to and serving the Master.

# Philemon

# PHILEMON

## Greetings from Paul

This letter is from Paul, in prison for preaching the Good News about Christ Jesus, and from our brother Timothy.

It is written to Philemon, our much loved co-worker, [2]and to our sister Apphia and to Archippus, a fellow soldier of the cross. I am also writing to the church that meets in your house.
[3]May God our Father and the Lord Jesus Christ give you grace and peace.

## Paul's Thanksgiving and Prayer

[4]I always thank God when I pray for you, Philemon, [5]because I keep hearing of your trust in the Lord Jesus and your love for all of God's people. **[6]You are generous because of your faith. And I am praying that you will really put your generosity to work, for in so doing you will come to an understanding of all the good things we can do for Christ.** [7]I myself have gained much joy and comfort from your love, my brother, because your kindness has so often refreshed the hearts of God's people.

## Paul's Appeal for Onesimus

[8]That is why I am boldly asking a favour of you. I could demand it in the name of Christ because it is the right thing for you to do, [9]but because of our love, I prefer just to ask you. So take this as a request from your friend Paul, an old man, now in prison for the sake of Christ Jesus.
[10]My plea is that you show kindness to Onesimus. I think of him as my own son because he became a believer as a result of my ministry here in prison. [11]Onesimus hasn't been of much use to you in the past, but now he is very useful to both of us. [12]I am sending him back to you, and with him comes my own heart. [13]I really wanted to keep him here with me while I am in these chains for preaching the Good News, and he would have helped me on your behalf. [14]But I didn't want to do anything without your consent. And I didn't want you to help because you were forced to do it but because you wanted to. [15]Perhaps you could think of it this way: Onesimus ran away for a little while so you could have him back for ever. [16]He is no longer just a slave; he is a beloved brother, especially to me. Now he will mean much more to you, both as a slave and as a brother in the Lord.
[17]So if you consider me your partner, give him the same welcome you would give me if I were coming. [18]If he has harmed you in any way or stolen anything from you, charge me for it. [19]I, Paul, write this in my own handwriting: "I will repay it." And I won't mention that you owe me your very soul!
[20]Yes, dear brother, please do me this favour for the Lord's sake. Give me this encouragement in Christ. [21]I am confident as I write this letter that you will do what I ask and even more!
[22]Please keep a guest room ready for me, for I am hoping that God will answer your prayers and let me return to you soon.

## Paul's Final Greetings

[23]Epaphras, my fellow prisoner in Christ Jesus, sends you his greetings. [24]So do Mark, Aristarchus, Demas, and Luke, my co-workers.
[25]The grace of the Lord Jesus Christ be with your spirit.

The soccer referee's whistle was introduced in 1878. Prior to this a referee had to rely on waving a handkerchief.

# Sports Specific Training:

Obviously a javelin thrower and a pole-vaulter will need unique and skill-specific training regimes. Ideally, a training programme should be individually tailored to meet the needs of each discipline or sport; however, many athletes train in a group or team flexibility programme. This team-centred programme is great for team building. However, in such cases, it is still essential that each individual athlete be properly instructed to concentrate on specific areas that need additional focus.

# Hebrews

In Hebrews we learn how wonderfully God's purpose and plan come together in Jesus. For two thousand years the church has debated the authorship of the book of Hebrews. Now we can answer the big question - God wrote the book! The whole Bible is God's autobiography, he merely used men to pen the manuscript. We really don't know who God used to write this great book, though a small majority of Biblical scholars arguably lean toward the Apostle Paul. That said, it was God's good pleasure that we should not know the identity of the author though he certainly writes with apostolic authority. Clearly it was intended for Jewish converts to the faith and probably focused on the converts in Jerusalem. These Christians were being torn by the rich tradition of their old Jewish system and culture and the emergence of Jesus as the fulfilment of the Old Testament.

Its purpose was to show the true meaning of the Mosaic system (the Old Covenant) and its representative and temporary character. It proves that the Levitical priesthood was a 'shadow' of that of Christ, and that the Old Testament sacrifices prefigured the great and all-perfect sacrifice, God's Son. In Hebrews we are shown how the Old Testament reveals God and his plan for ultimately redeeming his people: it all points to the cross.

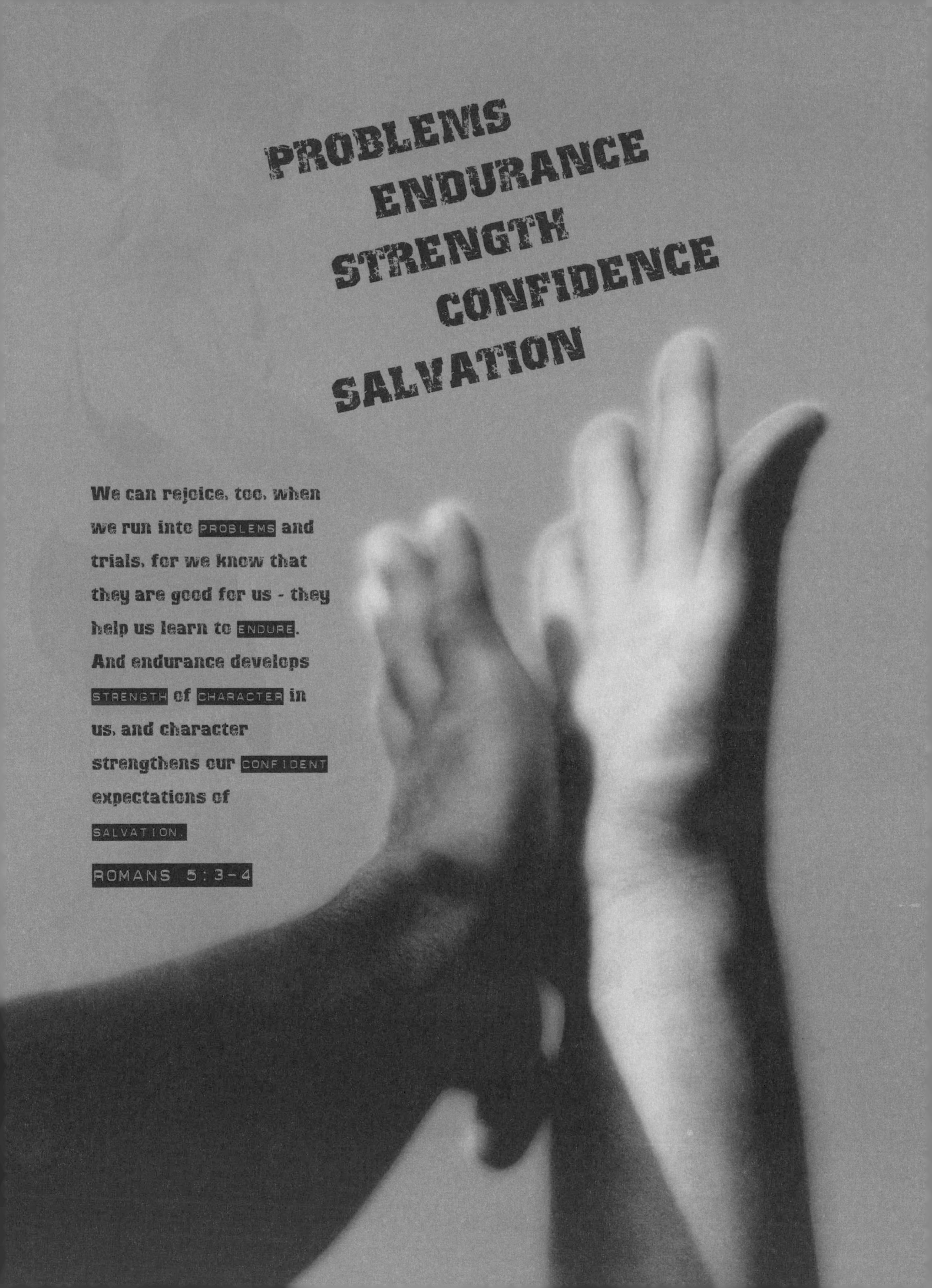

PROBLEMS
ENDURANCE
STRENGTH
CONFIDENCE
SALVATION

We can rejoice, too, when we run into `PROBLEMS` and trials, for we know that they are good for us - they help us learn to `ENDURE`. And endurance develops `STRENGTH` of `CHARACTER` in us, and character strengthens our `CONFIDENT` expectations of `SALVATION`.

`ROMANS 5:3-4`

# HEBREWS

## Jesus Christ Is God's Son

# 1

Long ago God spoke many times and in many ways to our ancestors through the prophets. [2]But now in these final days, he has spoken to us through his Son. God promised everything to the Son as an inheritance, and through the Son he made the universe and everything in it. [3]The Son reflects God's own glory, and everything about him represents God exactly. He sustains the universe by the mighty power of his command. After he died to cleanse us from the stain of sin, he sat down in the place of honour at the right hand of the majestic God of heaven.

## Christ Is Greater Than the Angels

[4]This shows that God's Son is far greater than the angels, just as the name God gave him is far greater than their names. [5]For God never said to any angel what he said to Jesus:
"You are my Son.
Today I have become your Father."
And again God said,
"I will be his Father,
and he will be my Son."
[6]And then, when he presented his honoured Son to the world, God said, "Let all the angels of God worship him."
[7]God calls his angels
"messengers swift as the wind,
and servants made of flaming fire."
[8]But to his Son he says,
"Your throne, O God, endures for ever and ever.
Your royal power is expressed in righteousness.
[9]You love what is right and hate what is wrong.
Therefore God, your God, has anointed you,
pouring out the oil of joy on you more than on anyone else."
[10]And,
"Lord, in the beginning you laid the foundation of the earth,
and the heavens are the work of your hands.
[11]Even they will perish, but you remain for ever.
They will wear out like old clothing.
[12]You will roll them up like an old coat.
They will fade away like old clothing.
But you are always the same;
you will never grow old."

**The verse Psalm 118:8 "It is better to trust the Lord than to put confidence in people" is in the exact middle of the complete Old and New Testament.**

[13]And God never said to an angel, as he did to his Son,
"Sit in honour at my right hand
until I humble your enemies,
making them a footstool under your feet."
[14]But angels are only servants. They are spirits sent from God to care for those who will receive salvation.

## A Warning against Drifting Away

# 2

So we must listen very carefully to the truth we have heard, or we may drift away from it. [2]The message God delivered through angels has always proved true, and the people were punished for every violation of the law and every act of disobedience. [3]What makes us think that we can escape if we are indifferent to this great salvation that was announced by the Lord Jesus himself? It was passed on to us by those who heard him speak, [4]and God verified the message by signs and wonders and various miracles and by giving gifts of the Holy Spirit whenever he chose to do so.

## Jesus, the Man

[5]And furthermore, the future world we are talking about will not be controlled by angels. [6]For somewhere in the Scriptures it says,
"What is man that you should think of him,
and the son of man that you should care for him?
[7]For a little while you made him lower than the angels,
and you crowned him with glory and honour.
[8]You gave him authority over all things."
Now when it says "all things," it means nothing is left out. But we have not yet seen all of this happen. [9]What we do see is Jesus, who "for a little while was made lower than the angels" and now is "crowned with glory and honour" because he suffered death for us. Yes, by God's grace, Jesus tasted death for everyone in all the world. [10]And it was only right that God—who made everything and for whom everything was made—should bring his many children into glory. Through the suffering of Jesus, God made him a perfect leader, one fit to bring them into their salvation.

[11]**So now Jesus and the ones he makes holy have the same Father. That is why Jesus is not ashamed to call them his brothers and sisters.** [12]For he said to God,
"I will declare the wonder of your name to my brothers and sisters.
I will praise you among all your people."
[13]He also said, "I will put my trust in him." And in the same context he said, "Here I am—together with the children God has given me."
[14]Because God's children are human beings—made of flesh and blood—Jesus also became flesh and blood by being born in human form. For only as a human being could he die, and only by dying could he break the power of the Devil, who had the power of death. [15]Only in this way could he deliver those who have lived all their lives as slaves to the fear of dying.

Be courageous. Courage allows you to be firm when facing danger and temptation. You may feel scared and be tempted to do bad things; that's a normal part of life. What courage does is allow you to live for God, to speak, react and perform whilst under pressure.
"Be on guard. Stand true to what you believe. Be courageous. Be strong." 1 Corinthians 16:13

[16]We all know that Jesus came to help the descendants of Abraham, not to help the angels. [17]Therefore, it was necessary for Jesus to be in every respect like us, his brothers and sisters, so that he could be our merciful and faithful High Priest before God. He then could offer a sacrifice that would take away the sins of the people. [18]Since he himself has gone through suffering and temptation, he is able to help us when we are being tempted.

## Jesus Is Greater Than Moses

# 3

And so, dear brothers and sisters who belong to God and are bound for heaven, think about this Jesus whom we declare to be God's Messenger and High Priest. [2]For he was faithful to God, who appointed him, just as Moses served faithfully and was entrusted with God's entire house. [3]But Jesus deserves far more glory than Moses, just as a person who builds a fine house deserves more praise than the house itself. [4]For every house has a builder, but God is the one who made everything.

[5]Moses was certainly faithful in God's house, but only as a servant. His work was an illustration of the truths God would reveal later. [6]**But Christ, the faithful Son, was in charge of the entire household. And we are God's household, if we keep up our courage and remain confident in our hope in Christ.** [7]That is why the Holy Spirit says,
"Today you must listen to his voice.
[8]Don't harden your hearts against him
as Israel did when they rebelled,
when they tested God's patience in the wilderness.
[9]There your ancestors tried my patience,
even though they saw my miracles for forty years.
[10]So I was angry with them, and I said,
'Their hearts always turn away from me.
They refuse to do what I tell them.'
[11]So in my anger I made a vow:
'They will never enter my place of rest.'"
[12]Be careful then, dear brothers and sisters. Make sure that your own hearts are not evil and unbelieving, turning you away from the living God. [13]You must warn each other every day, as long as it is called "today,"

so that none of you will be deceived by sin and hardened against God. [14]For if we are faithful to the end, trusting God just as firmly as when we first believed, we will share in all that belongs to Christ. [15]But never forget the warning:
"Today you must listen to his voice.
Don't harden your hearts against him
as Israel did when they rebelled."
[16]And who were those people who rebelled against God, even though they heard his voice? Weren't they the ones Moses led out of Egypt? [17]And who made God angry for forty years? Wasn't it the people who sinned, whose bodies fell in the wilderness? [18]And to whom was God speaking when he vowed that they would never enter his place of rest? He was speaking to those who disobeyed him. [19]So we see that they were not allowed to enter his rest because of their unbelief.

## Promised Rest for God's People

# 4

God's promise of entering his place of rest still stands, so we ought to tremble with fear that some of you might fail to get there. [2]For this Good News—that God has prepared a place of rest—has been announced to us just as it was to them. But it did them no good because they didn't believe what God told them. [3]For only we who believe can enter his place of rest. As for those who didn't believe, God said,
"In my anger I made a vow:
'They will never enter my place of rest,'"
even though his place of rest has been ready since he made the world. [4]We know it is ready because the Scriptures mention the seventh day, saying, "On the seventh day God rested from all his work." [5]But in the other passage God said, "They will never enter my place of rest." [6]So God's rest is there for people to enter. But those who formerly heard the Good News failed to enter because they disobeyed God. [7]So God set another time for entering his place of rest, and that time is today. God announced this through David a long time later in the words already quoted:
"Today you must listen to his voice.
Don't harden your hearts against him."
[8]This new place of rest was not the land of Canaan, where Joshua led them. If it had been, God would not have spoken later about another day of rest. [9]So there is a special rest still waiting for the people of God. [10]For all who enter into God's rest will find rest from their labours, just as God rested after creating the

world. ¹¹Let us do our best to enter that place of rest. For anyone who disobeys God, as the people of Israel did, will fall.

¹²**For the word of God is full of living power. It is sharper than the sharpest knife, cutting deep into our innermost thoughts and desires. It exposes us for what we really are.** ¹³Nothing in all creation can hide from him. Everything is naked and exposed before his eyes. This is the God to whom we must explain all that we have done.

**action**

**CH 4:14-16 WHAT'S IT SAYING?**

**WHAT AM I GOING TO DO ABOUT IT?**

## Christ Is Our High Priest

¹⁴That is why we have a great High Priest who has gone to heaven, Jesus the Son of God. Let us cling to him and never stop trusting him. ¹⁵This High Priest of

# WHAT DOES IT MEAN?

**Sport in scripture:**
Paul frequently draws on sporting analogies to help us better understand the Christian faith. Competitions like Grecian gymnastic contests (Gal. 2:2; 5:7; Phil. 2:16; 3:14; 1 Tim. 6:12; 2 Tim. 2:5; Heb. 12:1, 4, 12) and the numerous Greek Olympic, Pythian, Nemean, and Isthmian games were of great national importance, and the victors at any of these games of wrestling, racing, etc., were highly respected.

ours understands our weaknesses, for he faced all of the same temptations we do, yet he did not sin. ¹⁶So let us come boldly to the throne of our gracious God.

There we will receive his mercy, and we will find grace to help us when we need it.

## 5

Now a high priest is a man chosen to represent other human beings in their dealings with God. He presents their gifts to God and offers their sacrifices for sins. ²And because he is human, he is able to deal gently with the people, though they are ignorant and wayward. For he is subject to the same weaknesses they have. ³That is why he has to offer sacrifices, both for their sins and for his own sins. ⁴And no one can become a high priest simply because he wants such an honour. He has to be called by God for this work, just as Aaron was. ⁵That is why Christ did not exalt himself to become High Priest. No, he was chosen by God, who said to him,
"You are my Son.
Today I have become your Father."
⁶And in another passage God said to him,
"You are a priest for ever
in the line of Melchizedek."
⁷While Jesus was here on earth, he offered prayers and pleadings, with a loud cry and tears, to the one who could deliver him out of death. And God heard his prayers because of his reverence for God. ⁸So even though Jesus was God's Son, he learned obedience from the things he suffered. ⁹In this way, God qualified him as a perfect High Priest, and he became the source of eternal salvation for all those who obey him. ¹⁰And God designated him to be a High Priest in the line of Melchizedek.

## A Call to Spiritual Growth

¹¹There is so much more we would like to say about this. But you don't seem to listen, so it's hard to make you understand. ¹²**You have been Christians a long time now, and you ought to be teaching others. Instead, you need someone to teach you again the basic things a beginner must learn about the Scriptures. You are like babies who drink only milk and cannot eat solid food.** ¹³And a person who is living on milk isn't very far along in the Christian life and doesn't know much about doing what is right. ¹⁴Solid food is for those who are mature, who have

'A Strong and Trustworthy Anchor' Hebrews 6:16-20
Early Christians used to use the sign of an anchor (much like the fish sign) as a symbol for their faith in Christ. Don't flounder through life - hang on to God's assurance of a safe refuge. In the fickle world of sport it is nice to have an anchor, a strong promise from God that those that have faith in Christ are fastened securely to him.

# BIBLE HIT

# NOVEMBER M.A.P.

## 1
| S.D. | | P.L. | | P.G. | | S.G. | |
|---|---|---|---|---|---|---|---|
| P. | ☐ | F. | ☐ | F. | ☐ | T. | ☐ |
| F. | ☐ | W. | ☐ | W. | ☐ | P. | ☐ |
| B. | ☐ | P. | ☐ | C. | ☐ | C. | ☐ |

## 2
| S.D. | | P.L. | | P.G. | | S.G. | |
|---|---|---|---|---|---|---|---|
| P. | ☐ | F. | ☐ | F. | ☐ | T. | ☐ |
| F. | ☐ | W. | ☐ | W. | ☐ | P. | ☐ |
| B. | ☐ | P. | ☐ | C. | ☐ | C. | ☐ |

## 3
| S.D. | | P.L. | | P.G. | | S.G. | |
|---|---|---|---|---|---|---|---|
| P. | ☐ | F. | ☐ | F. | ☐ | T. | ☐ |
| F. | ☐ | W. | ☐ | W. | ☐ | P. | ☐ |
| B. | ☐ | P. | ☐ | C. | ☐ | C. | ☐ |

## 4
| S.D. | | P.L. | | P.G. | | S.G. | |
|---|---|---|---|---|---|---|---|
| P. | ☐ | F. | ☐ | F. | ☐ | T. | ☐ |
| F. | ☐ | W. | ☐ | W. | ☐ | P. | ☐ |
| B. | ☐ | P. | ☐ | C. | ☐ | C. | ☐ |

## 9
| S.D. | | P.L. | | P.G. | | S.G. | |
|---|---|---|---|---|---|---|---|
| P. | ☐ | F. | ☐ | F. | ☐ | T. | ☐ |
| F. | ☐ | W. | ☐ | W. | ☐ | P. | ☐ |
| B. | ☐ | P. | ☐ | C. | ☐ | C. | ☐ |

## 10
| S.D. | | P.L. | | P.G. | | S.G. | |
|---|---|---|---|---|---|---|---|
| P. | ☐ | F. | ☐ | F. | ☐ | T. | ☐ |
| F. | ☐ | W. | ☐ | W. | ☐ | P. | ☐ |
| B. | ☐ | P. | ☐ | C. | ☐ | C. | ☐ |

## 11
| S.D. | | P.L. | | P.G. | | S.G. | |
|---|---|---|---|---|---|---|---|
| P. | ☐ | F. | ☐ | F. | ☐ | T. | ☐ |
| F. | ☐ | W. | ☐ | W. | ☐ | P. | ☐ |
| B. | ☐ | P. | ☐ | C. | ☐ | C. | ☐ |

## 12
| S.D. | | P.L. | | P.G. | | S.G. | |
|---|---|---|---|---|---|---|---|
| P. | ☐ | F. | ☐ | F. | ☐ | T. | ☐ |
| F. | ☐ | W. | ☐ | W. | ☐ | P. | ☐ |
| B. | ☐ | P. | ☐ | C. | ☐ | C. | ☐ |

## 17
| S.D. | | P.L. | | P.G. | | S.G. | |
|---|---|---|---|---|---|---|---|
| P. | ☐ | F. | ☐ | F. | ☐ | T. | ☐ |
| F. | ☐ | W. | ☐ | W. | ☐ | P. | ☐ |
| B. | ☐ | P. | ☐ | C. | ☐ | C. | ☐ |

## 18
| S.D. | | P.L. | | P.G. | | S.G. | |
|---|---|---|---|---|---|---|---|
| P. | ☐ | F. | ☐ | F. | ☐ | T. | ☐ |
| F. | ☐ | W. | ☐ | W. | ☐ | P. | ☐ |
| B. | ☐ | P. | ☐ | C. | ☐ | C. | ☐ |

## 19
| S.D. | | P.L. | | P.G. | | S.G. | |
|---|---|---|---|---|---|---|---|
| P. | ☐ | F. | ☐ | F. | ☐ | T. | ☐ |
| F. | ☐ | W. | ☐ | W. | ☐ | P. | ☐ |
| B. | ☐ | P. | ☐ | C. | ☐ | C. | ☐ |

## 20
| S.D. | | P.L. | | P.G. | | S.G. | |
|---|---|---|---|---|---|---|---|
| P. | ☐ | F. | ☐ | F. | ☐ | T. | ☐ |
| F. | ☐ | W. | ☐ | W. | ☐ | P. | ☐ |
| B. | ☐ | P. | ☐ | C. | ☐ | C. | ☐ |

## 25
| S.D. | | P.L. | | P.G. | | S.G. | |
|---|---|---|---|---|---|---|---|
| P. | ☐ | F. | ☐ | F. | ☐ | T. | ☐ |
| F. | ☐ | W. | ☐ | W. | ☐ | P. | ☐ |
| B. | ☐ | P. | ☐ | C. | ☐ | C. | ☐ |

## 26
| S.D. | | P.L. | | P.G. | | S.G. | |
|---|---|---|---|---|---|---|---|
| P. | ☐ | F. | ☐ | F. | ☐ | T. | ☐ |
| F. | ☐ | W. | ☐ | W. | ☐ | P. | ☐ |
| B. | ☐ | P. | ☐ | C. | ☐ | C. | ☐ |

## 27
| S.D. | | P.L. | | P.G. | | S.G. | |
|---|---|---|---|---|---|---|---|
| P. | ☐ | F. | ☐ | F. | ☐ | T. | ☐ |
| F. | ☐ | W. | ☐ | W. | ☐ | P. | ☐ |
| B. | ☐ | P. | ☐ | C. | ☐ | C. | ☐ |

## 28
| S.D. | | P.L. | | P.G. | | S.G. | |
|---|---|---|---|---|---|---|---|
| P. | ☐ | F. | ☐ | F. | ☐ | T. | ☐ |
| F. | ☐ | W. | ☐ | W. | ☐ | P. | ☐ |
| B. | ☐ | P. | ☐ | C. | ☐ | C. | ☐ |

## Spiritual Disciplines

**Prayer**

**Faith Community**

**Bible Reading**

## Prayer List

**Friends**

**World**

**Personal**

Who am I....
Where am I going....
How am I going to get there?

# nt:sport
## MONTHLY ACTION PLAN

### 5
| S.D. | P.L. | P.G. | S.G. |
|---|---|---|---|
| P. ☐ | F. ☐ | F. ☐ | T. ☐ |
| F. ☐ | W. ☐ | W. ☐ | P. ☐ |
| B. ☐ | P. ☐ | C. ☐ | C. ☐ |

### 6
| S.D. | P.L. | P.G. | S.G. |
|---|---|---|---|
| P. ☐ | F. ☐ | F. ☐ | T. ☐ |
| F. ☐ | W. ☐ | W. ☐ | P. ☐ |
| B. ☐ | P. ☐ | C. ☐ | C. ☐ |

### 7
| S.D. | P.L. | P.G. | S.G. |
|---|---|---|---|
| P. ☐ | F. ☐ | F. ☐ | T. ☐ |
| F. ☐ | W. ☐ | W. ☐ | P. ☐ |
| B. ☐ | P. ☐ | C. ☐ | C. ☐ |

### 8
| S.D. | P.L. | P.G. | S.G. |
|---|---|---|---|
| P. ☐ | F. ☐ | F. ☐ | T. ☐ |
| F. ☐ | W. ☐ | W. ☐ | P. ☐ |
| B. ☐ | P. ☐ | C. ☐ | C. ☐ |

### 13
| S.D. | P.L. | P.G. | S.G. |
|---|---|---|---|
| P. ☐ | F. ☐ | F. ☐ | T. ☐ |
| F. ☐ | W. ☐ | W. ☐ | P. ☐ |
| B. ☐ | P. ☐ | C. ☐ | C. ☐ |

### 14
| S.D. | P.L. | P.G. | S.G. |
|---|---|---|---|
| P. ☐ | F. ☐ | F. ☐ | T. ☐ |
| F. ☐ | W. ☐ | W. ☐ | P. ☐ |
| B. ☐ | P. ☐ | C. ☐ | C. ☐ |

### 15
| S.D. | P.L. | P.G. | S.G. |
|---|---|---|---|
| P. ☐ | F. ☐ | F. ☐ | T. ☐ |
| F. ☐ | W. ☐ | W. ☐ | P. ☐ |
| B. ☐ | P. ☐ | C. ☐ | C. ☐ |

### 16
| S.D. | P.L. | P.G. | S.G. |
|---|---|---|---|
| P. ☐ | F. ☐ | F. ☐ | T. ☐ |
| F. ☐ | W. ☐ | W. ☐ | P. ☐ |
| B. ☐ | P. ☐ | C. ☐ | C. ☐ |

### 21
| S.D. | P.L. | P.G. | S.G. |
|---|---|---|---|
| P. ☐ | F. ☐ | F. ☐ | T. ☐ |
| F. ☐ | W. ☐ | W. ☐ | P. ☐ |
| B. ☐ | P. ☐ | C. ☐ | C. ☐ |

### 22
| S.D. | P.L. | P.G. | S.G. |
|---|---|---|---|
| P. ☐ | F. ☐ | F. ☐ | T. ☐ |
| F. ☐ | W. ☐ | W. ☐ | P. ☐ |
| B. ☐ | P. ☐ | C. ☐ | C. ☐ |

### 23
| S.D. | P.L. | P.G. | S.G. |
|---|---|---|---|
| P. ☐ | F. ☐ | F. ☐ | T. ☐ |
| F. ☐ | W. ☐ | W. ☐ | P. ☐ |
| B. ☐ | P. ☐ | C. ☐ | C. ☐ |

### 24
| S.D. | P.L. | P.G. | S.G. |
|---|---|---|---|
| P. ☐ | F. ☐ | F. ☐ | T. ☐ |
| F. ☐ | W. ☐ | W. ☐ | P. ☐ |
| B. ☐ | P. ☐ | C. ☐ | C. ☐ |

### 29
| S.D. | P.L. | P.G. | S.G. |
|---|---|---|---|
| P. ☐ | F. ☐ | F. ☐ | T. ☐ |
| F. ☐ | W. ☐ | W. ☐ | P. ☐ |
| B. ☐ | P. ☐ | C. ☐ | C. ☐ |

### 30
| S.D. | P.L. | P.G. | S.G. |
|---|---|---|---|
| P. ☐ | F. ☐ | F. ☐ | T. ☐ |
| F. ☐ | W. ☐ | W. ☐ | P. ☐ |
| B. ☐ | P. ☐ | C. ☐ | C. ☐ |

**Proverbs 20:24**

How can we understand the road we travel? It is the Lord who directs our steps.

## Personal Goals

**Family**

**Work/School/Social**

**Challenge**

## Sport Goals

**Training**

**Performance**

**Competition Results**

(For designing your MAP - Monthly Action Plan - see introduction pages)

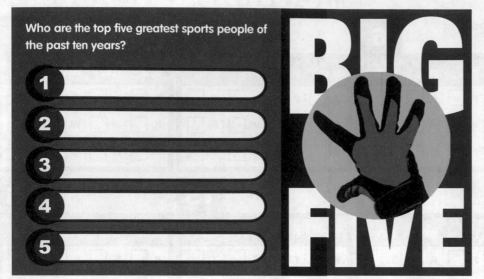

**Who are the top five greatest sports people of the past ten years?**

1 _____
2 _____
3 _____
4 _____
5 _____

**BIG FIVE**

trained themselves to recognize the difference between right and wrong and then do what is right.

# 6

So let us stop going over the basics of Christianity again and again. Let us go on instead and become mature in our understanding. Surely we don't need to start all over again with the importance of turning away from evil deeds and placing our faith in God. [2]You don't need further instruction about baptisms, the laying on of hands, the resurrection of the dead, and eternal judgement. [3]And so, God willing, we will move forward to further understanding.

[4]For it is impossible to restore to repentance those who were once enlightened—those who have experienced the good things of heaven and shared in the Holy Spirit, [5]who have tasted the goodness of the word of God and the power of the

age to come—[6]and who then turn away from God. It is impossible to bring such people to repentance again because they are nailing the Son of God to the cross again by rejecting him, holding him up to public shame.

[7]When the ground soaks up the rain that falls on it and bears a good crop for the farmer, it has the blessing of God. [8]But if a field bears thistles and thorns, it is useless. The farmer will condemn that field and burn it.

[9]Dear friends, even though we are talking like this, we really don't believe that it applies to you. We are confident that you are meant for better things, things that come with salvation. [10]**For God is not unfair. He will not forget how hard you have worked for him and how you have shown your love to him by caring for other Christians, as you still do.** [11]Our great desire is that you will keep right on loving others as long as life lasts, in order to make certain that what you hope for will come true. [12]Then you will not become spiritually dull and indifferent. Instead, you will follow the example of those who are going to inherit God's promises because of their faith and patience.

## God's Promises Bring Hope

[13]For example, there was God's promise to Abraham. Since there was no one greater to swear by, God took an oath in his own name, saying:
[14]"I will certainly bless you richly,
and I will multiply your descendants into countless millions."
[15]Then Abraham waited patiently, and he received what God had promised.

[16]When people take an oath, they call on someone greater than themselves to hold them to it. And without any question that oath is binding. [17]God also bound himself with an oath, so that those who received the promise could be perfectly sure that he would never change his mind. [18]So God has given us both his promise and his oath. These two things are unchangeable because it is impossible for God to lie. Therefore, we who have fled to him for refuge can take new courage, for we can hold on to his promise with confidence.

[19]This confidence is like a strong and trustworthy anchor for our souls. It leads us through the curtain of heaven into God's inner sanctuary. [20]Jesus has already gone in there for us. He has become our eternal High Priest in the line of Melchizedek.

## Melchizedek Is Compared to Abraham

# 7

This Melchizedek was king of the city of Salem and also a priest of God Most High. When Abraham was returning home after winning a great battle against many kings, Melchizedek met him and blessed him. [2]Then Abraham took a tenth of all he had won in the battle and gave it to Melchizedek. His name means "king of justice." He is also "king of peace" because Salem means "peace." [3]There is no record of his father or mother or any of his ancestors—no beginning or end to his life. He remains a priest for ever, resembling the Son of God.

[4]Consider then how great this Melchizedek was. Even Abraham, the great patriarch of Israel, recognized how great Melchizedek was by giving him a tenth of what he had taken in battle. [5]Now the priests, who are descendants of Levi, are commanded in the law of Moses to collect a tithe from all the people, even

## STAND POINT

**When you are not getting enough playing time.**

### 6:10

For God is not unfair. He will not forget how hard you have worked for him and how you have shown your love to him by caring for other Christians, as you still do.

**STATS**

Due to World Wars I and II, Summer Olympic Games were not held in 1916, 1940, or 1944.

## Winners are patient!

In sport you are constantly waiting and persisting - whether you are waiting for the season to begin, the match to start, a play to develop, an injury to heal, or to be called up for your country. Sport can teach you to persevere and be patient. Knowing God is in control and waiting peacefully is a great way to express faith and worship to God. Patience is a quality for strong people.

"Don't worry about anything: instead pray about everything. Tell God what you need, and thank him for what he has done". Philippians 4:6

### Winners can wait!

though they are their own relatives. ⁶But Melchizedek, who was not even related to Levi, collected a tenth from Abraham. And Melchizedek placed a blessing upon Abraham, the one who had already received the promises of God. ⁷And without question, the person who has the power to bless is always greater than the person who is blessed.

⁸In the case of Jewish priests, tithes are paid to men who will die. But Melchizedek is greater than they are, because we are told that he lives on. ⁹In addition, we might even say that Levi's descendants, the ones who collect the tithe, paid a tithe to Melchizedek through their ancestor Abraham. ¹⁰For although Levi wasn't born yet, the seed from which he came was in Abraham's loins when Melchizedek collected the tithe from him.

¹¹And finally, if the priesthood of Levi could have achieved God's purposes—and it was that priesthood on which the law was based—why did God need to send a different priest from the line of Melchizedek, instead of from the line of Levi and Aaron? ¹²And when the priesthood is changed, the law must also be changed to permit it. ¹³For the one we are talking about belongs to a different tribe, whose members do not serve at the altar. ¹⁴What I mean is, our Lord came from the tribe of Judah, and Moses never mentioned Judah in connection with the priesthood.

### Christ Is like Melchizedek

¹⁵The change in God's law is even more evident from the fact that a different priest, who is like Melchizedek, has now come. ¹⁶He became a priest, not by meeting the old requirement of belonging to the tribe of Levi, but by the power of a life that cannot be destroyed. ¹⁷And the psalmist pointed this out when he said of Christ,

"You are a priest for ever
in the line of Melchizedek."

¹⁸Yes, the old requirement about the priesthood was set aside because it was weak and useless. ¹⁹For the law made nothing perfect, and now a better hope has taken its place. And that is how we draw near to God. ²⁰God took an oath that Christ would always be a priest, but he never did this for any other priest. ²¹Only to Jesus did he say,

"The Lord has taken an oath
and will not break his vow:
'You are a priest for ever.'"

²²Because of God's oath, it is Jesus who guarantees the effectiveness of this better covenant.

²³Another difference is that there were many priests under the old system. When one priest died, another had to take his place. ²⁴But Jesus remains a priest for ever; his priesthood will never end. ²⁵**Therefore he is able, once and for ever, to save everyone who comes to God through**

him. He lives for ever to plead with God on their behalf.

²⁶He is the kind of high priest we need because he is holy and blameless, unstained by sin. He has now been set apart from sinners, and he has been given the highest place of honour in heaven. ²⁷He does not need to offer sacrifices every day like the other high priests. They did this for their own sins first and then for the sins of the people. But Jesus did this once for all when he sacrificed himself on the cross. ²⁸Those who were high priests under the law of Moses were limited by human weakness. But after the law was given, God appointed his Son with an oath, and his Son has been made perfect for ever.

### Christ Is Our High Priest

**8**

Here is the main point: Our High Priest sat down in the place of highest honour in heaven, at God's right hand. ²There he ministers in the sacred tent, the true place of worship that was built by the Lord and not by human hands.

³And since every high priest is required to offer gifts and sacrifices, our High Priest must make an offering, too. ⁴If he were here on earth, he would not even be a priest, since there already are priests who offer the gifts required by the law of Moses. ⁵They serve in a place of worship that is only a copy, a shadow of the real one in heaven. For when Moses was getting ready to build the Tabernacle, God gave him

### If You Coach, Coach Positively:

'The things that get rewarded get done.' Encourage the athletes that come prepared, ready to learn, and wanting to work, regardless of their skill. Give recognition for effort, not just results. Most improvements come about little by little. Note and reinforce the little victories on the way to the play that wins the championship game.

# profiles

Bible FACTS

## Moses:

'Who am I, that I should go to Pharaoh and bring the Israelites out of Egypt?' Exodus 3:11. Moses was a giant in history with a privileged upbringing yet when commanded to free the Israelites and bring them to the Promised Land of their ancestors, he felt inadequate. The sense of unworthiness or weakness is a huge power seen in many successful Bible heroes. We are inadequate, but when that knowledge forces us to beg God for power then great things can happen. Moses survived the death penalty given by Pharaoh, the ruler of Egypt, who had for years used the people of Joseph (Israelites) to be slaves for Egypt. Moses, after being given a privileged upbringing, eventually fled to the desert. But God had a huge task for Moses in freeing God's special people. Moses conceded and with the help of his brother and God's power led two million people out of slavery and into an odyssey which lasted forty years in the wilderness. Moses obeyed God and formed a nation that would influence the world in which we live today.

this warning: "Be sure that you make everything according to the design I have shown you here on the mountain." [6]But our High Priest has been given a ministry that is far superior to the ministry of those who serve under the old laws, for he is the one who guarantees for us a better covenant with God, based on better promises.

**What The Bible Says About Itself: "For the word of God is full of living power. It is sharper than the sharpest knife cutting deep into our innermost thoughts and desires." (Hebrews 4:12)**

[7]If the first covenant had been faultless, there would have been no need for a second covenant to replace it. [8]But God himself found fault with the old one when he said:

"The day will come, says the Lord,
when I will make a new covenant
with the people of Israel and Judah.
[9]This covenant will not be like the one
I made with their ancestors
when I took them by the hand
and led them out of the land of Egypt.
They did not remain faithful to my covenant,
so I turned my back on them, says the Lord.
[10]But this is the new covenant I will make
with the people of Israel on that day, says the Lord:
I will put my laws in their minds
so they will understand them,
and I will write them on their hearts
so they will obey them.
I will be their God,
and they will be my people.
[11]And they will not need to teach their neighbours,
nor will they need to teach their family,
saying, 'You should know the Lord.'
For everyone, from the least to the greatest,
will already know me.
[12]And I will forgive their wrongdoings,
and I will never again remember their sins."
[13]When God speaks of a new covenant, it means he has made the first one obsolete. It is now out of date and ready to be put aside.

## Old Rules about Worship

# 9

Now in that first covenant between God and Israel, there were regulations for worship and a sacred tent here on earth. [2]There were two rooms in this tent. In the first room were a lampstand, a table, and loaves of holy bread on the table. This was called the Holy Place. [3]Then there was a curtain, and behind the curtain was the second room called the Most Holy Place. [4]In that room were a gold incense altar and a wooden chest called the Ark of the Covenant, which was covered with gold on all sides. Inside the Ark were a gold jar containing some manna, Aaron's staff that sprouted leaves, and the stone tablets of the covenant with the Ten Commandments written on them. [5]The glorious cherubim were above the Ark. Their wings were stretched out over the Ark's cover, the place of atonement. But we cannot explain all of these things now.

[6]When these things were all in place, the priests went in and out of the first room regularly as they performed their religious duties. [7]But only the high priest goes into the Most Holy Place, and only once a year, and always with blood, which he offers to God to cover his own sins and the sins the people have committed in ignorance. [8]By these regulations the Holy Spirit revealed that the Most Holy Place was not open

count on it

**Brand New!**
When you give yourself to Christ you become brand new. You get a new set of clothes, a new race to run and a new finish line to run towards. "What this means is that those who become Christians become new persons. They are not the same any more, for the old life is gone. A new life has begun!" 2 Corinthians 5:17
**Count on it!**

to the people as long as the first room and the entire system it represents were still in use.

⁹This is an illustration pointing to the present time. For the gifts and sacrifices that the priests offer are not able to cleanse the consciences of the people who bring them. ¹⁰For that old system deals only with food and drink and ritual washing—external regulations that are in effect only until their limitations can be corrected.

## Christ Is the Perfect Sacrifice

¹¹So Christ has now become the High Priest over all the good things that have come. He has entered that great, perfect sanctuary in heaven, not made by human hands and not part of this created world. **¹²Once for all time he took blood into that Most Holy Place, but not the blood of goats and calves. He took his own blood, and with it he secured our salvation for ever.**

¹³Under the old system, the blood of goats and bulls and the ashes of a young cow could cleanse people's bodies from ritual defilement. ¹⁴Just think how much more the blood of Christ will purify our hearts from

The first Winter Olympics were in 1924 at Chamonix, France.

deeds that lead to death so that we can worship the living God. For by the power of the eternal Spirit, Christ offered himself to God as a perfect sacrifice for our sins. ¹⁵That is why he is the one who mediates the new covenant between God and people, so that all who

are invited can receive the eternal inheritance God has promised them. For Christ died to set them free from the penalty of the sins they had committed under that first covenant.

¹⁶Now when someone dies and leaves a will, no one gets anything until it is proved that the person who wrote the will is dead. ¹⁷The will goes into effect only after the death of the person who wrote it. While the person is still alive, no one can use the will to get any of the things promised to them.

¹⁸That is why blood was required under the first covenant as a proof of death. ¹⁹For after Moses had given the people all of God's laws, he took the blood of calves and goats, along with water, and sprinkled both the book of God's laws and all the people, using branches of hyssop bushes and scarlet wool. ²⁰Then he said, "This blood confirms the covenant God has made with you." ²¹And in the same way, he sprinkled blood on the sacred tent and on everything used for worship. ²²In fact, we can say that according to the law of Moses, nearly everything was purified by sprinkling with blood. Without the shedding of blood, there is no forgiveness of sins.

²³That is why the earthly tent and everything in it—which were copies of things in heaven—had to be purified by the blood of animals. But the real things in heaven had to be purified with far better sacrifices than the blood of animals.

²⁴For Christ has entered into heaven itself to appear now before God as our Advocate. He did not go into the earthly place of worship, for that was merely a copy of the real Temple in heaven. ²⁵Nor did he enter heaven to offer himself again and again, like the earthly high priest who enters the Most Holy Place year after year to offer the blood of an animal. ²⁶If that had been necessary, he would have had to die again and again, ever since the world began. But no! He came once for all time, at the end of the age, to remove the power of sin for ever by his sacrificial death for us.

²⁷And just as it is destined that each person dies only

STAND POINT

**When you are losing.**

**10:36**

Patient endurance is what you need now, so you will continue to do God's will. Then you will receive all that he has promised.

once and after that comes judgement, ²⁸so also Christ died only once as a sacrifice to take away the sins of many people. He will come again but not to deal with our sins again. This time he will bring salvation to all those who are eagerly waiting for him.

## Christ's Sacrifice Once for All

# 10

The old system in the law of Moses was only a shadow of the things to come, not the reality of the good things Christ has done for us. The sacrifices under the old system were repeated again and again, year after year, but they were never able to provide perfect cleansing for those who came to worship. ²If they could have provided perfect cleansing, the sacrifices would have stopped, for the worshippers would have been purified once for all time, and their feelings of guilt would have disappeared.

³But just the opposite happened. Those yearly sacrifices reminded them of their sins year after year. ⁴For it is not possible for the blood of bulls and goats to take away sins. ⁵That is why Christ, when he came into the world, said, "You did not want animal sacrifices and grain offerings. But you have given me a body so that I may obey you. ⁶No, you were not pleased with animals burned on the altar or with other offerings for sin.

**Sometimes I feel tempted to do some really bad things. I don't, but still feel bad. Is there a difference between temptation and sin?**

Yes, there is a BIG difference! Remember, Jesus was tempted in the desert by Satan. You will be tempted your whole life. Most of the time temptation will not be blatant and hideous but subtle and seductive. It is your response to temptation that is important. Jesus never gave in to temptation.

Be careful. Are you putting yourself into tempting situations? Be careful what you watch and who you hang around with and what you are putting into your mind.

⁷Then I said, 'Look, I have come to do your will, O God—just as it is written about me in the Scriptures.'"

⁸Christ said, "You did not want animal sacrifices or grain offerings or animals burned on the altar or other offerings for sin, nor were you pleased with them" (though they are required by the law of Moses). ⁹Then he added, "Look, I have come to do your will." He cancels the first covenant in order to establish the second. ¹⁰And what God wants is for us to be made holy by the sacrifice of the body of Jesus Christ once for all time.

¹¹Under the old covenant, the priest stands before the altar day after day, offering sacrifices that can never take away sins. ¹²But our High Priest offered himself to God as one sacrifice for sins, good for all time. Then he sat down at the place of highest honour at God's right hand. ¹³There he waits until his enemies are humbled as a footstool under his feet. ¹⁴For by that one offering he perfected for ever all those whom he is making holy.

¹⁵And the Holy Spirit also testifies that this is so. First he says,

¹⁶"This is the new covenant I will make
with my people on that day, says the Lord:
I will put my laws in their hearts
so they will understand them,
and I will write them on their minds
so they will obey them."

¹⁷Then he adds,

"I will never again remember
their sins and lawless deeds."

¹⁸Now when sins have been forgiven, there is no need to offer any more sacrifices.

## A Call to Persevere

¹⁹**And so, dear brothers and sisters, we can boldly enter heaven's Most Holy Place because of the blood of Jesus.** ²⁰This is the new, life-giving way that Christ has opened up for us through the sacred curtain, by means of his death for us.

²¹And since we have a great High Priest who rules over God's people, ²²let us go right into the presence of God, with true hearts fully trusting him. For our evil consciences have been sprinkled with Christ's blood to make us clean, and our bodies

## count on it

### Forgiveness!

Let's say you ask for forgiveness for doing a bad thing. You ask for forgiveness and it is gone! You still feel bad and you go back to God and ask forgiveness again. God will say, 'What bad thing? My son took it away; now go and live for me! When you are forgiven you are clean!'

"You know that Jesus came to take away our sins, for there is no sin in him." 1 John 3:5

**Count on it!**

have been washed with pure water. ²³Without wavering, let us hold tightly to the hope we say we have, for God can be trusted to keep his promise. ²⁴Think of ways to encourage one another to outbursts of love and good deeds. ²⁵And let us not neglect our meeting together, as some people do, but encourage and warn each other, especially now that the day of his coming back again is drawing near.

²⁶Dear friends, if we deliberately continue sinning after we have received a full knowledge of the truth, there is no other sacrifice that will cover these sins. ²⁷There

will be nothing to look forward to but the terrible expectation of God's judgement and the raging fire that will consume his enemies. ²⁸Anyone who refused to obey the law of Moses was put to death without mercy on the testimony of two or three witnesses. ²⁹Think how much more terrible the punishment will be for those who have trampled on the Son of God and have treated the blood of the covenant as if it were common and unholy. Such people have insulted and enraged the Holy Spirit who brings God's mercy to his people.

³⁰For we know the one who said,

"I will take vengeance.
I will repay those who deserve it."

He also said,

"The Lord will judge his own people."

³¹It is a terrible thing to fall into the hands of the living God.

³²Don't ever forget those early days when you first learned about Christ. Remember how you remained faithful even though it meant terrible suffering. ³³Sometimes you were exposed to public ridicule and were beaten, and sometimes you helped others who were suffering the same things. ³⁴You suffered along with those who were thrown into jail. When all you owned was taken from you, you accepted it with joy. You knew you had better things waiting for you in eternity.

³⁵Do not throw away this confident trust in the Lord, no matter what happens. Remember the great reward it brings you! ³⁶Patient endurance is what you need now, so you will continue to do God's will. Then you will receive all that he has promised.

³⁷"For in just a little while,
the Coming One will come and not delay.
³⁸And a righteous person will live by faith.
But I will have no pleasure in anyone who turns away."

³⁹But we are not like those who turn their backs on God and seal their fate. We have faith that assures our salvation.

---

'Discipline' Hebrews 12:6

Would you wilfully allow your children to do something that would hurt themselves? God can never function contrary to his own nature. He will never give you second best. He can't! His nature will not let him. You are his children and he wants his children to grow strong and healthy. Never mistake discipline for hatred. He will bring discipline, judgement and wrath on those who continue in sin and rebellion. His disciplines, however, are always fair and based on love and a desire for his children to have the best.

BIBLE HIT

# WHAT

# DOES IT MEAN?

## Fasting

It typically means going without food or drink for a set period of time. Our Lord rebuked the Pharisees for their show and hypocritical pretences in fasting (Matt. 6:16). He himself appointed no fast but it is recorded that he did fast. The early Christians, however, observed fasting especially during times of important decision-making. (Acts 13:3; 14:23; ).

## Great Examples of Faith

**11**

**What is faith? It is the confident assurance that what we hope for is going to happen. It is the evidence of things we cannot yet see.** ²God gave his approval to people in days of old because of their faith. ³By faith we understand that the entire universe was formed at God's command, that what we now see did not come from anything that can be seen.

⁴It was by faith that Abel brought a more acceptable offering to God than Cain did. God accepted Abel's offering to show that he was a righteous man. And although Abel is long dead, he still speaks to us because of his faith.

⁵It was by faith that Enoch was taken up to heaven without dying—"suddenly he disappeared because God took him." But before he was taken up, he was approved as pleasing to God. ⁶So, you see, it is impossible to please God without faith. Anyone who wants to come to him must believe that there is a God and that he rewards those who sincerely seek him.

⁷It was by faith that Noah built an ark to save his family from the flood. He obeyed God, who warned him about something that had never happened before. By his faith he condemned the rest of the world and was made right in God's sight.

⁸It was by faith that Abraham obeyed when God called him to leave home and go to another land that God would give him as his inheritance. He went without knowing where he was going. ⁹And even when he reached the land God promised him, he lived there by faith—for he was like a foreigner, living in a tent. And so did Isaac and Jacob, to whom God gave the same promise. ¹⁰Abraham did this because he was confidently looking forward to a city with eternal foundations, a city designed and built by God.

¹¹It was by faith that Sarah together with Abraham was able to have a child, even though they were too old and Sarah was barren. Abraham believed that God would keep his promise. ¹²And so a whole nation came from this one man, Abraham, who was too old to have any children—a nation with so many people that, like the stars of the sky and the sand on the seashore, there is no way to count them.

¹³All these faithful ones died without receiving what God had promised them, but they saw it all from a distance and welcomed the promises of God. They agreed that they were no more than foreigners and nomads here on earth. ¹⁴And obviously people who talk like that are looking forward to a country they can call their own. ¹⁵If they had meant the country they came from, they would have found a way to go back. ¹⁶But they were looking for a better place, a heavenly homeland. That is why God is not ashamed to be called their God, for he has prepared a heavenly city for them.

¹⁷It was by faith that Abraham offered Isaac as a sacrifice when God was testing him. Abraham, who had received God's promises, was ready to sacrifice his only son, Isaac, ¹⁸though God had promised him, "Isaac is the son through whom your descendants will be counted." ¹⁹Abraham assumed that if Isaac died, God was able to bring him back to life again. And in a sense, Abraham did receive his son back from the dead.

²⁰It was by faith that Isaac blessed his two sons, Jacob and Esau. He had confidence in what God was going to do in the future.

²¹It was by faith that Jacob, when he was old and dying, blessed each of Joseph's sons and bowed in worship as he leaned on his staff.

²²And it was by faith that Joseph, when he was about to die, confidently spoke of God's bringing the people of Israel out of Egypt. He was so sure of it that he commanded them to carry his bones with them when they left!

²³It was by faith that Moses' parents hid him for three months. They saw that God had given them an unusual child, and they were not afraid of what the king might do.

²⁴It was by faith that Moses, when he grew up, refused to be treated as the son of Pharaoh's daughter. ²⁵He chose to share the oppression of God's people instead of enjoying the fleeting pleasures of sin. ²⁶He thought it was better to suffer for the sake of the Messiah than to own the treasures of Egypt, for he was looking ahead to the great reward that God would give him.

## TIPS

## Strength Training and Flexibility:

Strength training is a vital component for athletes, although misconceptions exist regarding the relationship between strength training and flexibility. Research demonstrates that weight training does not decrease flexibility and in some instances actually improves it. With proper training that is technically correct, an athlete can improve both overall strength and flexibility.

²⁷It was by faith that Moses left the land of Egypt. He was not afraid of the king. Moses kept right on going because he kept his eyes on the one who is invisible. ²⁸It was by faith that Moses commanded the people of Israel to keep the Passover and to sprinkle blood on the doorposts so that the angel of death would not kill their first-born sons.

²⁹It was by faith that the people of Israel went right through the Red Sea as though they were on dry ground. But when the Egyptians followed, they were all drowned.

³⁰It was by faith that the people of Israel marched around Jericho seven days, and the walls came crashing down.

³¹It was by faith that Rahab the prostitute did not die with all the others in her city who refused to obey God. For she had given a friendly welcome to the spies.

³²Well, how much more do I need to say? It would take too long to recount the stories of the faith of Gideon, Barak, Samson, Jephthah, David, Samuel, and all the prophets. ³³By faith these people overthrew kingdoms, ruled with justice, and received what God had promised them. They shut the mouths of lions, ³⁴quenched the flames of fire, and escaped death by the edge of the sword. Their weakness was turned to strength. They became strong in battle and put whole armies to flight. ³⁵Women received their loved ones back again from death.

But others trusted God and were tortured, preferring to die rather than turn from God and be free. They placed their hope in the resurrection to a better life. ³⁶Some were mocked, and their backs were cut open with whips. Others were chained in dungeons. ³⁷Some died by stoning, and some were sawn in half; others were killed with the sword. Some went about in skins of sheep and goats, hungry and oppressed and mistreated. ³⁸They were too good for this world. They wandered over deserts and mountains, hiding in caves and holes in the ground.

³⁹All of these people we have mentioned received God's approval because of their faith, yet none of them received all that God had promised. ⁴⁰For God had far better things in mind for us that would also benefit them, for they can't receive the prize at the end of the race until we finish the race.

action

### CH 12:1-2 WHAT'S IT SAYING?

### WHAT AM I GOING TO DO ABOUT IT?

## God's Discipline Proves His Love

# 12

**Therefore, since we are surrounded by such a huge crowd of witnesses to the life of faith, let us strip off every weight that slows us down, especially the sin that so easily hinders our progress. And let us run with endurance the race that God has set before us.** ²We do this by keeping our eyes on Jesus, on whom our faith depends from start to finish. He was willing to die a shameful death on the cross because of the joy he knew would be his afterwards. Now he is seated in the place of highest honour beside God's throne in heaven. ³Think about

A soccer ball is made up of 32 leather panels, held together by 642 stitches.

all he endured when sinful people did such terrible things to him, so that you don't become weary and give up. ⁴After all, you have not yet given your lives in your struggle against sin.

⁵And have you entirely forgotten the encouraging words God spoke to you, his children? He said,

"My child, don't ignore it when the Lord disciplines you,

and don't be discouraged when he corrects you.

⁶For the Lord disciplines those he loves,

and he punishes those he accepts as his children."

⁷As you endure this divine discipline, remember that God is treating you as his own children. Whoever heard of a child who was never disciplined? ⁸If God doesn't discipline you as he does all of his children, it means that you are illegitimate and are not really his children after all. ⁹Since we respect our earthly fathers who disciplined us, should we not all the more cheerfully submit to the discipline of our heavenly Father and live for ever?

¹⁰For our earthly fathers disciplined us for a few years, doing the best they could. But God's discipline is always right and good for us because it means we will share in his holiness. ¹¹No discipline is enjoyable while it is happening—it is painful! But afterwards there will be a quiet harvest of right living for those who are trained in this way.

¹²So take a new grip with your tired hands and stand firm on your shaky legs. ¹³Mark out a straight path for your feet. Then those who follow you, though they are weak and lame, will not stumble and fall but will become strong.

### Is the Bible Trustworthy?

Aren't you glad God gave us this book! Great historians outside the Bible such as Tacitus and Josephus mention Jesus. Archaeological ruins around Israel verify Biblical records. The consistency of the Bible is convincing with some 66 books and 40 different authors spanning 1000 years, communicating the same general theme. It displays a remarkable unity and it claims to be inspired by the Spirit of God. Historians say it is the most authoritative book of its time. If God created us and loves us wouldn't it make sense that he would want to communicate with us? You can trust it!

## A Call to Listen to God

[14]Try to live in peace with everyone, and seek to live a clean and holy life, for those who are not holy will not see the Lord. [15]Look after each other so that none of you will miss out on the special favour of God. Watch out that no bitter root of unbelief rises up among you, for whenever it springs up, many are corrupted by its poison. [16]Make sure that no one is immoral or godless like Esau. He traded his birthright as the oldest son for a single meal. [17]And afterwards, when he wanted his father's blessing, he was rejected. It was too late for repentance, even though he wept bitter tears.

[18]You have not come to a physical mountain, to a place of flaming fire, darkness, gloom, and whirlwind, as the Israelites did at Mount Sinai when God gave them his laws. [19]For they heard an awesome trumpet blast and a voice with a message so terrible that they begged God to stop speaking. [20]They staggered back under God's command: "If even an animal touches the mountain, it must be stoned to death." [21]Moses himself was so frightened at the sight that he said, "I am terrified and trembling."

[22]No, you have come to Mount Zion, to the city of the living God, the heavenly Jerusalem, and to thousands of angels in joyful assembly. [23]You have come to the assembly of God's first-born children, whose names are written in heaven. You have come to God himself, who is the judge of all people. And you have come to the spirits of the redeemed in heaven who have now been made perfect. [24]You have come to Jesus, the one who mediates the new covenant between God and people, and to the sprinkled blood, which graciously forgives instead of crying out for vengeance as the blood of Abel did.

[25]See to it that you obey God, the one who is speaking to you. For if the people of Israel did not escape when they refused to listen to Moses, the earthly messenger, how terrible our danger if we reject the One who speaks to us from heaven! [26]When God spoke from Mount Sinai his voice shook the earth, but now he makes another promise: "Once again I will shake not only the earth but the heavens also." [27]This means that the things on earth will be shaken, so that only eternal things will be left.

[28]Since we are receiving a Kingdom that cannot be destroyed, let us be thankful and please God by worshipping him with holy fear and awe. [29]For our God is a consuming fire.

## Concluding Words

# 13

Continue to love each other with true Christian love. [2]Don't forget to show hospitality to strangers, for some who have done this have entertained angels without realizing it! [3]Don't forget about those in prison. Suffer with them as though you were there yourself. Share the sorrow of those being mistreated, as though you feel their pain in your own bodies.

[4]Give honour to marriage, and remain faithful to one another in marriage. God will surely judge people who are immoral and those who commit adultery.

[5]Stay away from the love of money; be satisfied with what you have. For God has said,
"I will never fail you.
I will never forsake you."
[6]That is why we can say with confidence,
"The Lord is my helper,
so I will not be afraid.
What can mere mortals do to me?"

[7]Remember your leaders who first taught you the word of God. Think of all the good that has come from their lives, and trust the Lord as they do.

[8]Jesus Christ is the same yesterday, today, and for ever. [9]So do not be attracted by strange, new ideas. Your spiritual strength comes from God's special favour, not from ceremonial rules about food, which don't help those who follow them.

[10]We have an altar from which the priests in the Temple on earth have no right to eat. [11]Under the system of Jewish laws, the high priest brought the blood of animals into the Holy Place as a sacrifice for sin, but the bodies of the animals were burned outside the camp. [12]So also Jesus suffered and died outside the city gates in order to make his people holy by shedding his own blood. [13]So let us go out to him outside the camp and bear the disgrace he bore. [14]**For this world is not our home; we are looking forward to our city in heaven, which is yet to come.**

[15]With Jesus' help, let us continually offer our sacrifice of praise to God by proclaiming the glory of his name. [16]Don't forget to do good and to share what you have with those in need, for such sacrifices are very pleasing to God.

[17]Obey your spiritual leaders and do what they say. Their work is to watch over your souls, and they know they are accountable to God. Give them reason to do this joyfully and not with sorrow. That would certainly not be for your benefit.

[18]Pray for us, for our conscience is clear and we want to live honourably in everything we do. [19]I especially need your prayers right now so that I can come back to you soon.

[20-21]And now, may the God of peace, who brought again from the dead our Lord Jesus, equip you with all you need for doing his will. May he produce in you, through the power of Jesus Christ, all that is pleasing to him. Jesus is the great Shepherd of the sheep by an everlasting covenant, signed with his blood. To him be glory for ever and ever. Amen.

[22]I urge you, dear brothers and sisters, please listen carefully to what I have said in this brief letter.

[23]I want you to know that our brother Timothy is now out of jail. If he comes here soon, I will bring him with me to see you.

[24]Give my greetings to all your leaders and to the other believers there. The Christians from Italy send you their greetings.

[25]May God's grace be with you all.

**STAND POINT**

**When you need confidence**
13:6

That is why we can say with confidence,
"The Lord is my helper, so I will not be afraid. What can mere mortals do to me?"

# Standing firm

'With all these things in mind, dear brothers and sisters, stand firm and keep a strong grip on everything we taught you both in person and by letter.'
2 Thessalonians 2:15

How encouraging it is to find someone standing firm in his or her faith in the world of sport. It is obvious that some people are drifting spiritually. Many athletes are looking for a new gimmick to improve their performance, so they try Jesus the same way they may try a lucky charm or a new colour of running shoes. Often a superstitious faith is a brand of religion that comes with feigned or half-hearted devotion to God. They do not want to obey their creator; they prefer to have a 'genie in a bottle' that will obey them. When it is convenient, they may go to church or read their Bibles, but they are often merely drifting with the current. Sometimes the drifters get anchored to God and sometimes they flounder and fade away.

An eccentric friend who annoyingly always talks in Christian jargon, asked a colleague of mine, 'When did you wake up?' The colleague was baffled and said, '6:00am.'

My friend was a bit frustrated that he did not catch his line of enquiry and again repeated the question with more emphasis, 'No man, when did you WAKE UP, WAKE UP SPIRITUALLY! When did you become a Christian?' My colleague was quick and fired back, 'Ah, I woke up in '76, but did not get out of bed until '80!' There are plenty of Christian weaklings getting pushed around by every new fad or temptation. We need some spiritual tough guys that will not get pushed around and that will hang on to their faith in times of adversity. So get out of bed! Stand firm in your faith, hang on tight to the word of God, and be a blessing to someone else, someone who has just woken up!

'This confidence is like a strong and trustworthy anchor for our souls.' Hebrews 6:19

### Reflection
I can stand firm because my feet are on a secure foundation.

### Prayer
Father, you are the rock on which I stand.

'The difference between a successful person and others is not a lack of strength, but a lack of will.'
Vince Lombardi

Nicked from:A Sporting Guide to Eternity, Steve Connor,
Christian Focus Publications - ISBN 1-85792-746-X

Imagine growing up with Jesus! He was not an only child - he had a big family and James was his half-brother. When the time came for Jesus to start his formal ministry James was not ready to follow his older brother. But after his resurrection we find James so changed that he ends up leading the strategic church in Jerusalem (see Acts 15) and later is recorded by the great historian Josephus as dying a painful death for his faith in Jesus - his brother, Lord and Saviour.

Faith works! Unlike the person who learns all about fishing but never goes fishing, you can't just read about it. James writes his relatively small book to encourage believers to 'live it'. No more lip-service - if you do not live out your faith, do you really have a faith? James shows us how to live our lives and that our actions (good deeds) reflect our faith. Throughout this book we hear echoes of Jesus' life and teachings: 'I assure you, when you refused to help the least of these my brothers and sisters, you were refusing to help me.' Matthew 25:45

# James

# JAMES

## Greetings from James

# 1

This letter is from James, a slave of God and of the Lord Jesus Christ.
It is written to Jewish Christians scattered among the nations. Greetings!

## Faith and Endurance

[2]Dear brothers and sisters, whenever trouble comes your way, let it be an opportunity for joy. [3]For when your faith is tested, your endurance has a chance to grow. [4]So let it grow, for when your endurance is fully developed, you will be strong in character and ready for anything. [5]If you need wisdom—if you want to know what God wants you to do—ask him, and he will gladly tell you. He will not resent your asking. [6]But when you ask him, be sure that you really expect him to answer, for a doubtful mind is as unsettled as a wave of the sea that is driven and tossed by the wind. [7]People like that should not expect to receive anything from the Lord. [8]They can't make up their minds. They waver back and forth in everything they do.

Be courageous. Courage allows you to be firm when facing danger and temptation. You may feel scared and be tempted to do bad things; that's a normal part of life. What courage does is allow you to live for God, to speak, react and perform whilst under pressure.
"Be on guard. Stand true to what you believe. Be courageous. Be strong." 1 Corinthians 16:13

## When you need direction:

### 1: 5-8

If you need wisdom—if you want to know what God wants you to do—ask him, and he will gladly tell you. He will not resent your asking. [6]But when you ask him, be sure that you really expect him to answer, for a doubtful mind is as unsettled as a wave of the sea that is driven and tossed by the wind. [7]People like that should not expect to receive anything from the Lord. [8]They can't make up their minds. They waver back and forth in everything they do.

[9]Christians who are poor should be glad, for God has honoured them. [10]And those who are rich should be glad, for God has humbled them. They will fade away like a flower in the field. [11]The hot sun rises and dries up the grass; the flower withers, and its beauty fades away. So also, wealthy people will fade away with all of their achievements.
[12]God blesses the people who patiently endure testing. Afterwards they will receive the crown of life that God has promised to those who love him. [13]And remember, no one who wants to do wrong should ever say, "God is tempting me." God is never tempted to do wrong, and he never tempts anyone else either. [14]Temptation comes from the lure of our own evil desires. [15]These evil desires lead to evil actions, and evil actions lead to death. [16]So don't be misled, my dear brothers and sisters.
[17]Whatever is good and perfect comes to us from God above, who created all heaven's lights. Unlike them, he never changes or casts shifting shadows. [18]In his goodness he chose to make us his own children by giving us his true word. And we, out of all creation, became his choice possession.

## Listening and Doing

[19]**My dear brothers and sisters, be quick to listen, slow to speak, and slow to get angry.** [20]Your anger can never make things right in God's sight.
[21]So get rid of all the filth and evil in your lives, and humbly accept the message God has planted in your hearts, for it is strong enough to save your souls.
[22]And remember, it is a message to obey, not just to listen to. If you don't obey, you are only fooling yourself. [23]For if you just listen and don't obey, it is like looking at your face in a mirror but doing nothing to improve your appearance. [24]You see yourself, walk away, and forget what you look like. [25]But if you keep looking steadily into God's perfect law—the law that sets you free—and if you do what it says and don't forget what you heard, then God will bless you for doing it.
[26]If you claim to be religious but don't control your tongue, you are just fooling yourself, and your religion is worthless.
[27]Pure and lasting religion in the sight of God our Father means that we must care for orphans and widows in their troubles, and refuse to let the world corrupt us.

## A Warning against Prejudice

# 2

My dear brothers and sisters, how can you claim that you have faith in our glorious Lord Jesus Christ if you favour some people more than others?
[2]For instance, suppose someone comes into your meeting dressed in fancy clothes and expensive jewellery, and another comes in who is poor and dressed in shabby clothes. [3]If you give special attention and a good seat to the rich person, but you say to the poor one, "You can stand over there, or else sit on the floor"—well, [4]doesn't this discrimination show that you are guided by wrong motives?
[5]Listen to me, dear brothers and sisters. Hasn't God chosen the poor in this world to be rich in faith? Aren't they the ones who will inherit the Kingdom he promised to those who love him? [6]And yet, you insult the poor man! Isn't it the rich who oppress you and drag you into court? [7]Aren't they the ones who slander Jesus Christ, whose noble name you bear?
[8]Yes indeed, it is good when you truly obey our Lord's

royal command found in the Scriptures: "Love your neighbour as yourself." [9]But if you pay special attention to the rich, you are committing a sin, for you are guilty of breaking that law.

[10]And the person who keeps all of the laws except one is as guilty as the person who has broken all of God's laws. [11]For the same God who said, "Do not commit adultery," also said, "Do not murder." So if you murder someone, you have broken the entire law, even if you do not commit adultery.

[12]So whenever you speak, or whatever you do, remember that you will be judged by the law of love, the law that set you free. [13]For there will be no mercy for you if you have not been merciful to others. But if you have been merciful, then God's mercy towards you will win out over his judgement against you.

**CH 2:14-26 WHAT'S IT SAYING?**

**WHAT AM I GOING TO DO ABOUT IT?**

## Faith without Good Deeds Is Dead

[14]Dear brothers and sisters, what's the use of saying you have faith if you don't prove it by your actions? That kind of faith can't save anyone. [15]Suppose you see a brother or sister who needs food or clothing, [16]and you say, "Well, goodbye and God bless you; stay warm and eat well"——but then you don't give that person any food or clothing. What good does that do?

**[17]So you see, it isn't enough just to have faith. Faith that doesn't show itself by good deeds is no faith at all—it is dead and useless.**

[18]Now someone may argue, "Some people have faith; others have good deeds." I say, "I can't see your faith if you don't have good deeds, but I will show you my faith through my good deeds."

[19]Do you still think it's enough just to believe that there is one God? Well, even the demons believe this, and they tremble in terror! [20]How foolish! When will you ever learn that faith that does not result in good deeds is useless?

[21]Don't you remember that our ancestor Abraham was declared right with God because of what he did when he offered his son Isaac on the altar? [22]You see, he was trusting God so much that he was willing to do whatever God told him to do. His faith was made complete by what he did—by his actions. [23]And so it happened just as the Scriptures say: "Abraham believed God, so God declared him to be righteous." He was even called "the friend of God." [24]So you see, we are made right with God by what we do, not by faith alone.

[25]Rahab the prostitute is another example of this. She was made right with God by her actions—when she hid those messengers and sent them safely away by a different road. **[26]Just as the body is dead without a spirit, so also faith is dead without good deeds.**

## Controlling the Tongue

# 3

Dear brothers and sisters, not many of you should become teachers in the church, for we who teach will be judged by God with greater strictness.

[2]We all make many mistakes, but those who control their tongues can also control themselves in every other way. [3]We can make a large horse turn around and go wherever we want by means of a small bit in its mouth. [4]And a tiny rudder makes a huge ship turn wherever the pilot wants it to go, even though the winds are strong. [5]So also, the tongue is a small thing, but what enormous damage it can do. A tiny spark can set a great forest on fire. [6]And the tongue is a flame of fire. It is full of wickedness that can ruin your whole life. It can turn the entire course of your life into a blazing flame of destruction, for it is set on fire by hell itself.

[7]People can tame all kinds of animals and birds and reptiles and fish, [8]but no one can tame the tongue. It

# WHAT DOES IT MEAN?

**Fall of man**

...is an expression arguably gleaned from the Apocryphal Book of Wisdom, to express the fact of the rebellion of Adam and Eve against God, and the consequent sin and misery which they and all their offspring inherited. The history of the Fall is recorded in Gen. 2 and 3. The effects of this first sin upon our first parents themselves were shame, a sense of humiliation and contamination. We inherited the disease of sin and are by our very nature 'Spiritually dead' and must be restored to life through faith in Christ.

is an uncontrollable evil, full of deadly poison. [9]Sometimes it praises our Lord and Father, and sometimes it breaks out into curses against those who have been made in the image of God. [10]And so blessing and cursing come pouring out of the same mouth. Surely, my brothers and sisters, this is not right! [11]Does a spring of water bubble out with both fresh water and bitter water? [12]Can you pick olives from a fig tree or figs from a grapevine? No, and you can't draw fresh water from a salty pool.

**'Spiritual fitness test'** James 1:2-4

Have you ever taken a fitness test? They can be pretty tough and revealing. James reminds us that our faith will be tested too. A test will reveal shortcomings and strengths and can create endurance. Troubles will come your way - it is a promise! Troubles will either pulverise or polish you. With God's strength, take on life's challenges with joy knowing they will transform you into a person that is ready for anything!

## True Wisdom Comes from God

[13]If you are wise and understand God's ways, live a life of steady goodness so that only good deeds will pour forth. And if you don't brag about the good you do, then you will be truly wise! [14]But if you are bitterly jealous and there is selfish ambition in your hearts, don't brag about being wise. That is the worst kind of lie. [15]For jealousy and selfishness are not God's kind of wisdom. Such things are earthly, unspiritual, and motivated by the Devil. [16]For wherever there is jealousy and selfish ambition, there you will find disorder and every kind of evil.

[17]But the wisdom that comes from heaven is first of all pure. It is also peace loving, gentle at all times, and willing to yield to others. It is full of mercy and good deeds. It shows no partiality and is always sincere. [18]**And those who are peacemakers will plant seeds of peace and reap a harvest of goodness.**

## Drawing Close to God

# 4

What is causing the quarrels and fights among you? Isn't it the whole army of evil desires at war within you? [2]You want what you don't have, so you scheme and kill to get it. You are jealous for what others have, and you can't possess it, so you fight and quarrel to take it away from them. And yet the reason you don't have what you want is that you don't ask God for it. [3]And even when you do ask, you don't get it because your whole motive is wrong—you want only what will give you pleasure. [4]You adulterers! Don't you realize that friendship with this world makes you an enemy of God? I say it again, that if your aim is to enjoy this world, you can't be a friend of God. [5]What do you think the Scriptures mean when they say that the Holy Spirit, whom God has placed within us, jealously longs for us to be faithful? [6]He gives us more and more strength to stand against such evil desires. As the Scriptures say,

"God sets himself against the proud,
but he shows favour to the humble."

[7]So humble yourselves before God. Resist the Devil, and he will flee from you. [8]**Draw close to God, and God will draw close to you.** Wash your hands, you sinners; purify your hearts, you hypocrites. [9]Let there be tears for the wrong things you have done. Let there be sorrow and deep grief. Let there be sadness instead of laughter, and gloom instead of joy. [10]When you bow down before the Lord and admit your dependence on him, he will lift you up and give you honour.

## Warning against Judging Others

[11]Don't speak evil against each other, my dear brothers and sisters. If you criticize each other and condemn each other, then you are criticizing and condemning God's law. But you are not a judge who can decide whether the law is right or wrong. Your job is to obey it. [12]God alone, who made the law, can rightly judge among us. He alone has the power to save or to destroy. So what right do you have to condemn your neighbour?

## Warning about Self-Confidence

[13]Look here, you people who say, "Today or tomorrow we are going to a certain town and will stay there a year. We will do business there and make a profit." [14]How do you know what will happen tomorrow? For your life is like the morning fog—it's here a little while, then it's gone. [15]What you ought to say is, "If the Lord wants us to, we will live and do this or that." [16]Otherwise you will be boasting about your own plans, and all such boasting is evil.

[17]Remember, it is sin to know what you ought to do and then not do it.

## Warning to the Rich

# 5

Look here, you rich people, weep and groan with anguish because of all the terrible troubles ahead of you. [2]Your wealth is rotting away, and your fine clothes are moth-eaten rags. [3]Your gold and silver have become worthless. The very wealth you were counting on will eat away your flesh in hell. This treasure you have accumulated will stand as evidence against you on the day of judgement. [4]For listen! Hear the cries of the field workers whom you have cheated of their pay. The wages you held back cry out against you. The cries of the reapers have reached the ears of the Lord Almighty.

What are the five most important skills for you sport?

1
2
3
4
5

BIG FIVE

⁵You have spent your years on earth in luxury, satisfying your every whim. Now your hearts are nice and fat, ready for the slaughter. ⁶You have condemned and killed good people who had no power to defend themselves against you.

**action**

CH 5:7-20 WHAT'S IT SAYING?

WHAT AM I GOING TO DO ABOUT IT?

## Patience in Suffering

⁷Dear brothers and sisters, you must be patient as you wait for the Lord's return. Consider the farmers who eagerly look for the rains in the autumn and in the spring. They patiently wait for the precious harvest to ripen. ⁸You, too, must be patient. And take courage, for the coming of the Lord is near. ⁹Don't grumble about each other, my brothers and sisters, or God will judge you. For look! The great Judge is coming. He is standing at the door!

¹⁰For examples of patience in suffering, dear brothers and sisters, look at the prophets who spoke in the name of the Lord. ¹¹We give great honour to those who endure under suffering. Job is an example of a man who endured patiently. From his experience we see how the Lord's plan finally ended in good, for he is full of tenderness and mercy.

¹²But most of all, my brothers and sisters, never take an oath, by heaven or earth or anything else. Just say a simple yes or no, so that you will not sin and be condemned for it.

### The Power of Prayer

¹³Are any among you suffering? They should keep on praying about it. And those who have reason to be thankful should continually sing praises to the Lord. ¹⁴Are any among you sick? They should call for the elders of the church and have them pray over them, anointing them with oil in the name of the Lord. ¹⁵And their prayer offered in faith will heal the sick, and the Lord will make them well. And anyone who has committed sins will be forgiven.

¹⁶Confess your sins to each other and pray for each other so that you may be healed. The earnest prayer of a righteous person has great power and wonderful results. ¹⁷Elijah was as human as we are, and yet when he prayed earnestly that no rain would fall, none fell for the next three and a half years! ¹⁸Then he prayed for rain, and down it poured. The grass turned green, and the crops began to grow again.

### Restore Wandering Believers

¹⁹My dear brothers and sisters, if anyone among you wanders away from the truth and is brought back again, ²⁰you can be sure that the one who brings that person back will save that sinner from death and bring about the forgiveness of many sins.

**I think about sex all the time. Am I messed-up?**
This is totally normal (although arguably more of a guy issue).
They say the average male adolescent thinks about sex one out of every seven seconds. It is hard to figure what they think about in the other six seconds! Probably sport and food! How you control and direct your thoughts is what counts. Hang in there and ask God to help you with this issue (you may have to ask for help one out of every six seconds!).

It's a long road

LIVE it

A sports writer reflecting on his long friendship with a particular boxer once wrote, 'He started out mean, inarticulate, narcissistic, and shallow. But after his conversion to Christianity he miraculously became generous, articulate, selfless and cared deeply for others.' Be careful - when you hang around Jesus, you change! Similarly Peter the fisherman - boastful, hasty, strong-tempered, inarticulate and at times cowardly - hung around Jesus and changed! Peter, now filled with the Holy Spirit (read Acts 1-3) became articulate, lion-hearted, thoughtful, and became missionary and spokesman for the Christian church. In 1 Peter he is strengthening the persecuted believers in their faith and reminding us that our worth, all of our significance and security, are found only in God who, out of love, has given us salvation through his son Jesus.

# 1 Peter

# 1 PETER

## Greetings from Peter

# 1

This letter is from Peter, an apostle of Jesus Christ.

I am writing to God's chosen people who are living as foreigners in the lands of Pontus, Galatia, Cappadocia, the province of Asia, and Bithynia. [2]God the Father chose you long ago, and the Spirit has made you holy. As a result, you have obeyed Jesus Christ and are cleansed by his blood. May you have more and more of God's special favour and wonderful peace.

## The Hope of Eternal Life

[3]All honour to the God and Father of our Lord Jesus Christ, for it is by his boundless mercy that God has given us the privilege of being born again. Now we live with a wonderful expectation because Jesus Christ rose again from the dead. [4]For God has reserved a priceless inheritance for his children. It is kept in heaven for you, pure and undefiled, beyond the reach of change and decay. [5]And God, in his mighty power, will protect you until you receive this salvation, because you are trusting him. It will be revealed on the last day for all to see. [6]So be truly glad! There is wonderful joy ahead, even though it is necessary for you to endure many trials for a while.

[7]These trials are only to test your faith, to show that it is strong and pure. It is being tested as fire tests and purifies gold—and your faith is far more precious to God than mere gold. So if your faith remains strong after being tried by fiery trials, it will bring you much praise and glory and

Jean Genevieve Garnerin was the first female parachutist, jumping from a hot air-balloon in 1799.

more about. They prophesied about this gracious salvation prepared for you, even though they had many questions as to what it all could mean. [11]They wondered what the Spirit of Christ within them was talking about when he told them in advance about Christ's suffering and his great glory afterwards. They wondered when and to whom all this would happen. [12]They were told that these things would not happen during their lifetime, but many years later, during yours. And now this Good News has been announced by those who preached to you in the power of the Holy Spirit sent from heaven. It is all so wonderful that even the angels are eagerly watching these things happen.

## A Call to Holy Living

[13]So think clearly and exercise self-control. Look forward to the special blessings that will come to you at the return of Jesus Christ. [14]Obey God because you are his children. Don't slip back into your old ways of

judge or reward you according to what you do. So you must live in reverent fear of him during your time as foreigners here on earth. [18]For you know that God paid a ransom to save you from the empty life you inherited from your ancestors. And the ransom he paid was not mere gold or silver. [19]He paid for you with the precious lifeblood of Christ, the sinless, spotless Lamb of God. [20]God chose him for this purpose long before the world began, but now in these final days, he was sent to the earth for all to see. And he did this for you. [21]Through Christ you have come to trust in God. And because God raised Christ from the dead and gave him great glory, your faith and hope can be placed confidently in God. [22]Now you can have sincere love for each other as brothers and sisters because you were cleansed from your sins when you accepted the truth of the Good News. So see to it that you really do love each other intensely with all your hearts.

[23]For you have be**en born again. Your new life did not come from your earthly parents because the life they gave you will end in death. But this new life w**ill last for ever because it comes from the eternal, living word of God. [24]As the prophet says,

"People are like grass that dies away;
their beauty fades as quickly as the beauty of wildflowers.
The grass withers,
and the flowers fall away.
[25]**But the word of the Lord will last for ever."**
**And that word is the Good News that was preached to you.**

## Overcome your Fear of Failure:

Many athletes do not fulfil their potential due to their inability to overcome their fear of failure. In order to succeed an athlete must accept that in order to learn and improve they must encounter failure. The process of learning how to handle their disappointment and how the lessons learnt can improve them will develop a healthy drive that does not like failure but at the same time does not fear it.

honour on the day when Jesus Christ is revealed to the whole world.

[8]You love him even though you have never seen him. Though you do not see him, you trust him; and even now you are happy with a glorious, inexpressible joy. [9]Your reward for trusting him will be the salvation of your souls.

[10]This salvation was something the prophets wanted to know

doing evil; you didn't know any better then. [15]But now you must be holy in everything you do, just as God— who chose you to be his children—is holy. [16]For he himself has said, "You must be holy because I am holy."

[17]And remember that the heavenly Father to whom you pray has no favourites when he judges. He will

# 2

So get rid of all malicious behaviour and deceit. Don't just pretend to be good! Be done with hypocrisy and jealousy and backstabbing. [2]You must crave pure spiritual milk so that you can grow into the fullness of your salvation. Cry out for this nourishment as a

# Winners are fair!

When someone is cheating on us fair play is important! But the quality of fairness comes in the measure that we are fair to others. Being truthful, keeping our promises, empathy, reporting cheats and playing by the rules are marks of a winner. Competing as hard as you can is totally fair, as long as you play within the confines of the rules. You may win or lose by one hundred points but don't scream 'it's not fair!' if both teams agreed to play under the same rules. What is unfair is when you try to win or lose outside of the rules. You may choose to keep the score under control, that may be wise. When you commit a foul, you must be honest - in the long term it will pay-off. **"The Lord hates cheating, but he delights in honesty."** Proverbs 11:1

## Winners live by the rules!

baby cries for milk, [3]now that you have had a taste of the Lord's kindness.

### Living Stones for God's House

[4]Come to Christ, who is the living cornerstone of God's temple. He was rejected by the people, but he is precious to God who chose him.

[5]And now God is building you, as living stones, into his spiritual temple. What's more, you are God's holy priests, who offer the spiritual sacrifices that please him because of Jesus Christ. [6]As the Scriptures express it,

"I am placing a stone in Jerusalem,
a chosen cornerstone,
and anyone who believes in him
will never be disappointed."

[7]Yes, he is very precious to you who believe. But for those who reject him,

"The stone that was rejected by the builders has now **become the cornerstone.**"

[8]And the Scriptures also say,

**"H**e is the stone that makes people stumble, the rock that will make them fall."

They stumble because they do not listen to God's word or obey it, and so they meet the fate that has been planned for them.

[9]But you are not like that, for you are a chosen people. You are a kingdom of priests, God's holy nation, his very own possession. This is so you can show others the goodness of God, for he called you out of the darkness into his wonderful light.

[10]"Once you were not a people;
now you are the people of God.
Once you received none of God's mercy;
now you have received his mercy."

[11]Dear brothers and sisters, you are foreigners and aliens here. So I warn you to keep away from evil desires because they fight against your very souls. [12]Be careful how you live among your unbelieving neighbours. Even if they accuse you of doing wrong, they will see your honourable behaviour, and they will believe and give honour to God when he comes to judge the world.

### Respecting People in Authority

[13]For the Lord's sake, accept all authority—the king as head of state, [14]and the officials he has appointed. For the king has sent them to punish all who do wrong and to honour those who do right.

[15]It is God's will that your good lives should silence those who make foolish accusations against you. [16]You are not slaves; you are free. But your freedom is not an excuse to do evil. You are free to live as God's slaves. [17]Show respect for everyone. Love your Christian brothers and sisters. Fear God. Show respect for the king.

### Slaves

[18]You who are slaves must accept the authority of your masters. Do whatever they tell you—not only if they are kind and reasonable, but even if they are harsh. [19]For God is pleased with you when, for the sake of your conscience, you patiently endure unfair treatment. [20]Of course, you get no credit for being patient if you are beaten for doing wrong. But if you suffer for doing right and are patient beneath the blows, God is pleased with you.

[21]This suffering is all part of what God has called you to. Christ, who suffered for you, is your example. Follow in his steps. [22]He never sinned, and he never deceived anyone. [23]He did not retaliate when he was insulted. When he suffered, he did not threaten to get even. He left his case in the hands of God, who always judges fairly. [24]He personally carried away our sins in his own body on the cross so we can be dead to sin and live for what is right. You have been healed by his wounds! [25]Once you were wandering like lost sheep. But now you have turned to your Shepherd, the Guardian of your souls.

Stay right with God. Forgiveness is a benefit that we should love to receive. Satan will try to tell you that you are not worthy to go to God for forgiveness. He is half right - we are not worthy, and we never will be worthy. But we must turn back to God when we sin and he will gladly and faithfully forgive us. Once forgiven we have a freedom that comes from purity. "But if we confess our sins to him, he is faithful and just to forgive us and to cleanse us from every wrong." 1 John 1:9

## Wives

## 3

In the same way, you wives must accept the authority of your husbands, even those who refuse to accept the Good News. Your godly lives will speak to them better than any words. They will be won over [2]by watching your pure, godly behaviour.

[3]Don't be concerned about the outward beauty that depends on fancy hairstyles, expensive jewellery, or beautiful clothes. **[4]You should be known for the beauty that comes from within, the unfading beauty of a gentle and quiet spirit, which is so precious to God.** [5]That is the way the holy women of old made themselves beautiful. They trusted God and accepted the authority of their husbands. [6]For instance, Sarah obeyed her husband, Abraham, when she called him her master. You are her daughters when you do what is right without fear of what your husbands might do.

## Husbands

[7]In the same way, you husbands must give honour to your wives. Treat her with understanding as you live together. She may be weaker than you are, but she is your equal partner in God's gift of new life. If you don't treat her as you should, your prayers will not be heard.

## All Christians

[8]Finally, all of you should be of one mind, full of sympathy towards each other, loving one another with tender hearts and humble minds. [9]Don't repay evil for evil. Don't retaliate when people say unkind things about you. Instead, pay them back with a blessing. That is what God wants you to do, and he will bless you for it. [10]For the Scriptures say,
"If you want a happy life and good days,
keep your tongue from speaking evil,
and keep your lips from telling lies.
[11]Turn away from evil and do good.
Work hard at living in peace with others.
[12]The eyes of the Lord watch over those who do right,
and his ears are open to their prayers.
But the Lord turns his face
against those who do evil."

## Suffering for Doing Good

[13]Now, who will want to harm you if you are eager to do good? [14]But even if you suffer for doing what is right, God will reward you for it. So don't be afraid and don't worry. [15]Instead, you must worship Christ as Lord of your life. And if you are asked about your Christian hope, always be ready to explain it. [16]But you must do this in a gentle and respectful way. Keep your conscience clear. Then if people speak evil against you, they will be ashamed when they see what a good

In 1976 Junko Tabei from Japan became the first woman to reach the top of Everest.

life you live because you belong to Christ. ¹⁷Remember, it is better to suffer for doing good, if that is what God wants, than to suffer for doing wrong!

¹⁸Christ also suffered when he died for our sins once for all time. He never sinned, but he died for sinners that he might bring us safely home to God. He suffered physical death, but he was raised to life in the Spirit. ¹⁹So he went and preached to the spirits in prison— ²⁰those who disobeyed God long ago when God waited patiently while Noah was building his boat. Only eight people were saved from drowning in that terrible flood. ²¹And this is a picture of baptism, which now saves you by the power of Jesus Christ's resurrection. Baptism is not a removal of dirt from your body; it is an appeal to God from a clean conscience.

²²Now Christ has gone to heaven. He is seated in the place of honour next to God, and all the angels and authorities and powers are bowing before him.

## Living for God

# 4

So then, since Christ suffered physical pain, you must arm yourselves with the same attitude he had, and be ready to suffer, too. For if you are willing to suffer for Christ, you have decided to stop sinning. ²And you won't spend the rest of your life chasing after evil desires, but you will be anxious to do the will of God. ³You have had enough in the past of the evil things that godless people enjoy—their immorality and lust, their feasting and drunkenness and wild parties, and their terrible worship of idols.

⁴Of course, your former friends are very surprised when you no longer join them in the wicked things they do, and they say evil things about you. ⁵But just remember that they will have to face God, who will judge everyone, both the living and the dead. ⁶That is why the Good News was preached even to those who have died—so that although their bodies were

Bible FACTS

**Today, the complete Bible is available in 400 of the 6,500 languages spoken in the world.**

punished with death, they could still live in the spirit as God does.

⁷The end of the world is coming soon. Therefore, be earnest and disciplined in your prayers. ⁸Most important of all, continue to show deep love for each other, for love covers a multitude of sins. ⁹Cheerfully share your home with those who need a meal or a place to stay.

¹⁰God has given gifts to each of you from his great variety of spiritual gifts. Manage them well so that God's generosity can flow through you. ¹¹Are you called to be a speaker? Then speak as though God himself were speaking through you. Are you called to help others? Do it with all the strength and energy that God supplies. Then God will be given glory in everything through Jesus Christ. All glory and power belong to him for ever and ever. Amen.

action

**CH 4:7–11 WHAT'S IT SAYING?**

**WHAT AM I GOING TO DO ABOUT IT?**

## Suffering for Being a Christian

¹²Dear friends, don't be surprised at the fiery trials you are going through, as if something strange were happening to you. ¹³Instead, be very glad—because these trials will make you partners with Christ in his suffering, and afterwards you will have the wonderful joy of sharing his glory when it is displayed to all the world.

STAND POINT

**When you need to listen to your coach**

5:5

You younger men, accept the authority of the elders. And all of you, serve each other in humility, for "God sets himself against the proud, but he shows favour to the humble."

¹⁴Be happy if you are insulted for being a Christian, for then the glorious Spirit of God will come upon you. ¹⁵If you suffer, however, it must not be for murder, stealing, making trouble, or prying into other people's affairs. ¹⁶But it is no shame to suffer for being a Christian. Praise God for the privilege of being called by his wonderful name! ¹⁷For the time has come for judgement, and it must begin first among God's own children. And if even we Christians must be judged, what terrible fate awaits those who have never believed God's Good News? ¹⁸And

"If the righteous are barely saved,
what chance will the godless and sinners have?"

¹⁹So if you are suffering according to God's will, keep on doing what is right, and trust yourself to the God who made you, for he will never fail you.

## Advice for Elders and Young Men

# 5

And now, a word to you who are elders in the churches. I, too, am an elder and a witness to the sufferings of Christ. And I, too, will share his glory and his honour when he returns. As a fellow elder, this is my appeal to you: ²Care for the flock of God entrusted to you. Watch over it willingly, not grudgingly—not for what you will get out of it, but because you are eager to serve God. ³Don't lord it over the people assigned to your care, but lead them by your good example. ⁴And when the head Shepherd comes, your reward will be a never-ending share in his glory and honour.

⁵You younger men, accept the authority of the elders. And all of you, serve each other in humility, for

"God sets himself against the proud,
but he shows favour to the humble."

⁶So humble yourselves under the mighty power of God, and in his good time he will honour you. ⁷Give all your worries

and cares to God, for he cares about what happens to you. [8]Be careful! Watch out for attacks from the Devil, your great enemy. He prowls around like a roaring lion, looking for some victim to devour. [9]Take a firm stand against him, and be strong in your faith. Remember that your Christian brothers and sisters all over the world are going through the same kind of suffering you are.

[10]In his kindness God called you to his eternal glory by means of Jesus Christ. After you have suffered a little while, he will restore, support, and strengthen you, and he will place you on a firm foundation. [11]All power is his for ever and ever. Amen.

## Peter's Final Greetings

[12]I have written this short letter to you with the help of Silas, whom I consider a faithful brother. My purpose in writing is to encourage you and assure you that the grace of God is with you no matter what happens. [13]Your sister church here in Rome sends you greetings, and so does my son Mark. [14]Greet each other in Christian love.

Peace be to all of you who are in Christ.

PERSONAL ASSESSMENTS

## SPIRITUAL GIFT SURVEY:

God has given us all unique ways to build his kingdom. **Pick out five from this list you feel you have or may have a special talent for.**

Ask God to help you develop these or other talents for his Kingdom.

## Spiritual Gifts Profile

**Missionary**: to use other spiritual gifts to minister in other unique cultures.
See 1 Corinthians 9:19-23.
**Healing**: gift whereby the Spirit works through Christians to restore health to the sick. See James 5:13-16, Luke 9:1-2.
**Intercession**: enables Christians to pray with great and unique positive effect for the building of the Kingdom. See 1 Thessalonians 3:10-13, 1 Timothy 2:1-2.
**Craftsmanship**: endows Christians to use hands and minds to build up the Kingdom through artistic, creative means. See Exodus 28:3-4.
**Hospitality**: utilizes Christians to cheerfully open their homes willingly and offer lodging, food and comfort to other people. See Genesis 18:1-15.
**Faith**: gives extraordinary confidence in God's promises, power and presence.
See Hebrews 11.
**Discernment**: to know with assurance whether some behaviour is of God or of Satan. See Acts 5:3-6, Acts 16:16-18.
**Mercy**: empathy and compassion for those who are suffering.
See Luke 10:30-37.

**Giving**: to cheerfully and liberally offer their material blessings for the work of the church.
See 2 Corinthians 8:1-5.
**Administration**: understand and effectively direct the goals and big picture of a given faith community. See Acts 15:12-21.
**Leadership**: to motivate, direct and inspire God's people in such a way that they harmoniously work together to do the Church's work effectively.
See Hebrews 13:7, Judges 3:10, Exodus 18:13-16.
**Helps**: to assist in bearing the burdens of other Christians and help them in such a way that they can do their tasks more effectively. See Acts 6:2-4, Galatians 6:1-2.
**Knowledge**: to understand in an exceptional way the great truths of God's word and to make them real to others.
See Ephesians 3:14-19.
**Wisdom**: an understanding of God's will and work as it relates to the life of the individual and faith community.
See James 3:13-17
**Exhortation**: to bring comfort, counsel and encouragement.
See Acts 11:23-24, Acts 14:21-22.
**Teacher**: to communicate the truths of God's word so that others can learn and apply it to their lives.
See Hebrews 5:12-14.
**Pastor**: taking responsibility for the spiritual welfare of a group of believers.
See 1 Peter 5:1-11.
**Evangelist**: to express faith in Christ to unbelievers in a spiritually effective manner.
See Acts 8:26-40.
**Prophet**: to interpret and apply God's revelation in a given situation.
See 1 Corinthians 14:1-5, 1 Corinthians 14:30-33, 1 Corinthians 14:37-40.

# 2 Peter

What is the biggest problem for a coach whose team is winning? It is keeping his players from becoming complacent and cocky. In his final words Peter reminds Christians at large not to become complacent. 'So make every effort to apply the benefits of these promises to your life', 'I plan to keep reminding you of these things…', 'Dear children, keep away from anything that might take God's place in your hearts.'

Our job as Christians is to keep God number one! Peter like a good coach encourages us to push on and have victory in Jesus. Allow God to take command in your life every day read the scriptures for encouragement, training and transformation. Allow Peter to 'keep reminding you'.

# 2 PETER

## Greetings from Peter

# 1

This letter is from Simon Peter, a slave and apostle of Jesus Christ.

I am writing to all of you who share the same precious faith we have, faith given to us by Jesus Christ, our God and Saviour, who makes us right with God.

[2]May God bless you with his special favour and wonderful peace as you come to know Jesus, our God and Lord, better and better.

## When you need discipline:

### 1:6

Knowing God leads to self-control. Self-control leads to patient endurance, and patient endurance leads to godliness.

## Growing in the Knowledge of God

[3]As we know Jesus better, his divine power gives us everything we need for living a godly life. He has called us to receive his own glory and goodness! [4]And by that same mighty power, he has given us all of his rich and wonderful promises. He has promised that you will escape the decadence all around you caused by evil desires and that you will share in his divine nature.

[5]**So make every effort to apply the benefits of these promises to your life.** Then your faith will produce a life of moral excellence. A life of moral excellence leads to knowing God better. [6]Knowing God leads to self-control. Self-control leads to patient endurance, and patient endurance leads to godliness. [7]Godliness leads to love for other Christians, and finally you will grow to have genuine love for everyone. [8]The more you grow like this, the more you will become productive and useful in your knowledge of our Lord Jesus Christ. [9]But those who fail to develop these virtues are blind or, at least, very shortsighted. They have already forgotten that God has cleansed them from their old life of sin.

[10]So, dear brothers and sisters, work hard to prove that you really are among those God has called and chosen. Doing

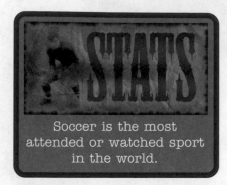

Soccer is the most attended or watched sport in the world.

this, you will never stumble or fall away. [11]And God will open wide the gates of heaven for you to enter into the eternal Kingdom of our Lord and Saviour Jesus Christ.

## Paying Attention to Scripture

[12]I plan to keep on reminding you of these things—even though you already know them and are standing firm in the truth. [13]Yes, I believe I should keep on reminding you of these things as long as I live. [14]But the Lord Jesus Christ has shown me that my days here on earth are numbered and I am soon to die. [15]So I will work hard to make these things clear to you. I want you to remember them long after I am gone.

[16]For we were not making up clever stories when we told you about the power of our Lord Jesus Christ and his coming again. We have seen his majestic splendour with our own eyes. [17]And he received honour and glory from God the Father when God's glorious, majestic voice called down from heaven, "This is my beloved Son; I am fully pleased with him." [18]We ourselves heard the voice when we were there with him on the holy mountain.

[19]Because of that, we have even greater confidence in the message proclaimed by the prophets. Pay close attention to what they wrote, for their words are like a light shining in a dark place—until the day Christ appears and his brilliant light shines in your hearts. [20]Above all, you must understand that no prophecy in Scripture ever came from the prophets themselves [21]or because they wanted to prophesy. It was the Holy Spirit who moved the prophets to speak from God.

## The Danger of False Teachers

# 2

But there were also false prophets in Israel, just as there will be false teachers among you. They will cleverly teach their destructive heresies about God and even turn against their Master who bought them. Theirs will be a swift and terrible end. [2]Many will follow

their evil teaching and shameful immorality. And because of them, Christ and his true way will be slandered. [3]In their greed they will make up clever lies to get hold of your money. But God condemned them long ago, and their destruction is on the way.

[4]For God did not spare even the angels when they sinned; he threw them into hell, in gloomy caves and darkness until the judgement day. [5]And God did not spare the ancient world—except for Noah and his family of seven. Noah warned the world of God's righteous judgement. Then God destroyed the whole world of ungodly people with a vast flood. [6]Later, he turned the cities of Sodom and Gomorrah into heaps of ashes and swept them off the face of the earth. He made them an example of what will happen to ungodly people.

[7]But at the same time, God rescued Lot out of Sodom because he was a good man who was sick of all the immorality and wickedness around him. [8]Yes, he was a righteous man who was distressed by the wickedness he saw and heard day after day.

[9]So you see, the Lord knows how to rescue godly people from their trials, even while punishing the wicked right up until the day of judgement. [10]He is especially hard on those who follow their own evil, lustful desires and who despise authority. These people are proud and arrogant, daring even to scoff at the glorious ones without so much as trembling. [11]But the angels, even though they are far greater in power and strength than these false teachers, never speak out disrespectfully against the glorious ones.

[12]These false teachers are like unthinking animals, creatures of instinct, who are born to be caught and killed. They laugh at the terrifying powers they know so little about, and they will be destroyed along with them. [13]Their destruction is their reward for the harm they have done. They love to indulge in evil pleasures in broad daylight. They are a disgrace and a stain among you. They revel in deceitfulness while they feast with you. [14]They commit adultery with their eyes, and their lust is never satisfied. They make a game of luring unstable people into sin. They train themselves to be greedy; they are doomed and cursed. [15]They have wandered off the right road and followed the way of Balaam son of Beor, who loved to earn money by doing wrong. [16]But Balaam was stopped from his mad course when his donkey rebuked him with a human voice.

[17]These people are as useless as dried-up springs of water or as clouds blown away by the wind—promising much and delivering nothing. They are doomed to blackest darkness. [18]They brag about themselves with empty, foolish boasting. With lustful

desire as their bait, they lure back into sin those who have just escaped from such wicked living. ¹⁹They promise freedom, but they themselves are slaves to sin and corruption. For you are a slave to whatever controls you. ²⁰And when people escape from the wicked ways of the world by learning about our Lord and Saviour Jesus Christ and then get tangled up with sin and become its slave again, they are worse off than before. ²¹It would be better if they had never known the right way to live than to know it and then reject the holy commandments that were given to them. ²²**They make these proverbs come true: "A dog returns to its vomit," and "A washed pig returns to the mud."**

## The Day of the Lord Is Coming

# 3

This is my second letter to you, dear friends, and in both of them I have tried to stimulate your wholesome thinking and refresh your memory. ²I want you to remember and understand what the holy prophets said long ago and what our Lord and Saviour commanded through your apostles.

³First, I want to remind you that in the last days there will be scoffers who will laugh at the truth and do every evil thing they desire. ⁴This will be their argument: "Jesus promised to come back, did he? Then where is he? Why, as far back as anyone can remember, everything has remained exactly the same since the world was first created."

⁵They deliberately forget that God made the heavens by the word of his command, and he brought the earth up from the water and surrounded it with water. ⁶Then he used the water to destroy the world with a mighty flood. ⁷And God has also commanded that the heavens and the earth will be consumed by fire on the day of judgement, when ungodly people will perish.

⁸**But you must not forget, dear friends, that a day is like a thousand years to the Lord, and a thousand years is like a day.** ⁹The Lord isn't really being slow about his promise to return, as some people think. No, he is being patient for your sake. He does not want anyone to perish, so he is giving more time for everyone to repent. ¹⁰But the day of the Lord will come as unexpectedly as a thief. Then the heavens will pass away with a terrible noise, and everything in them will disappear in fire, and the earth and everything on it will be exposed to judgement.

¹¹Since everything around us is going to melt away, what holy, godly lives you should be living! ¹²You should look forward to that day and hurry it along—the day when God will set the heavens on fire and the elements will melt away in the flames. ¹³But we are looking forward to the new heavens and new earth he has promised, a world where everyone is right with God.

¹⁴And so, dear friends, while you are waiting for these things to happen, make every effort to live a pure and blameless life. And be at peace with God. ¹⁵And remember, the Lord is waiting so that people have time to be saved. This is just as our beloved brother Paul wrote to you with the wisdom God gave him—¹⁶speaking of these things in all of his letters. Some of his comments are hard to understand, and those who are ignorant and unstable have twisted his letters around to mean something quite different from what he meant, just as they do the other parts of Scripture—and the result is disaster for them.

**CH 3:1-16 WHAT'S IT SAYING?**

**WHAT AM I GOING TO DO ABOUT IT?**

## Peter's Final Words

¹⁷I am warning you ahead of time, dear friends, so that you can watch out and not be carried away by the errors of these wicked people. I don't want you to lose your own secure footing.

¹⁸But grow in the grace and knowledge of our Lord and Saviour Jesus Christ.
To him be all glory and honour, both now and for evermore. Amen.

# WHAT DOES IT MEAN?

**Inspiration of Scripture**
Inspiration is the extraordinary or supernatural divine influence of those who wrote the Holy Scriptures, rendering their writings infallible. (2 Tim. 3:16). The writers were supernaturally guided and prompted to express exactly what God intended them to communicate as a revelation of his mind and will.

**The concept of HELL occurs 23 times in the New Testament.**

## Wearing the Uniform

'Quick! Bring the finest robe in the house and put it on him. Get a ring for his finger, and sandals for his feet. And kill the calf we have been fattening in the pen. We must celebrate with a feast, for this son of mine was dead and has now returned to life.' Luke 15:22-24

Do you remember receiving your first sports uniform? I didn't want to take mine off and probably wore it to bed! There is something about humans that loves definition, and validation. One of the great things about sport is that it sets margins. You're either part of the team or you're not. You win or lose. You have a low handicap or a high one. We enjoy being part of a group. The more others want to be part of a group the more esteemed the group is. Even anti-group types form their own counter-cultures and wear anti-social clothing (which is just another uniform), jewellery, haircuts, etc.... Ironically the anti-establishment uniform usually becomes the next generation's establishment kit. At one time not wearing a tie to watch a sporting event was considered socially outrageous!

DEVOTIONAL

Being adopted into God's family gives you certain rights, privileges and responsibilities. You wear a new uniform. If you are a Christian you have been adopted into God's family. You are now a princess or a prince. You belong to God and you have a new allegiance, a new title and new citizenship. And, like enjoying being part of a team, you also have new duties and responsibilities that come with the uniform.

'Now you are no longer a slave but God's own child. And since you are his child, everything he has belongs to you.' Galatians 4:7

Nicked from: A Sporting Guide to Eternity, Steve Connor,
Christian Focus Publications - ISBN 1-85792-746-X

# 1,2,3 John

John had seen it all: he witnessed Jesus' crucifixion, was banished to the isle of Patmos, his brother and many of his closest friends were martyred and legend has it that he was boiled in oil. Yet, at around one hundred years of age he was still going strong and his central theme is: love God and love others as 'dear children of God'. These three small letters are powerfully condensed; John does not waste a word.

Perhaps **1 John** is a supplement to his wonderful Gospel (see introduction to the Gospel of John). The letter gives us an intimate understanding of the privilege that those who follow Christ have: 'See how very much our heavenly Father loves us, for he allows us to be called his children...'(3:1). But it also contains strict warnings: 'Dear children, keep away from anything that might take God's place in your hearts' (5:21). As always the early church leaders are dogged by problems with bogus teachers trying to corrupt Christians and entire churches. And again we find John addressing the issue and correcting his 'dear children'. But this is no bad thing. If John, Paul and Peter did not have to deal with these idiots we would not have the rich, strong instruction in the Scriptures that we apply to our lives today.

**2 John and 3 John** are very intimate and concise letters, perhaps originally written on one sheet of papyrus each. Though they are short, meditate on them, allow God's power to transform your being and apply them to your life.

# 1 JOHN

## Introduction

# 1

The one who existed from the beginning is the one we have heard and seen. We saw him with our own eyes and touched him with our own hands. He is Jesus Christ, the Word of life. [2]This one who is life from God was shown to us, and we have seen him. And now we testify and announce to you that he is the one who is eternal life. He was with the Father, and then he was shown to us. [3]We are telling you about what we ourselves have actually seen and heard, so that you may have fellowship with us. And our fellowship is with the Father and with his Son, Jesus Christ.

[4]We are writing these things so that our joy will be complete.

**CH 1:5-10 WHAT'S IT SAYING?**

**WHAT AM I GOING TO DO ABOUT IT?**

## Living in the Light

[5]This is the message he has given us to announce to you: God is light and there is no darkness in him at all. [6]So we are lying if we say we have fellowship with God but go on living in spiritual darkness. We are not living in the truth. [7]But if we are living in the light of God's presence, just as Christ is,

# count on it

### You can't earn it!

There is nothing we can do to earn our way onto God's team. It is merely a "free gift". Our actions and lifestyle may be impressive in comparison to some. If we compare ourselves to Hitler or the hypocrite that goes to church we look pretty good. But when we try to make it on God's Team by the standard of a righteous life we "fall short". The good news is it is a free gift. You were chosen for the team because God loves you. He values you. He even likes you and wants you to spend time with him. But you do not make the team because of your skill as a player. "For all have sinned and fall short of God's glorious standard." Romans 3:23
**Count on it!**

then we have fellowship with each other, and the blood of Jesus, his Son, cleanses us from every sin.

[8]If we say we have no sin, we are only fooling ourselves and refusing to accept the truth. [9]But if we confess our sins to him, he is faithful and just to forgive us and to cleanse us from every wrong. [10]If we claim we have not sinned, we are calling God a liar and showing that his word has no place in our hearts.

# 2

My dear children, I am writing this to you so that you will not sin. But if you do sin, there is someone to plead for you before the Father. He is Jesus Christ, the one who pleases God completely. [2]He is the sacrifice for our sins. He takes away not only our sins but the sins of all the world.

[3]And how can we be sure that we belong to him? By obeying his commandments. [4]If someone says, "I belong to God," but doesn't obey God's commandments, that person is a liar and does not live in the truth. [5]But those who obey God's word really do love him. That is the way to know whether or not we live in him. [6]Those who say they live in God should live their lives as Christ did.

## A New Commandment

[7]Dear friends, I am not writing a new commandment, for it is an old one you have always had, right from the beginning. This commandment—to love one another—is the same message you heard before. [8]Yet it is also new. This commandment is true in Christ and is true among you, because the darkness is disappearing and the true light is already shining.

[9]If anyone says, "I am living in the light," but hates a Christian brother or sister, that person is still living in darkness. [10]Anyone who loves other Christians is living in the light and does not cause anyone to stumble. [11]Anyone who hates a Christian brother or sister is living and walking in darkness. Such a person is lost, having been blinded by the darkness.

[12]I am writing to you, my dear children, because your sins have been forgiven because of Jesus.

[13]I am writing to you who are mature because you know Christ, the one who is from the beginning.

I am writing to you who are young because you have won your battle with Satan.

[14]I have written to you, children, because you have known the Father.

I have written to you who are mature because you know Christ, the one who is from the beginning.

I have written to you who are young because you are strong with God's word living in your hearts, and you have won your battle with Satan.

[15]Stop loving this evil world and all that it offers you, for when you love the world, you show that you do not have the love of the Father in you. [16]For the world offers only the lust for physical pleasure, the lust for everything we see, and pride in our possessions. These are not from the Father. They are from this evil world. [17]And this world is fading away, along with everything it craves. But if you do the will of God, you will live for ever.

[18]Dear children, the last hour is here. You have heard that the Antichrist is coming, and already many such

antichrists have appeared. From this we know that the end of the world has come. ¹⁹These people left our churches because they never really belonged with us; otherwise they would have stayed with us. When they left us, it proved that they do not belong with us. ²⁰But you are not like that, for the Holy Spirit has come upon you, and all of you know the truth. ²¹So I am writing to you not because you don't know the truth but because you know the difference between truth and falsehood. ²²And who is the great liar? The one who says that Jesus is not the Christ. Such people are antichrists, for they have denied the Father and the Son. ²³Anyone who denies the Son doesn't have the

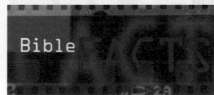

Bible FACTS

### The word 'gospel' means good news.

Father either. But anyone who confesses the Son has the Father also.

²⁴So you must remain faithful to what you have been

taught from the beginning. If you do, you will continue to live in fellowship with the Son and with the Father. ²⁵And in this fellowship we enjoy the eternal life he promised us.

²⁶I have written these things to you because you need to be aware of those who want to lead you astray. ²⁷But you have received the Holy Spirit, and he lives within you, so you don't need anyone to teach you what is true. For the Spirit teaches you all things, and what he teaches is true—it is not a lie. So continue in what he has taught you, and continue to live in Christ.

²⁸And now, dear children, continue to live in fellowship with Christ so that when he returns, you will be full of courage

STAND POINT

## When you need to feel loved

### 3:1

See how very much our heavenly Father loves us, for he allows us to be called his children, and we really are! But the people who belong to this world don't know God, so they don't understand that we are his children.

and not shrink back from him in shame. ²⁹Since we know that God is always right, we also know that all who do what is right are his children.

## Living as Children of God

# 3

See how very much our heavenly Father loves us, for he allows us to be called his children, and we really are! But the people who belong to this world don't know God, so they don't understand that we are his children. ²Yes, dear friends, we are already God's children, and we can't even imagine what we will be like when Christ returns. But we do know that when he comes we will be like him, for we will see him as he really is. ³And all who believe this will keep themselves pure, just as Christ is pure.

⁴Those who sin are opposed to the law of God, for all sin opposes the law of God. ⁵And you know that Jesus came to take away our sins, for there is no sin in him. ⁶So if we continue to live in him, we won't sin either. But those who keep on sinning have never known him or understood who he is.

⁷Dear children, don't let anyone deceive you about this: When people do what is right, it is because they are righteous, even as Christ is righteous. ⁸But when people keep on sinning, it shows they belong to the Devil, who has been sinning since the beginning. But the Son of God came to destroy these works of the Devil. ⁹Those who have been born into God's family do not sin, because God's life is in them. So they can't keep on sinning, because they have been born of God. ¹⁰So now we can tell who are children of God and who are children of the Devil. Anyone who does not obey God's commands and does not love other Christians does not belong to God.

## Love One Another

¹¹This is the message we have heard from the beginning: We should love one another. ¹²We must not be like Cain, who belonged to the evil one and killed his brother. And why did he kill him? Because Cain had been doing what was evil, and his brother had been doing what was right. ¹³So don't be surprised, dear brothers and sisters, if the world hates you.

¹⁴If we love our Christian brothers and sisters, it proves that we have passed from death to eternal life. But a person who has no love is still dead. ¹⁵Anyone who hates another Christian is really a murderer at heart. And you know that murderers don't have eternal life within them. ¹⁶We know what real love is because Christ gave up his life for us. And so we also ought to give up our lives for our Christian brothers and sisters. ¹⁷But if anyone has enough money to live well and sees a brother or sister in need and refuses to help—how can God's love be in that person?

¹⁸Dear children, let us stop just saying we love each other; let us really show it by our actions. ¹⁹It is by our actions that we know we are living in the truth, so we will be confident when we stand before the Lord, ²⁰even if our hearts condemn us. For God is greater than our hearts, and he knows everything.

²¹Dear friends, if our conscience is clear, we can come to God with bold confidence. ²²And we will receive whatever we request because we obey him and do the things that please him. ²³And this is his commandment: We must believe in the name of his Son, Jesus Christ, and love one another, just as he commanded us. **²⁴Those who obey God's commandments live in fellowship with him, and he with them. And we know he lives in us because the Holy Spirit lives in us.**

Bible FACTS

**A chariot imported from Egypt cost around 600 shekels of silver (that would be about the same cost as a luxury car today).**

## Discerning False Prophets

# 4

Dear friends, do not believe everyone who claims to speak by the Spirit. You must test them to see if the spirit they have comes from God. For there are many false prophets in the world. ²This is the way to find out if they have the Spirit of God: If a prophet acknowledges that Jesus Christ became a human being, that person has the Spirit of God. ³If a prophet does not acknowledge Jesus, that person is not from God. Such a person has the spirit of the Antichrist. You have heard that he is going to come into the world, and he is already here.

⁴But you belong to God, my dear children. You have

Who are five people you want to encourage this year?

1
2
3
4
5

BIG FIVE

## TIPS

### Fundamentals are Key:

The mental aspect of the game will, and does, affect your performance. For example, for various reasons, when golfers put a driver in their hands they tend to tense up. Before you begin to count on your driver to help you lower your score, you need to develop a comfort level with it. The same is true in all sport; work hard on fundamentals and slowly pull out the big plays (or clubs) as your confidence and skill develop.

already won your fight with these false prophets, because the Spirit who lives in you is greater than the spirit who lives in the world. [5]These people belong to this world, so they speak from the world's viewpoint, and the world listens to them. [6]But we belong to God; that is why those who know God listen to us. If they do not belong to God, they do not listen to us. That is how we know if someone has the Spirit of truth or the spirit of deception.

### Loving One Another

[7]Dear friends, let us continue to love one another, for love comes from God. Anyone who loves is born of God and knows God. [8]But anyone who does not love does not know God—for God is love.

[9]God showed how much he loved us by sending his only Son into the world so that we might have eternal life through him. [10]This is real love. It is not that we loved God, but that he loved us and sent his Son as a sacrifice to take away our sins.

[11]Dear friends, since God loved us that much, we surely ought to love each other. [12]No one has ever seen God. But if we love each other, God lives in us, and his love has been brought to full expression through us.

[13]And God has given us his Spirit as proof that we live in him and he in us. [14]Furthermore, we have seen with our own eyes and now testify that the Father sent his Son to be the Saviour of the world. [15]All who proclaim that Jesus is the Son of God have God living in them, and they live in God. [16]We know how much God loves us, and we have put our trust in him. God is love, and all who live in love live in God, and God lives in them. [17]And as we live in God, our love grows more perfect. So we will not be afraid on the day of judgement, but we can face him with confidence because we are like Christ here in this world.

[18]Such love has no fear because perfect love expels all fear. If we are afraid, it is for fear of judgement, and this shows that his love has not been perfected in us. [19]We love each other as a result of his loving us first.

[20]If someone says, "I love God," but hates a Christian brother

## STATS

Roger Bannister broke the 4-minute mile barrier in 1954.

# DECEMBER M.A.P.

## 1
| S.D. | P.L. | P.G. | S.G. |
|------|------|------|------|
| P. ☐ | F. ☐ | F. ☐ | T. ☐ |
| F. ☐ | W. ☐ | W. ☐ | P. ☐ |
| B. ☐ | P. ☐ | C. ☐ | C. ☐ |

## 2
| S.D. | P.L. | P.G. | S.G. |
|------|------|------|------|
| P. ☐ | F. ☐ | F. ☐ | T. ☐ |
| F. ☐ | W. ☐ | W. ☐ | P. ☐ |
| B. ☐ | P. ☐ | C. ☐ | C. ☐ |

## 3
| S.D. | P.L. | P.G. | S.G. |
|------|------|------|------|
| P. ☐ | F. ☐ | F. ☐ | T. ☐ |
| F. ☐ | W. ☐ | W. ☐ | P. ☐ |
| B. ☐ | P. ☐ | C. ☐ | C. ☐ |

## 4
| S.D. | P.L. | P.G. | S.G. |
|------|------|------|------|
| P. ☐ | F. ☐ | F. ☐ | T. ☐ |
| F. ☐ | W. ☐ | W. ☐ | P. ☐ |
| B. ☐ | P. ☐ | C. ☐ | C. ☐ |

## 9
| S.D. | P.L. | P.G. | S.G. |
|------|------|------|------|
| P. ☐ | F. ☐ | F. ☐ | T. ☐ |
| F. ☐ | W. ☐ | W. ☐ | P. ☐ |
| B. ☐ | P. ☐ | C. ☐ | C. ☐ |

## 10
| S.D. | P.L. | P.G. | S.G. |
|------|------|------|------|
| P. ☐ | F. ☐ | F. ☐ | T. ☐ |
| F. ☐ | W. ☐ | W. ☐ | P. ☐ |
| B. ☐ | P. ☐ | C. ☐ | C. ☐ |

## 11
| S.D. | P.L. | P.G. | S.G. |
|------|------|------|------|
| P. ☐ | F. ☐ | F. ☐ | T. ☐ |
| F. ☐ | W. ☐ | W. ☐ | P. ☐ |
| B. ☐ | P. ☐ | C. ☐ | C. ☐ |

## 12
| S.D. | P.L. | P.G. | S.G. |
|------|------|------|------|
| P. ☐ | F. ☐ | F. ☐ | T. ☐ |
| F. ☐ | W. ☐ | W. ☐ | P. ☐ |
| B. ☐ | P. ☐ | C. ☐ | C. ☐ |

## 17
| S.D. | P.L. | P.G. | S.G. |
|------|------|------|------|
| P. ☐ | F. ☐ | F. ☐ | T. ☐ |
| F. ☐ | W. ☐ | W. ☐ | P. ☐ |
| B. ☐ | P. ☐ | C. ☐ | C. ☐ |

## 18
| S.D. | P.L. | P.G. | S.G. |
|------|------|------|------|
| P. ☐ | F. ☐ | F. ☐ | T. ☐ |
| F. ☐ | W. ☐ | W. ☐ | P. ☐ |
| B. ☐ | P. ☐ | C. ☐ | C. ☐ |

## 19
| S.D. | P.L. | P.G. | S.G. |
|------|------|------|------|
| P. ☐ | F. ☐ | F. ☐ | T. ☐ |
| F. ☐ | W. ☐ | W. ☐ | P. ☐ |
| B. ☐ | P. ☐ | C. ☐ | C. ☐ |

## 20
| S.D. | P.L. | P.G. | S.G. |
|------|------|------|------|
| P. ☐ | F. ☐ | F. ☐ | T. ☐ |
| F. ☐ | W. ☐ | W. ☐ | P. ☐ |
| B. ☐ | P. ☐ | C. ☐ | C. ☐ |

## 25
| S.D. | P.L. | P.G. | S.G. |
|------|------|------|------|
| P. ☐ | F. ☐ | F. ☐ | T. ☐ |
| F. ☐ | W. ☐ | W. ☐ | P. ☐ |
| B. ☐ | P. ☐ | C. ☐ | C. ☐ |

## 26
| S.D. | P.L. | P.G. | S.G. |
|------|------|------|------|
| P. ☐ | F. ☐ | F. ☐ | T. ☐ |
| F. ☐ | W. ☐ | W. ☐ | P. ☐ |
| B. ☐ | P. ☐ | C. ☐ | C. ☐ |

## 27
| S.D. | P.L. | P.G. | S.G. |
|------|------|------|------|
| P. ☐ | F. ☐ | F. ☐ | T. ☐ |
| F. ☐ | W. ☐ | W. ☐ | P. ☐ |
| B. ☐ | P. ☐ | C. ☐ | C. ☐ |

## 28
| S.D. | P.L. | P.G. | S.G. |
|------|------|------|------|
| P. ☐ | F. ☐ | F. ☐ | T. ☐ |
| F. ☐ | W. ☐ | W. ☐ | P. ☐ |
| B. ☐ | P. ☐ | C. ☐ | C. ☐ |

## Spiritual Disciplines

**Prayer**

**Faith Community**

**Bible Reading**

## Prayer List

**Friends**

**World**

**Personal**

(For designing your MAP - Monthly Action Plan - see introduction pages)

Who am I....
Where am I going....
How am I going to get there?

# nt:sport
## MONTHLY ACTION PLAN

### 5
| S.D. | P.L. | P.G. | S.G. |
|------|------|------|------|
| P. ☐ | F. ☐ | F. ☐ | T. ☐ |
| F. ☐ | W. ☐ | W. ☐ | P. ☐ |
| B. ☐ | P. ☐ | C. ☐ | C. ☐ |

### 6
| S.D. | P.L. | P.G. | S.G. |
|------|------|------|------|
| P. ☐ | F. ☐ | F. ☐ | T. ☐ |
| F. ☐ | W. ☐ | W. ☐ | P. ☐ |
| B. ☐ | P. ☐ | C. ☐ | C. ☐ |

### 7
| S.D. | P.L. | P.G. | S.G. |
|------|------|------|------|
| P. ☐ | F. ☐ | F. ☐ | T. ☐ |
| F. ☐ | W. ☐ | W. ☐ | P. ☐ |
| B. ☐ | P. ☐ | C. ☐ | C. ☐ |

### 8
| S.D. | P.L. | P.G. | S.G. |
|------|------|------|------|
| P. ☐ | F. ☐ | F. ☐ | T. ☐ |
| F. ☐ | W. ☐ | W. ☐ | P. ☐ |
| B. ☐ | P. ☐ | C. ☐ | C. ☐ |

### 13
| S.D. | P.L. | P.G. | S.G. |
|------|------|------|------|
| P. ☐ | F. ☐ | F. ☐ | T. ☐ |
| F. ☐ | W. ☐ | W. ☐ | P. ☐ |
| B. ☐ | P. ☐ | C. ☐ | C. ☐ |

### 14
| S.D. | P.L. | P.G. | S.G. |
|------|------|------|------|
| P. ☐ | F. ☐ | F. ☐ | T. ☐ |
| F. ☐ | W. ☐ | W. ☐ | P. ☐ |
| B. ☐ | P. ☐ | C. ☐ | C. ☐ |

### 15
| S.D. | P.L. | P.G. | S.G. |
|------|------|------|------|
| P. ☐ | F. ☐ | F. ☐ | T. ☐ |
| F. ☐ | W. ☐ | W. ☐ | P. ☐ |
| B. ☐ | P. ☐ | C. ☐ | C. ☐ |

### 16
| S.D. | P.L. | P.G. | S.G. |
|------|------|------|------|
| P. ☐ | F. ☐ | F. ☐ | T. ☐ |
| F. ☐ | W. ☐ | W. ☐ | P. ☐ |
| B. ☐ | P. ☐ | C. ☐ | C. ☐ |

### 21
| S.D. | P.L. | P.G. | S.G. |
|------|------|------|------|
| P. ☐ | F. ☐ | F. ☐ | T. ☐ |
| F. ☐ | W. ☐ | W. ☐ | P. ☐ |
| B. ☐ | P. ☐ | C. ☐ | C. ☐ |

### 22
| S.D. | P.L. | P.G. | S.G. |
|------|------|------|------|
| P. ☐ | F. ☐ | F. ☐ | T. ☐ |
| F. ☐ | W. ☐ | W. ☐ | P. ☐ |
| B. ☐ | P. ☐ | C. ☐ | C. ☐ |

### 23
| S.D. | P.L. | P.G. | S.G. |
|------|------|------|------|
| P. ☐ | F. ☐ | F. ☐ | T. ☐ |
| F. ☐ | W. ☐ | W. ☐ | P. ☐ |
| B. ☐ | P. ☐ | C. ☐ | C. ☐ |

### 24
| S.D. | P.L. | P.G. | S.G. |
|------|------|------|------|
| P. ☐ | F. ☐ | F. ☐ | T. ☐ |
| F. ☐ | W. ☐ | W. ☐ | P. ☐ |
| B. ☐ | P. ☐ | C. ☐ | C. ☐ |

### 29
| S.D. | P.L. | P.G. | S.G. |
|------|------|------|------|
| P. ☐ | F. ☐ | F. ☐ | T. ☐ |
| F. ☐ | W. ☐ | W. ☐ | P. ☐ |
| B. ☐ | P. ☐ | C. ☐ | C. ☐ |

### 30
| S.D. | P.L. | P.G. | S.G. |
|------|------|------|------|
| P. ☐ | F. ☐ | F. ☐ | T. ☐ |
| F. ☐ | W. ☐ | W. ☐ | P. ☐ |
| B. ☐ | P. ☐ | C. ☐ | C. ☐ |

### 31
| S.D. | P.L. | P.G. | S.G. |
|------|------|------|------|
| P. ☐ | F. ☐ | F. ☐ | T. ☐ |
| F. ☐ | W. ☐ | W. ☐ | P. ☐ |
| B. ☐ | P. ☐ | C. ☐ | C. ☐ |

**Proverbs 21:30**

Human plans, no matter how wise or well advised, cannot stand against the Lord.

## Personal Goals

**Family**

**Work/School/Social**

**Challenge**

## Sport Goals

**Training**

**Performance**

**Competition Results**

# WHAT DOES IT MEAN?

### Jerusalem

Jerusalem is a city of contrasts, called at times the 'city of God' and the 'holy city'. It is one of the most famous cities in the world and considered sacred by Jews, Christians and Muslims and has a powerful mixture of East and West embodied at one time. The great city has been under siege for over four thousand years. It became King David's capital and after his death, his son, Solomon built the 'Temple', a house for God. Jerusalem has been rebuilt over and over on the immense beds of rubbish resulting from blockade, destruction and war. In Jesus' time, Jerusalem was the Jewish cultural centre and capital and a powder keg of tension because of Roman occupation and domination. Jesus visited as a boy, taught in the Temple, celebrated festivals, was crucified and showed himself after his resurrection in the 'Holy City'.

or sister, that person is a liar; for if we don't love people we can see, how can we love God, whom we have not seen? [21] And God himself has commanded that we must love not only him but our Christian brothers and sisters, too.

### action

CH 4:1–21 WHAT'S IT SAYING?

WHAT AM I GOING TO DO ABOUT IT?

## Faith in the Son of God

# 5

Everyone who believes that Jesus is the Christ is a child of God. And everyone who loves the Father loves his children, too. [2] We know we love God's children if we love God and obey his commandments. [3] Loving God means keeping his commandments, and really, that isn't difficult. [4] **For every child of God defeats this evil world by trusting Christ to give the victory.** [5] And the ones who win this battle against the world are the ones who believe that Jesus is the Son of God.

[6] And Jesus Christ was revealed as God's Son by his baptism in water and by shedding his blood on the cross—not by water only, but by water and blood. And the Spirit also gives us the testimony that this is true. [7] So we have these three witnesses—[8] the Spirit, the water, and the blood—and all three agree. [9] Since

we believe human testimony, surely we can believe the testimony that comes from God. And God has testified about his Son. [10] All who believe in the Son of God know that this is true. Those who don't believe this are actually calling God a liar because they don't believe what God has testified about his Son.

[11] And this is what God has testified: He has given us eternal life, and this life is in his Son. [12] So whoever has God's Son has life; whoever does not have his Son does not have life.

## Conclusion

[13] I write this to you who believe in the Son of God, so that you may know you have eternal life. [14] And we can be confident that he will listen to us whenever we ask him for anything in line with his will. [15] And if we know he is listening when we make our requests, we can be sure that he will give us what we ask for.

[16] If you see a Christian brother or sister sinning in a way that does not lead to death, you should pray, and God will give that person life. But there is a sin that leads to death, and I am not saying you should pray for those who commit it. [17] Every type of wrongdoing is sin, but not all sin leads to death.

[18] We know that those who have become part of God's family do not make a practice of sinning, for God's Son holds them securely, and the evil one cannot get his hands on them. [19] We know that we are children of God and that the world around us is under the power and control of the evil one. [20] And we know that the Son of God has come, and he has given us understanding so that we can know the true God. And now we are in God because we are in his Son, Jesus Christ. He is the only true God, and he is eternal life. [21] Dear children, keep away from anything that might take God's place in your hearts.

# 2 JOHN

## Greetings

This letter is from John the Elder.

It is written to the chosen lady and to her children, whom I love in the truth, as does everyone else who knows God's truth—[2] the truth that lives in us and will be in our hearts for ever.

[3] May grace, mercy, and peace, which come from God our Father and from Jesus Christ his Son, be with us who live in truth and love.

## Live in the Truth

[4] How happy I was to meet some of your children and find them living in the truth, just as we have been

commanded by the Father.

⁵And now I want to urge you, dear lady, that we should love one another. This is not a new commandment, but one we had from the beginning. ⁶Love means doing what God has commanded us, and he has commanded us to love one another, just as you heard from the beginning.

⁷Many deceivers have gone out into the world. They do not believe that Jesus Christ came to earth in a real body. Such a person is a deceiver and an antichrist. ⁸Watch out, so that you do not lose the prize for which we have been working so hard. Be diligent so that you will receive your full reward. **⁹For if you wander beyond the teaching of Christ, you will not have fellowship with God. But if you continue in the teaching of Christ, you will have fellowship with both the Father and the Son.**

¹⁰If someone comes to your meeting and does not teach the truth about Christ, don't invite him into your house or encourage him in any way. ¹¹Anyone who encourages him becomes a partner in his evil work.

## Conclusion

¹²Well, I have much more to say to you, but I don't want to say it in a letter. For I hope to visit you soon and to talk with you face to face. Then our joy will be complete.

¹³Greetings from the children of your sister, chosen by God.

# 3 JOHN

## Greetings

This letter is from John the Elder.

It is written to Gaius, my dear friend, whom I love in the truth.

²Dear friend, I am praying that all is well with you and that your body is as healthy as I know your soul is. ³Some of the brothers recently returned and made me very happy by telling me about your faithfulness and that you are living in the truth. ⁴I could have no greater joy than to hear that my children live in the truth.

## Caring for the Lord's Workers

⁵Dear friend, you are doing a good work for God when you take care of the travelling teachers who are passing through, even though they are strangers to you. ⁶They have told the church here of your friendship and your loving deeds. You do well to send them on their way in a manner that pleases God. ⁷For they are travelling for the Lord and accept nothing from those who are not Christians. ⁸So we ourselves should support them so that we may become partners with them for the truth.

⁹I sent a brief letter to the church about this, but Diotrephes, who loves to be the leader, does not acknowledge our authority. ¹⁰When I come, I will report some of the things he is doing and the wicked things he is saying about us. He not only refuses to welcome the travelling teachers, he also tells others not to help them. And when they do help, he puts them out of the church.

¹¹Dear friend, don't let this bad example influence you. Follow only what is good. Remember that those who do good prove that they are God's children, and those who do evil prove that they do not know God. ¹²But everyone speaks highly of Demetrius, even truth itself. We ourselves can say the same for him, and you know we speak the truth.

**V11-12 WHAT'S IT SAYING?**

**WHAT AM I GOING TO DO ABOUT IT?**

## Conclusion

¹³I have much to tell you, but I don't want to do it in a letter. ¹⁴For I hope to see you soon, and then we will talk face to face.

¹⁵May God's peace be with you. Your friends here send you their greetings. Please give my personal greetings to each of our friends there.

**My friends say that Christians are too uptight about watching movies and listening to music...**

Our intake affects our output. The goal of sport nutrition is to 'eat to compete' – to fuel the body for maximum performance. What we feed our minds on is just as important as what we feed our bodies. The kind of books we read, the people we hang out with, the music we listen to, and the films and television programmes we watch are all part of our mental diet. You are what you eat. **'A wise person is hungry for truth, while the fool feeds on foolishness'. Proverbs 15:14**

**find the power**
LIVE it

# Jude

Jude is the brother of James and half-brother of Jesus (see Mark 6:3). Plainly his target audience was the Christian movement that was spreading around the world. Like other Bible writers Jude has to stop the spread of false teaching which can spread like a cancer. We can feel his concern and the sense of urgency to stop the raging disease of lies. But in this struggle for the hearts of men, the adversity creates strength and endurance.

You do not become a champion by listening to and following liars. You cannot be successful and lazy. The same is true in your walk with God - it never says it will be easy and there is a spiritual evil that is going to wage war against you, 'dangerous reefs that can shipwreck you'. But we are not to be scared because we have a God that will 'keep us from stumbling' and bring us into his presence.

# JUⴅE

## Greetings from Jude

This letter is from Jude, a slave of Jesus Christ and a brother of James.

I am writing to all who are called to live in the love of God the Father and the care of Jesus Christ.

[2]May you receive more and more of God's mercy, peace, and love.

## The Danger of False Teachers

[3]Dearly loved friends, I had been eagerly planning to write to you about the salvation we all share. But now I find that I must write about something else, urging you to defend the truth of the Good News. God gave this unchanging truth once for all time to his holy people. [4]I say this because some godless people have wormed their way in among you, saying that God's forgiveness allows us to live immoral lives. The fate of such people was determined long ago, for they have turned against our only Master and Lord, Jesus Christ.

[5]**I must remind you—and you know it well—that even though the Lord rescued the whole nation of Israel from Egypt, he later destroyed every one of those who did not remain faithful.** [6]And I remind you of the angels who did not stay within the limits of authority God gave them but left the place where they belonged. God has kept them chained in prisons of darkness, waiting for the day of judgement. [7]And don't forget the cities of Sodom and Gomorrah and their neighbouring towns, which were filled with sexual immorality and every kind of sexual perversion. Those cities were destroyed by fire and are a warning of the eternal fire that will punish all who are evil.

[8]Yet these false teachers, who claim authority from their dreams, live immoral lives, defy authority, and scoff at the power of the glorious ones. [9]But even Michael, one of the mightiest of the angels, did not dare accuse Satan of blasphemy, but simply said, "The Lord rebuke you." (This took place when Michael was arguing with Satan about Moses' body.) [10]But these people mock and curse the things they do not understand. Like animals, they do whatever their instincts tell them, and they bring about their own destruction. [11]How

## STAND POINT

### When a friend is weak:

### vs 22

Show mercy to those whose faith is wavering.

terrible it will be for them! For they follow the evil example of Cain, who killed his brother. Like Balaam, they will do anything for money. And like Korah, they will perish because of their rebellion.

action

**V12-16 WHAT'S IT SAYING?**

**WHAT AM I GOING TO DO ABOUT IT?**

[12]When these people join you in fellowship meals celebrating the love of the Lord, they are like dangerous reefs that can shipwreck you. They are shameless in the way they care only about themselves. They are like clouds blowing over dry land without giving rain, promising much but producing nothing. They are like trees without fruit at harvest-time. They are not only dead but doubly dead, for they have been pulled out by the roots. [13]They are like wild waves of the sea, churning up the dirty foam of their shameful deeds. They are wandering stars, heading for everlasting gloom and darkness.

[14]Now Enoch, who lived seven generations after Adam, prophesied about these people. He said, "Look, the Lord is coming with thousands of his holy ones. [15]He will bring the people of the world to judgement. He will convict the ungodly of all the evil things they have done in rebellion

Bible FACTS

## The 10 plagues of Egypt:

1. **Water turns to blood**
2. **Frogs**
3. **Lice and fleas**
4. **Flies**
5. **Cattle die of diseases**
6. **Boils and sores**
7. **Hail**
8. **Locusts**
9. **Darkness**
10. **Death of first-born**

and of all the insults that godless sinners have spoken against him."

[16]These people are grumblers and complainers, doing whatever evil they feel like. They are loudmouthed braggarts, and they flatter others to get favours in return.

## A Call to Remain Faithful

[17]But you, my dear friends, must remember what the apostles of our Lord Jesus Christ told you, [18]that in the last times there would be scoffers whose purpose in life is to enjoy themselves in every evil way imaginable. [19]Now they are here, and they are the ones who are creating divisions among you. They live by natural instinct because they do not have God's Spirit living in them.

[20]**But you, dear friends, must continue to build your lives on the foundation of your holy faith. And continue to pray as you are directed by the Holy Spirit.** [21]Live in such a way that God's love can bless you as you wait for the eternal life that our Lord Jesus Christ in his mercy is going to give you. [22]Show mercy to those whose faith is wavering. [23]Rescue others by snatching them from the flames of judgement. There are still others to whom you need to show mercy, but be careful that you aren't contaminated by their sins.

## A Prayer of Praise

[24]And now, all glory to God, who is able to keep you from stumbling, and who will bring you into his glorious presence innocent of sin and with great joy. [25]All glory to him, who alone is God our Saviour, through Jesus Christ our Lord. Yes, glory, majesty, power, and authority belong to him, in the beginning, now, and for evermore. Amen.

# Revelation

Read this book if you want to be blessed! It expressly promises that all who 'read' and 'all who listen and obey' this book will be given blessing (Rev. 1:3). It also promises that anybody who 'adds to' or 'removes' anything from this book will be cursed! (Rev. 22:18). The word revelation means unveiling or revealing (Apocalypse is the Greek name). The book is a disclosure of truth that Jesus Christ possesses and is giving to us, his church. The central theme is Jesus Christ's reign and his complete and eternal victory over Satan. God gives us a glimpse at the end of the match and the scoreboard reads: God Wins!

The author of this book was undoubtedly John the apostle. As to the relation between this book and the Gospel of John, it has been well observed that the leading ideas of both are the same: the ultimate clash between good and evil and God's solution. The Gospel gives us a magnificent historical drama and the Revelation gives us the amazing vision and foretelling. In both Jesus Christ is the key figure, whose victory through the cross is central!

OUTLINE:
- 1        Jesus revealed in glory
- 2 & 3    Scope of church history
- 4 & 5    Christ and his church
- 6–17     Christ and the world
- 18–22    Christ's return

# REVELATION

## Prologue

# 1

This is a revelation from Jesus Christ, which God gave him concerning the events that will happen soon. An angel was sent to God's servant John so that John could share the revelation with God's other servants. ²John faithfully reported the word of God and the testimony of Jesus Christ—everything he saw.

³**God blesses the one who reads this prophecy to the church, and he blesses all who listen to it and obey what it says. For the time is near when these things will happen.**

## John's Greeting to the Seven Churches

⁴This letter is from John to the seven churches in the province of Asia. Grace and peace from the one who is, who always was, and who is still to come; from the sevenfold Spirit before his throne; ⁵and from Jesus Christ, who is the faithful witness to these things, the first to rise from the dead, and the commander of all the rulers of the world.

All praise to him who loves us and has freed us from our sins by shedding his blood for us. ⁶He has made us his Kingdom and his priests who serve before God his Father. Give to him everlasting glory! He rules for ever and ever! Amen!

⁷Look! He comes with the clouds of heaven. And everyone will see him—even those who pierced him. And all the nations of the earth will weep because of him. Yes! Amen!

⁸"I am the Alpha and the Omega—the beginning and the end," says the Lord God. "I am the one who is, who always was, and who is still to come, the Almighty One."

## Vision of the Son of Man

⁹I am John, your brother. In Jesus we are partners in suffering and in the Kingdom and in patient endurance. I was exiled to the island of Patmos for preaching the word of God and speaking about Jesus. ¹⁰It was the Lord's Day, and I was worshipping in the Spirit. Suddenly, I heard a loud voice behind me, a voice that sounded like a trumpet blast. ¹¹It said, "Write down what you see, and send it to the seven churches: Ephesus, Smyrna, Pergamum, Thyatira, Sardis, Philadelphia, and Laodicea."

¹²When I turned to see who was speaking to me, I saw seven gold lampstands. ¹³And standing in the middle of the lampstands was the Son of Man. He was wearing a long robe with a gold sash across his chest. ¹⁴His head and his hair were white like wool, as white as snow. And his eyes were

## count on it

**Christ came for you!**
Jesus Christ had a purpose, a focus and a finish line. He completed his race and the end result was that those who receive his love and forgiveness, in faith, will have eternal life. You are a sinner - but...
"This is a true saying, and everyone should believe it: Christ Jesus came into the world to save sinners."
1 Timothy 1:15
**Count on it!**

bright like flames of fire. ¹⁵His feet were as bright as bronze refined in a furnace, and his voice thundered like mighty ocean waves. ¹⁶He held seven stars in his right hand, and a sharp two-edged sword came from his mouth. And his face was as bright as the sun in all its brilliance.

¹⁷When I saw him, I fell at his feet as dead. But he laid his right hand on me and said, "Don't be afraid! I am

## STAND POINT

**When you face death**

**1:18**

I am the living one who died. Look, I am alive for ever and ever! And I hold the keys of death and the grave.

the First and the Last. ¹⁸I am the living one who died. Look, I am alive for ever and ever! And I hold the keys of death and the grave. ¹⁹Write down what you have seen—both the things that are now happening and the things that will happen later. ²⁰This is the meaning of the seven stars you saw in my right hand and the seven gold lampstands: The seven stars are the angels of the seven churches, and the seven lampstands are the seven churches.

## action

**CH 2:2-7 WHAT'S IT SAYING?**

**WHAT AM I GOING TO DO ABOUT IT?**

## The Message to the Church in Ephesus

# 2

"Write this letter to the angel of the church in Ephesus. This is the message from the one who holds the seven stars in his right hand, the one who walks among the seven gold lampstands:

²"I know all the things you do. I have seen your hard work and your patient endurance. I know you don't tolerate evil people. You have examined the claims of those who say they are apostles but are not. You have discovered they are liars.

³You have patiently suffered for me without giving up.

⁴But I have this complaint against you. You don't love

me or each other as you did at first! [5]Look how far you have fallen from your first love! Turn back to me again and work as you did at first. If you don't, I will come and remove your lampstand from its place among the churches. [6]But there is this about you that is good: You hate the deeds of the immoral Nicolaitans, just as I do.

[7]"Anyone who is willing to hear should listen to the Spirit and understand what the Spirit is saying to the churches. Everyone who is victorious will eat from the tree of life in the paradise of God.

## The Message to the Church in Smyrna

[8]"Write this letter to the angel of the church in Smyrna. This is the message from the one who is the First and the Last, who died and is alive:

[9]"I know about your suffering and your poverty—but you are rich! I know the slander of those opposing you. They say they are Jews, but they really aren't because theirs is a synagogue of Satan. [10]Don't be afraid of what you are about to suffer. The Devil will throw some of you into prison and put you to the test. You will be persecuted for 'ten days.' Remain faithful even when facing death, and I will give you the crown of life.

[11]"Anyone who is willing to hear should listen to the Spirit and understand what the Spirit is saying to the churches. Whoever is victorious will not be hurt by the second death.

## The Message to the Church in Pergamum

[12]"Write this letter to the angel of the church in Pergamum. This is the message from the one who has a sharp two-edged sword:

[13]"I know that you live in the city where that great throne of Satan is located, and yet you have remained loyal to me. And you refused to deny me even when Antipas, my faithful witness, was martyred among you by Satan's followers. [14]And yet I have a few complaints against you. You tolerate some among you who are like Balaam, who showed Balak how to trip up the people of Israel. He taught them to worship idols by eating food offered to idols and by committing sexual sin. [15]In the same way, you have some Nicolaitans among you—people who follow the same teaching and commit the same sins. [16]Repent, or I will come to you suddenly and fight against them with the sword of my mouth.

[17]"Anyone who is willing to hear should listen to the Spirit and understand what the Spirit is saying to the

**Give it to God:** When anything starts to bug you - anything - ask God for help. There is nothing too big or small for him to help you with. Worry should be an alarm bell ringing in your head to remind you to pray. "Don't worry about anything; instead, pray about everything. Tell God what you need, and thank him for all he has done. If you do this, you will experience God's peace, which is far more wonderful than the human mind can understand. His peace will guard your hearts and minds as you live in Christ Jesus." Philippians 4:6-7

# POWER HABITS

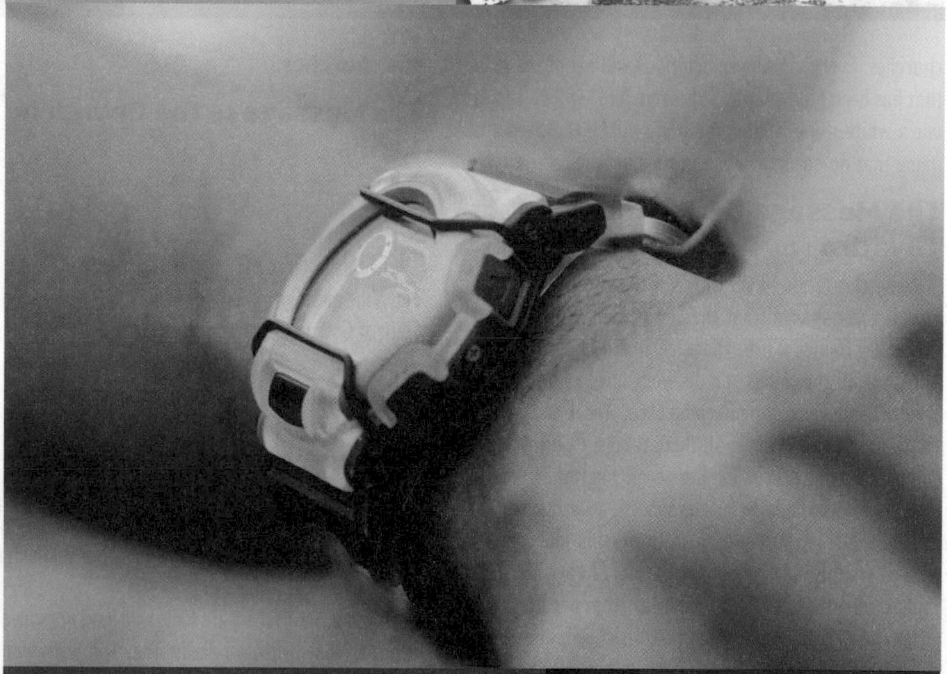

Who are the five coolest athletes under pressure?

1
2
3
4
5

# BIG FIVE

TIPS

## How to Improve your Anticipation:

Good anticipation is a PRIMARY reason why great players make the game look so easy. They always seem to be moving in the right direction toward their opponents' shots and rarely seem surprised by what is happening in competition. Many players think of anticipation as knowing exactly what type of delivery will come at them. Anticipation is not so much knowing the exact shot your opponent is about to throw you, but reducing the possibilities to a few of the likeliest ones. This comes with time and experience. Watch professionals, your opponents and team-mates compete. Don't just watch the game, put yourself in their shoes, feel their footwork and their responses. You will soon learn there are only a few realistic options that will come at you.

churches. Everyone who is victorious will eat of the manna that has been hidden away in heaven. And I will give to each one a white stone, and on the stone will be engraved a new name that no one knows except the one who receives it.

## The Message to the Church in Thyatira

[18]"Write this letter to the angel of the church in Thyatira. This is the message from the Son of God, whose eyes are bright like flames of fire, whose feet are like polished bronze: [19]"I know all the things you do—your love, your faith, your service, and your patient endurance. And I can see your constant improvement in all these things. [20]But I have this complaint against you. You are permitting that woman—that Jezebel who calls herself a prophet—to lead my servants astray. She is encouraging them to worship idols, eat food offered to idols, and commit sexual sin. [21]I gave her time to repent, but she would not turn away from her immorality. [22]Therefore, I will throw her upon a sickbed, and she will suffer greatly with all who commit adultery with her, unless they turn away from all their evil deeds. [23]I will strike her children dead. And all the churches will know that I am the one who searches out the thoughts and intentions of every person. And I will give to each of you whatever you deserve. [24]But I also have a message for the rest of you in Thyatira who have not followed this false teaching ('deeper truths,' as they call them—depths of Satan, really). I will ask nothing more of you [25]except that you hold tightly to what you have until I come.

[26]"To all who are victorious, who obey me to the very end, I will give authority over all the nations. [27]They will rule the nations with an iron rod and smash them like clay pots. [28]They will have the same authority I received from my Father, and I will also give them the morning star! [29]**Anyone who is willing to hear should listen to the Spirit and understand what the Spirit is saying to**

the churches.

## The Message to the Church in Sardis

# 3

"Write this letter to the angel of the church in Sardis. This is the message from the one who has the sevenfold Spirit of God and the seven stars:
"I know all the things you do, and that you have a reputation for being alive——but you are dead. [2]Now wake up! Strengthen what little remains, for even what is left is at the point of death. Your deeds are far from right in the sight of God. [3]Go back to what you heard and believed at first; hold to it firmly and turn to me again. Unless you do, I will come upon you suddenly, as unexpected as a thief.

[4]"Yet even in Sardis there are some who have not soiled their garments with evil deeds. They will walk with me in white, for they are worthy. [5]All who are victorious will be clothed in white. I will never erase their names from the Book of Life, but I will announce before my

STATS

Golf is the only sport to have been played on the moon - on 6 February 1971 Alan Shepard hit a golf ball.

Father and his angels that they are mine. [6]Anyone who is willing to hear should listen to the Spirit and understand what the Spirit is saying to the churches.

## The Message to the Church in Philadelphia

[7]"Write this letter to the angel of the church in Philadelphia. This is the message from the one who is holy and true. He is the one who has the key of David. He opens doors, and no one can shut them; he shuts doors, and no one can open them.

[8]"I know all the things you do, and I have opened a door for you that no one can shut. You have little strength, yet you obeyed my word and did not deny me. [9]Look! I will force those who belong to Satan—those liars who say they are Jews but are not—to come and bow down at your feet. They will acknowledge that you are the ones I love.

[10]"Because you have obeyed my command to persevere, I will protect you from the great time of testing that will come upon the whole world to test those who belong to this world. [11]Look, I am coming quickly. Hold on to what you have, so that no one will take away your crown. [12]All who are victorious will become pillars in the Temple of my God, and they will never have to leave it. And I will write my God's name on them, and they will be citizens in the city of my God—the new Jerusalem that comes down from heaven from my God. And they will have my new name inscribed upon them. [13]Anyone who is willing to hear should listen to the Spirit and understand what the Spirit is saying to the churches.

## The Message to the Church in Laodicea

[14]"Write this letter to the angel of the church in

Laodicea. This is the message from the one who is the Amen—the faithful and true witness, the ruler of God's creation:

<sup>15</sup>"I know all the things you do, that you are neither hot nor cold. I wish you were one or the other! <sup>16</sup>But since you are like lukewarm water, I will spit you out of my mouth! <sup>17</sup>You say, 'I am rich. I have everything I want. I don't need a thing!' And you don't realize that you are wretched and miserable and poor and blind and naked. <sup>18</sup>I advise you to buy gold from me— gold that has been purified by fire. Then you will be rich. And also buy white garments so you will not be shamed by your nakedness. And buy ointment for your eyes so you will be able to see. <sup>19</sup>I am the one who corrects and disciplines everyone I love. Be diligent and turn from your indifference.

<sup>20</sup>"Look! Here I stand at the door and knock. If you hear me calling and open the door, I will come in, and we will share a meal as friends. <sup>21</sup>I will invite everyone who is victorious to sit with me on my throne, just as I was victorious and sat with my Father on his throne. <sup>22</sup>Anyone who is willing to hear should listen to the Spirit and understand what the Spirit is saying to the churches."

## Worship in Heaven

# 4

Then as I looked, I saw a door standing open in heaven, and the same voice I had heard before spoke to me with the sound of a mighty trumpet blast. The voice said, "Come up here, and I will show you what must happen after these things." <sup>2</sup>And instantly I was in the Spirit, and I saw a throne in heaven and someone sitting on it! <sup>3</sup>The one sitting on the throne was as brilliant as gemstones—jasper and carnelian. And the glow of an emerald circled his throne like a rainbow. <sup>4</sup>Twenty-four thrones surrounded him, and twenty-four elders sat on them. They were all clothed in white and had gold crowns on their heads. <sup>5</sup>And from the throne came flashes of lightning and the rumble of thunder. And in front of the throne were seven lampstands with burning flames. They are the seven spirits of God. <sup>6</sup>In front of the throne was a shiny sea of glass, sparkling like crystal.

In the centre and around the throne were four living beings, each covered with eyes, front and back. <sup>7</sup>The first of these living beings had the form of a lion; the second looked like an ox; the third had a human face; and the fourth had the form of an eagle with wings spread out as though in flight. <sup>8</sup>Each of these living

beings had six wings, and their wings were covered with eyes, inside and out. Day after day and night after night they keep on saying,

"Holy, holy, holy is the Lord God Almighty— the one who always was, who is, and who is still to come."

<sup>9</sup>Whenever the living beings give glory and honour and thanks to the one sitting on the throne, the one who lives for ever and ever, <sup>10</sup>the twenty-four elders fall down and worship the one who lives for ever and ever. And they lay their crowns before the throne and say,

<sup>11</sup>"You are worthy, O Lord our God, to receive glory and honour and power. For you created everything, and it is for your pleasure that they exist and were created."

**CH 5:1-14 WHAT'S IT SAYING?**

**WHAT AM I GOING TO DO ABOUT IT?**

## The Lamb Opens the Scroll

# 5

And I saw a scroll in the right hand of the one who was sitting on the throne. There was writing on the inside and the outside of the scroll, and it was sealed

# profiles

**David:**

1 Samuel 17:45 - 'David shouted in reply, "You come to me with sword, spear, and javelin, but I come to you in the name of the Lord Almighty."' If you were to write a story for your own religion you would not constantly show yourself and your colleagues failing. But the Bible was written by God, not men, and God allows us to see that he will use flawed but faithful people for great things. David was fearless in the face of seemingly great odds. Have you ever faced a struggle that was apparently impossible to overcome? David faced these struggles over and over but instead of relying on his own strength he relied on God. Samuel the high priest and prophet was commissioned by God to find a good King to lead the Israelites. 1 Samuel 16:7 - 'But the Lord said to Samuel, "Don't judge by his appearance or height, for I have rejected him. The Lord doesn't make decisions the way you do! People judge by outward appearance, but the Lord looks at a person's thoughts and intentions."' David was a shepherd, poet, giant-killer, king, commander. But his failures include liar, adulterer, and murderer. He learned from his mistakes. The consequences of his sin were painful but the joy of his life was glorious.

**Should Christians consider themselves better or superior to those who aren't?**
Of course not. We should consider ourselves as beggars that have found a lasting source of food. Christians should be aware of their shortcomings. The classic answer to 'I don't want to go to church, it is full of hypocrites' should be, 'No it's not, there is always room for one more!' How do we know it is full of hypocrites? Because we are flawed people, falling down in our faith every day. Fortunately, we have a perfect redeemer.

with seven seals. ²And I saw a strong angel, who shouted with a loud voice: "Who is worthy to break the seals on this scroll and unroll it?" ³But no one in heaven or on earth or under the earth was able to open the scroll and read it. ⁴Then I wept because no one could be found who was worthy to open the scroll and read it. ⁵But one of the twenty-four elders said to me, "Stop weeping! Look, the Lion of the tribe of Judah, the heir to David's throne, has conquered. He is worthy to open the scroll and break its seven seals."

⁶I looked and I saw a Lamb that had been killed but was now standing between the throne and the four living beings and among the twenty-four elders. He had seven horns and seven eyes, which are the seven spirits of God that are sent out into every part of the earth. ⁷He stepped forward and took the scroll from the right hand of the one sitting on the throne. ⁸And as he took the scroll, the four living beings and the twenty-four elders fell down before the Lamb. Each one had a harp, and they held gold bowls filled with incense—the prayers of God's people!

⁹And they sang a new song with these words:
"You are worthy to take the scroll
and break its seals and open it.
For you were killed, and your blood has ransomed people for God
from every tribe and language and people and nation.
¹⁰And you have caused them to become God's Kingdom and his priests.
And they will reign on the earth."

¹¹Then I looked again, and I heard the singing of thousands and millions of angels around the throne and the living beings and the elders. ¹²And they sang in a mighty chorus:
"The Lamb is worthy—the Lamb who was killed.
He is worthy to receive power and riches
and wisdom and strength
and honour and glory and blessing."
¹³And then I heard every creature in heaven and on earth and under the earth and in the sea. They also sang:
"Blessing and honour and glory and power
belong to the one sitting on the throne
and to the Lamb for ever and ever."

¹⁴And the four living beings said, "Amen!" And the twenty-four elders fell down and worshipped God and the Lamb.

## The Lamb Breaks the First Six Seals

# 6

As I watched, the Lamb broke the first of the seven seals on the scroll. Then one of the four living beings called out with a voice that sounded like thunder, "Come!" ²I looked up and saw a white horse. Its rider carried a bow, and a crown was placed on his head. He rode out to win many battles and gain the victory. ³When the Lamb broke the second seal, I heard the second living being say, "Come!" ⁴And another horse appeared, a red one. Its rider was given a mighty sword and the authority to remove peace from the earth. And there was war and slaughter everywhere.

⁵When the Lamb broke the third seal, I heard the third living being say, "Come!" And I looked up and saw a black horse, and its rider was holding a pair of scales in his hand. ⁶And a voice from among the four living beings said, "A loaf of wheat bread or three loaves of barley for a day's pay. And don't waste the olive oil and wine."

⁷And when the Lamb broke the fourth seal, I heard the fourth living being say, "Come!" ⁸And I looked up and saw a horse whose colour was pale green like a corpse. And Death was the name of its rider, who was

**Revelation, written about 95 AD, is the youngest book in the New Testament.**

followed around by the Grave. They were given authority over one-fourth of the earth, to kill with the sword and famine and disease and wild animals. ⁹And when the Lamb broke the fifth seal, I saw under the altar the souls of all who had been martyred for the word of God and for being faithful in their witness. ¹⁰They called loudly to the Lord and said, "O Sovereign Lord, holy and true, how long will it be before you judge the people who belong to this world for what they have done to us? When will you avenge our blood against these people?" ¹¹Then a white robe was given to each of them. And they were told to rest a little longer until the full number of their brothers and sisters—their fellow servants of Jesus—had been martyred.

¹²I watched as the Lamb broke the sixth seal, and there was a great earthquake. The sun became as dark as black cloth, and the moon became as red as blood. ¹³Then the stars of the sky fell to the earth like green figs falling from trees shaken by mighty winds. ¹⁴And the sky was rolled up like a scroll and taken away. And all of the mountains and all of the islands disappeared. ¹⁵Then the kings of the earth, the rulers, the generals, the wealthy people, the people with great power, and every slave and every free person—all hid themselves in the caves and among the rocks of the mountains. ¹⁶And they cried to the mountains and the rocks, "Fall on us and hide us from the face of the one who sits on the throne and from the wrath of the Lamb. ¹⁷For the great day of their wrath has come, and who will be able to survive?"

# WHAT DOES IT MEAN?

## Judgement

Judgement is the sentence that will be passed on our actions at the last day (Matt. 25; Rom. 14:10,11; 2 Cor. 5:10; 2 Thess. 1:7-10). The judge is Jesus Christ. All judgement is committed to him (Acts 17:31; John 5:22,27; Rev. 1:7). The persons to be judged are: the whole race of Adam without a single exception (Matt. 25:31-46; 1 Cor. 15:51,52; Rev. 20:11-15); and the fallen angels (2 Pet. 2:4; Jude 1:6). The rule of judgement is the standard of God's law as revealed to men and written on their hearts (Luke 12:47,48; Rom. 2:12-16). As the Scriptures represent the final judgement as certain, universal, decisive and having eternal consequences (Heb. 6:2), let us be concerned for the welfare of our immortal interests and the interests of our friends. Let's run to Jesus' mercy, make the most of our time on earth, rely on Jesus' faithfulness to change us and stick close to his commands.

## God's People Will Be Preserved

# 7

Then I saw four angels standing at the four corners of the earth, holding back the four winds from blowing upon the earth. Not a leaf rustled in the trees, and the sea became as smooth as glass. [2]And I saw another angel coming from the east, carrying the seal of the living God. And he shouted out to those four angels who had been given power to injure land and sea, [3]"Wait! Don't hurt the land or the sea or the trees until we have placed the seal of God on the foreheads of his servants."

[4]And I heard how many were marked with the seal of God. There were 144,000 who were sealed from all the tribes of Israel:

| [5] | from Judah | 12,000 |
| | from Reuben | 12,000 |
| | from Gad | 12,000 |
| [6] | from Asher | 12,000 |
| | from Naphtali | 12,000 |
| | from Manasseh | 12,000 |
| [7] | from Simeon | 12,000 |
| | from Levi | 12,000 |
| | from Issachar | 12,000 |
| [8] | from Zebulun | 12,000 |
| | from Joseph | 12,000 |
| | from Benjamin | 12,000 |

## Praise from the Great Multitude

[9]After this I saw a vast crowd, too great to count, from every nation and tribe and people and language, standing in front of the throne and before the Lamb. They were clothed in white and held palm branches in their hands. [10]And they were shouting with a mighty shout, "Salvation comes from our God on the throne and from the Lamb!"

[11]And all the angels were standing around the throne and around the elders and the four living beings. And they fell face down before the throne and worshipped God. [12]They said,

"Amen! Blessing and glory and wisdom
and thanksgiving and honour and power and strength
belong to our God for ever and for ever. Amen!"

[13]Then one of the twenty-four elders asked me, "Who are these who are clothed in white? Where do they come from?"

[14]And I said to him, "Sir, you are the one who knows." Then he said to me, "These are the ones coming out of the great tribulation. They washed their robes in the blood of the Lamb and made them white. [15]That is why they are standing in front of the throne of God, serving him day and night in his Temple. And he who sits on the throne will live among them and shelter them. [16]They will never again be hungry or thirsty, and they will be fully protected from the scorching midday heat. [17]For the Lamb who stands in front of the throne will be their Shepherd. He will lead them to the springs of life-giving water. And God will wipe away all their tears."

## The Lamb Breaks the Seventh Seal

# 8

When the Lamb broke the seventh seal, there was silence throughout heaven for about half an hour. [2]And I saw the seven angels who stand before God, and they were given seven trumpets.

[3]Then another angel with a gold incense burner came and stood at the altar. And a great quantity of incense was given to him to mix with the prayers of God's people, to be offered on the gold altar before the throne. [4]The smoke of the incense, mixed with the prayers of the saints, ascended up to God from the altar where the angel had poured them out. [5]Then the angel filled the incense burner with fire from the altar and threw it down upon the earth; and thunder crashed, lightning flashed, and there was a terrible earthquake.

## The First Four Trumpets

[6]Then the seven angels with the seven trumpets prepared to blow their mighty blasts.

[7]The first angel blew his trumpet, and hail and fire mixed with blood were thrown down upon the earth, and one-third of the earth was set on fire. One-third of the trees were burned, and all the grass was burned.

[8]Then the second angel blew his trumpet, and a great

**STAND POINT**

### When you need guidance

**7:17**

"For the Lamb who stands in front of the throne will be their Shepherd. He will lead them to the springs of life-giving water. And God will wipe away all their tears."

mountain of fire was thrown into the sea. And one-third of the water in the sea became blood. [9]And one-third of all things living in the sea died. And one-third of all the ships on the sea were destroyed.

[10]Then the third angel blew his trumpet, and a great flaming star fell out of the sky, burning like a torch. It fell upon one-third of the rivers and on the springs of water. [11]The name of the star was Bitterness. It made one-third of the water bitter, and many people died because the water was so bitter.

[12]Then the fourth angel blew his trumpet, and one-third of the sun was struck, and one-third of the moon, and one-third of the stars, and they became dark. And one-third of the day was dark and one-third of the night also.

[13]Then I looked up. And I heard a single eagle crying loudly as it flew through the air, "Terror, terror, terror to all who belong to this world because of what will happen when the last three angels blow their trumpets."

## The Fifth Trumpet Brings the First Terror

# 9

Then the fifth angel blew his trumpet, and I saw a star that had fallen to earth from the sky, and he was given the key to the shaft of the bottomless pit. [2]When he opened it, smoke poured out as though from a huge furnace, and the sunlight and air were darkened by the smoke.

[3]Then locusts came from the smoke and descended on the earth, and they were given power to sting like scorpions. [4]They were told not to hurt the grass or plants or trees but to attack all the people who did not have the seal of God on their foreheads. [5]They were told not to kill them but to torture them for five months with agony like the pain of scorpion

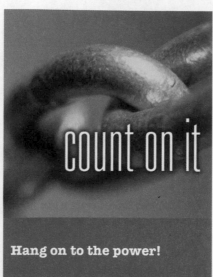

### Hang on to the power!

Like water skiing, you have to hang onto the rope - the power. It is not your power that will make you fly, it is God's! God's power is what will give you life. You will be pulled out of polluted water and your skill will improve, but Christ is the only source of power that pulls you out of your sin and evil. "Without wavering, let us hold tightly to the hope we say we have, for God can be trusted to keep his promise."
Hebrews 10:23
**Count on it!**

### When you feel like procrastinating

**10:6**

And he swore an oath in the name of the one who lives for ever and ever, who created heaven and everything in it, the earth and everything in it, and the sea and everything in it. He said, "God will wait no longer."

stings. [6]**In those days people will seek death but will not find it. They will long to die, but death will flee away!** [7]The locusts looked like horses armed for battle. They had gold crowns on their heads, and they had human faces. [8]Their hair was long like the hair of a woman, and their teeth were like the teeth of a lion. [9]They wore armour made of iron, and their wings roared like an army of chariots rushing into battle. [10]They had tails that stung like scorpions, with power to torture people. This power was given to them for five months. [11]Their king is the angel from the bottomless pit; his name in Hebrew is Abaddon, and in Greek, Apollyon—the Destroyer.

[12]The first terror is past, but look, two more terrors are coming!

## The Sixth Trumpet Brings the Second Terror

[13]Then the sixth angel blew his trumpet, and I heard a voice speaking from the four horns of the gold altar that stands in the presence of God. [14]And the voice spoke to the sixth angel who held the trumpet: "Release the four angels who are bound at the great River Euphrates." [15]And the four angels who had been prepared for this hour and day and month and year were turned loose to kill one-third of all the people on earth. [16]They led an army of 200 million mounted troops—I heard an announcement of how many there were.

[17]And in my vision, I saw the horses and the riders sitting on them. The riders wore armour that was fiery red and sky blue and yellow. The horses' heads were like the heads of lions, and fire and smoke and burning sulphur billowed from their mouths. [18]One-third of all the people on earth were killed by these three plagues—by the fire and the smoke and burning sulphur that came from the mouths of the horses. [19]Their power was in their mouths, but also in their tails. For their tails had heads like snakes, with the power to injure people.

[20]But the people who did not die in these plagues still refused to turn from their evil deeds. They continued to worship demons and idols made of gold, silver, bronze, stone, and wood—idols that neither see nor hear nor walk! [21]And they did not repent of their murders or their witchcraft or their immorality or their thefts.

## The Angel and the Small Scroll

# 10

Then I saw another mighty angel coming down from heaven, surrounded by a cloud, with a rainbow over his head. His face shone like the sun, and his feet were like pillars of fire. [2]And in his hand was a small scroll, which he had unrolled. He stood with his right foot on the sea and his left foot on the land. [3]And he gave a great shout, like the roar of a lion. And when he shouted, the seven thunders answered.

[4]When the seven thunders spoke, I was about to write. But a voice from heaven called to me: "Keep secret what the seven thunders said. Do not write it down." [5]Then the mighty angel standing on the sea and on the land lifted his right hand to heaven. [6]**And he swore an oath in the name of the one**

# Winners have that touch!

Self control - temperance: the skill of taking things only as far as is appropriate. Imagine Tiger Woods drops the ball six feet from the ninth hole at St. Andrews golf course. He walks up to the green, pulls out a wood and blasts the ball into the North Sea! That is intemperance! God gave us good things to enjoy, not to abuse. We can be intemperate about so many things: sport, clothes, work, sex…yes, there are certain things that are prohibited and things only to be done within God's plan. There are certain things that are better to stay away from because they will either influence or discourage others. Self-control is the attitude of keeping yourself together: to stay on God's path and enjoy the journey he has for you. "Carry out my instructions; do not forsake them. Guard them, for they will lead you to a fulfilled life." Proverbs 4:13

## Winners have self-control!

who lives for ever and ever, who created heaven and everything in it, the earth and everything in it, and the sea and everything in it. He said, "God will wait no longer. ⁷But when the seventh angel blows his trumpet, God's mysterious plan will be fulfilled. It will happen just as he announced it to his servants the prophets."

⁸Then the voice from heaven called to me again: "Go and take the unrolled scroll from the angel who is standing on the sea and on the land."

⁹So I approached him and asked him to give me the little scroll. "Yes, take it and eat it," he said. "At first it will taste like honey, but when you swallow it, it will make your stomach sour!" ¹⁰So I took the little scroll from the hands of the angel, and I ate it! It was sweet in my mouth, but it made my stomach sour. ¹¹Then he said to me, "You must prophesy again about many peoples, nations, languages, and kings."

## The Two Witnesses

# 11

Then I was given a measuring stick, and I was told, "Go and measure the Temple of God and the altar, and count the number of worshippers. ²But do not measure the outer courtyard, for it has been turned over to the nations. They will trample the holy city for 42 months. ³And I will give power to my two witnesses, and they will be clothed in sackcloth and will prophesy during those 1,260 days."

⁴These two prophets are the two olive trees and the two lampstands that stand before the Lord of all the earth. ⁵If anyone tries to harm them, fire flashes from the mouths of the prophets and consumes their enemies. This is how anyone who tries to harm them must die. ⁶They have power to shut the skies so that no rain will fall for as long as they prophesy. And they have the power to turn the rivers and oceans into blood, and to send every kind of plague upon the earth as often as they wish.

⁷When they complete their testimony, the beast that comes up out of the bottomless pit will declare war against them. He will conquer them and kill them. ⁸And their bodies will lie in the main street of Jerusalem, the city which is called "Sodom" and "Egypt," the city where their Lord was crucified. ⁹And for three and a half days, all peoples, tribes, languages, and nations will come to stare at their bodies. No one will be allowed to bury them. ¹⁰All the people who belong to this world will give presents to each other to celebrate the death of the two prophets who had tormented them.

¹¹But after three and a half days, the spirit of life from God entered them, and they stood up! And terror struck all who were staring at them. ¹²Then a loud voice shouted from heaven, "Come up here!" And they rose to heaven in a cloud as their enemies watched.

¹³And in the same hour there was a terrible earthquake that destroyed a tenth of the city. Seven thousand people died in that earthquake. And everyone who did not die was terrified and gave glory to the God of heaven.

¹⁴The second terror is past, but look, now the third terror is coming quickly.

## The Seventh Trumpet Brings the Third Terror

¹⁵Then the seventh angel blew his trumpet, and there were loud voices shouting in heaven: "The whole world has now become the Kingdom of our Lord and of his Christ, and he will reign for ever and ever."

¹⁶And the twenty-four elders sitting on their thrones before God fell on their faces and worshipped him. ¹⁷And they said, "We give thanks to you, Lord God Almighty,
the one who is and who always was,
for now you have assumed your great power
and have begun to reign.
¹⁸The nations were angry with you,
but now the time of your wrath has come.
It is time to judge the dead and reward your servants.
You will reward your prophets and your holy people,
all who fear your name, from the least to the greatest.
And you will destroy all who have caused destruction on the earth."

## STATS

The very first Olympic race, held in 776 BC, was won by Corubus, a chef.

•

About 42,000 tennis balls are used in the 650 or so matches in the Wimbledon Championship.

[19]Then, in heaven, the Temple of God was opened and the Ark of his covenant could be seen inside the Temple. Lightning flashed, thunder crashed and roared; there was a great hailstorm, and the world was shaken by a mighty earthquake.

## The Woman and the Dragon

# 12

Then I witnessed in heaven an event of great significance. I saw a woman clothed with the sun, with the moon beneath her feet, and a crown of twelve stars on her head. [2]She was pregnant, and she cried out in the pain of labour as she awaited her delivery.

[3]Suddenly, I witnessed in heaven another significant event. I saw a large red dragon with seven heads and ten horns, with seven crowns on his heads. [4]His tail dragged down one-third of the stars, which he threw to the earth. He stood before the woman as she was about to give birth to her child, ready to devour the baby as soon as it was born.

[5]She gave birth to a boy who was to rule all nations with an iron rod. And the child was snatched away from the dragon and was caught up to God and to his throne. [6]And the woman fled into the wilderness, where God had prepared a place to give her care for 1,260 days.

[7]Then there was war in heaven. Michael and the angels under his command fought the dragon and his angels. [8]And the dragon lost the battle and was forced out of heaven. [9]This great dragon—the ancient serpent called the Devil, or Satan, the one deceiving the whole world—was thrown down to the earth with all his angels.

[10]Then I heard a loud voice shouting across the heavens, "It has happened at last—the salvation and power and kingdom of our God, and the authority of his Christ! For the Accuser has been thrown down to earth—the one who accused our brothers and sisters before our God day and night. [11]And they have defeated him because of the blood of the Lamb and because of their testimony. And they were not afraid to die. [12]Rejoice, O heavens! And you who live in the heavens, rejoice! But terror will come on the earth and the sea. For the Devil has come down to you in great anger, and he knows that he has little time."

[13]And when the dragon realized that he had been thrown down to the earth, he pursued the woman who had given birth to the child. [14]But she was given two wings like those of a great eagle. This allowed her to fly to a place prepared for her in the wilderness, where she would be cared for and protected from the dragon for a time, times, and half a time. [15]Then the dragon tried to drown the woman with a flood of water that flowed from its mouth. [16]But the earth helped her by opening its mouth and swallowing the river that gushed out from the mouth of the dragon. [17]Then the dragon became

angry at the woman, and he declared war against the rest of her children—all who keep God's commandments and confess that they belong to Jesus.

## The Beast out of the Sea

[18]Then he stood waiting on the shore of the sea.

**action**

**CH 13:3–10 WHAT'S IT SAYING?**

**WHAT AM I GOING TO DO ABOUT IT?**

# 13

And now in my vision I saw a beast rising up out of the sea. It had seven heads and ten horns, with ten crowns on its horns. And written on each head were names that blasphemed God. [2]This beast looked like a leopard, but it had bear's feet and a lion's mouth! And the dragon gave him his own power and throne and great authority.

[3]I saw that one of the heads of the beast seemed wounded beyond recovery—but the fatal wound was healed! All the world marvelled at this miracle and followed the beast in awe. [4]They worshipped the dragon for giving the beast such power, and they worshipped the beast. "Is there anyone as great as the beast?" they exclaimed. "Who is able to fight against him?"

[5]Then the beast was allowed to speak great

blasphemies against God. And he was given authority to do what he wanted for forty-two months. [6]And he spoke terrible words of blasphemy against God, slandering his name and all who live in heaven, who are his temple. [7]And the beast was allowed to wage war against God's holy people and to overcome them. And he was given authority to rule over every tribe and people and language and nation. [8]And all the people who belong to this world worshipped the beast. They are the ones whose names were not written in the Book of Life, which belongs to the Lamb who was killed before the world was made.

[9]Anyone who is willing to hear should listen and understand. [10]The people who are destined for prison will be arrested and taken away. Those who are destined for death will be killed. But do not be dismayed, for here is your opportunity to have endurance and faith.

## The Beast out of the Earth

[11]Then I saw another beast come up out of the earth. He had two horns like those of a lamb, and he spoke with the voice of a dragon. [12]He exercised all the authority of the first beast. And he required all the earth and those who belong to this world to worship the first beast, whose death-wound had been healed. [13]He did astounding miracles, such as making fire flash down to earth from heaven while everyone was watching. [14]And with all the miracles he was allowed to perform on behalf of the first beast, he deceived all the people who belong to this world. He ordered the people of the world to make a great statue of the first beast, who was fatally wounded and then came back to life. [15]He was permitted to give life to this statue so that it could speak. Then the statue commanded that anyone refusing to worship it must die.

[16]He required everyone—great and small, rich and poor, slave and free—to be given a mark on the right hand or on the forehead. [17]And no one could buy or sell anything without that mark, which was either the name of the beast or the number representing his

**Bible**

**In Old Testament times the Mediterranean Sea was called the Great Sea.**

STAND POINT

**When you need endurance**

**14:12**

And I heard a sound from heaven like the roaring of a great waterfall or the rolling of mighty thunder. It was like the sound of many harpists playing together.

## The Lamb and the 144,000

# 14

Then I saw the Lamb standing on Mount Zion, and with him were 144,000 who had his name and his Father's name written on their foreheads. ²And I heard a sound from heaven like the roaring of a great waterfall or the rolling of mighty thunder. It was like the sound of many harpists playing together.

³This great choir sang a wonderful new song in front of the throne of God and before the four living beings and the twenty-four elders. And no one could learn this song except those 144,000 who had been redeemed from the earth. ⁴For they are spiritually undefiled, pure as virgins, following the Lamb wherever he goes. They have been purchased from among the people on the earth as a special offering to God and to the Lamb. ⁵No falsehood can be charged against them; they are blameless.

## The Three Angels

⁶And I saw another angel flying through the heavens, carrying the everlasting Good News to preach to the people who belong to this world—to every nation, tribe, language, and people. ⁷"Fear God," he shouted. "Give glory to him. For the time has come when he will sit as judge. Worship him who made heaven and earth, the sea, and all the springs of water."

name. ¹⁸Wisdom is needed to understand this. Let the one who has understanding solve the number of the beast, for it is the number of a man. His number is 666.

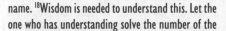

## Tactical Knowledge:

Players should develop a broad tactical understanding of the game to quickly assess situations on the field and make the correct choices for their team. Rigid team roles and positions will not succeed in the future; therefore players will be required to be flexible in where and how they play.

[8]Then another angel followed him through the skies, shouting, "Babylon is fallen—that great city is fallen—because she seduced the nations of the world and made them drink the wine of her passionate immorality."

[9]Then a third angel followed them, shouting,

"Anyone who worships the beast and his statue or who accepts his mark on the forehead or the hand [10]must drink the wine of God's wrath. It is poured out undiluted into God's cup of wrath. And they will be tormented with fire and burning sulphur in the presence of the holy angels and the Lamb. [11]The smoke of their torment rises for ever and ever, and they will have no relief day or night, for they have worshipped the beast and his statue and have accepted the mark of his name. [12]Let this encourage God's holy people to endure persecution patiently and remain firm to the end, obeying his commands and trusting in Jesus."

[13]And I heard a voice from heaven saying, "Write this down: Blessed are those who die in the Lord from now on. Yes, says the Spirit, they are blessed indeed, for they will rest from all their toils and trials; for their good deeds follow them!"

## The Harvest of the Earth

[14]Then I saw the Son of Man sitting on a white cloud. He had a gold crown on his head and a sharp sickle in his hand. [15]Then an angel came from the Temple and called out in a loud voice to the one sitting on the cloud, "Use the sickle, for the time has come for you to harvest; the crop is ripe on the earth." [16]So the one sitting on the cloud swung his sickle over the earth, and the whole earth was harvested.

[17]After that, another angel came from the Temple in heaven, and he also had a sharp sickle. [18]Then another angel, who has power to destroy the world with fire, shouted to the angel with the sickle, "Use your sickle now to gather the clusters of grapes from the vines of the earth, for they are fully ripe for judgement." [19]So the angel swung his sickle on the earth and loaded the grapes into the great winepress of God's wrath. [20]And the grapes were trodden in the winepress outside the city, and blood flowed from the winepress in a stream about three hundred kilometres long and as high as a horse's bridle.

## The Song of Moses and of the Lamb

# 15

Then I saw in heaven another significant event, and it was great and marvellous. Seven angels were holding the seven last plagues, which would bring God's wrath to completion. [2]I saw before me what seemed to be a crystal sea mixed with fire. And on it stood all the people who had been victorious over the beast and his statue and the number representing

**WHAT DOES IT MEAN?**

**Bethlehem and Nazareth:**
Jesus' birthplace and home-town. The birth of our Lord took place at the time and town predicted by the Old Testament prophets. Joseph and Mary were providentially led to go up to Bethlehem because Joseph was a descendant of King David and had to register for an official census in Bethlehem. He travelled with his fiancée Mary who was heavily pregnant and there the baby Jesus was born. For more on Jesus' birth read: Matthew 2 & Luke 2.

Though Jesus was destined to be born in Bethlehem he was raised approximately 60 miles to the north in the town of Nazareth, in the region of Galilee. This was the home of Joseph and Mary (Luke 2:39), and here the angel announced to the 'virgin' the birth of the Christ (1:26-28). Jesus grew up from his infancy to manhood (4:16) and here he began his public ministry in the synagogue (Matt. 13:54).

his name. They were all holding harps that God had given them. [3]And they were singing the song of Moses, the servant of God, and the song of the Lamb:

"Great and marvellous are your actions,
Lord God Almighty.
Just and true are your ways,
O King of the nations.
[4]Who will not fear, O Lord, and glorify your name?
For you alone are holy.
All nations will come and worship before you,
for your righteous deeds have been revealed."

## The Seven Bowls of the Seven Plagues

[5]Then I looked and saw that the Temple in heaven, God's Tabernacle, was thrown wide open! [6]The seven angels who were holding the bowls of the seven plagues came from the Temple, clothed in spotless white linen with gold belts across their chests. [7]And one of the four living beings handed each of the seven angels a gold bowl filled with the terrible wrath of God, who lives for ever and for ever. [8]The Temple was filled with smoke from God's glory and power. No one could enter the Temple until the seven angels had completed pouring out the seven plagues.

# 16

Then I heard a mighty voice shouting from the Temple to the seven angels, "Now go and empty out the seven bowls of God's wrath on the earth."

[2]So the first angel left the Temple and poured out his bowl over the earth, and horrible, malignant sores broke out on everyone who had the mark of the beast and who worshipped his statue.

[3]Then the second angel poured out his bowl on the sea, and it became like the blood of a corpse. And everything in the sea died.

[4]Then the third angel poured out his bowl on the rivers and springs, and they became blood. [5]And I heard the angel who had authority over all water saying, "You are just in sending this judgement, O Holy One, who is and who always was. [6]For your holy people and your prophets have been killed, and their blood was poured out on the earth. So you have given their murderers blood to drink. It is their just reward." [7]And I heard a voice from the altar saying, "Yes, Lord God Almighty, your punishments are true and just." [8]Then the fourth angel poured out his bowl on the sun, causing it to scorch everyone with its fire. [9]Everyone was burned by this blast of heat, and they cursed the name of God, who sent all of these plagues.

They did not repent and give him glory.

[10]Then the fifth angel poured out his bowl on the throne of the beast, and his kingdom was plunged into darkness. And his subjects ground their teeth in anguish, [11]and they cursed the God of heaven for their pains and sores. But they refused to repent of all their evil deeds.

[12]Then the sixth angel poured out his bowl on the great River Euphrates, and it dried up so that the kings from the east could march their armies westward without hindrance. [13]And I saw three evil spirits that looked like frogs leap from the mouth of the dragon, the beast, and the false prophet. [14]These miracle-working demons caused all the rulers of the world to gather for battle against the Lord on that great judgement day of God Almighty.

[15]"Take note: I will come as unexpectedly as a thief! Blessed are all who are watching for me, who keep their robes ready so they will not need to walk naked and ashamed."

[16]And they gathered all the rulers and their armies to a place called Armageddon in Hebrew.

[17]Then the seventh angel poured out his bowl into the air. And a mighty shout came from the throne of the Temple in heaven, saying, "It is finished!" [18]Then the thunder crashed and rolled, and lightning flashed. And there was an earthquake greater than ever before in human history. [19]The great city of Babylon split into three pieces, and cities around the world fell into heaps of rubble. And so God remembered all of Babylon's sins, and he made her drink the cup that was filled with the wine of his fierce wrath. [20]And every island

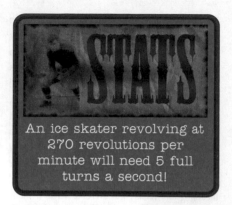

An ice skater revolving at 270 revolutions per minute will need 5 full turns a second!

disappeared, and all the mountains were levelled. [21]There was a terrible hailstorm, and hailstones weighing thirty-four kilograms fell from the sky onto the people below. They cursed God because of the hailstorm, which was a very terrible plague.

## The Great Prostitute

# 17

One of the seven angels who had poured out the seven bowls came over and spoke to me. "Come with me," he said, "and I will show you the judgement that is going to come on the great prostitute, who sits on many waters. [2]The rulers of the world have had immoral relations with her, and the people who belong to this world have been made drunk by the wine of her immorality."

[3]So the angel took me in spirit into the wilderness. There I saw a woman sitting on a scarlet beast that had seven heads and ten horns, written all over with blasphemies against God. [4]The woman wore purple and scarlet clothing and beautiful jewellery made of gold and precious gems and pearls. She held in her hand a gold goblet full of obscenities and the impurities of her immorality. [5]A mysterious name was written on her forehead: "Babylon the Great, Mother of All Prostitutes and Obscenities in the World." [6]I could see that she was drunk—drunk with the blood of God's holy people who were witnesses for Jesus. I stared at her completely amazed.

[7]"Why are you so amazed?" the angel asked. "I will tell you the mystery of this woman and of the beast with seven heads and ten horns. [8]The beast you saw was alive but isn't now. And yet he will soon come up out of the bottomless pit and go to eternal destruction. And the people who belong to this world, whose names were not written in the Book of Life from before the world began, will be amazed at the reappearance of this beast who had died.

[9]"And now understand this: The seven heads of the beast represent the seven hills of the city where this woman rules. They also represent seven kings. [10]Five kings have already fallen, the sixth now reigns, and the seventh is yet to come, but his reign will be brief. [11]The scarlet beast that was alive and then died is the eighth king. He is like the other seven, and he, too, will go to his doom. [12]His ten horns are ten kings who have not yet risen to power; they will be appointed to their kingdoms for one brief moment to reign with the beast. [13]They will all agree to give their power and authority to him. [14]Together they will wage war against the Lamb, but the Lamb will defeat them because he is Lord over all lords and King over all kings, and his people are the called and chosen and faithful ones."

[15]And the angel said to me, "The waters where the prostitute

**I have faith in Jesus, but how do I answer my friends when they say all religions lead to the same thing?**

We are commanded to love everyone, but we were not commanded to believe everyone. Look up John 14:6, 'Jesus told him, "I am the way, the truth and the life. No one can come to the Father (God) except through me."' Jesus said he was mutually exclusive (the only way to God): that makes him a liar, a lunatic, or the real deal - 'The Lord'. Many world religions:

- agree that God made the earth and the rules
- agree that mankind broke the rules and the consequence is separation from God
- depart from Christianity at the step needed to get back to God.
- say, 'Do this, this and this, and you will attain a higher place near heaven.'

Christianity tells us the truth. We will never attain reconciliation with God in anything we do. **'For all have sinned and fall short of God's glorious standard.'** Yet now God in his gracious kindness declares us not guilty. He has done this through Christ Jesus, who has freed us by taking away our sins. **'For God sent Jesus to take the punishment for our sins and to satisfy God's anger against us.'** Romans 3:23-25

is sitting represent masses of people of every nation and language. ¹⁶The scarlet beast and his ten horns—which represent ten kings who will reign with him—all hate the prostitute. They will strip her naked, eat her flesh, and burn her remains with fire. ¹⁷For God has put a plan into their minds, a plan that will carry out his purposes. They will mutually agree to give their authority to the scarlet beast, and so the words of God will be fulfilled. ¹⁸And this woman you saw in your vision represents the great city that rules over the kings of the earth."

**CH 18:1-24 WHAT'S IT SAYING?**

**WHAT AM I GOING TO DO ABOUT IT?**

## The Fall of Babylon

# 18

After all this I saw another angel come down from heaven with great authority, and the earth grew bright with his splendour. ²He gave a mighty shout, "Babylon is fallen—that great city is fallen! She has become the hideout of demons and evil spirits, a nest for filthy buzzards, and a den for dreadful beasts. ³For all the nations have drunk the wine of her passionate immorality. The rulers of the world have committed adultery with her, and merchants throughout the world have grown rich as a result of her luxurious living."

⁴Then I heard another voice calling from heaven,

"Come away from her, my people. Do not take part in her sins, or you will be punished with her. ⁵For her sins are piled as high as heaven, and God is ready to judge her for her evil deeds. ⁶Do to her as she has done to your people. Give her a double penalty for all her evil deeds. She brewed a cup of terror for others, so give her twice as much as she gave out. ⁷She has lived in luxury and pleasure, so match it now with torments and sorrows. She boasts, 'I am queen on my throne. I am no helpless widow. I will not experience sorrow.' ⁸Therefore, the sorrows of death and mourning and famine will overtake her in a single day. She will be utterly consumed by fire, for the Lord God who judges her is mighty."

⁹And the rulers of the world who took part in her immoral acts and enjoyed her great luxury will mourn for her as they see the smoke rising from her charred remains. ¹⁰They will stand at a distance, terrified by her great torment. They will cry out, "How terrible, how terrible for Babylon, that great city! In one single moment God's judgement came on her."

¹¹The merchants of the world will weep and mourn for her, for there is no one left to buy their goods. ¹²She bought great quantities of gold, silver, jewels, pearls, fine linen, purple dye, silk, scarlet cloth, every kind of perfumed wood, ivory goods, objects made of expensive wood, bronze, iron, and marble. ¹³She also bought cinnamon, spice, incense, myrrh, frankincense, wine, olive oil, fine flour, wheat, cattle, sheep, horses, chariots, and slaves—yes, she even traded in human lives.

¹⁴"All the fancy things you loved so much are gone," they cry. "The luxuries and splendour that you prized so much will never be yours again. They are gone for ever."

¹⁵The merchants who became wealthy by selling her these things will stand at a distance, terrified by her great torment. They will weep and cry. ¹⁶"How terrible, how terrible for that great city! She was so beautiful—like a woman clothed in finest purple and scarlet linens, decked out with gold and precious stones and pearls! ¹⁷And in one single moment all the wealth of the city is gone!"

And all the shipowners and captains of the merchant ships and their crews will stand at a distance. ¹⁸They will weep as they watch the smoke ascend, and they will say, "Where in all the world is there another city like this?" ¹⁹And they will throw dust on their heads to show their great sorrow. And they will say, "How terrible, how terrible for the great city! She made us all rich from her great wealth. And now in a single

hour it is all gone."

²⁰**But you, O heaven, rejoice over her fate. And you also rejoice, O holy people of God and apostles and prophets! For at last God has judged her on your behalf.**

²¹Then a mighty angel picked up a boulder as large as a great millstone. He threw it into the ocean and shouted, "Babylon, the great city, will be thrown down as violently as I have thrown away this stone, and she will disappear for ever. ²²Never again will the sound of music be heard there—no more harps, songs, flutes, or trumpets. There will be no industry of any kind, and no more milling of corn. ²³Her nights will be dark, without a single lamp. There will be no happy voices of brides and grooms. This will happen because her merchants, who were the greatest in the world, deceived the nations with her sorceries. ²⁴In her streets the blood of the prophets was spilled. She was the one who slaughtered God's people all over the world."

## Songs of Victory in Heaven

# 19

After this, I heard the sound of a vast crowd in heaven shouting, "Hallelujah! Salvation is from our God. Glory and power belong to him alone. ²His judgements are just and true. He has punished the great prostitute who corrupted the earth with her immorality, and he has avenged the murder of his servants." ³Again and again their voices rang, "Hallelujah! The smoke from that city ascends for ever and for ever!"

⁴Then the twenty-four elders and the four living beings fell down and worshipped God, who was sitting on the throne. They cried out, "Amen! Hallelujah!"

⁵And from the throne came a voice that said, "Praise our God, all his servants, from the least to the greatest, all who fear him."

⁶Then I heard again what sounded like the shout of a huge crowd, or the roar of mighty ocean waves, or the crash of loud thunder: "Hallelujah! For the Lord our God, the Almighty, reigns. ⁷Let us be glad and rejoice and honour him. For the time has come for the wedding feast of the Lamb, and his bride has prepared herself. ⁸She is permitted to wear the finest white linen." (Fine linen represents the good deeds done by the people of God.)

⁹**And the angel said, "Write this: Blessed are those who are invited to the wedding feast of the Lamb." And**

he added, "These are true words that come from God."

¹⁰Then I fell down at his feet to worship him, but he said, "No, don't worship me. For I am a servant of God, just like you and other brothers and sisters who testify of their faith in Jesus. Worship God. For the essence of prophecy is to give a clear witness for Jesus."

## The Rider on the White Horse

¹¹Then I saw heaven opened, and a white horse was standing there. And the one sitting on the horse was named Faithful and True. For he judges fairly and then goes to war. ¹²His eyes were bright like flames of fire, and on his head were many crowns. A name was written on him, and only he knew what it meant. ¹³He was clothed with a robe dipped in blood, and his title was the Word of God. ¹⁴The armies of heaven, dressed in pure white linen, followed him on white horses. ¹⁵From his mouth came a sharp sword, and with it he struck down the nations. He ruled them with an iron rod, and he trod the winepress of the fierce wrath of almighty God. ¹⁶On his robe and thigh was written this title: King of kings and Lord of lords.

¹⁷Then I saw an angel standing in the sun, shouting to the vultures flying high in the sky: "Come! Gather together for the great banquet God has prepared. ¹⁸Come and eat the flesh of kings, captains, and strong warriors; of horses and their riders; and of all humanity, both free and slave, small and great."

¹⁹Then I saw the beast gathering the kings of the earth and their armies in order to fight against the one sitting on the horse and his army. ²⁰And the beast was captured, and with him the false prophet who did mighty miracles on behalf of the beast—miracles that deceived all who had accepted the mark of the beast and who worshipped his statue. Both the beast and his false prophet were thrown alive into the lake of fire that burns with sulphur. ²¹Their entire army was killed by the sharp sword that came out of the mouth of the one riding the white horse. And all the vultures of the sky gorged themselves on the dead bodies.

## The Thousand Years

# 20

Then I saw an angel come down from heaven with the key to the bottomless pit and a heavy chain in his hand. ²He seized the dragon—that old serpent, the Devil, Satan—and bound him in chains for a thousand years. ³The angel threw him into the bottomless pit, which he then shut and locked so Satan

**The Bible, the world's best-selling book, is also the world's most shoplifted book.**

could not deceive the nations any more until the thousand years were finished. Afterwards he would be released again for a little while.

⁴Then I saw thrones, and the people sitting on them had been given the authority to judge. And I saw the souls of those who had been beheaded for their testimony about Jesus, for proclaiming the word of God. And I saw the souls of those who had not worshipped the beast or his statue, nor accepted his mark on their forehead or their hands. They came to life again, and they reigned with Christ for a thousand years. ⁵This is the first resurrection. (The rest of the dead did not come back to life until the thousand years had ended.) ⁶Blessed and holy are those who share in the first resurrection. For them the second death holds no power, but they will be priests of God and of Christ and will reign with him a thousand years.

## The Defeat of Satan

⁷When the thousand years end, Satan will be let out of his prison. ⁸He will go out to deceive the nations from every corner of the earth, which are called Gog and Magog. He will gather them together for battle—a mighty host, as numberless as sand along the shore. ⁹And I saw them as they went up on the broad plain of the earth and surrounded God's people and the beloved city. But fire from heaven came down on the attacking armies and consumed them.

¹⁰Then the Devil, who betrayed them, was thrown into the lake of fire that burns with sulphur, joining the beast and the false prophet. There they will be tormented day and night for ever and ever.

## The Final Judgement

¹¹And I saw a great white throne, and I saw the one who was sitting on it. The earth and sky fled from his presence, but they found no place to hide. ¹²I saw the dead, both great and small, standing before God's throne. And the books were opened, including the Book of Life. And the dead were judged according to the things written in the books, according to what they

had done. ¹³The sea gave up the dead in it, and death and the grave gave up the dead in them. They were all judged according to their deeds. ¹⁴And death and the grave were thrown into the lake of fire. This is the second death—the lake of fire. ¹⁵And anyone whose name was not found recorded in the Book of Life was thrown into the lake of fire.

## The New Jerusalem

# 21

Then I saw a new heaven and a new earth, for the old heaven and the old earth had disappeared. And the sea was also gone. ²And I saw the holy city, the new Jerusalem, coming down from God out of heaven like a beautiful bride prepared for her husband.

³I heard a loud shout from the throne, saying, "Look, the home of God is now among his people! He will live with them, and they will be his people. God himself will be with them. ⁴**He will remove all of their sorrows, and there will be no more death or sorrow or crying or pain. For the old world and its evils are gone for ever.**"

⁵And the one sitting on the throne said, "Look, I am making all things new!" And then he said to me, "Write this down, for what I tell you is trustworthy and true." ⁶And he also said, "It is finished! I am the Alpha and the Omega—the Beginning and the End. To all who are thirsty I will give the springs of the water of life without charge! ⁷All who are victorious will inherit all these blessings, and I will be their God, and they will be my children. ⁸But cowards who turn away from me, and unbelievers, and the corrupt, and murderers, and the immoral, and those who practise witchcraft, and idol worshippers, and all liars—their doom is in the lake that burns with fire and sulphur. This is the

**STAND POINT**

**When you need something to look forward to**

**21:4**

"He will remove all of their sorrows, and there will be no more death or sorrow or crying or pain. For the old world and its evils are gone for ever."

second death."

[9]Then one of the seven angels who held the seven bowls containing the seven last plagues came and said to me, "Come with me! I will show you the bride, the wife of the Lamb." [10]So he took me in spirit to a great, high mountain, and he showed me the holy city, Jerusalem, descending out of heaven from God. [11]It was filled with the glory of God and sparkled like a precious gem, crystal clear like jasper. [12]Its walls were broad and high, with twelve gates guarded by twelve angels. And the names of the twelve tribes of Israel were written on the gates. [13]There were three gates on each side—east, north, south, and west. [14]The wall of the city had twelve foundation stones, and on them were written the names of the twelve apostles of the Lamb.

[15]The angel who talked to me held in his hand a gold measuring stick to measure the city, its gates, and its wall. [16]When he measured it, he found it was a square, as wide as it was long. In fact, it was in the form of a cube, for its length and width and height were each 2,220 kilometres. [17]Then he measured the walls and found them to be 66 metres thick (the angel used a standard human measure).

[18]The wall was made of jasper, and the city was pure gold, as clear as glass. [19]The wall of the city was built on foundation stones inlaid with twelve gems: the first was jasper, the second sapphire, the third agate, the fourth emerald, [20]the fifth onyx, the sixth carnelian, the seventh chrysolite, the eighth beryl, the ninth topaz, the tenth chrysoprase, the eleventh jacinth, the twelfth amethyst.

[21]The twelve gates were made of pearls—each gate from a single pearl! And the main street was pure gold, as clear as glass.

[22]No temple could be seen in the city, for the Lord God Almighty and the Lamb are its temple. [23]And the city has no need of sun or moon, for the glory of God illuminates the city, and the Lamb is its light. [24]The nations of the earth will walk in its light, and the rulers of the world will come and bring their glory to it. [25]Its gates never close at the end of day because there is no night. [26]And all the nations will bring their glory and honour into the city. [27]Nothing evil will be allowed to enter—no one who practises shameful idolatry and dishonesty—but only those whose names are written in the Lamb's Book of Life.

# 22

And the angel showed me a pure river with the water of life, clear as crystal, flowing from the throne of God and of the Lamb, [2]coursing down the centre of the main street. On each side of the river grew a tree of life, bearing twelve crops of fruit, with a fresh crop each month. The leaves were used for medicine to heal the nations.

[3]No longer will anything be cursed. For the throne of God

and of the Lamb will be there, and his servants will worship him. [4]And they will see his face, and his name will be written on their foreheads. [5]And there will be no night there—no need for lamps or sun—for the Lord God will shine on them. And they will reign for ever and ever.

[6]Then the angel said to me, "These words are trustworthy and true: 'The Lord God, who tells his prophets what the future holds, has sent his angel to tell you what will happen soon.'"

CH 22:7-21 WHAT'S IT SAYING?

WHAT AM I GOING TO do ABOUT IT?

## Jesus Is Coming

[7]"Look, I am coming soon! Blessed are those who obey the prophecy written in this scroll."

[8]I, John, am the one who saw and heard all these things. And when I saw and heard these things, I fell

down to worship the angel who showed them to me. [9]But again he said, "No, don't worship me. I am a servant of God, just like you and your brothers the prophets, as well as all who obey what is written in this scroll. Worship God!"

[10]Then he instructed me, "Do not seal up the prophetic words you have written, for the time is near. [11]Let the one who is doing wrong continue to do wrong; the one who is vile, continue to be vile; the one who is good, continue to do good; and the one who is holy, continue in holiness."

[12]"See, I am coming soon, and my reward is with me, to repay all according to their deeds. [13]I am the Alpha and the Omega, the First and the Last, the Beginning and the End."

[14]Blessed are those who wash their robes so they can enter through the gates of the city and eat the fruit from the tree of life. [15]Outside the city are the dogs—the sorcerers, the sexually immoral, the murderers, the idol worshippers, and all who love to live a lie.

[16]"I, Jesus, have sent my angel to give you this message for the churches. I am both the source of David and the heir to his throne. I am the bright morning star."

[17]The Spirit and the bride say, "Come." Let each one who hears them say, "Come." Let the thirsty ones come—anyone who wants to. Let them come and drink the water of life without charge. [18]And I solemnly declare to everyone who hears the prophetic words of this book: If anyone adds anything to what is written here, God will add to that person the plagues described in this book. [19]And if anyone removes any of the words of this prophetic book, God will remove that person's share in the tree of life and in the holy city that are described in this book.

[20]He who is the faithful witness to all these things says,

"Yes, I am coming soon!"

Amen! Come, Lord Jesus!

[21]The grace of the Lord Jesus be with you all.

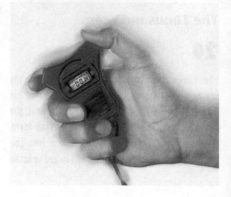

# notes

# resource

## To The Next Level

**To The Next Level is a ministry dedicated to educate, inspire and motivate athletes and coaches, and all whom they influence to achieve their full human, spiritual, and athletic potential in reaching to the next level through a life changing relationship with Jesus Christ.**

**Performance Principles**  www.TOTHENEXTLEVEL.org

What does it take to be a champion? Countless athletes take to the pitch, court, rink, pool and mat each year - all hoping to be crowned a champion. But few actually achieve their goals. Athletic Performance Principles for Life are the keys to being a champion - not only in athletics, but in life as well. Study these areas and plug this wisdom into your own life - you'll be glad you did!

www.tothenextlevel.org

# Monthly Action Plan: Goals List M.A.P.

**SPIRITUAL DISCIPLINES:**

_____

Prayer:

_____

Faith Community:

_____

Bible Reading:

_____

**PRAYER LIST**

_____

Friends:

_____

World:

_____

Personal:

_____

# Monthly Action Plan: Goals List

## M.A.P.

## PERSONAL GOALS

Family:

Work/Social/School:

Challenge:

## SPORTS GOALS:

Training:

Performance:

Competition Results:

# notes